Teach Yourself®
Microsoft® Active
Server Pages 3

Teach Yourself®
Microsoft® Active Server Pages 3

Sandra E. Eddy

Simon St.Laurent

W. Scott Kallmeyer

IDG Books Worldwide, Inc.

An International Data Group Company

Foster City, CA • Chicago, IL • Indianapolis, IN • New York, NY

Teach Yourself® Microsoft® Active Server Pages 3

Published by
IDG Books Worldwide, Inc.
An International Data Group Company
919 E. Hillsdale Blvd., Suite 400
Foster City, CA 94404
`www.idgbooks.com` (IDG Books Worldwide Web site)

Library of Congress Control Number: 00-104427

ISBN: 0-7645-4601-5

Printed in the United States of America

10 9 8 7 6 5 4 3 2 1

1V/ST/QV/QQ/IN

Distributed in the United States by IDG Books Worldwide, Inc.

Distributed by CDG Books Canada Inc. for Canada; by Transworld Publishers Limited in the United Kingdom; by IDG Norge Books for Norway; by IDG Sweden Books for Sweden; by IDG Books Australia Publishing Corporation Pty. Ltd. for Australia and New Zealand; by TransQuest Publishers Pte Ltd. for Singapore, Malaysia, Thailand, Indonesia, and Hong Kong; by Gotop Information Inc. for Taiwan; by ICG Muse, Inc. for Japan; by Intersoft for South Africa; by Eyrolles for France; by International Thomson Publishing for Germany, Austria and Switzerland; by Distribuidora Cuspide for Argentina; by LR International for Brazil; by Galileo Libros for Chile; by Ediciones ZETA S.C.R. Ltda. for Peru; by WS Computer Publishing Corporation, Inc., for the Philippines; by Contemporanea de Ediciones for Venezuela; by Express Computer Distributors for the Caribbean and West Indies; by Micronesia Media Distributor, Inc. for Micronesia; by Chips Computadoras S.A. de C.V. for Mexico; by Editorial Norma de Panama S.A. for Panama; by American Bookshops for Finland.

For general information on IDG Books Worldwide's books in the U.S., please call our Consumer Customer Service department at 800-762-2974. For reseller information, including discounts and premium sales, please call our Reseller Customer Service department at 800-434-3422.

For information on where to purchase IDG Books Worldwide's books outside the U.S., please contact our International Sales department at 317-572-3337 or fax 317-572-4002.

For consumer information on foreign language translations, please contact our Customer Service department at 800-434-3422, fax 317-572-4002, or e-mail rights@idgbooks.com.

For information on licensing foreign or domestic rights, please phone +1-650-653-7098.

For sales inquiries and special prices for bulk quantities, please contact our Sales department at 800-434-3422 or write to the address above.

For information on using IDG Books Worldwide's books in the classroom or for ordering examination copies, please contact our Educational Sales department at 800-434-2086 or fax 317-572-4005.

For press review copies, author interviews, or other publicity information, please contact our Public Relations department at 650-653-7000 or fax 650-653-7500.

For authorization to photocopy items for corporate, personal, or educational use, please contact Copyright Clearance Center, 222 Rosewood Drive, Danvers, MA 01923, or fax 978-750-4470.

ABOUT IDG BOOKS WORLDWIDE

Welcome to the world of IDG Books Worldwide.

IDG Books Worldwide, Inc., is a subsidiary of International Data Group, the world's largest publisher of computer-related information and the leading global provider of information services on information technology. IDG was founded more than 30 years ago by Patrick J. McGovern and now employs more than 9,000 people worldwide. IDG publishes more than 290 computer publications in over 75 countries. More than 90 million people read one or more IDG publications each month.

Launched in 1990, IDG Books Worldwide is today the #1 publisher of best-selling computer books in the United States. We are proud to have received eight awards from the Computer Press Association in recognition of editorial excellence and three from Computer Currents' First Annual Readers' Choice Awards. Our best-selling ...For Dummies® series has more than 50 million copies in print with translations in 31 languages. IDG Books Worldwide, through a joint venture with IDG's Hi-Tech Beijing, became the first U.S. publisher to publish a computer book in the People's Republic of China. In record time, IDG Books Worldwide has become the first choice for millions of readers around the world who want to learn how to better manage their businesses.

Our mission is simple: Every one of our books is designed to bring extra value and skill-building instructions to the reader. Our books are written by experts who understand and care about our readers. The knowledge base of our editorial staff comes from years of experience in publishing, education, and journalism — experience we use to produce books to carry us into the new millennium. In short, we care about books, so we attract the best people. We devote special attention to details such as audience, interior design, use of icons, and illustrations. And because we use an efficient process of authoring, editing, and desktop publishing our books electronically, we can spend more time ensuring superior content and less time on the technicalities of making books.

You can count on our commitment to deliver high-quality books at competitive prices on topics you want to read about. At IDG Books Worldwide, we continue in the IDG tradition of delivering quality for more than 30 years. You'll find no better book on a subject than one from IDG Books Worldwide.

John Kilcullen
Chairman and CEO
IDG Books Worldwide, Inc.

Eighth Annual
Computer Press
Awards ⪴1992

Ninth Annual
Computer Press
Awards ⪴1993

Tenth Annual
Computer Press
Awards ⪴1994

Eleventh Annual
Computer Press
Awards ⪴1995

IDG is the world's leading IT media, research and exposition company. Founded in 1964, IDG had 1997 revenues of $2.05 billion and has more than 9,000 employees worldwide. IDG offers the widest range of media options that reach IT buyers in 75 countries representing 95% of worldwide IT spending. IDG's diverse product and services portfolio spans six key areas including print publishing, online publishing, expositions and conferences, market research, education and training, and global marketing services. More than 90 million people read one or more of IDG's 290 magazines and newspapers, including IDG's leading global brands — Computerworld, PC World, Network World, Macworld and the Channel World family of publications. IDG Books Worldwide is one of the fastest-growing computer book publishers in the world, with more than 700 titles in 36 languages. The "...For Dummies®" series alone has more than 50 million copies in print. IDG offers online users the largest network of technology-specific Web sites around the world through IDG.net (http://www.idg.net), which comprises more than 225 targeted Web sites in 55 countries worldwide. International Data Corporation (IDC) is the world's largest provider of information technology data, analysis and consulting, with research centers in over 41 countries and more than 400 research analysts worldwide. IDG World Expo is a leading producer of more than 168 globally branded conferences and expositions in 35 countries including E3 (Electronic Entertainment Expo), Macworld Expo, ComNet, Windows World Expo, ICE (Internet Commerce Expo), Agenda, DEMO, and Spotlight. IDG's training subsidiary, ExecuTrain, is the world's largest computer training company, with more than 230 locations worldwide and 785 training courses. IDG Marketing Services helps industry-leading IT companies build international brand recognition by developing global integrated marketing programs via IDG's print, online and exposition products worldwide. Further information about the company can be found at www.idg.com.   1/26/00

Credits

Acquisitions Editor
   Debra Williams Cauley

Project Editor
   Barbra Guerra

Technical Editor
   Robert Murdoch

Copy Editor
   Eric Hahn

Project Coordinator
   Amanda Foxworth

Graphics and Production Specialists
   Amy Adrian
   Karl Brandt
   Brian Drumm
   Jacque Schneider

Quality Control Specialists
   Laura Albert
   Chris Weisbart

Book Designers
   Daniel Ziegler Design
   Cátálin Dulfu
   Kurt Krames

Proofreading and Indexing
   York Production Services

Cover Design
   Sarah Barnes

Special Help
   E. Shawn Aylsworth

About the Author

Sandra E. Eddy specializes in writing both how-to and reference books about the Internet, Windows, and Windows applications. Until she became a full-time freelance writer in 1993, Ms. Eddy was a documentation manager and technical writer for a major software company. From 1984 to 1993, she wrote and edited user and technical manuals for both PC- and mainframe-based computer programs. Ms. Eddy is the author of the following books from IDG Books Worldwide: *HTML in Plain English, XML in Plain English, The GIF Animator's Guide,* and *Teach Yourself XML.*

Simon St.Laurent is a Web developer, network administrator, computer book author, and XML troublemaker living in Ithaca, New York. His books include *XML: A Primer, XML Elements of Style, Building XML Applications, Cookies,* and *Sharing Bandwidth.* He is a contributing editor to *xmlhack* and an occasional contributor to *XML.com.*

Scott Kallmeyer is a Web developer, Internet instructor, yoga student, and ASP author living in Ellicott City, Maryland. He is also a contributing author to the *ASPAlliance for the Wise ASP* column, writing articles for those desperately seeking JScript advice.

For Linda Bernat, Natalie Dyen, and Carole Shankin. — *SEE*
For Tracey, love. — *SSL*
For Ellen and our family. Thanks. — *WSK*

Welcome to
Teach Yourself

Welcome to *Teach Yourself*, a series read and trusted by millions for a decade. Although you may have seen the *Teach Yourself* name on other books, ours is the original. In addition, no *Teach Yourself* series has ever delivered more on the promise of its name than this series. That's because IDG Books Worldwide has transformed *Teach Yourself* into a new cutting-edge format that gives you all the information you need to learn quickly and easily.

Readers have told us that they want to learn by doing and that they want to learn as much as they can in as short a time as possible. We listened to you and believe that our new task-by-task format and suite of learning tools deliver the book you need to successfully teach yourself any technology topic. Features such as our Personal Workbook, which lets you practice and reinforce the skills you've just learned, help ensure that you get full value out of the time you invest in your learning. Handy cross-references to related topics and online sites broaden your knowledge and give you control over the kind of information you want, when you want it.

More Answers . . .

In designing the latest incarnation of this series, we started with the premise that people like you, who are beginning to intermediate computer users, want to take control of your own learning. To do this, you need the proper tools to find answers to questions so you can solve problems now.

In designing a series of books that provide such tools, we created a unique and concise visual format. The added bonus: *Teach Yourself* books actually pack more information into their pages than other books written on the same subjects. Skill for skill, you typically get much more information in a *Teach Yourself* book. In fact, *Teach Yourself* books, on average, cover twice the skills covered by other computer books — as many as 125 skills per book — so they're more likely to address your specific needs.

Welcome to Teach Yourself

...In Less Time

We know you don't want to spend twice the time to get all this great information, so we provide lots of time-saving features:

▶ A modular task-by-task organization of information: any task you want to perform is easy to find and includes simple-to-follow steps

▶ A larger size than standard makes the book easy to read and convenient to use at a computer workstation. The large format also enables us to include many more illustrations — 500 screen illustrations show you how to get everything done!

▶ A Personal Workbook at the end of each chapter reinforces learning with extra practice, real-world applications for your learning, and questions and answers to test your knowledge

▶ Cross-references appearing at the bottom of each task page refer you to related information, providing a path through the book for learning particular aspects of the software thoroughly

▶ A Find It Online feature offers valuable ideas on where to go on the Internet to get more information or to download useful files

▶ Take Note sidebars provide added-value information from our expert authors for more in-depth learning

▶ An attractive, consistent organization of information helps you quickly find and learn the skills you need

These *Teach Yourself* features are designed to help you learn the essential skills about a technology in the least amount of time, with the most benefit. We've placed these features consistently throughout the book, so you quickly learn where to go to find just the information you need — whether you work through the book from cover to cover or use it later to solve a new problem.

You will find a *Teach Yourself* book on almost any technology subject — from the Internet to Windows to Microsoft Office. Take control of your learning today, with IDG Books Worldwide's *Teach Yourself* series.

Teach Yourself
More Answers in Less Time

Go to this area if you want special tips, cautions, and notes that provide added insight into the current task.

Search through the task headings to find the topic you want right away. To learn a new skill, search the contents, chapter opener, or the extensive index to find what you need. Then find — at a glance — the clear task heading that matches it.

Defining Entities

A s you learned in the introduction to entities in Chapter 6, an entity is a named chunk of information that is referred to from within a document and placed in the document during processing.

HTML entities are predefined in the HTML specification. In fact, without entities, the HTML specification would be much longer than its current 300-plus pages. As you browse through the specification, you'll find many instances of entities. Examples include %heading;, which represents the six heading elements; %coreattrs;, which lists the declarations for the commonly-used id (identifier), class (classifications), style (stylesheet), and title (element title) attributes; and %i18n;, which lists the lang (language code) and dir (text direction). For example, the events entity lists ten dynamic HTML attributes that trigger scripts when a certain event — such as clicking, double-clicking, or pressing a particular key — occurs. When you specify an events attribute in an HTML document, you can link an event, such as clicking a mouse or pressing a key, with a particular action, such as changing a color. Most HTML elements support the events attributes, so you can imagine the size of the HTML DTD without these shortcuts.

In XML, you can declare parameter entities (PEs) within the DTD and general entities in the non-DTD portions of a document. The HTML code on the preceding facing page illustrates the use of PEs in a DTD. You'll learn about declaring entities in Chapter 8.

A program that processes an XML document runs straight down the document — from the top line to the bottom line. When the program encounters an entity reference, it quickly replaces the entity reference with *replacement text*, the text enclosed within the entity declaration. The processor does this before processing other parts of the document. So, it's important to place entity declarations near the top of the DTD. If an entity declaration is located after an element in which that entity appears, the parser cannot correctly interpret the element's contents.

Learn the concepts behind the task at hand and, more important, learn how the task is relevant in the real world. Time-saving suggestions and advice show you how to make the most of each skill.

After you learn the task at hand, you may have more questions, or you may want to read about other tasks related to the topic. Use the cross-references to find different tasks to make your learning more efficient.

TAKE NOTE

DECLARING DATA ENTITIES

The XML specification states that you can include unparsed external general entities, also known as *data entities*, in your documents. Data entities are produced by external programs that are not related to XML in any way. For example, you can declare a graphic, audio or video file, or a word-processing document in any format — anything that an XML parser will not process. Data entity files are usually binary. However, if you want to import but not process an external text (ASCII) file, you can declare it as a data entity. When you declare a data entity, you must include the NDATA keyword and the file type (such as GIF, AVI, PDF, DOC, JPEG or JPG, MPEG, and so forth). For example:

```
<!ENTITY robin-pic
  SYSTEM ../grafix/robin.gif"
  NDATA gif >
```

This example declares a GIF file called robin.gif. When you declare a data entity, it must be an element attribute with an attribute type of ENTITY (for a single file) or ENTITIES (for a list of files).

REFERRING TO COMMON DELIMITERS IN HTML OR XML TEXT

When you want to insert a <, >, &, or " character as character-data text, think of how a processor will misinterpret the character: it will think that you are starting or ending a tag, or beginning an entity or string. So, in both HTML and XML, use <, >, &, and " respectively, to represent these characters within character data.

CROSS-REFERENCE

For an overview of entities, read the "Utilizing Entities" task in Chapter 6.

106

FIND IT ONLINE

Find a long paper on SGML DTD structure at http://etext.virginia.edu/bin/tei-tocs?div=DIV1&id=ST.

Use the Find It Online element to locate Internet resources that provide more background, take you on interesting side trips, and offer additional tools for mastering and using the skills you need. (Occasionally you'll find a handy shortcut here.)

The current chapter name and number always appear in the top right-hand corner of every task spread, so you always know exactly where you are in the book.

Building the Underlying Structure of a Document

CHAPTER 7

Entity	Parsed/Unparsed	Internal/External	Description
Table 7-4: HTML AND XML ENTITIES			
General	Parsed	Internal	An embedded string that will appear as document content
General	Parsed	External	An imported file that will appear as document content
Character	Parsed	Internal/External	A type of general entity used to represent special characters
Data	Unparsed	External	A type of general entity used to import a non-XML file defined as binary
Parameter (PE)	Parsed	Internal	An embedded string used to enhance a DTD
Parameter (PE)	Parsed	External	An imported file used to enhance a DTD

Listing 7-8: Examples of Entities

```
<!DOCTYPE HTML PUBLIC
  "-//W3C//DTD HTML 4.0//EN">
<HTML><HEAD>
<TITLE>Examples of Entities</TITLE>
</HEAD><BODY>
<FONT SIZE=+2>
The less-than symbol looks like &lt;. 1
<P>The greater-than symbol looks like
&gt;.</P> 2 3
<P>The ampersand looks like &amp;.</P>
<P>The quotation mark looks like &quot;.</P>
</FONT> 4
</BODY></HTML>
```

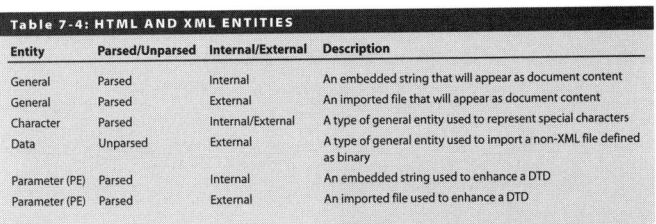

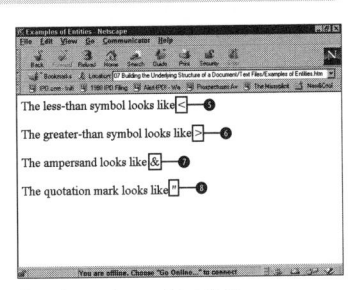

The less-than symbol looks like < 5
The greater-than symbol looks like > 6
The ampersand looks like & 7
The quotation mark looks like " 8

1 Insert the < entity into a block of characters.
2 Enter the > entity to display >.
3 Insert the & entity to display the ampersand.
4 The " entity represents the quotation mark.

5 In a document, the < entity looks like this.
6 The processor interprets > as >.
7 The & entity is displayed as an ampersand.
8 The " entity looks like this.

107

Who This Book Is For

This book is written for you, a beginning to intermediate PC user who isn't afraid to take charge of his or her own learning experience. You don't want a lot of technical jargon; you *do* want to learn as much about PC technology as you can in a limited amount of time. You need a book that is straightforward, easy to follow, and logically organized, so you can find answers to your questions easily. And, you appreciate simple-to-use tools such as handy cross-references and visual step-by-step procedures that help you make the most of your learning. We have created the unique *Teach Yourself* format specifically to meet your needs.

Ultimately, people learn by doing. Follow the clear, illustrated steps presented with every task to complete a procedure. The detailed callouts for each step show you exactly where to go and what to do to complete the task.

Personal Workbook

It's a well-known fact that much of what we learn is lost soon after we learn it if we don't reinforce our newly acquired skills with practice and repetition. That's why each *Teach Yourself* chapter ends with your own Personal Workbook. Here's where you can get extra practice, test your knowledge, and discover ideas for using what you've learned in the real world. There's even a Visual Quiz to help you remember your way around the topic's software environment.

Feedback

Please let us know what you think about this book, and whether you have any suggestions for improvements. You can send questions and comments to the *Teach Yourself* editors on the IDG Books Worldwide Web site at **www.idgbooks.com**.

Personal Workbook

Q & A

1 What do HTML and XML stand for?

_____

_____

_____

_____

2 What is a hypertext link?

_____

_____

_____

3 What is a DTD?

_____

_____

_____

4 What is the difference between HTML and XML?

_____

_____

_____

5 What is an element?

_____

_____

_____

_____

6 What are start tags and end tags?

_____

_____

_____

7 What are attributes?

_____

_____

_____

8 What is the difference between markup and character data?

_____

_____

_____

ANSWERS: PAGE 497

76

After working through the tasks in each chapter, you can test your progress and reinforce your learning by answering the questions in the Q&A section. Then check your answers in the Personal Workbook Answers appendix at the back of the book.

Another practical way to reinforce your skills is to do additional exercises on the same skills you just learned without the benefit of the chapter's visual steps. If you struggle with any of these exercises, it's a good idea to refer to the chapter's tasks to be sure you've mastered them.

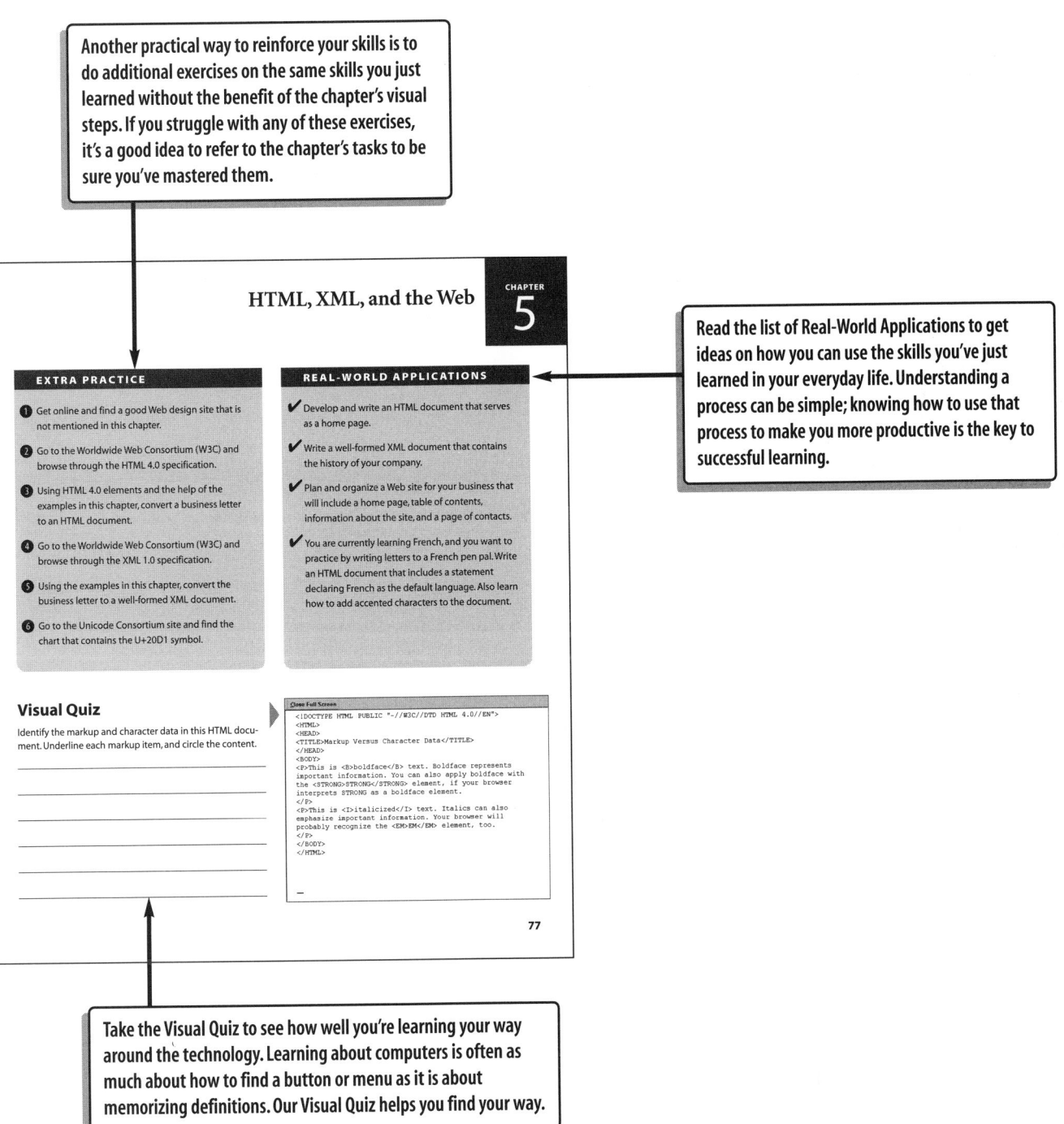

HTML, XML, and the Web

CHAPTER 5

Read the list of Real-World Applications to get ideas on how you can use the skills you've just learned in your everyday life. Understanding a process can be simple; knowing how to use that process to make you more productive is the key to successful learning.

EXTRA PRACTICE

1. Get online and find a good Web design site that is not mentioned in this chapter.

2. Go to the Worldwide Web Consortium (W3C) and browse through the HTML 4.0 specification.

3. Using HTML 4.0 elements and the help of the examples in this chapter, convert a business letter to an HTML document.

4. Go to the Worldwide Web Consortium (W3C) and browse through the XML 1.0 specification.

5. Using the examples in this chapter, convert the business letter to a well-formed XML document.

6. Go to the Unicode Consortium site and find the chart that contains the U+20D1 symbol.

REAL-WORLD APPLICATIONS

✔ Develop and write an HTML document that serves as a home page.

✔ Write a well-formed XML document that contains the history of your company.

✔ Plan and organize a Web site for your business that will include a home page, table of contents, information about the site, and a page of contacts.

✔ You are currently learning French, and you want to practice by writing letters to a French pen pal. Write an HTML document that includes a statement declaring French as the default language. Also learn how to add accented characters to the document.

Visual Quiz

Identify the markup and character data in this HTML document. Underline each markup item, and circle the content.

_____

_____

_____

_____

_____

_____

```
Close Full Screen
<!DOCTYPE HTML PUBLIC "-//W3C//DTD HTML 4.0//EN">
<HTML>
<HEAD>
<TITLE>Markup Versus Character Data</TITLE>
</HEAD>
<BODY>
<P>This is <B>boldface</B> text. Boldface represents
important information. You can also apply boldface with
the <STRONG>STRONG</STRONG> element, if your browser
interprets STRONG as a boldface element.
</P>
<P>This is <I>italicized</I> text. Italics can also
emphasize important information. Your browser will
probably recognize the <EM>EM</EM> element, too.
</P>
</BODY>
</HTML>
```

77

Take the Visual Quiz to see how well you're learning your way around the technology. Learning about computers is often as much about how to find a button or menu as it is about memorizing definitions. Our Visual Quiz helps you find your way.

Acknowledgments

Creating an Internet or computer book requires many hands — from the editors who lead the way to those who lay out the pages — in order to produce the book that you are reading. In this section, we would like to thank all whose support has been so important.

A thank you to our acquisitions editor, Debra Williams Cauley, for your patience throughout these months and to project editor, Barb Guerra, for your professionalism and good humor. Thanks also to copy editor, Eric Hahn; project coordinator, Amanda Foxworth; acquisitions assistant, Christy Clinton; and other members of the team at IDG Books. For his technical knowledge and great attention to detail, thanks very much to our technical editor, Rob Murdoch.

Finally, thanks to the readers of *Teach Yourself ASP*. Please let us know what you think of the book and how we can make the next edition even better.

And on a personal note . . .

Thanks to Matt Wagner of Waterside Productions. For their continued encouragement, thanks to my family and friends. For their important and continuing contributions — Toni and Eli. And in loving memory of Indy and Bart.

Sandra E. Eddy (`eddygrp@sover.net`)

Thanks very much to Tracey Cranston for supporting me throughout this project. Thanks also to my co-authors for their extraordinary work.

Simon St.Laurent (`simonstl@simonstl.com`)

A special thank you to Debra for giving a new author an opportunity to join this team.

W. Scott Kallmeyer (`wsk@rocketmail.com`)

Contents

Contents

CONTENTS

CONTENTS

CONTENTS

CONTENTS

Appendixes

Teach Yourself®
Microsoft® Active
Server Pages 3

PART

I

Getting Ready for ASP

In the good old days — just two or three years ago — pages on the World Wide Web were composed of black, static text and a few graphics on a gray background. You didn't have to worry about formatting, alignments, foreground and background colors, dynamic page objects, animation, or any page design whatsoever — you hadn't even heard of most of the above. The language of choice was one of the many early versions of HTML.

These days, a multitude of technologies — as well as new acronyms — are entering the world of Web-document development at a breakneck pace: You have a menu of markup languages (HTML, XML,

and custom XML-based languages); designer graphics and animation; a bevy of stylesheets (CSS, DSSSL-O, and, soon, the first official XSL recommendation); dynamic and static objects; scripting (JavaScript, JScript, VBScript, Perl, and so forth); database handling; and much more. Now, along comes Active Server Pages (ASP) to make your life a little easier. ASP manages all of the technologies, executes them, and converts them to HTML code that almost any browser can handle.

This part of the book introduces you to ASP, the servers on which ASP executes, and the operating systems that support those servers.

CHAPTER 1

ASP Building Blocks

Active Server Pages, which is a technology developed by the Microsoft Corporation, enables developers to create Web pages that can be viewed with a Web browser after executing on the following: the Microsoft Internet Information Server (IIS) on a Windows NT computer; Personal Web Manager on your own personal computer or on the Windows NT Workstation; and other servers. This approach is in contrast to HTML pages, which are viewed using a browser. Although HTML documents can include scripts, applets, and multimedia objects, the ASP technology is dedicated to the creation of dynamic pages on a base of HTML or XML markup.

You can make an ASP page from a static HTML document: Just change the file extension from `.htm` or `.html` to `.asp`, and you have an ASP document. However, the best ASP pages incorporate a variety of Web technologies, including the VBScript and JScript scripting languages, ActiveX Data Objects (ADO) and ActiveX Server Components, server-side objects (six of which are predefined), and the Microsoft Scripting Runtime library.

ASP documents require both a server and a browser. Supported servers include Internet Information Server (IIS), Personal Web Server (PWS), or any server supported by Chili!Soft ASP. At the time of this writing, Chili!Soft ASP supports the AIX, HP-UX, Linux, OS/390, Solaris, and Windows NT.

ASP makes it easier to enable database transactions. You can replace your CGI scripts with ASP codes and make SQL queries to obtain information from e-commerce and other databases.

This chapter starts by providing an overview of ASP and many of the technologies with which it is bundled. In the following two tasks, you'll learn about how various Windows operating systems (Windows NT, Windows NT Workstation, Windows 98, and Windows 95) support the use of ASP. The IIS server is bundled with Windows NT, and the PWS server is on the Windows 98 installation CD-ROM. You'll be introduced to both servers in this chapter. You'll also find out how to obtain PWS for Windows 95.

After setting up the operating system-server combination, you can get started with ASP. The penultimate task introduces you to converting your HTML documents to ASP pages. Finally, you'll be provided an overview of Hypertext Transfer Protocol (HTTP), which is the set of rules by which Web servers and Web clients communicate.

Introducing ASP

Using Active Server Pages (ASP) technology, you can wrap programming-language code and scripts within standard HTML documents, thereby making your pages dynamic and interactive. You probably know that HTML 4.0 already supports scripting, embedded applets, and interactive forms. However, compared to HTML, ASP is capable of being much more dynamic and interactive.

An ASP document can contain *server-side scripts* — scripts that are interpreted and executed by the server rather than the browser, which is located on the client computer. One advantage of using the server as a base for applications and scripts is that the user's computer is free of excess programs and applets. Another benefit is that the server is often a more powerful computer than the client. Perhaps the most important advantage is that ASP pages are run on the server, and after processing these pages are completely HTML. As a result, most browsers will be able to display the entire content of your pages. To learn more about clients and servers, refer to the following Take Note.

ASP supports and bundles versions of both VBScript and JScript, thereby assuring that your pages are dynamic. In addition, even browsers that do not support scripting can handle your ASP documents. You'll learn more about scripting in Part 3, "Adding Scripts to Documents."

An ASP document can include predefined objects that enable you to transfer information between the browser and the server. You can also extend ASP with additional objects and ActiveX Data Objects (ADO). ASP includes six built-in objects that enable interaction between the server and the browser. The Request and Response objects handle requests and responses to requests. The Server object enables you to create new objects, convert text into HTML, and perform other common tasks. Application manages information about the active application, and Session manages *sessions*, the times when applications are active. The ObjectContext object is used with MTS. ASP also includes Active Server Pages Scripting Objects (Dictionary,

FileSystemObject, and TextStream) in a library named Microsoft Scripting Runtime. Chapters 19, 20, and 21 discuss using objects in your ASP pages.

ASP also supports Active Server Components, which are COM components provided by Microsoft and other companies. Predefined controls include Ad Rotator, Browser Capabilities, Content Linking, and Database Access.

Electronic commerce is an increasingly important component of the Web. Because ASP supports the use of SQL queries, you can use ASP pages to gather information using interactive input forms, place the information in databases, and even ask for more information or send messages to users filling in the forms. To enable transactions, the Microsoft Transaction Server (MTS) is bundled with IIS 4.0. You'll learn about ASP and databases in Chapters 21, 23, and 24.

TAKE NOTE

▶ CLIENT VERSUS SERVER

To differentiate between clients and servers, think of the meaning of the words *client* and *server*. Another term for client is customer. A server *serves* the client. A client computer, which *belongs* to the user (and contains the browser program), makes requests of a server program or server computer. ASP technology, which is based on the server, uses both the server and the client to present Web pages efficiently. In contrast, HTML documents are based completely on the client computer. So, it follows that *client-side* applications run on the client computer, and *server-side* applications run on the server. An interesting article about client-side and server-side objects is located at **http://msdn.microsoft. com/workshop/ essentials/geekspeak/clientvserver.asp**.

CROSS-REFERENCE

Newcomers to HTML can learn about creating documents in Chapters 5 through 13.

FIND IT ONLINE

To link to many ASP resources, go to **http://support.microsoft. com/support/default.asp?PR=asp&FR=0&SD=SO&**.

Listing 1-1: An HTML Document with a Simple Script

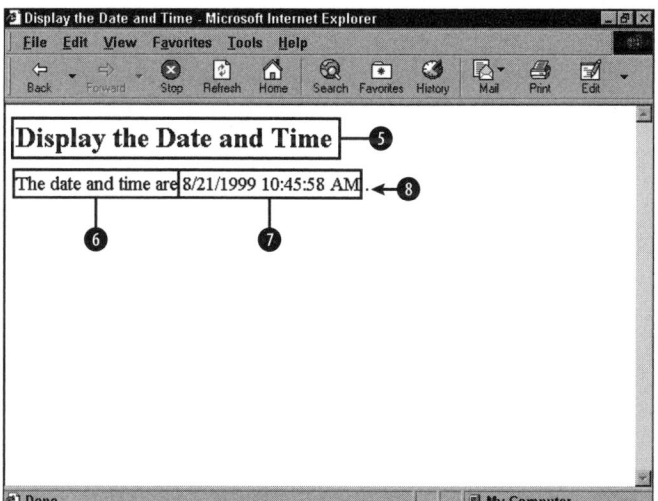

```
<HTML>
<HEAD>
<TITLE>Display the Date and Time</TITLE>
</HEAD>
<BODY>
<H2>Display the Date and Time</H2>
<P>The date and time are
<SCRIPT LANGUAGE="VBSCRIPT">    ← ❷
<!--
Document.Write(Now)    ← ❸
//-->
</SCRIPT>    ← ❹
.
</BODY></HTML>
```

Listing 1-2: An ASP Document with a Simple Script

```
<HTML>
<HEAD>
<TITLE>Display the Date and Time</TITLE>
</HEAD>
<BODY>
<H2>Display the Date and Time</H2>
<P>The date and time are
<%Response.Write(Now)%>.    ← ⓬
</BODY></HTML>
  ❾    ❿              ⓫
```

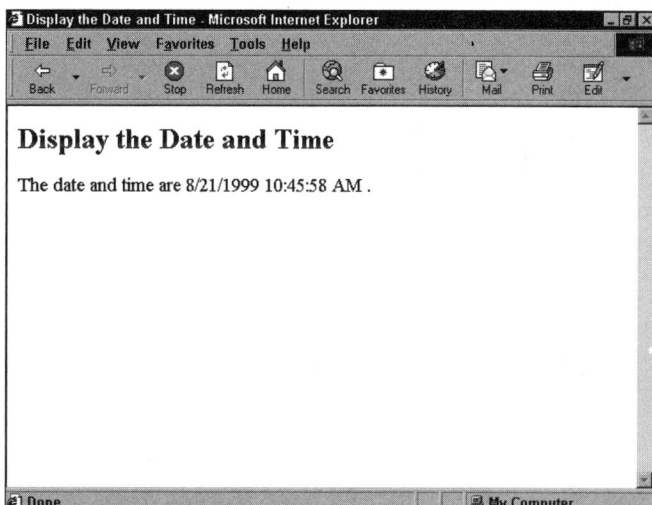

❶ Start a document with HTML.

❷ Identify the scripting language, VBScript.

❸ Insert a script that writes the current date and time.

❹ End the script and add a period to complete the sentence.

❺ Start with an HTML heading.

❻ Insert the start of a sentence written in HTML.

❼ Display the current date and time using a short script.

❽ End the sentence with a period.

❾ Start the script with the <% delimiter.

❿ Change Document to Response, an ASP keyword.

⓫ Complete the script with the %> delimiter.

⓬ End the sentence with a period outside the script.

▶ As you can see, you achieve the same results: ASP understands that the script is written in VBScript.

Learning about Windows Operating Systems and ASP

As you have learned, ASP is primarily a Windows-based technology: ASP runs either on a Windows NT computer using Internet Information Server, or on a Windows NT Workstation or a Windows 98 or 95 PC using the PWS server. (Note that the Chili!Soft ASP application enables ASP to run on servers running other operating systems — such as UNIX, LINUX, HP-UX, Solaris, and so forth. For more information about Chili!Soft ASP, see Chapter 4.) Selecting a computer and a particular type of Windows operating system determines the server that you use, as well as the capacity, speed, and behavior of your Web site. This task examines the various Windows operating systems and discusses their strengths. Note that Table 1-1 (on the facing page) summarizes system requirements for each operating system.

Windows NT Server, which is the most powerful Windows operating system, is capable of handling almost any type of Internet demand. The Windows NT Server includes the Microsoft Transaction Server (MTS), Microsoft Message Queue Server, the Internet Connection Services for Microsoft RAS, and the IIS server. For an overview of the IIS server, see the "Finding Out about the Internet Information Server" task; for additional IIS information (including installation instructions), refer to Chapter 2.

Microsoft recommends Windows NT Workstation for all new business PCs. All desktop PCs with Windows NT Workstation should have Advanced Configuration and Power Interface (ACPI), and notebook computers should have plug-and-play and power management. The Windows NT Workstation includes a version of the PWS server, Version 4.0, that supports service on the World Wide Web and File Transfer Protocol (FTP). PWS includes the Microsoft Transaction Server (MTS), Microsoft Message Queue Server, Microsoft FrontPage Server Extensions, and Microsoft Data Access Components. For an overview of the PWS server, see the "Finding Out about the Personal Web Server" task; for additional information (including installation instructions), refer to Chapter 3.

Microsoft considers Windows 98 to be a consumer operating system. However, you can use Windows 98 with PWS to host a small Web site or a test site.

ASP Versus CGI

The Common Gateway Interface (CGI), which has been a Web mainstay for years, specifies communications between servers and host computers. Both ASP documents and CGI scripts either create dynamic pages or respond to a user filling in a form. However, ASP has several advantages over CGI:

▶ ASP is a technology embedded in HTML documents. Its scripts are processed by the server and displayed by the browser. In contrast, a CGI script calls and executes a separate CGI program on an HTTP server. Unlike CGI, ASP does not need a separate program to run its scripts.

▶ ASP runs on the server and its results are sent to the browser. In contrast, the CGI program is triggered on the browser, processed on the server, and its results may be sent back to the browser. This means that CGI causes more browser-server interaction, which slows processing and may introduce errors.

▶ ASP is *multithreaded*: several scripts can run almost simultaneously. On the other hand, every time a CGI script is run, a new session of a CGI program must start.

▶ ASP developers can get good results from easy-to-use scripting languages such as VBScript or JScript. To get the best results from CGI, a Web page developer should know a full-blown programming language such as Perl, Visual Basic, C, or C++.

CROSS-REFERENCE

Chapters 2 covers IIS, and Chapter 4 discusses PWS — including installation and features.

FIND IT ONLINE

Link to over 60 ASP-related Web sites from http://mavweb.net/asp_links.asp.

ASP Building Blocks

Table 1-1: MINIMUM/RECOMMENDED REQUIREMENTS FOR WINDOWS OPERATING SYSTEMS

Component	Windows NT	Windows NT Workstation	Windows 98
Processor	Intel Pentium 66MHz; 32MB RAM *or* Risc Alpha; 48MB RAM (minimum)	Intel Pentium 66MHz; 32MB RAM *or* Risc Alpha; 48MB RAM (minimum)	Intel Pentium 33MHz; 16MB RAM (minimum)
	Intel Pentium 90MHz; 64MB RAM *or* Risc Alpha; 64MB RAM (recommended)	Intel Pentium 90MHz; 64MB RAM *or* Risc Alpha; 64MB RAM (recommended)	Intel Pentium 90MHz; 32MB RAM (recommended)
Hard Drive	200MB	100MB to 200MB	190MB to 400MB
Monitor	VGA (minimum)	VGA (minimum)	VGA (minimum)
	Super VGA or one that is compatible with Windows NT Server 4.0 (recommended)	Super VGA or one that is compatible with Windows NT Server 4.0 (recommended)	Super VGA (recommended)
Upgrade from: /Used for:	Windows NT/Business of any size	Windows 95 or Windows 3.x/Small business	Windows 95 or Windows 3.x/Consumers

Finding Out about the Internet Information Server

The Internet Information Server (IIS) installed on a Windows NT Server computer combines two powerful Web technologies. Using IIS, you can set up a Web site for your business. According to Microsoft's Internet Information Server 4.0 Data Sheet (**http://www.microsoft.com/ntserver/web/exec/feature/Datasheet.asp**), IIS can support "Web sites that receive millions of hits per day." IIS extends Windows NT features — *scalability* (an application's ability to expand the system to allow for higher numbers of pages and/or visitors to the site), strong security, and integrated applications.

▶ IIS enables you to develop Web pages, publish to both Web and FTP sites, handle file and data sharing, and use the Index Server, which is a sophisticated indexing and search tool.

▶ IIS enables the development and maintenance of Web-based applications using any programming language and full-featured debugging tools. The Java Virtual Machine, which is bundled with IIS, enables developers to use Java applications in ASP.

▶ Because each Web application is run in its own area of memory, each is protected from any applications that crash or degenerate. Once again, scalability is important: it allows applications to handle any number of visitors at one time.

▶ IIS provides tools that make networks, intranets, and Internet sites easy to manage, and you can configure IIS to fit your particular needs. For example, you can use wizards or scripts to create Web sites and directory structures. Or you can use IIS-created log files to analyze activity at your site.

On the facing page, Table 1-2 lists the software and hardware requirements for installing IIS successfully, and Table 1-3 includes the components that are bundled with IIS.

ISAPI Versus CGI

When you install the IIS server or PWS server, the `asp.dll` file is copied onto the target computer. `asp.dll` is compiled into a *dynamic link library* (a file that stores an executable routine that is called by a particular Windows application), which interprets your ASP scripts to access your Web server. `asp.dll` is officially known as an Internet Server Application Programming Interface (ISAPI) extension. An *Application Programming Interface (API)* is a set of tested and stable modules used by an application to interface with the operating system. A programmer simply plugs an API into an application, thereby avoiding the re-creation of commonly-used code.

ISAPI is an improvement on CGI (which is discussed in the previous Take Note). The advantages of ISAPI over CGI include the following:

▶ Tests have shown that ISAPI runs much faster than CGI because a new instance of a CGI program must be opened whenever there is a command. However, the ISAPI DLL is loaded once as part of the HTTP server and enables the use of multiple commands.

▶ As part of the HTTP server, ISAPI can access HTTP resources.

▶ Because ISAPI is bundled with IIS and PWS, it can take advantage of both servers' features — especially their security features.

▶ You can convert CGI scripts to ISAPI easily.

▶ ISAPI can be either an application or a filter. As part of an HTTP server, an ISAPI filter can aid in security and log-in routines. CGI does not provide a filter option.

CROSS-REFERENCE

Chapter 2 covers the installation and explores the features of the Internet Information Server.

FIND IT ONLINE

A Windows intranetting presentation starts at **http://slatertech.com/intranetting/sld001.htm.**

ASP Building Blocks

Table 1-2: REQUIREMENTS FOR IIS

Component	Minimum	Recommended
Operating System	Windows NT Server 4.0 (or later) and Windows NT 4.0 Service Pack 3 (or greater)	Windows NT Server 4.0 (or later) and Windows NT 4.0 Service Pack 3 (or greater)
Required Program	Internet Explorer 4.01 (or later)	Internet Explorer 4.01 (or later)
Microprocessor	90MHz, Pentium; 200MHz, Alpha	90MHz, Pentium; 200MHz, Alpha
Random Access Memory	32MB (Pentium); 64MB (Alpha)	64MB (Pentium and Alpha)
Hard drive storage	200MB	200MB
Monitor	VGA	SVGA

Table 1-3: SELECTED COMPONENTS INSTALLED WITH IIS

Component	Description
Active Directory Services Interface (ADSI)	Helps programmers develop directory-enabled applications
Active Server Pages	Enables server-side scripts using the bundled VBScript, JScript, and other features
Internet Database Connector	Creates, updates, or obtains in ODBC and OLE DB database records
Internet Information Server	Enables you to host any size Web site
Microsoft Certificate Server	Authenticates users of the Web site via digital certificates
Microsoft Index Server	Searches for and retrieves Web information
Microsoft Transaction Server	Enables the development of server (especially database) applications
Windows Media Technologies	Transmits multimedia content to users

Finding Out about the Personal Web Server

The Personal Web Server (PWS) is a server for everyone — from the novice user to the experienced developer. You can install PWS on your Windows 98 and Windows 95 machine, or a slightly different version on your Windows NT Workstation computer. Because PWS is a compact version of IIS, you can upload Web documents from a PWS computer to a Windows NT computer — located either at your office or at your Internet service provider (ISP) — with IIS up and running.

Documents uploaded from PWS computers to IIS computers are completely compatible. This means that you can develop, test, and maintain Web documents on a computer that is entirely separate from the computer on which your Web site or intranet is active. If you operate a small business, you can even use a computer with PWS installed to run a small Web site or corporate intranet.

PWS supports important technologies that enable you to create and serve up dynamic pages that include the latest bells and whistles. PWS-supported technologies include ASP, two popular scripting languages (VBScript and JScript), Server-Side Includes, CGI, Internet Server API, and ActiveX.

The Personal Web Manager is PWS's user-friendly interface. With the Personal Web Manager, you can control PWS completely. For example, you can stop or pause the server or start it again. You can view site statistics, including the number of visitors and requests, the number of bytes transferred, and the number of active connections to your site.

The Personal Web Manager includes two wizards: one for automating the creation of a home page, and another for publishing Web pages. The sophisticated Home Page Wizard enables you to style the home page and include a guest book, a personal inbox, and links to your e-mail address and to other Web pages. You can use advanced features to secure individual directories and to maintain a structure of directories.

On the facing page, Table 1-4 lists the software and hardware requirements for installing PWS successfully, and Table 1-5 includes the components that are bundled with PWS.

The more powerful version of PWS for the Microsoft Windows NT Workstation includes all the Windows 98 PWS features and some from IIS. Extra features include scripting debugging, FTP publishing, and the Internet Service Manager, which is part of the Microsoft Management Console. Both the Internet Service Manager and the Microsoft Management Console help you to administer your Web site.

However, because PWS is regarded as a personal Web tool and should not be used to host large Web sites, it does not include IIS features such as the Microsoft Certificate Server, Microsoft Index Server, or Microsoft Site Server Express.

TAKE NOTE

EVOLVING THE PERSONAL WEB SERVER AND PEER WEB SERVICES

Earlier versions of Windows NT, Windows NT Workstation, and Windows 95 each had their own Web server: Internet Information Server (IIS), Peer Web Services (PWS), and Personal Web Server (PWS), respectively. Personal Web Server evolved from Vermeer, the company that created FrontPage. When Microsoft acquired Vermeer, Microsoft's Personal Web Server replaced Vermeer's Web server. Both IIS and Peer Web Services were developed by Microsoft. Both PWSs were merged as a result of Microsoft's acquisition of ResNova, which had developed a Macintosh-based Web server with a user-friendly interface. After Microsoft developers adapted the ResNova server into Personal Web Server for the Macintosh, they decided that both PWSs should benefit from the user interface to become the Personal Web Server.

CROSS-REFERENCE

Chapter 3 covers the installation and explores the features of the Personal Web Server.

FIND IT ONLINE

View Personal Web Server features at **http://www.microsoft. com/NTServer/web/exec/feature/PWS.asp**.

Table 1-4: REQUIREMENTS FOR PWS

Component	Minimum	Recommended
Operating System	Windows 95, Windows 98 (or later), Windows NT Workstation 4.0 (or later)	Windows 98 (or later), Windows NT Workstation 4.0 (or later)
Required Program	Internet Explorer 4.01 (or later)	Internet Explorer 4.01 (or later)
Microprocessor	33MHz, 486	90MHz, Pentium
Random Access Memory	16MB	20 to 32MB (or greater)
Hard drive storage	20MB (for a Minimum installation)	40MB
Monitor	VGA	SVGA

Table 1-5: COMPONENTS INSTALLED WITH PWS

Component	Installation Type	Description
Active Server Pages	Minimum/Typical	Enables server-side scripts using the bundled VBScript, JScript, and many other features
FrontPage Server Extension	Typical	Enables you to use FrontPage to run your Web site
Microsoft Data Access Components	Minimum/Typical	Supports ActiveX Data Objects and the Microsoft Access driver
Microsoft Message Queue Client	Custom	Enables applications to both process and send messages about transaction completion
Microsoft Transaction Server	Minimum/Typical	Enables the development of server applications, especially related to database processing
Personal Web Server	Minimum/Typical	Enables you to host a small Web site
Visual InterDev RAD Remote Deployment	Custom	Enables you to use Microsoft Visual InterDev to deploy applications on your Web server

Converting Web Pages to ASP

It's quite simple to convert your HTML (and XML) documents to ASP pages. For static, non-scripted Web documents, just change the file extension from .htm or .html to .asp. Of course, to take full advantage of ASP's ability to present dynamic pages, you should add scripts to your pages. You'll learn about writing HTML and XML documents in Part 2, and find out about scripting in Part 3.

When you convert a scripted segment of an HTML document such as this:

```
<SCRIPT LANGUAGE="VBSCRIPT">
<!--

   Document.Write(Now)

//-->
</SCRIPT>
```

to an ASP page, you actually simplify it:

```
<%  Response.Write(Now)  %>
```

The <% and %> delimiters mark the beginning and end of ASP code and replace the <SCRIPT> and </SCRIPT> tags in HTML documents. The comments allow older non-script browsers to ignore the script altogether. (See the following Take Note.)

The most important difference between HTML documents and ASP pages is the location in which processing takes place. As you know, HTML documents run on the browser, which is located on the client (user) computer. ASP pages run on the server, which passes the results to the browser. So, you cannot open an ASP page on the browser and expect dynamic results.

How do you get an ASP page to run? First, you must make sure that the file has an .asp extension, rather than .htm or .html. Then, you must store it in a directory that the server recognizes. (You'll learn more about this for the IIS and PWS servers in Chapters 2 and 4, respectively.) Next, make sure that your server is running. Finally, open your browser program, enter the proper URL (which includes the path to the location of the file), and view the results.

TAKE NOTE

▶ COMMENTING YOUR DOCUMENTS AND SCRIPTS

Comments are an important part of HTML, XML, and ASP documents. Without comments, you or those maintaining Web pages could have problems understanding particular lines of code. To insert a comment in an HTML, XML, or ASP document, enter the <!-- delimiter, type the comment, and end with the --> delimiter. When a browser or processor interprets the document, the comment will not be displayed.

Comments play another part in enclosing scripts in HTML documents. Older browsers may not support scripting. Instead of interpreting a script, a browser may display it as plain text — obviously an unwelcome addition to a Web page. To avoid that situation, surround a script with comments. Newer browsers will ignore the comments and interpret the script.

▶ BUILDING A QUICK TEST DOCUMENT

When you develop ASP pages, you'll want to test them — probably over and over again. One way to do this is to create an HTML page with a set of links to a set of test ASP pages. If you plan to test a maximum of five pages at a time, create five links — whether or not the pages actually exist. For example, you can set up links to testpg01.asp, testpg02.asp, testpg03.asp, testpg04.asp, and testpg05.asp pages. (Remember to include a complete path and to place the files in a directory that the server recognizes. Also make sure that your server is running.) Because the link page is an HTML document, you can use your browser to view the linked-to ASP pages.

CROSS-REFERENCE
In Chapter 14, you can learn more about how scripts and content make up ASP documents.

FIND IT ONLINE
You can link to many ASP resources from http://www.chilisoft.com/sitemap.asp.

Listing 1-3: Another HTML Scripting Example

```
<HTML>
<HEAD>
<TITLE>A Scripted HTML Page</TITLE>  ◄━❶
</HEAD>
<BODY>
<SCRIPT LANGUAGE="VBSCRIPT">  ◄━❷
<!--

     Dim Hello
     Hello = "Hello, World"
     Document.Write Hello

-->
                    ❸
</SCRIPT>
</BODY></HTML>

     ❹
```

Listing 1-4: Another ASP Scripting Example

```
<HTML>
<HEAD>
<TITLE>A Scripted HTML Page</TITLE>
</HEAD>
<BODY>
<% Dim Hello
     Hello = "Hello, World"
     Response.Write Hello   %>  ◄━❼
</BODY></HTML>
              ❻
    ❺
```

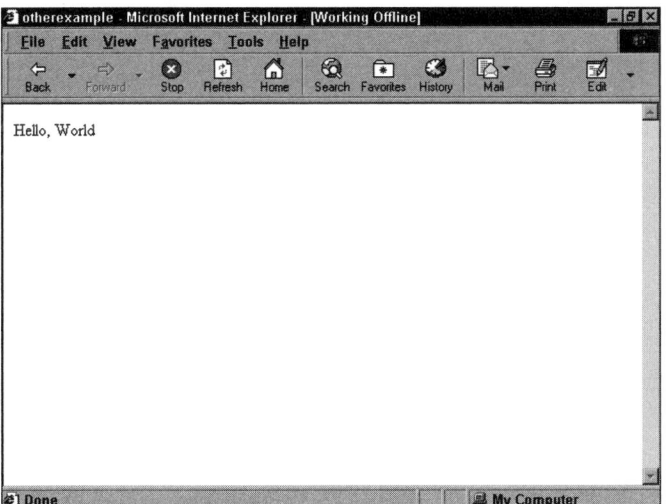

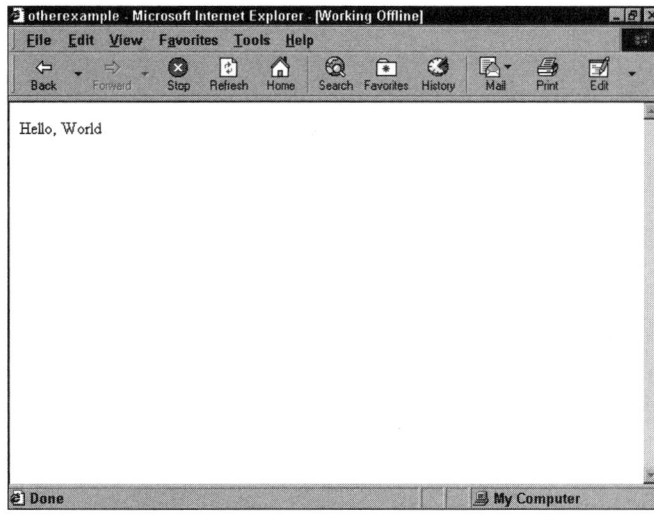

❶ Start a document with HTML.

❷ Identify the scripting language, VBScript.

❸ Insert a script.

❹ End the script and HTML code.

▶ The only text that appears onscreen is generated by the script.

❺ Insert the <% delimiter to start the script section.

❻ ASP recognizes the Response.Write command.

❼ End the script with %>.

▶ In Explorer, the ASP version of the HTML document looks the same onscreen as the HTML-scripted document.

Enabling Transactions Using HTTP

Communications across networks such as the Internet are controlled by *protocols*, which are sets of rules that allow computers running various operating systems to send and receive accurate data. For example, if you want to download a file from an FTP site, the site and your computer use the File Transfer Protocol to communicate and to check for the accuracy of the data being transmitted. Hypertext Transport Protocol (HTTP) is the protocol that enables one computer to send a hypertext document to another. So, HTTP controls the communications between browsers and servers across the Internet. Both IIS and PWS support HTTP. The current version is HTTP/1.1.

HTTP provides several important features:

▶ It enables communications with any number of resources (that is, you can jump from one site to another), while other Internet protocols enable communications with one site only. For example, FTP enables you to transfer files from one site. Then, if you want to transfer another file, you must start another FTP session.

▶ You can use HTTP to perform non-HTTP transfers. So, a Web-page developer can include links to FTP sites — if the server and other software allow it. (The IIS server supports FTP, but PWS does not.) HTTP/1.1 supports transfers by SMTP, NNTP, FTP, Gopher, and WAIS.

▶ HTTP supports data types named in the Multipart Internet Mail Extension (MIME) specification. This ranges from e-mail and plain-text to multimedia data types.

▶ HTTP/1.1 supports *persistent connections*, using a single TCP connection to fetch multiple addresses. Persistent connections make for more efficient sessions using *caching*, which is special storage in memory, and *pipelining*, which enables a user to

request multiple addresses without waiting for responses from each address.

▶ HTTP/1.0 assigned each domain name to different URLs. Now, HTTP/1.1 allows servers to assign a single URL to many Web sites.

You can learn more about HTTP/1.1 by visiting the resources listed in Table 1-6.

TAKE NOTE

▶ LEARNING ABOUT HTTP-NG

HTTP supports client-server communications. Even if an application needs only a small part of HTTP, its developer may have to use much more HTTP code than is required. The Internet Engineering Task Force (IETF) has been discussing how to "modularize" HTTP and make other important improvements. For example, HTTP-Next Generation (HTTP-NG) will add more data types to those currently supported by HTTP/1.1. At the same time, HTTP-NG will not be rewritten on top of previous versions; it will be developed under a new architecture.

According to the HTTP-NG Overview, November 17, 1998: "Modularity is an important kind of simplicity, and HTTP/1.x isn't very modular. If we look carefully at HTTP/1.x, we can see it addresses three layers of concerns, but in a way that does not cleanly separate those layers: message transport, general-purpose remote method invocation, and a particular set of methods historically focused on document processing (broadly construed to include things like forms processing and searching)."

If these three layers were separated into separate modules, HTTP would run much more efficiently and quickly.

CROSS-REFERENCE

Chapter 19 discusses request and response objects, which handle the transmission of queries and forms.

FIND IT ONLINE

The home page for HTTP documents, news, and activities is at **http://www.w3.org/Protocols**.

Table 1-6: SELECTED HTTP/1.1 RESOURCES

Resource	Address	Description
Key Differences between HTTP/1.0 and HTTP/1.1	http://www.research.att.com/~bala/papers/h0vh1.html	A lengthy paper discussing the nine areas of difference between HTTP/1.0 and HTTP/1.1
FAQ — HTTP 1.1 Protocol	http://websitecreations.net/faqhttp.htm	A short FAQ on improving Web performance and learning about HTTP/1.1
Network Performance Effects of HTTP/1.1, CSS1, and PNG	http://www.w3.org/Talks/9704WWW6-WebPerf/overview.htm	A presentation on improving network performance
Preliminary HTTP/1.1 Performance Evaluation	http://www.w3.org/Talks/970115HTTP/overview.htm	A presentation covering an evaluation of HTTP/1.1
HTTP-NG Overview	http://www.w3.org/Protocols/HTTP-NG/1998/11/draft-frystyk-httpng-overview-00	An expired Internet draft that provides an overview of HTTP-NG
Win32 Internet HTTP Functions in Visual Basic	http://msdn.microsoft.com/library/techart/msdn_vbhttp.htm	An article, with a sample application, on using Visual Basic to show HTTP functions
Microsoft Support for Web Standards	http://msdn.microsoft.com/standards/top150/webstandardwp.asp	A white paper on Microsoft's role in open industry standards for the World Wide Web
Top 150 Open Standards & Specifications: Networking	http://msdn.microsoft.com/standards/top150/network.asp	A table — with links — of technologies that Microsoft supports

Personal Workbook

Q & A

1 What does ASP mean? What does it do?

_____

_____

_____

_____

2 What does IIS represent? What is IIS?

_____

_____

_____

3 What does PWS represent? What is PWS?

_____

_____

_____

4 How do HTML documents and ASP pages differ?

_____

_____

_____

5 What is a server-side script?

_____

_____

_____

_____

6 What is scalability?

_____

_____

_____

7 What delimiters do you use to identify ASP code to a server?

_____

_____

_____

8 What does HTTP represent? What does HTTP do?

_____

_____

_____

ANSWERS: PAGE 495

EXTRA PRACTICE

1. Go online and locate an online Web encyclopedia or glossary. Then, find meanings for the following acronyms: HTML, XML, CSS, DSSSL, DSSSL-O, and XSL.

2. Evaluate your computer. Does it meet the minimum or recommended computer and operating-system specifications for running Active Server Pages?

3. Using the Windows help facility, find out about the Personal Web Server or the Internet Information Server.

4. Go online to the Microsoft home page. Search for "Active Server Pages" resources for developers.

5. Go online and find a .PDF version of the HTTP/1.1 specification.

6. Go online and learn about dynamic link libraries.

REAL-WORLD APPLICATIONS

✔ You are a Web page developer who likes to test new technologies on your personal computer. Prepare to set up your PC for running ASP pages.

✔ Your non-profit organization is proud of having had a multipage Web site for four years. However, now the site is looking old and creaky. Choose a new PC with an appropriate server.

✔ Your company plans to set up an intranet. Research and write a report that discusses the selection of computers and operating systems.

✔ You are a Web site consultant. A catalog company with a small, slow-running HTML e-commerce site has requested a report on upgrading its computer system so that it can serve its customers more quickly and post dynamic Web pages.

Visual Quiz

Circle the beginning of the scripting code. Circle the end.

_____

_____

_____

_____

_____

_____

```
<HTML>
<HEAD>
<TITLE>Visual Quiz 1</TITLE>
</HEAD>
<BODY>
<%
    Dim City01, City02, City03, City04
    City01 = "New York"
    City02 = "Los Angeles"
    City03 = "Chicago"
    City04 = "Houston"
%>
<H3>Cities</H3>
<P>These are four top cities in the U.S.
<%
    response.write City01 & " " & City02
    response.write City03 & " " & City04
%>
</BODY>
</HTML>
```

CHAPTER 2

MASTER THESE SKILLS

▶ Planning a Successful IIS Installation

▶ Configuring TCP/IP on Windows NT

▶ Installing IIS and ASP on Windows NT Server

▶ Configuring IIS and ASP on Windows NT Server

▶ Managing IIS and Windows NT Security

▶ Monitoring Internet Information Server Performance

Setting Up Windows NT and Internet Information Server for ASP

In this chapter, you'll learn how to plan for a successful installation of Microsoft Internet Information Server 4.0 and Active Server Pages support on a computer running Windows NT 4.0 Server. In the preceding chapter, you learned about the general relationships between Windows NT 4.0 and Internet Information Server.

You'll also learn about setting up TCP/IP for Windows NT, a key networking protocol that you'll need to have in order to use Active Server Pages and the Web. If you manage your own server, you'll be able to set up a basic configuration for development and deployment. If you have a system administrator who handles that task, you'll know what to request.

In this chapter, you'll install and configure the key application that makes Active Server Pages work: Internet Information Server, part of the Windows NT Option Pack. You'll also explore the management tools you can use to enable (and disable) ASP.

As the Web has provided access to more and more information, the security considerations involved in setting up a Web server have grown enormously. You'll get a guided tour of potential security issues and ways to prevent problems.

Finally, you'll learn how to watch your server in action, simplifying the task of detecting (and eliminating) performance bottlenecks as they occur.

Planning a Successful IIS Installation

Even if you're a developer just setting up a test implementation on a local machine, planning your Internet Information Server installation carefully can save you lots of work later, when you make your site "live" and open it for business. Whether your server is an old PC in the corner or a multiprocessor monster in a carefully-monitored environment, having a clear road map will reduce your frustration levels and increase your chances of having a successful installation the first time around.

First, check that you are using hardware that is up to the task. While serving static Web pages doesn't make too many demands on a server, the processing involved in creating "live" Web pages with Active Server Pages is much more significant. Older and slower computers that seemed perfectly happy running a Web server before you began using ASP will suddenly show their age if you force them to run multiple simultaneous transactions.

While Microsoft claims that any Pentium or Alpha-based computer with 32MB (48MB for Alpha) of RAM is sufficient to run the Option Pack that includes Internet Information Server, even the Microsoft Management Console interface for managing IIS will feel incredibly slow on an older system with too little memory. The actual amount of processing power and memory you need will depend on the traffic you plan to support, but a 200Mhz processor and 64MB of RAM is a reasonable minimum for any server hosting Active Server Pages for multiple simultaneous clients. (A testing system may be able to get away with less.)

The other key factors you'll need to consider are the Web server's role and position in your network. Typically, NT servers used for IIS are configured as plain servers, not as primary domain controllers or backup domain controllers. If someone breaks into your Web server, at least your security and account information is stored someplace else. You can, however, use a domain controller to run IIS if necessary, though performance and security may suffer.

Your Web server also needs a permanent IP address — not the more flexible addresses most clients use. Changing addresses are fine if your computer is the one making requests and finding things, but a terrible inconvenience if your computer is the one being sought. Check with whomever controls your network — your network administrator, your ISP, or yourself — and make sure to get a static IP address.

Finally, you need to know how your Web server is going to relate to the resources it needs to present its information. In the simplest case (shown on the opposite page), a single client (possibly even run on the server itself) will be accessing content generated solely on a single server. In a more complex case, clients will access information created by accessing resources on an entire network behind the server, requiring considerably more infrastructure planning and resource allocation.

TAKE NOTE

▶ PLANNING THE PEOPLE AS WELL AS THE COMPUTERS

A large-scale ASP implementation will require oversight on a regular basis. The sooner you can bring in the network administrators, system administrators, developers, and content providers who will be involved in using your site, the better. Managing the political end of a dynamic site is often as complex as managing the technical end.

▶ USING WINDOWS NT WORKSTATION

If you have a Windows NT Workstation, you can run Peer Web Services, which provides most of the functionality of Internet Information Server, but only supports ten concurrent users. For development, or for very small installations, that may be acceptable.

CROSS-REFERENCE

If you plan to include database resources in your ASP application, be sure to check Chapter 21.

FIND IT ONLINE

Microsoft's general site for information on Internet Information Server, including deployment, is at **http://www.microsoft.com/ ntserver/web/default.asp**.

Setting Up Windows NT and Internet Information Server for ASP

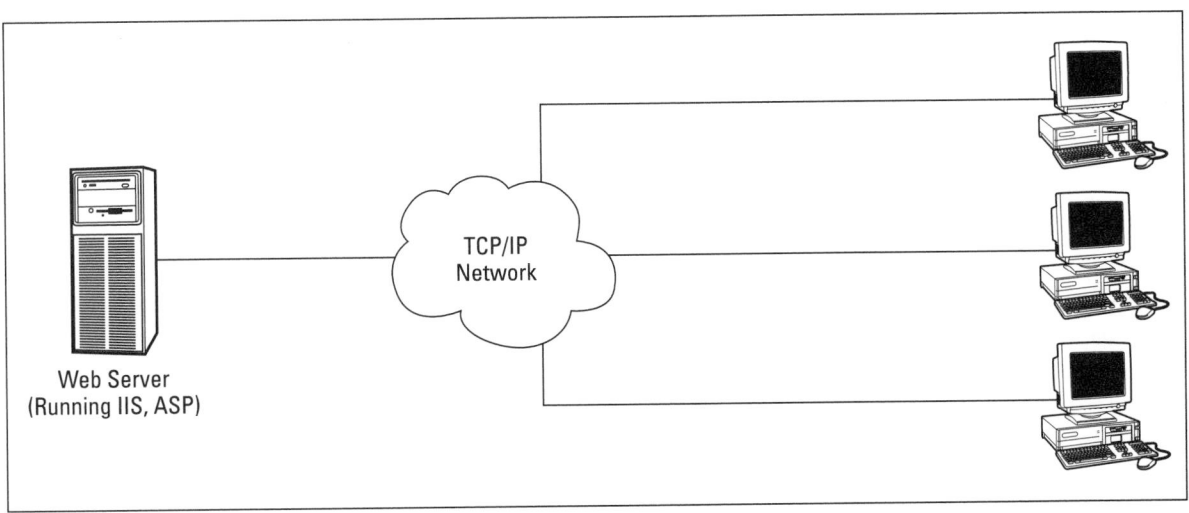

▶ *An ASP deployment may involve a single server connected to clients via TCP/IP.*

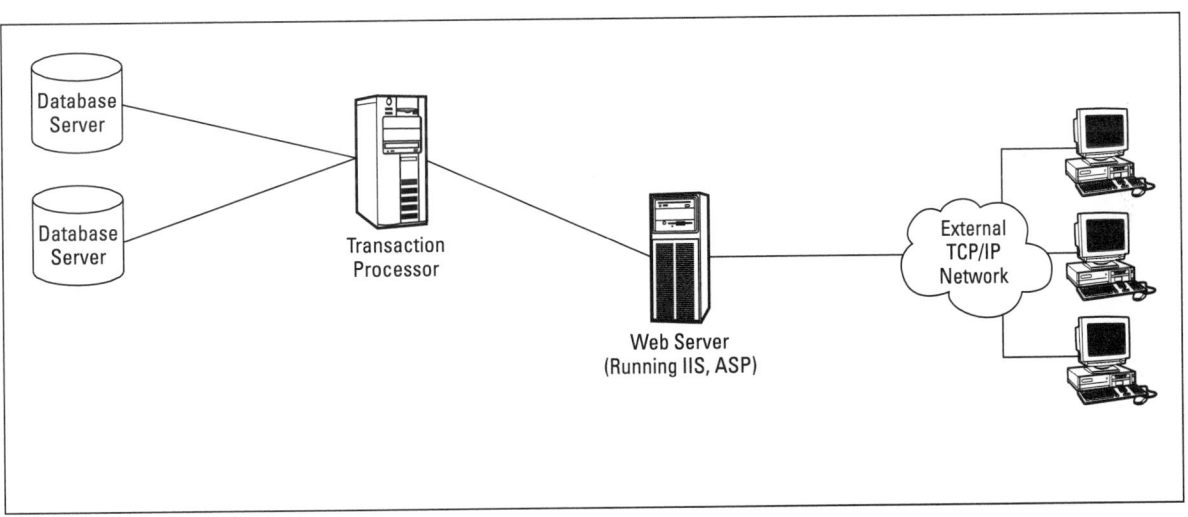

▶ *More complex ASP deployments may use a server and various data sources intricately connected to produce pages for clients.*

Configuring TCP/IP on Windows NT

Using Active Server Pages requires the coordination of a number of subsystems, the most fundamental of which is network connectivity. A server with a misconfigured network is typically invisible to the world, frustrating users and content owners alike. Fortunately, setting up network settings correctly isn't that difficult, though it sometimes takes coordination with a number of other people, primarily your network administrator.

Servers that run IIS must have the TCP/IP protocol installed on them, which is typically done when the server is first installed. (If not, the Add... button on the Protocols tab of the Network control panel will enable you to add TCP/IP.) Servers usually need to have fixed IP addresses.

The simple way to fix an IP address is to enter the address directly in the Network control panel's TCP/IP protocol area, as shown on the opposite page. Using the Advanced IP Addressing area, you can even assign multiple IP addresses to the same adapter card, making it easy to create a server that hosts multiple sites. (Be certain to get the IP addresses, subnet masks, and gateway addresses you use from your network administrator or ISP. Otherwise, you can cause conflicts all over the network.)

If you have an ISP that insists on keeping control over your IP address even though it's fixed, you can select the "Obtain an IP address from a DHCP server" option. (Most DHCP servers can be told to assign the same IP address to a particular computer every time.)

If you need to find out your computers current IP address, the `ipconfig` utility can be very handy. Typing the `ipconfig` command in a command box produces a brief description of your computer's network identity, whether it was fixed in the control panel or acquired dynamically.

```
C:>ipconfig
Windows NT IP Configuration
Ethernet adapter CpqNF31:
IP Address. . . . . . . . : 192.168.124.14
Subnet Mask . . . . . . . : 255.255.255.0
Default Gateway . . . . . : 192.168.124.1
```

Another handy tool for checking on your IP network's status is `netstat`. This command will show you the open connections your computer has with other systems (and sometimes with itself). Using the `-a` switch, making the full command `netstat -a`, displays all of the service ports that are listening, waiting for other computers on the network to contact them and initiate a connection.

TAKE NOTE

NAMING YOUR SERVER WITH DNS

Most Web servers identify themselves by name — like **www.simonstl.com** — rather than by a number. Domain Name Services (DNS) are typically handled by network administrators and ISPs. Contact your ISP or network administrator if you want to refer to your server by name.

ADDRESSES, PORTS, AND SOCKETS

IP addresses are composed of four bytes, typically written as decimal numbers separated by periods. Each IP address identifies a particular computer. Ports are numbered references to programs that ease the task of figuring out which information goes where, and are numbered from 0 to 65535. The combination of an address and a port is called a *socket*, identifying a unique program listening on a host with a particular IP address. Sockets are labeled with the name or number of the host, followed by a colon and the port number, like 127.0.0.1:80.

LOCALHOST

You should always be able to connect to the computer you're currently using at the name "localhost" or at the address 127.0.0.1.

CROSS-REFERENCE

Network configuration will be an issue again when we discuss security in a following section.

FIND IT ONLINE

The comp.protocols.tcp-ip FAQ is available at **http://www.cis. ohio-state.edu/hypertext/faq/bngusenet/comp/protocols/ tcp-ip/top.html**.

Setting Up Windows NT and Internet Information Server for ASP

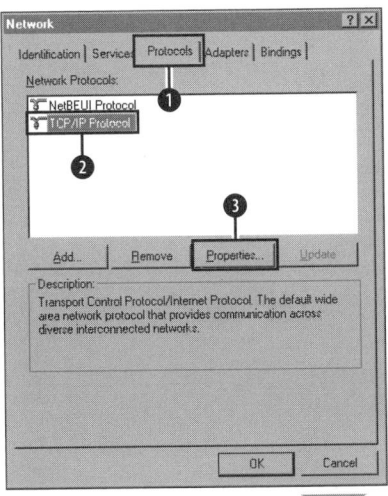

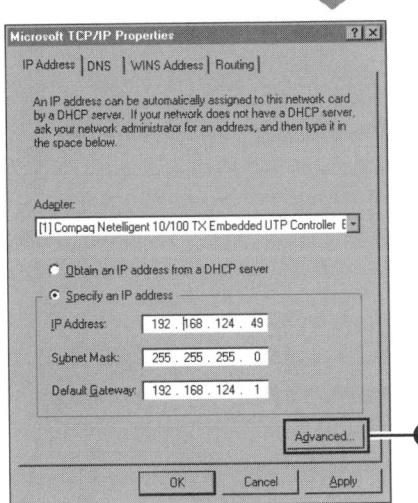

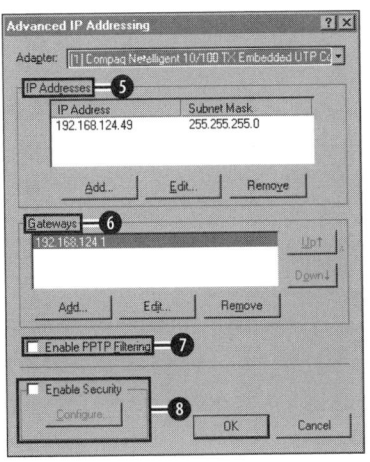

❶ The protocols tab of the Network control panel is the place to start when managing TCP/IP on Windows NT Server.

❷ Double-click the name "TCP/IP Protocol" or select it.

❸ Click the "Properties..." button to open the Microsoft TCP/IP Properties dialog.

▶ The Microsoft TCP/IP Properties dialog provides a quick way to enter a single IP address for each network adapter.

❹ If you need to assign multiple IP addresses, click the "Advanced..." button.

❺ The Advanced IP Addressing dialog enables you to enter multiple IP addresses for each network adapter.

❻ You can also select multiple gateways for traffic leaving this server.

❼ If necessary, enable PPTP filtering. (Note: You typically don't enable PPTP filtering on a Web server.)

❽ This dialog also gives you access to some basic security functionality.

❾ If your network administrator or ISP insists on keeping control of your IP address, select "Obtain an IP address from a DHCP server" and let them do all the work.

25

Installing IIS and ASP on Windows NT Server

Microsoft Internet Information Server 4.0 is a part of the Windows NT Option Pack, available as a free download (though they want lots of information about you) from Microsoft at **http://www. microsoft.com/ntserver/nts/downloads/recommended/N T4OptPk/default.asp**. Windows NT Option Pack also comes with some recently packaged copies of Windows NT Server, so check your CD before beginning a long download of the Option Pack.

The Option Pack includes much more than IIS. Fortunately, the Microsoft site doesn't require you to download everything. All you really need to download is Internet Information Server.

The Option Pack also requires that its host server have Internet Explorer 4.01 or later and Windows NT Service Pack 3 or later installed before the installation of IIS. If you haven't installed these, download them if necessary and install them before attempting to install the Option Pack. (Service Pack 3 is offered as an option during the Option Pack download.)

Warning: You'll need to reboot your server at the end of this installation (and the Internet Explorer installation as well). Be prepared!

Once you have a copy of the Option Pack, you'll need to run the Option Pack Setup program (setup.exe) in the directory holding the Option Pack files. After the usual introduction and license acceptance screens, you may be asked if you want to "Upgrade Only" or "Upgrade Plus," as shown at top left. Select "Upgrade Plus" so you can make sure you've got all the parts you need. (You can always run the setup program again if you missed anything.)

Next, you'll see the screen for selecting the components you want to install or remove, as shown in at top right. Even if you only downloaded Internet Information Server, you'll see a number of options at the top level, including Front Page Extensions, IIS itself, the Microsoft Data Access Components, the Microsoft Management Console (required), and the Microsoft Script Debugger.

Most of these top-level pieces contain a number of subcomponents, which you can select by clicking the "Show Subcomponents" button when the component is highlighted. IIS itself contains a large number of subcomponents, as shown at bottom left. You need to install the World Wide Web Server, which provides HyperText Transfer Protocol (HTTP) services, and the Internet Service Manager to run Active Server Pages. The rest of the components are more or less optional. The SMTP server may be useful if your Web server will be sending out e-mail messages, you may need FTP to upload new files (though it's not a very secure protocol), and the NNTP server can handle basic newsgroup services if you need a news server for your site.

The other area that deserves exploration is the Microsoft Data Access Components, shown at bottom-right. If you don't plan to use a database in conjunction with your Active Server Pages, you don't need to install these, but typically you'll want to make sure that all the subcomponents in this area are selected.

Once you've selected all the components and subcomponents for your needs, click the OK button. After decompressing and installing files, the setup program will need to restart your server. When it comes back up, Internet Information Server should be installed and running.

TAKE NOTE

▶ **OLDER VERSIONS OF IIS**

Internet Information Server 2.0 comes with Windows NT Server 4.0, and Internet Information Server 3.0, which was the first server to support ASP, was available as a download before the arrival of IIS 4.0. If you have one of these older versions (especially IIS 2.0), it's worth the effort to install the update if you plan to use ASP extensively.

CROSS-REFERENCE

You can come back to Option Pack setup and install extra components at any time in the course of this book or your own development.

FIND IT ONLINE

If you have problems with Internet Information Server, you can search the Microsoft Knowledge Base at **http://www.microsoft. com/ntserver/support/searchkb/default.asp**.

Setting Up Windows NT and Internet Information Server for ASP

CHAPTER
2

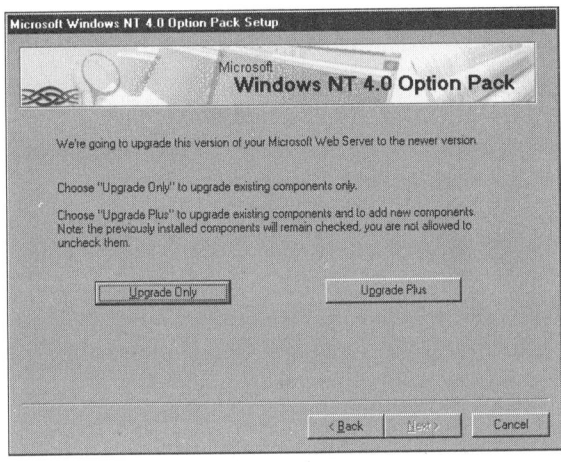

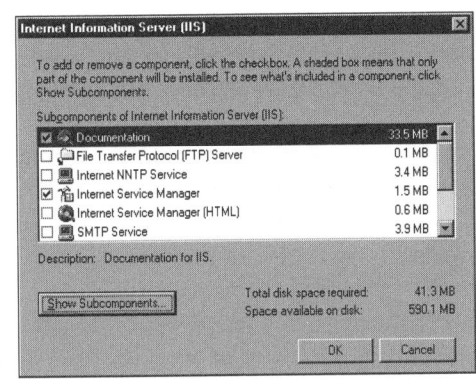

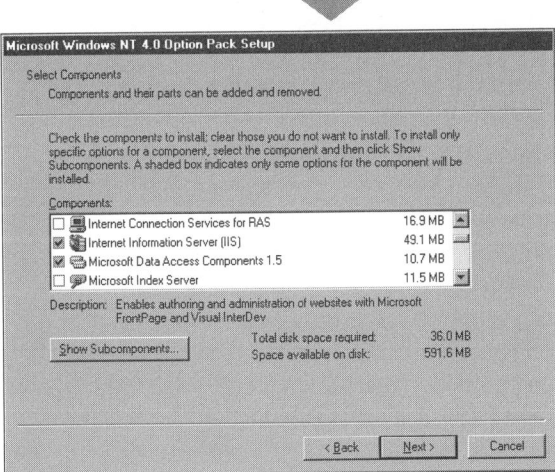

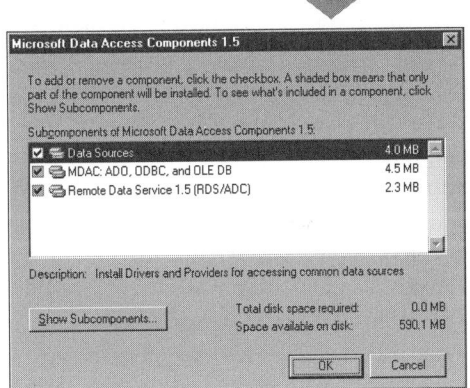

▶ When you install IIS 4.0 on a computer that has an older version installed, you'll see this message. Click "Upgrade Plus."

▶ The Option Pack includes many components that you may choose to install or leave out.

▶ Internet Information Server 4.0 itself includes a wide variety of components.

▶ Be sure to select all of the Data Access Components if you plan to use ASP with databases.

27

Configuring IIS and ASP on Windows NT Server

Active Server Pages is enabled when Internet Information Server 4.0 is installed, and (if you like) you can skip ahead a few chapters and start building Active Server Pages immediately. However, if your site has any security concerns or if you want to manage IIS more tightly, you should definitely become familiar with the Microsoft Management Console (MMC) and the Internet Service Manager that operates inside its framework.

Internet Service Manager enables you to specify where Active Server Pages can operate, what to do if they have bugs, and set parameters governing the behavior of scripts and sessions. Internet Service Manager looks a lot like Windows Explorer; it uses the same set of nested folders and documents to enable you to explore your Web sites rather than your hard drive. You won't see every directory on your system; instead, you'll see the directories, files, and resources relevant to the Web site your server is hosting.

To start managing your Web server, select Internet Service Manager from Start ⇨ Programs ⇨ Windows NT 4.0 Option Pack ⇨ Microsoft Internet Information Server. (You may want to move a copy of the shortcut someplace more convenient.) The Microsoft Management Console will start up, and you'll see a window much like that on the opposite page. (Your particular view may vary, and you'll need to click some of the + signs to expand the tree.)

The MMC gives you the power to change the way ASP applications behave, as shown on the opposite page. If you don't plan to use ASP's Session object to keep track of users as they move through your application, you can tell ASP not to track sessions, thereby reducing your overhead and avoiding sending users "cookies" that they may not want. You can modify the Session timeout, increasing or reducing how frequently a user must visit your site for their information to be kept. Visitors who come by less often than this value will "lose their place" in your application and may have to start some transactions over again. Reducing the value may bother your slower users, but will improve server performance when lots of users are visiting your site. You can change the default scripting language ASP uses; VBScript is the default, and JScript is another built-in option. Finally, the ASP Script timeout lets you tell IIS when to stop processing a script that may have gone into an endless loop or become stuck waiting for a resource, letting it give up and return an error message rather than tying up server resources.

The App Debugging tab has additional options for managing Active Server Pages when things go wrong. Here, you can enable ASP server- or client-side script debugging if you installed Microsoft's Script Debugging tools. (If you didn't, you can go back to the Option Pack installer and add them.) Perhaps more importantly, you can tell IIS how much information to provide when a script has an error. While you're debugging a site, it makes sense to send detailed error messages to clients. When a site goes live, sending those error messages to the public may expose more information about your site than is necessary, and invite hackers to take a closer look. Make certain you tell IIS to "Send text error message to client" when you make a site public.

CROSS-REFERENCE

For more on the Session object and session management, see Chapter 26.

Setting Up Windows NT and Internet Information Server for ASP

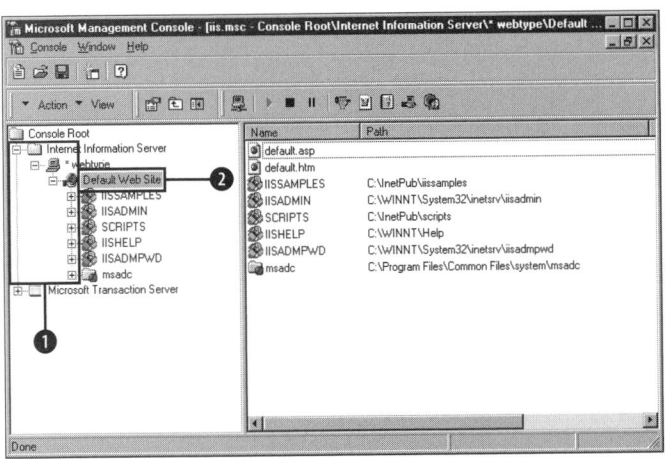

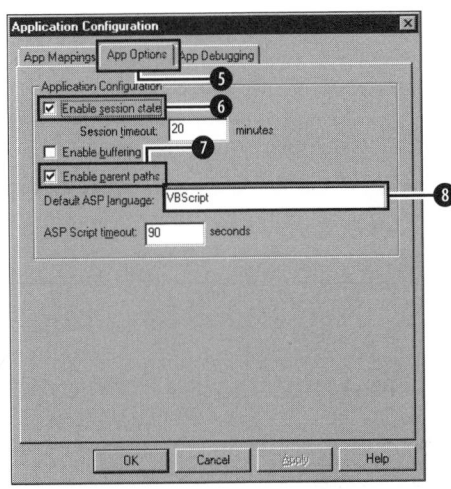

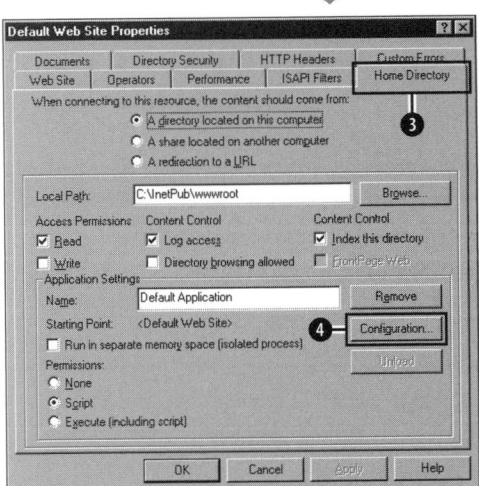

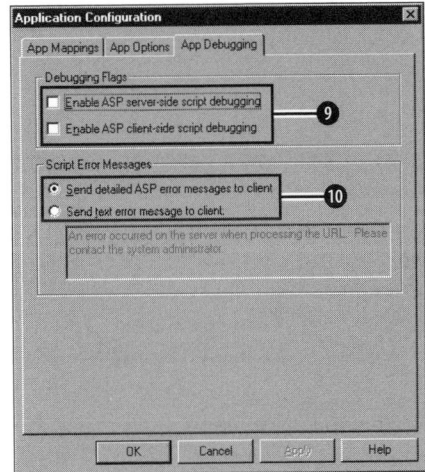

1 The Internet Service Manager presents your Web site configuration. You can navigate by clicking the plus and minus icons.

2 To manage the Active Server Pages settings for a site or a directory, right-click the site or directory name (such as "Default Web Site") and select the Properties... option.

3 The "Home Directory" tab (or just "Directory") enables you to modify how IIS processes Active Server Pages for that site or directory. The Home Directory tab of the site or directory properties dialog enables you to turn scripting on and off, as well as choose directory settings.

4 Clicking the Configuration... button will bring up the Application Configuration dialog box.

5 The App Options tab of the Application Configuration dialog gives you specific control over how Active Server Pages are processed.

6 You can turn off session tracking by unchecking "Enable session status."

7 "Enable parent paths" opens a potential security hole, allowing ASP scripts to reference programs in the directories above their immediate parent paths.

8 The Default ASP language textbox enables you to enter your preferred scripting language.

9 These Debugging Flags checkboxes enable you to enable and disable Microsoft's server- and client-side debugging tools. Make sure that they are unchecked on public sites.

10 The Script Error Messages buttons enable you to select how much information is sent to the client. **29**

Managing IIS and Windows NT Security

Opening a server to the public — even on an internal network — can potentially expose your data and even your databases to unfriendly forces, such as disgruntled employees who take information or crackers (hostile hackers) who graffiti your site quietly and leave you with a mess to clean up (and worse, explain to users and supervisors).

Windows NT, Internet Information Server, and Active Server Pages have had security problems exposed throughout the course of their development, but (hopefully) the current versions of these three critical tools are both safer and more stable than they have been in the past. Many holes have been sealed, though the nature of scripting makes it possible to reopen some of them. The tools are reasonably safe, but developers and administrators still need to be vigilant.

The network architecture you use to connect your site to a public network (whether it is the Internet or an intranet) can provide a first line of defense against intruders. Depending on the scale of your site, a complete firewall solution, a simple proxy server, or some network configuration changes may be enough to protect your information while still allowing the Web server to have some connections to developers and critical resources like databases. The general approach involves closing down the connections your server will accept from the outside, limiting your server's risk.

In a large-scale installation, a firewall or proxy server may insulate the Web server from the outside world, as shown at the top of the opposite page. Even if crackers assault your network, they have to break through the firewall or proxy server first, possibly setting off alarms and providing you with additional time to defend your site. A well-configured firewall or proxy server limits the connections that external systems can establish, providing more flexibility for the systems on the inside.

An alternate approach, shown at the bottom of the opposite page, directly exposes the Web server to the outside world but strictly locks down the connection between that server and external networks. All connectivity to the server outside of its public "Web" face has to come through a separate internal network without a direct connection to the outside world. By limiting the server's communications to a single open Web port (80) and possibly a secure Web port (443), you can minimize the damage that crackers can do to the system.

To block ports on a network card, select the network adapter card that will be facing the public network and follow the steps shown in "Configuring IIS and ASP" to reach the Advanced window's security configuration. Then follow the steps on the opposite page. You'll have to restart the server for these changes to take effect.

You may still have additional work to do. If your server is supporting other protocols, like IPX or NetBIOS, you'll need to disable them, at least for the network adapter facing the public. On the private network, you'll still want to implement regular Windows NT security, making certain that passwords are difficult to crack, directory privileges are limited to those who genuinely need access, and the administrator account's password remains as private as possible. Within IIS, grant the "Execute" privilege to as few directories as possible (preferably none) and make sure that your ASP pages transmit no sensitive information, such as passwords for network resources and databases.

FIND IT ONLINE

For more on Windows NT Server security, visit **http://www.microsoft.com/ntserver/security/default.asp**.

CROSS-REFERENCE

Script security is an issue we'll deal with throughout this book, especially in the sections on databases.

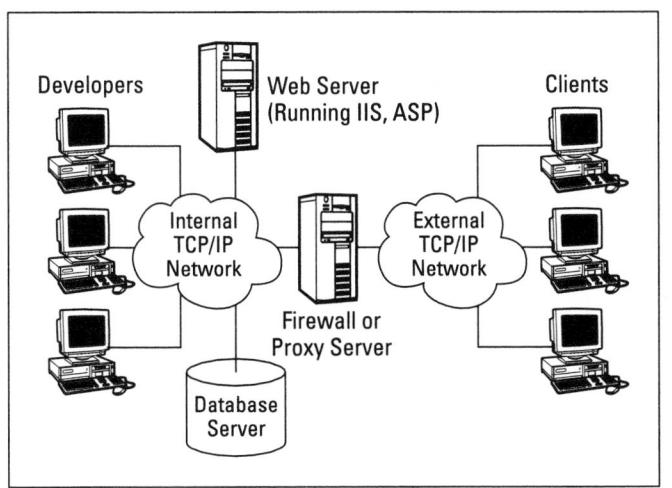

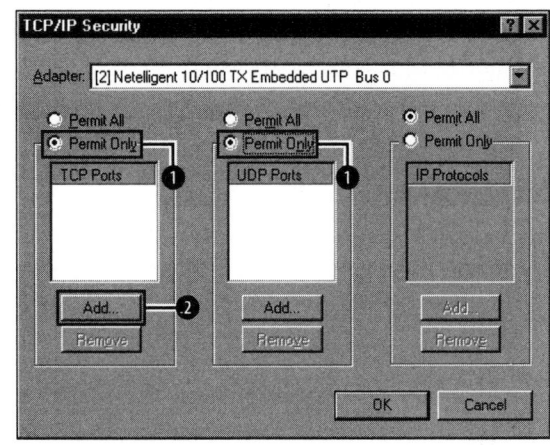

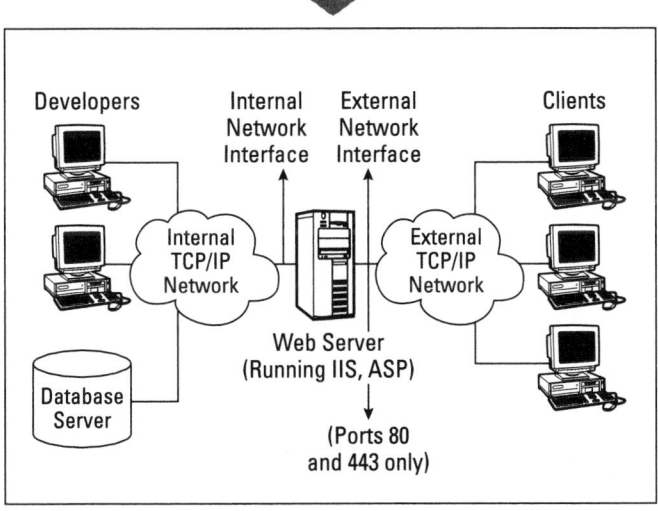

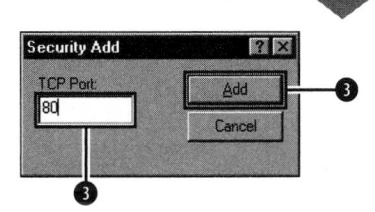

▶ *Using a dedicated firewall or proxy server can simplify and strengthen your security setup, allowing somewhat more flexibility on the internal network.*

▶ *A simpler setup that uses two network adapters in the server requires more vigilance on the public network but can be appropriate for small-scale implementations.*

❶ *The TCP/IP Security dialog enables you to limit IP traffic to approved ports. Select "Permit Only" for the TCP Ports and UDP Ports. (You can do this for IP Protocols as well, though your server will no longer respond to ping, a common network testing utility.) At this point, all TCP/IP network services are cut off.*

❷ *To regain HTTP service, click the "Add..." button underneath the TCP Ports list.*

❸ *Add port 80 to the list, using this dialog box. (If you will be providing secure transactions on this server, you may want to add port 443 here as well, opening up that port.)*

Monitoring Internet Information Server Performance

Throughout the development cycle, and after implementation, you may need to know how healthy your server is feeling. Figuring out ahead of time when your server is overburdened (and from where that burden is coming) can help manage your server and your scripts, enabling you to move from crisis cleanup to crisis prevention. "Ordinary" Web servers (those that don't serve up dynamic content) are fairly easy to monitor, as input/output (I/O) and network traffic bottlenecks can be fixed in a relatively simple manner. When Active Server Pages (and the objects that accompany them) move on to a server, however, performance can vary for an enormous number of reasons, ranging from bad code to an ever-growing set of data that needs to be processed.

Windows NT Server's Administrative Tools include Performance Monitor, a fairly simple (though highly configurable) piece of software for watching your server and its many processes. Internet Information and Active Server Pages connect directly into this framework, becoming components whose appetites for processing and memory can be closely watched. You can even run Performance Monitor remotely, tracking the performance of multiple computers over a network. (You need administrative privileges on those computers to do so, however.)

Performance Monitor can be started from the Start button at the bottom of the Windows NT interface, at Start ➪ Programs ➪ Administrative Tools (Common) ➪ Performance Monitor. The program starts up with an empty screen. To monitor performance, you'll need to tell Performance Monitor what it should be watching.

The Add to Chart dialog box offers a wide variety of options for monitoring your NT server system and Internet Information Server. The Active Server Pages options enable you to monitor ASP closely, separating its performance from the rest of IIS. Monitoring IIS (using the Internet Information Service Global and the Web Service entries) and ASP simultaneously, perhaps with other general measurements of server performance, can give you a good idea of how the different tasks performed by a system are interacting.

The Performance Monitor chart offers lots of customization. Administrators can choose the appearance of the line displaying the measurement, modifying its color, width, and appearance. Perhaps more important is the Scale choice, which enables you to choose a multiplier for the measurement to keep it within the bounds of the chart, which stretch from zero to 100. Requests per second are reasonably measured at a scale of 1 to 1 (unless, of course, you have more than 100 requests per second), but Request Bytes Out Total may need to be scaled down periodically to keep it within bounds.

Once you've chosen the counters you wish to track, Performance Monitor will display a graph updated periodically that displays the most recent status. A red line scans the graph from left to right, leaving behind the most recent information. By default, it moves once per second, though this value can be changed by selecting the Chart... menu item from the Options... menu. You can save and restore your chart options from the File Menu as well, and log performance counters for long-term performance analysis.

TAKE NOTE

▶ WINDOWS NT TASK MANAGER

If you just need a quick snapshot of your system's current status, press Ctrl+Shift+Esc to launch the Windows NT Task Manager. This tool provides a much simpler graph than Performance Monitor of both CPU and memory usage, and its Processes tab provides a process-by-process guide to resource consumption. It has another huge advantage — you can get into it, even when your CPU is pegged at 100%, and shut down misbehaving processes.

CROSS-REFERENCE

For more information about Windows NT optimization, see *Essential Windows NT System Administration* by Aleeen Frisch (O'Reilly, 1998).

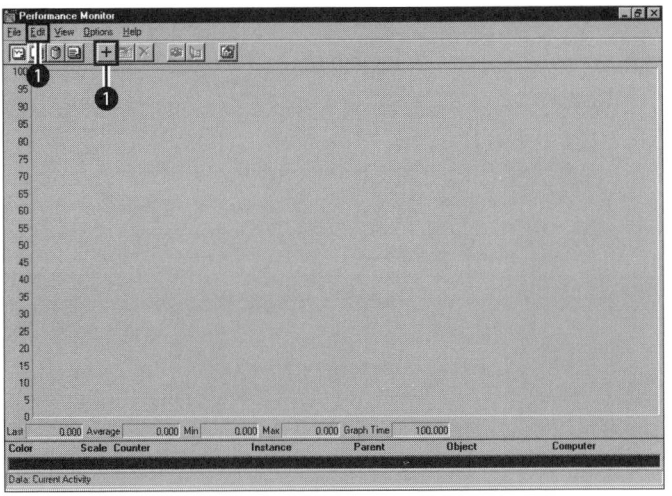

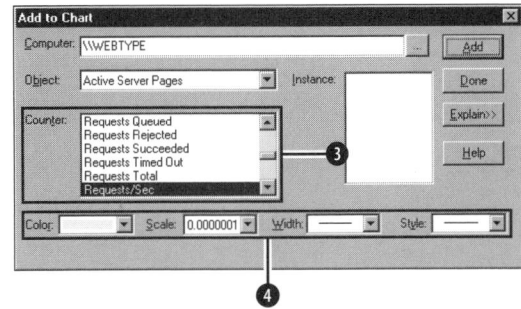

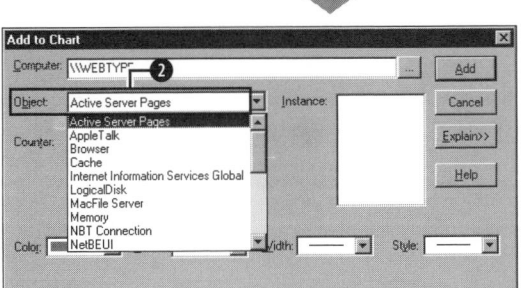

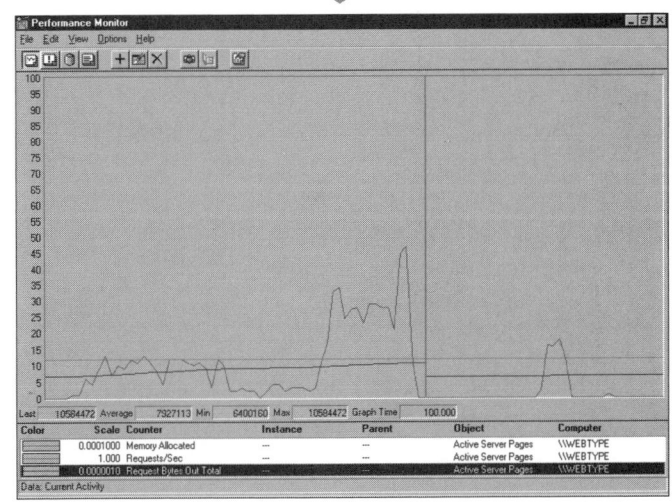

❶ The Windows NT Performance Monitor provides a window into your server's current resource consumption. To add an item to the chart, click the plus sign (+) in the toolbar or choose Add to Chart... from the Edit menu.

❷ To add additional lines on Active Server Pages information, select "Active Server Pages" from the Object drop-down menu.

❸ To choose a particular aspect of ASP performance, select an option from the Counter list.

❹ The options at the bottom of the Add to Chart dialog box enable you to choose how the information will be presented on the chart — color, scale, line width, and line style.

▶ Once you've selected your counters, Performance Monitor will track their values and present them as a changing graph.

Personal Workbook

Q & A

1 Who needs to be involved in planning an Internet Information Server installation?

_____

_____

_____

2 Where can you download and learn about Internet Information Server?

_____

_____

_____

3 Which protocol does NT Server use to transmit information over the Internet?

_____

_____

_____

4 Which protocol does Internet Information Server use to support Web traffic?

_____

_____

_____

5 Which scripting language does Active Server Pages use by default?

_____

_____

_____

6 What tool do you run to administer Internet Information Server?

_____

_____

_____

7 Why do you need to secure Web servers on internal networks?

_____

_____

_____

8 What TCP/IP port does HTTP use? What TCP/IP port does secure HTTP use?

_____

_____

_____

ANSWERS: PAGE 495

1 Install the sample sites that come with IIS and explore them from the Internet Service Manager and a Web browser.

2 Plan Internet Information Server installations for a public site and an internal site.

3 Explore the Internet security advisory systems, such as the **www.cert.org** site.

4 Explore the bindings tab of the network control panel to learn how to connect and disconnect protocols and adapters.

5 Use Performance Monitor to watch NT servers supporting different levels of processing and different types of load.

✔ You are a developer who needs to create an ASP-based Web site using an old computer running NT server. Figure out what you need to connect this computer to your network and install IIS.

✔ You are a network administrator who needs to add a Web server to an existing internal network. What questions do you have for the system administrator and developers?

✔ Your old Web site is looking ancient, and its host server is becoming too slow for the load. Present a transition strategy that will improve your site and make it more exciting using a new NT server and Internet Information Server.

Visual Quiz

Microsoft Management Console enables you to control much more than just ASP. Given the opening screen below, how would you zero in on the ASP controls for your Web site named "WowScript" and turn off the display of full debugging messages for ASP?

_____

_____

_____

_____

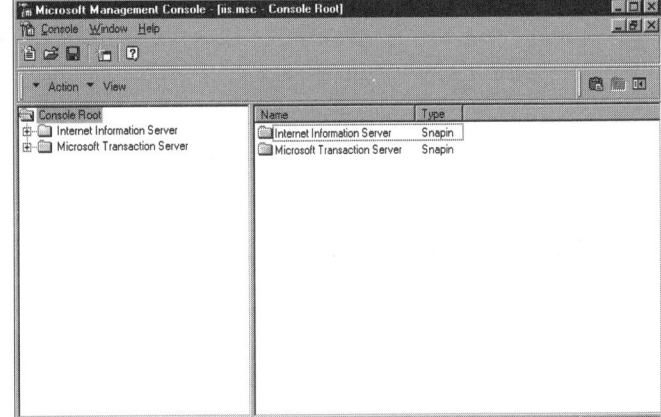

CHAPTER 3

MASTER
THESE
SKILLS

▶ **Fine-Tuning Windows 98 Internet Connections**
▶ **Obtaining and Installing PWS**
▶ **Touring PWS**
▶ **Securing PWS**
▶ **Creating and Publishing Pages in PWS**

Setting Up Windows 98 and the Personal Web Server for ASP

As you learned in the first chapter, PWS is a Web server for the Windows NT Workstation, Windows 98, and Windows 95. You can use PWS to host a small Web site or to test the HTML documents or ASP pages that you will post to the IIS server (or another server that supports HTML, ASP, or both). Having a separate test server means that you can maintain and test your Web pages thoroughly before posting them to your everyday server.

PWS 4.0, the current version of the server, is bundled with ASP technology so you won't have to find, download, and install ASP separately. When you install PWS, you also install ASP. PWS also supports CGI, ISAPI (Internet Server API), ActiveX, JScript, VBScript, and Server-Side Includes. Other technologies bundled with PWS 4.0 include Microsoft Transaction Server, Microsoft Data Access Component, and Microsoft Message Queue Server. When you use PWS, you'll be able to use many popular technologies to make your Web pages dynamic as well as feature up-to-date technologies.

This chapter covers the installation of the Personal Web Server (PWS) and a tour of its features. The first task in the chapter provides information about configuring Windows 98 for PWS. After you configure your computer, you can go ahead with the installation of PWS. Because PWS 4.0 is included on your Windows 98 CD-ROM, you won't have to worry about finding PWS online. The second task covers installation and provides download information for those using Windows 95. In the third task, you'll get an overview of the Personal Web Manager, which is the user interface for PWS. When you allow visitors to access your computer, you must protect your files. Using PWS security features, which are covered in the fourth task, you can prevent visitors from browsing through the contents of your PC. Finally, the final task shows how to create a home page and move it and your other Web pages to the proper directories. Throughout the chapter, the Take Notes will provide additional information about certain technical topics as well as PWS features.

Fine-Tuning Windows 98 Internet Connections

In Chapter 2, the "Configuring TCP/IP on Windows NT" task shows you how to set up network connectivity on a Windows NT server. You'll configure a PC running Windows 98 and PWS in much the same way. In fact, if your computer is set up for the Internet, you have already completed this task. If this is the case, you can move on to the following task.

"Configuring TCP/IP on Windows NT" states that servers that run IIS must have TCP/IP installed. The same is true for servers running PWS. To check that the current TCP/IP settings for an individual Internet connection are correct, click the Start button to open the Start menu and select Programs, Accessories, Communications, and Dial-Up Networking — in that order. Double-click the icon for your current dial-up connection. In the dialog box for your connection, click the TCP/IP Settings button, and review the contents of the TCP/IP Settings dialog box. (For an illustration of this process, see the figures and descriptions on the facing page.)

Unlike earlier versions of PWS, the 4.0 version automates most of the configuration for you: the appropriate directories are either shared or not shared, the directory structure is in place, and so forth.

TAKE NOTE

▶ FINDING OUT TCP/IP BASICS

Transmission Control Protocol/Internet Protocol (TCP/IP) originated in the Advanced Projects Research Agency (ARPA) of the U.S. Department of Defense. TCP/IP is two sets (TCP and IP) of *protocols*, or rules, for communications between computers — even those using various operating systems. One computer can always send data to another computer. The important factor is whether accurate data is received. TCP/IP checks for accuracy and ensures that the data is received in the proper order.

An *IP address*, which is a binary number made up of four bytes (for example, 208.199.65.40), identifies a host computer to computers that request communications. Typically, the first three bytes are assigned to a network and the last byte identifies a host computer on that network.

▶ FINE-TUNING WINDOWS 95 INTERNET CONNECTIONS

Checking to see if TCP/IP is set up on a Windows 95 computer is similar to checking Windows NT. To do so, click the Start button, select Settings, and then select Control Panel. In the Control Panel window, double-click the Network icon. In the Network window, select TCP/IP and click the IP Address tab. Then, use "Configuring TCP/IP on Windows NT" as your guide to the proper TCP/IP settings.

CROSS-REFERENCE

Browse through Chapter 2 to learn more about the background of server configuration.

FIND IT ONLINE

At **http://www.helmig.com/j_helmig/pws.htm**, review how PWS is set up on a Windows 95 PC.

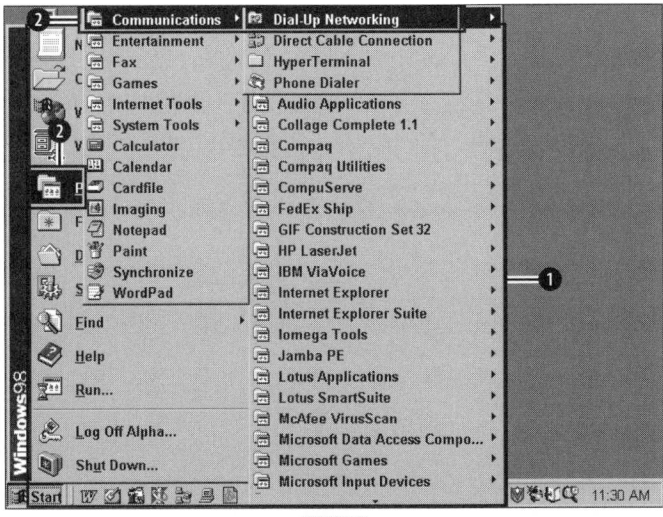

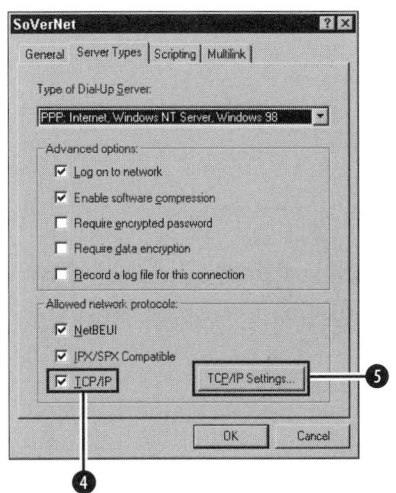

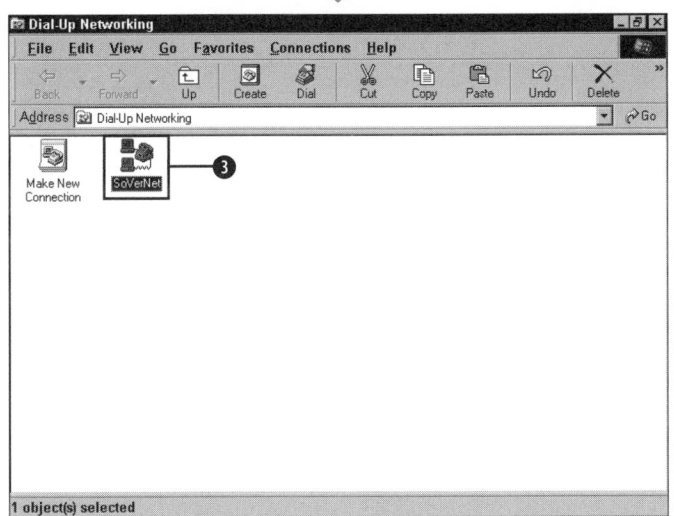

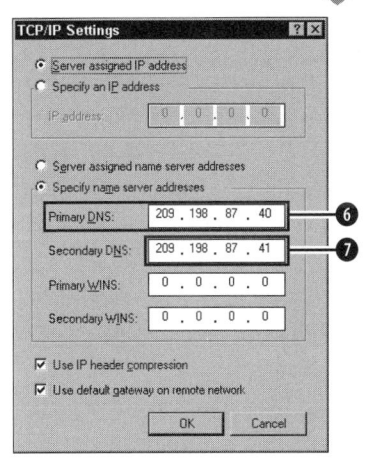

① Open the Start menu.

② Select Programs, Accessories, Communications, and Dial-Up Networking.

③ Double-click the icon for your Internet connection.

④ Make sure that the TCP/IP checkbox is checked.

⑤ Click the TCP/IP Settings button.

⑥ Enter a primary domain name system (DNS) identifier for the host.

⑦ Optionally, enter a second DNS.

Obtaining and Installing PWS

If you are running Windows 98 on your computer, it's simple to find and install PWS. Its setup file is located in the addins\pws folder on the Windows 98 CD-ROM.

If, however, you are using Windows 95 and want to install PWS, you will have to download the NT 4 (or greater) Option Pack for Windows 95/NT Workstation, which contains PWS. To do so, go to **http://www.microsoft.com/ NTServer/all/Downloads.asp** or **http://www.microsoft. com/windows/ie/pws/main.htm**. Then, follow the instructions for downloading.

To install PWS properly, Internet Explorer 4.01 (or greater) must be installed on your computer first. If you are using Windows 98, Internet Explorer is installed automatically. Still, you should make sure that the version is at least 4.01. (A Windows 95 computer may have an outdated version or lack Internet Explorer altogether.)

To install PWS from the Windows 98 CD-ROM, follow these steps:

1 Turn on your computer, make sure that Windows 98 is running, and insert the Windows 98 CD-ROM in your CD-ROM drive. If a Windows 98 CD-ROM startup screen appears, click Browse This CD-ROM, double-click the Add-Ons icon, and double-click the PWS icon. Then go to Step 3.

2 If the startup screen does not appear, open Windows Explorer. Then display the succeeding folder contents: click the icon representing your CD-ROM drive, click the icon for the add-ons folder, and click the icon for the pws folder.

3 In the pws folder, double-click the setup icon. After initializing for a few seconds, the Microsoft Personal Web Server Setup window appears (see figures on facing page).

4 Click Next. The next Setup window appears. Continue to follow the prompts until the installation is complete. The remaining figures on the

facing page illustrate the dialog boxes that are displayed before the installation begins.

5 At the conclusion of installation, click Finish. Then, answer Yes to restart your computer.

6 If your computer is not part of a network, rename \windows\hosts.sam to \windows\hosts.

TAKE NOTE

▶ SELECTING AN INSTALLATION TYPE

Windows-based programs often offer three types of installation: Minimum, Custom, or Typical. *Minimum* installation is the best choice if your hard drive space is limited. However, you may miss some important features. *Custom* installation is for experienced users who know the options to select. If you are a novice, selecting Custom can lead to problems such as missing but required components. The safest installation choice is *Typical*, which includes the features and options that the program developers think that you will need.

▶ INTRODUCING THE MICROSOFT TRANSACTION SERVER

One of the components in the Personal Web Server download is the Microsoft Transaction Server (MTS), with which you can develop server applications. In the computer world, *transactions* are single activities in a computer system — typically, related to database processing. MTS supports the use of the Microsoft Component Object Model (COM) technologies and can run under servers such as IIS, PWS, the Microsoft Message Queue Server (MSMQ), and the Microsoft SNA Server. For more information about MTS and how to use it, refer to Chapter 24.

CROSS-REFERENCE

Chapter 1 introduces you to the Windows 98 operating system and the Personal Web Server.

FIND IT ONLINE

Learn how to install and set up PWS at **http://support.microsoft. com/support/kb/articles/Q195/3/48.ASP**.

Setting Up Windows 98 and the Personal Web Server for ASP

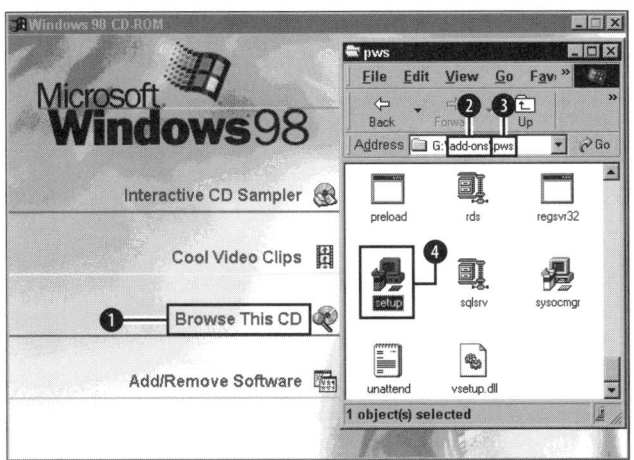

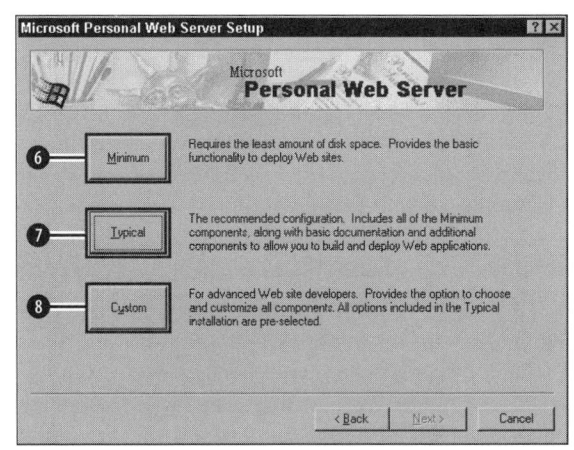

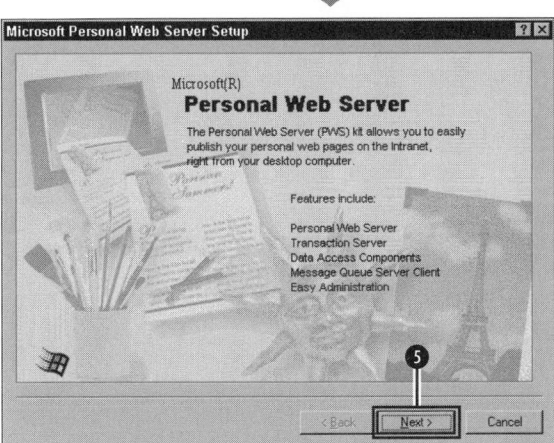

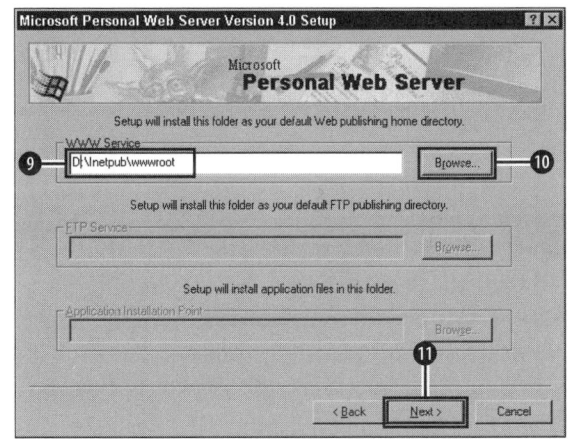

1. *Click Browse This CD.*

2. *Then, double-click the Add-Ons icon.*

3. *Double-click the PWS icon.*

4. *Finally, double-click the Setup icon.*

5. *Click Next.*

6. *Select Minimum to install the minimum number of files — perhaps too few.*

7. *Choose Typical to install minimum files, documentation, and other components.*

8. *Select Custom to choose the files — if you are an expert.*

9. *Either accept or overtype the Web-publishing home directory.*

10. *Or click the Browse button and find an appropriate folder.*

11. *Click Next to move on to the actual installation.*

Touring PWS

Once you start your computer and Windows, PWS also starts automatically. PWS is a terminate-and-stay-resident (TSR) program, which means that it runs constantly in the background—unless you have stopped it during the current computer session. PWS is represented by an icon in the system tray, or task bar, at the bottom of your Desktop and by a shortcut icon on your Desktop. If you can't find the taskbar icon, move your mouse pointer over the task bar, pausing at each icon until you see the following message: *Personal Web Server is running*. To display the main Personal Web Manager window, the user interface with which you control PWS, double-click the icon in the task bar or the shortcut icon.

The Personal Web Manager has five windows (Main, Publish, Web Site, Tour, and Advanced) located on the left side of every Personal Web Manager window. Click an icon to open a particular window.

- ▶ The **Main** window enables you to make your Web site available to anyone who can access the computer on which PWS is installed. You can also monitor the connections to your site and view other related statistics.
- ▶ The **Publish** window features the Publishing Wizard, which enables you to post select files to a Web server. The Wizard also places links on your home page. Note that you must have created a home page before having full use of the Wizard.
- ▶ The **Web Site** window provides the Home Page Wizard, which helps you create a home page without having to learn HTML or scripting.
- ▶ The **Tour** window provides a guided tour to PWS. It's a good idea to use the tour to find out about PWS before you start working on your Web site.
- ▶ The **Advanced** window shows the directories in which pages are stored. The window also enables you to make your site and selected directories

available to visitors and set three types of permissions for selected directories. You can also add, edit, or remove directories in the Advanced window. To learn more about using the Advanced window, refer to the following task, "Securing PWS."

CROSS-REFERENCE

To learn how to use ASP on servers other than IIS and PWS, read Chapter 4.

FIND IT ONLINE

Read an article about using FrontPage and PWS at **http://abiglime. com/webmaster/articles/frontpage/092697.htm**.

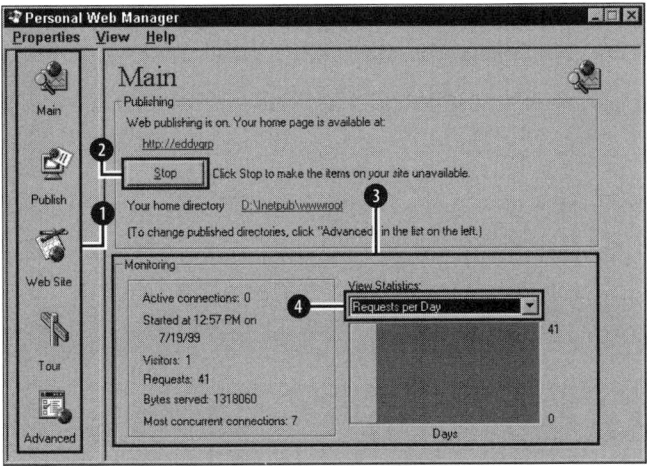

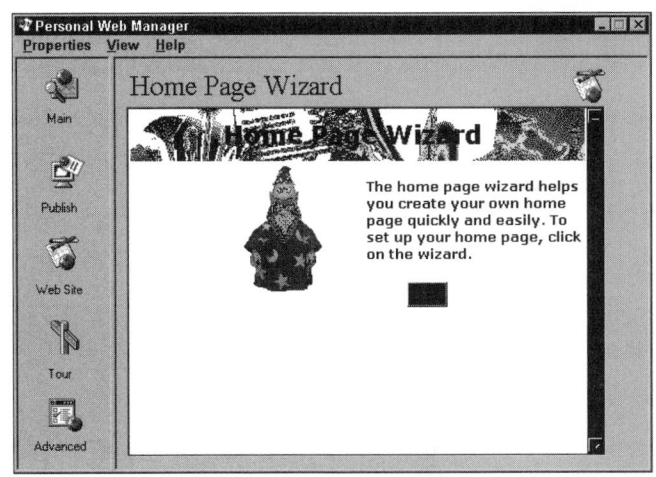

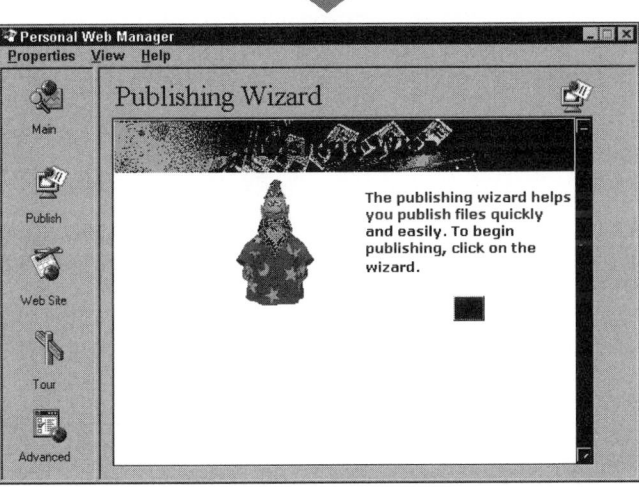

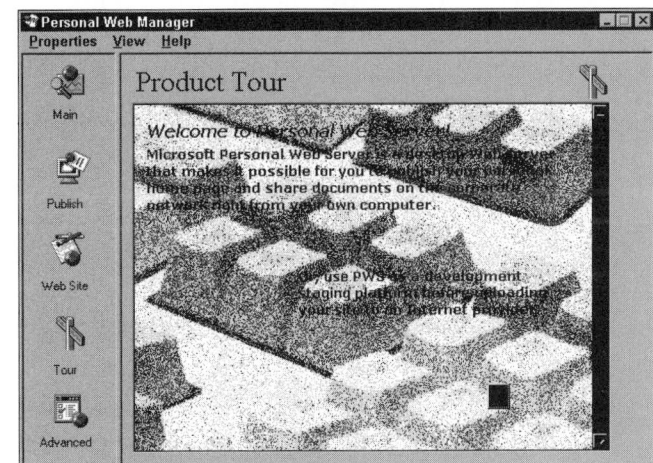

① Click an icon to reveal another Personal Web Manager window.

② Click Stop to make your site unavailable to visitors.

③ Monitor your site in the Monitoring section.

④ Open to view one of four types of statistics.

▶ Publish your HTML and ASP pages using the Publishing Wizard.

▶ Start the Home Page Wizard to create a home page. Then publish it from The Personal Web Manager's Publish window.

▶ Learn about PWS by taking a tour.

Securing PWS

PWS provides several ways to protect your Web site and selected directories — as well as the files stored within them.

- ▶ Control all access to your entire Web site from the Main section of the Personal Web Manager. To stop access, click the Stop button, which then changes to the Start button. To restore access, click Start. (See the top-left figure on the facing page.)
- ▶ Hide or allow access to the contents of a selected directory by clearing or checking the Allow Directory Browsing checkbox in the Advanced section of the Personal Web Manager. By default, the checkbox is cleared (all directories are hidden). (See the top-right figure on the facing page.)
- ▶ Set one of three levels of permissions for those individuals allowed to access a selected directory by going to the Advanced section of the Personal Web Manager, clicking the Edit Properties button, and selecting options in the Edit Directory dialog box. (See the bottom figures on the facing page.)

The first two of these options provide a simple choice of an on-off switch. However, the third option needs further explanation. You can allow visitors to have one, two, or three types of access: Read, Execute, and Scripting.

- ▶ **Read** allows visitors to your site to read or download files stored in an available directory. Give Read permission to directories that contain HTML files. Note that if a directory does not have Read permission, its ASP pages cannot be run.
- ▶ **Execute** controls whether applications (including script engines) can run in the selected directory. Pages that contain only text and graphics should *not* have Execute permission.
- ▶ **Scripts** controls whether script engines can run in the selected directory. Granting Scripts permission without also giving Execute permission means that scripts can run — but applications cannot. This makes Scripts permission ideal for directories that contain ASP scripts only.

If a particular type of permission has not been granted, the visitor who attempts access will see an error message instead of the requested page.

TAKE NOTE

▶ CREATING A NEW DIRECTORY IN PWS

As you start to personalize the PWS directories, you'll want to create subdirectories in which to store documents. To do so, go to the Advanced section of the Personal Web Manager. Select the <Home> directory at the top of the Virtual Directories window. Click Add. In the Add Directory dialog box, click Browse and select the \Inetpub\wwwroot directory (if you accepted the default settings during installation). In the Directory text box, type the new directory name after \Inetpub\wwwroot (see the bottom-right figure on the facing page). After setting permissions and giving an alias (see the following Take Note), click OK. When you create a new directory, that directory is given Read and Script permissions.

▶ NICKNAMING A DIRECTORY

We all have seen URLs so long that they stretch well beyond the limits of your browser window. To create a shorter URL, give it an *alias*, or a nickname. Note that the alias does not replace the original; it's just an alternative. To give an alias to a selected PWS directory, open the Edit Directory or Add Directory dialog box, type the alias in the Alias text box, and click OK.

CROSS-REFERENCE

The "Managing IIS and Windows NT Security" task in Chapter 2 shows you how to secure a server.

FIND IT ONLINE

Go to **http://www.chem.hope.edu/discus/server95.html** to read about recommended servers for Windows 95/98.

Setting Up Windows 98 and the Personal Web Server for ASP

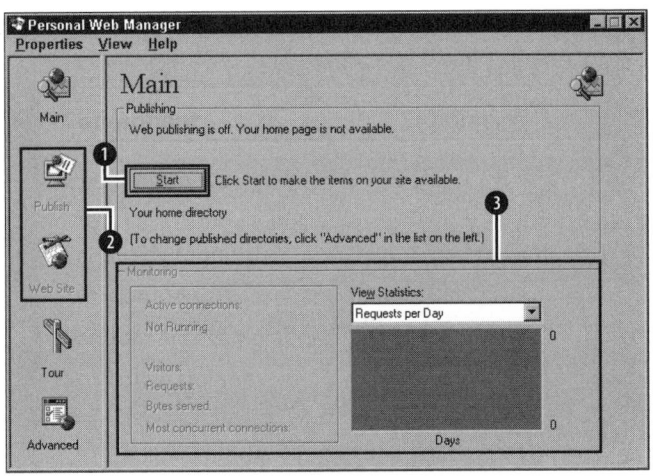

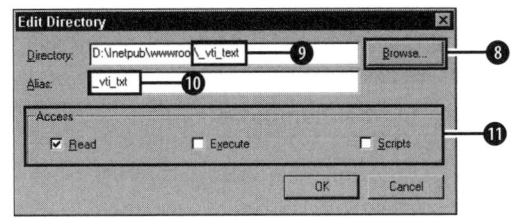

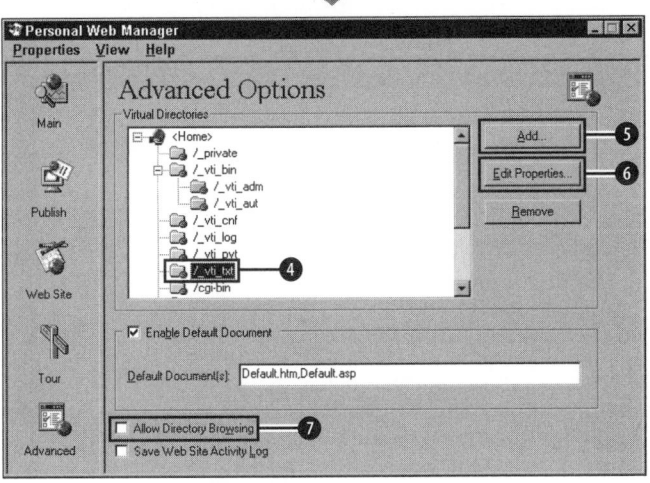

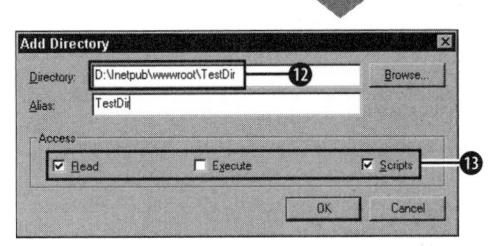

❶ Click the Start button to open your site to visitors.

❷ Publish and Web Site are not available.

❸ Monitoring pauses until you click Start.

❹ Select a directory to work on it.

❺ Add a subdirectory below the selected directory...

❻ Or, edit the selected directory.

❼ Clear to allow the browsing of its contents, or check to prevent browsing.

❽ Click Browse to select a directory.

❾ If necessary, append a subdirectory.

❿ Type an alias.

⓫ Select access to the directory and its contents.

⓬ You can type a directory path.

⓭ You can grant one, two, or three permissions.

45

Creating and Publishing Pages in PWS

PWS provides a Home Page Wizard with which you can create a home page for your Web site. The Wizard enables you to add a guest book (which visitors to your site can use to register their names and addresses) and a drop box (in which visitors can leave messages to you). You can also include as many links as you wish, including one to your e-mail address.

To use the Home Page Wizard, start the Personal Web Manager and click the Web Site icon. Through several screens, the Wizard prompts you to build your home page step by step. First, you can choose a look for your page (by attaching a cascading stylesheet) and decide whether to include the guest book and drop box. Then, fill in text boxes in order to add a title, your name, address, and telephone information to the page. When you have finished filling in the text boxes, click a button and the Wizard completes, saves, and displays your page in an Internet Explorer window. If you wish, you can edit the page by using the Home Page Wizard or by opening the source code in a text editor.

When you publish a page using the Publishing Wizard, you actually copy the page to a chosen directory. The only difference between the Publishing Wizard and Windows Explorer is that the Wizard automates the process and prompts you to add a description. To use the Publishing Wizard, open the Personal Web Manager and click the Publish icon. Click the right-arrow button to open the window on which you will provide information about the file to be published. In the Path text box, either type the complete path — including the file name — or click the Browse button to "build" the path, directory by directory. If the drive in which the file is located is *not* C:, you must type the drive identifier. As a result, you will have access to the desired drive. Type a description of the page in the Description text box. Then, click the Add button to copy the file.

A much easier way of copying the file is to use Windows Explorer. After copying the file, you can continue to work in Windows Explorer, creating directories and subdirectories as well as moving, copying, and even deleting files from your Web site.

CROSS-REFERENCE

The "Monitoring Internet Information Server Performance" task in Chapter 2 discusses IIS monitoring.

FIND IT ONLINE

Use the PWS Knowledge Base (**http://www.studiodeluxe. net/pws/pwsfaq4.htm**) to answer PWS questions.

Setting Up Windows 98 and the Personal Web Server for ASP

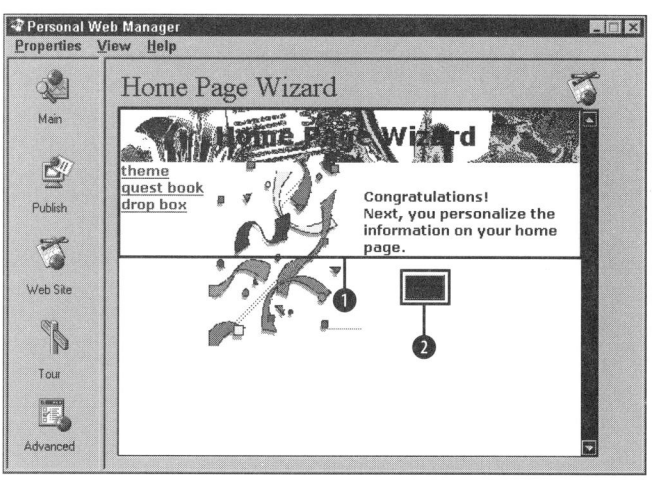

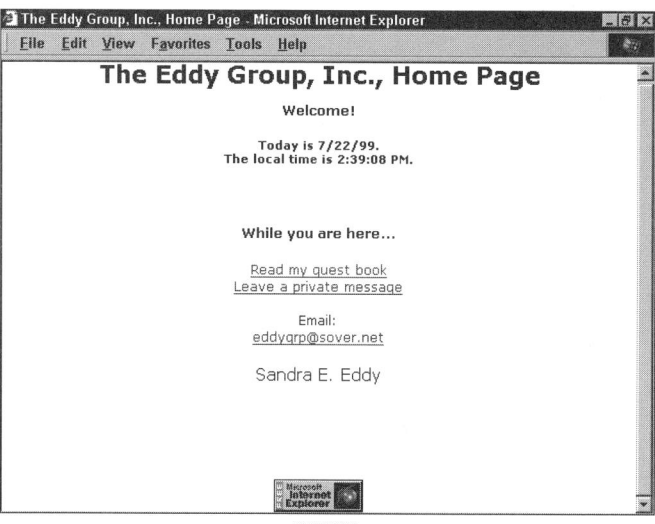

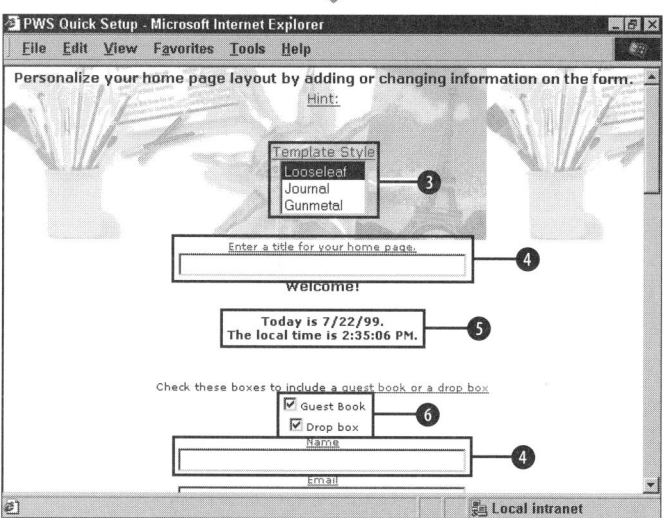

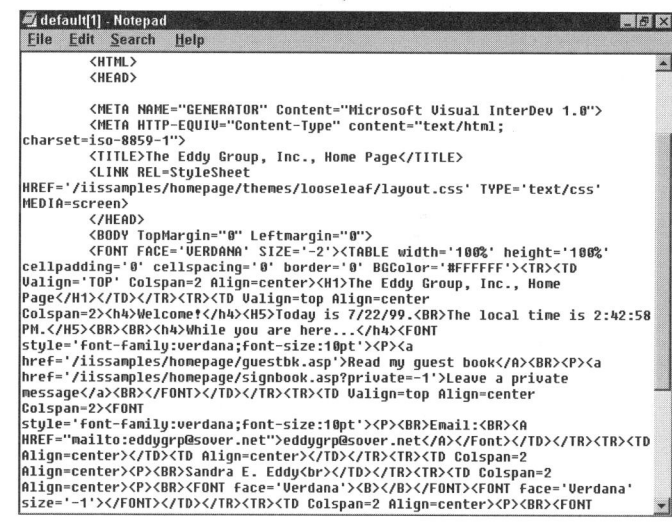

① *A Home Page Wizard window shows your selections.*

② *Click the button to fill in the home page.*

③ *You have a second chance to choose a template style.*

④ *Enter the home page title and your name.*

⑤ *Notice the date and time, which the Wizard added.*

⑥ *To add or exclude components, check or clear.*

▶ *The completed home page includes the components that you or the Wizard included.*

▶ *You can edit the source code displayed in the Notepad window.*

Personal Workbook

Q & A

1 On what platforms can you use the Personal Web Server?

_____

_____

_____

2 What are two ways that you can use PWS?

_____

_____

_____

3 What is TCP/IP and what does it do?

_____

_____

_____

4 What program do you need to install on your computer before installing PWS?

_____

_____

_____

5 What is the name of the user interface for PWS?

_____

_____

_____

_____

6 How do you start a guided tour of PWS?

_____

_____

_____

_____

7 Are the PWS help files stored at an online site?

_____

_____

_____

8 How do you control access to your entire Web site?

_____

_____

_____

ANSWERS: PAGE 496

EXTRA PRACTICE

1 Configure your computer for PWS and then install PWS.

2 Plan a Web site with three levels of directories. How would you change the current PWS directory structure?

3 Use the PWS help system to learn about directory browsing and how to enable it.

4 Go online and find three PWS sites that are not referenced in this chapter or Chapter 1.

5 Create your own home page using the Home Page Wizard and then place it in the proper directory.

6 Using the Personal Web Manager, ensure that the home page directory is available to visitors.

REAL-WORLD APPLICATIONS

✔ You are in charge of your corporate Web site. Plan and design a test site on which new pages will be developed and existing pages will be maintained.

✔ You run a small non-profit organization and want to create, run, and maintain your own informational Web site. Plan a PWS-based Web site.

✔ Your small company currently has HTML documents on its Web site. Create an initial plan to convert to ASP pages on a PWS server.

✔ You are a freelance Web site developer who plans and creates Web sites for small organizations. Write a business plan for Web sites based on your clients' PCs.

Visual Quiz

Look at the figure and answer these questions. How would you make your Web site unavailable? How would you take a tour of PWS? When did the current PWS session start? How would you display a chart that illustrates the requests per hour? How would you set permissions for a particular directory?

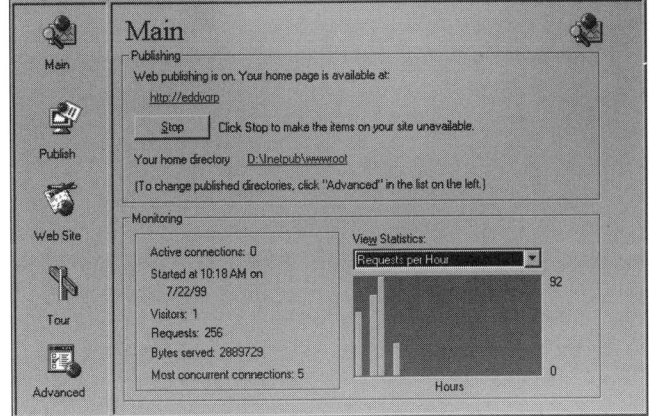

_____

_____

_____

_____

CHAPTER 4

MASTER THESE SKILLS

▶ An Overview of Chili!Soft ASP

▶ Chili!Soft ASP Capabilities and Limitations

▶ Installing Chili!Soft ASP on Windows NT

▶ Additional ASP Alternatives

Using Chili!Soft ASP

In this chapter, you'll learn about several alternatives to Microsoft's environments for running Active Server Pages. You'll also embark on a guided tour of Chili!Soft ASP, an ASP platform that has been available for a number of years. If you have no need to run ASP outside of Windows NT or Windows 95/98, then you can probably skip this chapter safely. If you run a mixed environment where multiple Web servers and/or multiple operating systems are used to host active sites, this chapter can help you make your Active Server Pages sites portable.

You'll start with an overview of Chili!Soft ASP, an environment for running Active Server Pages on Windows NT and Solaris (the UNIX flavor from Sun Microsystems). Chili!Soft has re-created Windows-specific and IIS-specific components to reproduce the object and scripting models on which Active Server Pages rely.

Moving beyond the overview, we'll kick the tires a bit and explore the costs and benefits of running ASP outside of its home Microsoft environments.

Chili!Soft has put an enormous amount of effort into keeping its ASP compatible with Microsoft's, but there are a few things of which Chili!Soft's product is capable that IIS can't do and vice versa.

After you're familiar with the general architecture of Chili!Soft ASP, we'll move to deployment planning. We'll explore issues ranging from compatibility to scalability to personnel and training to help you figure out how best to add Chili!Soft ASP to your existing Web infrastructure or plan a server around it. Chili!Soft ASP comes in a variety of flavors for different operating environments. We'll demonstrate how to install and configure Chili!Soft ASP under Netscape's Enterprise Web Server running on Windows NT.

After we've explored Chili!Soft ASP, we'll conclude with information on several other implementations of ASP, each of which takes its own approach to supporting Active Server Pages in different environments. While Active Server Pages technology originated at Microsoft, developers are slowly getting a wider variety of choices for ASP hosting environments.

An Overview of Chili!Soft ASP

Active Server Pages has definitely been Microsoft's turf for a long while, but they're willing to share with Chili!Soft, a fellow Seattle-area software development company. Chili!Soft's Active Server Pages implementations have been available nearly as long as Microsoft's, and have long been a staple on Microsoft Developer Network, MSDN.

Chili!Soft ASP is the senior contender to Microsoft in the ASP arena, providing developers with a complete environment for hosting Active Server Pages on Windows NT and UNIX (primarily Sun Solaris and IBM AIX, though additional support for platforms including Linux, HP-UX, and OS/390 may appear). Chili!Soft ASP is a set of components you can add to other Web servers, not a complete Web server in itself, making it easy to integrate your ASP applications with your existing server environment. Chili!Soft has spent an enormous amount of time, especially on the UNIX side, on ensuring complete compatibility with ASP components like Microsoft's Active Data Objects for database access.

Chili!Soft provides a complete ASP development environment. VBScript and JavaScript are both supported, and all of the objects built into the Active Server Pages engine are available for use. Chili!Soft goes well beyond these core components in its Solaris editions, providing versions of the database tools for ASP that work on that platform. The same database calls that were built for the Windows environment can be used on Solaris. (On Windows servers, the database objects are available as part of the operating system.) Chili!Soft also includes additional tools that let it mimic Microsoft Web servers, including FrontPage 2000 support. By combining technology supported by Microsoft with the wider variety of platforms available beyond Microsoft, Chili!Soft takes advantage of the best of both worlds.

The Chili!Soft ASP software supplements its host Web server with ASP functionality. The host server — which can be from Apache, Netscape, O'Reilly, IBM, or Lotus, and run on a variety of operating systems — doesn't need to know anything about Active Server Pages itself. Chili!Soft ASP processes the contents of ASP files and returning the results to the Web server. The Web server just needs to know that Chili!Soft ASP will be used to process all ASP files. ASP applications can work in their own space, without having to interact directly with the host server. The Chili!Soft ASP module connects to the host server to process Active Server Pages, but should otherwise remain out of the way, avoiding possible conflicts with other content-providing mechanisms.

Chili!Soft ASP may not be appropriate for every ASP installation, but offers an easy migration path for sites that have used and are using Active Server Pages to yield a new level of scalability and performance.

TAKE NOTE

▶ CULTURE SHOCK

Using Chili!Soft ASP often involves bridging Microsoft- and non-Microsoft platforms. Developers may use the Windows 95/98 Personal Web Server to build their pages, and then upload them to a UNIX server hosting the Chili!Soft ASP environment. You may need to teach your UNIX administration staff about Active Server Pages and your development staff about UNIX to make things go smoothly.

▶ DEVELOPMENT AND PRODUCTION ENVIRONMENTS

Chili!Soft ASP is designed for high-volume production deployment, and its cost may discourage its use in development-only settings. Plan your development strategy carefully, and allow some time for moving between development environments and final production. Make certain that you test all your work in the final production environment before exposing it to the public. At the same time, make certain your developers understand the rules for Chili!Soft ASP deployment and don't create components that only work in the development environment.

FIND IT ONLINE

Chili!Soft is at: **http://www.chilisoft.com/**.

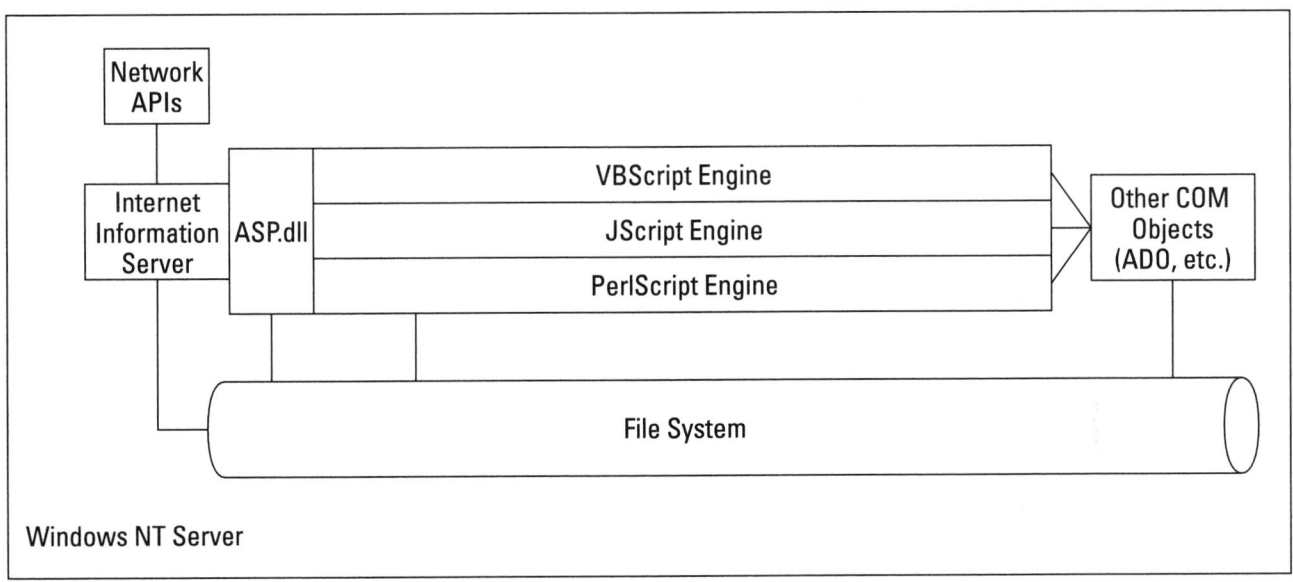

▶ *Even in Microsoft's IIS, Active Server Pages are handled by a set of software modules that add ASP functionality to the core Web server.*

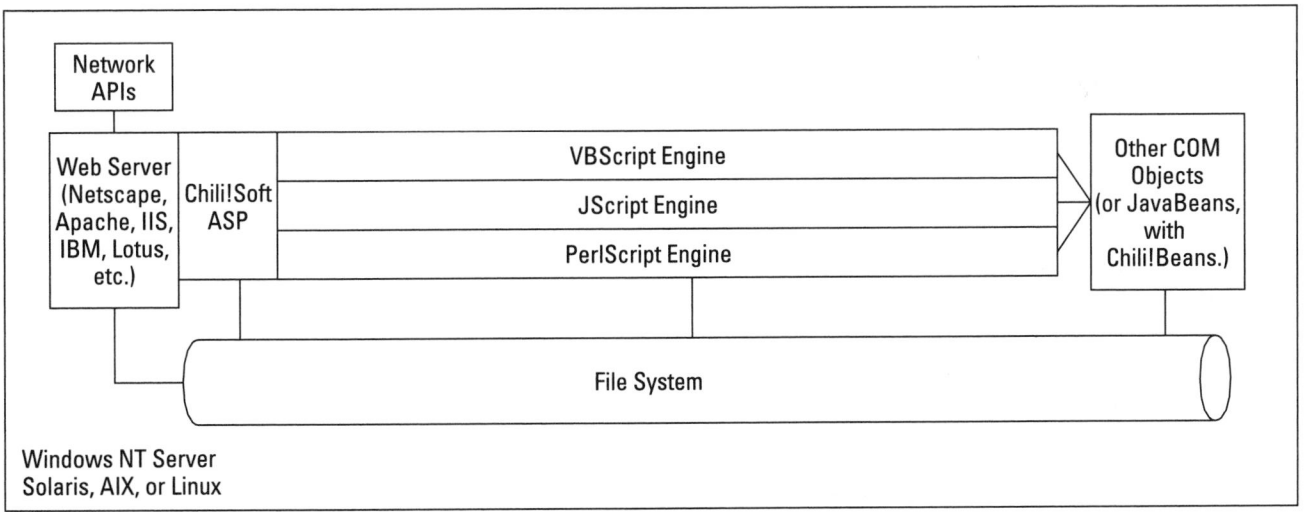

▶ *Chili!Soft ASP uses a similar model to add ASP functionality to a variety of different Web servers.*

Chili!Soft ASP Capabilities and Limitations

Chili!Soft has focused primarily on making Chili!Soft ASP as compatible as possible with Microsoft's implementation of Active Server Pages, and has built a similar set of tools. Chili!Soft does have a few advantages and limitations that are slightly different from those in Microsoft's version, however, and developers should be aware of the extra features as well as the few missing parts.

The main missing features are some of the extras that come in the Windows NT Option pack, notably Microsoft Transaction Server, which Microsoft integrated fairly tightly with ASP in the release of Internet Information Server 4.0. If your site doesn't use databases or if those database needs are simple, this may not be a drawback. On the other hand, if your site acts as an interface to enormous amounts of new and modified data coming in from users, you may need to custom-craft connectivity between your Active Server Pages running on Chili!Soft ASP and a transaction server. The transaction facilities built into Active Server Pages won't work on other platforms, at least not in the current version.

Some of the other components of Internet Information Server, such as the SMTP support and NNTP support, are also missing in Chili!Soft ASP. Building this support into applications isn't difficult, especially on a Web server with general Internet support built into it, but it won't be compatible across other implementations of ASP.

Another set of information that ASP exposes is the server variables for each request. The precise set of variables available changes from server to server. The ASP objects provide a "safe" wrapper around these variables that works across platforms and servers, but some applications may reach into the server variables directly to collect information not provided by the wrappers. If your application depends on certain variables provided by a particular

server and not by others (which can happen, for instance, if your application relies on Windows NT Authentication), you can encounter problems when you move the application to a different Web server that doesn't provide those variables or calls them something different. While the core server variables are fairly consistent, variations in the overall set are common. Sticking to the Request object's interpretation of the server information rather than accessing it directly should avoid these problems entirely.

A few problems may arise because of differences among platforms, not just Web servers. All file names in UNIX are case-sensitive, for example, and use the forward-slash separator (/) instead of the backward-slash separator (\) between directory and file names. Writing code that checks the platform before attempting to access files using a particular convention will help get you out of this trap. Similarly, not all databases are available on all platforms. You can't read and write a Microsoft Access database on a Solaris machine. Choose database formats that work with the system you'll be using, or host your databases on separate machines connected over the network.

Chili!Soft ASP also provides some functionality that doesn't come with Internet Information Server. In particular, Chili!Beans allow developers to access Java code — particularly Enterprise Java Beans — within the scripts of Active Server Pages, much like ASP normally uses COM objects. (Chili!Soft also provides extensive support for COM objects that run outside of Windows using Mainsoft's Mainwin package — you will need to have the source for the components, however, making third-party ports difficult.) Chili!Beans provides a convenient bridge between Active Server Pages and Java, but it may make it more difficult to move your applications back to Microsoft's IIS implementation.

CROSS-REFERENCE

For more on transactions, see Chapter 26. For more about server variables, see Chapter 20.

▶ *Chili!Soft ASP can work with COM objects (either native Windows NT or ported with Mainsoft's Mainwin) just like Microsoft's ASP.*

▶ *If it fits your needs, Chili!Soft's Chili!Beans package will let you use JavaBeans from ASP instead of COM objects, giving you cross-platform access to your logic.*

Installing Chili!Soft ASP on Windows NT

Installing Chili!Soft ASP on Windows NT is a fairly straightforward process, as the installation software does most of the work. For the most part, you just have to tell it where to install its software and select among options. You can choose to skip some components, but for the most part, installation is an automated process.

Make sure that you've installed your Web server before you install Chili!Soft ASP, and then start the Chili!Soft installer. (You can download a 30-day demonstration from **http://www.chilisoft.com**, and Chili!Soft will be more than happy to sell you a longer-term license.) It's easiest if you stop your Web server before installing Chili!Soft ASP, and you will need to restart your NT server at the end of the installation, so try to schedule your installation for a time when the server doesn't need to be available. (Often that's 3 A.M. on production servers, and even that may be difficult.)

After the usual splash screen to welcome you and tell you what software you're installing, the Chili!Soft ASP installer will ask you to accept the license. Next, you'll need to enter your name and organization. The next step lets you choose where in your file system to install Chili!Soft ASP. Chili!Soft ASP isn't particular about where it is installed, so just make sure you put it someplace where there is room and your system administrator approves.

The next two screens let you choose which components to install and which Web server will be acting as host to Chili!Soft ASP. There isn't much point in installing less than the full installation, unless your application has no use for databases, you're paranoid about sample applications, or you have the user guide installed on another machine and don't need it on the production server. The choice of Web server may be more important, especially if

your server is a test server running multiple Web servers simultaneously. (Checking the "Show all supported web servers" checkbox gives you a glimpse at how many servers Chili!Soft ASP supports as well.)

The next few screens tell you to stop your Web server before installing, which gives Chili!Soft ASP unfettered access to your configuration files and lets it connect to your Web server. You'll be notified of the progress of the installation, and at the end you'll be notified that you need to restart the server. You don't have to restart immediately, but you can't use the Chili!Soft ASP functionality until you do.

After you've restarted, it's probably best to check out the samples and make sure that everything is working. (On the Start Menu, select Programs/Chili!ASP/Samples.) Your Web browser will start, and you'll see a selection of examples, all of which use ASP. Choosing any example will start it up. Showing source in your Web browser will only show you the HTML produced by Chili!Soft ASP, but the "View ASP Source" image at the bottom of each example will take you to the code used to generate the page.

TAKE NOTE

▶ REMOVING IIS

If Internet Information Server was installed on the server that will be used for Chili!ASP, you probably want to make sure that it has been removed before beginning the installation of the Web server software you will be using, in order to free port 80 (the standard Web server port) for your use.

CROSS-REFERENCE

All of the network configuration performed in Chapter 2 is applicable to Chili!Soft ASP installations on Windows NT.

FIND IT ONLINE

Information on installing and configuring Chili!Soft ASP on UNIX systems is available at **http://www.chilisoft.com/caspdoc/**.

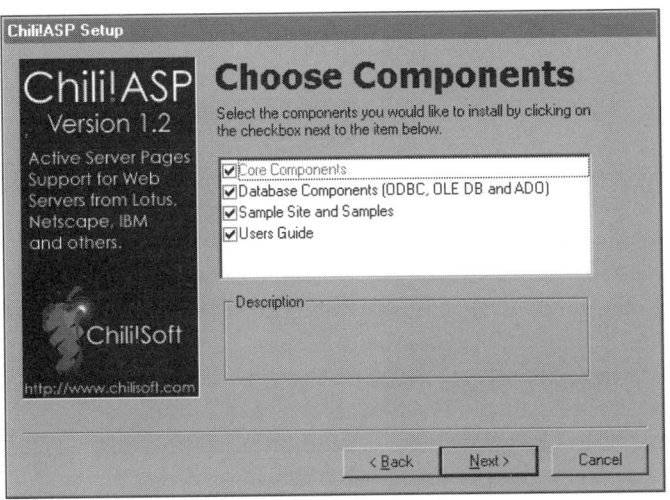

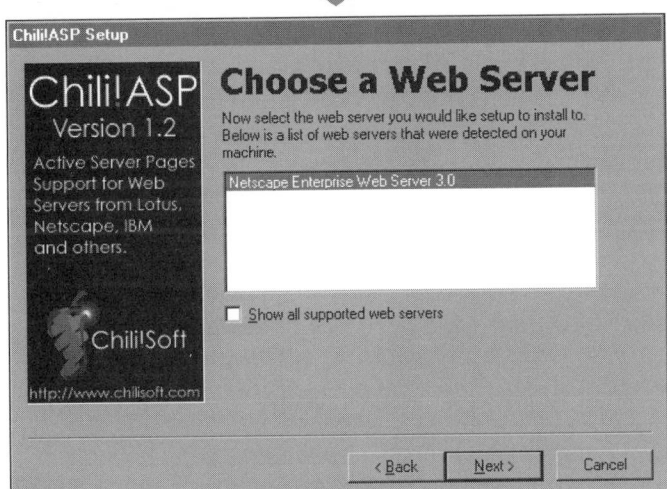

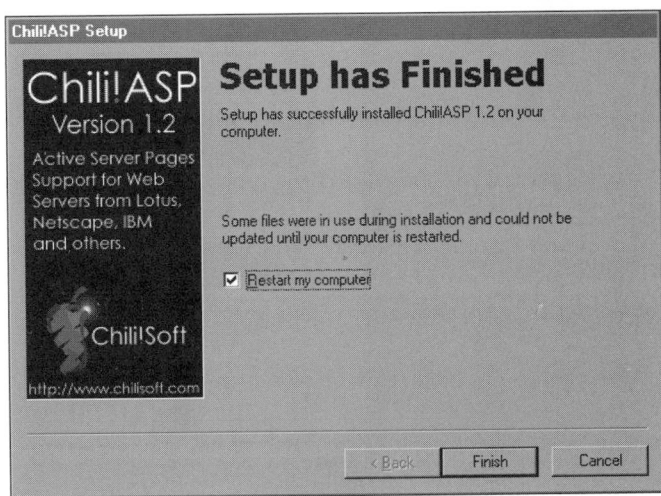

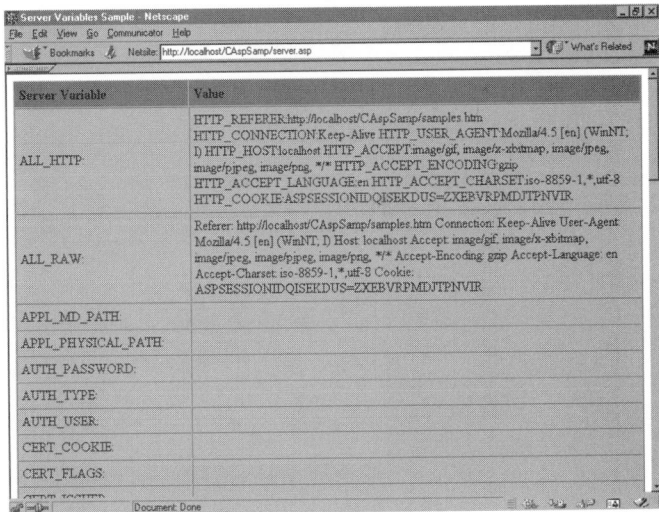

▶ Chili!Soft ASP will need to know which components you want to install. Typically, you'll just install everything, unless you have multiple server installations and don't need extra copies of documentation.

▶ The Chili!Soft ASP installer will search your computer for Web servers and list the servers that can host it.

▶ After you've finished installing Chili!Soft ASP, you'll need to restart your server. You can either reboot from the startup program or reboot manually, but you won't be able to use ASP on your server until after the restart.

▶ Once you've restarted the computer, you can visit the ASP sample pages (from the Start Menu ⇨ Programs ⇨ Chili!Soft ⇨ Samples). This page shows all of the HTTP environment variables in a request.

Additional ASP Alternatives

While Chili!Soft ASP is the oldest alternative to Microsoft's ASP-hosting products, it isn't the only one. The other contenders in the ASP field take different approaches, making them appropriate to a different set of needs and environments. Additional contenders may yet appear as ASP becomes more common; the two solutions in this section are merely the most active alternatives.

Instant ASP (iASP) from Halcyon Software executes Active Server Pages through a Java servlet. This arrangement makes it possible to use ASP on any server supporting Java servlets (including Internet Information Server, if you add a third-party servlet runner). Halcyon Software has combined scripting engines with code supporting ASP's core objects in a Java environment. Unlike Java applets, which often require download and compilation times that get in the way of users, Java servlets are loaded and compiled once, on the server, and then run without additional overhead.

Instant ASP supports the core ASP objects, and can also connect to third-party ASP components using R-JAX, a Java technology that allows Instant ASP processing to access and use COM objects on the local machine (if it happens to be running Windows) or on a remote Windows machine (if necessary). Most Active Server Pages applications should be able to move smoothly from the Microsoft IIS environment to the Instant ASP environment without any modification, unless additional COM objects are involved (in this case, minor modifications to use R-JAX may be required).

Instant ASP also gives ASP pages access to Java-specific components like Enterprise Java Beans, as well as to CORBA (a competitor to COM) objects. Future versions will provide support for Java Server Pages (JSP), enabling developers to mix JSP and ASP on the same server. Halcyon Software also provides a set of Java components for handling tasks like sending e-mail and creating charts and graphics dynamically within iASP.

OpenASP, from the ActiveScripting organization, is providing a free module for using ASP with the open source Apache Web server or the Netscape Web Servers. The same code base is used for both an Apache module and a Netscape NSAPI component. OpenASP is itself open source, and is distributed under the Summit Public License. The host Web server needs to be running the Apache or Netscape servers, but these servers are available for a wide variety of platforms. Because source code is provided, you may be able to custom-compile it to a platform that isn't supported. If OpenASP is missing functionality you need, and you can write the code to provide it, you can make changes yourself (and publish them to other users as well).

OpenASP is still under development, but is already capable of running a wide variety of ASP applications. It doesn't yet support the complete set of core ASP objects — be certain to check the `readme.txt` that comes with the distribution. Also, the `global.asa` file (described in Chapter 22) is not supported as of this writing.

TAKE NOTE

ACTIVESCRIPTING ON THE CLIENT

The ActiveScripting Organization is also working on an open source port of Microsoft's client-side scripting architecture for Mozilla, the next generation of Netscape's browser software.

CROSS-REFERENCE

If you use one of these tools, be sure to check the documentation provided by the tool vendor to be certain all the objects you need are supported.

FIND IT ONLINE

For more information about iASP, including a free version for developers, visit **http://www.halcyonsoft.com**. For more on OpenASP, visit **http://www.activescripting.org**.

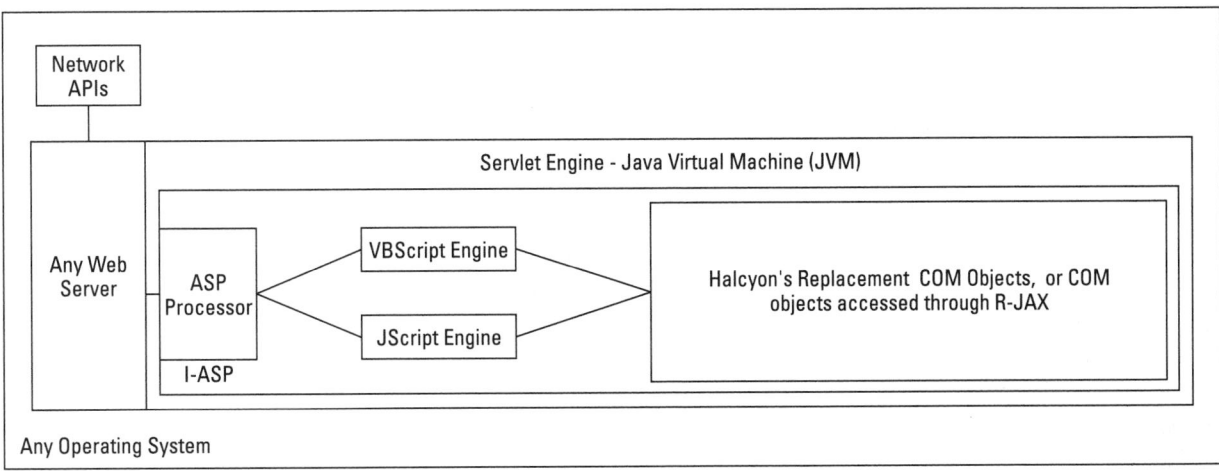

▶ *OpenASP can connect to the Apache Web Server as a module.*

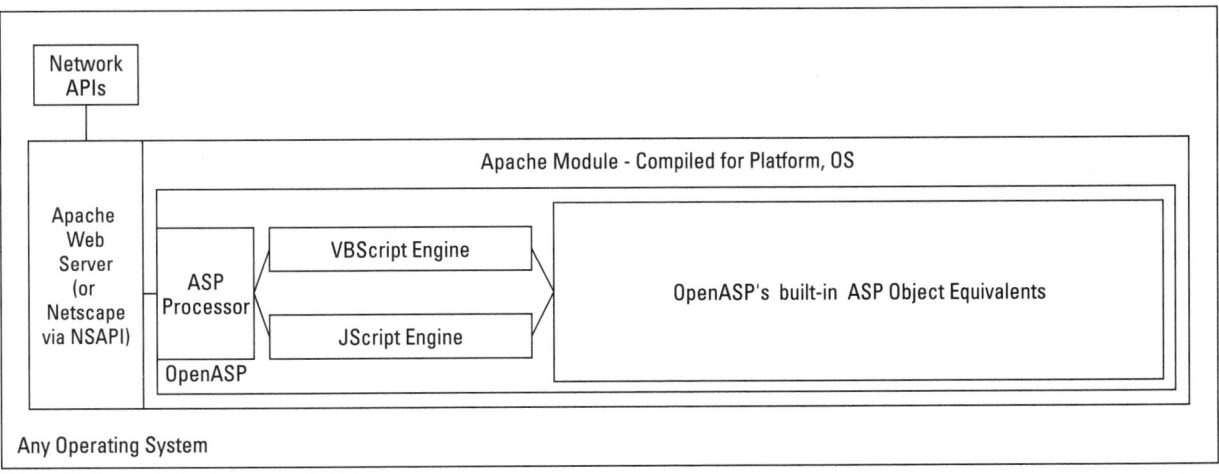

▶ *Halcyon's iASP uses the Java servlet architecture to connect to the Web server in a manner independent of the particular operating system and Web server.*

Personal Workbook

Q & A

1 Who needs to be involved in choosing your ASP deployment environment (operating system, server, and so forth)?

_____

_____

_____

2 Where can you download and learn about Chili!Soft ASP?

_____

_____

_____

3 What services does Chili!Soft ASP provide to non-Microsoft Web servers?

_____

_____

_____

4 What extra functionality does Chili!Beans provide?

_____

_____

_____

5 What ASP features may vary among different Web server platforms?

_____

_____

_____

6 How does Halcyon Software's iASP work across different servers and platforms without platform- or server-specific configurations?

_____

_____

_____

7 Which of the ASP alternatives explored in this chapter is open source?

_____

_____

_____

8 Why is it a good idea to install Chili!Soft ASP on off-hours?

_____

_____

ANSWERS: PAGE 497

EXTRA PRACTICE

1. Download a sample copy of Chili!Soft ASP and install it.

2. Copy some simple ASP applications from an Internet Information Server installation to one of these alternatives and test compatibility.

3. Explore Java and Java beans at the JavaSoft site (**http://java.sun.com**).

4. Visit Halcyon Software's site and learn about ASP, JSP, and servlets.

5. Use Performance Monitor to compare the load created by different ASP engines on a Windows NT Server.

6. Visit large sites that use ASP and check the HTTP headers to see what kind of Web server they're using.

REAL-WORLD APPLICATIONS

✔ You are a developer who needs to create an ASP-based Web site using a Sun Solaris-based server. Evaluate your alternatives.

✔ You are a network administrator who needs to move an IIS-based ASP application to a larger system because of load problems. How do you choose between a larger NT installation and the alternatives?

✔ Your databases are stored on remote servers. Do you need to modify the database access when you move to a different Web server?

✔ Your old Web site is looking ancient, and the server holding it is becoming too slow for the load that it is carrying. Using an alternative ASP implementation, present a transition strategy that will improve your site and make it more exciting.

Marking up Web Pages

At this point in *Teach Yourself Microsoft Active Server Pages 3*, you have received a detailed overview of Active Server Pages and have set up your operating system and server. In this part of the book, you will learn how to create the HTML and XML documents into which you will insert the scripts that will make your Web pages dynamic.

In the nine chapters that compose this part, you'll get an overview of the HTML and XML markup languages, find out about the basic building blocks of Web documents, and learn how to plan, design, and create basic documents. In addition, you'll also find out how to combine these documents into a well-organized Web site that your visitors will be able to navigate easily. After completing these chapters, you'll know how to assemble a single document or set of documents gradually by adding both the underlying structure and the content. You also will find out how to insert forms and add database information to a document. Finally, you will learn how to style your document pages, paragraphs, components, and selected blocks of text and characters.

CHAPTER 5

HTML, XML, and the Web

Both *HyperText Markup Language* (HTML) and *Extensible Markup Language* (XML) enable you to issue instructions that combine text, images, and whitespace to present sophisticated and aesthetically pleasing Web pages. In addition, HTML and XML documents can contain *hypertext links*, underlined or highlighted text that someone browsing through a document can click to jump to other parts of the same document or a completely different document. Both HTML and XML are closely related to *Standard Generalized Markup Language* (SGML), the International Standardization Organization (ISO) standard. SGML is a standard that commercial and government organizations around the world use to publish and distribute their documents. Each SGML document is controlled by a *document type definition* (DTD), which specifies the rules for creating documents and contains declarations for markup, default values, and ranges of values. Every component of the HTML language is defined in an SGML DTD. The structure of HTML is set and unchangeable. On the other hand, XML is a subset of SGML, so you can use XML to create DTDs and, therefore, to develop custom markup languages for particular industries, occupations, or types of documents.

In this chapter, you'll get an overview of both HTML and XML—how these markup languages are similar and how they differ. You'll get your first glimpse of HTML and XML documents and be introduced to some of the components that comprise those documents.

Later in the chapter, you'll learn how to plan and design the most effective documents and the best-organized Web sites. After all, if visitors to a site encounter difficulties moving from page to page or run into dead ends and obsolete pages, they won't stay long.

Finally, you will learn about the international nature of the Web and its documents. In your travels around the Web, you have most likely seen pages from sites all around the world as well as pages in various languages. In this chapter's final task, you'll get an overview of the way that non-English alphabets and special characters are supported in HTML and XML. Both languages support the International Standard ISO 10646-1, or the Unicode Standard, which not only includes tens of thousands of international characters and symbols (ranging from the characters in the English alphabet to the Euro and other currency symbols), but also the setting of left-to-right and right-to-left output of text.

Exploring HTML

HTML is designed to enable a Web page developer to produce a document that not only includes text and graphics but also contains hypertext links to other Web documents and files. A *link* addresses a location within the document displayed onscreen or to any other document posted on a Web site worldwide. When an individual viewing the document clicks a link, the browser program opens the linked section or document in the current window or a new one.

Using HTML, a developer can format or enhance any type of document and selected text, display a page's text and graphics on a background color or graphic, insert fixed or animated graphics or graphical links, and add sound files that play when a page opens or a visitor clicks. A developer can add tables and forms to a page, and can use *frames* to display multiple small windows simultaneously.

An HTML document is a text-only file that you can create using a text editor, word processor, or an HTML editor. Note that when you save an HTML file, it is limited to a certain number of document types: the most popular documents have an `.HTM` or `.HTML` extension. Other popular Web document types include `.SHTML`, `.CFM`, `.PHP`, and — as is shown throughout this book — `.ASP`.

The main difference between an HTML document and another text file is the *element*, the markup (see the following Take Note) that instructs the Web browser or processor how to use particular chunks of the document. *Start tags* and *end tags* enclose element names and mark the beginning and end of selected pieces of the document. For example:

```
<P>This is <B>important</B>.</P>
```

The example starts and ends with the P paragraph element, which marks the beginning and end of a paragraph. The B element applies boldface to the text that is enclosed within the `<B>` start tag and the `</B>` end tag.

In addition to element names, start tags can contain *attributes*, which fine-tune the behavior of an element. With attributes, you can change a color, set a value, name the selection, or provide a URL. The left column on the facing page contains two examples of HTML documents. You'll find illustrations of the examples on the right side of the page.

TAKE NOTE

▶ DIFFERENTIATING BETWEEN MARKUP AND CHARACTER DATA

HTML documents — as well as documents created using other markup languages, such as XML and SGML — are comprised of markup and character data. *Markup*, which makes up the underlying structure of the document, instructs browsers and other processing programs on how to organize and format selected parts of the document. Markup is the *logical structure*, which consists of lines and pieces of code that tell how to process the document or selected parts. The remaining non-markup content of a document is known as *character data*. The character data is what you will see on a printed or displayed page — the *physical structure* of the document. As you continue reading through this part of the book, you'll learn more about markup and character data.

CROSS-REFERENCE
To learn more about markup languages and their components, browse through Chapter 6.

FIND IT ONLINE
Go to **http://www.w3.org/TR/REC-html40/** to review or download the current HTML specification.

Listing 5-1: A Small HTML Document

```
<!DOCTYPE HTML PUBLIC
    "-//W3C//DTD HTML 4.0//EN">          ◄─❶
<HTML>          ◄─❷
<HEAD>
<TITLE>Examples of Tags</TITLE>
</HEAD>
<BODY>
<P>This is <B>important</B>.</P>
<P>This is <I>italicized</I>.</P>          ◄─❸
<P>This is a <SUB>subscript</SUB>.</P>
<P>This is a <SUP>superscript</SUP>.</P>
</BODY></HTML>          ◄─❹
```

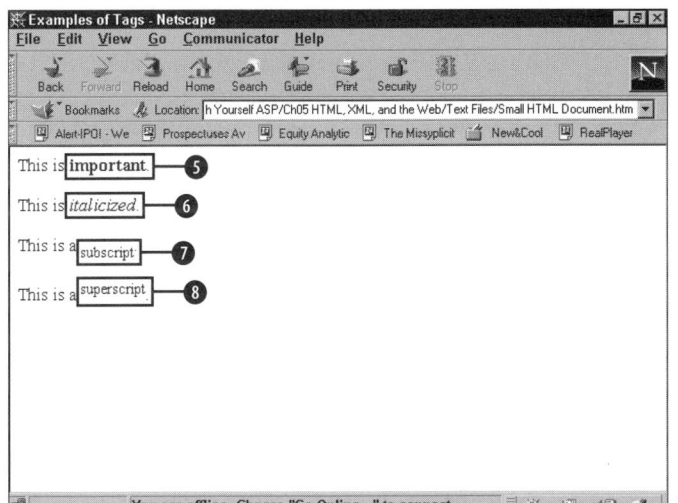

❶ *This markup statement instructs using the 4.0 version of HTML.*

❷ *Begin an HTML document with an <HTML> start tag.*

❸ *Insert the content after the <BODY> start tag.*

❹ *End the document with the </BODY> and </HTML> end tags.*

❺ *The B element enhances a selection with boldface.*

❻ *The I element italicizes a selection.*

❼ *The SUB element applies subscript to selected text.*

❽ *Use SUP to format text with superscript.*

Listing 5-2: Adding a Heading and Links

```
<!DOCTYPE HTML PUBLIC
    "-//W3C//DTD HTML 4.0//EN">
<HTML><HEAD>
<TITLE>Headings and Links</TITLE></HEAD>
<BODY><H1>Research Starting Points</H1>          ◄─1
This page lists three of my favorites.
<P><A HREF="http://www.altavista.com/">          ◄─3
AltaVista</A> (http://www.altavista.com/)
</P>          2          4
<P><A HREF="http://www.yahoo.com/">Yahoo
</A> (http://www.yahoo.com/)</P>
<P><A HREF="http://www.lycos.com/">Lycos
</A> (http://www.lycos.com/)</P>
</BODY></HTML>
```

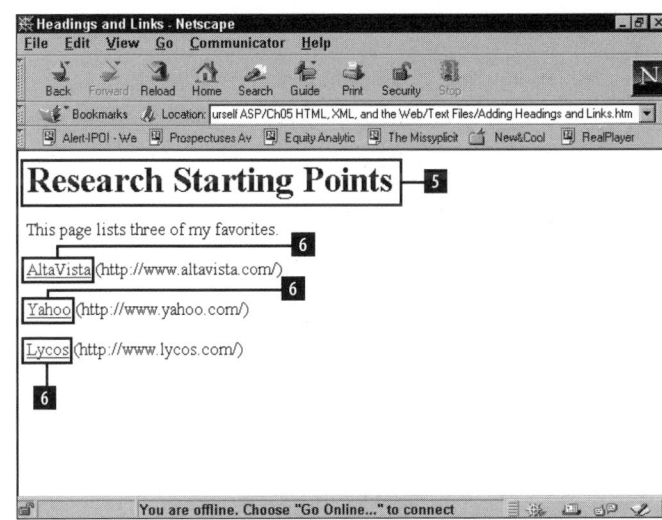

1 *Enclose a top-level heading within the <H1> and </H1> tags.*

2 *Use the <A> start tag to begin a link.*

3 *Insert the HREF attribute and specify a URL.*

4 *End the link with the </A> end tag.*

5 *Display a top-level heading.*

6 *Click on the blue, underlined text to link to a resource.*

67

Introducing XML

XML documents are structured in the same manner as HTML documents: In an XML document, you combine markup (such as start tags and end tags) and content to produce Web pages and other documents. With the exception of the first lines, XML and HTML documents should look the same.

The primary difference between HTML and XML is whether you can define elements, attributes, other markup, and their values or whether these components are predefined for you. Remember that the document type definition (DTD) contains declarations for markup, values, ranges of values, and behavior. HTML's DTD is predefined; you cannot edit any part of it. In contrast, you can create any number of DTDs for your XML documents. With XML, you can define sets of custom elements to organize and describe the information in a document, and then use style sheets (see Chapter 13) to display it.

An XML document does not always require a DTD. A *well-formed* document must follow XML rules but is not necessarily associated with a DTD. On the other hand, a *valid* document must follow XML rules and always has an associated DTD — either internal or external. An *internal DTD subset* is part of the document whose elements, attributes, and other markup it defines. An *external DTD subset* is a separate document, which is referred to from one or more documents. The facing page provides examples of XML documents.

rules, limitations, and values for each of the components. So, when a browser, parser, or other processing program reads a document, it compares the markup and content with the declarations and rules in the DTD. The document type declaration — the top lines in a document — provides information about the DTD. Look at the following top of an HTML document:

```
<!DOCTYPE HTML PUBLIC
"-//W3C//DTD HTML 4.0//EN">
```

!DOCTYPE is a reserved keyword that indicates the start of the document type declaration, which in combination with the HTML keyword simply states that this is an HTML document. The PUBLIC keyword indicates that the DTD is stored in a location that the public can access. The remaining code, enclosed within quotation marks, names the location of the DTD file, its version number, and the language, English (EN), in which it is written.

As you have learned, an XML document can access an internal DTD (stored at the beginning of the document) or an external DTD (a separate document). Within an XML document, the pointer to the DTD is known as a document type declaration. An XML document type declaration looks like this if the DTD is an internal subset:

```
<?xml version = "1.0"?>
<!DOCTYPE document [
```

or this, if the DTD is an external subset:

```
<!DOCTYPE test SYSTEM "test.dtd">
```

In the prior examples, document and test are the document names. It is important to note that a document type declaration is *never* known as a DTD. DTD always refers to a document type definition.

TAKE NOTE

▶ LEARNING ABOUT DOCUMENT TYPE DECLARATIONS

Using Extended Backus-Naur Form (EBNF) notation, a developer writes a DTD to specify the elements, attributes, entities, and special characters for one document or a document set. A DTD also sets the

CROSS-REFERENCE

In Chapter 7, you'll learn about how to view the structure of a DTD and how to write an XML DTD.

FIND IT ONLINE

You can find the official XML specification at
http://www.w3.org/TR/1998/REC-xml-19980210.

Listing 5-3: A Well-Formed XML Document

```
<?xml version="1.0"?>   ←❶
<HTML>
<HEAD>
<TITLE>Examples of Tags</TITLE>
</HEAD>
<BODY>
<P>This is <B>important</B>.</P>
<P>This is <I>italicized</I>.</P>    ←❷
<P>This is a <SUB>subscript</SUB>.</P>
<P>This is a <SUP>superscript</SUP>.</P>
</BODY>
</HTML>
```

Listing 5-4: Converting to a Valid XML Document

```
<?xml version="1.0"?>
<!DOCTYPE text [←❸
<!ELEMENT text (p*|b*|i*|sub*|sup*)>   ←❹
<!ELEMENT p    ( #PCDATA)>
<!ELEMENT b      (#PCDATA)>
<!ELEMENT i      (#PCDATA)>   ←❺
<!ELEMENT sub  (#PCDATA)>
<!ELEMENT sup  (#PCDATA)>
]>←❻
<text><p>This is <b>important</b>.</p>
<p>This is <i>italicized</i>.</p>
<p>This is a <sub>subscript</sub>.</p>
<p>This is a <sup>superscript</sup>.</p>
</text>
```

Listing 5-5: Converting Another Document to XML

```
<?xml version="1.0"?>
<!DOCTYPE document [   ←🄵
<!ELEMENT document
(title,(h1|p|link)*>   ←🄶
<!ELEMENT title   ( #PCDATA)>
<!ELEMENT h1      (#PCDATA)>
<!ELEMENT p       (#PCDATA)>
<!ELEMENT link    ANY>
<!ATTLIST link
    xml:link   CDATA    #FIXED "simple"
    href       CDATA           #REQUIRED   ←🄷
    id         ID              #REQUIRED>
]>
<document>
<title>Headings and Links</title>
<h1>Research Starting Points</h1>
<p>This page lists three of my favorites.
</p>
<p><link href="http://www.altavista.com/">
    AltaVista</link>                          ←🄸
    (http://www.altavista.com/)</p>
<p><link href="http://www.yahoo.com/">
    Yahoo</link>
    (http://www.yahoo.com/)</p>
<p><link href="http://www.lycos.com/">
    Lycos</link>
    (http://www.lycos.com/)
</p></document>
```

❶ Begin the document with the XML declaration.

❷ The remaining lines can duplicate an HTML document (see Listing 5-1).

❸ State the document type and start the DTD ([).

❹ Declare the main (root) element and list its child elements.

❺ Declare the child elements and their data types.

❻ End the DTD with].

🄵 Start the DTD and declare the main (root) element.

🄶 Set the child-element order using the comma (required order) and pipe (any order).

🄷 The !ATTLIST keyword starts an attribute list for the simple link, link.

🄸 Insert a simple link (see Chapter 8) in the document.

Planning and Designing a Document

As you have seen in the prior two tasks, XML documents and HTML documents use essentially the same structure for presenting content. It follows that both types of documents — especially those that will be posted on the Web or on an intranet — should follow the same design. (Note that, as pointed out in the following Take Note, XML documents are not always developed as Web pages.) So, you can use many online Web-page design resources as a guide for designing both HTML and XML documents. For a list of selected resources, refer to Table 5-1 on the facing page. Or, you can find a well-designed Web document, view the underlying source code to see how the document was constructed, and use it as a template for your documents.

The best-designed pages use an underlying grid for layout. This invisible grid provides a structure for inserting text, graphics, and whitespace for single pages or pairs of facing pages. *Whitespace*, which is any "empty" non-text, non-graphical part of a page, accentuates the text and graphics.

Another excellent resource of page design is a full-featured word processor. Most word processors provide templates for standard documents, including Web pages. Books on desktop publishing, printing, and typography are also good sources.

TAKE NOTE

OUTPUTTING XML DOCUMENTS

In addition to the differences that you have already learned about HTML and XML, there is one more important fact. XML documents will not always be displayed on the Web. You can write XML documents that produce output that you'll never see: an XML parser can send output information to an intermediate program for further processing. Perhaps the most important alternate output is the information that is sent to a database program. For example, a processor can send fields to a retail database to accumulate data about customers and to update an inventory system. XML parsers can also send information to a program that converts text to audio or submits instructions to a robot that manufactures an automobile.

DIFFERENTIATING BETWEEN HTML AND XML ELEMENTS

When you read through about the XML specification for the first time, you'll quickly find out that XML is a case-sensitive language: each of the components used to construct DTDs have a special mix of uppercase and/or lowercase characters. For example, components that have an initial uppercase letter indicate a *regular expression* (a way of grouping characters or options); all other components are lowercase. In addition, some reserved keywords are completely uppercase.

However, when many developers create documents using predefined elements (in HTML) or custom elements (in XML) or combine HTML and XML in a single document, they often follow this informal standard: all HTML elements are expressed in uppercase, and all XML elements are entered in lowercase.

CROSS-REFERENCE

You'll learn about using page-layout grids in the "Laying Out Pages Using Tables" task in Chapter 10.

FIND IT ONLINE

Access many HTML and Web links from the comprehensive directory at **http://html.miningco.com/index.htm**.

Table 5-1: SELECTED WEB DESIGN RESOURCES

Page	Description	URL
HTML home page	Links to Web design help and the HTML specification	**http://www.w3.org/MarkUp/**
Guide to Web Style	A "cookbook for helping people create better Web pages"	**http://www.sun.com/styleguide/**
D. J. Quad's Ultimate HTML Site	Many links to HTML authoring and design resources	**http://www.quadzilla.com/**
Adding a Touch of Style	Dave Raggett's introductory guide to styling Web pages	**http://www.w3.org/MarkUp/Guide/**
Desktop Publishing, Web Design, and Marketing Links	Links to desktop publishing and Web design sites	**http://ideabook.com/links.htm**
BigNoseBird.Com Site Guide	Links to resources, articles, and tutorials about Web page creation	**http://bignosebird.com/siteguide.shtml**
Graphion's Online Type Museum	An online typography and typesetting museum	**http://www.slip.net/~graphion/museum.html**
TYPE*links	Links to information about typography	**http://www.truetype.demon.co.uk/links.htm**
Will-Harris House	Links to design, typography, computer, and many more resources	**http://www.will-harris.com/**
HTML Station	Links to Web page development resources	**http://www.december.com/html/**
The Mining Co.	A directory of links to Web design resources	**http://html.miningco.com/internet/design**
HTML Writers Guild	Resources for Web page designers and developers	**http://www.hwg.org/**
Beyond the Bones of HTML	Web page design resources	**http://www.avalon.net/~librarian/bones/bones.html**

Planning and Designing a Web Site

If you plan a Web site carefully and logically, your visitors will be able to find their way around your pages easily—without hitting dead ends and trying to link to obsolete or missing pages. As your site grows, its planning and design becomes more important. Without careful organization, a massive set of Web pages can become a hodgepodge consisting of pages that don't link to any other pages—especially if the site has gone through many changes and additions. Some of the older or obsolete pages may still exist but link only to other pages that are either obsolete or have been deleted.

Most Web sites—both good and bad—start with a *home page*, which is the entrance to the site. The home page usually includes a welcome message and links to the main pages at the site. For example, a corporate site's home page may include links to pages on the company history, names and addresses of contacts, product and service information, the site's copyright information, and a *site map*, which is a textual or graphical representation of the table of pages.

You can organize your Web site in various ways. Perhaps the most common is a top-down, organization-chart arrangement. At the top is a single home page, under that is the first layer of pages, and each of those pages can have subsidiary pages. (See the diagram on the facing page.)

Another type of site may start with a home page, but then follow a different organization: For example, pages are arranged sequentially with a single page linking to the page before it and to the page after it. In addition, all pages usually link back to the home page and sometimes link to a table of contents or a site map. Or, a site can look like a wheel composed of pages that are all linked to a hub home page.

A relatively new method of organizing a Web site is holding pages in a set of *frames*, which are fixed or sizeable windows organized on the desktop. Start with a non-frame home page, and organize the remaining pages within frames. HTML supports several frame elements and attributes, which you'll learn about in Chapter 11. The current XML 1.0 recommendation does not support the use of frames; however, it is possible to write a Java program to enable frames for an XML site. To keep up with changes to XML, check **http://www.w3.org/XML/** from time to time.

TAKE NOTE

▶ HONORING COPYRIGHTS

If you see a copyright notice on a book, document, or Web page, you cannot use that book, document, or page without explicit permission from its author. Copyright laws protect all types of creative people from infringement of their work. To learn about U.S. copyright law and to link to related sites, go to the United States Copyright Office (**http://lcweb.loc. gov/copyright/**).

CROSS-REFERENCE

Chapter 14 introduces you to the structure of an ASP document, which is based on what you've learned here.

FIND IT ONLINE

The WDVL Site Map (**http://www.stars.com/Location/Maps/ ToC.html**) contains links to site design and other pages.

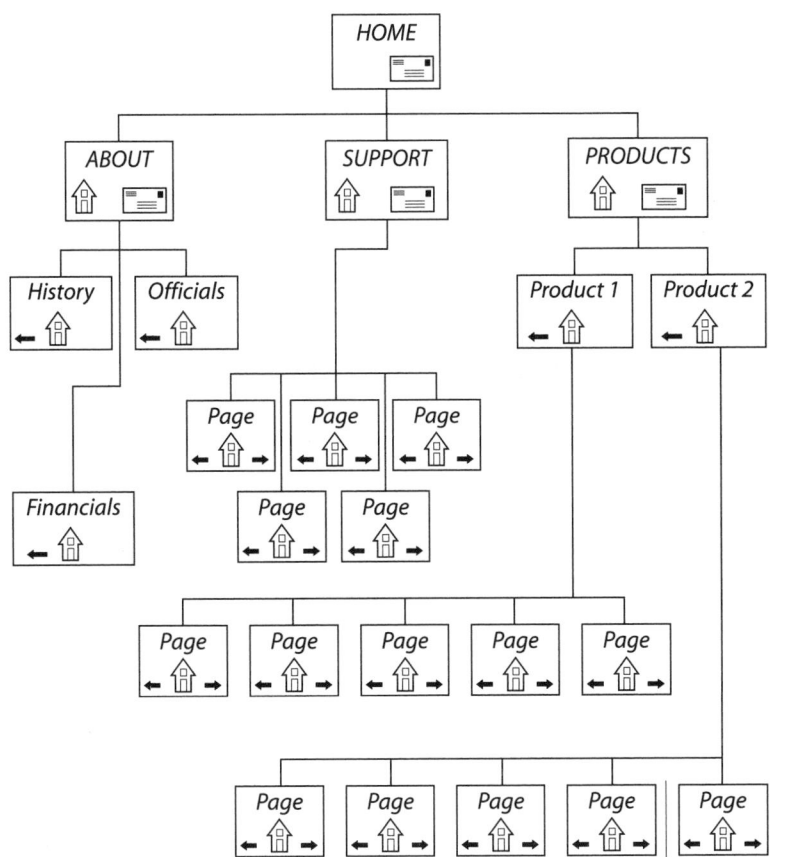

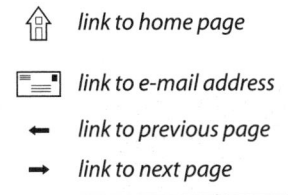

link to home page

link to e-mail address

link to previous page

link to next page

Managing International Pages

The Web has always been international in scope: as you know, the Web's original purpose was for scientists around the world to share research information. Now, as the Web has grown to encompass many other sites — commercial, educational, organizational, and personal — the developers of the Web have addressed the issue of *internationalization*, the support of non-English alphabets and special characters.

In the 2.0 and 3.2 versions of HTML, the supported character code was the International Standard ISO-8859, which was comprised of Latin character sets and special characters. Many international character sets and special symbols were not supported at all. By the time HTML 4.0 was under development, its Working Group decided to support the International Standard ISO 10646-1, which includes ISO 8859, adds international characters and symbols, and supports the explicit setting of the direction of text output. Supported character sets include alphabets for many languages, punctuation marks, technical and mathematical characters, arrows, dingbats, and *diacritics*, which are marks that are added to a letter. Diacritics include acute and grave accents, breves, cedillas, circumflexes, macrons, tildes, and so forth.

From the start of XML development, its Working Group also stated support for ISO 10646-1.

Founded in 1991, the Unicode Consortium is an international group of software companies and researchers. The Unicode Standard, which is a subset of the International Standard ISO/IEC 10646-1, is comprised of codes for almost 39,000 characters as well as scripts and other character sets. All the characters in HTML and XML documents must be supported by the Unicode Standard. The Unicode Consortium's Web site (**http://www.unicode.org/**) provides information about the characters in the newest version, 2.1. Table 5-2, on the facing page, lists some of the pages at the Unicode site.

TAKE NOTE

▶ SPECIFYING A LANGUAGE FOR AN HTML OR XML DOCUMENT

You can name a language for either an HTML or XML document using a two-letter language code. (For a list of supported language codes, see Appendix E.)

To set a language code for an entire HTML document, edit the document's first line:

```
<!DOCTYPE HTML PUBLIC
    "-//W3C//DTD HTML 4.0//EN">
```

The EN (at the end of the line) represents English.

Many HTML elements support the LANG attribute, with which you can name the language used within the element's start tag and end tag:

```
<P LANG="DE">Erzeugnisse und Dienste</P>
```

As you may have guessed, the DE represents German.

In XML documents, use the xml:lang attribute to name a language:

```
<frenchtext xml:lang=fr>
babouin et chimpanzé
</frenchtext>
```

The language code fr specifies that the text within the start tag and end tag is to be processed as French.

In both HTML and XML documents, you can also specify country codes (see Appendix F) and subcodes, which refine a language or country (for example, British English versus American English or French French versus Canadian French).

CROSS-REFERENCE
Chapter 8 teaches you how to create a basic HTML or XML document, using elements, attributes, and so forth.

FIND IT ONLINE
To link to information and discussions about internationalization, go to **http://www.w3.org/International/**.

Table 5-2: SELECTED PAGES AT THE UNICODE WEB SITE

Page	Description	URL
Unicode Home Page (graphical version)	A graphical home page	**http://www.unicode.org/**
Unicode Home Page (text version)	A text-only home page	**http://www.unicode.org/textonly.html**
Unicode Copyright	Copyright information about the pages at the Unicode site	**http://www.unicode.org/unicode/copyright.html**
Contents	A list of page links at the Unicode site	**http://www.unicode.org/unicode/contents.html**
What's New?	A list of new or changed features, arranged from the newest to oldest date	**http://www.unicode.org/unicode/wnew.html**
The Unicode Consortium	Information about the Unicode Consortium and its members	**http://www.unicode.org/unicode/consortium/consort.html**
The Unicode Standard	Links to information about the Unicode Standard, scripts, code charts, proposed scripts and codes, and related publications	**http://www.unicode.org/unicode/standard/standard.html**
Unicode 2.1 Character Charts	The home page for code charts:names lists and glyphs	**http://charts.unicode.org/charts.html**
Supported Scripts	A list of scripts (such as alphabets, character sets) supported in the Unicode Standard	**http://www.unicode.org/unicode/standard/supported.html**
The Unicode(r) Standard: A Technical Introduction	Eight pages of concise information about the Unicode Standard	**http://www.unicode.org/unicode/standard/principles.html**
Online Data	Links at the Unicode site and other sources, including the Unicode FTP site, language codes, and country codes	**http://www.unicode.org/unicode/onlinedat/online.html**
Unicode Publications	Links to information about printed and electronic publications	**http://www.unicode.org/unicode/publications.html**
Technical Work	The home page of links to technical work, publications, data, and conferences of the Unicode Technical Committee (UTC)	**http://www.unicode.org/unicode/techwork.html**
Technical Reports	Links to electronic technical reports that are not part of the Unicode Standard	**http://www.unicode.org/unicode/reports/techreports.html**
Related Standards Organizations	Links to other standards organizations throughout the world	**http://www.unicode.org/unicode/onlinedat/related.html**
Updates & Errata	An index of updates to the Unicode Standard, Version 2.0	**http://www.unicode.org/unicode/uni2errata/UnicodeErrata.html**

Personal Workbook

Q & A

1 What do HTML and XML stand for?

_____

_____

_____

_____

2 What is a hypertext link?

_____

_____

_____

3 What is a DTD?

_____

_____

_____

4 What is the difference between HTML and XML?

_____

_____

_____

5 What is an element?

_____

_____

_____

_____

6 What are start tags and end tags?

_____

_____

_____

7 What are attributes?

_____

_____

_____

8 What is the difference between markup and character data?

_____

_____

_____

ANSWERS: PAGE 497

EXTRA PRACTICE

1. Get online and find a good Web design site that is not mentioned in this chapter.

2. Go to the Worldwide Web Consortium (W3C) and browse through the HTML 4.0 specification.

3. Using HTML 4.0 elements and the help of the examples in this chapter, convert a business letter to an HTML document.

4. Go to the Worldwide Web Consortium (W3C) and browse through the XML 1.0 specification.

5. Using the examples in this chapter, convert the business letter to a well-formed XML document.

6. Go to the Unicode Consortium site and find the chart that contains the U+20D1 symbol.

REAL-WORLD APPLICATIONS

✔ Develop and write an HTML document that serves as a home page.

✔ Write a well-formed XML document that contains the history of your company.

✔ Plan and organize a Web site for your business that will include a home page, table of contents, information about the site, and a page of contacts.

✔ You are currently learning French, and you want to practice by writing letters to a French pen pal. Write an HTML document that includes a statement declaring French as the default language. Also learn how to add accented characters to the document.

Visual Quiz

Identify the markup and character data in this HTML document. Underline each markup item, and circle the content.

_____

_____

_____

_____

_____

_____

```
Close Full Screen
<!DOCTYPE HTML PUBLIC "-//W3C//DTD HTML 4.0//EN">
<HTML>
<HEAD>
<TITLE>Markup Versus Character Data</TITLE>
</HEAD>
<BODY>
<P>This is <B>boldface</B> text. Boldface represents
important information. You can also apply boldface with
the <STRONG>STRONG</STRONG> element, if your browser
interprets STRONG as a boldface element.
</P>
<P>This is <I>italicized</I> text. Italics can also
emphasize important information. Your browser will
probably recognize the <EM>EM</EM> element, too.
</P>
</BODY>
</HTML>

—
```

CHAPTER 6

The Building Blocks of Markup Languages

This chapter introduces you to the basic components of a markup language (such as HTML or XML) and its documents. You'll learn about language building blocks and how to use them to construct Web documents. In the prior chapter, you were introduced to markup and character data. With the first task in this chapter, you'll learn more about the differences between markup and character data.

You'll also find out about elements, which are the essential building blocks of both HTML and XML documents. An *element* identifies a chunk of a document to be processed in a particular way. In a document, the beginning of an occurrence of an element is marked with a start tag; the end is indicated with an end tag. You'll learn about start tags and end tags in this chapter. As you read through the chapter and learn about document components, you'll see examples of their use in Web documents as well as important reference information.

In this chapter, you'll also get an overview of *attributes*, with which you can specify, or refine, characteristics of elements. With attributes, you can set the appearance of a selected document component (such as its height and width, color, or the presence or absence of a border) or an initial value (such as the default color of a component or the name of your documents' primary editor). In both HTML and XML, you can use an attribute to give a particular element a name. This means that you can link to that element, style it, or process it in some way. In XML, you can also require that an element be used or make its use optional.

Use *entities* as nicknames for long names, technical terms, or even separate files. For example, you can use a three- or four-character word to refer to a company name or difficult-to-type phrase that appears throughout your documents. Or, in a computer manual or employee handbook, you can use a set of entity references to "call" the chapters that make up the book.

To conclude the chapter, you'll find out how to put all these components together in a document type definition (DTD), in which you define elements, attributes, and entities for a single document or set of related documents.

Recognizing Markup and Character Data

Whether they are written in HTML or XML, documents are comprised of two main components: markup and character data. As you learned in the "Differentiating between Markup and Character Data" Take Note in the previous chapter, *markup* makes up the logical structure that underlies a document, and *character data* comprises the visible physical structure. Markup instructs a processor on how to format and/or display the character data.

In Chapter 5, you also were introduced to DTDs, which specify the rules and contain declarations for the markup components of the documents with which the DTDs are associated. You'll learn more about DTDs in the "Introducing DTDs" task at the end of this chapter as well as in Chapter 7.

How does a browser or document processor recognize the difference between markup and character data? In the examples in Chapter 5, you saw this difference for yourself. Whether you are looking at an HTML or XML document, delimiters, such as < and >, point to the beginning and end of markup sections. Look at this line:

```
<P>This is a <SUB>subscript</SUB>.</P>
```

The < and > delimit the P and SUB elements and separate them from the content that they enclose. For example, <P> marks the beginning of a paragraph, and </P> marks the end.

In a DTD, reserved keywords, such as !ELEMENT and !DOCTYPE, indicate particular types of markup, such as the start of the definition of an element or the type of document. As you continue reading this chapter, you'll find out more about elements and delimiters.

TAKE NOTE

▶ LEARNING ABOUT EXTENDED BACKUS-NAUR FORM (EBNF) NOTATION

EBNF is the standard syntax for HTML and XML DTDs and document markup. In the standard HTML DTD and custom XML DTDs, developers use EBNF syntax to define the elements, attributes, entities, and other components. EBNF enables you to specify components, valid values and ranges of values, and the location of particular elements in the hierarchy of declared elements. EBNF uses special characters to delimit or connect components. For example, the less-than symbol (<) marks the beginning of components, such as declarations, start tags, and end tags. Quotation marks (") and single-quote marks (') indicate the beginning and end of strings, and sets of parentheses (( )) group parts of expressions. Sets of brackets ([ ]) group optional ranges of characters or other components. Other characters connect components in various ways. For example, the pipe (|) or comma (,) connects components from which you can choose or specifies the order in which elements can be used. The not symbol (^) precedes grouped characters that are not allowed in a particular instance (for example, to state that certain characters are not permitted as values). Tables 6-1 and 6-2 summarize EBNF syntax. As you read the remaining tasks in this chapter, you'll learn much more about EBNF.

CROSS-REFERENCE

In Chapter 7, you'll learn about developing DTDs to define the behavior of markup and content.

FIND IT ONLINE

Review EBNF at **http://www.cs.man.ac.uk/~pjj/bnf/ebnf_rjb93a_xbnf.mth**.

Table 6-1: EXTENDED BACKUS-NAUR FORM (EBNF) NOTATION

Syntax	Description
`#xN`	Enter `#x` and `N`, a hexadecimal integer matching any UCS-4 code value in ISO/IEC 10646 standard.
`[ ]`	Brackets indicate that the grouped content within is optional.
`[a-zA-Z]`, `[#xN-#xN]`	Enter one of the characters within the range a to z, A to Z, or #xN to #xN.
`[^a-z]`, `[^#xN-#xN]`	Do *not* enter any of the characters within the range adjacent to the NOT character.
`[^abc]`, `[^#xN#xN#xN]`	Do *not* enter any of the characters adjacent to the NOT character.
`"string"|'string'`	Enter the literal string enclosed within the quotation marks or single quote marks. Do *not* mix quotation marks and single quote marks in an expression.
`( )`	Parentheses contain an expression in the same way that you would write a mathematical expression.
`(expression)`	Enter an expression consisting of a combination of the previously listed parts of XML syntax and using the syntax in Table 6-2, where A represents an expression.

Table 6-2: EXTENDED BACKUS-NAUR FORM (EBNF) EXPRESSION SYNTAX

Syntax	Description
`A?`	An expression followed by a question mark indicates that the expression is optional.
`A B`	One expression followed by another must be matched exactly.
`A|B`	Expressions separated by pipe symbols indicate ORs. Choose one expression OR the other — in other words, just choose one. In this book, pipes appear in a larger point size to differentiate them from pipe characters within elements.
`A - B`	The first expression must be present, and the expression following the minus sign must be absent. Note that a range (for example, A-B) contains no spaces, but the minus sign indicating an absent expression (A – B) is both preceded and succeeded by a space.
`A+`	An expression followed by a plus sign indicates that the expression *must* appear one or more times.
`A*`	An expression followed by an asterisk indicates that the expression *may* appear one or more times.

Learning about Elements

Perhaps the most important markup component of an HTML or XML document is the element. An *element* defines selected parts of a document and marks the boundaries for formatting or future processing. For example, you can use an element to identify and format a heading, body text, or a note or warning. Or, you can use an element as a placeholder for a document's future content, such as a graphic (see the following Take Note).

In both HTML and XML documents, individual elements are part of an ordered system of elements. The top element is known as the *root element* or the *document element*; all other elements are children or descendants of the root. In HTML, the HTML element is at the top of the hierarchy, and HEAD and BODY are the child elements of HTML. On the other hand, you define and name the root element in XML. If you convert an HTML document to XML, you can simply use the HTML or BODY elements as the root. (The HEAD element usually marks a small section at the top of the document, so it's not practical to use HEAD as the root.)

Child elements can have child elements of their own. For example, an XML element that defines a chapter can contain elements for various types of paragraphs or text. Look at some of the levels of elements that might make up a typical book:

```
book
    chapter
        heading1
        heading2
        bodytext
            boldface
            italics
            quotation
```

In HTML, you choose from a set of predefined elements. For example, HTML provides six levels of heading elements — H1 through H6. In the prior task, you saw the B (boldface) and I (italics) elements used in example documents. HTML supports two quotation elements: BLOCKQUOTE, for long block quotations, and Q, for short inline ones.

The structure of elements within a document is like a tree, with a trunk (root element) and various sizes of branches (child elements).

TAKE NOTE

▶ DIFFERENTIATING BETWEEN HTML'S INLINE AND BLOCK ELEMENTS

HTML provides both inline and block elements. An *inline element*'s content flows from the previous element to the following element without a line break, unless there isn't enough room on the current line. A *block element*'s content starts on a new line and triggers another line break at the end of its display.

▶ DEFINING ELEMENT TERMS

As you get into the technical details of markup languages, you'll find terms that initially could be considered to be interchangeable. For example, what's the difference between an element and an element type? An *element* is the actual physical occurrence of the element — its start tag, attributes, content, and end tag (for example, <P>This is a paragraph</P>) — in one location in a document. An *element type* is the defined element (for example, P, B, I, and more), which can occur numerous places in a document. In addition, an *element name* or *generic identifier* is the name that is assigned to an element.

CROSS-REFERENCE

In the "Declaring Root and Child Elements" task in Chapter 7, find out how to define XML elements.

FIND IT ONLINE

The Webpedia (**http://www.webpedia.com/**) provides links to many Web building articles, resources, and downloads.

Listing 6-1: A Sample HTML Memo

```
<!DOCTYPE HTML PUBLIC
    "-//W3C//DTD HTML 4.0//EN">        ❶
<HTML>
<HEAD>        ❷
<TITLE>Memo to All Employees</TITLE>        ❷
</HEAD>
<BODY>
All Employees<BR>
The Boss<BR>
Holiday
<P><B>Congratulations!</B></P>
<P>
To celebrate our latest numbers, take the
Wednesday before Thanksgiving off.        ❸
<I>This is in addition to the usual
days off: Thanksgiving and the day
after.</I>
</P>
<P>
<B>Thanks for your help.</B>
</P>
</BODY>        ❹
</HTML>
```

❶ Name the document type and version, HTML 4.0, and start the
document.

❷ Insert the HEAD section.

❸ Enter the document body.

❹ Close the last paragraph, the body, and the document.

Listing 6-2: A Counterpart XML Memo

```
<?xml version="1.0"?>        ❺
<!DOCTYPE memo [        ❻
<!ELEMENT memo (to, from, subject, text*)>        ❼
<!ELEMENT to        (#PCDATA)>
<!ELEMENT from      (#PCDATA)>
<!ELEMENT subject   (#PCDATA)>
<!ELEMENT text      (bold*|ital*)>        ❽
    <!ELEMENT bold  (#PCDATA)>
    <!ELEMENT ital  (#PCDATA)>
]>
<memo>
<to>All Employees</to>
<from>The Boss</from>
<subject>Holiday</subject>
<text>
<bold>Congratulations!</bold>
</text>
<text>
To celebrate our latest numbers, take the
Wednesday before Thanksgiving off.
<ital>This is in addition to the usual
days off: Thanksgiving and the day
after.</ital>
</text>
<text>
<bold>Thanks for your help.</bold>
</text>
</memo>
```

❺ Name the document type and version, XML 1.0.

❻ Start a DTD and declare the root element.

❼ List child elements of the root. The commas force their selection
order.

❽ List child elements of a child. The pipe allows any order, and the
asterisk enables any number of elements.

Using Start Tags and End Tags

In prior tasks in this chapter and Chapter 5, you have learned about markup and character and also have seen sample HTML and XML documents. You have noticed document components such as `<BODY>`, `<bold>`, `</BODY>`, and `</bold>`. These components are probably the most commonly-used markup: start tags and end tags.

In HTML and XML documents, an element starts with a start tag (for example, `<element>`) and ends with an end tag (for example, `</element>`). The less-than (`<`) character marks the beginning of both start and end tags, and the greater-than (`>`) character marks the end of them. Both the `<` and `>` characters are known as *delimiters*: they mark the limits of the tags. The only difference between the start tag and end tag is the slash (`/`), which identifies the end tag and is placed between the less-than character and the first character in the element name. Then, the content (if applicable) resides between the start tag and end tag. For example:

`<P>This is a short paragraph.</P>`

The example starts with the `<P>` start tag, contains content of one sentence, and ends with the `</P>` end tag. Note that HTML's P element type represents a paragraph.

In XML, start tags and end tags *must* come in matching sets: for every start tag, there must be an end tag. The pairing of tags enables you and programs that process XML to track the proper construction of a document, element by element. In addition to their other work, XML processors check to ensure that all elements are composed of pairs of start tags and end tags and that the tags contain all the required delimiters and characters. You'll learn about XML's special format for empty elements in the following Take Note.

Between the start tag and end tag, most elements contain nested child elements, character data, or both. Note that any attributes, which define elements further, are located within the start tag — after the element is named and before the `>`, which ends the start tag. In the following "Understanding Attributes" task, you'll learn about attributes and how they are used.

TAKE NOTE

▶ USING EMPTY ELEMENTS

Both HTML and XML have elements that do not have current content but serve as placeholders for a future component of a Web page. These are known as *empty elements*. In HTML, a commonly-used placeholder element is IMG, which refers to a graphic image. XML provides a special syntax for empty elements, which combines the start and end tags into a single tag. For example:

`<graphic pict="bicycle.jpg"/>`

The beginning of the line is a start tag with a `<` and the pict element name. The line continues with the name of a JPEG file. The end of the line contains the `/`, which represents an end tag, and finishes with the `>` delimiter.

CROSS-REFERENCE

Find out how to add elements to an HTML or XML document in the "Entering Elements" task in Chapter 8.

FIND IT ONLINE

HTML Help (**http://www.htmlhelp.com/**) is a comprehensive Web resource for HTML tools, guides, links, and more.

Listing 6-3: A Sample HTML Letter

```
<!DOCTYPE HTML PUBLIC
    "-//W3C//DTD HTML 4.0//EN">          ← ❶
<HTML>
<HEAD>
<TITLE>A Boilerplate Letter</TITLE>     ← ❷
</HEAD>
<BODY>
John Q. Doe<BR>
123 Main Street<BR>
Anytown, NY  12000
<P>Dear John:</P>
<P>I'd like to advise you of an important
company-wide sale of our rafts.
</P>
<P>Until the end of this month, we are
offering 20% off selected rafts.</P>
<P>As always, thank you for your business,
and good luck with your upcoming whitewater
season.
</P>
<P>
Victor C. Vikk</P>
</BODY>      ← ❹
</HTML>
```

❶ Start the document with a document type statement.
❷ Insert a title in the HEAD section.
❸ In the BODY section, add a series of paragraphs.
❹ Use end tags to complete the body and the document.

Listing 6-4: A Counterpart XML Letter

```
?xml version="1.0"?>                    ← ❺
<!DOCTYPE letter [
<!ELEMENT letter (name, address, para*,
                  signature)>
<!ELEMENT name              (#PCDATA)>
<!ELEMENT address (street, city, state,
                   zip)>
   <!ELEMENT city           (#PCDATA)>  ← ❻
   <!ELEMENT state          (#PCDATA)>
   <!ELEMENT zip            (#PCDATA)>
<!ELEMENT para              (#PCDATA)>
<!ELEMENT signature         (#PCDATA)>
]>
<letter>
<name>John Q. Doe</name>
<address>123 Main Street</address>
<city>Anytown</city><state> NY</state>  ← ❼
<zip>12000</zip>
<para>Dear John:</para>
<para>I'd like to advise you of an
important company-wide sale of our rafts.
</para>
<para>Until the end of this month, we are
offering 20% off selected rafts.</para>   ← ❽
<para>As always, thank you for your
business, and good luck with your upcoming
whitewater season.
</para>
<signature>Victor C. Vikk</signature>
</letter>
```

❺ Start the document by declaring the XML version.
❻ Declare the root and child elements in the DTD.
❼ Address the letter.
❽ Enter a series of paragraphs, and end with a signature.

Understanding Attributes

M any elements have associated *attributes*, which specify characteristics (such as size, color, or dimensions), limitations (such as whether an element's use is required or optional), or initial values or list of possible values. In HTML, all attributes are predefined in the HTML 4.0 DTD.

In XML, you can define the attributes associated with a particular element. Use an attribute-list (starting with the required `!ATTLIST` keyword) declaration to do so.

In both HTML and XML, you can use child elements to define the characteristics of higher-level elements, thereby eliminating some attributes. For example, you have already seen the use of the `B` (boldface) and `I` (italics) elements, which affect the enhancement of selected text within paragraphs.

Later in this book, you will learn how to use stylesheets (see Chapter 13) to format and enhance Web documents. Sometimes, a style serves the same purpose as an attribute. So, if you associate a stylesheet with a document, you will not need to use as many attributes as in pre-stylesheet days.

Remember that XML documents do not always end up as Web pages; the processing program can send the results to an intermediate program. So, if you want to format XML documents for display on your Web site, you must associate the document with a stylesheet.

Whenever you add attributes and attribute values to an HTML or XML document, they are located within the start tag. The start tag for an HTML element with an added attribute and an attribute value looks like this:

```
<P ALIGN="justify">
```

The `ALIGN` attribute justifies the text within the paragraph. Until the `</P>` end tag, all enclosed text is aligned with both the left and right margins.

Although empty elements cannot contain content, they can have attributes. Look at the XML example from the Take Note in the prior task:

```
<graphic pict="bicycle.jpg"/>
```

The `graphic` element has at least one attribute, `pict`. In this example, the value of `pict` is the URL of a JPEG file. HTML's `IMG` element, which is also used to insert graphics in documents, has many attributes. You can use IMG attributes to format a graphic in various ways — to set its vertical and horizontal alignment, specify height and width, and add a border — and to name it, start and end dynamic effects with a mouse click or keystroke, and much more.

TAKE NOTE

▶ REQUIRING END TAGS IN XML

In HTML, some elements allow you to omit the end tag. In XML, the end tag is *always* required. So, if you currently work with HTML documents but plan to convert to XML in the future, you should add both required and optional end tags to your HTML documents for future XML compatibility.

CROSS-REFERENCE
Chapter 8's "Entering Attributes" task teaches you how to add attributes to an HTML or XML document.

FIND IT ONLINE
Learn about HTML tables, forms, frames, and more at **http://www.virtualbusiness.com/wim2/wim3.html**.

Listing 6-5: An HTML Document with Attributes

```
<!DOCTYPE HTML PUBLIC
 "-//W3C//DTD HTML 4.0//EN">
<HTML><HEAD><TITLE>The Bart Page</TITLE>
</HEAD><BODY>
<H1><I>Bart</I></H1>
<IMG SRC="bart.jpg" height="124"
width="150" alt="bart.jpg" border="6">
<P><FONT SIZE="4">Bart was a handsome
golden retriever who loved to watch
television, especially advertisements that
featured animals. When he discovered the
nature segment of the CBS Sunday Morning
show, he was on his way.
</FONT></P></BODY></HTML>
```

Listing 6-6: Horizontal Rules and Their Attributes

```
<!DOCTYPE HTML PUBLIC
 "-//W3C//DTD HTML 4.0//EN">
<HTML><HEAD>
<TITLE>Horizontal Rules</TITLE>
</HEAD><BODY>
<H2>Examples of Horizontal Rules</H4>
<B>The default horizontal rule:</B>
<HR>
<BR><B>A short, left-aligned rule:</B>
<HR width="300" align="left">
<BR><B>A rule with some height:</B>
<HR size="10">
<BR><B>A rule with no shading:</B>
<HR noshade></BODY></HTML>
```

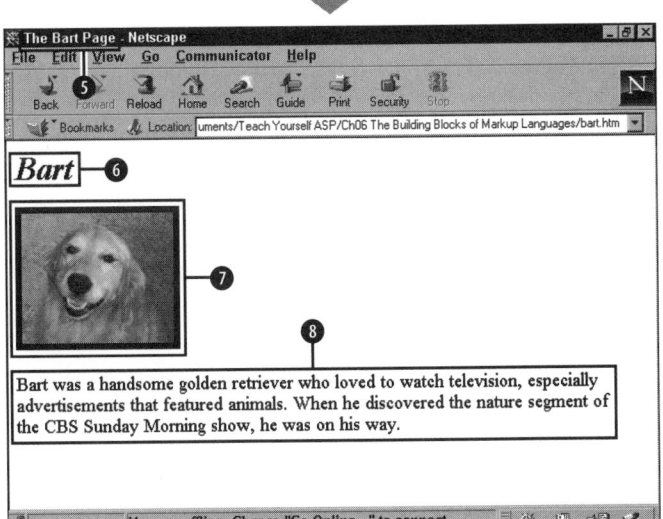

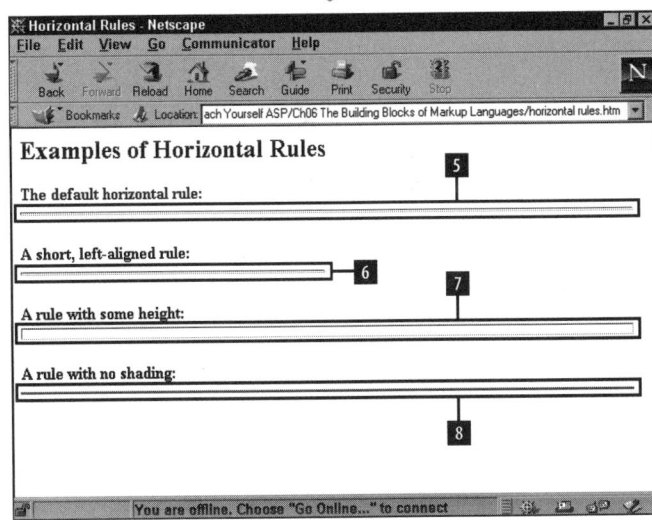

❶ The source file is `bart.jpg`.

❷ Set the height at 124 pixels.

❸ Set the width to 150 pixels.

❹ The alternate name is `bart.jpg`, and the border is 6 pixels.

❺ The title is entered in the document's HEAD section.

❻ The top-level heading appears before the graphic.

❼ The graphic's dimensions are attributes of the IMG element.

❽ Increase the text size using the SIZE attribute of the FONT element.

1 The default rule stretches from the left to right margin.

2 Use the `width` attribute to set the width.

3 Increase the rule's height using the `size` attribute.

4 Use the `noshade` attribute to remove the rule's shading.

5 The default rule stretches from the left to right margin.

6 The rule is less than the default width.

7 The rule is 10 pixels high.

8 A "noshade" rule is all one color.

Utilizing Entities

Both HTML and XML support the use of *entities*, which are sets of characters from the supported International Standard ISO 10646-1, or Unicode Standard. Entities can range from a single character to an entire document. Within a document, a reference to an entity causes the program that processes the document to replace the reference with replacement text. An entity reference is usually a shortcut to a larger chunk of text.

Entity references and the entities with which they are associated work in the same way as a word processor's search-and-replace function: the program searches for a word or phrase (the entity reference) and replaces it with another word, phrase, or document (the entity).

Use entity references to substitute for a difficult-to-spell technical term or a long company name — especially those terms and names that you use many times in one or more documents. For example, the entity reference `bop` could stand for `byte-oriented protocol`, or `ldc` could represent the `Lotus Development Corporation`. In a DTD, you define an entity reference as follows:

```
<!ENTITY bop "byte-oriented protocol"
```

Then, when you specify `bop` in an XML document:

```
<para>Transmit data as a character string
  using &bop;.</para>
```

the XML processor replaces it:

Transmit data as a character string using byte-oriented protocol.

You can also use entities to insert several documents (such as a group of chapters or files making up a report) into a master document. You may have created each of the documents yourself, or each member of a working group could work on an individual document.

HTML and XML support various types of entity references. To differentiate among the types, precede each with one or more special characters. All types of entity references end with a semicolon (;). Table 6-3 lists entity references. Under each entry, you'll find a brief description and example.

Both HTML and XML reserve the general entities listed in Table 6-4. Notice that each reserved entity represents a commonly-used delimiter.

TAKE NOTE

▶ LEARNING ABOUT THE VARIETY OF ENTITIES

HTML and XML share several types of entities:

▶ A *general entity*, which is named within the character data in a document.

▶ A *parameter entity* (PE) is named within DTD markup. Remember that the HTML DTD has already been defined and cannot be modified by the general Web development population. However, you can add PEs to your XML DTDs.

▶ A *parsed entity*, which is processed (parsed) only if it is used in a document. A parsed entity can include both character data and markup. In contrast, an *unparsed entity* is never parsed.

▶ An *internal entity*, which is declared in the same document from which it is referenced. In contrast, an *external entity* is in an external document and is referred to by using a URL.

CROSS-REFERENCE
To learn more about adding entities to documents, refer to the "Entering General Entities" task in Chapter 8.

FIND IT ONLINE
The Unicode Organization (**http://www.unicode.org/**) presents many pages that show) the characters supported by HTML and XML.

The Building Blocks of Markup Languages

Table 6-3: RESERVED CHARACTERS FOR ENTITY REFERENCES

Entity references	Start with	Refers to	Example
Decimal character	`&#`	a decimal character inserted in a document	`&#226;`
Hexadecimal character	`&#x`	a hexadecimal character inserted in a document	`&#x00E2;`
Parsed general	`&`	alphanumeric characters inserted in a document	`&ldc;`
Parameter entity (PE)	`%`	alphanumeric characters inserted in an XML DTD	`%ldc;`

Table 6-4: RESERVED ENTITIES

To produce this character	Insert this entity
ampersand (&)	`&amp;`
apostrophe (!)	`&apos;`
greater-than (>)	`&gt;`
less-than (<)	`&lt;`
quotation mark (")	`&quot;`

Listing 6-7: An Example of an XML Master Document

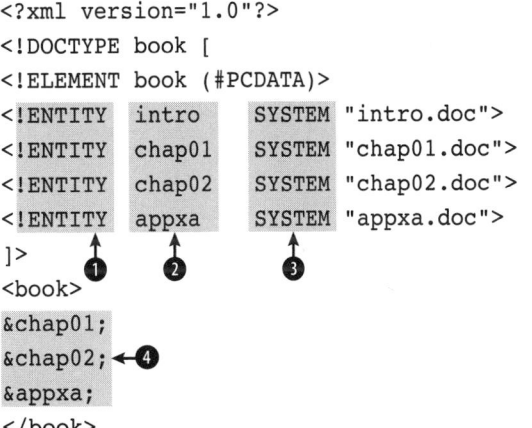

```
<?xml version="1.0"?>
<!DOCTYPE book [
<!ELEMENT book (#PCDATA)>
<!ENTITY   intro    SYSTEM "intro.doc">
<!ENTITY   chap01   SYSTEM "chap01.doc">
<!ENTITY   chap02   SYSTEM "chap02.doc">
<!ENTITY   appxa    SYSTEM "appxa.doc">
]>
<book>
&chap01;
&chap02;
&appxa;
</book>
```

❶ Start an entity declaration with the `!ENTITY` keyword.
❷ Name the entity references.
❸ `SYSTEM` indicates that the files are on your local network.
❹ Insert the entity references in the body of the document.

Introducing DTDs

As you have already learned, a DTD defines the markup components of one or more documents with which it is associated. The components include elements, attributes, and entities. An accurate HTML document is always associated with the predefined HTML DTD. However, an XML document may or may not be associated with a DTD (see the following Take Note).

Up to this point in the book, sample XML documents have always started with a DTD — starting with the [in the document type declaration:

```
<!DOCTYPE memo [
```

and ending with the]> delimiters after all the components, such as elements, attributes, and entities, have been defined. A DTD that is part of the document that it defines is known as an *internal DTD subset*. An internal DTD defines the components of only one document — the one in which it is included. XML DTDs can also be separate files or *external DTD subsets*. Because it is a document unto itself, an external DTD subset can control one or more documents. For example, you can develop one DTD to define all the document components for your letters, another to control all your reports, and so forth.

An external DTD starts the same way as any other XML document:

```
<?xml version="1.0"?>
<!DOCTYPE root_element [
```

and is referred to from within the XML document that it controls. The first two lines of a document with an external DTD looks something like this:

```
<?xml version="1.0"?>
<!DOCTYPE book SYSTEM "book.dtd">
```

Occasionally, an XML document can contain an internal DTD and be associated with an external DTD. In this situation, the declarations in the internal DTD override those in the external DTD.

Actually, all XML documents associated with a DTD include an internal DTD subset; if an external DTD is connected to a document, the internal subset names the external DTD.

TAKE NOTE

LEARNING ABOUT WELL-FORMED AND VALID XML DOCUMENTS

XML documents come in two flavors — well-formed and valid. A *well-formed document* is not associated with a DTD. However, the document must be well-organized and follow all the rules for XML documents. For example, it must have one root element and all its elements must have matching start tags and end tags. A well-formed document is checked for accuracy by a nonvalidating XML parser.

Like a well-formed document, a *valid document* is accurate and can be parsed by a nonvalidating parser. However, to be valid, a document must include an internal or external DTD. A valid document must follow all XML rules and accurately follow the declarations specified in the DTD. In order to test the document against its DTD, it should be parsed against a validating parser.

CROSS-REFERENCE

You'll learn more about working with internal DTD subsets and external DTD subsets in Chapter 7.

FIND IT ONLINE

The Developer Shed (**http://www.devshed.com/**) provides many "tools to build a better website."

Listing 6-8: A Small Well-Formed XML Document

```
<?xml version="1.0"?>  ←❶
<doc>  ❷
<head>A Well-Formed Document</head>  ←❹
<text>  ←❷        ❸
A <ital>well-formed</ital> document does
not have a DTD. However, it must meet all
the rules of an accurate XML document. But,
how does a processor know how to treat
undeclared elements?
</text>  ←❹
</doc>
```

❶ Start a well-formed document with an XML declaration.
❷ Begin each element with a start tag.
❸ End each element with an end tag.
❹ Nest child elements completely within higher-level elements.

Listing 6-9: A Well-Formed Document with an Empty Element

```
<?xml version = "1.0"?>
<doc>
<title>A Document with a Graphic</title>
<pic src="sky.gif"/>
<poem>
When the lamp is shattered
The light in the dust lies dead—
When the cloud is scattered
The rainbow's glory is shed.
</poem>
<author>Percy Bysshe Shelley</author>
</doc>
```

▶ This example of a well-formed XML document shows that you can include an empty element such as a graphic.

Listing 6-10: A Valid Document with an Internal DTD

```
         ❶        ❷
<?xml version="1.0"?>
<!DOCTYPE document [  ←❸
<!ELEMENT document (head|para)*>
<!ELEMENT head     (#PCDATA)>
<!ELEMENT para     (#PCDATA)>
<!ELEMENT ital     (#PCDATA)>]>
                            ↑❹
<document>
<head>A Well-Formed Document</head>
<para>A <ital>valid</ital> document has an
internal or external DTD. Its elements are
defined, so the processor can interpret
document content properly.</para>
```

❶ Start a document type declaration with the !DOCTYPE keyword.
❷ Make sure that the !DOCTYPE and root element names match.
❸ Begin the DTD with a left bracket ([).
❹ End the DTD with a right bracket (]).

Listing 6-11: The Same Document with an External DTD

```
<?xml version="1.0"?>
<!DOCTYPE document SYSTEM "/dtds/doc.dtd">
<document>
<head>A Well-Formed Document</head>
<para>A <ital>valid</ital> document has an
internal or external DTD. Its elements are
defined, so the processor can interpret
document content properly.</para>
<para>Associate a style sheet to format
various elements.</para></document>
```

▶ An XML with an external DTD has a document type declaration that refers to the DTD and its storage location. All the element declarations are in the external file.

Personal Workbook

Q & A

1 How does a browser or processor identify markup in a document?

_____

_____

_____

2 How does a processor identify a particular type of markup?

_____

_____

_____

3 What does EBNF stand for?

_____

_____

_____

4 List five EBNF delimiters or connectors.

_____

_____

_____

5 What is the root element?

_____

_____

_____

6 What are child elements?

_____

_____

_____

7 What is an inline element?

_____

_____

_____

8 What is a block element?

_____

_____

_____

ANSWERS: PAGE 498

1 Go to the Unicode site and find the Latin 1 Supplementary chart.

2 Using the chart that you found in the previous question, write entities for all the characters with umlauts.

3 Convert any of the HTML listings in this chapter to an XML document with an internal DTD.

4 Go to the HTML 4.0 specification and find the entity declarations for inline elements and block elements.

5 In the HTML 4.0 specification or in this book, find all the elements that enhance text.

6 Using the example DTDs and HTML's text-enhancement elements as a guide, write a DTD that includes child elements that enhance text.

✔ You have been assigned to set up a corporate intranet. Your first step is to design a well-organized HTML-based Web site.

✔ For your intranet, plan a home page, which will link to one or more pages from every department.

✔ Plan how to convert your corporate telephone list to a Web document.

✔ Plan and develop a home page for your family. Be sure that the photographs are small to ensure that they will load quickly.

Visual Quiz

Identify components in this XML document. Where is the XML version? Mark the symbol that starts the DTD and the symbol that ends the DTD. What is the name of the root element? Circle the root's child element declarations. Circle the children of one of the child elements. Circle the part of the document that will be displayed. Mark one start tag and one end tag. Identify the empty element and show its location in the output text. Circle the entity references.

```
Close Full Screen
<?xml version = "1.0"?>
<!DOCTYPE report [
<!ENTITY  file01   SYSTEM "file01.doc">
<!ENTITY  file02   SYSTEM "file02.doc">
<!ELEMENT report  (logo|head1|head2|text*)>
<!ELEMENT logo    EMPTY>
<!ELEMENT head1   (#PCDATA)>
<!ELEMENT head2   (#PCDATA)>
<!ELEMENT text    (bold|ital)>
]>
<report>
<head1>Sample Report</head1>
<logo src="corplogo.gif"/>
<head2>Introduction</head2>
<text>Our company has big plans for this year. The
following report will go into the details.
</text>
&file01;
&file02;
</report>
```

CHAPTER 7

MASTER THESE SKILLS

▶ Learning about Internal and External Subsets
▶ Declaring Root and Child Elements
▶ Controlling Element Content
▶ Declaring Empty Elements
▶ Adding Attribute Lists
▶ Defining Entities

Building the Underlying Structure of a Document

This chapter teaches the fine points of interpreting or building DTDs. Here, you'll find out about the major DTD components, which make up HTML and XML documents.

As you know, the HTML DTD is predefined for you. However, in order to use HTML elements and attributes properly, you will sometimes have to review the DTD to understand a particular element or attribute-list declaration — especially declaration structure, reserved keywords, delimiters, and so forth.

In the prior chapter, you were introduced to internal DTD subsets and external DTD subsets, which are either part of the document whose components it declares or a separate, external file. In the first task in this chapter, you'll build on this knowledge. You'll also see an example of a multi-generational DTD and an example of a document that refers to that external DTD and includes an internal DTD.

The second task discusses root elements and their child elements. You'll find out how to use certain characters to require or make optional the order in which child elements are chosen as well as how to require or make optional the selection of particular child elements. The following task shows how you can determine or limit the content of a particular element: to child elements only, to future content only, to a mix of child elements and character data, or to any elements that have been declared elsewhere in the DTD. Then, you'll discover how to use empty elements as placeholders for future content. If you want to "decorate" a document with external files, you'll have to know exactly how empty elements work in both HTML and XML documents.

The last two tasks discuss attributes and entities. Attributes enable you to refine elements as well as set values or ranges of values. Entities are shortcuts for long or complicated words, phrases, or even entire files. Using entities, you can insert special non-keyboard characters in documents or assemble long documents made up of separate files.

Learning about Internal and External Subsets

In the previous chapter, you were introduced to internal DTD subsets and external DTD subsets. Remember that every HTML and XML document contains an internal DTD: at minimum, it refers to the URI of an external DTD. HTML documents *always* contain an opening line that "calls" an external DTD — a predefined DTD that declares all of HTML's elements, attributes, and entities:

```
<!DOCTYPE HTML PUBLIC
    "-//W3C//DTD HTML 4.0//EN">
```

The example line calls the HTML 4.0 DTD.

As you know, XML documents can either have a minimal internal DTD that only refers to an external DTD subset or an internal DTD in which all the elements, attributes, entities, and other markup components are declared:

```
<!DOCTYPE book SYSTEM "book.dtd">
<!DOCTYPE root_element [
```

The first document type declaration refers to an external DTD subset, and the second starts an internal DTD.

Remember that an internal DTD subset for an XML document starts with a left bracket ([) immediately after the !DOCTYPE declaration and ends with a right bracket and greater-than symbol (]>). The DTD is contained completely within the brackets.

It is important to note that an internal DTD defines elements only for the document in which it is contained. This means that you cannot use an internal DTD to specify the elements for a set of documents. So, if you plan to develop a lengthy DTD in which many elements and attributes are declared, try to make it an external DTD. Further, external DTDs enable you to set corporate or department standards for groups of related documents such as memoranda, mass-mailing letters, reports, and so forth.

You can combine external and internal DTDs. If you do so, the components of the internal DTD have priority over those of the external DTD. For an example, see Listing 7-2 on the facing page.

TAKE NOTE

VARYING YOUR XML DECLARATIONS

The first line in an XML document states the version of XML that will control processing. For example:

```
<?xml version = "1.0"?>
```

The sample line says that an XML parser should use the 1.0 version of XML when it processes the document. (At this point, 1.0 is the only version. However, you can count on the W3C, which develops XML, to announce other XML recommendations in the future.)

You can add other information to the XML declaration:

```
<?xml version = "1.0"
    standalone="no"?>
```

The example line includes the standalone="no" statement, which indicates that external DTDs may be associated with the current document. The value standalone="no" is the default if there is an external DTD. Therefore, you can consider standalone="no" a document comment. If your document uses an internal DTD to declare its markup components, you can add standalone="yes" to the XML declaration. The value standalone="yes" is the default, so you are not required to add it to the declaration.

An XML declaration can also include an encoding declaration:

```
<?xml version = "1.0"
    encoding="UTF-8"?>
```

UTF-8 represents the UTF-8 character codes. This is the XML default. Other supported encodings include UTF-16 and ISO-8859-*n*, where *n* represents ASCII plus language variations (1 through 15) of the Latin character set.

CROSS-REFERENCE

To learn about organizing international Web pages, see "Managing International Pages" in Chapter 5.

FIND IT ONLINE

CNET Builder.com (**http://www.builder.com/**) provides links to a variety of Web site tips, tutorials, and downloads.

Building the Underlying Structure of a Document

Listing 7-1: A Four-Generation External DTD

```
<?xml version="1.0"?>   ◀—❶
                              ❷
<!DOCTYPE book [
<!ELEMENT book (front,chap+,apps+,index)>
  <!ELEMENT front        (titlepg,copyrt)>   ❸
    <!ELEMENT titlepg      (title,author,loc)>
      <!ELEMENT title    (#PCDATA)>
      <!ELEMENT author   (#PCDATA)>
      <!ELEMENT loc      (#PCDATA)>
    <!ELEMENT copyrt     (#PCDATA)>
  <!ELEMENT chap  (intro,(head+|body+|sum))>
  <!ELEMENT apps  (intro,(head+|body+))>
  <!ELEMENT index        (#PCDATA)>
    <!ELEMENT intro      (#PCDATA)>
    <!ELEMENT head   (h1|h2|h3|h4)>
      <!ELEMENT h1       (#PCDATA)>
      <!ELEMENT h2       (#PCDATA)>
      <!ELEMENT h3       (#PCDATA)>
      <!ELEMENT h4       (#PCDATA)>
    <!ELEMENT body   (normal*|bold*|ital*)>
      <!ELEMENT normal   (#PCDATA)>
      <!ELEMENT bold     (#PCDATA)>
      <!ELEMENT ital     (#PCDATA)>
    <!ELEMENT sum        (#PCDATA)>
]>  ◀—❹
```

❶ Start with the XML and document type declarations.
❷ List four child elements for the root element, book.
❸ Define two levels of children for the front element.
❹ Close the DTD with the]> delimiters.

Listing 7-2: A Document with Two DTDs

```
<?xml version="1.0"?>                  ▮1
<!DOCTYPE manual SYSTEM "book.dtd" [ ◀—▮2
<!ELEMENT manual                ▮3
        (front,chap+,apps+,glos,index,offices)>
  <!ELEMENT front (read1st,titlepg,copyrt)>
    <!ELEMENT read1st (normal*|bold*|ital*)>
    <!ELEMENT titlepg (title,program)> ◀—▮4
  <!ELEMENT chap
      (subtoc,intro, (head+|body+|sum))>
    <!ELEMENT subtoc (#PCDATA)>
    <!ELEMENT body
      (normal*|bold*|ital*|warn*|note*|tip*)>
      <!ELEMENT warn (#PCDATA)>
      <!ELEMENT note (#PCDATA)>
      <!ELEMENT tip (#PCDATA)>
  <!ELEMENT glos (intro,dl)>
    <!ELEMENT dl ((dt,dd)+)>
      <!ELEMENT dt (bold)>
      <!ELEMENT dd (#PCDATA)>
  <!ELEMENT offices
      (name,addrss+,city,state,zip)>
      <!ELEMENT name (#PCDATA)>
      <!ELEMENT addrss (#PCDATA)>
      <!ELEMENT city (#PCDATA)>
      <!ELEMENT state (#PCDATA)>
      <!ELEMENT zip (#PCDATA)>
]>
```

▮1 In the !DOCTYPE statement, refer to the external DTD.
▮2 Start the internal DTD, whose elements have priority over the external DTD.
▮3 The front element now includes the read1st element.
▮4 The titlepg element omits two elements and adds the program element.

Declaring Root and Child Elements

Whether written in HTML or XML, every document has a root element, which is the top element. All other elements in the document are children or descendants of the root. As you learned in Chapter 6, HTML is the root element in every HTML document: HTML marks the start and end of the document. In addition, the predefined HTML DTD sets the structure of the root, child, and other descendant elements. Table 7-1 summarizes generations of elements.

In XML documents, the DTD developer declares the root element as well as all the child elements. For example:

```
<?xml version="1.0"?>
<!DOCTYPE memo [
<!ELEMENT memo (to, from, subj, body)>
```

In the example, memo is the root element. The element declaration starts with the ELEMENT keyword, a valid XML element name (starting with a letter or underscore character), and is followed by a list of all the child elements, enclosed within parentheses. The commas that separate the children indicate that each of the elements must be used in a particular order: to, followed by from, followed by subject, and ending with body. A document writer can select each of the listed child elements once. You can add the *, ?, or + symbols to an element to control its use. Look at the following element declaration:

```
<!ELEMENT memo (to*, from, subj?, body+)>
```

If you follow a child element's name with an asterisk (*), the element is optional but can be used more than once in a document. A question mark (?) indicates that the element is optional but can only be used once in a document. A plus sign (+) means that the element must be used at least once in a document.

The pipe symbol (|) allows latitude in element selection. For example:

```
<!ELEMENT text (bold*| ital*)>
```

The sample declaration states that the bold and ital elements are children of the text element. You can use each of these elements any number of times in a document, and you can select each in any order. (If you separated the elements with a comma, you would be forced to select bold before using ital.

You can combine commas and pipes within an element declaration. When you do so, use parentheses to group like elements. For example:

```
<!ELEMENT plan (logo,(text*|chart?))>
```

In this example, the logo must occur first. The rest of the document can be made up of any number of text chunks accompanied by optional charts.

TAKE NOTE

FINDING DTDS ONLINE

You don't always have to develop an XML DTD from scratch. You can find many XML and SGML DTDs on the World Wide Web or at FTP sites. Simply use your favorite search engine and keywords such as *dtd*, *"xml dtd"*, or *"sgml dtd"*. (Remember to enclose phrases within quotation marks.) If your industry has an XML-based custom markup language, see if you can adapt the underlying DTD. Make sure that you use DTDs that do not contain typographic and spelling errors. Errors are the mark of an inaccurate DTD.

CROSS-REFERENCE
For an overview of HTML and XML elements, refer to the "Learning about Elements" task in Chapter 6.

FIND IT ONLINE
Robin Cover's XML site, at **http://www.oasis-open.org/cover/xml.html**, is a comprehensive XML directory.

Table 7-1: ELEMENTS GENERATIONS

Generation	Description
Root	The top-level element in a document; the *document element* within which all other elements for the current document are nested.
Child	An element that is nested under a parent element. In HTML and XML documents, all elements other than the root are child elements.
Parent	An element under which its child elements are nested.
ancestor	A higher-level element, such as a parent element or the root, in a family tree of elements.
descendant	All generations of elements nested under a parent element or the root.

Listing 7-3: Examples of Root Element Declarations

```
<!ELEMENT report
   (cover, title, abstract, intro,
   section+, summary)>
                   └─❶

<!ELEMENT manual (cover, title, abstract,
    TOC, intro, chapter+, appendix*, index)>
         ❸                         ↑
                                   ❷
<!ELEMENT paper (title, abstract,
    (head,body)+, appendix*, footnotes)>

<!-- text child elements -->←❹
<!ELEMENT text (normal*|bold*|italics*)>
```

❶ *+ means that at least one instance of an element must appear.*

❷ *An asterisk (*) allows an element to occur more than once.*

❸ *This pair of elements must appear at least once.*

❹ *Use comments to explain a declaration.*

Listing 7-4: Business Plan Elements

```
<?xml version="1.0"?>
<!DOCTYPE busplan [
<!ELEMENT busplan (cover, title, abstract,
    intro, section+, summary)>              ←❶
  <!ELEMENT cover (#PCDATA)>
  <!ELEMENT title (#PCDATA)>
  <!ELEMENT abstract (#PCDATA)>
  <!ELEMENT intro (#PCDATA)>          ❷        ❸
  <!ELEMENT section ((logo*|chart*),(exec_sum,
     bus_descr, ind_info, compete,market_plan,
     operations, manage, finances))>
  <!ELEMENT logo EMPTY>
  <!ELEMENT chart EMPTY>
  <!ELEMENT exec_sum (head+|text+)>
  <!ELEMENT bus_descr (head+|text+)>
  <!ELEMENT ind_info (head+|text+)>
  <!ELEMENT compete (head+|text+)>
  <!ELEMENT market_plan (head+|text+)>
  <!ELEMENT operations (head+|text+)>
  <!ELEMENT manage (head+|text+)>
  <!ELEMENT finances (head+|text+)>
  <!ELEMENT summary (head*|text+)>
      <!ELEMENT head (h1|h2|h3|h4)>
        <!ELEMENT h1 (#PCDATA)>            ❹
        <!ELEMENT h2 (#PCDATA)>
        <!ELEMENT h3 (#PCDATA)>
        <!ELEMENT h4 (#PCDATA)>
      <!ELEMENT text (norm|bold|ital)>
        <!ELEMENT norm (#PCDATA)>
        <!ELEMENT bold (#PCDATA)>
        <!ELEMENT ital (#PCDATA)>
]>
```

❶ *Declare the root element and list the first generation of children.*

❷ *Allow any number of logos and charts throughout the report.*

❸ *Use commas to force an order of report components.*

❹ *Each child must contain at least one heading and body text.*

Controlling Element Content

As you have seen in prior tasks and examples, a root element lists its child elements as contents — unless the root element has no children. Elements can have three other types of content: ANY, which is a reserved keyword stating that the content includes any declared elements, including itself; mixed character data and child elements; and EMPTY, which is a reserved keyword stating that there is no content. (You can see examples of empty elements on the facing page; you'll learn more about empty elements and how to declare them in the following task.)

In many of the examples you have seen thus far, the following element declaration has been most common:

```
<!ELEMENT bird      (#PCDATA)>
```

This declaration means that the bird element can contain parsed character data, which is character data that will be processed when the document is processed. Because the element declaration occurs within the DTD, the actual character data is not included in the declaration; the declaration simply states that character data can be contained within the element tags in the future XML document.

To indicate that an element can contain a mix of character data and child elements, code the declaration as follows:

```
<!ELEMENT bird      (#PCDATA|egg)>
```

The declaration states that the bird element could include parsed character data or the child element, egg. The element declaration could also look like this:

```
<!ELEMENT bird      ANY>
```

The element can have any content but *must* have at least one child element that has already been declared elsewhere in the DTD. Note that you cannot declare the same element type (such as bird) more than once in a DTD; however, you can declare attributes and entities more than once.

TAKE NOTE

► LEARNING MORE ABOUT GENERATIONS

Element generations are similar to family generations: they both include parents (that is, roots), ancestors (all elements above the parents), descendants (all elements below the parents), and children.

Several generations of child elements can exist within a document: the first generation of child elements are immediately under the root, the second generation of child elements (analogous to grandchildren) are under the original child elements, the third generation of child elements (analogous to great-grandchildren) are under the second generation, and so forth. These generations form a tree of elements — from the root to the first generation of children to each succeeding generation. For example:

```
root-element
    generation 1
        generation 2
        generation 2
            generation 3
                generation 4
            generation 3
                generation 4
```

The hierarchy of elements in both HTML and XML documents has an effect on certain attributes. For example, say the text element has two children: warning and caution. If text is in the Courier font and has a point size of 12, both warning and caution will have the same settings — unless you explicitly specify a different font, point size, or both. When you read Chapter 13, you'll find out how stylesheet properties for a child element are either inherited or not inherited from its parent.

CROSS-REFERENCE

Learn the difference between markup and character data in "Recognizing Markup and Character Data" in Chapter 6.

FIND IT ONLINE

Go to **http://www.w3.org/Provider/Style/** to browse through a classic article on creating HTML documents.

Listing 7-5: Samples of Empty Elements

```
<!DOCTYPE HTML PUBLIC
      "-//W3C//DTD HTML 4.0//EN">
<HTML><HEAD>
<TITLE>Empty Elements</TITLE>
</HEAD><BODY>①              ②
<H2>Directional Arrows</H2>
<IMG SRC="redarrow.jpg"> ←③
<BR><B><I>red down arrow</B></I></IMG>
<P><IMG SRC="bluearrow.jpg"> ┌④
<BR><B><I>blue up arrow</B></I></IMG>
<P><IMG SRC="greenarrow.jpg">
<BR><B><I>green left arrow</B></I></IMG>
<P><IMG SRC="cyanarrow.jpg">
<BR><B><I>cyan right arrow</B></I></IMG>
</BODY></HTML>
```

① *Start an empty element with the* IMG *start tag.*
② *Refer to the source file.*
③ *End the start tag with >.*
④ *If you wish, break and add a caption.*

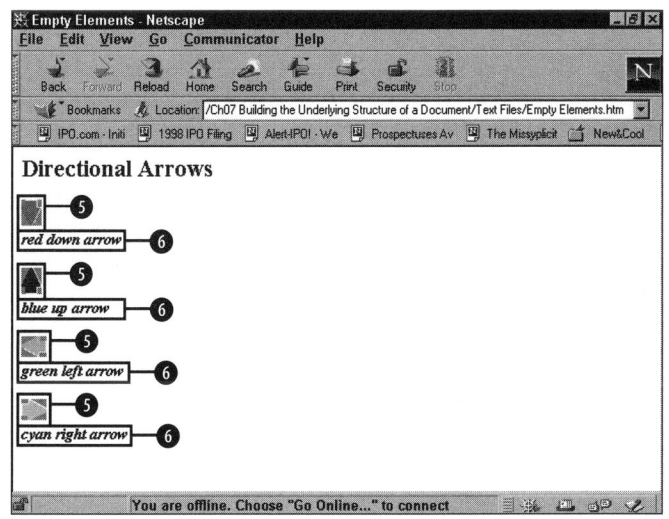

⑤ *The browser inserts the source-file image.*
⑥ *After a line break, a caption appears.*

Listing 7-6: The First Draft of a DTD

```
<?xml version = "1.0"?>
<!DOCTYPE document [
<!ELEMENT document (title,intro,page+)> ←■1
   <!ELEMENT title (#PCDATA)> ←■2
   <!ELEMENT intro (in_text|#PCDATA)> ←■3
      <!ELEMENT in_text (#PCDATA)>
   <!ELEMENT page (head,pg_text+)> ←■4
      <!ELEMENT head (#PCDATA)>
      <!ELEMENT pg_text (#PCDATA)>
   ]>
```

■1 *Root element lists child elements.*
■2 *Element accepts parsed character data.*
■3 *Element mixes a child element and parsed character data.*
■4 *A child element can contain its own children.*

Listing 7-7: XML Document with an Empty Element

```
<?xml version="1.0"?>
<!DOCTYPE library [
<!ELEMENT library
      (text|(figure,caption)+)>
  <!ELEMENT text (#PCDATA)>
  <!ELEMENT figure EMPTY> ←①
  <!ATTLIST figure
      src      CDATA      #REQUIRED> ←②
  <!ELEMENT caption (#PCDATA)>
]>
<library><text>introductory text</text>
<figure src="renoir1.gif"/> ←③
<caption>Young Girl</caption>
</library>
```

① *Declare the* figure *element, which is a placeholder for an image.*
② *The required* src *attribute provides the URI for the image.*
③ *Enter the URI within the* <figure> *start tag.*

Declaring Empty Elements

In the "Using Empty Elements" Take Note in Chapter 6, you were introduced to empty elements, which do not have current content but serve as placeholders for a future component of an HTML- or XML-based Web page. In HTML, the most commonly-used placeholder element is IMG, whose start tag contains the URI of a graphic image to be inserted in the document when it is displayed or printed and, optionally, other attributes. The IMG element declaration in the HTML 4.0 recommendation looks like this:

```
<!ELEMENT IMG - O EMPTY>
```

The declaration starts with the familiar ELEMENT keyword and continues with the IMG element name. The hyphen indicates that the start tag is required. According to the HTML 4.0 recommendation, "The hyphen and the following 'O' indicate that the end tag can be omitted, but together with the content model 'EMPTY,' this is strengthened to the rule that the end tag *must* be omitted. The 'EMPTY' keyword means that instances of this type must not have content." HTML 4.0 empty elements are AREA, BASE, BASEFONT, BR, COL, FRAME, HR, IMG, INPUT, ISINDEX, LINK, META, and PARAM.

As you know, XML always requires an end tag. So, you would expect to write code for an empty XML element using the following format:

```
<image uri="buffalo.gif"></image>
```

This example is completely valid. However, XML provides a special shortcut syntax that combines the start tag and end tag:

```
<image src="buffalo.gif"/>
```

Notice that the usual end tag is missing, but its ending slash (/) and > delimiter close the statement. When the XML browser or parser encounters the empty-element tag, it should be programmed to interpret it correctly.

To declare an empty element, use the following syntax:

```
<!ELEMENT image EMPTY>
```

You'll learn how to declare attributes for empty elements in the following task.

TAKE NOTE

USING END TAGS IN XML

In HTML, end tags come in three categories: some are required, some are optional, and others must be omitted. In XML, the end tag is *always* present. So, if you currently work with HTML documents but plan to convert to XML in the future, you should add both required and optional end tags to your HTML documents for future compatibility with XML.

FINDING MULTIMEDIA FILES ONLINE

You don't have to be an artist or musician to enhance your Web pages. As always, the Web is a major resource of graphics and audio files. To search for multimedia on the Web, start up a search engine, enter keywords (such as *icons* or *graphics*) or key phrases (such as *"free graphics,"* *"downloadable music",* or *"sound effects"*) and click the Search or Go button. (Remember to enclose phrases within quotation marks.) Before you download or save a file, make sure that it is copyright-free. Table 7-2 lists several sources of multimedia content and information.

CROSS-REFERENCE

In the "Adding Multimedia Content" task in Chapter 8, you'll find out how to use empty elements.

FIND IT ONLINE

Learn about HTML and XML at **http://www.cs.caltech. edu/~adam/papers/xml/ascent-of-xml.html**.

Table 7-2: MULTIMEDIA SOURCES ON THE WEB

Name	URL	Description
VL-WWW: Images_and_Icons	http://www.wdvl.com/Vlib/Multimedia/Images_and_Icons.html	Several pages of links to graphics galleries
Yahoo! Computers and Internet:Graphics	http://dir.yahoo.com/Computers_and_Internet/Graphics/	Links to a variety of graphics-related sites
Yahoo! Arts:Design Arts: Graphic Design:Web Page Design and Layout:Graphics	http://dir.yahoo.com/Arts/Design_Arts/Graphic_Design/Web_Page_Design_and_Layout/Graphics/	Links to backgrounds, clip art, icons, transparent images, animated GIFs, and archives of graphics
MSDN Online Design: Multimedia Gallery	http://msdn.microsoft.com/workshop/design/creative/mmgallry.asp	Downloadable backgrounds, banners, navigation controls, images, and sounds
IliCons	http://www.ilicon.com/	A directory to primarily Macintosh icons
Creative Box	http://skyscraper.fortunecity.com/memphis/824/	Links to many icons as well as Macintosh resources
Color Manipulation Device	http://www.meat.com/software/cmd/body.html	A Windows shareware utility that aids in selecting Web page colors
RGB Color Chart	http://www.phoenix.net/~jacobson/rgb.html	A comprehensive chart of RGB color values and links to other resources
Multimedia for the Web – Web Design Net Links	http://webdesign.miningco.com/msubmultimedia.htm	Pages of links to audio, video, and chat resources
Audio Browser: Sound Files	http://www.webplaces.com/html/sounds.htm	Links to many categories of sound files

Adding Attribute Lists

Elements and attributes work hand in hand — especially in HTML documents and to a lesser extent in XML documents. Now that stylesheets are becoming more popular in both XML and HTML documents, attributes will become less important.

An *attribute* is an option or characteristic that further defines an element and affects its behavior or value. Attributes can specify formats or enhancements of selected text, paragraphs, pages, or an entire document. In the HTML specifications, attributes have been defined for you. In XML, a DTD developer declares lists of attributes for all (or almost all) elements.

A sample element declaration and attribute list looks like this:

```
<!ELEMENT image EMPTY>
<!ATTLIST image
    src      CDATA                  #REQUIRED
    id       ID                     #IMPLIED
    align    (left|right|center)    "left"
    border   (yes|no)               "no"
    height   CDATA                  #IMPLIED
    width    CDATA                  #IMPLIED>

    or

<!ELEMENT image EMPTY>
<!ATTLIST image id      ID            #IMPLIED>
<!ATTLIST image src     CDATA         #REQUIRED>
<!ATTLIST image align   (left|right|center)
                                     "left">
<!ATTLIST image border  (yes|no)      "no">
<!ATTLIST image height  CDATA         #IMPLIED>
<!ATTLIST image width   CDATA         #IMPLIED>
```

Notice that this attribute list is for an empty XML element. (Remember that an empty element cannot have content but is allowed to have attributes.) The name of the attribute list is the same as the element name. Each entry includes an individual, unique attribute name, followed by the attribute type (see the following Take Note) or one or more values from which you can choose, and ending with

the default value or whether the attribute is required (#REQUIRED) or optional (#IMPLIED). Table 7-3 lists XML's attribute defaults.

Table 7-3: XML ATTRIBUTE DEFAULTS

Default	Description
#IMPLIED	This default is optional. If the document developer does not supply an attribute value, the processing application should.
#REQUIRED	This default requires that the attribute be used.
#FIXED default_value	This default provides a fixed attribute value. The individual working on the document cannot enter a different value. If no value is entered, the attribute takes the default value.
Default_value	This default provides a default value for the attribute. If no value is entered, the attribute takes the default value.

HTML 4.0: The HTML Element and Its Components

```
<!ENTITY % LanguageCode "NAME"
   -- a language code, as per [RFC1766] -->        ◄─❶


<!ENTITY % i18n
 "lang         %LanguageCode; #IMPLIED  -- language code --        ◄─❷
  dir          (ltr|rtl)      #IMPLIED  -- direction for weak/neutral text --"

<!ENTITY % html.content "HEAD, BODY">◄─❸

<!ELEMENT HTML O O (%html.content;)     -- document root element -->
<!ATTLIST HTML
  %i18n;                                -- lang, dir --◄─❹
>
```

❶ *The* LanguageCode *entity contributes to the* i18n *entity.*
❷ *The* i18n *entity also sets the text direction.*
❸ *The* html.content *entity is part of the* HTML *element declaration.*
❹ *The* i18n *entity is the only entry on* HTML*'s attribute list.*

CROSS-REFERENCE
To learn how to add attributes to a document, see the
"Entering Attributes" task in Chapter 8.

FIND IT ONLINE
Link to XML and SGML information from the experts at
**http://www.arbortext.com/Think_Tank/think_tank.
html.**

Defining Entities

As you learned in the introduction to entities in Chapter 6, an entity is a named chunk of information that is referred to from within a document and placed in the document during processing.

HTML entities are predefined in the HTML specification. In fact, without entities, the HTML specification would be much longer than its current 300-plus pages. As you browse through the specification, you'll find many instances of entities. Examples include `%heading;`, which represents the six heading elements; `%coreattrs;`, which lists the declarations for the commonly-used `id` (identifier), `class` (classifications), `style` (stylesheet), and `title` (element title) attributes; and `%i18n;`, which lists the `lang` (language code) and `dir` (text direction). For example, the `events` entity lists ten dynamic HTML attributes that trigger scripts when a certain event — such as clicking, double-clicking, or pressing a particular key — occurs. When you specify an events attribute in an HTML document, you can link an event, such as clicking a mouse or pressing a key, with a particular action, such as changing a color. Most HTML elements support the `events` attributes, so you can imagine the size of the HTML DTD without these shortcuts.

In XML, you can declare parameter entities (PEs) within the DTD and general entities in the non-DTD portions of a document. The HTML code on the preceding facing page illustrates the use of PEs in a DTD. You'll learn about declaring entities in Chapter 8.

A program that processes an XML document runs straight down the document — from the top line to the bottom line. When the program encounters an entity reference, it quickly replaces the entity reference with *replacement text*, the text enclosed within the entity declaration. The processor does this before processing other parts of the document. So, it's important to place entity declarations near the top of the DTD. If an entity declaration is located after an element in which that entity appears, the parser cannot correctly interpret the element's contents.

TAKE NOTE

DECLARING DATA ENTITIES

The XML specification states that you can include unparsed external general entities, also known as *data entities*, in your documents. Data entities are produced by external programs that are not related to XML in any way. For example, you can declare a graphic, audio or video file, or a word-processing document in any format — anything that an XML parser will not process. Data entity files are usually binary. However, if you want to import but not process an external text (ASCII) file, you can declare it as a data entity. When you declare a data entity, you must include the NDATA keyword and the file type (such as GIF, AVI, PDF, DOC, JPEG or JPG, MPEG, and so forth). For example:

```
<!ENTITY robin-pic
  SYSTEM "../grafix/robin.gif"
  NDATA gif >
```

This example declares a GIF file called `robin.gif`. When you declare a data entity, it must be an element attribute with an attribute type of ENTITY (for a single file) or ENTITIES (for a list of files).

REFERRING TO COMMON DELIMITERS IN HTML OR XML TEXT

When you want to insert a <, >, &, or " character as character-data text, think of how a processor will misinterpret the character: it will think that you are starting or ending a tag, or beginning an entity or string. So, in both HTML and XML, use `&lt;`, `&gt;`, `&amp;`, and `&quot;` respectively, to represent these characters within character data.

CROSS-REFERENCE

For an overview of entities, read the "Utilizing Entities" task in Chapter 6.

FIND IT ONLINE

Find a long paper on SGML DTD structure at **http://etext.virginia.edu/bin/tei-tocs?div=DIV1&id=ST**.

Table 7-4: HTML AND XML ENTITIES

Entity	Parsed/Unparsed	Internal/External	Description
General	Parsed	Internal	An embedded string that will appear as document content
General	Parsed	External	An imported file that will appear as document content
Character	Parsed	Internal/External	A type of general entity used to represent special characters
Data	Unparsed	External	A type of general entity used to import a non-XML file defined as binary
Parameter (PE)	Parsed	Internal	An embedded string used to enhance a DTD
Parameter (PE)	Parsed	External	An imported file used to enhance a DTD

Listing 7-8: Examples of Entities

```
<!DOCTYPE HTML PUBLIC
 "-//W3C//DTD HTML 4.0//EN">
<HTML><HEAD>
<TITLE>Examples of Entities</TITLE>
</HEAD><BODY>
<FONT SIZE=+2>
The less-than symbol looks like &lt;.
<P>The greater-than symbol looks like
 &gt;.</P>
<P>The ampersand looks like &amp;.</P>
<P>The quotation mark looks like &quot;.</P>
</FONT>
</BODY></HTML>
```

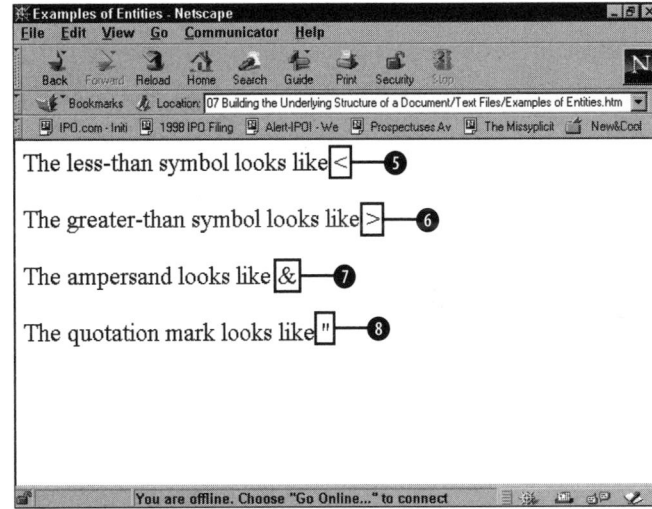

1. Insert the < entity into a block of characters.
2. Enter the > entity to display >.
3. Insert the & entity to display the ampersand.
4. The " entity represents the quotation mark.

5. In a document, the < entity looks like this.
6. The processor interprets > as >.
7. The & entity is displayed as an ampersand.
8. The " entity looks like this.

Personal Workbook

Q & A

1 Does an HTML document ever include an internal DTD?

_____

_____

_____

2 Do XML documents always include an internal DTD?

_____

_____

_____

3 What does the first line of an HTML document look like?

_____

_____

_____

4 What does the document type declaration of an XML document with an external DTD look like?

_____

_____

_____

5 What delimiters mark the beginning and end of an internal XML DTD?

_____

_____

_____

6 What declarations can the XML declaration contain?

_____

_____

_____

7 In a list of child elements, what does the comma separator indicate? What does the pipe indicate?

_____

_____

_____

8 What happens when an XML parser encounters an entity reference in a document?

_____

_____

_____

ANSWERS: PAGE 499

EXTRA PRACTICE

1. Plan and write an HTML document for a fax cover sheet.

2. Plan and create the first draft of an XML DTD for the same fax cover sheet.

3. Edit the fax-cover-sheet DTD so that you must use boldface for the To, From, and Subject elements and can use boldface and italics within body text.

4. Go online and find a DTD for the Math Markup Language.

5. Plan and write an HTML document that refers to at least five graphics.

6. Go to the Unicode Consortium Web site (**www.unicode.org/**), and find the codes for the English alphabet.

REAL-WORLD APPLICATIONS

✔ You are converting your Web documents from HTML to XML. Schedule the creation of XML DTDs and the document conversions.

✔ Your company is planning to set up an intranet. Design its site map.

✔ You head a small group of writers and graphic artists that will convert your marketing materials to HTML documents. Assign each member of your work group conversion tasks.

✔ Plan and create a DTD that will serve as a template for your employee handbook.

Visual Quiz

Mark the many things that are wrong with this DTD.

_____

_____

_____

_____

_____

_____

```
W Microsoft Word - Visual Quiz 7                    _ 8 X
File  Edit  View  Insert  Format  Tools  Table  Window  Help   _ 8 X

<?xml version="1.2"
<!DOCTYPE story [
<!ELEMENT storey (intro,chap,chap)>
   <!ELEMENT intro      (#PDATA)>
   <!ELEMENT chap      (head1\head2|text)>
     <!ELEMENT heading1   (#PCDATA)>
     <!ELEMENT h2         (#PCDATA)>
     <!ELEMENT text       (normal,bold,ital)>
       <!ELEMENT norm    (#PCDATA)>
       <!ELEMENT bold   (#PCDATA)>
       <!ELEMENT italics (#PCDATA)>
     <!ELEMENT sum        (#PCDATA)>
  [>>
```

CHAPTER **8**

MASTER
THESE
SKILLS

▶ **Starting a Document**
▶ **Entering Elements**
▶ **Entering Attributes**
▶ **Entering General Entities**
▶ **Adding Multimedia Content**
▶ **Adding Links to a Document**
▶ **Parsing a Document**

Creating a Basic Document

In this part's preceding chapters, you have learned about various components that make up HTML and XML documents. Now, you'll find out how to combine all the components into accurate and well-designed documents.

As you know, the DTD is the basis for the underlying structure and the look of all HTML and most XML documents. In HTML, the DTD is predefined. Because you cannot edit the DTD and its declaration, you must abide by it. In XML, you can either use a preexisting DTD or design your own. This flexibility gives you more latitude in constructing and refining documents, but you can also get into more trouble unless you plan ahead.

For both HTML and XML documents, you set the look of the pages and also provide the information used as contents. You can choose a combination of elements, attributes, attribute values, and other components that individualize the document.

In the first task of the chapter, you'll learn about the required lines with which you start an HTML or XML document — lines that tell the program that processes the document what version of HTML or XML to use and where that version is located. For XML documents, the lines can also indicate whether the document contains an internal DTD or a standalone external DTD, as well as the character set that is used.

The following tasks tell you, step by step, how to add components to the document. You'll learn how to use start tags and end tags to mark the beginning and end of inserted elements. Then, you'll find out how to use attributes and general entities. Next, you will learn how to enhance a document using multimedia content, such as graphics, sound files, and video files. In the penultimate task, you'll get an overview of HTML and XML's hypertext links that enable your document's visitors to travel to other parts of the current document, your Web site, and other sites around the world.

The final task in the chapter discusses document processing. For HTML documents, you have two choices of processors: those within HTML editors and those built into Web browsers. For XML documents, you can use nonvalidating parsers to check well-formed documents and validating parsers for valid documents. In addition, certain Web browsers also process both HTML and XML documents. More of these browsers are on their way.

Starting a Document

A document — whether it uses HTML or XML as its markup language — contains a combination of markup and character data. An HTML document uses its top line to refer to the predefined DTD that declares its elements, attributes, and other document components; otherwise, the rest of the document uses markup to set its structure and character data to form its content. As you know, XML documents are based on custom-made DTDs. So, a typical XML document either contains an internal DTD in which the element, attributes, and other document components are declared or, at minimum, refers to an external DTD.

When you actually start adding content to a document, you should have spent a great deal of time deciding how the document will be structured and formatted: the number of heading levels, the placement of graphics, the default typefaces and point sizes, and so forth. When you actually create the document, you should only have to worry about its content; the structure should almost take care of itself. In the case of XML documents, if you write the DTD at the same time that you add content, you are only setting yourself up for trouble. The best plan is to write and test the DTD thoroughly before you add the first word to the document.

Note that XML parsers are not programmed to be as forgiving as HTML-only browsers. If you code an XML DTD inaccurately, you'll encounter warning messages and errors that may stop processing altogether.

Start an HTML document with the following line:

```
<!DOCTYPE HTML PUBLIC
    "-//W3C//DTD HTML 4.0//EN">
```

which refers to the HTML 4.0 DTD and its location. Then, add the top-level start tags and end tags:

```
<HTML><HEAD>
</HEAD>
<BODY>
</BODY>
</HTML>
```

The HEAD section contains lines that are not displayed in the document, and the BODY section includes the actual document content. HEAD section elements include BASE, LINK, META (see a following Take Note), SCRIPT, STYLE, TITLE, and ISINDEX (which is deprecated and should be used sparingly if at all).

The top two lines of an XML document should be an XML declaration:

```
<?xml version="1.0"?>
```

followed by the document type declaration:

```
<!DOCTYPE root_element [
```

for an internal DTD, or:

```
<!DOCTYPE book SYSTEM|PUBLIC "dtdname.dtd">
```

for an external DTD file on your local network (SYSTEM) or a publicly-available folder (PUBLIC).

Note that the document type declaration at the top of HTML and XML documents tells browsers and other processors that this is an HTML or XML document, names the supported HTML or XML version, and states its location.

TAKE NOTE

▶ SETTING DOCUMENT STANDARDS

One of the marks of well-planned corporate documents — both internal (memos and timely reports) and external (manuals, proposals, and marketing) — is a uniform design. An important benefit of set standards is that those working on the documents know where the graphics go, what fonts to use, and what enhancements to apply for specific sections: Everything is planned ahead.

CROSS-REFERENCE
To learn about the two types of XML DTDs, see "Learning about Internal and External Subsets" in Chapter 7.

FIND IT ONLINE
To follow the development of new versions of HTML, go to http://www.w3.org/MarkUp/.

Listing 8-1: First Lines of a Sample HEAD Section

```
<!DOCTYPE HTML PUBLIC
    "-//W3C//DTD HTML 4.0//EN">    ◄──❶
<HTML>  ◄──❷
<HEAD>
<TITLE>Colors in HTML Documents</TITLE>    ❸
<META name "description" content="The color
 names and codes for HTML documents">
<META name="author" content="Sandra E. Eddy">
<META name="create-date" content="4/10/00">
<META name="keywords" content="HTML colors,
colors, background colors, table colors, cell
colors, row colors, column colors, page
colors">
</HEAD>  ◄──❹
```

❶ Start a document with the HTML location, version, and language.

❷ Start the HTML document, and open the HEAD section.

❸ Include META statements with the title, author, date, and keywords.

❹ End the HEAD section.

Listing 8-2: First Lines of Several XML Documents

```
<?xml version="1.0"?>
<!DOCTYPE article [
<!ELEMENT article (#PCDATA)>    ◄──■1
]>
```

```
<?xml version="1.0"? standalone="yes"?>
<!DOCTYPE article [
<!ELEMENT article (#PCDATA)>    ■2
]>
```

```
                                ■3
<?xml version="1.0" standalone="no"?>
<!DOCTYPE book SYSTEM "book.dtd">
```

```
<?xml version="1.0" encoding="UTF-16"◄──■4
    standalone="no"?>
<!DOCTYPE book SYSTEM "book.dtd">
```

TAKE NOTE

▶ LEARNING ABOUT METADATA

Metadata (that is, data about data) is author, date, or keyword information about the current document entered in the HEAD section at the top of the document. In HTML, use one or more META (metadata) elements to name the author or editor, the creation date, or latest edit date for those who will work on the document in the future. For example:

```
<META name="Author"
       content="Sandra E. Eddy">
```

You can also use META to list keywords that can help search indexes match the keywords that users enter. When the metadata and user-entered keywords match, search indexes will assign a rank to your document and include it in a list that users can browse and jump to your document. For example:

```
<META name="keywords"
       content="computer, computers,
    internet, windows, html, xml, asp,
    active server pages, coding"
```

Because you declare your own XML metadata elements in a DTD, you can include any other information that you wish. The W3C (**http://www.w3.org/**) supports two working drafts that will most likely become standards for XML metadata: the Resource Description Framework (RDF) Model and Syntax Specification and the Resource Description Framework (RDF) Schema Specification. RDF will enable XML developers to support a variety of metadata.

■1 Declare the version and name the document type and root.

■2 Indicate that the document stands by itself.

■3 Say that the document does not stand alone, and name the DTD.

■4 State that the document uses the UTF-16 character set.

Entering Elements

As you know, elements are the basic components of your HTML and XML documents. Using elements, you mark selected parts of your documents for present formatting or future styling and enhancements. Whether you use an existing DTD (in HTML or XML) or create your own (in XML), element declarations include information about how to use the elements as well as what you must or must not do when using the elements. Remember that HTML and XML documents contain one root element and an underlying hierarchy of child and descendant elements. Note that a child element must be completely enclosed within its parent; elements should never overlap.

The hierarchy also determines the look and behavior of content within the root, children, and other descendants. For example, a high-level child element might include an attribute that sets the typeface and point size for enclosed text. This attribute, by default, controls the typeface and size of text for child elements. However, those elements can have attributes that explicitly set different typefaces, point sizes, or both.

To insert an element in a document, enter a start tag and an end tag. The start tag marks the beginning of the element and its content, and the end tag marks the end. Note that in HTML, end tags are required, optional, or forbidden. In XML, end tags are always required. In both HTML and XML, child elements are completely nested within its parent; elements should never overlap. For example:

```
<P>This is
<B><I>bold and italicized</B></I>
text.</P>
```

is invalid because the `</B>` and `</I>` are transposed. You have to end the inner element (`</I>`) before ending the outer one (`</B>`).

You have already learned that you can handle XML empty elements with separate start tags and end tags as well as a combination of tags:

```
<img src="sample.gif"/>
```

As you can see, an empty element can contain attributes; in this case, the attribute refers to the GIF file that will be inserted in the document during processing.

It is important to note that when using empty elements in XML documents, both types of syntaxes work properly. However, when those who maintain the tags in the XML document see the special format, they immediately know that the element is empty.

TAKE NOTE

SETTING ASP CONVENTIONS

The best ASP pages are valid documents; that is, the HTML specification or XML DTD is faithfully and carefully followed. For example, where they are required, start and end tags are always supplied, required attributes and attribute values always appear, attribute values are enclosed within quotation marks, and so on.

When you are responsible for setting Web document standards, it is extremely important to specify how you want specific elements and attributes utilized as well as how your documents should be constructed. For example, you may want the title of each document to follow certain standards, the head section to always include the author's name and the creation date. In addition, you probably want all documents thoroughly commented; that is, every line of a document should be clear to future writers and developers.

When you add scripts (see Part 3) to ASP pages to make them dynamic and interactive, consider following certain conventions. You might want to state the language in which a particular script is written and follow certain indention conventions.

CROSS-REFERENCE
To find out about using start and end tags, see the "Using Start Tags and End Tags" task in Chapter 6.

FIND IT ONLINE
Use the tutorial at **http://www.w3.org/MarkUp/Guide** as a guide to creating your first documents.

Listing 8-3: An HTML Document with a Variety of Content

```
<!DOCTYPE HTML PUBLIC
      "-//W3C//DTD HTML 4.0//EN">
<HTML><HEAD>
<TITLE>A Potpourri of Content</TITLE>
</HEAD><BODY>
<H2>An Image</H2>
<IMG SRC="house.gif" height="45" width="100">
<H4>An Image</H4>
<IMG SRC="redarrow.jpg" height="25"     ◄❶
width="25">
<H4>A Bulleted List</H4>
<UL TYPE="square">
<LI>Rural</LI>
<LI>Rustic</LI>      ◄❷
<LI>Cape</LI>
</UL>
<H4>A Table</H4>      ❸
<TABLE BORDER>
<TR><TH>Jan</TH><TH>Feb</TH><TH>Mar</TH></TR>
<TR><TD>81</TD><TD>95</TD><TD>99</TD></TR>
<TR><TD>75</TD><TD>96</TD><TD>101</TD></TR>
</TABLE>
<H4>A Link</H4>
Click on <A HREF="http://www.altavista.com/">
Altavista</A> to search for documents.
</BODY></HTML>
                  ❹
```

❶ Start with an image.
❷ Then, add a bulleted list with square bullets.
❸ Insert a small table.
❹ Conclude by adding a link.

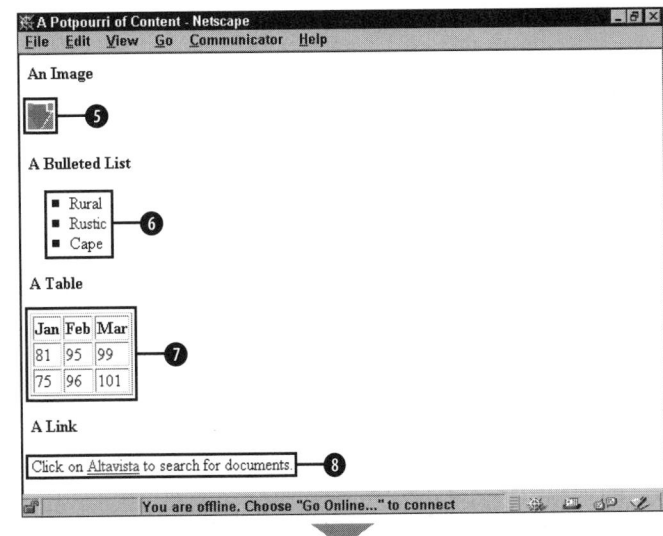

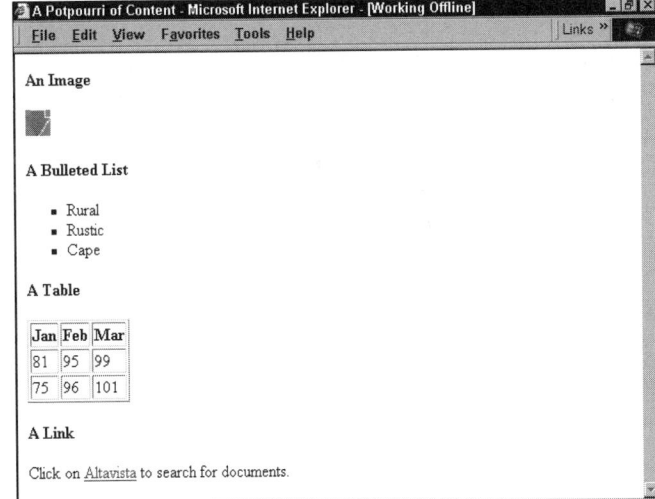

❺ Start with an image.
❻ Then, add a bulleted list with square bullets.
❼ Insert a small table.
❽ Conclude by adding a link.

▶ This figure shows the same Web document in the Internet Explorer window, (the prior figure was captured in the Netscape Navigator window).

Entering Attributes

You can find attributes in start tags and in empty-element tags. Attributes, which are made up of attribute names and attribute values, are associated with elements. While a declaration for a particular element must be unique in its DTD, you can declare the same attribute under one or more elements. For example, in HTML, you can use the align attribute to align a variety of elements with or between the margins of a page.

An attribute refines the element with which it is associated. For example, an attribute may name or identify a particular occurrence of an element. Then, you can use that element in a unique way from other elements of the same type: you could format or enhance it or link to it.

When an attribute is given one or a range of values, the DTD developer sets a limit for document writers. For example, the HTML DTD limits the number of color names and color codes that can be applied to various parts of a document. When you declare attributes in an XML DTD, you can: force the use of an attribute by using the #REQUIRED keyword or offer the attribute as an option by using the #IMPLIED keyword; set a default value for an attribute; or offer a list of valid values from which a document writer can choose.

As you learned in the prior chapter, an element can have more than one attribute. Each attribute in a document must also include its value, enclosed within quotation marks or single quote marks. HTML browsers may allow you to get away without the quotes, but XML parsers do not.

CROSS-REFERENCE

To learn attribute basics, see "Understanding Attributes" in Chapter 6 and "Adding Attribute Lists" in Chapter 7.

FIND IT ONLINE

The HTML Activity Statement (**http://www.w3.org/MarkUp/Activity.html**) shows new documents and meetings.

Listing 8-4: An HTML-Based Press Release

```
<!DOCTYPE HTML PUBLIC
   ❶  "-//W3C//DTD HTML 4.0//EN">
<HTML><HEAD><TITLE>Star Screen ◀❶
</TITLE></HEAD><BODY>
<H1 TITLE="Star Screen" CLASS="gss001"> ◀❸
Announcing the Star Screen</H1> ◀❷
<P>The Glamooroose Screen Company
   announces its newest design: the Star
   Screen.</P>
<P>The Star Screen is decorated with
   gold and silver stars on a navy or black
   background.</P>                            ◀❹
<P>Call your representative today!</P>
</BODY></HTML>
```

❶ In the HEAD section, insert the title.
❷ The press-release title is formatted as a heading.
❸ Insert a document title and class identifier.
❹ Each paragraph is formatted with the default font.

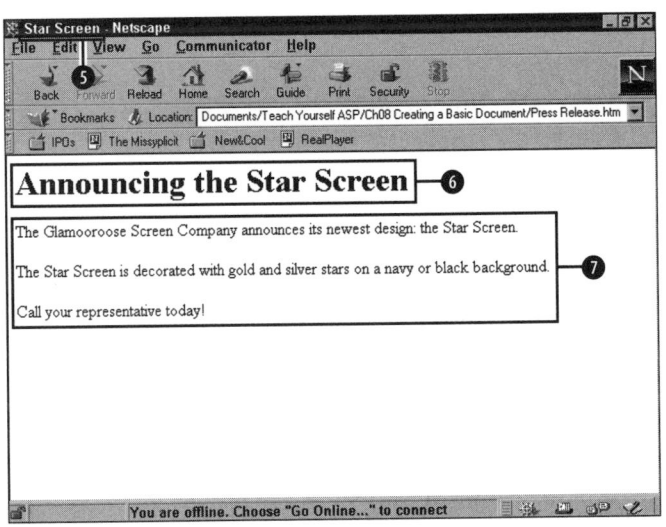

❺ Notice the title in the title bar.
❻ The press-release title is formatted as a heading.
❼ Each paragraph is formatted with the default font.

Listing 8-5: A Press-Release DTD

```
<?xml version = "1.0"?>
<!DOCTYPE pressrel [
<!ELEMENT pressrel (title,para+)>
  <!ELEMENT    title (#PCDATA)>
  <!ATTLIST title
          name    CDATA      #REQUIRED ◀❶
          id      ID         #REQUIRED
          font    CDATA      "Helvetica" ◀❷
          size    CDATA      "14"> ◀❸
  <!ELEMENT    para (#PCDATA)>
  <!ATTLIST para
          font    CDATA      "Times New Roman"
          size    CDATA      "10">
]>                              ❹
```

❶ Require the use of the name and id attributes.
❷ Name the default font, Helvetica, for the title element.
❸ Set the default point size to 14.
❹ Set the default font and point size for the para element.

Listing 8-6: The Content of an XML-Based Press Release ❷

```
<title name="Star Screen" id="gss001">
Announcing the Star Screen</title> ◀❶
<para>The Glamooroose Screen Company
   announces its newest design: the Star
   Screen.</para>
<para>The Star Screen is decorated with
   gold and silver stars silkscreened on a navy
   or black background.</para>
<para>Call your representative today!</para>
```
❸

❶ Enter the press-release title.
❷ Because the name and id attributes are required, insert them.
❸ By default, each paragraph (para) has its font and size preset.

117

Entering General Entities

As you have already learned, entities are shortcuts for information — ranging from one character to an entire file. In general, when a processor goes through the lines in a document, it looks for entity references and replaces them with the contents of the entities. When entities are declared in a DTD, they are known as parameter entities (PEs). When entities are included in a document, they are called general entities.

In HTML, the use of both types of entities is limited. For example, PEs are included in the predefined HTML DTD. Because you cannot edit the HTML DTD, you can't declare your own PEs. As you know, HTML (along with XML) supports the International Standard ISO 10646-1, or the Unicode Standard, which includes tens of thousands of international characters and symbols. So, you can incorporate general entities based on Unicode characters in your HTML documents. (See the first example on the facing page.)

XML provides greater support for entities; it supports both PEs and general entities. In addition, XML's general entities come in two flavors: they can be parsed or unparsed. A processor acts on *parsed entities* and interprets them; a processor simply passes *unparsed entities* in their original form to the output document. Both PEs and general entities remain in their original positions, either in the DTD or the non-DTD part of the document.

In XML, you can use entities as shortcuts. You can declare an entity that provides a short reference to a technical term, company name, or long name. For example:

```
<!ENTITY anti "antidisestablishmentarianism">
```

In a document, you can refer to the term as follows:

```
<italpara>I won't use the term
<bold>&anti;</bold>
very often, because do you really want to know
about the opposition to the withdrawal of
support from an established church in an
Internet book?</italpara>
```

The example will look like this on your screen:

*I won't use the term **antidisestablishmentarianism** very often, because do you really want to know about the opposition to the withdrawal of support from an established church in an Internet book?*

TAKE NOTE

▶ LEARNING ABOUT OTHER GENERAL ENTITIES

XML supports two general entities: character and data. A character entity represents special characters and symbols. Learn more about these entities in the Take Note entitled "Referring to Common Delimiters in HTML or XML Text" in Chapter 7. A data entity represents an imported non-XML file usually defined as binary. Learn more about data entities in the "Declaring Data Entities" Take Note, also in Chapter 7.

▶ LEARNING ABOUT NUMBER SYSTEMS

General entities can use two number systems for its special characters. The *decimal system*, also known as the base-10 system, consists of the numbers 0 through 9. In a decimal number, each digit position is a power of 10. To express a decimal character, precede it with &# and end it with a semicolon (for example, an uppercase E with a circumflex above is Ê).

The *hexadecimal system*, also known as the base-16 system, consists of the numbers 0 through 9 and the letters A through F (10 through 15). The advantage of using the hexadecimal system is that two hexadecimal digits can fit into a single eight-bit byte, thereby saving storage space on a computer. To express a hexadecimal character, precede it with &#x and end it with a semicolon (the uppercase E with a circumflex above is Ê).

CROSS-REFERENCE

The "Utilizing Entities" task in Chapter 6 provides an introduction to entities in HTML and XML.

FIND IT ONLINE

At **http://home.netscape.com/computing/webbuilding/index.html**, learn how to build Web pages and sites.

Listing 8-7: General Entities in an HTML Document

```
<!DOCTYPE HTML PUBLIC
    "-//W3C//DTD HTML 4.0//EN">
<HTML><HEAD><TITLE>Decorated Lewis Carroll
</TITLE></HEAD><BODY>
<H2>Jabberwocky</H2>
Tw&#225;s br&#238;ll&#238;g, &#225;nd the
slithy t&#171;&#187;v&#233;s<BR>
Did g&#165;re &#225;nd g&#238;mble &#237;n the
w&#228;be;<BR>
All m&#239;msy were the
b&#176;r&#176;g&#176;ves,<BR>
And the m&#248me r&#224;ths outgr&#229;be.
</BODY></HTML>
```

▶ To add special characters to a document, replace the usual
alphabetic characters with general entities, such as á,
î, «, and so forth.

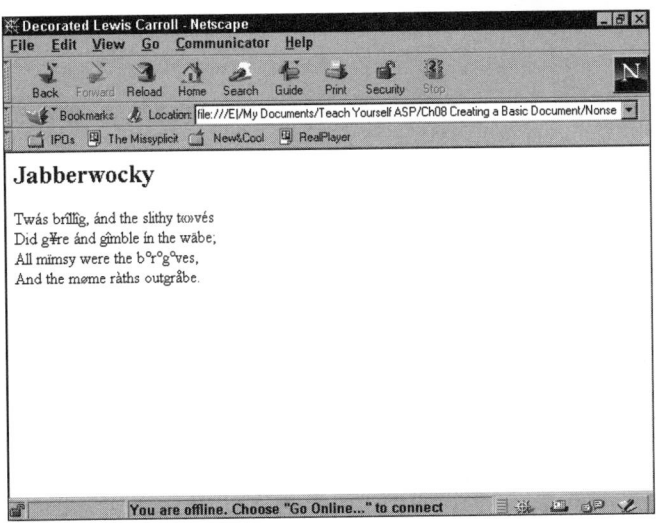

Jabberwocky

Twás brillig, ánd the slithy tœvés
Did gŧre ánd gîmble ín the wäbe;
All mímsy were the bᵒrᵒgᵒves,
And the møme räths outgråbe.

▶ One or two special characters replace many letters in this
nonsense poem by Lewis Carroll.

Listing 8-8: PEs from the HTML DTD

```
<!ENTITY % InputType
"(TEXT | PASSWORD | CHECKBOX | RADIO
        | SUBMIT | RESET | FILE | HIDDEN      —❶
        | IMAGE | BUTTON)"
>
```

```
<!ENTITY % inline "#PCDATA | %fontstyle;
            | %phrase; | %special;           —❷
            | %formctrl;"
>
```

❶ The % InputType PE lists the choices for the INPUT element.

❷ The % inline PE includes parsed character data and four
entities.

Listing 8-9: Declaring and Using General Entities in XML

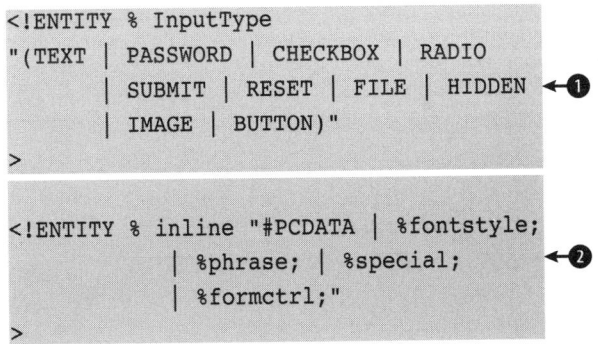

```
<!ENTITY rem "Rembrandt">
<!ENTITY sen "Sennelier">   ◀❶
<!ENTITY hol "Holbein">
```

```
<para>When I order pastels, I choose from
these brands: &hol;, &rem;, and &sen;.
&rem; is the brand that I use most often.
&sen; pastels are almost as soft as oil
paints. &hol; are harder than &rem; and
&sen;.<para>
```

❶ Declare the entity reference and the text of the entity.

❷ In a document, "sandwich" the reference between & and ;.

Adding Multimedia Content

You can add multimedia content to your HTML pages in several ways: You can insert graphics using the IMG element, which is dedicated to importing images, add a variety of multimedia types using the OBJECT element, or create links to multimedia files using the A element. This task covers the IMG and OBJECT elements. You'll learn about the A element in the following task.

As you know, IMG is an empty element that is a place-holder for an image that will be inserted in the output.

```
<IMG src="sample.gif" alt="A Sample GIF File>
```

According to the HTML 4.0 specification (see the facing page), both the src and alt attributes are required. As you can see, the IMG element provides several optional attributes. Note that the IMG element must appear in the BODY section, and the end tag is forbidden.

The OBJECT element not only enables you to insert graphical images into a document but also allows the addition of other multimedia objects, such as text, applets, scripts, form controls, and so forth. The following sample code appears in the HTML 4.0 specification:

```
<P><OBJECT
classid="http://www.miamachina.it
/analogclock.py">
An animated clock</OBJECT>
```

The classid attribute names the location of an analog clock, which is coded in Python (denoted by the py extension).

Note that the OBJECT element normally appears in the BODY section but occasionally can be placed in the HEAD section without content. Also note that both the start tag and end tag are required, and you can embed an OBJECT element within another OBJECT element. This makes OB-JECT statements easy to convert to XML. You'll find the complete OBJECT element and attribute-list declarations on the facing page.

Sometimes, you'll need to *initialize* an object, which means that its values must be reset to one or more default values. To initialize, use the PARAM element, a child of OBJECT. As with other empty elements, PARAM's attributes make the element work. Here's an example adapted from the HTML 4.0 specification:

```
<P><OBJECT
classid="http://www.miamachina.it
/analogclock.py">
<PARAM name="height" value="40"
valuetype="data">
<PARAM name="width" value="40"
valuetype="data"></OBJECT>
```

CROSS-REFERENCE

To learn how to design good Web pages, see the "Planning and Designing a Document" task in Chapter 5.

FIND IT ONLINE

To link to FAQs about the World Wide Web and Web development, go to http://www.boutell.com/faq/.

HTML 4.0: The IMG Element

```
<!ELEMENT IMG - O EMPTY◄-❷        -- Embedded image -->
<!ATTLIST IMG  ↑
                ❶
   %attrs;                         --%coreattrs, %i18n, %events --
   src       %URI;      ❸►#REQUIRED  -- URI of image to embed --
   alt       %Text;        #REQUIRED  -- short description --
   longdesc  %URI;         #IMPLIED   -- link to long description --
   height    %Length;      #IMPLIED   -- override height --
   width     %Length;   ❹►#IMPLIED   -- override width --
   usemap    %URI;         #IMPLIED   -- use client-side image map --
   ismap     (ismap)       #IMPLIED   -- use server-side image map --
```

❶ IMG *requires the start tag and allows the end tag.*
❷ *The* IMG *element is empty.*
❸ *You must use the* src *and* alt *attributes.*
❹ *You can use the remaining attributes.*

HTML 4.0: The OBJECT Element

```
             ┌1   ┌2      ┌3
<!ELEMENT OBJECT - - (PARAM | %flow;)*
  -- generic embedded object -->
<!ATTLIST OBJECT
                        4
   %attrs;                        --%coreattrs, %i18n, %events —
   declare   (declare)    #IMPLIED  -- declare but don't instantiate flag --
   classid   %URI;        #IMPLIED  -- identifies an implementation --
   codebase  %URI;        #IMPLIED  -- base URI for classid, data, archive--
   data      %URI;        #IMPLIED  -- reference to object's data --
   type      %ContentType; #IMPLIED -- content type for data --
   codetype  %ContentType; #IMPLIED -- content type for code --
   archive   %URI;        #IMPLIED  -- space separated archive list --
   standby   %Text;       #IMPLIED  -- message to show while loading --
   height    %Length;     #IMPLIED  -- override height --
   width     %Length;     #IMPLIED  -- override width --
   usemap    %URI;        #IMPLIED  -- use client-side image map --
   name      CDATA        #IMPLIED  -- submit as part of form --
   tabindex  NUMBER       #IMPLIED  -- position in tabbing order --
```

1 OBJECT *requires both the start tag and end tag.*
2 *The* PARAM *element is a child of* OBJECT.
3 *The* %flow; *entity includes block and inline elements.*
4 *All attributes are optional.*

Adding Links to a Document

Hypertext links mark the major difference between Web pages and plain text files. Normally, when individuals read the page of a book or article, they start at the top of the first page and finish at the bottom of the last page. If they need to look up a word or term, they consult a dictionary or another book. When readers browse through Web documents, they can learn about some words or terms by clicking them. The click activates the link and displays new information from the same document or an entirely different document onscreen.

Regardless of the type of link, its most important attribute is the URI, which gives the absolute or relative address of the target of the link. An *absolute URI* starts with the name of an Internet protocol, such as `http:`, `ftp:`, `gopher:`, `file:`, `mailto:`, and so forth, continues with the name of the computer on which the resource is located, and concludes with the file name and extension of the resource. A relative URI is a less-than-complete name. For example, if the file is located on your computer, there is no need to furnish the computer name. Instead, the URI may contain a combination of the folder name (if it differs from the current one), the file name and extension (if they differ), and the name of a location within the file. It doesn't matter whether you write an absolute or relative URI: If the link works properly, the URI is valid.

Use the A element to construct the only type of link supported by HTML. A typical HTML link is as follows:

```
<P>Click on <A HREF="http://www.xxx.com/">XXX
</A> to link to our home page.</P>
```

In the output document, the link will look something like *Click on XXX to link to our home page.*

XML supports several types of links: simple, extended, locator, group, and document. The XML Linking Language and XML Pointer Language (XPointer) working drafts set the specifications for XML links. Note that a working draft is under development and subject to change. A working draft is *not* the final version of a specification. So, before you start working through this chapter, get a copy of the latest working draft.

A *simple link*, which is analogous to an HTML link, uses the following syntax for its element and attribute-list declarations:

```
<!ELEMENT simp_link ANY>
<!ATTLIST simp_link
    xml:link   CDATA   #FIXED "simple"
```

The `xml:link` attribute declaration in the example ensures that only simple links are allowed for the `simp_link` element. Note that you can declare other attributes for the element. Be sure to close any attribute-list declaration with the > delimiter.

Extended links enable you to define many links in one or more XML documents. When you use extended links, you can jump from any link in any document to a link resource in any document. You can identify the content associated with a particular link so that if the content changes but the identifier remains the same, you can still access the link. Element and attribute-list declarations for extended links look like this:

```
<!ELEMENT ext_link ANY>
  xml:link   CDATA   #FIXED    "extended"
```

For this example, the `"extended"` value of the `xml:link` attribute allows only extended links for the element. You'll find out why the URI is missing in the following part of this task.

Continued

Continued

TAKE NOTE

TRAVERSING LINKS

Traverse is an important term in linking. When you click on a link, you activate it and access a target resource. This entire process is called *traversing* the link.

CROSS-REFERENCE
Chapter 18 discusses how the display of Web documents can change, depending on the browser.

FIND IT ONLINE
The W3C XML Linking Language working draft is located at **http://www.w3.org/TR/WD-xlink**.

HTML 4.0: The A Element

```
<!ELEMENT A - - (%inline;)* -(A)      -- anchor -->
<!ATTLIST A
  %attrs;                         --%coreattrs, %i18n, %events --
  charset     %Charset;     #IMPLIED  -- char encoding of linked resource --
  type        %ContentType; #IMPLIED  -- advisory content type --
  name        CDATA         #IMPLIED  -- named link end --
  href        %URI;         #IMPLIED  -- URI for linked resource --
  hreflang    %LanguageCode; #IMPLIED -- language code --
  rel         %LinkTypes;   #IMPLIED  -- forward link types --
  rev         %LinkTypes;   #IMPLIED  -- reverse link types --
  accesskey   %Character;   #IMPLIED  -- accessibility key character --
  shape       %Shape;       rect      -- for use with client-side image maps --
  coords      %Coords;      #IMPLIED  -- for use with client-side image maps --
  tabindex    NUMBER        #IMPLIED  -- position in tabbing order --
  onfocus     %Script;      #IMPLIED  -- the element got the focus --
  onblur      %Script;      #IMPLIED  -- the element lost the focus --
>
```

❶ *The inline* A *element anchors a simple HTML link.*
❷ *Use the* href *keyword to indicate a URI.*
❸ *The* rel *keyword indicates the forward relationship from URI to anchor.*
❹ *The* rev *keyword indicates the backward relationship from anchor to URI.*

Listing 8-10: A Three-Link HTML Document

```
<!DOCTYPE HTML PUBLIC
1   "-//W3C//DTD HTML 4.0//EN">
<HTML><HEAD><TITLE>Some Famous Web Sites
</TITLE></HEAD><BODY>
<H1>Famous Web Sites</H2>
<A href="http://www.yahoo.com/">
Yahoo</A> (http://www.yahoo.com/)
<P><A href="http://home.netscape.com/">
Netscape</A> (http://home.netscape.com/)</P>
<P><A href="http://www.microsoft.com/">
Microsoft</A> (http://www.microsoft.com/)</P>
</BODY></HTML>
```

1 *Enter the* A *start tag.*
2 *Add the* href *attribute and a URI.*
3 *End the start tag.*
4 *Insert the text of the link and the end tag.*

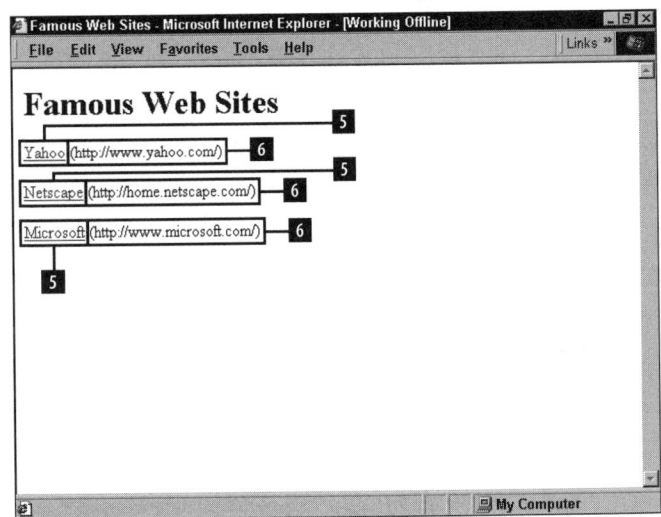

5 *By default, a link is underlined.*
6 *If text is not underlined, it is probably regular text.*

123

Adding Links to a Document

Continued

An extended link is made up of a parent element and one or more child elements, which are known as locator elements. The locator elements contain the URI information, target resource information, and other attributes. The parent element contains the locator elements and its attributes can set characteristics of the entire extended link. Element and attribute-list declarations for a locator can be coded as follows:

```
<!ELEMENT locator ANY>
<!ATTLIST locator
 xml:link     CDATA     #FIXED     "locator"
 href         CDATA                #REQUIRED>
```

Be sure to end the attribute-list declaration with >. Extended links in XML can be inline or out-of-line. An *inline link* is an internal link within the current document. Note that child elements of inline links are part of the link element. An *out-of-line* link specifies the location of the link in an external file. Out-of-line links are particularly useful for extended link groups. Inline links and out-of-line links follow the same syntax.

An *extended link group*, which has a similar structure to the extended link and is a special kind of extended link, refers a set of related documents that can contain links to all the other documents in the set, as well as other documents outside the set. An extended link group is made up of nested extended link document elements, each referring to a single document in the document set. Each document in the set may or may not include simple, extended, or other extended link groups. Element and attribute-list declarations for a typical extended link group and its document element can look like this:

```
<!ELEMENT group (document*)>
 xml:link     CDATA     #FIXED     "group"

<!ELEMENT document EMPTY>
<!ATTLIST document
```

```
 xml:link     CDATA     #FIXED     "document"
 href         CDATA     #REQUIRED
>
```

Extended pointers, or XPointers, use location terms to find a specific location or component in a target document. You can use one or more absolute location terms, relative location terms, spanning location terms, attribute location terms, and string location terms — separately or in combination — to pinpoint a particular location to which to link. To specify an XPointer, simply add a *fragment identifier*, which starts with the pound sign (#) symbol, to a URI. You'll see an example of an XPointer on the facing page. Note that in HTML, fragment identifiers also start with the pound sign and match the value of the NAME attribute of the target resource's A element.

TAKE NOTE

▶ LEARNING MORE ABOUT LINKING

All HTML and simple XML links operate in one direction — from the link to the target resource. Some XML links can be *multidirectional,* which means that you can jump to several target locations simultaneously from within a single XML link. Note that multidirectional does *not* mean that you can jump from a target resource back to its link.

▶ DECLARING LINKING ELEMENT CONTENTS

When you declare a linking element, two types of contents — ANY and EMPTY — are valid. Use the ANY keyword to specify a non-empty element with any content, including a link. Use EMPTY to specify an empty element. Remember that an empty element can contain attributes, such as URIs and a link. For any linking element, include the xml:link attribute.

CROSS-REFERENCE

Chapter 19 covers how to use Dynamic HTML and ASP to create dynamic documents.

FIND IT ONLINE

The W3C XML Pointer Language working draft is located at http://www.w3.org/TR/WD-xptr.

Listing 8-11: Samples of Simple XML Links

```
<text id="para503" xml:link="simple"  ←❶
href="/names/adams.xml" show="new"
title="prez">The Second</text>


<graphic id="pic-c01-12"
xml:link="simple" inline="true"  ←❷
caption="Bart"  ←❶
href="/pics/bart.jpg"  ←❸
title="retrievers" show="new"/>
                      ❹
```

❶ An XML link must include the xml:link attribute.
❷ An inline link has a value of true.
❸ The graphic file is bart.jpg, which is in the pics folder.
❹ The show attribute creates a new window.

Listing 8-12: An Example of an XML Extended Link

```
                          ❶
                              ❷
<interview xml:link="extended"
                      inline="true">
  <locator href="emcee001.txt"
                 role="thesis"/>
  <locator href="smith001.txt"
                 role="reply"/>    ←❸
  <locator href="emcee002.txt"
                 role="response"/>
  <locator href="smith002.txt"
                 role="explain"/>
</interview>  ←❹
```

❶ Define the extended link.
❷ Specify that this is an inline link.
❸ Add empty locator elements and URIs.
❹ Conclude the extended link with an end tag.

Listing 8-13: An Example of an XML Extended Link Group ❶

```
<group xml:link="group" steps="2">
  <document xml:link="document"  ←❷
    href="http://www.xxx.com/doc1.doc"  ←❸
  />  ←❹
  <document xml:link="document"  ←❷
    href="http://www.xxx.com/doc2.doc"  ←❸
  />  ←❹
  <document xml:link="document"  ←❷
    href="http://www.xxx.com/doc3.doc"  ←❸
  />  ←❹
  <document xml:link="document"  ←❷
    href="http://www.xxx.com/doc4.doc"  ←❸
  />  ←❹
</group>  ←❹
```

❶ Insert the xml:link attribute and use a value of "group".
❷ Insert the xml:link attribute and use a value of "document".
❸ Enter the href attribute and the URL of the document.
❹ Insert the end tag.

Listing 8-14: Examples of Absolute and Relative XML Extended Pointers

```
<anchor xml:link="extended"  ←🔲1
 href="http://x.com/test.xml#ID(sect_01)">
 Sample Document               🔲2
</anchor>


<anchor xml:link="extended"  ←🔲1
 href="/test.xml#child(3,#element,art,5)">
 Sample Document          🔲3
</anchor>     🔲4
```

🔲1 Declare an extended link.
🔲2 Add the fragment identifier (#) and specify the extended pointer: sect-01.
🔲3 Insert a relative URI.
🔲4 Choose the third child element, and art must equal 5.

Parsing a Document

This final task in the chapter discusses document processing. For HTML documents, you can choose from two types of processors. If you use a sophisticated HTML editor or suite of development programs to create your documents, a processor is built in. Most sophisticated HTML editors spot errors automatically as you enter lines of markup and content. When an error occurs, simply make corrections and move on. Web browsers for all types of operating-system platforms process your documents. When it finds an error, it will either display a special symbol, the error-free part of the document, or actually try to display the entire document, errors and all. Typically, a Web browser will adjust automatically for errors and display a document as best it can. This adjustment means that you can get away with missing end tags, overlapping elements, and mismatched delimiters.

It's a different story with XML documents. You must follow the rules or your documents will be neither well-formed nor valid. Inaccurate XML documents may not be processed at all. *Parsing* is the act of analyzing the text in an XML document, both markup and content, using the information in the document prolog (analogous to an HTML HEAD section) as a guide. XML supports two main types of parsers: nonvalidating and validating. A *nonvalidating parser* processes a document against XML rules and associated external documents, but is not programmed to interpret the document against its DTD. A *validating parser* finds a DTD, external files, *and* XML rules. A validating parser ensures that a document follows the declarations specified in the DTD. For a list of XML parsers, refer to Table 8-1.

However, without a DTD to define markup components, the parser and any target applications reach certain limits of processing accuracy beyond which they cannot go. If an XML document that is not associated with a DTD includes a custom element, there is no way for the parser to interpret the element. For example, does an element named TEXT represent all body text, a specially-formatted block of text, or a citation from a religious document? This ambiguity illustrates the importance of DTDs to XML documents. After all, if HTML documents always rely on the HTML DTD for its structure and formats, why should XML documents be less fortunate?

As XML becomes more popular, more XML editors will enable you to check for accuracy in real-time. Plus, you'll find Web browsers that support custom XML languages that process XML documents in the same way that HTML editors and browsers do.

TAKE NOTE

▶ PARSING ELEMENT GENERATIONS

When a validating XML parser processes a document, it evaluates the hierarchy of declared elements. It creates an *element tree* that shows the root element, its child elements, and other generations of elements. The parser is programmed to recognize tag delimiters, and interprets delimiters for various types of entities, and inserts the contents of entities in the proper locations in the document. After processing, the parser sends the completed document to a target application for further processing. The target application creates output that will be displayed, printed, or sent to another application.

▶ USING CONDITIONAL SECTIONS IN XML

While you are testing a document, you can use conditional sectioning to include or ignore a chunk of the DTD. Use the <![INCLUDE keyword and delimiters to start an included section, and <![IGNORE to ignore a section. End each type of section with the]]> delimiters. For more information, see the XML specification or one of the XML books by the authors.

CROSS-REFERENCE

For a review of the building blocks of HTML and XML documents, refer to all the tasks in Chapter 6.

FIND IT ONLINE

Parser Central (http://www.finetuning.com/parse.html) lists XML editors, parsers, and utilities.

Table 8-1: SELECTED XML PARSERS

Parser Name	URL	Description
Ælfred	http://www.microstar.com/aelfred.html	A validating parser for Java programmers who want to add XML support to their applets
expat (EXtensible markup language PArser Toolkit)	http://www.jclark.com/xml/expat.html	A non-validating, C-based XML browser
Lark and Larval	http://www.textuality.com/Lark/	Non-validating and validating XML parsers
NXP	http://www.edu.uni-klu.ac.at/~nmikula/NXP/	A validating Java-based parser in the public domain
SP	http://www.jclark.com/sp/	A C++-based SGML parser that can parse well-formed XML documents
Tcl (Tool Command Language) Toolkit	http://tcltk.anu.edu.au/XML/	A toolkit for parsing XML documents and DTDs
XAF	http://www.megginson.com/XAF/home.html	A Java-based, SAX-conformant XML parser
XML for Java	http://www.alphaworks.IBM.com/formula/xml/	A validating XML parser written in Java
xmlproc	http://www.stud.ifi.uio.no/~larsga/download/python/xml/index	A Python-based validating XML parser
XP	http://www.jclark.com/xml/xp/index.html	A Java-based parser that tests for well-formed documents
Xparse	http://www.jeremie.com/Dev/XML/	A JavaScript-based XML parser that tests for well-formed documents

Personal Workbook

Q & A

1 What sets the structure of all HTML and most XML documents?

_____

_____

_____

2 What is the name of the first line in an HTML document and the second line in an XML document?

_____

_____

3 What is metadata? What HTML element do you use to mark metadata?

_____

_____

_____

4 How do you insert an element in a document? Where do you place attributes and attribute values? Where do you insert character data?

_____

_____

_____

5 What is the basic rule for embedding a child element under a parent element?

_____

_____

_____

6 Write a sample empty element as it appear in an XML document.

_____

_____

_____

7 Where is a general entity located? Where is a parameter entity?

_____

_____

_____

8 What is a locator?

_____

_____

_____

ANSWERS: PAGE 500

EXTRA PRACTICE

1 In the prior chapter, you created a fax cover sheet. Add a logo to the document.

2 Go online, find the HTML 4.0 specification, and find two HTML elements that enable you to strike through selected text.

3 Write an HTML document that displays five versions of a graphic, each height and width ten pixels greater than the previous one.

4 In the previous chapter, you found the codes for the English alphabet. Now, write an HTML document that displays each character and its counterpart entity code.

5 Go online, find a Web document that you like, save it on your computer, and revise it. (Note: Remember to abide by copyright regulations.)

REAL-WORLD APPLICATIONS

✔ For your company intranet, you have been assigned to create a document template that includes the corporate logo and a paragraph on the company history.

✔ Now that you have created an employee-handbook template (see Chapter 7), write an outline of all the chapters.

✔ In this chapter, you saw an example of a press-release DTD. Now, write an HTML or XML site map for all of this year's press releases.

✔ You are in charge of maintaining a library of the art department's graphics. Write an illustrated intranet-based directory of those graphics.

Visual Quiz

How would you write this HTML document? Use the H1, H3, H6, IMG, P, and A elements. Note that the image is 40 pixels by 40 pixels. (Hint: The URI for Dell is **http://www.dell.com/**, and the URI for Compaq is **http://www.compaq.com/**.)

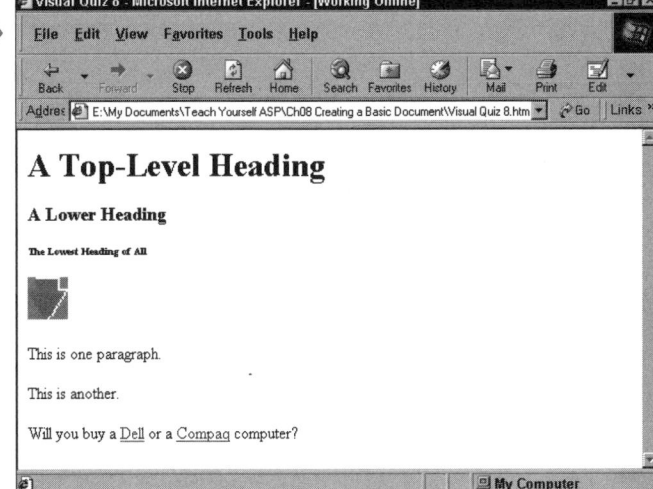

_____

_____

_____

_____

_____

CHAPTER 9

MASTER THESE SKILLS

▶ **Using Lists in Your Documents**
▶ **Constructing Ordered Lists**
▶ **Building Unordered Lists**
▶ **Nesting Ordered and Unordered Lists**
▶ **Adding a Glossary to Your Document**

Adding Lists to Documents

This chapter discusses the structure and presentation of lists in Web documents. Because of the predefined DTD, lists in HTML are not easily modified. For example, items on ordered lists are preceded by a number or a letter, and unordered list items are headed by one of three bullet types. The structure of each type of list, including the sizes of breaks before and after each item, distances between numbers or bullets and list text, and alignments, is set by default. However, you can make some format and enhancement changes by using stylesheets, which you will learn about in Chapter 13.

On the other hand, the structure and look of XML lists can vary, depending on the DTD developer. You can use the basic structure of HTML lists as a guide for XML list elements and attributes. Or, you can declare several sets of list elements that are dedicated to various list formats and designs.

In this chapter, the first task introduces you to the four types of HTML lists, their basic construction, and their underlying structure. HTML lists are ordered (numbered), unordered (bulleted), definition (glossaries), and simple. You'll compare list types —

especially the most common, ordered and unordered — and find out when to select a particular list type for a specific purpose. For example, if you want to present list items in a particular order (such as an instruction list), you'll want to use an ordered list. In contrast, if you want to highlight several items that can be arranged or used in any order (such as a list of features), you'll create an unordered list. The second and third tasks present the structure of ordered and unordered lists and how to compose them.

You can embed one list within another. So, you can nest a child ordered or unordered list within an ordered list or unordered list. The following task discusses and demonstrates how to nest lists.

Instead of single items, definition lists are made up of pairs of items: terms and definitions. In the last task, you will learn about the structure of definition lists and how to construct them.

Each task in the chapter contains a Take Note on a particular list topic. You'll see how to declare particular types of list elements in XML DTDs. The chapter also contains element and attribute-list declarations from the HTML 4.0 DTD.

Using Lists in Your Documents

HTML supports the use of several types of lists: ordered, unordered, definition, and simple.

Ordered lists, also known as numbered lists, contain list items that are arranged in a specific sequence. A list of instructions, where each step depends on the prior one, is a good example of an ordered list. Each item is preceded by a number. You can use attributes or stylesheet properties to change the number type for a particular list or all the lists in a document. To mark an ordered list in an HTML document, begin with the <OL> start tag and end with the </OL> end tag. Use the <LI> and </LI> tags to start and end individual list items. To learn how to create an ordered list, refer to the following task, "Constructing Ordered Lists."

Unordered lists, also known as bulleted lists, contain list items that appear in any sequence, such as a checklist. Items on an unordered list typically are preceded by a bullet. You can use attributes or stylesheet properties to change the bullet symbol for a particular list or all the lists in a document. To mark an unordered list in an HTML document, begin with the <UL> start tag and end with the </UL> end tag. Use the <LI> and </LI> tags to start and end individual list items. To learn how to create an unordered list, refer to the "Building Unordered Lists" task.

Definition lists, also known as glossaries, contain two components: terms and definitions. To mark a definition list in an HTML document, begin with the <DL> start tag and end with the </DL> end tag. Use the <DT> and </DT> tags to start and end individual definition terms, and the <DD> and </DD> tags to start and end individual definition descriptions. Note that each definition term must be paired with a definition description. To learn how to create a definition list, refer to the "Adding a Glossary to Your Document" task.

Simple lists contain individual items that are not preceded by numbers or bullets. HTML elements used to create simple lists are DIR and MENU, both of which are deprecated. The reason for the deprecation is that you can use stylesheets to format simple lists without having to select specific list elements. Simple lists are not covered in this book.

In markup terms, a list is an element that contains a repeating, embedded child element (for ordered and unordered lists) or pairs of child elements (for definition lists). You'll learn more about each type of list as you continue to read through this chapter.

TAKE NOTE

▶ DIFFERENTIATING HTML AND XML LISTS

In XML, you define the elements that make up a list. Because XML and HTML lists won't vary from each other except for the format, consider using the HTML list element and attribute declarations as the basis for your custom list elements (see the facing page). In XML, when you define a list or list-item element, you can give it any name. However, remember that some processors or browsers may have an eight-character limit.

▶ DECIDING ON ORDERED OR UNORDERED LISTS

Both ordered and unordered lists contain ordered list items. The document writer enters one list item, followed by another and another, and so forth, in the order in which he or she wants them to appear on the page or screen. The true difference between ordered and unordered lists is whether order matters. For example, if you are installing a program, order can be quite important: you must insert a CD before you can execute the installation program. On the other hand, if you are shopping in a supermarket, the first item on your grocery list could just as well be your last.

CROSS-REFERENCE

Learn about nesting one list within another in "Nesting Ordered and Unordered Lists" in this chapter.

FIND IT ONLINE

The HTML 4.0 Easy Reference (**http://www.sbrady.com/hotsource/html/htmleasy.html**) contains links to HTML tasks.

HTML 4.0: The OL and LI Elements and Related Entities

```
<!ENTITY % OLStyle "CDATA">              -- constrained to: "(1|a|A|i|I)"  -->
<!ELEMENT OL - - (LI)+                   -- ordered list -->
<!ATTLIST OL
  &attrs;                                -- %coreattrs, %i18n, %events -->       ←❶
  type             %OLStyle;   #IMPLIED  -- numbering style --
  compact          (compact)   #IMPLIED  -- reduced interitem spacing --
  start            NUMBER      #IMPLIED  -- starting sequence number -->
```

```
<!ENTITY % LIStyle "CDATA">         -- constrained to: "(%ULStyle;|%OLStyle;)" -->
<!ELEMENT LI - O (%flow;)           -- list item -->
<!ATTLIST LI
  &attrs;                                -- %coreattrs, %i18n, %events --        ←❷
  type             %LIStyle;   #IMPLIED  -- numbering style --
  value            NUMBER      #IMPLIED  -- reset sequence number -->
```

❶ *Use the* OL *element to mark an ordered list.*
❷ *The* LI *element specifies a list item.*

HTML 4.0: The UL, DL, DT, DD Elements and Related Declarations

```
<!ENTITY % ULStyle "(disc|square|circle)">
<!-- Unordered Lists (UL) bullet styles -->
<!ELEMENT UL - - (LI)+                   -- unordered list -->
<!ATTLIST UL
  &attrs;                                -- %coreattrs, %i18n, %events --        ←1
  type     %ULStyle;   #IMPLIED          -- bullet style --
  compact  (compact)   #IMPLIED          -- reduced interitem spacing -->
```

```
<!ELEMENT DL - - (DT|DD)+                -- definition list -->
<!ATTLIST DL                                                                      ←2
  &attrs;                                -- %coreattrs, %i18n, %events -->
```

```
<!ELEMENT DT - O (%inline;)*             -- definition term -->
<!ELEMENT DD - O (%flow;)*               -- definition description -->
<!ATTLIST DT|DD)                                                                  ←3
  &attrs;                                -- %coreattrs, %i18n, %events -->
```

1 *Use the* UL *element to mark an unordered list.*
2 *The* DL *element starts and ends a definition list.*
3 DT *and* DD *define pairs of terms and descriptions.*

Constructing Ordered Lists

Ordered lists are composed of items preceded by numbers. In an HTML document, a short ordered list is coded like this:

```
<OL>
  <LI>Do this.</LI>
  <LI>Then, do it again.</LI>
</OL>
```

Notice that the individual list items are nested within the `<OL>` and `</OL>` tags. When the browser processes the list, it precedes each list item with a number:

1. Do this.
2. Then, do it again.

If you look at the HTML 4.0 OL element declaration on the preceding page, you'll notice that the `type` attribute contains the `%OLStyle;` entity. `%OLStyle;` constrains the numbering style for ordered lists or items within ordered lists to 1, a, A, i, or I:

```
<OL type="A">
```

The default is 1, which represents the standard (1, 2, 3, and so forth) numbering system. The a and A values assign lowercase or uppercase alphabetic characters, and the i and I items assign lowercase or uppercase Roman numerals.

Another ordered-lists characteristic is that you can explicitly state the starting number using the `start` attribute:

```
<OL start="5">
```

Obviously, the default starting number is 1 (or the starting number of its number type counterpart). But, think of a numbered list that is interrupted by a paragraph of narrative. You may have had to close the list with an end tag, but when you resume the list, you want to have the latitude of setting the starting number yourself. Note that you can reset the sequence number for a list item using the `value` attribute.

TAKE NOTE

USING ORDERED LISTS IN XML

In XML documents, you insert ordered lists in the same way that you do in HTML documents. However, because you (or a developer) creates the DTD, you can custom-design list elements, their attributes, and their attribute values. In an XML DTD, specify the element structure for an ordered list as follows:

```
<!ELEMENT order (item+)>
   <!ELEMENT item (#PCDATA)>
```

The `item` element is a child of the `order` element. Remember that the plus sign indicates that one or more `item` elements must be included in the list. Once you have declared the elements, you can declare attribute lists for each. For example, you could ensure that each list using the order element has an identifier:

```
<!ATTLIST order
   id   ID              #REQUIRED>
```

DIFFERENTIATING ONE LIST FROM ANOTHER USING ATTRIBUTES

In HTML, you can use the value of attributes — such as CLASS, ID, or TYPE — to identify one or several lists for special treatment. For example, you could format a particular ordered list in a different way from all the other ordered lists in a document. The CLASS attribute specifies one or more classifications for its element, ID gives a unique name that identifies its element, and TYPE specifies a valid Internet Media Type (MIMETYPE) for the element. Because you control the contents of the DTD in XML, you can actually declare several list elements. For example, you can define an attribute that has the ID attribute type to differentiate one element from another.

CROSS-REFERENCE

Find out how to style lists and list items in the "Styling Text" and "Styling Page Elements" tasks in Chapter 13.

FIND IT ONLINE

Go to **http://www-pcd.stanford.edu/mogens/intro/ tutorial.html** for a three-part tutorial and many HTML links.

Listing 9-1: An Ordered List in an HTML Document

```
<!DOCTYPE HTML PUBLIC
    "-//W3C//DTD HTML 4.0//EN">
<HTML><HEAD>
<TITLE>An Ordered List</TITLE></HEAD>
<BODY>
<H1>An Ordered List</H2>
<OL>  ←❶
   <LI>Clean garage.</LI>
   <LI>Paint garage floor.</LI>
   <LI>Wait for paint to dry.</LI>  ←❷
   <LI>Drive car into garage.</LI>
   <LI>Close garage door.</LI>
</OL>  ←❸
</BODY></HTML>
```

❶ Begin an ordered list with the <OL> start tag.

❷ Insert one or more list items.

❸ Complete the list with the </OL> end tag.

❹ The list begins with the default starting number 1.

❺ The last item on the list is the fifth.

Listing 9-2: An XML DTD for an Ordered List

```
<?xml version="1.0"?>
<!DOCTYPE document [
<!ELEMENT document (heading,olist*)>  ←❶
<!ELEMENT heading  (#PCDATA)>
<!ELEMENT olist (item+)>  ←❷
<!ATTLIST olist
     id     ID           #IMPLIED
     title  CDATA        #IMPLIED
>
    <!ELEMENT item (#PCDATA)>  ←❸
]>
```

Listing 9-3: The Ordered List Written in XML

```
<document>
                        ❺
   <heading>An Ordered List</heading>
   <olist title="List of Chores">
                        ❹
     <item>Clean garage.</item>
     <item>Paint garage floor.</item>
     <item>Wait for paint to dry.</item>  ←❻
     <item>Drive car into garage.</item>
     <item>Close garage door.</item>
   </olist>  ←❼
</document>
```

❶ Declare the root element, document, which encompasses the entire document.

❷ Nest the olist (ordered list) child element.

❸ Embed olist's child element, item.

❹ Begin the ordered list with the <olist> start tag.

❺ Add the title attribute.

❻ Insert one or more list items.

❼ Complete the list with the </olist> end tag.

Building Unordered Lists

U nordered lists are composed of items preceded by bullets. The presence of the bullets implies that the list items don't have to be read or performed in a particular order. In an HTML document, a typical unordered list can look like this:

```
<UL>
   <LI>Do this.</LI>
   <LI>Do that before or after.</LI>
   <LI>Do this any time.</LI>
</UL>
```

Notice that the list is structured in the same way as an ordered list: Once again, the individual list items are nested within the <UL> and </UL> tags. When the browser processes the list, it precedes each list item with a bullet:

▶ Do this.
▶ Do that before or after.
▶ Do this any time.

Notice that the UL element declaration on a preceding page includes its own version of the type attribute. Instead of specifying the number type as it does for the OL element, the %ULStyle; entity within the type attribute determines the bullet style: disc, square, or circle. To use the type attribute for an unordered list, include the attribute in the start tag:

```
<UL type="disc">
```

The default is disc, which is a filled circle. The square type is a filled square, and the circle type is an unfilled circle.

Because items on an unordered list are preceded by bullets, there is no need to be able to start numbering. Therefore, there is no start attribute for unordered lists.

TAKE NOTE

▶ USING UNORDERED LISTS IN XML

In XML, you include unordered lists in a document using the same element structure as you do with ordered lists in both HTML and XML documents. So, it follows that in XML you also declare unordered list elements in the same way that you define ordered list elements:

```
<!ELEMENT ulist (item+)>
   <!ELEMENT item (#PCDATA)>
```

Then, declare attribute lists for either or both elements.

▶ SUBSTITUTING SMALL GRAPHICS FOR BULLETS

If you want to insert small graphics in place of unordered list bullets, you can do so. Just be prepared to spend some time and effort on the task. The trick is to simulate a list and to combine graphics and relatively short list items. If list items overflow to multiple lines, you may have an alignment problem. However, solve this by attaching a stylesheet to set alignment and to add white space between the graphic and the text.

To code the list in this task and to change the bullets to graphics, enter lines similar to the following:

```
<P><IMG src="gif.gif">Do this.</P>
<P><IMG src="gif.gif">Do that before
 or after.</P>
<P><IMG src="gif.gif">Do this any
 time.</P>
```

By default, images are left-aligned. Make sure that graphics are sized properly — no more than about 10 pixels square. When you simulate unordered lists and work with custom bullets, be prepared to fine-tune the list, the graphics, and your formats a few times.

CROSS-REFERENCE

In the "Managing International Pages" task in Chapter 5, learn how to obtain the codes for special characters.

FIND IT ONLINE

The **http://www.coedu.usf.edu/inst_tech/publications/html/** page starts an interactive HTML tutorial.

Listing 9-4: An Unordered List in an HTML Document

```
<!DOCTYPE HTML PUBLIC
   "-//W3C//DTD HTML 4.0//EN">
<HTML><HEAD>
<TITLE>An Unordered List</TITLE></HEAD>
<BODY>
<H1>An Unordered List</H2>
<UL>   ←❶
   <LI>Prepare for dinner party.</LI>
   <LI>Clean garage.</LI>
   <LI>Sweep basement floor.</LI>    ←❷
   <LI>Buy candles.</LI>
   <LI>Fix kitchen sink.</LI>
   <LI>Replace bathroom faucet gasket.</LI>
</UL>   ←❸
</BODY></HTML>
```

❶ Begin an unordered list with the <UL> start tag.

❷ Insert one or more list items.

❸ Complete the list with the </UL> end tag.

▶ All items on an unordered list are preceded by the same symbol — in this case, the default filled bullet.

Listing 9-5: An XML DTD for an Unordered List

```
<?xml version="1.0"?>
<!DOCTYPE document [
<!ELEMENT document (heading,ulist*)>
<!ELEMENT heading   (#PCDATA)>
<!ELEMENT ulist (item+)>
<!ATTLIST ulist
      id      ID           #IMPLIED
      title   CDATA        #IMPLIED
>
   <!ELEMENT item (#PCDATA)>
]>
```

▶ *If you compare this listing with Listing 9-2 (for an ordered list), you'll find that the DTDs are almost identical — except for one element name.*

Listing 9-6: The Unordered List Written in XML

```
1
<document>          2
<heading>An Unordered List</heading>
                                              3
<ulist title="Getting Ready">
   <item>Prepare for dinner party.</item>
   <item>Clean garage.</item>
   <item>Sweep basement floor.</item>
   <item>Buy candles.</item>
   <item>Fix kitchen sink.</item>
   <item>Replace bathroom faucet gasket.</item>
</ulist>   ←4
</document>
```

1 Begin the unordered list with the <ulist> start tag.

2 Add the title attribute.

3 Insert one or more list items.

4 Complete the list with the </ulist> end tag.

Nesting Ordered and Unordered Lists

In your documents, you can nest one or more lists of any type within another list. For example, you could create the outline of a document using a different type of number (such as levels of A, 1, a, and so forth) for each level that you enter. Or, you could emphasize "subpoints" within an unordered or ordered list, using two types of bullets.

Nesting a list is easy to do. Simply place a list — beginning with its start tag and concluding with its end tag — completely within the start tags and end tags of its parent list. Remember that you cannot overlap elements in documents, so it's important to reiterate that the child list must be entirely within the boundaries of the parent list. Look at the following ordered list, which contains a completely embedded unordered list:

```
<OL>
  <LI>Unwrap the CD-ROM.</LI>
  <LI>Insert the CD-ROM into the carousel.</LI>
    <UL>
      <LI>Your player must be turned on.</LI>
      <LI>Preset the volume to 3.</LI>
    </UL>
  <LI>Press the Play button.</LI>
  <LI>Sit back and listen.</LI>
</OL>
```

In this example, the bullets emphasize important points that can be performed at any time.

TAKE NOTE

MAKING YOUR DOCUMENTS EASIER TO UNDERSTAND

Comments are an important part of both HTML and XML documents. Without comments, you or your successors could have problems understanding particular lines of code. To insert a comment in an HTML or XML document, enter the <!-- delimiter, type the comment, and end with the --> delimiter. When a browser or processor interprets the document, the comment will not be displayed.

▶ DECLARING NESTED-LIST ELEMENTS IN XML

Because you can define all the custom elements you could ever desire in an XML DTD, you can actually declare list elements that are dedicated to specific types of nested lists. For example, you could declare several generations of parent-child elements:

```
<!ELEMENT toplist (no_one+)>
  <!ELEMENT no_one (no_two+)>
    <!ELEMENT no_two (no_three+)>
      <!ELEMENT no_three (no_four+)>
```

By declaring additional XML elements to differentiate among list types, you can produce more readable nested listings. For example, think about creating an outline comprised of nested lists. First, define a series of list elements as follows: the top-level list under which all other lists are nested is named nest1; the second, which is nested within nest1 lists, is nest2; and so forth. Then, you structure each list to indent it properly and to apply other distinctive formats and enhancements. Of course, this can work against you, too. When you create lists using different element names, make sure that you track nesting levels. Every time you add or remove a nesting level or change the order of nesting, you have to edit the tags carefully.

A better way to change the look of a list is to use a stylesheet. Then, you can stick with a few list elements. When you declare an attribute list, make sure that you include an identifier with which you can make a particular list unique.

CROSS-REFERENCE

In the "Planning and Designing a Document" task in Chapter 5, learn how to outline a new document.

FIND IT ONLINE

http://www.pageresource.com/html/hclist.htm links to many HTML tutorials and other resources.

Listing 9-7: A Nested Outline of This Chapter

```
<!DOCTYPE HTML PUBLIC
    "-//W3C//DTD HTML 4.0//EN">
<HTML>
<HEAD>
<TITLE>Nested Lists</TITLE>
</HEAD>
<BODY>
<H3>Chapter 9: Adding Lists to Documents</H3>
<OL TYPE="A">    ①
  <LI>Master These Skills</LI>
  <LI>Introduction</LI>
  <LI>Using Lists in Your Documents</LI>
  <LI>Constructing Ordered Lists</LI>
  <LI>Building Unordered Lists</LI>
  <LI>Nesting Ordered and Unordered Lists</LI>
  <LI>Adding a Glossary to Your Document</LI>
  <LI>Personal Workbook</LI>
  <OL TYPE="1">    ②
    <LI>Q&A</LI>
    <LI>Extra Practice</LI>
    <LI>Real World Application</LI>
    <LI>Visual Quiz</LI>
  </OL>    ③
</OL>    ④
</BODY>
</HTML>
```

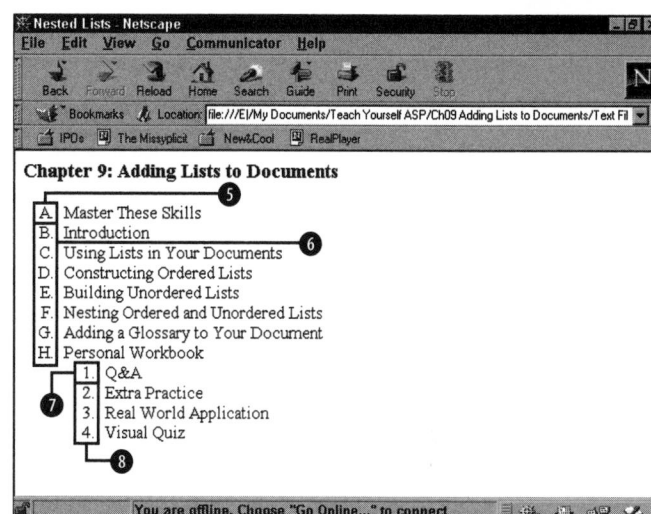

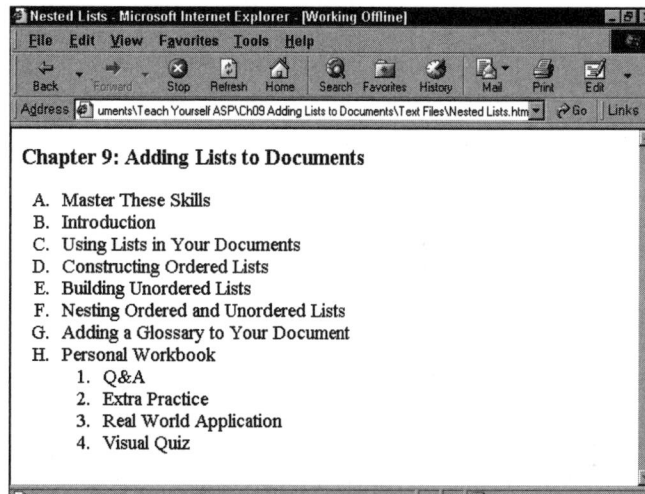

① Start an ordered list and set the type to A.

② Start a nested ordered list and set the type to 1.

③ Close the child list.

④ Close the parent list.

⑤ The first ordered list starts with the letter A.

⑥ Each item on the list is iterated by one alphabetic character.

⑦ The child ordered list starts numbering with 1.

⑧ Each list item is preceded by a number.

▶ As you can see, this Web page is slightly different when displayed in the Internet Explorer window. This difference emphasizes the importance of testing your pages in several browsers.

139

Adding a Glossary to Your Document

The *definition list* is a different type of list: It contains pairs of nested elements, each of which are composed of a definition term and a definition description. A glossary, such as the one following the last chapter in this book, is the most common example of a definition list.

In HTML, definition lists are composed of three elements: DL, DT, and DD. The DL element encloses the entire definition list; the DT element marks the beginning and end of the term; and the DD element marks the description. (Refer to the DL, DT, and DD element and attribute-list declarations on the facing page in the "Using Lists in Your Documents" task.)

A typical definition list looks something like this example from *The Devil's Dictionary*, by Ambrose Bierce:

```
<DL>
   <DT>bore</DT>
   <DD>a person who talks when you wish him to
listen</DD>
   <DT>cynic</DT>
   <DD>a blackguard whose faulty vision sees
things as they are, not as they ought to
be</DD>
</DL>
```

In an HTML document, the sample definition list might be formatted as follows:

bore   A person who talks when you wish him to listen

cynic   A blackguard whose faulty vision sees things as they are, not as they ought to be

The actual appearance of a definition list depends on the browser that processes the document.

Getting Writing and Editing Help from the Web

From time to time, everyone encounters problems with writing and editing documents. If you want to answer questions about proper sentence structure, punctuation, and so forth, visit these sites: The Editorial Eye (**http://www.eeicom.com/eye/eyeindex.html**) provides ten pages of links to articles and references resources. Subjects include E-Mail Etiquette, Essential Home Page Details, Editing All the Legalese the Law Allows, and Untangling the Web. The University of Illinois at Urbana-Champaign offers the Online Writing Guide (**http://www.english.uiuc.edu/cws/wworkshop/mainmenu.html**), which contains links to The Grammar Handbook, The Writing Techniques Handbook, and The Bibliography Handbook. The Purdue On-line Writing Lab (OWL) has a long history on the Web. Its OWL: Writing Resources page (**http://owl.english.purdue.edu/writers/introduction.html**) includes links to over 120 online writing handouts as well as other online resources (at OWL and elsewhere) under ten categories. The California Lutheran University's Virtual Library (**http://robles.callutheran.edu/iss/vlib2.html**) is a directory of links to Internet search tools, reference information (including dictionaries, thesauri, quotations, style guides, and statistics), and other resources arranged by subject — ranging from arts and humanities to business and economics.

CROSS-REFERENCE

In Chapter 10, you'll find out about tables, with which you can also format selected contents of a document.

FIND IT ONLINE

Use the HTML 4.0 tag reference at **http://developer.netscape.com/docs/manuals/htmlguid/content.htm**.

Listing 9-8: A Short Glossary of Terms

```
<!DOCTYPE HTML PUBLIC
       "-//W3C//DTD HTML 4.0//EN">
<HTML><HEAD>
<TITLE>A Definition List</TITLE>
</HEAD><BODY>
<H1>Glossary of Terms</H1>
<DL>  ①
<DT>address</DT>  ②                     ③
<DD>An electronic location to which e-mail is
sent; an electronic location on the Internet
or on a network.</DD>
<DT>ancestor</DT>  ②                    ③
<DD>A higher-level element, such as a parent,
in a family tree of elements.</DD>
<DT>archive</DT>
<DD>A collection of information, usually from
the past but sometimes from the present.</DD>
<DT>ASCII file</DT>
<DD>A text file or a text-only file.</DD>
<DT>ATTLIST</DT>
<DD>In a document type definition (DTD), a
list of attributes (that is, options or
characteristics) defined for an element.</DD>
<DT>attribute</DT>
<DD>A term for an option, which is a setting
that affects the behavior of and further
defines an element.</DD>
<DT>AU</DT>  ②
<DD>A UNIX-based sound file format.</DD>  ③
</DL></BODY></HTML>  ④
```

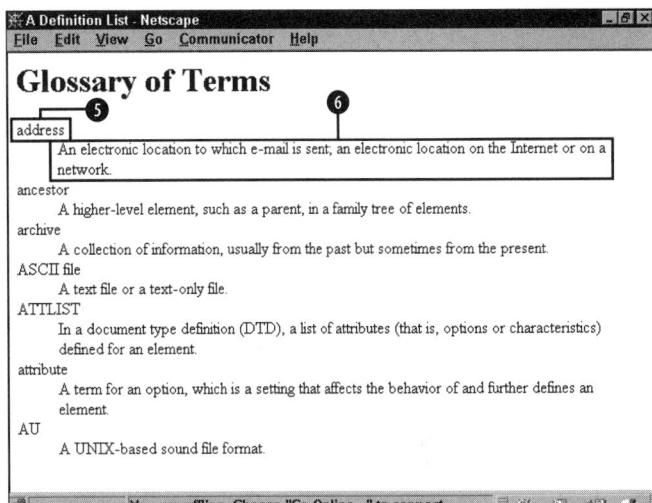

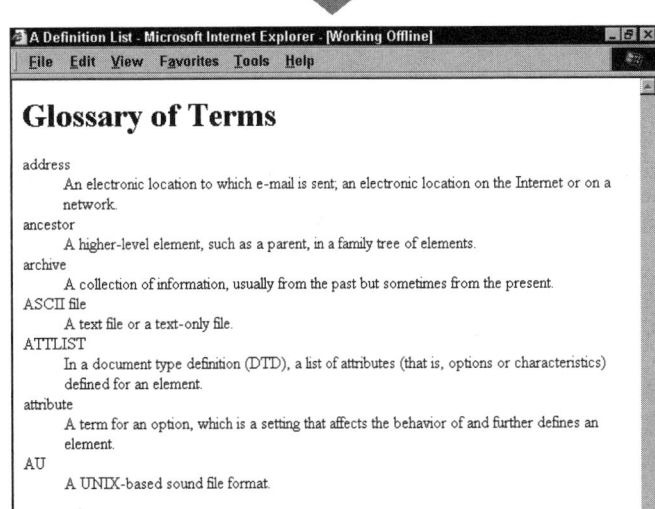

① Start the definition list.

② Add a definition term.

③ Enter the definition description.

④ End the definition list.

⑤ The definition term hugs the left margin.

⑥ After a break, the definition description is indented.

▶ A definition list in Microsoft Internet Explorer looks just about the same as a list in Netscape Navigator. Apply boldface by enclosing terms within <B> and </B> tags.

Personal Workbook

Q & A

1 What are the basic components of a list?

_____

_____

_____

2 What is the difference in the appearance of items on ordered and unordered lists?

_____

_____

_____

3 Should items on an ordered list be arranged in a particular order?

_____

_____

_____

4 Can you nest a combination of ordered and unordered lists?

_____

_____

_____

5 How do you change the number type or bullet type for a list?

_____

_____

_____

6 How do you insert a list in an HTML or XML document?

_____

_____

_____

7 What is another name for a definition list?

_____

_____

_____

8 What are the two child elements of a definition list?

_____

_____

_____

ANSWERS: PAGE 501

EXTRA PRACTICE

1. Create an HTML document for a basic recipe using an unordered list for the ingredients and an ordered list for the instructions.
2. Plan and design an XML DTD for the recipe document.
3. Prepare an HTML document to list your thoughts about why your boss should give you a raise.
4. Write an HTML document that lists the instructions for getting up from a chair, walking across the room to the TV set, and changing the channel from 2 to 4.
5. Develop an XML DTD that will list an inventory of your residence, room by room.
6. Write an XML document based on the DTD that you developed in the previous question.

REAL-WORLD APPLICATIONS

- ✔ You run a restaurant and must post a list of health and safety requirements for employees who prepare food. Write an HTML document that lists those requirements.
- ✔ Your department will plan and develop a glossary of terms for the product or service that you sell. Create a boilerplate document with at least 30 terms and descriptions.
- ✔ You have been assigned to teach a course on basic HTML. Plan five lessons based on Chapters 5 to 9 in this book. Develop an HTML document with at least two lists, one parent and one child.
- ✔ You are publishing an XML dictionary of slang terms. Design and create a DTD with definition-list elements as well as other elements.

Visual Quiz

How would you code this HTML document?

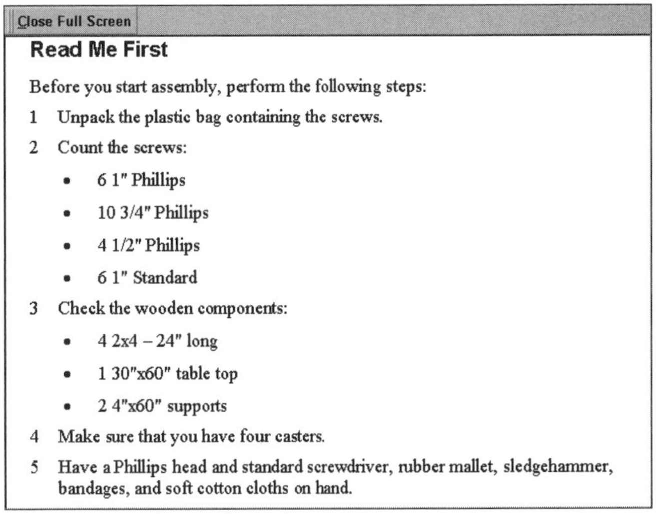
Close Full Screen
Read Me First
Before you start assembly, perform the following steps:
1 Unpack the plastic bag containing the screws.
2 Count the screws:
• 6 1" Phillips
• 10 3/4" Phillips
• 4 1/2" Phillips
• 6 1" Standard
3 Check the wooden components:
• 4 2x4 – 24" long
• 1 30"x60" table top
• 2 4"x60" supports
4 Make sure that you have four casters.
5 Have a Phillips head and standard screwdriver, rubber mallet, sledgehammer, bandages, and soft cotton cloths on hand.

CHAPTER 10

MASTER
THESE
SKILLS

▶ **Using Tables in Your Documents**

▶ **Building Tables**

▶ **Breaking Tables into Sections**

▶ **Varying the Width of Columns and Height of Rows**

▶ **Laying Out Pages Using Tables**

Adding Tables to Documents

A table is composed of horizontal rows and vertical columns. The *cells*, which are the intersections of rows and columns, contain the actual data.

The spreadsheet is probably the most commonly used table in the computer world. Most spreadsheets are made up of the following components:

▶ A heading usually spreads across several cells at the top. Headings are usually bold, large point size.

▶ The *column labels*, which are the subheadings in one or two rows under the heading, identify the contents of the columns below. Column labels are usually boldface or bold-italicized type.

▶ The *row labels*, which are the subheadings in one or two leftmost columns, identify the contents of the rows to the right. Row labels are usually formatted the same way as the column labels.

▶ The actual data comprise the remaining cells in the sheet.

Tables usually contain the same four components. You can use HTML or XML tables to organize and present information, such as monthly or quarterly income and expenses or a set of names and addresses. You can also use tables to lay out your Web pages in a series of invisible grids.

In this chapter, you will learn how to create tables for your Web documents. The first task provides an overview of the HTML elements with which you form elements and an overview of XML tables. The second task shows the markup used to create a simple table. In the next task, you will find out how to separate sections of rows and columns so that you can apply different formats to different sections of your tables. The following task shows how to combine cells — to change the height of certain rows and width of selected columns. The final task in the chapter provides an overview of how to lay out Web pages using sets of table cells as an underlying grid.

To help complete your knowledge of tables, throughout the chapter you'll be able to view selected table-element productions from the HTML 4.0 specification. These productions show the declarations of parent-and-child elements and attributes with which you construct and format HTML tables. Use these productions as a guide for declaring custom elements and attributes for XML tables. In addition, as you browse through the chapter, you'll find illustrated examples of tables.

Using Tables in Your Documents

The HTML specification contains five main elements with which you can specify the components of a table. (You'll learn about other table-related elements as this chapter continues.)

▶ TABLE, which defines the entire table, is the root table-creation element. The other four main elements are embedded within the <TABLE> start tag and </TABLE> end tag; that is, the elements are children of TABLE. (See the HTML 4.0 TABLE element declaration on the facing page.)

▶ The CAPTION element specifies the title of a table — above, below, to the left, or to the right of the table. Be sure to embed the <CAPTION> and </CAPTION> tags within the table. For more information, see the Take Note in the following task.

▶ The TR (table row) element defines a single row in the table. (See the HTML 4.0 TR element declaration on the facing page.)

▶ The TH (table heading) element defines a single heading cell within a defined row. So, it follows that TH is a child element of TR. By default, a table-heading is formatted in boldface. (See the HTML 4.0 TH element declaration on the facing page in the following task.)

▶ The TD (table data) element, the exact and non-heading counterpart of TH and the other child element of TR, defines a single data cell nested within a table row. (See the HTML 4.0 TD element declaration on the facing page in the following task.)

HTML table elements are *row-centric:* information is added to a table row by row.

TAKE NOTE

▶ **USING TABLES IN XML**

Because you define the elements in XML, an XML table can be either row-centric, *column-centric* (information is added column by column), or neither. Commonly used column-centric tables are accountants' balance sheets. Examples of tables that are neither row-centric nor column-centric are multiplication tables and the period table of elements.

So in XML, you can declare table elements as follows:

```
<!ELEMENT table (row+)>
<!ELEMENT row (cell+)>
<!ELEMENT cell (#PCDATA)>
  or
<!ELEMENT table (col+)>
<!ELEMENT col (cell+)>
<!ELEMENT cell (#PCDATA)>
```

The first example is row-centric and the second is column-centric. In the first case, the cell element is a child of row, and in the second, cell is a child of col.

▶ **LEARNING ABOUT BACKGROUND COLOR PRECEDENCES IN HTML TABLES, ROWS, AND CELLS**

When you add background color to a table, table row, or table cell using the BGCOLOR attribute or the background-color style, you should be aware of the order of precedence in which one color overrides another. The order of precedence for background color values is table cells (highest), table rows, and table (lowest). So, the color that you specify for a cell overrides that of the row or table in which it is located, and the color of a row overrides that of its table.

CROSS-REFERENCE

Chapter 5 presents an overview of HTML and XML, as well as the plan and design of Web sites and documents.

FIND IT ONLINE

For an old but useful summary of HTML tables, go to
http://home.netscape.com/assist/net_sites/tables.html.

HTML 4.0: The TABLE Element ❶

```
<!ELEMENT TABLE - - (CAPTION?, (COL*|COLGROUP*), THEAD?, TFOOT?, TBODY+)>
<!ATTLIST TABLE                        -- table element --
  %attrs;                    ❷        -- %coreattrs, %i18n, %events --
  summary      %Text;     #IMPLIED    -- purpose/structure for speech output --
  width        %Length;   #IMPLIED    -- table width --
  border       %Pixels;   #IMPLIED    -- controls frame width around table --
  frame        %TFrame;   #IMPLIED    -- which parts of frame to render --
  rules        %TRules;   #IMPLIED    -- rulings between rows and cols --
  cellspacing  %Length;   #IMPLIED    -- spacing between cells --
  cellpadding  %Length;   #IMPLIED    -- spacing within cells --
  align        %TAlign;   #IMPLIED    -- table position relative to window --
  bgcolor      %Color;    #IMPLIED    -- background color for cells --
  %reserved;              #IMPLIED    -- reserved for possible future use --
  datapagesize CDATA      #IMPLIED    -- reserved for possible future use --
>
```

❶ The TABLE *element contains several child elements.*
❷ All *the attributes of the* TABLE *element are optional.*

HTML 4.0: The TR Element ❶

```
<!ELEMENT TR       - O (TH|TD)+        -- table row -->
<!ATTLIST TR
  %attrs;                         ❷-- %coreattrs, %i18n, %events --
  %cellhalign;                      -- horizontal alignment in cells --
  %cellvalign;                      -- vertical alignment in cells --
  bgcolor      %Color;  #IMPLIED    -- background color for row -->
```

❶ The TR *element has two child elements,* TH *and* TD.
❷ Align *the contents of cells horizontally or vertically.*

Building Tables

Whether you are using HTML or XML, the process of building a table is similar: the difference is that in XML, the names of the elements may vary from those in HTML, and you may have declared a different set of attributes in your DTD. In addition, your XML elements may force you (or the individual constructing the Web document) to create a column-centric table, a table that contains a limited number of columns and/or rows, or a table that is styled or formatted in a particular way.

Assuming that — for now — you use the HTML model of five basic elements presented in the prior task, define a table that contains markup and content that looks something like this:

```
<TABLE>
  <CAPTION>caption text</CAPTION>
  <TR>
    <TH>header cell text</TH>
    <TH>header cell text</TH>
  </TR>
  <TR>
    <TD>data cell text</TD>
    <TD>data cell text</TD>
  </TR>
</TABLE>
```

Of course, you can format the code in a table document any way you want: you can omit the indentions, change the amount of indention, or place the TH or TD tags side by side. No doubt, your table will contain more rows and columns than the two of each in the example.

You can also insert attributes and attribute values and/or styles within the start tag. In HTML, you can use attributes to change the appearance of an entire table, one or more rows, one or more cells, and/or their contents. To

learn more about HTML table attributes, either view the HTML 4.0 specification or the contents of the prior or following facing pages. For more information about attributes, browse through Chapters 6 and 7.

You can replace some formatting attributes with styles, so it's probably a good idea to attach a stylesheet to your HTML document. In fact, to present a formatted XML document online or to print it in the proper format, you must attach a stylesheet. You'll learn more about cascading stylesheets and Extensible Style Language (XSL) stylesheets in Chapter 13.

Remember that many developers use uppercase HTML elements and attributes and lowercase XML elements and attributes — as an informal indication of whether elements and/or attributes belong to the HTML specification or an XML DTD. This is especially useful when you mix HTML and XML in the same document.

TAKE NOTE

LEARNING MORE ABOUT TABLE CAPTIONS

The CAPTION element, which is a child of the TABLE element, enables you to add one caption above, below, to the left, or to the right of a table. A table caption is not required, but it's a good idea to use a caption to identify the table and its contents. Then you can use the captions to create a table of tables that you can include in your site map. If you wish to add a caption to a table, CAPTION and its attributes must occur immediately after the <TABLE> start tag. For most browsers, the default position of a caption is above the table.

CROSS-REFERENCE

To learn about using EBNF, see the "Recognizing Markup and Character Data" task in Chapter 6.

FIND IT ONLINE

See examples of HTML tables at **http://home.netscape. com/assist/net_sites/table_sample.html**.

HTML 4.0: The TH and TD Elements

```
<!ELEMENT (TH|TD)   - O (%flow;)*      -- table header cell, table data cell -->
<!ATTLIST (TH|TD)                      -- header or data cell --
  %attrs;                              -- %coreattrs, %i18n, %events --
  abbr           %Text;   #IMPLIED -- default number of columns in group --
  axis           CDATA    #IMPLIED -- names groups of related headers --
  headers        IDREFS   #IMPLIED -- list of ids for header cells --
  scope          %Scope;  #IMPLIED -- scope covered by header cells --
  rowspan        NUMBER   1        -- number of rows spanned by cell --
  colspan        NUMBER   1        -- number of columns spanned by cell --
  %cellhalign;                     -- horizontal alignment in cells --
  %cellvalign;                     -- vertical alignment in cells --
  nowrap         (nowrap) #IMPLIED -- suppress word wrap --
  bgcolor        %Color;  #IMPLIED -- cell background color --
  width          %Pixels; #IMPLIED -- width for cell --
  height         %Pixels; #IMPLIED -- height for cell -->
```

❶ The TH and TD elements share the same set of attributes.

Listing 10-1: Your First Table

```
<!DOCTYPE HTML PUBLIC
    "-//W3C//DTD HTML 4.0//EN">
<HTML><HEAD>
<TITLE>Your First Table</TITLE></HEAD>
<BODY><TABLE BORDER>
<CAPTION>Your first table</CAPTION>
<TR>
 <TH> </TH>
 <TH>Quarter 1</TH><TH>Quarter 2</TH>
</TR>
<TR>
 <TD>Sales</TD><TD>1200</TD><TD>1500</TD>
</TR>
<TR>
 <TD>Expenses</TD><TD>900</TD><TD>950</TD>
</TR></TABLE></BODY></HTML>
```

❶ Specify a table with borders.
❷ Add a caption immediately after starting the table.
❸ The   entity inserts a non-breaking space into the cell.
❹ End the table, document body, and the document itself.

❺ The caption is in the default position, above the table.
❻ The table and cells are surrounded by borders.
❼ The empty cell contains a non-breaking space.
❽ By default, table heading cells are bold.

Breaking Tables into Sections

Earlier in this chapter, you learned that tables are sets of rows and columns. Typically, the top row of a table and its leftmost column indicate the type of content stored in the rest of the table. The contents of each cell in the top row label the columns, and the contents of the cells in the leftmost column label the rows. Use the TH and TD elements to divide a table into heading cells and data cells, respectively.

You can break a table into sections in other ways. For example, you can use the THEAD, TFOOT, and TBODY elements (see the listing on the facing page) to split a table into sets of one or more rows that include a table head, a table foot, and one or more table bodies. Simply mark the beginning of a section with a start tag and the end with an end tag. You must place the TFOOT section before the TBODY section so that the browser can plan for the placement of the foot section.

You can also separate a table into individual columns and column groups, or both using the COL and COLGROUP elements. The COL element groups attributes for one or more columns but does not set a column group. COL is empty, which means that it has no content. However, COL can have attributes — which is its sole purpose. COLGROUP defines an explicit column group. If a table does not include one or more explicitly-defined column groups, the entire table is a single column group.

TAKE NOTE

▶ EMPHASIZING COLUMNS AND ROWS

To emphasize the importance of column and row labels, they should look different from the rest of the table contents. To format selected cells or rows, you can apply combinations of boldface, italics, and other emphasis using the B, I, STRONG, EM, FONT, and other HTML elements. You can also use various attributes to apply color, borders, and dynamic effects or style selected elements using style sheets.

▶ STYLING XML TABLE COLUMNS USING ATTRIBUTES

In XML, tables can be row-centric or column-centric, depending on how you declare your table elements. For example, you can define a set number of columns by requiring particular attributes. Look at the following element and attribute-list declarations:

```
<!ELEMENT table (row+ | caption?)>
<!ELEMENT row (heading*, cell+)>
<!ELEMENT caption (#PCDATA)>
<!ELEMENT heading (#PCDATA)>
<!ELEMENT cell (#PCDATA)>
<!ATTLIST cell column (column1|column2|
                       column3) #REQUIRED>
```

In the example, you require that three columns be used — in any order. This requirement means that you can style each of the columns in a different way. Unfortunately, when you want to start another table with a different number of columns, you'll have to edit the attribute list in the DTD.

CROSS-REFERENCE

To find out about attributes, see the "Understanding Attributes" task in Chapter 6.

FIND IT ONLINE

The WDVL: Tables site (http://www.stars.com/Authoring/HTML/Tables/) briefly covers HTML table elements.

HTML 4.0: The THEAD, TFOOT, and TBODY Elements

```
<!ELEMENT THEAD    - O (TR)+              -- table header -->
<!ELEMENT TFOOT    - O (TR)+              -- table footer -->
<!ELEMENT TBODY    O O (TR)+              -- table body -->
<!ATTLIST (THEAD|TBODY|TFOOT)            -- table section --
  %attrs;                                -- %coreattrs, %i18n, %events --
  %cellhalign;                           -- horizontal alignment in cells --
  %cellvalign;                           -- vertical alignment in cells --
>
```

▶ *Each of the element's attributes lists also include other commonly used attributes —* id, class, lang, title, style, align, char, charoff, *and* valign *— as well as the* onclick, ondblclick, onmousedown, onmouseup, onmouseover, onmousemove, onmouseout, onkeypress, onkeydown, *and* onkeyup *intrinsic events.*

HTML 4.0: The COLGROUP and COL Elements

```
<!ELEMENT COLGROUP    - O (col)*         -- table column group -->
<!ATTLIST COLGROUP
  %attrs;                                -- %coreattrs, %i18n, %events --
  span          NUMBER         1         -- default number of columns in group --
  width         %MultiLength;  #IMPLIED  -- default width for enclosed COLs --
  %cellhalign;                           -- horizontal alignment in cells --
  %cellvalign;                           -- vertical alignment in cells --
>
```

```
<!ELEMENT COL        - O   EMPTY         -- table column -->
<!ATTLIST COL                            -- column groups and properties --
  %attrs;                                -- %coreattrs, %i18n, %events --
  span          NUMBER         1         -- COL attributes affect N columns --
  width         %MultiLength;  #IMPLIED  -- column width specification --
  %cellhalign;                           -- horizontal alignment in cells --
  %cellvalign;                           -- vertical alignment in cells --
>
```

▶ *Each element includes the same set of commonly used attributes used by* THEAD, TFOOT, *and* TBODY.

Varying the Width of Columns and Height of Rows

The TH and TD elements support the use of the colspan and rowspan attributes, which enable you to combine several columns or rows to increase the width or height of a particular cell. Each of these attributes specifies the number of cells in the span. Using the colspan and rowspan attributes erases the borders between the combined cells and extends the contents from the leftmost to the rightmost margins of the combined cell. In the HTML 4.0 DTD, the attribute declarations are as follows:

```
colspan          NUMBER    1
rowspan          NUMBER    1
```

As you can see, the valid value for each of the attributes is a number; the default value is 1. If colspan="0", the span extends through the remaining columns in the table; if rowspan="0", the span extends through the remaining rows in the table.

As you can see in the listing and figures on the facing page, the main use of the colspan and rowspan attributes is to improve the look of a table. In the example, which is based on an example in the HTML 4.0 specification, the heading *Average* applies to both the subheadings, *height* and *weight*. Because the heading is comprised of a main heading (*Average*) and two subheadings (*height* and *weight*), it takes up two rows. So, the leftmost empty area must explicitly encompass two rows. Then, rather than have *Average* appear twice — over *height* and *weight* — you can use a single instance of the term, which spans two columns. To balance the table further, the final heading, *Red eyes*, breaks into two one-word lines (that is, rows).

CROSS-REFERENCE

"Entering Elements," in Chapter 8, teaches you how to insert start tags, end tags, and content in a document.

FIND IT ONLINE

Go to **http://www.w3.org/TR/PR-html40/struct/tables.html** to read about HTML 4.0 tables in detail.

Listing 10-2: A Table with Merged Cells

```
<!DOCTYPE HTML PUBLIC
    "-//W3C//DTD HTML 4.0//EN">
<HTML><HEAD>
<TITLE>A Table with Merged Cells</TITLE>
</HEAD>
<BODY><TABLE border="1">
<CAPTION>
  <EM>A test table with merged cells</EM>
</CAPTION>
<TR><TH rowspan="2"></TH>
    <TH colspan="2">Average</TH>
    <TH rowspan="2">Red<BR>eyes</TH></TR>
<TR><TH>height</TH><TH>weight</TH></TR>
<TR><TH>Males</TH>
    <TD>1.9</TD><TD>0.003</TD><TD>40%</TD>
</TR>
<TR><TH>Females</TH>
    <TD>1.7</TD><TD>0.002</TD><TD>43%</TD>
</TR>
</TABLE>
</BODY></HTML>
```

❶ Span two empty rows.
❷ Place "Average" in the second and third cells.
❸ The last column spans two rows.
❹ The remaining rows and columns span one cell each.

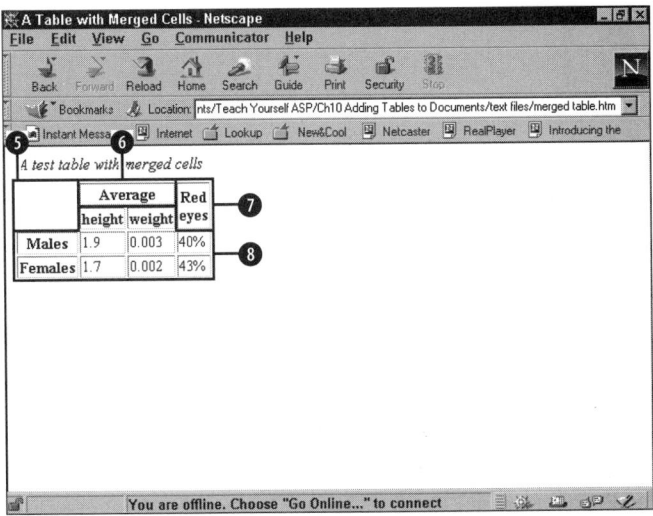

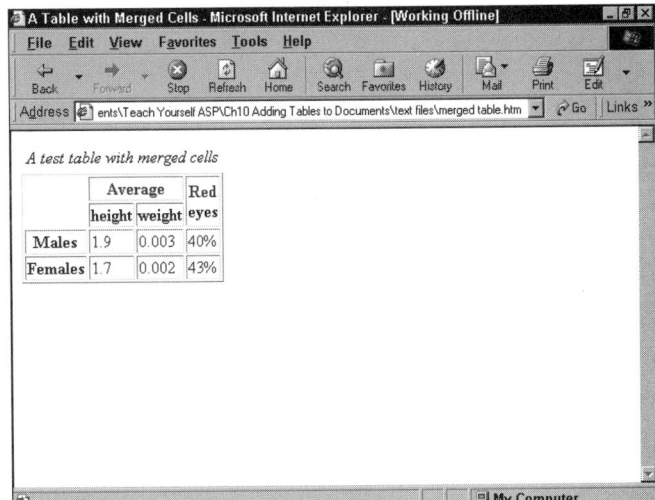

❺ The empty area spans two empty rows and two empty columns.

❻ "Average" spans the cells in the second and third columns.

❼ "Red eyes" spans two rows.

❽ The remaining rows and columns span one cell each.

▶ In the Microsoft Internet Explorer window, the table looks the same as it does in the Netscape Navigator window; it contains a combination of bold table heading cells and regular table data cells.

Laying Out Pages Using Tables

The typical way to lay out a Web document is to style it with a stylesheet. However, there is an alternate method: create a table in which you set up an invisible grid of cells. With this approach, you use tables to format and organize page elements within the borders of cells. You can use the `rowspan` and `colspan` attributes (see the preceding task) to change the dimensions of particular cells, or you can just let the amount of body text in a cell control the location of the following row on the page. For example, you can break a page into two columns. The right column might contain several cells with headings-and-text pairs on a white background. The left column could be made up of one long cell with a list of links or highlights of your site on a red or blue background. Or you can ensure that a corporate logo is located in the upper right corner of a page and that a link to corporate information stretches across the bottom of the page.

The example on the facing page uses three columns. The leftmost column contains all the headings except for the main heading at the top of the page. These headings are right-aligned and vertically aligned with the top of the cells in which they are located. The middle column simply inserts a vertical space on the page. The third column, which represents the remaining width of the page, holds all the body text. Each text block is left-aligned and aligned with the top of their cells.

CROSS-REFERENCE

Read "Planning and Designing a Document" in Chapter 5 to learn how to create an effective Web document.

FIND IT ONLINE

The HTML Tables site (http://viablesoftware.com/mvd/style2.htm) discusses table styles and design.

Listing 10-3: Part of a Page-Layout Table

```
<!DOCTYPE HTML PUBLIC
    "-//W3C//DTD HTML 4.0//EN">
<HTML><HEAD>
<TITLE>A Table for Page Layout</TITLE>
<BODY><H1>Big Heading</H1>
<HR width=95% align="left"></HR>
<TABLE width=95%>
<TR>
  <TD width="90" align="right"
  valign="top"><B>First Things</B><BR>
  <I><FONT size="2">Get this done first.
  </FONT></I></TD>
  <TD width="60"</TD>
  <TD align="left">This page provides
  instructions for installing a program.
  Before installing the program, you
  should have installed an operating
  system. Your computer should also have
  a mouse, printer, and a modem. If you
  have installed from a CD-ROM, make sure
  that you have stored it in a place from
  which you can retrieve it later.</TD>
</TR>
<TR>
  <TH align="right" valign="top">
  Requirements</TH><TD></TD>
  <TD align="left" valign="top">Minimum
  requirements for installing the program
  are:</TD></TR>
```

❶ Make the table 95% of the page width.
❷ The first column contains headings and summary text.
❸ The second column inserts space between the first and third columns.
❹ The third column contains body text.

Listing 10-4: Continuing the Page-Layout Table

```
<TR>
  <TD align="right" valign="top"><I>
  <FONT size="2">You'll need this
  hardware and software to run the
  program.</I></FONT></TD><TD></TD>
  <TD align="left"><UL>
  <LI>An IBM or 100% compatible PC with an
  80486 (or greater) microprocessor.</LI>
  <LI>Windows 95 or 98 (or greater)</LI>
  <LI>At least 16 megabytes of RAM</LI>
  <LI>A CD-ROM drive for installation</LI>
  </UL></TD>
</TR></TABLE></BODY></HTML>
```

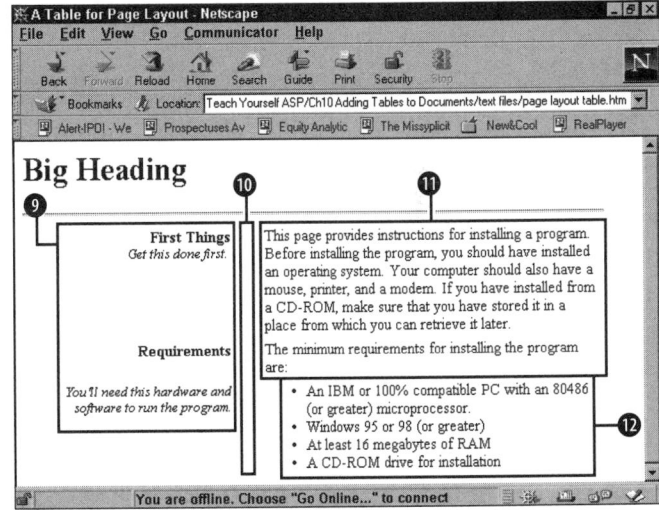

❺ Insert the first and second columns.
❻ Start the third column and an unordered list.
❼ Add four list items to the table-data cell in the third column.
❽ End the list, table-data cell, last row, table, and body.
❾ The first column contains headings and summary text.
❿ The second column inserts space between the first and third columns.
⓫ The third column contains body text.
⓬ The list items are indented from the column's left margin.

Personal Workbook

Q & A

1 What components make up a table?

_____

_____

_____

2 What are the main table elements in the HTML 4.0 specification?

_____

_____

_____

3 What is the characteristic of a row-centric table?

_____

_____

_____

4 What is the primary difference between an HTML table and an XML table?

_____

_____

_____

5 When you include both HTML and XML markup in the same document, how should you show the difference?

_____

_____

_____

6 What elements do you use to define table cells?

_____

_____

_____

7 How do you split a table into head, foot, and body sections?

_____

_____

_____

8 What attribute of the TABLE element shows or hides borders around a table and its cells?

_____

_____

_____

ANSWERS: PAGE 502

EXTRA PRACTICE

1. Design a table that shows five days of evening (8 P.M. to 11 P.M.) television programs.

2. Create a table showing the prices of computers from several vendors. Include general specifications about the computer.

3. Add formatting attributes to the price table.

4. Go online and find a table tutorial not mentioned in this chapter.

5. Create a table that presents four quarters of income and expenses for 1999. Use the `colspan` attribute to center 1999 above the quarter columns.

6. Using the example in the last task in this chapter as your basis, design a page containing your favorite recipe.

REAL-WORLD APPLICATIONS

✔ You have been assigned the job of creating a Web page of your international company's departments and their locations. Design and create a two-column table for this purpose.

✔ As the manager of a project, you want to track its progress. Each row should contain a task, its starting and ending dates, and the names of assigned employees.

✔ You want to post a glossary of terms for your industry online. Use a two-column table to lay out the page.

✔ You are searching for a new job and want to post your résumé at your Web site. Lay out the document using an underlying table.

Visual Quiz

How would you construct this table? (Make sure to align the contents of every cell properly.)

_____

_____

_____

_____

_____

_____

Visual Quiz 10 - Microsoft Internet Explorer - [Working Offline]

File   Edit   View   Favorites   Tools   Help

Back   Forward   Stop   Refresh   Home   Search   Favorites   History   Mail   Print   Edit

Employee	Address	Distance		
		Tom	Dick	Harry
Tom	Main Street	-	2 miles	4 miles
Dick	Maple Lane	2 mile	-	6 miles
Harry	Ray Way	4 miles	6 miles	-

Car Pooling Table

Done   My Computer

CHAPTER **11**

MASTER
THESE
SKILLS

▶ Defining Framesets
▶ Setting Up Frames
▶ Filling Frames
▶ Targeting Frames
▶ Modifying Frames
▶ Allowing for No Frames

Framing Documents

HTML provides several elements with which you can divide the browser window into a set of smaller windows, each displaying an entire or partial Web document. These small windows are called *frames*, and the sets of windows are known as *framesets*.

The current version of XML does not support the use of frames. Until a future XML specification supports frames, you'll have to depend on a programmer to write a custom frames application or applet. Note that enabling frames using programming is beyond the scope of this book.

In this chapter, you will learn about framesets and the frames within — how to create them, how to control their characteristics, and how to load them with content. The two most important frames elements in HTML are FRAMESET and FRAME. Using the FRAMESET element, you can define the number of frames in a frameset, set the percentage of the window devoted to each frame, and specify certain characteristics for the set. Then, specify each frame in the set using the FRAME element, which names the URI for the target document that will appear in the frame. The FRAME element also provides attributes with which you can affect the look and content of the frame.

This chapter contains several tasks devoted to framesets, frames, and the characteristics that you can apply to each. The first task teaches you how to define a frameset and specify the dimensions and location of each frame within. Next, you'll learn how to control the content and appearance of a specific frame within the set. Included in this task is a discussion of how to structure a frameset document. The third task goes further into the content of frames and the frameset as well as the logic of how framesets are arranged onscreen. Using the information in the fourth task, you will be able to load content into a particular frame. You can use a keyword and/or a frame name to fine-tune document displays. In the penultimate task, you will learn about attributes with which you can set the appearance and behavior of frames.

Finally, note that a few Web browsers do not support frames. So, whenever you design a set of frames-based Web documents, you should always include a "no-frames" section using HTML's NOFRAMES element. The NOFRAMES element is covered in the last task.

Defining Framesets

Use HTML's FRAMESET element to divide a browser window into two or more smaller windows so that you can simultaneously display separate parts of one document or a few individual documents. FRAMESET controls the structure of frames onscreen, the percentage of the entire screen set for each frame, and overall appearance of the frameset. (See the FRAMESET element declaration and attribute list on the facing page.)

FRAMESET's rows and cols attributes are programmed to divide the browser window into virtual rows and columns, respectively, as percentages of the entire window. An entire window measures 100% from top to bottom (rowwise), and 100% from side to side (columnwise). Take a look at the following start tag, attributes, and attribute values:

```
<FRAMESET rows=25%,25%,50% cols=50%,*>
```

The example defines a frameset composed of three rows that divide the screen into 25%, 25%, and 50% horizontally aligned segments. Notice that the sum of the three rows is 100%. The vertical dimension of the screen is divided into two columns: the first 50% and the second the remaining amount of space, which adds up to 100% again. The asterisk (*) tells the browser to calculate the rest of the value. You actually could have coded the frameset as follows:

```
<FRAMESET rows=25%,25%,50% cols=50%,50%>
```

but the asterisk prevents human calculation errors that result in a value under or over 100% of a particular horizontal or vertical dimension. So, the best way to express the statement is actually:

```
<FRAMESET rows=25%,25%,* cols=50%,*>
```

or

```
<FRAMESET rows=25%,*,50% cols=*,50%>
```

Note that the asterisk can be placed in any position.

You can also specify the dimensions of a frame in absolute measurements, in pixels. For example:

```
<FRAMESET rows=300,*,300 cols=600,*>
```

The first and last row (that is, the first and last frame) are 300 pixels from top to bottom. The middle row (the second frame) encompasses the remaining part of the screen. The width of the first frame is 600 pixels, and the remaining frame takes up the remainder.

You can combine absolute numbers with asterisks. For example:

```
<FRAMESET rows=1*,2*,3*>
```

In this case, the second row is twice the length of the first, and the third row is three times the length of the first. You can combine percentages, absolute measurements, and asterisks in your frameset rows and columns.

Design framesets with great care. Many users dislike frames — especially if the frames in the framesets are improperly sized. Carefully size a frame that contains a heading, table of contents, or set of buttons. If a subsidiary frame is too large, it will take valuable space from the main frame, which holds the most important document. If a frame is too small, some of its contents may be hidden. (Imagine what can happen if a link to an important page is not visible or usable.) In general, the best frameset design is to have one frame dominate the browser window.

TAKE NOTE

USING FRAMES IN XML

If you can get a programmer to write an application or applet that enables XML frames, you can use the HTML frames elements and attributes as a guide for your XML elements and attributes. The programmer will know how the application will process the frames.

CROSS-REFERENCE

You can learn about using tables for page design in the "Laying Out Pages Using Tables" task in Chapter 10.

FIND IT ONLINE

Access several tutorials on frames basics at **http://www.bfree.on.ca/HTML/Frame2.htm**.

HTML 4.0: The FRAMESET Element

```
<![ %HTML.Frameset; [
<!ELEMENT FRAMESET - - ((FRAMESET|FRAME)+ & NOFRAMES?) -- window subdivision-->
<!ATTLIST FRAMESET
  %coreattrs;                        -- id, class, style, title --
  rows           %MultiLengths; #IMPLIED  -- list of lengths,
                                             default: 100% (1 row) --
  cols           %MultiLengths; #IMPLIED  -- list of lengths,
                                             default: 100% (1 col) --
  onload         %Script;       #IMPLIED  -- all the frames have been loaded --
  onunload       %Script;       #IMPLIED  -- all the frames have been removed -->
]]>
```

① *The* `%HTML.Frameset;` *entity implicitly specifies an* INCLUDE *section.*

② *You can compose a frameset with another frameset or frames with optional "noframes."*

③ *The* `rows` *attribute specifies the layout of horizontal frames.*

④ *The* `cols` *attribute specifies the layout of vertical frames.*

Listing 11-1: A Simple Frames Example

```
<!DOCTYPE HTML PUBLIC
      "-//W3C//DTD HTML 4.0//EN">
<HTML>
<HEAD><TITLE>A Frameset Example</TITLE>
</HEAD>
<FRAMESET cols=30%,40%,*>
   <FRAME src="frame1.htm">
   <FRAME src="frame2.htm">
   <FRAME src="frame3.htm">
</FRAMESET>
</HTML>
<!DOCTYPE HTML PUBLIC
      "-//W3C//DTD HTML 4.0//EN">
<HTML><HEAD><TITLE>frame1</TITLE></HEAD>
<BODY LINK="#0000ff" VLINK="#800080"
BGCOLOR="#ffff99">
<I><P>Frame 1</P></I></BODY></HTML>
```

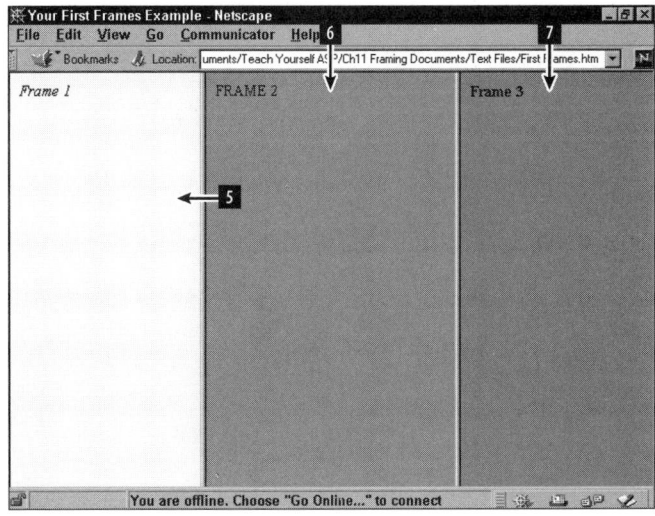

5 *The* `frame1.htm` *document appears in 30% of the window.*

6 *The* `frame2.htm` *document appears in 40% of the window.*

7 *The* `frame3.htm` *document appears in the remaining 30%.*

1 *Define three columns, at 30%, 40%, and the remaining width.*

2 *Refer to the* `frame1.htm`, `frame2.htm`, *and* `frame3.htm` *documents as content.*

3 *End the frameset.*

4 *Code the* `frame1.htm` *document.*

161

Setting Up Frames

Use the FRAME element to control the content and appearance of a specific frame. For example:

```
<FRAMESET rows=20%,*>
    <FRAME src="title.htm"></FRAME>
    <FRAME src="main.htm""></FRAME>
</FRAMESET>
```

The two frames in this frameset contain documents referenced by the src attribute. FRAMESET's rows attribute sets one frame at 20% of the screen rowwise; the other frame encompasses the remaining rows. Because the <FRAMESET> and <FRAME> start tags in the example contain no other attributes, the browser displays and formats the frameset using the default settings. (A complete list of the other attributes for the HTML 4.0 FRAME element appears on the facing page.)

The FRAME element provides several attributes that control the look and behavior of a specific frame. You can choose to display or omit a border for a particular frame using the frameborder attribute. You can choose from two possible values for frameborder: frameborder="1" turns on a three-dimensional border, and frameborder="0" omits the border. By omitting the border, you can produce framesets that look like non-frame documents. For example:

```
<FRAME src="frame1.htm" frameborder="0">
</FRAME>
```

The marginwidth and marginheight attributes control the size of the space between the margin borders and the contents of the frame. The marginwidth attribute specifies the size (in pixels) of the left and right margins, and marginheight sets the size of the top and bottom margins. For example:

```
<FRAME src="frame1.htm" marginwidth="8"
marginheight="5"></FRAME>
```

As you can see in the attribute declaration on the facing page, both marginwidth and marginheight contain the %Pixels; entity. The value %Pixels; simply is an absolute integer that represents the number of horizontal or vertical pixels on the computer screen or printed paper. A *pixel* is a dot that represents the smallest part of an image.

TAKE NOTE

▶ STRUCTURING A FRAMESET

A typical HTML document includes three main sets of start tags and end tags: <HTML></HTML>, <HEAD></HEAD>, and <BODY></BODY>, all of which set the main structure of the document. As you know, the HTML element, which is HTML's root element, instructs the browser that it is about to process a document supported by the current HTML DTD. The HEAD and BODY elements, which are the children of the HTML element, mark the beginning and end of the HEAD and BODY sections, respectively. However, when you use frames, the basic HTML document structure changes. According to the HTML 4.0 standard, the document is called a *frameset document*. In a frameset document, the <FRAMESET> and </FRAMESET> tags replace the <BODY> and </BODY> tags.

▶ DISPLAYING FRAMES IN XML DOCUMENTS

In HTML, the order of frames for formatting and adding content is strictly row-centric: rows take priority over columns. Row-centric document components are defined row by row — across the top row, down to the next row, across that row, down to the next, and so on. However, in XML — depending on the application or applet that controls framesets and frames — framesets and frames may be row-centric or column-centric. Check with the programmer who developed the application or applet.

CROSS-REFERENCE

Get an overview of the HTML markup language in the "Exploring HTML" task in Chapter 5.

FIND IT ONLINE

Harvillo's Finest HTML Help (**http://members.aol.com/ harvillo/index.html**) provides help and HTML utilities.

HTML 4.0: The FRAME Element

```
<![ %HTML.Frameset; [
<! - reserved frame names start with "_" otherwise starts with letter -->
<!ELEMENT FRAME - O EMPTY ◀─❶        -- subwindow -->
<!ATTLIST FRAME
  %coreattrs;                        -- id, class, style, title --
  longdesc      %URI;       #IMPLIED -- link to long description
                                        (complements title) --
  name          CDATA       #IMPLIED -- name of frame for targeting --◀─❷
  src           %URI;       #IMPLIED -- source of frame content --
  frameborder   (1|0)       1        -- request frame borders? --◀─❸
  marginwidth   %Pixels;    #IMPLIED -- margin widths in pixels --
  marginheight  %Pixels;    #IMPLIED -- margin height in pixels --◀─❹
  noresize      (noresize)  #IMPLIED -- allow users to resize frames? --
  scrolling     (yes|no|auto) auto   -- scroll bar or none --
  >
]]>
```

❶ *In HTML, the* FRAME *element is empty.*
❷ *You can name a frame so that you can activate it.*
❸ *Turn on (1) a border, or suppress it (0).*
❹ *Set the width and/or height of a frame margin.*

Listing 11-2: An Embedded Frameset

```
<!DOCTYPE HTML PUBLIC
      "-//W3C//DTD HTML 4.0//EN">
<HTML><HEAD>
<TITLE>An Embedded Frameset</TITLE>
</HEAD>
<FRAMESET cols=20%,*>◀─1
    <FRAME src="frame1.htm">◀─2
    <FRAMESET rows=30%,*>◀─3
        <FRAME src="frame2.htm">
        <FRAME src="frame3.htm"> ◀─4
    </FRAMESET>
</FRAMESET></HTML>
```

1 *Start the first frameset, which is columnwise.*
2 *Insert a document into the first frame.*
3 *Code the embedded frameset, which is rowwise.*
4 *Add two frame documents.*

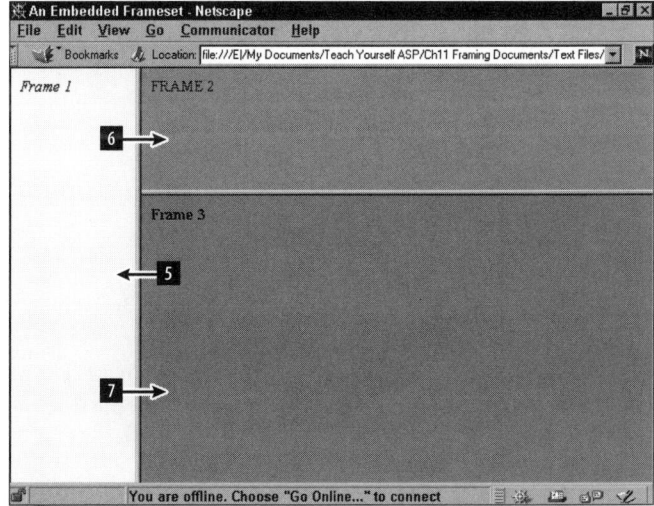

5 *The* frame1.htm *document appears in a 20% column.*
6 *The* frame2.htm *document appears in the top 30% of the right column.*
7 *The* frame3.htm *document appears in the remaining 70% of the column.*

Filling Frames

The most important part of a frame is the content within — documents that are composed of any combination of text, graphics, links, and other objects. As you learned in the preceding task and examples, the `src` attribute points to the URI of the document to be displayed in the frame.

All the frames in a frameset should usually contain material that is related in some way. For example, the current document may appear in the large, main frame. The rest of the frames may include a variety of subsidiary information, such as a table of links to all the site's documents (similar to the table of contents for a book) on the left side of the browser window, the site title at the top of the window, and, at the bottom, buttons linking to the home page, the pages before and after the current page, copyright or corporate information, and so forth.

The statements that set up this four-frame frameset might look something like this:

```
<FRAMESET cols=30%,*>
  <FRAME src="toc.htm"></FRAME>
  <FRAMESET rows=15%,*,15%>
    <FRAME src=title.htm"></FRAME>
    <FRAME src=main.htm"></FRAME>
    <FRAME src=buttons.htm"></FRAME>
  </FRAMESET>
</FRAMESET>
```

Notice that the parent frameset contains an embedded child frameset. The parent defines the two columns, the leftmost of which contains the `toc.htm` document. The embedded frameset controls the dimensions of the three remaining frames, which are all located in the second column. As you will learn in the following tasks in this chapter, you would probably include other attributes to control the appearance and behavior of individual frames within the parent and child framesets.

CROSS-REFERENCE

"Recognizing Markup and Character Data" in Chapter 6 shows the differences between markup and character data.

Listing 11-3: Three Generations of Framesets

```html
<!DOCTYPE HTML PUBLIC
      "-//W3C//DTD HTML 4.0//EN">
<HTML>
<HEAD>
<TITLE>Three Generations of Framesets</TITLE>
</HEAD>
<FRAMESET cols=20%,60%,*>      ❶
    <FRAME src="frame1.htm" scrolling="yes">      ❷
    <FRAMESET rows=15%,*>      ❸
        <FRAME src="frame2.htm">
        <FRAME src="frame3.htm"
              scrolling="yes">
    </FRAMESET>
    <FRAMESET cols=100%>      ❹
        <FRAME src="frame4.htm"
              scrolling="yes">
    </FRAMESET>
</FRAMESET>
</HTML>
```

❶ Specify three columns of frames in the top frameset.

❷ Add a scroll bar to the frame that contains frame1.htm.

❸ Code a second frameset for the two middle frames.

❹ Insert another frameset for the rightmost frame.

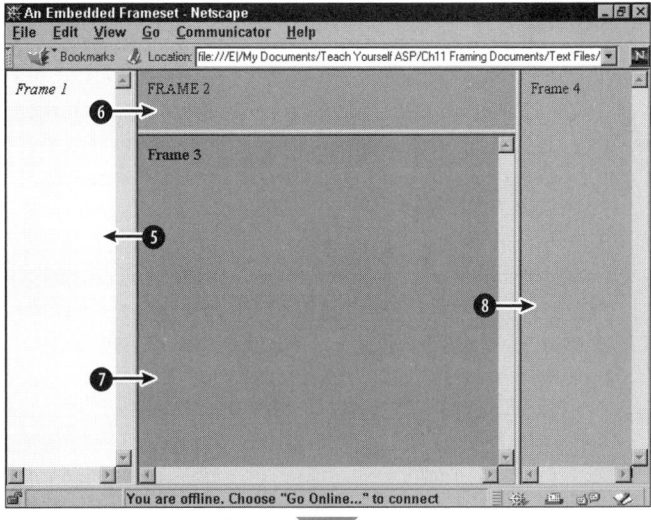

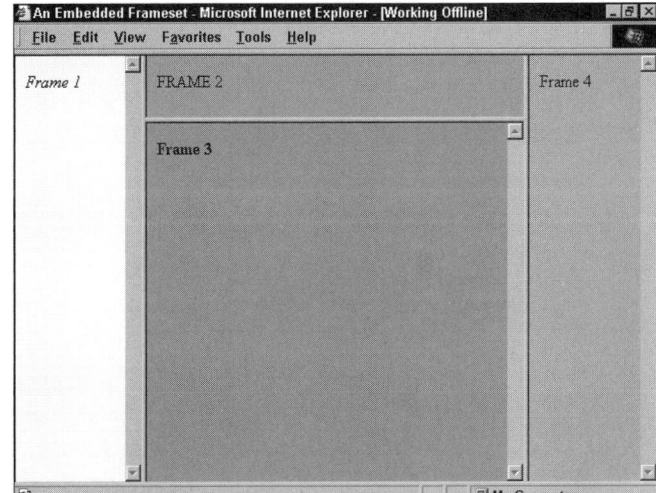

❺ The frame1.htm document appears in the leftmost, 20% column.

❻ The frame2.htm document appears in the top frame in the middle.

❼ The frame3.htm document appears in the remaining 85% frame.

❽ The frame4.htm document appears in the rightmost frame.

▶ In Microsoft Internet Explorer, the frameset document looks slightly different. The first, third, and fourth frames have only vertical scroll bars (scrolling="yes"). Netscape Navigator shows both vertical and horizontal scroll bars.

165

Targeting Frames

HTML enables you to place specific content in a particular window or frame. Use the FRAME element's name attribute to target a named frame. The value of the name attribute determines whether a document appears in a new, blank frame, or in a particular frame based on the hierarchy of frames that a user has browsed while visiting your site.

The value of the name attribute can either be a valid HTML name, which must begin with an uppercase or lowercase character from the current alphabet, or a reserved keyword. Reserved keywords are:

- ▶ _blank, which loads the contents into a blank frame
- ▶ _parent, which loads the contents into the frame that is one level above the current frame
- ▶ _self, which replaces the contents of the current frame with the new document
- ▶ _top, which loads the content into the top frame in the frameset

Look at the following line containing a FRAME element:

```
<FRAME src="toc.htm" name="toc">
```

In the example, the URI refers to the toc.htm document, which loads a table of contents into the frame. The name of the frame is toc, which also refers to the document.

The following lines all make the window (or frame) named main the target:

```
<A href="intr.htm" target="main">Introduction
</A>
<A href="ch1.htm" target="main">An Overview
 of Markup Languages</A>
<A href="ch2.htm" target="main">Learning
 about HTML</A>
```

These lines enable a user to click a table-of-contents link to place a document in the main frame.

TAKE NOTE

▶ LEARNING ABOUT HTML IMAGEMAPS

HTML provides a graphical way to add links to a document. You can use the AREA element to define the shape of the graphic, and the MAP element to name an image map on the client computer. AREA is a child element of MAP. Most maps contain several AREA elements. Each area is associated with a link to a particular target. For example:

```
<MAP name="Sample Map">
  <AREA shape="rect"
   coords="9,148,168,209"
   href="rect.htm">
  <AREA shape="circ"
   coords="86,45,19 href="circ.htm">
  <AREA shape="poly"
   coords="118,76,74,80,99,75,105,60,
   118,76" href="polygon.htm">
  <AREA shape="default" nohref>
</MAP>
```

The three AREA elements specify a rectangle, circle, and polygon, respectively.

You can learn more about image maps by visiting one of the following sites: Clickable Image Support in W3C httpd (**http://www.w3.org/Daemon/User/CGI/HTImageDoc.html**), NCSA Imagemap Tutorial (**http://hoohoo.ncsa.uiuc.edu/docs/tutorials/imagemapping.html**), several pages at the Imagemap Authoring Guide and Tutorial Sites (**http://www.cris.com/~automata/tutorial.shtml**), and several imagemap pages (**http://www.webcom.com/~webcom/html/tutor/imagemaps.shtml**) in the Web Communications HTML Guide, and Advanced HTML Programming (**http://www.intergalact.com/hp/part2/part2.html**).

CROSS-REFERENCE

The "Adding Links to a Document" task in Chapter 8 instructs you how to add links to documents.

FIND IT ONLINE

Advanced HTML — Frames (**http://www.wave.co.nz/pages/dklynn/frames.html**) is an overview of HTML frames.

Framing Documents

CHAPTER

11

Listing 11-4: An Online Document in Two Frames

```
<!DOCTYPE HTML PUBLIC
      "-//W3C//DTD HTML 4.0//EN">
<HTML>
<HEAD>
<TITLE>HTML in Plain English - Online</TITLE>
</HEAD>
<FRAMESET COLS=30%,*>     ◄①
   <FRAME src="toc.htm" name="toc">     ◄②
   <FRAME src="intro.htm" name="main"
         scrolling="yes">     ◄③
</FRAMESET>     ◄④
</HTML>
```

① *Specify a two-frame columnwise frameset.*
② *Place a table of contents in the left frame.*
③ *Name the main window* main, *and add a scroll bar.*
④ *End the frameset.*

Listing 11-5: Part of the Table of Contents

```
<!DOCTYPE HTML PUBLIC
      "-//W3C//DTD HTML 4.0//EN">
<HTML><HEAD>
<TITLE>Table of Contents</TITLE>     ⑤
</HEAD><BODY bgcolor="yellow" alink="blue"
   vlink="black">
<H2>Contents</H2>     ⑥
<FONT face="book antigua" size="2">     ⑦
<A href="intro.htm" target="main">
Introduction</A>
<A href="ch01.htm" target="main">Chapter 1
</A>
<BR><A href="ch02.htm" target="main">Chapter 2
</A></BODY></HTML>
```

⑤ *Make the background color yellow, and set links colors.*
⑥ *Set the default font face and point size.*
⑦ *Link to documents, and place them in the* main *window.*

Listing 11-6: The Top of the Introduction Document

```
<!DOCTYPE HTML PUBLIC
      "-//W3C//DTD HTML 4.0//EN">
<HTML><HEAD>
<TITLE>HTML in Plain English - Online</TITLE>
</HEAD><BODY>     ◄⑧
<H1>Introduction</H1>
<FONT face="book antigua" size="2">     ◄⑨
Welcome to <I>HTML in Plain English</I>. I
hope that you enjoy using this book as much as
I have enjoyed researching and writing it.
```

⑧ *A standard HTML document has a BODY section.*
⑨ *Set the default font and point size.*

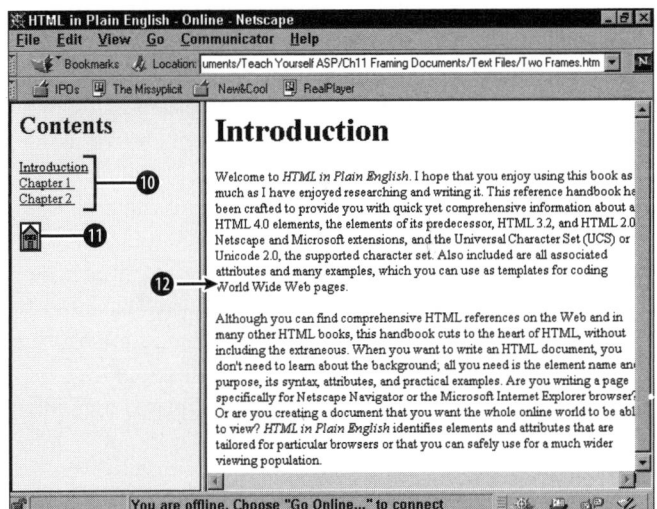

⑩ *Build a link to each chapter in the document.*
⑪ *Click to go to the top window (see the Escaping from Frames Sites take note section).*
⑫ *The introduction is currently in the main window.*

167

Modifying Frames

Placing frames onscreen should be just the beginning of your work. As with other HTML documents, your frames documents should be attractive and inviting. In addition, you should be able to tweak the behavior of individual frames, too. As you learned in a previous task in this chapter, you can turn on or off a frame border and you can set vertical and horizontal margins of individual frames. The FRAME element also has attributes with which you can determine whether frames are resizeable and can be scrolled. This task reviews frames attributes.

You can prevent individuals from resizing frames by entering the noresize attribute. Because individual frames are part of a frameset, in some cases, the effect of setting noresize on a frame prevents other frames in the frameset from being resized, too. For example, let's say that you have a frameset consisting of three frames and taking 100% of the space onscreen. If frames one and two do not include the noresize attribute, you may be able to resize the common border between frames one and two. If frame three is set to noresize, any common borders between frame three and the other two frames cannot be resized.

Scrolling enables a user to move the content within a frame using a horizontal or vertical scroll bar. The value of the scrolling attribute either displays or hides scroll bars on a frame's right or bottom border. So, scrolling="yes" indicates that the current frame always has scroll bars, and scrolling="no" states that the current frame doesn't have scroll bars. When scrolling="auto", the size of the content determines whether the scroll bar is displayed or hidden.

TAKE NOTE

▶ QUOTING CHARACTER DATA

What about incorporating a quotation with enclosed quotation marks within a string? Look at the following example:

```
<!ENTITY dickens1 'In Nicholas
Nickleby, Charles Dickens wrote, "Bring
in the bottled lightning, a clean
tumbler, and a corkscrew."'>

<!ENTITY dickens1 "In Nicholas
Nickleby, Charles Dickens wrote, 'Bring
in the bottled lightning, a clean
tumbler, and a corkscrew.'">
```

Both examples are correct. Just remember not to enclose a quotation within a mismatched set of a quotation mark and a single quote.

▶ UNDERSTANDING XML PIS

You may have wondered what the <? and ?> delimiters in the XML declaration actually indicate. The delimiters mark the beginning and end of a *processing instruction* (PI), which tells an application, such as an XML parser, how to process the enclosed code. So, <?xml version="1.0"?> tells the XML parser to use Version 1.0 of the XML language to process this document.

PIs are not limited to XML parsers. You can include a PI to tell another program to process a selection in a certain way. For example: <?xpert red text?> instructs a program called xpert to display selected text in a red color.

The combination of the ?xml characters is reserved for current and future versions of XML. This means that you cannot use ?xml within XML documents.

CROSS-REFERENCE

Learn how to add graphics and sound files to documents by reading "Adding Multimedia Content" in Chapter 8.

FIND IT ONLINE

HTML/Web Programming Resources (**http://normandy.sandhills. cc.nc.us/html.html**) is a gigantic links directory.

Listing 11-7: Two Frames, No Resizing

```
<!DOCTYPE HTML PUBLIC
    "-//W3C//DTD HTML 4.0//EN">
<HTML>
<HEAD>
<TITLE>HTML in Plain English - Online</TITLE>
</HEAD>
<FRAMESET COLS=30%,*>
  <FRAME src="toc.htm" name="toc" noresize>
  <FRAME src="intro.htm" name="main" noresize>
</FRAMESET>
</HTML>
```

▶ This example, which is adapted from Listing 11-4, does not allow resizing of either frame.

Listing 11-8: Two Frames, Both with Scrolling

```
<!DOCTYPE HTML PUBLIC
    "-//W3C//DTD HTML 4.0//EN">
<HTML>
<HEAD>
<TITLE>HTML in Plain English - Online</TITLE>
</HEAD>
<FRAMESET COLS=30%,*>
  <FRAME src="toc.htm" name="toc"
scrolling="yes">      ❷
    <FRAME src="intro.htm" name="main"
scrolling="auto">
</FRAMESET>          ❸
</HTML>
```

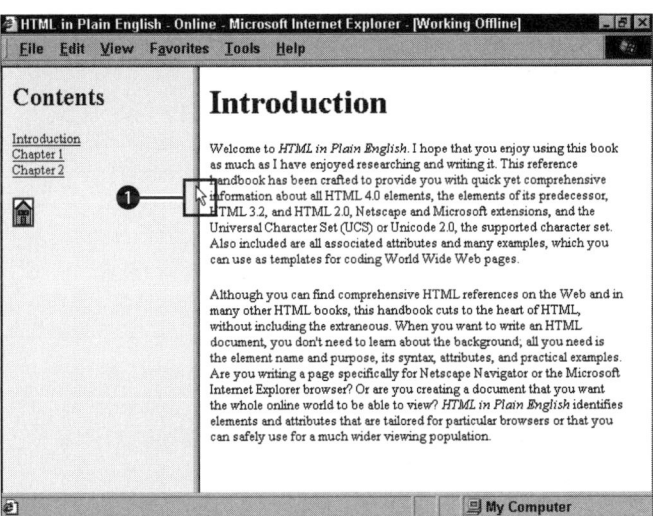

❶ If you could resize, the mouse pointer would be a double-pointed arrow.

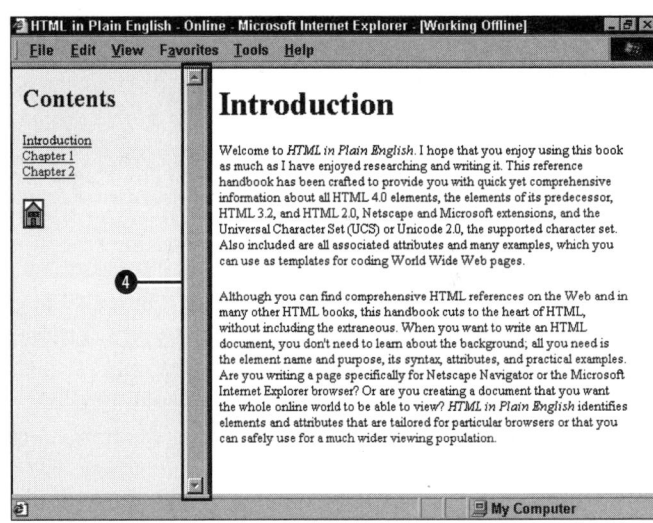

❷ The setting scrolling="yes" adds a scroll bar to the frame.

❸ The setting scrolling="auto" enables an optional scroll bar.

❹ The optional scroll bar is missing because the contents are completely visible.

Allowing for No Frames

Some HTML browsers do not support the use of frames — although HTML 4.0 does. When a particular browser does not support frames, it is not programmed to understand the FRAMESET and FRAME elements and their attributes. You can be sure that some future XML browsers will not recognize frames either. You cannot force visitors to your site to tour the Web using certain browsers, so you should always allow for alternate non-frames content.

Use the HTML NOFRAMES element to mark the beginning and end of non-frames content. You should define framesets and frames first and then complete your frameset document by adding a section starting with a <NOFRAMES> start tag and ending with a </NOFRAMES> end tag. Use the following structure:

```
<FRAMESET attributes>
    <FRAME attributes></FRAME>
    <FRAME attributes></FRAME>
</FRAMESET>
<NOFRAMES>
    content
</NOFRAMES>
```

When a non-frames browser encounters FRAMESET and FRAME tags, the browser drops through the FRAMESET and FRAME statements. When it reaches the NOFRAMES section, the browser displays the content of this NOFRAMES section.

Frames are not always easy to use — especially for users who have small-screen monitors and low graphic-resolution settings. Plus, some people just don't like frames. So, a developer of frame documents should offer their users the choice between frames and non-frames.

Maintaining a Review Cycle for a Workgroup

Whether your workgroup sets document standards or produces actual documents, the most efficient way of completing the project is to develop a list of review tasks, such as the following:

▶ Plan overall schedules for the entire group and for each member. Add milestones to mark progress along the way.

▶ Keep a paper trail of all meetings and milestones. Make sure that each document contains the creation date, modification date, and creator's name.

▶ Set up editing guidelines. How detailed or superficial do you want the review?

▶ One individual should make decisions to accept or reject suggestions.

▶ Make sure that each member of the group has a unique method of identifying his or her comments. For example, individuals can use unique ink or revision-mark colors or can write or type their initials.

▶ Schedule timely group meetings. However, make sure that you don't schedule too often. After all, meetings take valuable time.

▶ Communicate with every member of the group regularly.

▶ Develop a system of circulating drafts of the standards or document, ensuring that everyone uses the same version. One method is to insert the revision date and, optionally, the revision number in the footer. Another method is to circulate the version through the group, one member at a time.

▶ When you incorporate changes, immediately update the revision date.

CROSS-REFERENCE

The "Parsing a Document" task in Chapter 8 discusses the processing of both HTML and XML documents.

FIND IT ONLINE

The http://www.math.tamu.edu/~mpilant/math489/top-100.html page links to the top 100 Web sites.

HTML 4.0: The NOFRAMES Element

```
<![ %HTML.Frameset; [
<!ENTITY % noframes.content "(BODY) -(NOFRAMES) ">
]]>
```
← ❶

```
<!ENTITY % noframes.content "(%flow;)*">
```
← ❷

```
<!ELEMENT NOFRAMES - - %noframes.content;
 -- alternate content container for non frame-based rendering -->
<!ATTLIST NOFRAMES
    %attrs;                                    -- %coreattrs, %i18n, %events --
>
```
← ❸

❶ *The* %HTML.Frameset; *entity marks an* INCLUDE *section.*
❷ *The* NOFRAMES *element includes* % noframes.content *entity.*
❸ *The attribute list contains commonly used HTML attributes.*

Listing 11-9: An XML NOFRAMES Example

```
<frameset rows=50%,*>
    <frame href="frame2.xml"/>
    <frame href="frame3.xml"/>
</frameset>
<noframes>
```
← **1**
```
<head2>You Should Be Looking at Two
Frames!</head2>
<para>If you are reading this message, you are
using an XML browser
that does not support frames. Try again with a
different browser.
</para>
<img href="/pics/disappoint.gif"/>
</noframes>
```
← **2**

1 *The* <noframes> *start tag marks the beginning of alternate content.*
2 *The* </noframes> *end tag marks the end.*

Personal Workbook

Q & A

1 What is a frame?

_____

_____

_____

2 What is a frameset?

_____

_____

_____

3 Does XML support the use of frames and framesets?

_____

_____

_____

4 What does the HTML FRAMESET element do?

_____

_____

_____

5 What does the HTML FRAME element do?

_____

_____

_____

6 What start and end tags do the <FRAMESET> and </FRAMESET> tags replace in HTML frameset documents?

_____

_____

_____

7 What attribute do you use to control the display of a scroll bar in a frame? From what values can you choose for this attribute?

_____

_____

_____

8 When you have a frames site, how do you deal with browsers that do not support frames?

_____

_____

ANSWERS: PAGE 503

EXTRA PRACTICE

1. Create a frame site that contains links to Web directories in one frame and the first page of the linked directory in the other frame.

2. Add a fixed frame containing a title to the directory site.

3. Go online and find a frames tutorial that is not mentioned in this chapter.

4. Create a frame site that contains one frame for each member of your family, or a group of friends or colleagues.

5. Go online and find a frame site that is poorly designed. List the reasons.

6. Design a frame site that is composed of a large center frame surrounded by four outer frames.

REAL-WORLD APPLICATIONS

✔ Your corporate intranet currently consists of non-frame pages. You have been assigned to convert to a frames site. Design a site with a title frame, a content frame, and a navigation frame.

✔ Your catalog company sells children's toys, books, and clothing online. Your new frames site features two frames that divide the screen vertically into a narrow table of site pages and a wider frame with the current catalog page.

✔ You have volunteered to plan, design, and develop an online yearbook of the members of your group. This three-frames site will include a title frame, a "noresize" page of graphic links for each member, and a page of biographic information about the linked member.

Visual Quiz

How would you code this frameset?

_____

_____

_____

_____

_____

_____

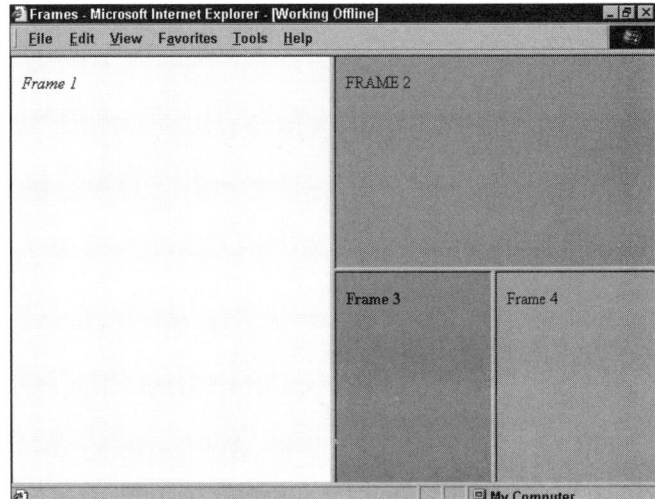

CHAPTER **12**

MASTER
THESE
SKILLS

▶ **Introducing Web-Based Databases**
▶ **Learning about Forms and Controls**
▶ **Creating a Form**
▶ **Getting Ready for User Input**
▶ **Processing a Form**
▶ **Converting Existing Database Information into a Document**

Placing Forms in Documents

In this chapter, you will learn about fill-in forms, which are the heart of this part of the book. The tasks here provide an overview of fill-in forms and the HTML elements and attributes with which you create them. You'll also learn the basics of databases. Note that in other chapters, you'll learn how to transfer information between users' computers and your databases.

If you have ever used HTML, you may have already learned about creating fill-in forms. However, when you create XML-based forms, you not only develop DTDs containing custom elements, attributes, and other components, but you also need to master stylesheets (see the following chapter) to format and enhance your forms.

Whether you use HTML or XML, the real purpose of a form is to gather information from visitors to your site and process it in some way. As a result, you should design easy-to-use forms that will attract visitors and encourage them to give you information. By using Active Server Pages (ASP) or CGI scripts and the HTTP protocol, you can send the supplied information to a server for further processing.

In the first task, you are introduced to online databases, which ultimately contain the information

that are entered in forms. You'll also learn about the components that comprise databases. The following task presents forms and controls, which are the components from which forms are composed. You'll find out about the HTML elements and attributes that define individual controls. Using the information in the third task, you'll be able to plan and design workable and easy-to-use forms. The next task teaches you how to prepare for user input by thorough testing. Following that task is a discussion on how a form is processed and what happens when a visitor clicks a Submit button.

Transferring information from a client computer to a server computer requires the use of programs and scripts to enable communications. You'll be introduced to Hypertext Transfer Protocol (HTTP) and the Common Gateway Interface (CGI). Note that you'll find out more about these and other means of communication later in the book. In the last task, you'll find out how to convert database information — particularly that developed in programs other than database management systems — into Web documents.

Introducing Web-Based Databases

I n its initial years, the World Wide Web was most important to educational and research institutions. Now, the Web is more business-oriented. More corporations are using the Web for advertising and selling.

As the Internet becomes more important to business enterprises, software companies have made it a point to develop Internet-ready programs and to add Internet features to their existing applications. Internet-ready applications should provide the following features:

▶ They should support the standard file types for that type of application. For example, word processors should support the .doc and .txt file types, spreadsheets should support .xls and .wk* types, and database programs should support the .dbf file type.

▶ They should also support Internet file types, such as .htm, .html, .asp, .shtml, .xml, and so forth, depending on the type of application and its purpose. This makes it easier to convert word-processing documents, spreadsheets, and databases to Web pages and Web-based forms.

▶ They should incorporate various Internet technologies, such as the ability to transfer files (such as Web pages) to and from servers and should support the use of e-mail. This means that some level of communications should be enabled within the applications.

▶ Suites of programs should not only be able to communicate with each other but should also be Internet-ready. For example, spreadsheets and databases should be able to transfer sheets and database information between applications as well as convert the information to online documents.

▶ Applications should start supporting sophisticated technologies, such as scripting, Dynamic HTML, and — of course — Active Server Pages.

Databases have already become an important part of the Web. For example, any commercial site at which goods are sold should have one or more underlying databases, which include both customer information and inventory information. The customer database produces lists of contacts for catalog mailings and e-mail contacts, and the inventory database allows for instantaneous checking for the availability of merchandise and ordering when quantities drop to a certain level. Often, Web-based marketing sites ask prospective customers to enter information into fill-in forms. Then that information is exported into databases for later processing as mailing lists or contacts lists.

TAKE NOTE

▶ STRUCTURE OF A DATABASE

Databases are made up of records, which are in turn composed of fields. A *field*, which is the smallest unit of information in a record, contains one piece of information, such as a city or telephone number. A *record* is composed of a group of related fields, such as all the appropriate information about a customer, an employee, or an inventory item. Use *forms*, or input forms, to enter information into the records in a database program.

▶ ADVANTAGES OF XML DATABASES

Using XML, developers can not only declare elements to build a fill-in form but can also use parsers to transfer input information directly into the database record. Another advantage of XML databases is the associated DTD, with which you can require certain elements, force elements to be used in a particular order, ensure that attributes have particular values, set a hierarchy of root, child, and other descendant elements, and more.

CROSS-REFERENCE

Learn all about Web sites at the "Planning and Designing a Web Site" task in Chapter 5.

FIND IT ONLINE

The WebCom Forms Guide (http://www.webcom.com/~webcom/html/tutor/forms/) is a forms tutorial.

Listing 12-1: A Simple Form

```
<!DOCTYPE HTML PUBLIC
     "-//W3C//DTD HTML 4.0//EN">
<HTML><HEAD>
<TITLE>A Simple Form</TITLE>
</HEAD><BODY>
<FORM action="cgi-bin/form-example"     ◄─❶
     method="post">
Type your name:<BR>
<INPUT type="text" name="name" size="40"><BR>
Type your email address:<BR>                ◄─❷
<INPUT type="text" name="email" size="30">
<BR>
Type your street address:<BR>           ❸
<TEXTAREA name="address" rows="3" cols="35">
</TEXTAREA>
<P><INPUT type="submit">◄─❹
<INPUT type="reset"></P></FORM>
</BODY></HTML>
```

❶ *Mark the beginning of the form with the* <FORM> *start tag.*
❷ *Insert two* INPUT *areas.*
❸ *Add a larger text area.*
❹ *Conclude with a submit button and a reset button.*

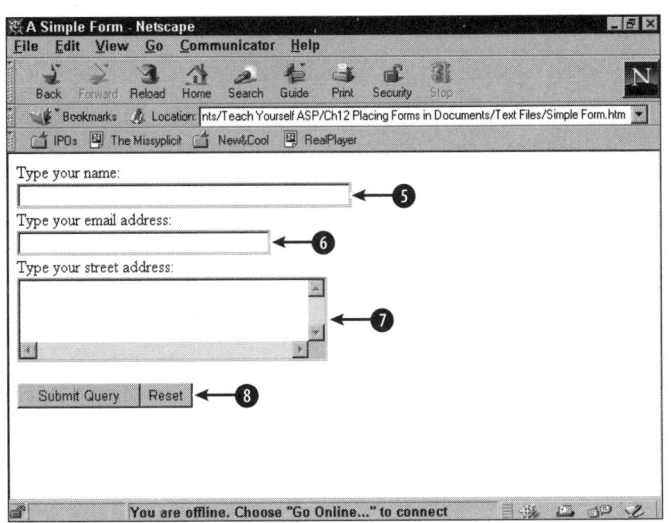

Planning for a Database

Before building a database, ask yourself the following questions:

▶ What is the purpose of this database? To compile information about future customers or contacts? To track your employees and changes in their status?

▶ What information will you want to display on-screen? Will you prepare monthly or weekly reports for your intranet or for printing? Will you create mailing lists and form letters from selected records? Will the processed information go to an intermediate application that processes it and sends it to another application for output?

▶ What formatting and enhancements will be applied to the output? Will the output be converted to a particular file format?

▶ What specific information do you need to compile? What fields does this database require?

▶ Are you planning the database for future changes and growth? Are you properly securing the information? Will you define reserved fields or can you add fields at a later time?

▶ How can you ensure that certain types of information belong in the fields for which they were defined?

▶ How will you sort records in this database? Will you have to pay special attention to sorting fields?

To learn more about database administration and design implementation, refer to a book or online site devoted to databases.

❺ *The first input area is 40 characters wide.*
❻ *The second input area is 30 characters wide.*
❼ *The* TEXTAREA *text box is 3 rows high and 35 columns wide.*
❽ *The buttons are side by side with no breaks.*

Learning about Forms and Controls

As you know, a form (or input form) is a part of a database into which information is entered for a particular record. Full-featured database programs enable individuals to enter information in a variety of ways — by typing into text boxes, by selecting items from lists, clicking option buttons, checking check boxes, and so forth. After inserting information into a form, the individual either clicks an OK button or presses the Enter key. At that point, the database program adds the record to the database. Input forms on the Web provide the same types of input choices, and an underlying program processes information in the same way as any other database application.

HTML forms are composed of *controls*, which are individual components supported by combinations of elements and attributes. HTML 4.0 provides the following control types, which are attributes that are usually under the INPUT element:

▶ The Checkbox control type is a small square box that represents an on or off status. Specify a checkbox by using the INPUT element and the TYPE="CHECKBOX" attribute.

▶ The File select control type is a file-uploading control. Specify the file select control type by using the INPUT element and the TYPE="FILE" attribute.

▶ The Hidden control type is a field that is not displayed on the form. It is used to transfer information between the client and the server. Specify the hidden control type by using the INPUT element and the TYPE="HIDDEN" attribute.

▶ The Menu control type is a list box or, sometimes, a pull-down menu. Specify the menu control type by using the SELECT element and either the OPTGROUP or OPTION element.

▶ The Object control type is any type of multimedia object (image, video file, or sound file) within a form. Specify the object control type by using the

OBJECT element. A multimedia object can also be located outside a form.

▶ The Radio button control type is a small round button in a group of buttons from which you can select only one at a time. Specify a radio button by using the INPUT element and the TYPE="RADIO" attribute and value.

▶ The Reset button control type is a push (command) button that you click to clear a form. Specify a Reset button by using the INPUT element and the TYPE="RESET" attribute.

▶ The Submit button control type is a push (command) button that you click to submit a form. Specify a Submit button by using the INPUT element and the TYPE="SUBMIT" attribute.

▶ A multiple-line text box control type has a defined height and width. Specify a multiple-line text box control type by using the TEXTAREA element.

▶ A single-line text box control type has just one line with no height or width settings. Specify a single-line text box control type by using the INPUT element and the TYPE="TEXT" attribute.

TAKE NOTE

▶ VARYING FORMS FOR DATA ENTRY

Many forms — even in a single database — are designed to include some, but not all, fields in a record. For example, some fields contain the results of a calculation performed after the data are entered into a record. Other forms enable only some parts of a record (such as an employee name and telephone extension for a telephone list, or the name and personal address and telephone number for an address book) to be entered.

CROSS-REFERENCE

Find out how to develop Web documents at the "Planning and Designing a Document" task in Chapter 5.

FIND IT ONLINE

The HTML tutorial at **http://www.2kweb.net/html-tutorial/** covers forms, frames, tables, and other HTML topics.

Placing Forms in Documents

HTML 4.0: The FORM and LABEL Elements

```
<!ELEMENT FORM - - (%block;|SCRIPT)+ -(FORM) -- interactive form -->
<!ATTLIST FORM
  %attrs;                          -- %coreattrs, %i18n, %events --
  action        %URI;        #REQUIRED -- server-side form handler -- ◄❶
  method        (GET|POST)   GET       -- HTTP method used to submit the form-- ◄❷
  enctype       %ContentType; "application/x-www-form-urlencoded" ◄❸
  onsubmit      %Script;     #IMPLIED  -- the form was submitted --
  onreset       %Script;     #IMPLIED  -- the form was reset --      ◄❹
  accept-charset %Charsets;  #IMPLIED  -- list of supported charsets --
>


<! — Each label must not contain more than ONE field -->
<!ELEMENT LABEL - - (%inline;)* -(LABEL) —form field label text -->
<!ATTLIST LABEL
  %attrs;                          -- %coreattrs, %i18n, %events --
  for           IDREF        #IMPLIED  -- matches field ID value --
  accesskey     %Character;  #IMPLIED  -- accessibility key character --
  onfocus       %Script;     #IMPLIED  -- the element got the focus --
  onblur        %Script;     #IMPLIED  -- the element lost the focus --
>
```

❶ Use the `action` attribute to specify the server's form handler.
❷ Specify the HTTP method for submitting the form.
❸ The encoding type specifies the content.
❹ Run a script when the form is submitted or reset.

Creating a Form

Before you start developing any Web document, you must spend a great deal planning and designing it. Use the same philosophy when creating a form. Laying out a form is similar to laying out the pages for a Web document. However, you should think about factors that are unique to form design: forms should be easy to use and attractive to the eye. Keep the following points in mind:

▶ Users entering information should be able to move from control to control in a logical order.

▶ Make sure that the purpose of each control is completely clear to users entering data.

▶ Controls should be not too far apart or too close to each other for easier data entry.

▶ Select easy-to-read fonts for the labels (displayed names of controls) as well as the data being entered and displayed.

▶ Don't vary point sizes too much. Labels should be slightly larger or the same size as data.

Use the FORM element to mark the start (<FORM>) and end (</FORM>) of a form. (See the element and attribute-list declarations on the prior facing page.) Then, insert controls and optional labels for those controls.

The INPUT element sets the type of user input: characters that are typed, buttons that are clicked, and boxes and buttons that are selected. (For details, see the INPUT element and the attribute-list declarations on the facing page.)

The last type of control, the menu, is controlled by the SELECT, OPTGROUP, and OPTION elements. Use <SELECT> and </SELECT> to mark the beginning and end of the menu. Then, specify each item on the menu using the OPTION element. You can also group menu items with the OPTGROUP element. (See the element and attribute-list declarations on a following facing page.)

TAKE NOTE

▶ CREATING AN XML DATABASE DTD

Planning, laying out, and creating a database DTD for an XML document or set of documents requires more effort than if you created a new database using a program developed specifically for that purpose. For example, you won't have the help in automatically adding or defining fields that you would have if you were using a standard database program. However, once you have designed one database DTD, you can probably apply it to other similar types of DTDs.

Typically, each field in a database matches with an element in a database DTD. When you start compiling the list of potential elements, factor in the position of a particular element within the generations of elements. For example, in a database of name and address information, will you define a parent name element under which fall child elements for the first name, last name, and so forth? Your other choice is to eliminate name altogether and just have one level of first-name, last-name, and middle-initial elements, and so forth. You'll have to answer the same "generational" question about address elements and telephone elements. Your decision not only affects the way that the DTD is laid out but also the design of the database associated with the DTD. In addition, the way you specify generations may also affect the processing of output as well as the ease with which future developers understand the DTD's structure. Consider laying out the database on paper, and *then* developing the DTD.

CROSS-REFERENCE
Learn about both HTML and XML elements in the "Learning about Elements" task in Chapter 6.

FIND IT ONLINE
The Form Tutor (**http://junior.apk.net/~jbarta/tutor/forms/index.html**) is one of a series of Web tutorials.

HTML 4.0: The INPUT Element

```
<!ENTITY % InputType
  "(TEXT | PASSWORD | CHECKBOX |
    RADIO | SUBMIT | RESET |
    FILE | HIDDEN | IMAGE | BUTTON)"          ← ❶
```

```
<!--attribute name required for all but submit & reset -->
<!ELEMENT INPUT - O EMPTY ← ❷          -- form control -->
<!ATTLIST INPUT
  %attrs;                               -- %coreattrs, %i18n, %events --
  type         %InputType;  TEXT        -- what kind of widget is needed -- ← ❸
  name         CDATA        #IMPLIED    -- submit as part of form --         ❹
  value        CDATA        #IMPLIED    -- required for radio and checkboxes --
  checked      (checked)    #IMPLIED    -- for radio buttons and check boxes --
  disabled     (disabled)   #IMPLIED    -- unavailable in this context --
  readonly     (readonly)   #IMPLIED    -- for text and passwd ← ❹          ❹
  size         CDATA        #IMPLIED    -- specific to each type of field --
  maxlength    NUMBER       #IMPLIED    -- max chars for text fields -- ← ❹
  src          %URI;        #IMPLIED    -- for fields with images --
  alt          CDATA        #IMPLIED    -- short description --
  usemap       %URI;        #IMPLIED    -- use client-side image map --
  tabindex     NUMBER       #IMPLIED    -- position in tabbing order --
  accesskey    %Character;  #IMPLIED    -- accessibility key character --
  onfocus      %Script;     #IMPLIED    -- the element got the focus --
  onblur       %Script;     #IMPLIED    -- the element lost the focus --
  onselect     %Script;     #IMPLIED    -- some text was selected --
  onchange     %Script;     #IMPLIED    -- the element value was changed --
  accept       %ContentTypes; #IMPLIED  -- list of MIME types for file upload --
  %reserved;                            -- reserved for possible future use --
>
```

❶ The entity declaration incorporates all the input types.
❷ The INPUT element is empty.
❸ Specify the type of input with the type attribute.
❹ Certain attributes apply to only some input types.

Getting Ready for User Input

Once you have completed a fill-in form, you should test it by entering information into each text box, clicking the buttons in the form, and evaluating each of the remaining controls. Each control should work as planned and appear as designed. Also, test the form using as many Web browsers as possible. (Some browsers will work a little differently than others, but all should behave within your design parameters.) Go through many series of tests and edits until the form meets all your design and processing requirements.

Check the forms by answering the following questions:

▶ Is each of the text boxes the proper dimensions? In your judgment, can you see enough of the text that you enter for a user to understand the contents in the text boxes? Have you allowed for the greatest amount of information that will ever be entered in the text boxes? Are all the typefaces and point sizes in text boxes easy to read?

▶ Do check boxes alternately clear and check with each click under every browser with which you test a form?

▶ How many radio buttons can you select in any of the browsers with which you test? No more than one button in a group should be filled at any particular time.

▶ Are preselected options the proper choices? Are they highlighted properly?

▶ Are labels spelled correctly? Do labels appear in the selected font and point size? Consider emphasizing all labels with boldface, so that they will properly contrast with input information.

TAKE NOTE

▶ JUDGING CONTROLS ON THEIR SUCCESS

The measure of a control is whether it can be submitted to an application. In HTML, a control always has a name (use the name attribute), an initial value (usually set with the value attribute), and a current value (which a user might have set). A valid control whose content can be submitted to an application is successful. The HTML 4.0 recommendation states that a control is successful or unsuccessful under one or more of the following circumstances:
▶ If it is outside the form, it is unsuccessful.
▶ A control with its name paired with its current value is successful.
▶ If the value of the disabled attribute is "disabled", it is unsuccessful.
▶ If a form has more than one submit button, the activated button is successful.
▶ If a checkbox is checked, it is probably successful.
▶ If one radio button is filled, it is the successful radio button in the set.
▶ If a menu option is selected, it is successful.
▶ Reset buttons are not successful.

▶ LEARNING FROM THE NETSCAPE AND MICROSOFT EXTENSIONS

Both Netscape Communications Corporation, now a subsidiary of America Online, and Microsoft Corporation have contributed to the development of HTML. In HTML, Netscape and Microsoft have developed *extensions* — elements that *extend* beyond the current HTML version but are not "official" parts of the version. For example, all the frames elements started as Netscape extensions, and were enhanced by both Netscape and Microsoft attributes. Now frames are an official part of HTML 4.0.

CROSS-REFERENCE

Find out how to use tags in the "Using Start Tags and End Tags" task in Chapter 6.

FIND IT ONLINE

The VL-WWW: Forms site (**http://www.stars.com/Vlib/°Providers/Forms.html**) contains links to forms sites.

Placing Forms in Documents

HTML 4.0: The SELECT, OPTGROUP, and OPTION Elements

```
<!ELEMENT SELECT - -  (OPTGROUP|OPTION)+ -- option selector -->
<!ATTLIST SELECT
                                    ❶
  %attrs;                                -- %coreattrs, %i18n, %events --
  name       CDATA         #IMPLIED  -- field name --
  size       CDATA         #IMPLIED  -- rows visible --
  multiple   (multiple)    #IMPLIED  -- default is single selection --
  disabled   (disabled)    #IMPLIED  -- unavailable in this context --
  tabindex   NUMBER        #IMPLIED  -- position in tabbing order --
  onfocus    %Script;      #IMPLIED  -- the element got the focus --
  onblur     %Script;      #IMPLIED  -- the element lost the focus --
  onchange   %Script;      #IMPLIED  -- the element value was changed -->


<!ELEMENT OPTGROUP - -  (OPTION)+        -- option group -->◀❷
<!ATTLIST OPTGROUP
  %attrs;                                -- %coreattrs, %i18n, %events --
  disabled   (disabled)    #IMPLIED  -- unavailable in this context --
  label      %Text;        #IMPLIED  -- for use in hierarchical menus -->


<!ELEMENT OPTION - O  (#PCDATA)          -- selectable choice -->◀❸
<!ATTLIST OPTION
  %attrs;                                -- %coreattrs, %i18n, %events --
  selected   (selected)    #IMPLIED
  disabled   (disabled)    #IMPLIED  -- unavailable in this context --
  label      %Text;        #IMPLIED  -- for use in hierarchical menus --
  value      CDATA         #IMPLIED  -- defaults to element content -->
```

❶ The SELECT element's child elements are OPTGROUP and OPTION.

❷ The OPTGROUP element, whose child is OPTION, forms an option group.

❸ Use the OPTION element to mark one menu choice.

Processing a Form

For a fill-in form to work, its information must be transferred from a browser program to a form-handling application that processes it. So, once a visitor to your site has filled in the form and clicked a Submit button, the browser with which the user is viewing and editing the form transfers the information from the user's (client) computer to the URI specified in the `action` attribute in the `<FORM>` start tag. The form-handling program loads the form into a database, places it into an e-mail message, formats it for displaying online — or some combination of all three.

In every version of HTML — including the current Version 4.0 — forms developers have used the `method` attribute to specify the Hypertext Transfer Protocol (HTTP) or CGI script by which the form is submitted to a server, which contains a program that processes the form. *HTTP* is a protocol for both clients and servers. *CGI*, or Common Gateway Interface, is a communications specification.

The `method` attribute can have two values: `get` and `post`. `METHOD="GET"` appends the submitted form information to a newly created URI named by the `action` attribute using an *environment variable*, which is stored information about a particular program that other programs, including browsers, can use. The HTML 4.0 specification states that `method="get"` is deprecated, so plan to use `method="post"` most of the time. `METHOD="POST"` specifies the form to be sent to a server for processing. This method, which is recommended, is difficult to use — according to some form experts. Look at the following statement:

```
<FORM action="/cgi-bin/form-alpha"
      method="post">
```

The `action` attribute specifies a relative URI for the location of a *cgi-bin* (CGI binaries) folder that contains the script or program (`form-alpha`) that processes the form information. Once the connection is made to the server, the server takes over and searches for the `form-alpha` script or program. The script or program then processes the information and sends a message back to the server.

Note that `cgi-bin` is not only a folder, but is also a reserved word for a folder that stores one or more cgi-bin programs. Applications that are categorized as cgi-bin use the Common Gateway Interface (CGI) protocol to create HTML in response to user requests. HTTP is programmed to understand the hypertext links in the documents that it transfers.

TAKE NOTE

USING THE BUTTON OR INPUT ELEMENT

The `BUTTON` element, which is new to HTML 4.0, is designed specifically to create command buttons. In contrast, `INPUT` is an all-purpose element with which you can create a variety of controls, including buttons. According to the HTML 4.0 recommendation, the `BUTTON` element "offers richer rendering capabilities than the `INPUT` element."

COMPARING INPUT FORMS AND DIALOG BOXES

In many ways, you can compare a typical HTML input form to a standard dialog box. In fact, dialog boxes are actually forms that enable a user to enter information, select options, and click buttons. As you know, both forms and dialog boxes contain a variety of controls, ranging from command buttons to lists and checkboxes to radio buttons. Forms and dialog boxes can contain lists of items from which you can select one and sometimes more than one option. To create a list of options in an HTML form, use the `SELECT` element. Then, use the `OPTGROUP` and `OPTION` child elements to specify groups of options and individual options, respectively. The `OPTION` element provides the `SELECTED` attribute with which you can highlight the option that you wish to set as the default.

CROSS-REFERENCE
Get an overview of attributes at the "Understanding Attributes" task in Chapter 6.

FIND IT ONLINE
Read an article on Web forms and CGIs at **http://www.nlc-bnc.ca/pubs/netnotes/notes19.htm**.

Listing 12-2: A Form with a List Box

```
<!DOCTYPE HTML PUBLIC
    "-//W3C//DTD HTML 4.0//EN">
<HTML><HEAD><TITLE>A Simple Form</TITLE>
</HEAD><BODY>
<P>Select a breed:</P>
<FORM action="cgi-bin/form-example"
method="post">❷
<SELECT name="dogs" size="3" multiple>◀❶
<OPTION selected>Golden Retriever</OPTION>
<OPTION>Labrador Retriever</OPTION>
<OPTION>Newfoundland</OPTION></SELECT>◀❸
<P>Type your dog's name:  <INPUT type="text"
        size="30"></P>❹
<INPUT type="submit"><BR><INPUT type="reset">
</FORM></BODY></HTML>
```

❶ Mark the beginning of the list with the <SELECT> start tag.
❷ Make the first option the default selection.
❸ Insert two more options, and complete the list with the end tag.
❹ Add a Submit button, break the line, and insert the Reset button.

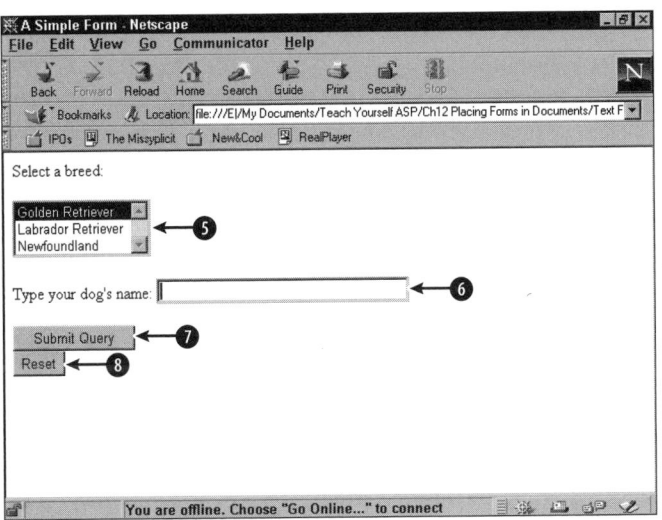

❺ Click to select one of three choices.
❻ Enter information in the text box.
❼ Click Submit Query to submit the form.
❽ Or, click Reset to clear the form.

Listing 12-3: Elements in an XML Database DTD

```
<?xml version="1.0"?>
<!DOCTYPE database [
<!ELEMENT database (record+)>◀❶
  <!ELEMENT record
    (name,occupation,address,city,state,zip)>
    <!ELEMENT name (prefix, first_name,◀❷
      last_name, suffix)>
    <!ELEMENT occupation (#PCDATA)>
    <!ELEMENT address (address_1,   ◀❸
      address_2)>
    <!ELEMENT city (#PCDATA)>
    <!ELEMENT state (#PCDATA)>◀❹
    <!ELEMENT zip (#PCDATA)>
]>
```

❶ Declare the root element, and list its child elements.
❷ Under the name element, list its four child elements.
❸ The address element has two children.
❹ The city, state, and zip elements have no child elements.

Listing 12-4: Part of Associated XML Document

```
<record>
    <prefix>Mr.</prefix>
    <first_name>Jackie</first_name>
    <last_name>Rogers</last_name>
    <suffix>Jr.</suffix>
    <occupation>Entertainer</occupation>
    <address_1>100 Roxy Drive</address_1>
    <address_2>Penthouse</address_2>
    <city>Vegas</city>
    <state>NV</state>
    <zip>80000</zip>
</record>
```

▶ Note elements that represent individual fields.

185

Converting Existing Database Information into a Document

I f a database has existed for several years, it probably predates the Web. This means that you have probably used a database management system to build the database. Even if the database is brand new, you may have created it using a database program, spreadsheet, word processor, or even a text editor. This task discusses the simple conversion of databases into HTML documents and XML documents. As you continue to work through the book, you'll find much more information about databases, including other database technologies (for example, SQL and ActiveX Data Objects) and enhancements (such as dynamic fill-in forms, transactions, and so forth).

Both HTML and XML documents are actually text (ASCII) documents with no hidden formatting characters. So, even if you are working with a database that does not originate from a database program, you can move information into a Web document quite easily. First, edit the file containing the information to prepare it for conversion. Then save the file as a text file. You can now edit the text file, adding prolog lines; elements, attributes, and other markup; and content until the file is an accurate HTML or XML document.

One of the most important factors in a smooth conversion operation is to prepare the material being moved. For example, if you want to move names and addresses that you have typed into a word-processing document, make sure that each field is separated from the next by a separator character (such as a comma or semicolon) and that each record is on a single line — even if you have to increase the measurement between the left and right margins. Sometimes, you can convert the text as you edit into a word-processing table so that you can detect easily whether all fields are completed. (After completing your work within the table, change back to a text format before the conversion.) Another way to ensure that the information is properly prepared is to insert tabs, which add extra space between each field so that you can view the information more easily.

When you move records from a database application — even if you convert the file to a text format — the first row may contain field labels instead of an actual record. So, editing is not complete until you have checked the converted file for accuracy.

When you finally incorporate all the database information into the Web document, you will have to continue editing. For example, you may find that lines don't break the way you want them to, you may detect random characters that should have been removed earlier or crept in during the conversion, and you will probably want to indent elements to show nesting. In addition, you will want to add attributes, entities, and other components to the document.

TAKE NOTE

REVIEWING THE ASCII CHARACTER SET

ASCII, which is an acronym for the American Standard Code for Information Interchange, is either a 128- or 256-character system — depending on whether it is an original or extended character set. The original ASCII character set is arranged in four 32-character groups. The first group consists of the uppercase alphabet and commonly used punctuation characters. The second group contains digits, spaces, and more punctuation symbols. The third group is composed of the lowercase alphabet and the less common punctuation characters. The fourth group features control characters, such as line feeds (known as LF) and carriage returns (CR).

ASCII coincides with the ANSI (American National Standards Institute) coding standard for characters, numbers, and other symbols. ANSI is a U.S. organization related to the International Organization for Standardization (ISO). ASCII, which is the International Standard ISO/IEC 10646, is an integral part of computing.

CROSS-REFERENCE
Read "Starting a Document" in Chapter 8 to find out how to start an HTML document.

FIND IT ONLINE
Go on a tour of HTML forms and CGI scripts at http://www.speakeasy.org/~cgires/cgi-tour.html.

Placing Forms in Documents

Listing 12-5: An Inventory Database DTD for XML

```
<?xml version="1.0"?>
<!DOCTYPE invent [
<!ELEMENT invent (record+)>  ←❶
   <!ELEMENT record (name, itemno, dept, warehse+, pdate, onhand, reorder)>  ←❷
      <!ELEMENT name (#PCDATA)>
      <!ATTLIST name
               id              ID                    #REQUIRED>
      <!ELEMENT itemno (#PCDATA)>
      <!ATTLIST itemno
               id              ID                    #REQUIRED>
      <!ELEMENT dept (#PCDATA)>
      <!ATTLIST dept
               name     (nails|bolts|tools)      "bolts"
               id              ID                    #REQUIRED>
      <!ELEMENT warehse (#PCDATA)>                              ←❸
      <!ATTLIST warehse
               location   (Miami|Erie|Troy)        "Troy"
               id              ID                    #REQUIRED>
      <!ELEMENT pdate (year,month,day)>
      <!ATTLIST pdate
               id              ID                    #REQUIRED>
         <!ELEMENT year (#PCDATA)>
         <!ATTLIST year                                    ❹
                 value    CDATA                    #FIXED  "2000">
         <!ELEMENT month (#PCDATA)>
         <!ELEMENT day (#PCDATA)>
      <!ELEMENT onhand (#PCDATA)>
      <!ELEMENT reorder (#PCDATA)>
]>
```

❶ *Declare the root and list its only child element.*
❷ *Declare the child element and its children.*
❸ *Offer a choice of department and warehouse locations and default values.*
❹ *Fix the year value to 2000. (Next year, change to 2001.)*

Personal Workbook

Q & A

1 What types of databases should online retailers use at their sites?

_____

_____

_____

2 What is a database field?

_____

_____

_____

3 What is a database record?

_____

_____

_____

4 What is a form?

_____

_____

_____

5 What is a control in an HTML form?

_____

_____

_____

6 List the HTML control types.

_____

_____

_____

7 What HTML element starts and ends a form?

_____

_____

_____

8 What is an extension?

_____

_____

_____

ANSWERS: PAGE 504

Placing Forms in Documents

EXTRA PRACTICE

1. Create an HTML document with which visitors can enter their names, addresses, telephone numbers, and e-mail address. (Hint: At this point, don't worry about getting information transfers to work.)

2. Develop an XML DTD that contains elements and attributes for the prior name-and-address database.

3. Create an XML document for the address book.

4. Go online and tour a well-known retailing site. What types of customer databases do you think they use?

5. Design a customer database form based on improvements to the retailing site that you just visited.

6. For your CD or tape collection, create an online database.

REAL-WORLD APPLICATIONS

✔ You are the human resources manager of your company. Write a specification for an HTML or XML employee database.

✔ You have been assigned to plan and design an HTML questionnaire form for your industry or business.

✔ You have decided to plan and design an XML DTD to track the inventory of your home.

✔ You own a small antique store and are now planning to establish an online retail site. Plan the pages at your site. Be sure to design an order form that will use two databases: customer and inventory. Gather customer information for future e-mail and form-letter contact, and use the inventory database to track your merchandise.

Visual Quiz

How would you code this HTML input form? Use the checked attribute for the American radio button. Use the value attribute to label the command buttons. (Hint: For other help, look at the element declarations on some of the facing pages in this chapter.)

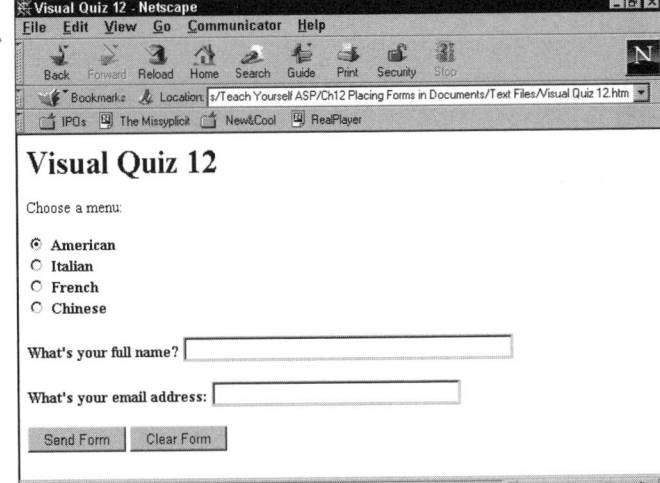

189

CHAPTER **13**

MASTER
THESE
SKILLS

▶ Learning about Cascading Stylesheets
▶ Learning about XSL
▶ Attaching a Stylesheet to a Document
▶ Laying Out Pages
▶ Setting Page and Element Borders
▶ Putting Elements into Position
▶ Styling Text

Styling Documents

In the preceding chapters in this part, you have learned how to use HTML and XML elements to control the structure and content of your documents. When you associate a stylesheet with a document, you can govern the appearance of that document.

As you know, HTML includes elements and attributes that enable you to format and enhance your documents. However, XML does not allow for formatting and enhancing elements and attributes: all the XML documents designed for output onscreen or in printed format *must* be associated with stylesheets. HTML documents actually improve when you use styles rather than styling attributes.

If you have any experience with word-processing programs, you know that each document is automatically associated with a default stylesheet or a stylesheet that you customize. A word-processing stylesheet applies standard formats (such as left alignment, the Times New Roman font, and a point size of 10) to each paragraph of body text in a document, and applies a font such as Helvetica, a boldface enhancement, and a higher point size to headings. Using stylesheets, you can develop well-formatted documents using a set of predefined standards, thereby controlling the look of each type of document. Stylesheets also enable

users to apply several styles at once to one or more paragraphs, which saves a great deal of time in document creation. For example, a stylesheet can use the same fonts and point sizes for the headings and body text of all corporate press releases, and different sets of fonts and point sizes for employee manuals — assuming that the people who create and edit the documents follow the stylesheet standards. Stylesheets for HTML and XML work in the same way as word-processing stylesheets.

In this chapter, you will get an overview of two types of stylesheets: cascading stylesheets (CSS) and Extensible Stylesheet Language (XSL). You can use CSS stylesheets to apply styling properties to both HTML and XML documents. CSS is now in its second version, so it is relatively stable — although neither CSS1 nor CSS2 is fully accepted by many browsers. XSL is an XML-based grammar, which is a working draft. A working draft is subject to change; you can expect many changes until the draft becomes an official specification. To obtain up-to-date information about any note, working draft, or specification supported by the World Wide Web Consortium (W3C), browse the W3C Technical Reports page (**http://www.w3.org/TR**).

Learning about Cascading Stylesheets

Cascading stylesheets are made up of sets of rules that are applied to elements. A stylesheet rule is composed of two parts: The *selector* is the HTML or XML element to which the rule applies, and the *declaration* consists of the property (similar to an attribute) and the value — both within brackets. Look at the following example:

```
P { FONT: 12pt "Century Schoolbook",
 "Times New Roman", serif}
```

In the example, `P` is the selector, `FONT` is the CSS property, `12pt` is the point size, `"Century Schoolbook"` and `"Times New Roman"` are specific typefaces, and `serif` is a generic typeface type. The font size value of `12pt` (12 points) is an approximation. The font size probably depends on the editor with which you create the document, the browser with which you view the paragraph, or the printer with which you print it. The browser tries to use the first typeface in the list. If that is not available on the client computer, the browser attempts to use the second typeface. If that typeface is also unavailable, the browser finds a serif typeface with which to display the selected text.

A stylesheet enables a document developer to specify universal formats for all identical elements in a document type (such as memoranda or cover letters). For example, all top-level headings should always look the same, and lower-level headings should vary so that each descending level has a gradually reduced point size and different enhancements (through changing combinations of boldface, italics, bold italics, and so forth) to make the organization more distinct. Using a stylesheet, a writer can change the font, font size, and color of all level-one headings by using a single style rule. Without a stylesheet, a writer would have to accept the default styles or redefine the look of every level-one heading.

Currently, some Web browsers support stylesheets — completely or partially — and many other browsers will support stylesheets soon.

TAKE NOTE

STYLESHEET RESOURCES AT W3C

The W3C offers several stylesheet resources starting at the home page (**http://www.w3.org/style/**). The W3C Core Styles site (**http://www.w3.org/StyleSheets/Core/**) offers several predefined stylesheets. Use them in your documents or use them as aids when you construct stylesheets. Dave Raggett's article, "Adding a Touch of Style" (**http://www.w3.org/MarkUp/Guide/style/**), is an introductory guide to styling Web pages. You can validate your stylesheet by downloading the W3C CSS Validation Service (**http://jigsaw.w3.org/css-validator/**).

LEARNING THE FINE POINTS OF CHARACTER SIZE

Measuring the size of a character and its position in a line can be complex. Certain terms enable you to differentiate the parts of a character and the line on which it rests. For example, the invisible line on which a character sits in a line of text is the *baseline*. A character above the baseline is *superscript*; a character below the baseline is *subscript*.

Then, analyze the character piece by piece. The *x-height* is the measurement of the body of a lowercase character from the top of the character down to the baseline. The *cap height* marks the difference between lowercase (for example, *w*) and uppercase (for example, *W*) characters; it is the measurement from the top of the x-height to the top of the uppercase character. If you add the x-height and cap height (in other words, all parts of the character above the baseline), the result is the *ascender*. The part of a character below the baseline (for example, a lowercase *p* or *q*) is the *descender*.

CROSS-REFERENCE

"Parsing a Document" in Chapter 8 provides an overview of how HTML and XML documents are processed.

FIND IT ONLINE

The current official cascading stylesheet specification is located at **http://www.w3.org/TR/REC-CSS2/**.

Listing 13-1: A Styled Document

```
<!DOCTYPE HTML PUBLIC
 "-//W3C//DTD HTML 4.0//EN">
<HTML><HEAD>
<TITLE>The Styled Bart Page</TITLE>
<STYLE TYPE="text/css">
BODY { margin: .75in;
font: 12pt "Century Schoolbook",
"Times New Roman", serif }
H1 { font: 20pt Arial, "Gill Sans",
sans-serif; font-style: italic;
font-weight: bold }
IMG { border: black solid thin;
margin-right: 24pt; float: left }
</STYLE>
</HEAD>
<BODY>
<H1>Bart</H1>
<IMG SRC="bart.jpg" alt="bart.jpg">
<P>Bart was a handsome golden retriever
who loved to watch television, especially
advertisements that featured animals.
When he discovered the nature segment of
the CBS Sunday Morning show, he was on
his way.
</P></BODY></HTML>
```

1 Start styles in the HEAD section with the `<STYLE>` tag.
2 Set page margins and font characteristics for the body.
3 Specify all the font attributes for top-level headings.
4 Add a border and right margin and float the element.

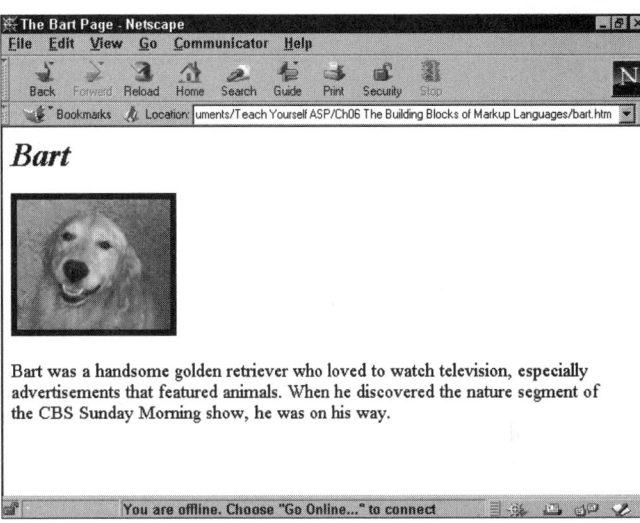

▶ This figure, from Listing 6-5, shows an unstyled version of this document.

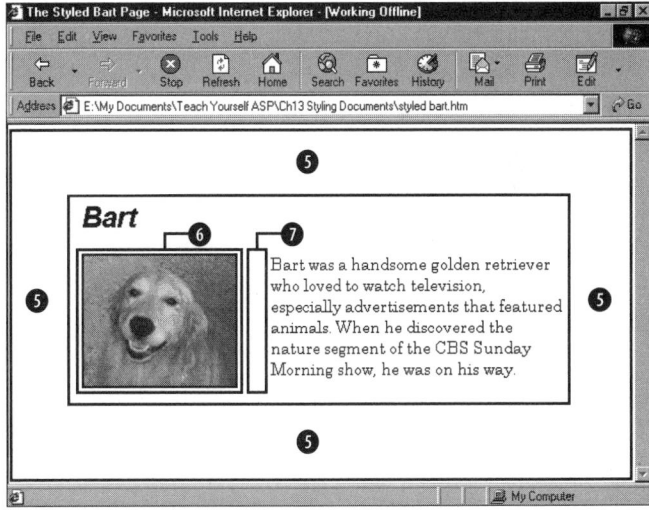

5 The page's margins add white space around the contents.
6 The image floats on the left.
7 Separate the image from text with a wide right margin.

Learning about XSL

At this writing, the Extensible Stylesheet Language (XSL) is in the working draft stage of development. (It is very important to note that working drafts are subject to change before they evolve into final recommendations.) XSL, which provides style properties for XML documents, is an XML-like language. XSL enables writers and editors to write documents that format and enhance XML document output using nested Document Style Semantics and Specification Language Online (DSSSL-O) rules and incorporating CSS and CSS-like properties. *DSSSL* is a comprehensive language (the ISO/IEC 10179: 1996 standard) with which you can *transform* (change raw markup and character data to output) and style documents. Its online version is a subset that enables developers to style online documents.

XSL documents are produced in the same way as XML documents; once you have learned how to use XML, you will be able to create properly-constructed and accurate XSL documents. As its DSSSL-O parent, XSL consists of two parts: a language that transforms XML documents and a vocabulary for formatting XML elements. XSL documents must be well-formed — according to the rules in the XML specification. (Remember that *well-formed* means that a document must follow the rules of XML but does not have an associated DTD).

XSL uses declarations to build an external XSL document for both individual elements and generations of elements. For example, you can define all top-level headings as bold, in the Helvetica typeface, and 16-point size. Or, you can make all heading elements bold and Helvetica, but vary individual point sizes. With XSL, you can also style elements by their position and value, generate text and graphics, and define formatting macros. You can write XSL documents for all types of printed and electronic output. (Note that XSL components can be included in an HTML or ASP document.)

To process an XSL stylesheet against an XML document, certain steps are followed. First, the XML document is analyzed to produce a *source tree*, which contains all the elements and attributes defined in the XML document's DTD — the root, generations of elements, and each element's attributes. Then, the XSL stylesheet is run against the source tree, which concludes with a *result tree* (a tree of elements that result from processing). The result tree is then interpreted, using XSL's formatting language to produce formatted output. Note that all four listings on the facing page appear in the current XSL working draft.

TAKE NOTE

LEARNING ABOUT THE DETAILS OF XSL PROCESSING

When you declare an XSL style, you define a template (comprised of a pattern and an action) for each format or enhancement. The *pattern* is a string that uses various criteria to match input element types (known as *nodes*) in the source tree. The *action* specifies a *subtree* (that is, the elements that match the pattern) and results in the application of *formatting objects* (in DSSSL, flow objects), styled objects that fill defined areas in the output. Formatting objects include hyperlinks, pages, groups of adjacent pages, and graphics.

USING XSL AND CSS TOGETHER

XSL goes a few steps beyond CSS in applying styles to generations of elements: It can also create new document contents and perform sophisticated selection techniques. Although CSS does not have an effect on this type of data, XSL can. So, you can use XSL and CSS together for these two purposes: use XSL to transform information, then style the information with CSS. For more information, see the W3C note "Using XSL and CSS Together" at **http://www.w3.org/TR/NOTE-XSL-and-CSS**.

CROSS-REFERENCE

All the tasks in Chapter 6 introduce you to the building blocks of all markup languages.

FIND IT ONLINE

The official XSL home page (**http://www.w3.org/Style/XSL/**) contains more than five pages of links.

Listing 13-2: Part of a Sample XSL Stylesheet

```
<xsl:stylesheet                        ❶
  xmlns:xsl="http://www.w3.org/TR/WD-xsl"
  xmlns:fo="http://www.w3.org/TR/WD-xsl/FO"
  result-ns="fo">              ❷        ❸
  <xsl:template match="/">
    <fo:basic-page-sequence font-family="serif">
      <xsl:apply-templates/>
                                        ❹
    </fo:basic-page-sequence>
  </xsl:template>
```

Listing 13-4: A Processing Example

```
<xsl:template match="chapter/title">
   <fo:rule-graphic/>
   <fo:block space-before="2pt">    ❶
      <xsl:text>Chapter </xsl:text>  ❷
      <xsl:number/>
      <xsl:text>: </xsl:text>        ❸
      <xsl:apply-templates/>
   </fo:block>
   <fo:rule-graphic/>               ❹
</xsl:template>
```

Listing 13-3: Creating a Set of Attributes

```
<xsl:attribute-set name="title-style">   ▣1
    <xsl:attribute name="font-size">
          12pt</xsl:attribute>           ◀2
    <xsl:attribute name= "font-weight">bold
    </xsl:attribute>
</xsl:attribute-set>
<xsl:template match="chapter/heading">    ◀3
  <fo:block quadding="start">
   <xsl:use attribute-set="title-style"/>
4  <xsl:apply-templates/>
  </fo:block>
</xsl:template>
```

Listing 13-5: Sample Macro Code

```
<macro name="warning-para">
  <fo:block-level-box>
    <fo:block>
      <text>Warning! </text>
      <contents/>
    </fo:block>
  </fo:block-level-box>
</macro>


<template match="warning">
  <invoke macro="warning-para">
    <apply-templates/>
  </invoke>
</template>
```

❶ Use the xmlns (XML namespace) declaration to access a URI.

❷ The result tree uses the formatting object vocabulary.

❸ The desired match is on the root element.

❹ The rule specifies a page sequence formatted with a serif font.

▣1 Declare and name an attribute set.

▣2 Declare and name individual attributes.

▣3 Match the chapter heading.

▣4 Apply the style for the attribute set.

❶ Set a rule formatting object above the text.

❷ Specify the word Chapter as text and add a space.

❸ Calculate a chapter number and add a colon.

❹ Set a rule formatting object below the text.

▶ You can write and apply macros for styles. Start the definition with the macro element, and specify the definition by applying a block format and enclosing the text in a box. Finally, invoke the macro.

Attaching a Stylesheet to a Document

Y ou can associate styles with the elements in an HTML document in several ways: by linking an external stylesheet, by inserting styles in a document or overriding an attached external stylesheet, or by defining an attribute for a particular element. The W3C recommends using external stylesheets.

To specify styles for an entire document, you can attach one or more external stylesheet documents using the `LINK` element in the HEAD section. For example:

```
<LINK href="styler.css" rel="stylesheet"
type="text/css">
```

The `href` attribute names a stylesheet, and the `type` attribute names an Internet Media Type. The `rel` attribute, which specifies the type of relationship of the link from the current document to the stylesheet, uses a variety of keywords (such as `stylesheet`) to identify the type of link.

To embed styles within the current document or to override an attached external stylesheet, use one or more `STYLE` elements in the HEAD section of a document. For example:

```
<STYLE TYPE="text/css">
BODY { margin: .75in;
font: 12pt "Century Schoolbook",
"Times New Roman", serif }
</STYLE>
```

The example shows that the boundaries of a style section are marked by a `<STYLE>` start tag and a `</STYLE>` end tag. The `TYPE` attribute names the Internet Media Type — in this case, text and cascading style sheet. The three following lines set margin and font style properties for the entire body of the HTML document.

To override stylesheet properties for a particular element, use the `STYLE` attribute. The following example appears in the HTML 4.0 specification:

```
<P style="font-size: 12pt; color: fuchsia">
Aren't style sheets wonderful?
```

Most HTML elements support the `STYLE` attribute. The two listings on the facing page are based on examples in the HTML specification.

Associating a Stylesheet with an XML Document

To associate a stylesheet with an XML document, insert the `xml-stylesheet` processing instructions (PI) anywhere within the XML document prolog. For example:

```
<?xml-stylesheet href="styler.css"
title="Stylesheet" type="text/css"?>
```

The keyword `xml-stylesheet` indicates that the attached external document is either a CSS (in this case, a cascading stylesheet) or XSL stylesheet. The following pseudo attributes are supported for `xml-stylesheet`:

href	CDATA	#REQUIRED
type	CDATA	#REQUIRED
title	CDATA	#IMPLIED
media	CDATA	#IMPLIED
charset	CDATA	#IMPLIED
alternate	(yes|no)	"no"

The attribute `href` specifies a URI link for the stylesheet. `type` specifies that the document is a cascading stylesheet (css). `title` specifies a title name of the external stylesheet document, `media` indicates the type of destination, and `charset` names the character set used in the stylesheet. `alternate="no"` associates the main stylesheet with the document, and `alternate="yes"` associates an alternate stylesheet.

CROSS-REFERENCE

Chapter 11 teaches you how to create and target HTML documents within frames.

FIND IT ONLINE

Learn about associating stylesheets with XML documents at **http://www.w3.org/TR/xml-stylesheet**.

HTML 4.0: The STYLE and LINK Elements

```
<!ELEMENT STYLE - - %StyleSheet; ←❶      -- style info -->
<!ATTLIST STYLE
  %i18n;                                 -- lang, dir, for use with title --
  type         %ContentType;  #IMPLIED  -- advisory content type --
  media        %MediaDesc; ←❷ #IMPLIED  -- designed for use with these media -->
  title        %Text;         #IMPLIED  -- advisory title --
>


<!ELEMENT LINK  - O EMPTY ←❸             -- a media-independent link -->
<!ATTLIST LINK
  %attrs;                                -- %coreattrs, %i18n, %events --
  charset      %Charset;      #IMPLIED  -- char encoding of linked resource --
  href         %URI; ←❹       #IMPLIED  -- URI for linked resource --
  hreflang     %LanguageCode; #IMPLIED  -- language code --
  type         %ContentType;  #IMPLIED  -- advisory content type --
  rel          %LinkTypes;    #IMPLIED  -- forward link types --
  rev          %LinkTypes;    #IMPLIED  -- reverse link types --
  media        %MediaDesc;    #IMPLIED  -- for rendering on these media --
>
```

❶ The %StyleSheet; *entity contains character-data information.*
❷ The %MediaDesc; *entity enables you to list media such as* screen *and* tv.
❸ *The* LINK *element is empty.*
❹ *Provide a URI for a linked external stylesheet.*

Listing 13-6: Limiting Styles with Class

```
<HEAD><STYLE type="text/css">               【1】
  #myclass {border-width: 1; border: solid;
      text-align: center}</STYLE>
</HEAD>
<BODY>                        【2】
<H1 class="myclass"> This is affected.</H1>
<H1>Not by the myclass style.</H1>
                      【3】
```

1 *Set styles for the* myclass *classification.*
2 *This top-level heading contains the* myclass *classification.*
3 *This top-level heading does not; it uses default styles.*

Listing 13-7: Limiting Styles with Identifiers

```
<HEAD><STYLE type="text/css">
  #myid {border-width: 1; border: solid;
      text-align: center}</STYLE>  ←【4】
</HEAD>
<BODY>
<H1 class="myclass">This is not affected.
</H1>                                      ←【5】
<H1 id="myid">This is affected.</H1>←【6】
<H1>Not affected.</H1>←【7】
```

4 *Set styles for the* myid *identifier.*
5 *This top-level heading uses other styles.*
6 *This top-level heading with the* myid *identifier is styled.*
7 *This default heading uses default styles.*

Laying Out Pages

Cascading stylesheets provide several properties for the background of all the pages in a document. For example, you can choose from five individual background properties or select one property that combines the five properties. For example:

```
BODY { background-image: url(bear.gif);
       background-color: red;
       background-attachment: fixed;
       background-position: 50% 50%;
       background-repeat: repeat; }
```

You don't need to include explicitly each of the background properties shown in the example. The following example shows that the `background` property combines some individual background properties into a single property. According to the Cascading Style Sheets, Level 2, recommendation, "The background property first sets all the individual background properties to their initial values, then assigns explicit values given in the declaration." For example:

```
BODY {background: url(bear.gif)
          red repeat fixed }
```

A browser should be able to interpret the unique values for each property. Note that Tables 13-1, 13-2, and 13-3 on the following three facing pages list CSS properties. Each entry includes a brief description and an example.

Using style properties, you can control two components at the edges of pages: the margin and padding. A *margin* is the outermost part of a page measured from the edge; and *padding* is between the margin but outside the text, graphic content, and any borders. The margin and padding properties work in much the same way as the background properties: You can set margins and padding using four specific properties — one each for the bottom, left, right, and top margin or padding — or you can combine some or all properties. You can turn on or off individual margins and padding or set specific margin or padding widths.

For example, you can use the `margin` property to combine the individual margin properties: `margin-top`, `margin-right`, `margin-bottom`, and `margin-left` — in that order. If you supply one value for the `margin` property, all margins are set to that value. If you supply two values, the browser supplies values from the opposite sides of the element: top and bottom, right and left. Three values set the top, right, and bottom margins. The left margin obtains its value from its opposite, the right margin.

If you want to set all four margins to the same width, all you need to do is provide a single value. For example:

```
BIGPAGE {margin: 0.5in}
```

is equivalent to:

```
BIGPAGE {margin: 0.5in 0.5in 0.5in 0.5in }
```

To specify an absolute measurement for one, two, three, or four margins, specify a value followed by a two-letter abbreviation representing the unit of measure. To specify a percentage of the parent element's margins, enter a value followed by the percent sign. You can enter the `auto` keyword to have the browser automatically calculate a minimum value for one, two, three, or four margins.

TAKE NOTE

▶ MAKING A STYLE MORE IMPORTANT

The CSS ! `important` keyword enables you to make the current style more important than those of the same priority. To use ! `important`, simply add it to the end of a style declaration. CSS provides two categories of declarations: *author-defined* and *user-defined*. An author-defined declaration that is *not* important overrides a user-defined declaration that is *not* important. An author-defined important declaration overrides a user-defined important declaration. A user-defined important declaration overrides an author declaration that is *not* important.

CROSS-REFERENCE
Chapter 6's task "Understanding Attributes" teaches you about some styling predecessors of elements.

FIND IT ONLINE
The HTML Writers Guild (**http://www.hwg.org/**) provides many resources for over 85,000 Web authors worldwide.

Table 13-1: CASCADING STYLESHEET PROPERTIES (FIRST OF THREE TABLES)

Property Name	Property/Properties Affected	Example
background	One or more background properties: background-attachment, background-color, background-image, background-position, background-repeat	{ background: url(fish.gif) silver repeat }
background-attachment	A fixed or scrolled background image	{ background-attachment: fixed }
background-color	The background color	{ background-color: cyan }
background-image }	The URL of the background image	{ background-image: url(fish.gif)
background-position	The background-image position	{ background-position: 0% 50% }
background-repeat	The number of times the background image appears	{ background-repeat: repeat }
border	One or more border's border-color, border-style, and/or border-width	{ border: blue solid medium }
border-bottom border-left border-right border-top	A border's border-color, border-style, border-bottom-width	{ border-bottom: silver dotted thick }
border-bottom-width border-left-width border-right-width border-top-width	A border width	{ border-top-width: thick }
border-color	The colors of one to four borders	{ border-color: blue }
border-style	One to four border-line styles	{ border-style: solid double }
border-width	The widths of one to four borders	{ border-width: thin }

Setting Page and Element Borders

As you know, properties apply to elements, so you can add styled borders to every page in a document (by styling the BODY element) as well as individual elements. The following code specifies border, right-margin, and float properties for all IMG elements in the document:

```
IMG { border-color: black ;
 border-style: solid; border-width: thin;
 margin-right: 24pt; float: left }
```

As with the various background, margin, and padding styles, you can combine several border properties — width, color, and style — into one, or specify several distinct properties for one, two, three, or four borders.

The border-bottom-width, border-left-width, border-right-width, and border-top-width properties set the width of the bottom, left, right, and top borders, respectively. You can set each of the border-width properties with a keyword — thin, medium (the default), or thick — or with an absolute measurement. To set an absolute border width, enter a positive value followed by a two-letter abbreviation representing the unit of measure.

You can set one, two, three, or four border widths by using the border-width property, which recognizes specified widths in the following order: border-width-top, border-width-right, border-width-bottom, and border-width-left. If you supply one width, all borders are set to that width. If you supply two or three widths, the browser supplies widths from the opposite sides of the element. Elements are paired as follows: top and bottom, left and right.

The border-color property sets colors of one, two, three, or four borders with a choice of five color-identifying options: The color name (red, maroon, yellow, green, lime, teal, olive, aqua, blue, navy, purple, fuchsia, black, gray, silver, or white); A three-digit hexadecimal color code (ranging from 0 to F, where one digit represents red, the next

green, and the last blue); A six-digit hexadecimal color code (where red, green, and blue are represented by two digits — 00 to FF — each); The keyword rgb, followed by a three-digit absolute decimal red-green-blue value (ranging from 000 to 255); The keyword rgb, followed by a relative red-green-blue value (each ranging from 0.0% to 100.0%, the equivalent of an absolute value of 000 to 255, respectively).

The border-style property enables you to select the look of one, two, three, or four border lines from nine styles: dotted, dashed, solid, double, groove, ridge, inset, outset, or none.

You can combine border properties by using the border style. The following example, which creates a thin, black, solid-line border, combines the border properties shown in the first example in this task:

```
IMG { border: black solid thin}
```

TAKE NOTE

▶ INHERITING STYLES

Elements embedded within other elements usually inherit style properties from their parent elements. So, if you apply the following styles to the BODY element:

```
BODY { font-family: "times new
roman", "century schoolbook", serif;
font-size: 12pt }
```

all the text within the <BODY> and </BODY> tags will be either Times New Roman or Century Schoolbook (depending on the fonts installed on your computer) and have a size of 12 points — unless elements that control the output or display of text have their own styles.

CROSS-REFERENCE

The "Declaring Empty Elements" task in Chapter 7 compares empty elements with "non-empty" ones.

FIND IT ONLINE

At **http://www.zeldman.com/askdrweb/css.html**, you can read a tutorial on using cascading stylesheets.

Table 13-2: CASCADING STYLESHEET PROPERTIES (SECOND OF THREE TABLES)

Property Name	Property/Properties Affected	Example
clear	The position of a floating element	{ clear: left }
color	The foreground color	{ color: blue }
display	The type of element display: inline or in a box	{ display: block }
float	The position of an element: floating or fixed in place	{ float: left }
font	Selected text's properties: font-style, font-variant, font-weight, font-size, line-height, font-family	{ font: small-caps/90% "courier", sans-serif }
font-family	The typeface of selected text	{ font-family: "Times New Roman" "Book Antigua", serif }
font-size	The point size of selected text	{ font-size: 12pt }
font-style	The "angle" of selected text	{ font-style: italic }
font-variant	Small caps or normal text	{ font-variant: small-caps }
font-weight	The level of boldness for text	{ font-weight: bold }
height	The height of an element	{ height: 200px }
letter-spacing	Spacing between characters	{ letter-spacing: 2pt }
line-height	The height of a line from baseline to baseline	{ line-height: 95% }
list-style	A list's properties: list-style-image, list-style-position, list-style-type	{ list-style: url(ab.gif) disk inside }
list-style-image	The URL of an image for a list's bullets	{ list-style-image: url(snp.gif }
list-style-position	Alignment of all but the first list items: with the left margin or as a hanging indent	{ list-style-position: outside }
list-style-type	The type of number or bullet for a list	{ list-style-type: decimal }

Putting Elements into Position

Certain CSS properties enable you to align elements vertically or set spacing between words and characters.

Use the `vertical-align` property to set the up-and-down alignment of the element with which it is associated. You can choose from several keywords (`baseline`, `sub`, `super`, `top`, `middle`, `bottom`, `text-top`, and `text-bottom`), or you can enter a percentage value (followed by a percent symbol). Enter the `baseline` (the default) keyword to align the element vertically with the baseline of the current element, or with the baseline of the parent element if the current element has no baseline. Remember that the *baseline* is the invisible line on which a non-subscript or non-superscript character sits in a line of text. The `sub` and `super` keywords make the element a subscript (that is, it sits below the baseline) and superscript (that is, it sits above the baseline), respectively. The `top` keyword aligns the top of the element with the top of the highest element on the current line; the `bottom` keyword aligns the bottom of the element with the lowest element; and the `middle` keyword aligns the element with the middle of the element. The `text-top` and the `text-bottom` keywords align the element with the top and bottom, respectively, of the parent element's typeface.

Kern is a printing term that indicates the adjustment of space between two adjacent letters. Typically, the larger the size of a particular typeface (for example, those used for headings), the farther apart some characters appear on-screen or on the printed page. The `letter-spacing` property sets spacing between characters using a keyword or measurement. Enter the `normal` keyword (the default) to represent the normal spacing between characters. You can also specify a positive or negative measurement, followed by a two-letter abbreviation representing the unit of measure, for the space between the characters. A positive value represents an increase in spacing, and a negative value indicates a decrease.

You can also compress and expand spacing between words. This enables you to fit more words on a single line (for example, to force the last word of a heading to join all the other words on a single line), to space out the words on a line (for example, to have text take up more room on a page), or to simulate justification — if you are prepared to spend a great deal of time on the task. You can also combine word spacing and line spacing to control the position of every character in a paragraph. The `word-spacing` property works in the same way as `letter-spacing`. Use the `normal` keyword (the default) to represent the normal spacing between words, or specify positive or negative values to increase or decrease spacing.

TAKE NOTE

SETTING WHITE SPACE IN HTML DOCUMENTS

By choosing one of three keywords, you can specify whether white space is eliminated, as in normal HTML documents, or preformatted. For example:
`BLOCKQUOTE { white-space: pre }`
treats the element as preformatted content in the same way that the `PRE` element works. The other keywords are `normal` (the default), which does not add white space to an element, and `nowrap`, which does not wrap text.

USING WHITE SPACE IN XML DOCUMENTS

The `xml:space` processing instruction either preserves or turns off the white space in an XML document, using the following syntax:
`xml:space (default|preserve)`
The `default` keyword allows a target application to set its own white space values; `preserve` keeps the white space values (as the HTML `PRE` element).

CROSS-REFERENCE
Chapter 9 teaches you how to add prestyled lists to your documents.

FIND IT ONLINE
Read Section 14 of the HTML 4.0 specification (**http://www.w3.org/markup**) to learn how to set HTML styles.

Table 13-3: CASCADING STYLESHEET PROPERTIES (THIRD OF THREE TABLES)

Property Name	Property/Properties Affected	Example
margin	The presence or size of one to four margins	{ margin: 1in 0.5in }
margin-bottom		
margin-left		
margin-right		
margin-top	The presence or size of a margin	{ margin-bottom: 12pt }
padding	The presence or size of one to four paddings	{ padding: 6pt 8pt }
padding-bottom		
padding-left		
padding-right		
padding-top	The presence or size of padding	{ padding-bottom: 0 }
text-align	Text's horizontal alignment: left, right, justified, or centered	{ text-align: justify }
text-decoration	Text decoration using lines or blinking	{ text-decoration: underline }
text-indent	A first-line text indention	{ text-indent: 1in }
text-transform	Change of case: initial caps, uppercase, lowercase, or normal	{ text-transform: capitalize }
vertical-align	An element's vertical alignment — with the baseline, an element, or text	{ vertical-align: top }
white-space	The format of white space	{ white-space: pre }
width	The width of an element	{ width: auto }
word-spacing	Spacing between words	{ word-spacing: 3pt }

Styling Text

As you may guess, the font properties control the appearance of selected text. The six font properties work in the same way as most of the other properties covered in this chapter: You can specify five individual font properties (`font-family`, `font-size`, `font-style`, `font-variant`, and `font-weight`) or combine each of these properties under one (`font`).

The `font-family` property specifies a typeface by one or more particular names (such as "Times New Roman" or Arial), a generic family name (such as `serif`, `sans-serif`, `cursive`, `fantasy`, and `monospace`), or a combination of both. Use quotation marks to enclose family names comprised of two or more words that are separated by spaces (for example, "Times New Roman" or "Bookman Old Style"). When you use the `font-family` property, it is best to list more than one typeface name. This approach ensures that you can define a font family even if a specific font is not available on your computer.

The `font-size` property specifies an absolute or relative point size using a value or a keyword. Either enter an absolute measurement, followed by a two-letter abbreviation for the unit of measure, or specify a percentage of the parent element's point size, followed by the percentage sign. You can type a keyword that represents a size relative to the current point size: `larger`, which is larger than the current point size; or `smaller`, which is smaller; or a keyword that represents an absolute size (determined by the browser): `xx-small`, `x-small`, `small`, `medium`, `large`, `x-large`, and `xx-large`.

The `font-style` property enables you to enter a keyword to specify the degree that text "leans." Valid keywords are `normal` (the default), which is unitalicized text; `oblique`, which is slightly italicized text; and `italic`, which is italicized. If you choose italic and the current typeface does not offer italics, text may be oblique instead.

Use the `font-variant` property to specify normal text (in this case, a mix of uppercase and lowercase characters that you typed) or *small caps*, which are uppercase characters that are smaller in size than standard uppercase characters. Enter the `normal` keyword for normal text or the `small-caps` keyword, respectively.

The weight of a font is the degree of boldness or lightness. Set the weight of selected text by using the `font-weight` property and a keyword or number. Choose from `normal`, which is the standard, non-bold, non-light text weight; `bold`, which is the standard boldface text; `bolder`, which is a relative value that is bolder than standard boldface and the equivalent of ultra-bold or heavy text; or `lighter`, which is a relative value that is the equivalent of light text. Valid numbers range from `100` to `900`, where `100` is the lightest weight and `900` is the boldest.

The `font` property combines multiple font properties in the same way that `margin` and `border` combine multiple margin and border properties. The `font` property specifies rules for the `font-style`, `font-variant`, `font-weight`, `font-size`, `line-height`, and `font-family` properties — in that order.

TAKE NOTE

▶ SETTING THE HEIGHT OF A TEXT LINE

The `line-height` property specifies the height of the text line from baseline to baseline. Either use a keyword or enter a value using this syntax:

```
line-height: {
normal|number|length|percent% }
```

Use `normal` (the default) to accept the parent element's line height or enter a number by which the current font size is multiplied for a new line height. You can set the length, which is a positive value followed by a two-letter unit-of-measure abbreviation. You can enter a positive percentage, followed by a percentage sign, to specify a relative line height.

CROSS-REFERENCE

The "Planning and Designing a Document" task in Chapter 5 teaches you how to set up a document.

FIND IT ONLINE

Cascading Style Sheets, Level 1 (http://www.w3.org/TR/REC-CSS1) introduces cascading stylesheets.

Listing 13-8: Examples of Font Properties

```
#ID=1234 { font-variant: small-caps;
           font-weight: bolder }     ◀❶

H2, H4 { font-style: italic;
              font-weight: bold}     ◀❷

.warn { font-weight: 800 } ◀❸

P {font: small-caps/90%
   "times new roman", serif }     ◀❹
```

Listing 13-9: Special Heading Styles

```
BODY { font-family: Braggadocio, Impact, ◀❚1
sans-serif }
H1    { font-size: 72pt;
        font-weight: 900 } ◀❚2

H2    { font-size: 48pt;
        font-weight: 800 }

H3    { font-size: 36pt;
        font-weight: 700 } ◀❚3

H4    { font-size: 24pt;
        font-weight: 600 }
```

Listing 13-10: Examples of Styled Paragraphs

```
BODY { font-family: "Times New Roman",
 "Book Antigua", serif;              ◀❶
       font-size: 12pt }
P.note { white-space: pre;
    ❷       text-decoration: underline; ◀❸
            text-decoration: overline;
            font-weight: bold           ◀❹
            font-size: 14pt;
            color: red }
<BODY>To install this program, double-click on
the setup icon.
<P class="note">To be able to click, you must
have a mouse and proper software installed on
your computer.</P>
<P>Then, let the installation program take
over. Follow the instructions on each message
box.</P>
```

❶ *Set the default formats for the body of the document.*
❷ *Start styling the* note *class of paragraph.*
❸ *The underline appears both under and over the text.*
❹ *The font is bold and large.*

❶ *This example sets font properties for the* 1234 *identifier.*

❷ *These two headings will be in bold italics.*

❸ *The* warn *classification will be extremely bold.*

❹ *The* font *property selects typefaces and sets 90% line height.*

❚1 *Specify high-impact fonts for the document body.*

❚2 *Set the largest size and boldest weight for the top-level heading.*

❚3 *Gradually decrease the size and weight for other headings.*

Personal Workbook

Q & A

1 When you associate a stylesheet with an HTML or XML document, what happens?

_____

_____

_____

2 What is the main difference between stylesheets for HTML documents and those for XML documents?

_____

_____

_____

3 What does CSS represent?

_____

_____

_____

4 What does XSL represent?

_____

_____

_____

5 What does a stylesheet rule consist of?

_____

_____

_____

6 What is the baseline?

_____

_____

_____

7 What is the x-height?

_____

_____

_____

8 What CSS properties set spaces between words and between characters?

_____

_____

_____

ANSWERS: PAGE 505

EXTRA PRACTICE

1. Go online and find a stylesheet tutorial at the W3C.

2. Find the Chocolate stylesheet at the W3C.

3. Write styles that set the left and right margins of all body text to 8 points and the top margin to 1 inch.

4. Specify a 12-point margin around an image with the classification of 12image.

5. Write two styles that set thin top and bottom borders and thick left and right borders.

6. Write one style that incorporates both styles in the preceding exercise.

REAL-WORLD APPLICATIONS

✔ Your corporate intranet is comprised of unstyled pages from five departments. Write an external stylesheet that standardizes all your intranet pages.

✔ You have been assigned to standardize all your corporation's Web-based memos and press releases. Write stylesheets for these corporate documents.

✔ Your company's newsletter will now be completely redesigned and posted on your corporate Web site. After evaluating the existing design, create an external stylesheet.

✔ Your company wants you to create external stylesheets for informal and formal business letters. Both versions contain a graphical letterhead. The informal letter is completely left-aligned in a block format. The formal letter's paragraphs are indented.

Visual Quiz

Identify the bad syntax in this stylesheet.

_____

_____

_____

_____

_____

_____

```
BODY { background-image: url(funny.doc)
                         border: big;
       margin: 80%:
       text_indent: 1in }
P:title { font-family: Helvetica, Arial Black, sans-serif;
       font-size: 24pt;
       font-weight: bold;
       margin: 2in 1in 0.5in 1in 1in }
P.#135 { font-family: "Tms New", "Courier", serif;
       font-size: 14pt;
       margin: 2in }
```

PART

III

Contents of 'Desktop'

Name

My Computer

Network Neigh

Internet Explore

Microsoft Outloo

Recycle Bin

My Briefcase

3252-9

3259-6

3261-8

3262-6

3281-2

3286-3

DE Phone List

Device Manager

In

Iomega Tools

Adding Scripts to Documents

In this part, you'll learn the difference between plain and static documents and dynamic and interactive pages — namely scripts. When you add a script to an HTML document or an ASP page, you introduce the concept of pages that change with user actions or on-the-spot computations.

You can write scripts in various languages. This part will provide overviews of three of the most popular languages: VBScript, which is based on Microsoft Visual Basic; JScript and its close relatives (JavaScript and ECMAScript), which are based on the Java programming language; and PerlScript, which is based on C and some UNIX utilities.

By building on the HTML tutorials in the preceding part, the chapters in this part show you how to transform your HTML documents into ASP pages. After you have completed this part, you'll know about the two types of scripts (client-side and server-side) and how to use both in your Web documents, you'll have been exposed to several scripting languages, and you'll find out about tools that can help you develop outstanding Web pages in a quick and efficient manner.

CHAPTER **14**

MASTER
THESE
SKILLS

▶ Learning about ASP Content
▶ Using Server-Side Includes
▶ Learning about Scripting
▶ Learning about HTTP Document Transmission
▶ Building Interfaces: Scripts on the Client
▶ Building Documents: Scripts on the Server
▶ Learning about the Windows Scripting Host

The Anatomy of an ASP Document: Scripts + Content = Pages

Now that you have reviewed your HTML skills or gained new ones, it's time to move on to ASP pages, which can be renamed plain HTML documents or can combine HTML statements and scripts. In the "Converting Web Pages to ASP" task in Chapter 1, you read an overview of how to transform your HTML documents to ASP. This chapter is loaded with pages and pages of information.

Starting with the first task in this chapter, you'll learn more about the similarities and differences between HTML documents and ASP pages. You'll get a hint of what's to come in the subsequent task on server-side includes — one component of the many special components, applets, and other objects added to your computer system when you install the server on which ASP pages will be interpreted. The third task introduces you to scripting and its benefits to your documents. You will learn that you can use many scripting languages to write scripts that will enhance your ASP pages. (Later in this part, you'll be introduced to three of the most popular scripting languages: VBScript, JScript, and PerlScript.)

In the following task, you'll find out how documents are transmitted between the user's client computer and the Web server using HTTP. (Remember that the last task in Chapter 1 introduced you to HTTP.) Next, building on the client-server knowledge that you gained in several preceding chapters, you'll explore the differences between client-side scripts, which run on the client computer, and server-side scripts, which are rendered by the server.

The best Web pages are well-designed and load quickly. The penultimate task discusses application architecture — how to plan and construct properly structured Web pages using all the technologies that you'll know before you finish this book.

Finally, you'll learn about the Windows Scripting Host (WSH), with which you can execute VBScript and JScript scripts to automate tasks related to the operation of Windows itself. WSH includes two components to execute scripts: one that you can run from the MS-DOS windows under Windows, and another that is a Windows applet.

Learning about ASP Content

In the preceding chapters, you were introduced to ASP and its building blocks, and you learned about the most basic to the most advanced HTML (and some XML) document content. With these fundamental concepts in place, you'll now learn how to turn HTML documents into ASP pages using increasingly complex technologies.

As the title of this chapter suggests, an ASP document is composed of both scripts and HTML content: To make an ASP page, simply take a standard HTML document — with content composed of markup, text, and graphics — and add scripts. The result is a dynamic, interactive ASP page. At this point, the only difference between HTML documents and ASP pages is the computer on which they are processed: HTML documents are run on the client, and ASP pages are run on the server.

Scripting languages, such as VBScript and JScript (covered in Chapters 15 and 16, respectively), are officially known as HTML extensions: They both *extend* the HTML language into new territory.

Many Web documents contain forms that users fill in and send to a computer serving a Web site. Scripts can enhance forms by making them interactive. So, when a user submits a form, the receiving Web site can send a thank-you message to the person at the other end. Or, a script can go even further: If the user submits certain information (such as a zip code), a script can check the entry against a database of zip codes. If the zip code and street address and/or city match, a thank-you message is sent. However, if the zip code seems to be inaccurate, the user can be prompted to correct the form and resubmit. Another example is missing information. If the user leaves a required field empty, the script can send a message to the user and redisplay the form. Although scripts can be embedded in both HTML documents and ASP pages, there are advantages of using ASP. You'll learn much more about

the differences between plain HTML documents and ASP pages, and the advantages of using ASP, as you continue reading this chapter.

TAKE NOTE

REVIEWING THE HISTORY OF CLIENT-SERVER ARCHITECTURE

As you know, HTML documents are processed by a Web browser, which is located on the client. Using a client computer is a relatively new concept, which came into being with IBM's personal computer. Before the PC, an earlier form of client-server — dumb terminals and mainframes — was the rule of the day. Many terminals (and several noisy printers) could be networked to one, two, or several mainframes, depending on the size and budget of the company or educational institution. This type of network had some big disadvantages: The centralized storage was tight, as was processing power for all those plugged-in people who wanted to perform a variety of tasks, from word processing to spreadsheets to mathematical calculations. The next step was to decentralize into PCs for individuals or groups. The main disadvantage was hooking a printer and other peripherals up to each PC. As soon as storage media became inexpensive, management started networking PCs into workgroups. Although mainframes are still up and running today — mainly for their superior processing power — most companies rely on scores of PCs to get the job done. The first client-server architecture was skewed toward the client: The server was simply a central hub to which peripherals were attached and on which many files could be stored and accessed by members of the workgroup.

CROSS-REFERENCE

Chapter 19 discusses built-in ASP objects (request, response, and server) and object-oriented development.

FIND IT ONLINE

At **http://support.microsoft.com/support/activeserver/links.asp**, you'll find links to ASP Web sites.

The Anatomy of an ASP Document: Scripts + Content = Pages

Listing 14-1: A Sample Scripted HTML Document

```
<HTML>
<HEAD>
<TITLE>Sample HTML</TITLE>     ←❶
</HEAD>
<BODY>
<H2>A Simple Calculation</H2>
<SCRIPT LANGUAGE="VBSCRIPT"
      RUNAT=SERVER>             ←❷

Dim A, B
A = 2     ←❸
B = A + A
Response.write A & " + " & A & " = " & B   ←❹
</SCRIPT>
</BODY>
</HTML>
```

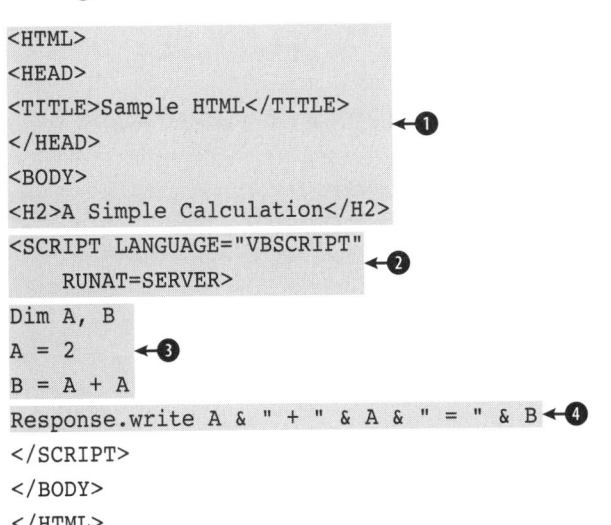

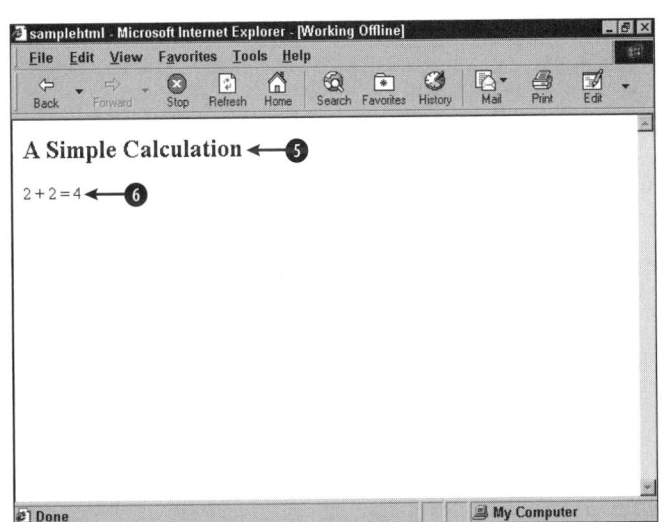

Listing 14-2: A Scripted ASP Page Counterpart

```
<HTML>
<HEAD>
<TITLE>Sample HTML</TITLE>     ←❼
</HEAD>
<BODY>
<H2>A Simple Calculation</H2>
<%  ←❽
Dim A, B
A = 2     ←❾
B = A + A
response.write A & " + " & A & " = " & B  ←❿
%>
</BODY>
</HTML>
```

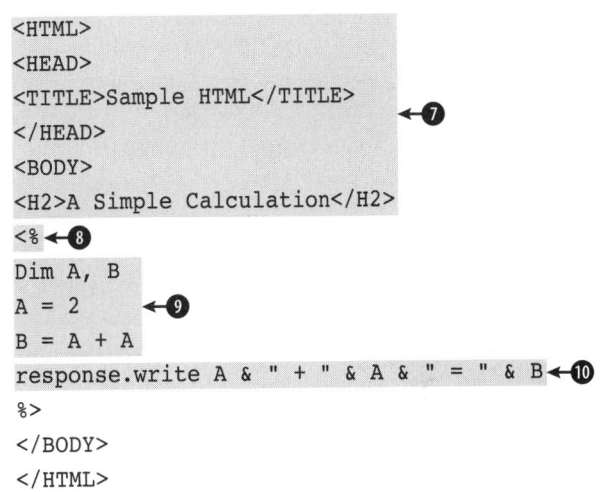

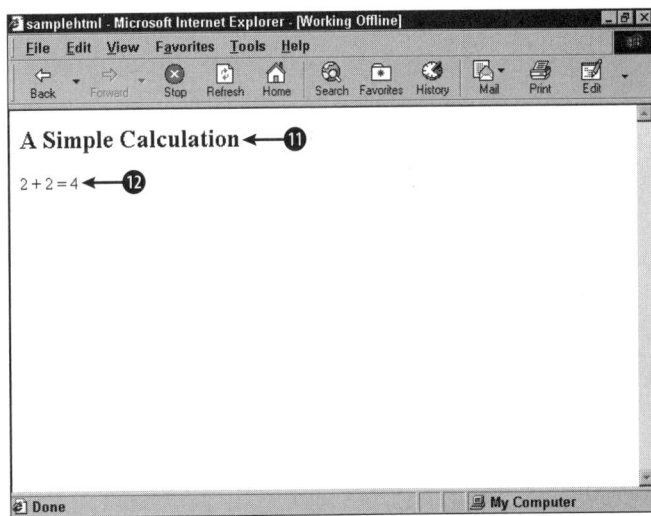

❶ Start an HTML document as you usually do.

❷ Start the script by specifying the scripting language.

❸ Declare the variables and set their values.

❹ Write the calculation on the page.

❺ Start an HTML document as you usually do.

❻ Write the calculation on the page.

❼ Start an HTML document as you usually do.

❽ Start the script by using ASP's <% delimiter.

❾ Declare the variables and set their values.

❿ The server responds by writing the calculation on the page.

⓫ Start an ASP page in the way you start an HTML document.

⓬ The server responds by writing the calculation on the page.

213

Using Server-Side Includes

S erver-side includes (SSIs) are commands with which you can add a file, provide information, or specify how to use an object in your ASP pages. SSIs are in the server object category: They are included with the server software.

To call an SSI, simply enter a keyword preceded by a hash mark (#) at the top of the ASP page and provide a variable, keyword, string, or other information.

The SSI line is located at the top of the page because it must be processed before any ASP code is interpreted. The only SSI supported by ASP is #INCLUDE.

The #INCLUDE SSI includes an external file in the same way that a Web document includes an external stylesheet. A typical #INCLUDE directive looks something like the two following examples:

```
<!-- #include file="C:\incs\vex.inc" -->
```

and

```
<!-- #include virtual="layout.inc" -->
```

#INCLUDE is the reserved name of an SSI directive. The file keyword represents a path and filename in a standard Windows folder, and virtual represents a path and filename in a virtual directory.

When you install the IIS and PWS servers, several SSIs are added to your computer in subfolders of \windows\system\inetsrv\iisadmin and \Inetpub\iissamples\homepage (for PWS installations). SSIs are text files, so you can create your own. If you always include certain lines (for example, your name and your company's name or the same metadata) in your documents, place those lines in an SSI. You can also write documents that include commonly-used scripts or entities — anything that you insert in most documents.

TAKE NOTE

▶ LEARNING ABOUT OTHER SERVER-SIDE INCLUDES

Your server probably supports all or most of these other SSIs: #CONFIG (directs how to format error messages, file sizes, and combinations of dates and times); #ECHO, which is related to the old DOS ECHO command (displays HTTP header, authentication, server, and other system information); #EXEC (executes a program, script, or DOS shell command), #FLASTMOD (returns the last modification time for the named file), and #FSIZE (returns the size of the named file).

▶ LEARNING ABOUT OBJECTS AND OBJECT-ORIENTED SCRIPTING

Objects are variables made up of their definitions and any associated data. For example, a single element on your Desktop is itself and its characteristics (such as a square red and black shortcut icon). An *object-oriented script* looks like any other script. However, the way that it is evaluated is different: The script is made up of sets of related objects that are calculated as sets. ASP pages can include *scripting objects* that are predefined within a scripting language and used within the language and predefined scripting objects that can be used by any scripting language. This brings up an interesting point: Some (but not all) scripting objects are supported or supplied by some scripting languages. This condition results in variations among languages: If you learn one language, you'll find that some aspects are related or even identical to other languages, but other parts are missing from other languages. Other objects include those that you define and *server objects*, such as SSIs, which are included in the server software.

CROSS-REFERENCE
Chapter 20 specifies how to install objects that further extend ASP beyond its built-in objects.

FIND IT ONLINE
CNET Builder.com (**http://www.builder.com/**) provides many links, including free downloads, for site builders.

Listing 14-3: Lines from a PWS Server-Include

```
<% If myinfo.Theme = "looseleaf" Then
     response.write "<FONT FACE='VERDANA' SIZE='-2'>"
     '        $Date: 9/11/97 5:07p $
     '        $ModTime: $
     '        $Revision: 8 $
     '        $Workfile: layout.inc $
     response.write "<TABLE width='100%' height='100%' "_
  & "cellpadding='0' cellspacing='0' border='0' BGColor='#FFFFFF'>"
  response.write "<TR><TD Valign='TOP' Colspan=2 Align=center><H1>"
     call Title
  response.write "</H1></TD></TR><TR><TD Valign=top Align=center Colspan=2>"
   call page_datetime
  response.write "<BR>"
     call page_messaging
     call file_check                'Checks for published files
  response.write "</TD></TR>"_
     & "<TR><TD Valign=top Align=center Colspan=2>"
     call layout_Email
     response.write "</TD></TR><TR><TD Align=center>"
     call Phone
     response.write "</TD><TD Align=center>"
     call faxPhone
     response.write "</TD></TR><TR><TD Colspan=2 Align=center>"
     call Address
     For num = 1 to 4
     response.write "</TD></TR><TR><TD Colspan=2 Align=center>"
     response.write Heading(num)
     Next
     response.write "</TD></TR><TR><TD Colspan=2 Align=center>"
     call ie_logo
     response.write "</TD></TD></TR></TABLE></FONT>"
  End If %>
```

▶ *The* layout.inc *server-include for the loose-leaf theme combines HTML markup and content in a script.*

Learning about Scripting

You have learned that scripts are small sections of programming code that make your Web pages more dynamic or interactive. A script can display different values for a variable, depending on calculations of other variables, or display the date, time, or both values.

HTML 4.0 supports a set of built-in *intrinsic events* that trigger a script when there is an action such as the click of a mouse button, the movement of the mouse pointer, the press of a keyboard key, the loading of a window, the click of a form button, and so forth. Intrinsic events are attributes of HTML elements; you can use many events with most elements, but others are limited to one or two. To check whether an event is associated with an element, refer to the HTML 4.0 specification — in particular, the DTD — or look at a book such as *HTML in Plain English*, written by Sandra E. Eddy, a co-author of this book, and also published by IDG Books Worldwide. Table 14-1 on the facing page lists and describes HTML 4.0's intrinsic events. Note that Microsoft and Netscape have defined additional events — not included in Table 14-1 — that may become part of a future HTML version.

As you learned in Chapter 1, an HTML document can include client-side scripts, which are run on the browser (located on the client computer), and an ASP document can contain server-side scripts, which are run on the server. In HTML, the beginning and end of a script is marked by the `<SCRIPT>` start tag and the `</SCRIPT>` end tag, respectively. ASP scripts are marked by the `<%` start delimiter and the `%>` end delimiter. The scripts within are expressed in exactly the same way — using the same syntax, depending on the language. In the following "Building Interfaces: Scripts on the Client" and "Building Documents: Scripts on the Server" sections, you'll learn more about client-side and server-side scripting.

Two scripts — VBScript and JScript — are bundled with the ASP technology. However, ASP is an open technology, so you can use any type of scripting or programming language in your pages.

Discovering what the HTML 4.0 specification says about scripts

According to the HTML 4.0 specification: "Scripts offer authors a means to extend HTML documents in highly active and interactive ways. For example:

▶ Scripts may be evaluated as a document loads to modify the contents of the document dynamically.

▶ Scripts may accompany a form to process input as it is entered. Designers may dynamically fill out parts of a form based on the values of other fields. They may also ensure that input data conforms to predetermined ranges of values, that fields are mutually consistent, etc.

▶ Scripts may be triggered by events that affect the document, such as loading, unloading, element focus, mouse movement, etc.

▶ Scripts may be linked to form controls (e.g., buttons) to produce graphical user interface elements."

CROSS-REFERENCE

To get an overview of VBScript, JScript, and PerlScript, see Chapters 15, 16, and 17, respectively.

FIND IT ONLINE

The Developer Shed (**http://www.devshed.com/**) has links to news, talk, resources, and tools.

Table 14-1: HTML 4.0'S INTRINSIC EVENTS

Event	The script runs when:	Use within these elements:
onblur	The current object is no longer the active object	BUTTON, INPUT, LABEL, SELECT, TEXTAREA
onchange	The current object is no longer the active object *and* has had a value change	INPUT, SELECT, TEXTAREA
onclick	A user clicks an object	most elements
ondblclick	A user double-clicks an object	most elements
onfocus	The current object becomes active through some user action	BUTTON, INPUT, LABEL, SELECT, TEXTAREA
onkeydown	A user presses and holds down a key over an object	most elements
onkeypress	A user presses and releases a key over an object	most elements
onkeyup	A user releases a key	most elements
onload	A window or frameset has loaded	BODY, FRAMESET
onmousedown	A user presses and holds down a mouse button	most elements
onmousemove	The mouse moves over an object	most elements
onmouseout	The mouse moves away from an object	most elements
onmouseover	A user moves the mouse over an object for the first time	most elements
onmouseup	A pressed-down mouse button is released	most elements
onreset	A user clicks a Reset button	FORM
onselect	A user selects text in a form's text box	INPUT, SELECT, TEXTAREA
onsubmit	A user clicks a Submit button	FORM
onunload	A document is removed from the screen	BODY, FRAMESET

Learning about HTTP Document Transmission

Remember that Hypertext Transfer Protocol is the protocol that enables one computer to send a document to another computer on the Web. When you enter `http://` and the rest of a URL, you are actually signaling an HTTP program installed on a remote computer that you wish to use that program to load a Web page onto your Desktop. Or, after a visitor to a Web site clicks a Submit button, an HTTP program transmits fill-in form information from the client computer to a server computer. These examples demonstrate that HTTP is capable of transmitting files in both directions: from the client to the server and from the server to the client.

An HTML form's first line:

```
<FORM METHOD="POST" ACTION="/forms/ex1"
    ENCTYPE="multipart/form-data" >
```

contains form-handling attributes. `METHOD="POST"` incorporates the form data in the form itself and sends the entire file to the HTTP processor. The `ACTION` attribute specifies an absolute or relative URL of a program that will process the form. The `ENCTYPE` attribute specifies the content type — the valid Internet Media Type (MIMETYPE) that is used to encode the form. The second example on the facing page is from the HTML 4.0 specification.

Before a client sends information to a server, it asks the server, using the TCP open request, whether it is ready to communicate and prepared to accept information. When the server answers that it is ready, both computers establish a connection, which is known as a *handshake*. At this point, the client starts to send the information in the form of IP *packets*, which are simply bundles of data of varying sizes. If a browser uses HTTP/1.0, after the transmission of a packet is completed, the server must acknowledge receiving the packet before the next one is sent. However, HTTP/1.1 speeds the process through *pipelining*. All the packets are sent, and the server acknowledges the entire group.

HTTP is also known as a request and response protocol. A client generates a request and a server responds. ASP includes two built-in objects, the Request object and the Response object. Request and Response conform to HTTP's requests and responses. For more information about the Request and Response objects, refer to Chapter 19.

TAKE NOTE

► TRANSMITTING INFORMATION IN THE FUTURE VERSION OF HTTP

HTTP-NG, which is the next generation of the protocol, primarily addresses adding new data types, such as XML and multimedia. However, HTTP-NG packet transmissions should become more efficient. According to the HTTP-NG Overview (the HTTP home page is **http://www.w3.org/Protocols/**), the following transmission issues will be addressed: batching and pipelining of messages, chunking and multiplexing of messages, and efficient record marking to determine the message length.

► INTRODUCING COOKIES

Cookies are a way for a Web site to check that a user has visited the site previously. Cookies also can help the user who visits a site again and again: Cookies may contain user information so that the user can be directed to a particular page or may not have to register again.

Cookies are text files stored on the client computer. The information in a cookie file is sent from the Web site server to the client computer through an HTTP transaction. Of course, in order for cookies to work, the user must not have turned them off in his or her browser. For more information about cookies, refer to Chapter 25.

CROSS-REFERENCE

For information about posting forms using built-in ASP Request objects, refer to Chapter 19.

FIND IT ONLINE

RFC1867 (**http://info.internet.isi.edu/in-notes/rfc/files/rfc1867.txt**) contains the latest HTTP upload methods.

Listing 14-4: A Sample Form

```
<FORM ACTION="cgi-bin/form-example" ←❶
METHOD="POST"> ←❷                                ❸
<B>Name: </B><INPUT TYPE="text" NAME="name"
SIZE="59"><BR>
<B>E-Mail Address: </B><INPUT TYPE="text"
NAME="email" SIZE="50"><BR>
<B>Street Address: </B><INPUT TYPE="text"
NAME="addr1" SIZE="51"><BR>
<B>City: </B><INPUT TYPE="text" NAME="city"
SIZE="61">
<P><INPUT TYPE="submit" VALUE="Send Data">
<INPUT TYPE="reset" VALUE="Clear Data">
</FORM>
                                  ❹
```

Listing 14-5: An Example of a Multipart Form

```
<HTML><HEAD>
<TITLE>A Sample Form</TITLE>
</HEAD><BODY>
<FORM action="http://server.dom/cgi/handle"
      enctype= "multipart/form-data" ←❶
      method="post">
<P>What is your name?
<INPUT type="text" name="sub_name">        ←❷
<BR>What files are you sending?
<INPUT type="file" name="sub_files">        ←❸
<P><INPUT type="submit" value="Send Now"> ←❹
<INPUT type="reset" value="Start Over">
</FORM>
</BODY></HTML>
```

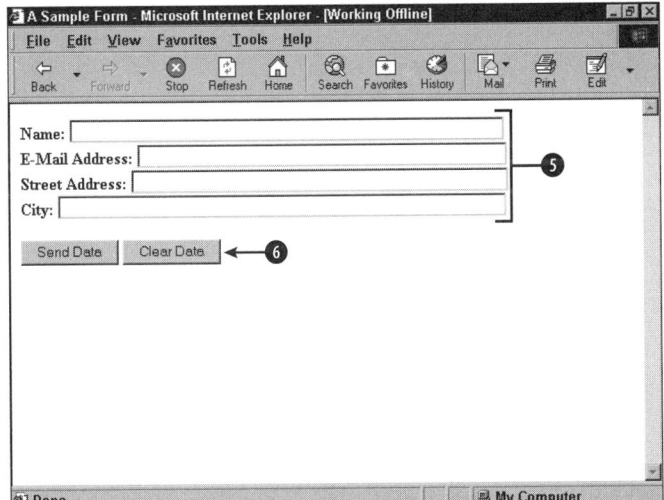

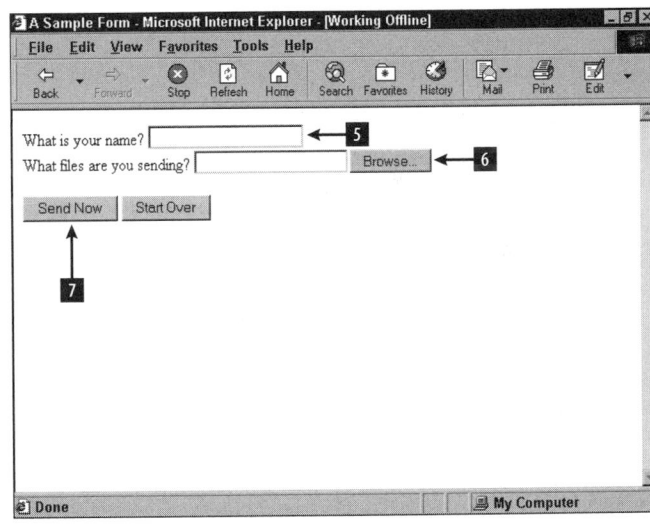

❶ This is the name of the processing file.

❷ This method posts the form and its data to the processor.

❸ Create, name, and size the form fields.

❹ Insert the buttons and add button values.

❺ Create, name, and size the form fields.

❻ Insert the buttons and add button values.

1 This encoding type defines forms that contain files or binary data.

2 Type your name.

3 Select a file to be submitted.

4 Send the form.

5 Type your name.

6 Select a file to be submitted.

7 Click on the Submit button.

219

Building Interfaces: Scripts on the Client

According to the HTML 4.0 recommendation, "a *client-side script* is a program that may accompany an HTML document or be embedded directly in it. The program executes on the client's machine when the document loads, or at some other time such as when a link is activated. HTML's support for scripts is independent of the scripting language." So, a client-side script runs on a browser that is installed and active on the user's computer.

When you develop HTML documents, success depends on many factors — ranging from the simple to complex. For example, it's critical (but not particularly challenging) to spell the names of elements correctly, use the proper delimiters, and add attributes that are supported by the latest version of HTML. If you design your documents to run only on the client side (that is, on the user's browser), you should make sure that the most popular browsers support all the technologies that you implement.

What is the process by which a user accesses a Web page with one or more client-side scripts? First, the user clicks a link or types in a URL to request the page. The Web site's server transmits the page to the user's browser, which must be able to recognize the language in which the script was written to interpret the script. The browser interprets the HTML code, executes scripts, and displays the page in the browser's application window. If a user has to perform an action (such as clicking a mouse button or pressing a key on the keyboard) to display part of the page, that processing occurs after the action — but still in the browser window. As you can see, this process involves very little interaction with the server — just the request for the page and the transmittal to the client. The client machine does most of the work and uses many more resources than the server. So, using client-side scripts provides one definite advantage: the server does very little processing. However, older client computers may have a difficult time handling large chunks of client-side scripts. Typically, server computers are more powerful than client computers. So, if

you're concerned about the ability of some of your user's computers to handle your scripts, you may have to consider the alternative: server-side scripts. Read on.

TAKE NOTE

▶ COMMENTING YOUR SCRIPTED DOCUMENTS

In Chapter 9, the "Making Your Documents Easier to Understand" Take Note discusses the importance of adding comments to your documents. As a document grows more complex, comments become much more important. You may have noticed the lack of comments in the examples in this book. This is not a case of "do as I say, not as I do." It's simply a space-saving maneuver; we'd like to show you as many lines of code as possible.

▶ EXPLORING THE DOCUMENT OBJECT AND document.write STATEMENT

In client-side scripting, *document object* is the name for an element in a document. So, when you want to display a document object onscreen, you issue the document.write command (in other words, *write* this *document* object). In VBScript, use the following syntax:

```
document.write "a string"
```

And in JScript, use this syntax:

```
document.write("a string");
```

Note that VBScript is case-insensitive, but JScript is case-sensitive.

In the "Learning How to Write in ASP" Take Note in the following task, you will find out about response.write, which is the ASP version of document.write.

CROSS-REFERENCE

To enhance your knowledge of components of HTML and XML documents, read Chapter 6.

FIND IT ONLINE

The miningco.com HTML home page (**http://html.miningco.com/ index.htm**) has many links to other HTML-related pages.

Listing 14-6: Client-Side Scripted Greetings

```
<HTML>
<HEAD>
<TITLE>Testing Scripts</TITLE>
</HEAD>
<BODY>
<H2>What languages does this browser support?
</H2>
<SCRIPT>
document.write("Hello world! This is the
default language: VBScript, JavaScript, or
JScript.")
</SCRIPT>
<BR>
<SCRIPT LANGUAGE="VBSCRIPT">
document.write("Hello again! This is
VBScript.")
</SCRIPT>
<BR>
<SCRIPT LANGUAGE="JavaScript">
document.write ("Hi! Can you read
JavaScript?");
</SCRIPT>
<BR>
<SCRIPT LANGUAGE="JScript">
document.write ("Aloha! I'm talking in
JScript.");
</SCRIPT>
</BODY>
</HTML>
```

❶ Write a script without naming the language.

❷ Create a VBScript script.

❸ Produce a JavaScript script.

❹ Write a JScript script.

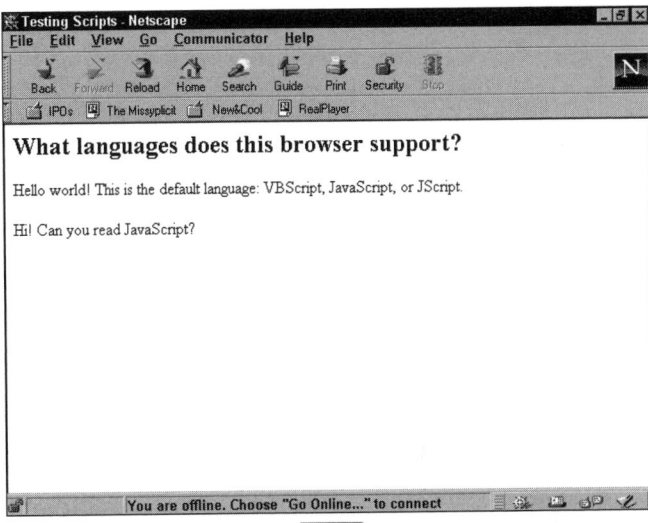

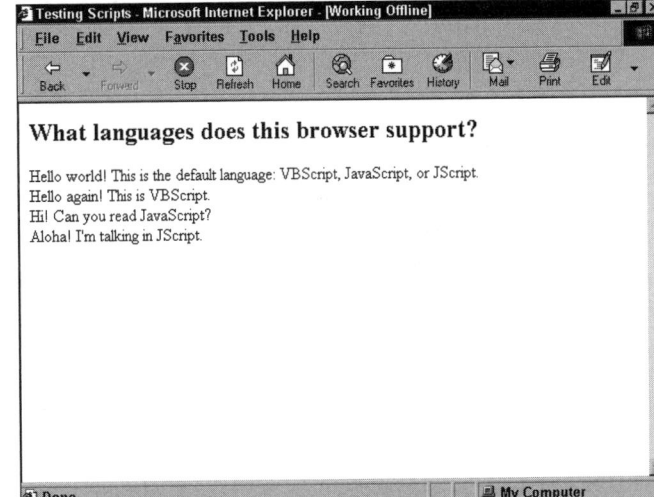

▶ Netscape Navigator obviously recognizes JavaScript, but there's a space where the VBScript greeting should be. So, JavaScript must be the default.

▶ Internet Explorer supports all three languages, so it's impossible to know the default language.

Building Documents: Scripts on the Server

On the surface, client-side scripts and server-side scripts look exactly alike — except for the delimiters: The beginning and end of a client-side script is marked by the `<SCRIPT>` and `</SCRIPT>` tags, and the section of server-side script starts with the `<%` delimiter and ends with `%>`. The main difference between the two types of scripts is the way in which they are interpreted. Server-side scripts are rendered in a different way than client-side scripts. Before the user clicks a link or types in a URL, the server has already executed the scripts. So, the browser does not have to support the language in which the script is written. When the user requests the page, the final results appear in the browser window.

Browser compatibility for client-side scripts is worth its own paragraph. For example, at the time that this book was written, Netscape Navigator supported JavaScript but did not support VBScript. In contrast, Microsoft Internet Explorer supported both JavaScript and VBScript. So, client-side processing of VBScript scripts would result in very different pages for these two popular browsers: Navigator would ignore the VBScript scripts, leaving empty space onscreen, but Internet Explorer would interpret them completely — if they were written properly. The "Detecting Browser Versions from the Server" task in Chapter 18 contains more information about testing browser compatibility.

You can combine client-side and server-side scripts in the same document. The main advantage of this strategy is that you can let the user's computer perform some of the resource-heavy scripting, such as loading large images and using time to obtain user information. If you make the server interpret every bit of script in a document, you may overtax a very busy computer. One example of mixing client-side and server-side scripts is an e-commerce site that asks every first-time customer to complete an electronic sales slip with information that might help the marketing department target special offers to the customer. Client-side scripts can take care of collecting and validating customer information. Then, server-side scripts can transmit the information to the server at which the receiving database is stored.

TAKE NOTE

▶ LEARNING HOW TO DISPLAY OUTPUT IN ASP

In the "Exploring the Document Object and `Document.Write Statement`" Take Note in the preceding task, you found out about the document object and how to use the `document.write` command to display that object online or on the printed page. When you convert your client-side HTML documents to server-side ASP pages, you'll have to convert all your `document.write` lines to `response.write` lines. ASP's Response object transmits information from the server to the browser on the client computer, and `write` is a method of Response. (See the "Learning about JScript Methods" Take Note in Chapter 16.) So, `response.write` means write this response online or on the printed page. In VBScript, use the following syntax:

```
response.write "a string"
```

And in JScript, the `document.write` syntax is as follows:

```
response.write("a string");
```

Note that VBScript is case-insensitive, but JScript is case-sensitive.

▶ SCRIPTING IN SECRET

One of the side advantages of using server-side scripts is that your final code is hidden from those who might want to copy it. Remember that server-side scripts are interpreted before the user requests the page. When the page appears onscreen, its source code has been stripped of all server-side scripts.

CROSS-REFERENCE
To learn how to integrate databases and Web pages, see Chapters 23 and 24.

FIND IT ONLINE
An ASP site with many valuable site-development links is located at **http://www.iwebs.net/asp.asp**.

Listing 14-7: Server-Side Scripted Random Numbers

```
<HTML><HEAD>
<TITLE>Doing the Randomize Statement</TITLE>
</HEAD><BODY>
<% ←❶
Dim AValue ←❷
Randomize ←❸
For I = 1 to 10
   AValue = Int((8 * Rnd) + 1)
   response.write AValue          ←❹
   response.write "<BR>"
Next
%>
</BODY></HTML>
```

Listing 14-8: A Server-Side Array Example

```
<HTML><HEAD>
<TITLE>Displaying an Array</TITLE>
</HEAD><BODY>  ❶
<% Dim CurValue      ❷
CurValue = Array("Smith", "Green", "Taylor")
Name = CurValue(0) ← ❸
response.write "The current name is " + Name
response.write ".<BR>"
Name = CurValue(1)
response.write "The current name is " + Name
response.write ".<BR>"
Name = CurValue(2)
response.write "The current name is " + Name
response.write ".<BR>" %> ← ❹
</BODY></HTML>
```

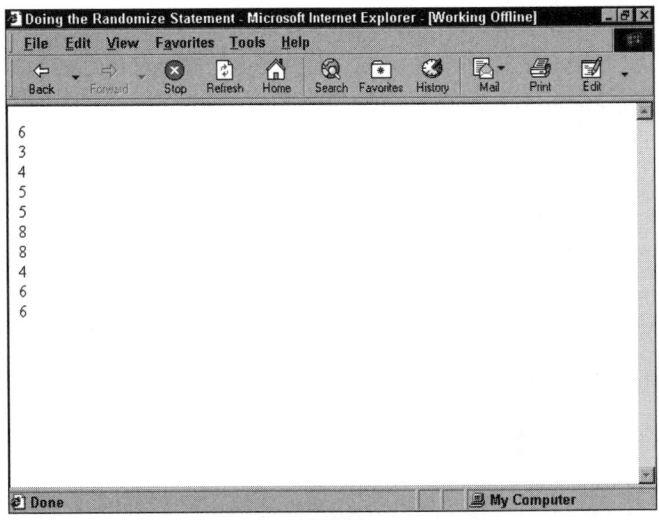

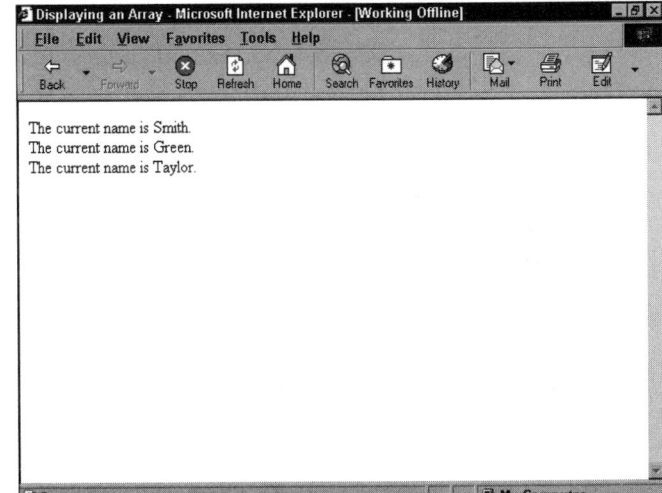

❶ Use <% and %> delimiters.

❷ Write a script without naming the language.

❸ Issue the Randomize statement.

❹ Generate and write ten random numbers.

❶ Use <% and %> delimiters.

❷ Declare an array consisting of three names.

❸ Arrays start with 0.

❹ Write the name, add a period, and break to the next line.

▶ The scripts run on the server, not the browser, so the user's computer resources are saved.

▶ The three names from the array appear onscreen.

223

Learning about the Windows Scripting Host

W hen DOS ruled the PC world, it was common practice to execute certain standard sets of commands with *batch files* or *batch programs*. Instead of entering commonly used commands one by one, you would enter them as lines in a batch file, save it with a .bat extension, and then execute it. The file would execute each of the commands for you. Batch files (and DOS) still exist under the fancy Windows user interface. For example, when you turn on a Windows 98 computer, the autoexec.bat and config.sys batch files, which specify basic settings for the computer, automate startup. Rather than entering each of these settings individually, you let the files do it.

The Windows Scripting Host (WSH), which is already installed on Windows 98 and Windows NT systems, is a scripting engine that can execute VBScript and JScript scripts (but not the Web pages in which the scripts are embedded) and supports all VBScript and JScript features and functions. In addition, WSH includes predefined functions that you can use to automate tasks related to Windows. For example, you can write scripts that include commands for adding, modifying, deleting, reading, and writing entries in the Registry; map network devices; and create or edit Windows shortcuts. You can also write a script that logs in to a network and connects all the servers.

WSH is one of Microsoft's Windows Script components, which include VBScript, JScript, the Windows or ActiveX Scripting Engine, COM Automation, and the Windows Script Components. WSH comes in two flavors: CSCRIPT, which is a DOS-like command-line utility, and WSCRIPT, which is a Windows applet.

To run CSCRIPT, open the MS-DOS window from within Windows, enter **CD \windows\command** to change to the folder in which CSCRIPT is stored, type **CSCRIPT**, and press Enter. (See the figure on the facing page.)

To run WSCRIPT, double-click one of the sample scripts stored in the \windows\Samples\WSH folder. (See the figures on the facing page.)

TAKE NOTE

▶ DOWNLOADING A COPY OF WSH

If you are running Windows 98 or Windows NT 4.0, a copy of WSH is already on your computer. However, if you have been running the same version of Windows for a while or you have an older Windows operating system that does not include a version of WSH (such as Windows 95), consider downloading a new version of WSH, which is included in the Windows Script Components (along with the latest versions of VBScript, JScript, and Windows Script Runtime). If you are using Windows 2000, a new, enhanced version of WSH is bundled.

To install WSH successfully, you must have already installed either Internet Explorer 4.0 (or greater), OSR2, or DCOM. After downloading the Windows Script Components executable file, open the folder in which it is located, and double-click the file to install the components.

The Windows Script download page is **http://www.microsoft.com/msdownload/vbscript/scripting.asp**. You can reach the WSH home page by linking to **http://msdn.microsoft.com/scripting/default.htm** and clicking Windows Script Host.

▶ VIEWING WSH SAMPLE SCRIPTS

After you use WSCRIPT to execute a sample script, you may want to look at the script. To view a sample script, click the Start button; select Programs, Accessories, and Notepad. In Notepad, choose Open from the File menu, change the Notepad's file type to All Files (*.*), go to the \windows\samples\WSH folder, and double-click the desired filename.

CROSS-REFERENCE

To get overviews of VBScript and JScript, see the first tasks in Chapters 15 and 16.

FIND IT ONLINE

The Windows Script Host page (**http://wsh.glazier.co.nz/home.asp**) contains WSH and scripting links.

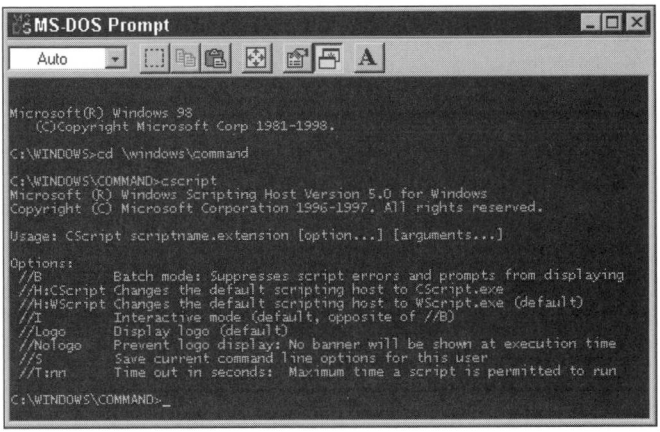

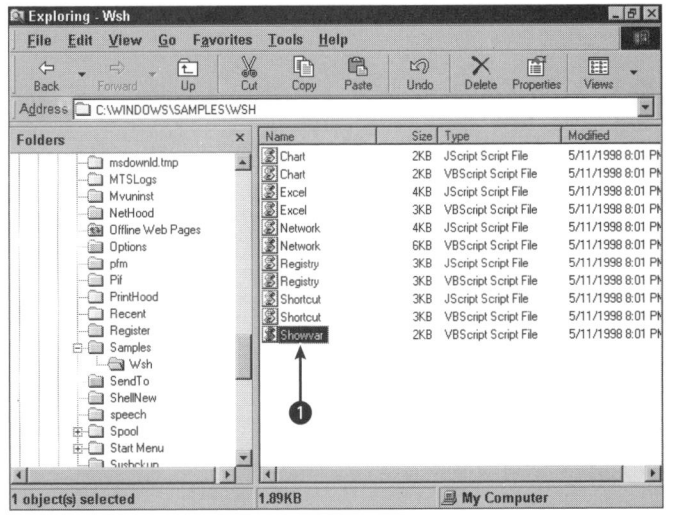

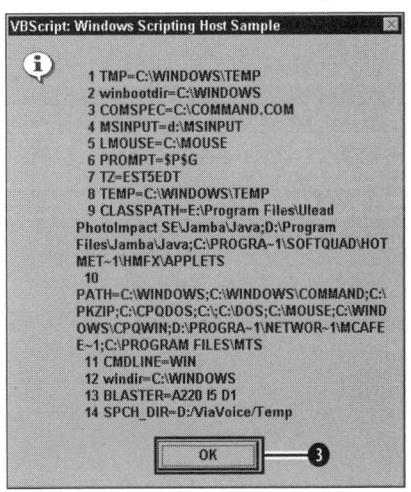

▶ To run a script, enter **cscript**, the filename, options, and arguments.

❶ Double-click the script's filename.

❷ Click OK.

❸ View the results, and click OK.

Personal Workbook

Q & A

1 What is the main difference between HTML documents and ASP pages?

_____

_____

_____

2 What are Server-Side includes?

_____

_____

_____

3 What is the only SSI supported by ASP?

_____

_____

_____

4 What are objects?

_____

_____

_____

5 Name five of HTML 4.0's intrinsic events.

_____

_____

_____

6 What are packets?

_____

_____

_____

7 What does the `document.write` command do?

_____

_____

_____

8 What is ASP's counterpart to the `document.write` command?

_____

_____

_____

ANSWERS: PAGE 506

EXTRA PRACTICE

1 Create a skeleton HTML document into which you will insert future scripts.

2 Prepare a timeline of client-server history.

3 Go online and do research on HTTP document transmission.

4 Go online and find tutorials for VBScript and JScript.

5 Go online and search for Web pages that use events to trigger actions. View or save the source code.

6 Go online and find a white paper on Web application architecture.

REAL-WORLD APPLICATIONS

✔ Your company has assigned you to write a report on when to use client-side scripts and when to use server-side scripts.

✔ Your small e-commerce site sells CDs to a young audience. You have decided to associate scripts with intrinsic events. Make a list of events and resulting actions that will become standards at your site.

✔ Now, you want to enhance forms-handling at your CD e-commerce site. Whenever a customer submits an order, you want to display a page that contains the completed form — except for the credit card number.

✔ You are in charge of Web-page development for your corporate intranet. Design a set of standards for converting paper reports to weekly and monthly Web-based reports.

Visual Quiz

Here is an HTML document that needs improvement with its architecture. Edit the document so that it is easier to understand.

_____

_____

_____

_____

_____

_____

```
Close Full Screen
<HTML><HEAD>
<TITLE>A Sample HTML Document</TITLE></HEAD>
<BODY BGCOLOR="white">
<H1>Lists</H1>
Thanks for visiting. On this page, you'll see an <A
HREF="http://www.eddygrp.com/OL">ordered list</A> and
an
<A HREF="http://www.eddygrp.com/UL">unordered
list.</A>
<H3>An Ordered List</H3>
<OL><LI>Do this step.
<LI>Then do this step.
<LI>Do it all over again starting at the top.</OL>
<H3>An Unordered List</H3>
<UL><LI>Planes
<LI>Trains
<LI>Automobiles
</UL>
<CENTER><IMG SRC="scene.gif"></CENTER>
</BODY></HTML>
```

CHAPTER **15**

MASTER
THESE
SKILLS

▶ **Learning about VBScript**

▶ **Including VBScript in Your Documents**

▶ **Using VBScript Variables**

▶ **Using VBScript Control Structures**

▶ **Building VBScript Programs**

Introducing VBScript

Visual Basic Scripting (VBScript) is a subset of Microsoft's Visual Basic, which in turn is an updated and sophisticated version of the BASIC programming language. Whether you are developing HTML documents or ASP pages, when you embed VBScript scripts, your documents can become dynamic and interactive. VBScript, which is bundled with both PWS (see Chapter 3) and IIS (see Chapter 4), is supported by Windows and Macintosh computers.

VBScript, which is both easy to learn and to use, is probably the most popular scripting language for novice to advanced ASP programmers. If you become familiar with VBScript, you can easily move up to Visual Basic in order to develop a variety of applications.

It's important to note that this chapter merely provides an overview of VBScript. For more detailed information about VBScript, go to Microsoft's scripting site (**http://msdn.microsoft.com/scripting/**) and click the VBScript link. At the VBScript site, you'll find a tutorial and a comprehensive language reference.

The tasks in this chapter introduce the basic VBScript components — starting with the most fundamental and ending with general programming concepts. So, in the first task, you'll be introduced to VBScript and discover the variety of VBScript scripts that you can use in your Web documents. The second task discusses how to include scripts in your HTML and ASP pages using combinations of elements, attributes, and delimiters. In the next task, you will learn about using variables in your VBScript scripts and differentiating among the three variable-declaring statements.

By default, when a script is executed, processing starts at the first line of code and finishes at the last line. In the fourth task, you will learn how to use conditional statements and looping statements to change the top-to-bottom flow when necessary. For example, you can write a script that runs one set of lines if a variable has a certain value and runs another set if the variable has a different value. Finally, in the last task in the chapter, you'll be ready to write simple VBScript programs by combining all the information that you have learned in the preceding tasks.

Throughout the chapter, Take Notes cover VBScript features as well as other important highlights of creating Web pages. You'll also learn the meaning of terms related to scripting and see plenty of real-life examples of VBScript at work.

Learning about VBScript

To make your HTML and ASP pages dynamic (for example, including buttons that change color when you move the mouse pointer over them) or interactive (for example, enabling a form to respond to a user's input), you can include VBScript scripts within your HTML documents. The scripts within a document are definitely not HTML, so you must identify them by using the SCRIPT element in HTML pages or unique delimiters (<% and %>) in ASP pages. You can include a script almost anywhere in a Web document. VBScript scripts run either on the client computer or the server; therefore, both HTML (which runs on the client) and ASP (which runs on the server) support VBScript. However, because this book is devoted to ASP, the scripting examples are server-side.

You can use VBScript scripts within the HEAD and BODY sections of your Web documents. For example, scripts that name variables that apply to the entire document or scripts that *initialize* (set initial values) belong in the HEAD section. In addition, scripts that always act in the same way on certain page elements (for example, in response to a mouse click on a element such as a button or list item) should be placed in the HEAD section. However, scripts that apply to a particular part of the document (for example, those that apply colors to bullets that are pointed to or those that change the size of text) should be inserted in the BODY section.

A document that includes a VBScript script requires special handling: It must be processed by an application that understands VBScript. Internet Explorer 4 (or greater) includes a VBScript processor that can interpret HTML documents with VBScript scripts; Netscape Navigator does not. ASP contains built-in support for VBScript (and JScript, which is covered in the following chapter). Without a VBScript processor, you and visitors to your site won't be able to view the results of your VBScript scripts.

CROSS-REFERENCE

To get an introduction to HTML and XML, look at "Exploring HTML" and "Introducing XML" in Chapter 5.

FIND IT ONLINE

Start to read the VBScript Language Reference at **http://msdn. microsoft.com/scripting/vbScript/doc/vbstoc.htm**.

Listing 15-1: A Scripted HTML Document

```
<HTML>
<HEAD>
<TITLE>Display the Date and Time</TITLE>
</HEAD>
<BODY>
<H2>Display the Date and Time</H2>
<P>The date and time are
<SCRIPT LANGUAGE="VBSCRIPT">
<!--
Document.Write(Now)
//-->
</SCRIPT>
.
</BODY></HTML>
```

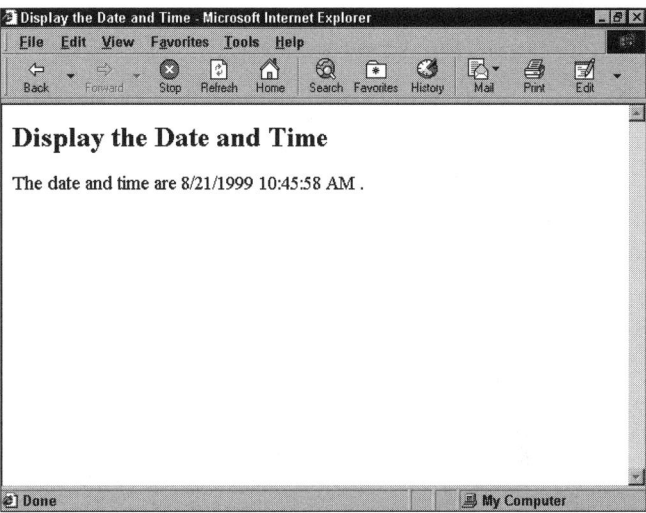

▶ *The resulting document displays the sentence, which combines text and scripting results and ends with a period — all on one line.*

1 Start the script with the SCRIPT element.
2 Identify the language as VBScript.
3 Now *displays the date and time automatically.*
4 End the sentence with a period outside the script.

Listing 15-2: A Counterpart ASP Page

```
<HTML>
<HEAD>
<TITLE>Display the Date and Time</TITLE>
</HEAD>
<BODY>
<H2>Display the Date and Time</H2>
<P>The date and time are
<%Response.Write(Now)%>.
</BODY></HTML>
```

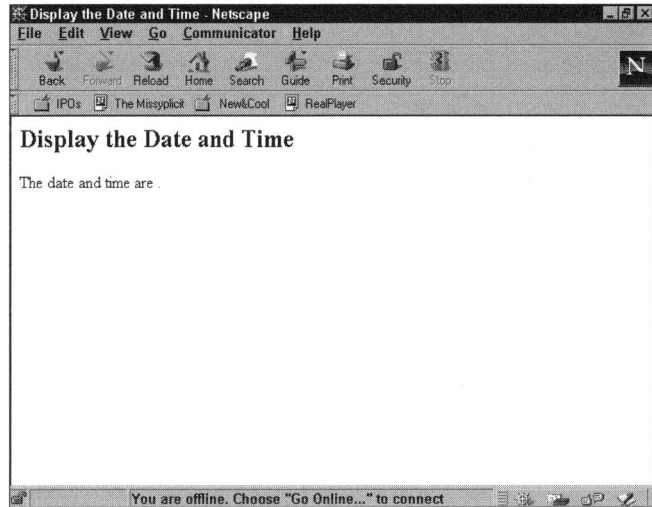

▶ *Without PWS or IIS running, Netscape Navigator does not support ASP. So, this figure shows incomplete results.*

5 Start the script with the <% delimiter.
6 Change Document *to* Response, *an ASP keyword.*
7 Complete the script with the %> delimiter.
8 End the sentence with a period outside the script.

Including VBScript in Your Documents

In HTML or ASP pages, you include VBScript scripts in different ways. In HTML documents, you identify the name of the scripting language, optionally state the location at which the script should run, and embed scripts using the SCRIPT element. For example:

```
<SCRIPT LANGUAGE="VBSCRIPT"
    RUNAT=SERVER>
<!-
    Const ConHello = "Hello, World!"
    Const ConNum01 = 123456
    Const ConDate01 = #8-6-70#
//->
</SCRIPT>
```

In the example, the `<SCRIPT>` start tag and `</SCRIPT>` end tag mark the beginning and end of the script. The LANGUAGE attribute names the scripting language, VBScript. The RUNAT attribute states that the script is run on the server. (By default, the script is run on the client computer.) The `<!–` and `//–>` delimiters represent comments. Comments that enclose scripts prevent older browsers, which do not support scripting, from displaying the script as document text. For more information about comments, see the "Commenting Your Documents and Scripts" Take Note in Chapter 1.

In ASP pages, you don't need to identify the language — VBScript is bundled with ASP. In addition, ASP always runs on the server, so there is no need for a RUNAT attribute and value. The prior HTML code would look like this in ASP:

```
<%
    Const ConHello = "Hello, World!"
    Const ConNum01 = 123456
    Const ConDate01 = #8-6-70#
%>
```

The `<%` and `%>` characters are *delimiters*, which indicate the start and end of the script and take the place of the `<SCRIPT>` and `</SCRIPT>` tags in HTML documents.

TAKE NOTE

USING VBSCRIPT CONSTANTS

A *constant* is a value that never changes. VBScript has predefined intrinsic constants: Empty, Nothing, Null, True, and False. A user can specify constants by using the Const statement. For example:

```
Const ConHello = "Howdy"
```

Notice that a literal is enclosed within quotation marks. A number does not require quotes:

```
Const ConFive = 5
```

Enclose a constant date or time within pound signs. For example:

```
Const ConStart = #5-16-88#
```

LEARNING ABOUT VBSCRIPT OPERATORS

Programming languages incorporate operators with which you can calculate or test values. VBScript provides arithmetic, comparison, and logical operators — which are evaluated in that order and from left to right within expressions. Expressions within parentheses are processed before expressions outside parentheses. Arithmetic operators are evaluated in the following order: exponentiation (^), unary negation (–), multiplication (*) and division (/), integer division (\), modulus arithmetic (Mod), addition (+) and subtraction (–), and string concatenation (&). Comparison operators are evaluated in this order: equal to (=), not equal to (<>), less than (<), greater than (>), less than or equal to (<=), greater than or equal to (>=), and equivalent to (Is) and like. Logical operators are evaluated in the following order: Not, And, Or, Xor, Eqv, and Imp.

CROSS-REFERENCE

Chapter 6 contains information about elements, attributes, and other components of Web documents.

FIND IT ONLINE

To access the Microsoft VBScript Language Reference and Tutorial, go to **http://asp-help.com/vbscript.asp**.

Listing 15-3: Displaying Various Values

```
<HTML><HEAD>
<TITLE>Show Various Values</TITLE>
</HEAD><BODY> <%  ←❶
Dim Hello
Hello = "Hello, World"        ❷
Response.Write Hello %>
<P> <%  ←❶          ❹
Dim FixNum              ❷
FixNum = 1000000
Response.Write FixNum %>
<P> <%  ←❶          ❹
Dim DateA               ❷
DateA = #4-17-67#
Response.Write DateA %>
</BODY></HTML>
                ❸
```

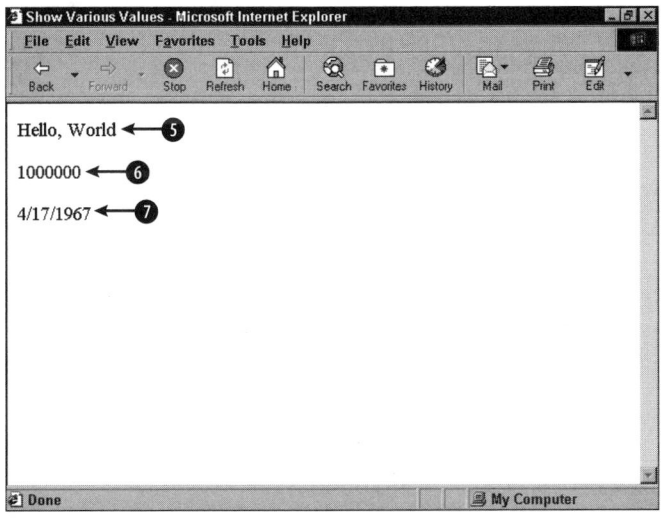

❶ Mark the beginning of the script.
❷ Declare a variable and give it a value.
❸ Write the variable in your document.
❹ Insert a paragraph break.
❺ Write a string.
❻ Show an integer.
❼ Display a date.

Listing 15-4: A Simple Calculation

```
<HTML><HEAD>
<TITLE>Calculate Some Numbers</TITLE>
</HEAD><BODY>
<% Dim Salary, Bonus, Income
Salary = 50000              ←❶
Bonus = 900
Income = Salary + Bonus ←❷
Response.Write Salary %>
<BR>+      ❹            ❹
<% Response.Write Bonus %>
<HR NOSHADE ALIGN="LEFT" WIDTH="45"> ←❸
<% Response.Write Income %>
</BODY></HTML>        ❹
```

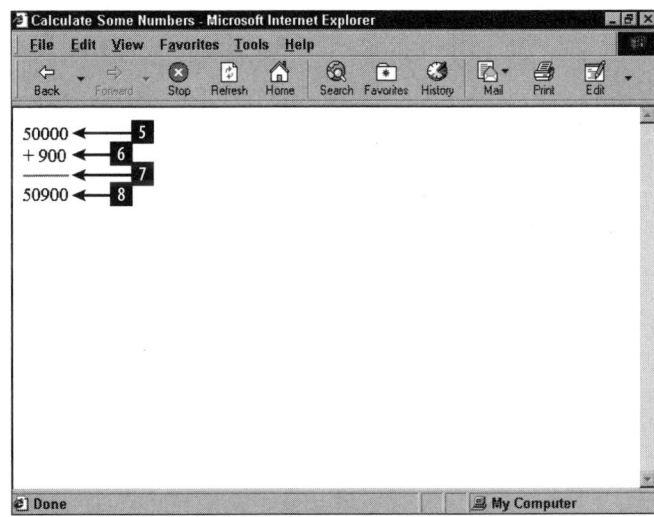

❶ Declare three variables and give values to two of them.
❷ Income is the result of adding Salary and Bonus.
❸ Insert a horizontal-rule underline.
❹ Write a variable.
❺ Write the salary.
❻ Include the bonus.
❼ Insert a horizontal-rule underline.
❽ Display the results of the calculation.

Using VBScript Variables

When you use a variable in your scripts, you don't have to enter the actual data itself; when the script is processed, the client or server program does it for you. Variables enable you to use "nicknames" or shortcuts to represent data, to allow a script to calculate value changes, and to enable you to replace one value with another quickly rather than "hard-coding" each instance of a value.

VBScript provides three statements — `Dim`, `Private`, and `Public` — with which you can declare variables.

The `Dim` statement declares an *array* (a list of one or more data values in one or more *dimensions*). Think of an array as a table of rows and columns of values. For example, a two-dimensional array has two columns of values.

```
Dim Terms(4)
Dim Terms()
Dim date01
```

The first line declares an array of five terms, starting at 0 and ending at 4. The second line declares a dynamic array, which is a list that can contain any number of values and dimensions. The third line declares a single element. Use the `ReDim` (*resize dim*ensions) statement to change the number of values and dimensions.

```
ReDim Terms(5, 3)
ReDim Preserve Terms (7, 2)
```

The first `ReDim` statement specifies an array of 6 rows and 4 columns, and the second declares 8 rows and 3 columns.

The optional `Preserve` keyword retains the original values of the array.

The `Private` statement declares a list of variables that are available only in the script in which it is coded. For example:

```
Private PrivNum
```

The `Public` statement declares one or more variables that are available to all scripting procedures in a document. It is very important to note that you must declare `Public`

statements outside specific procedures — for example, before any procedures are declared.

In the following example, three numbers are declared:

```
Public PubNum1, PubNum2, PubNum3
```

Names of variables, such as `Terms`, `PrivNum`, and so forth, must follow certain rules. A name must start with an alphabetic character, must not be longer than 255 characters, cannot contain a period (.), and must be unique.

After you declare a variable, you should give it a value. So, the value of a single variable can look like this:

```
PubNum1 = 246
```

TAKE NOTE

LEARNING ABOUT VBSCRIPT VARIANTS

In VBScript, the only possible data type is *variant*, which actually can contain a variety of data, ranging from character strings to numbers with various formats. VBScript is programmed to know the difference between characters and numbers. VBScript supports the following variants: **Boolean**, which has a value of either True or False; **Byte**, which is an integer with a value from 0 to 255; **Currency**, a negative or positive floating-point number with up to four places after the decimal point; **Date(Time)**, a number representing a date and an optional time; **Double**, a double-precision, floating-point, negative or positive number; **Empty**, which is either 0 or a null string (""); **Error**, an error number returned by the script; **Integer**, a positive or negative integer; **Long**, a positive or negative integer; **Null**, which represents no valid data; **Object**, which indicates an object; **Single**, a single-precision, floating-point, negative or positive number; and **String**, a variable length character string.

CROSS-REFERENCE

To learn how to place interactive fill-in forms in your Web documents, see Chapter 12.

FIND IT ONLINE

Distinguish between VBScript and JScript at **http://msdn. microsoft.com/library/techart/msdn_vbnjscrpt.htm.**

Listing 15-5: Concatenated Strings

```
<HTML>
<HEAD>
<title>Examples of Strings</title>
</HEAD>
<BODY>
<% Dim StrFirst, StrMiddle, StrLast, _  ←❶
   StrName
StrFirst = "Sandra"
StrMiddle = "E."  ←❷
StrLast = "Eddy"
StrName = StrFirst & StrMiddle & StrLast
Response.Write StrName %>
<P>
              ❸  ❹
<% StrName = StrFirst & " " & _  ←❶
   StrMiddle & " " & StrLast
Response.Write StrName %>
</BODY></HTML>
              ❹  ❸
        ❸
```

❶ Continue long lines with the underscore character.

❷ Give a string value to each variable.

❸ Join the strings by using ampersands (&).

❹ Insert spaces between the strings.

Listing 15-6: A Single String

```
<HTML>
<HEAD>
<TITLE>Another String Example</TITLE>
</HEAD>
<BODY>
<% Dim StrJoined
StrJoined = "Sandra E. Eddy"
Response.Write StrJoined %>
</BODY></HTML>
```

▶ If a string will always be joined in one way, why not name it as a single variable? Then, you can include the proper spaces within the string.

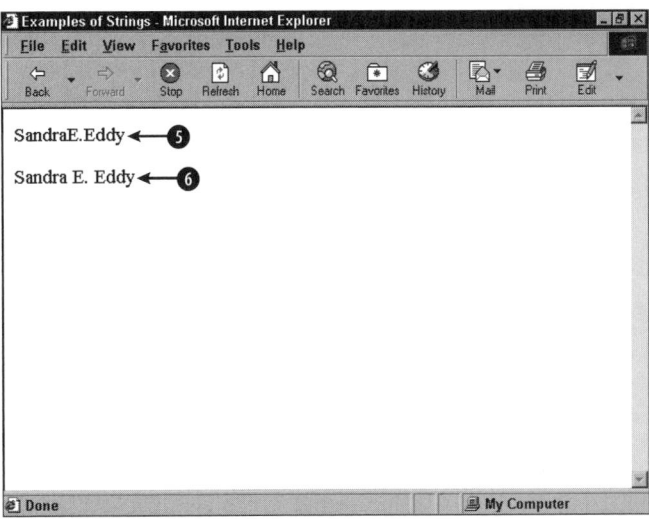

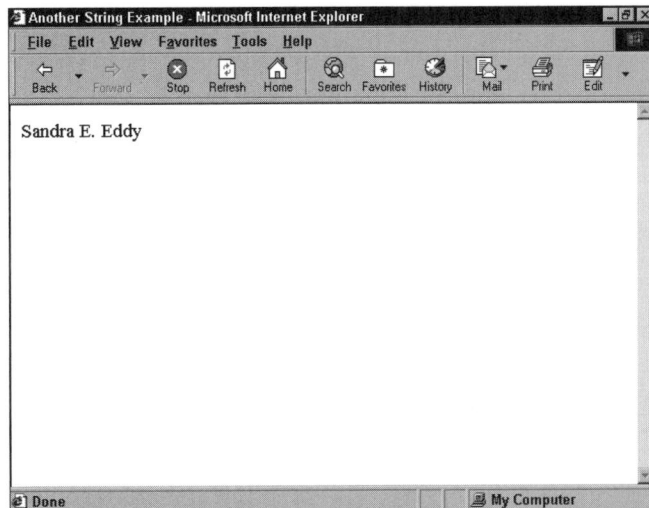

❺ These strings that run together are joined by ampersands.

❻ These strings are separated by spaces and ampersands.

▶ This figure displays the single string. There is no need to concatenate strings if one string will do.

Using VBScript Control Structures

In Web documents, processing normally flows from the top line of code to the bottom line. *Conditional statements* include branches to different sections of a script, thereby breaking the top-to-bottom flow. If a certain condition is met, one section of the script is processed; if an alternate condition is met, another section is processed. So, a script could branch to one section and process it if a value is greater than 5 or to another section if that value is less than 5. This example from Microsoft's VBScript Tutorial shows a simple conditional statement:

```
Sub FixDate()
    Dim myDate
    myDate = #2/13/95#
    If myDate < Now Then myDate = Now
End Sub
```

In the first line, the Sub keyword indicates the beginning of a *subroutine*, a section of script that is processed as a unit. The second line declares the myDate variable. The following line gives myDate a date value. The fourth line sets the conditions for processing: If myDate is less than the current system date and time, set myDate to the current system date and time. Otherwise, go to the End Sub line, which is the end of the subroutine. Then, processing continues — at the line following the line from which the subroutine was called. VBScript also provides another conditional statement, Select Case.

Looping statements repeatedly calculate a formula nested within the loop until a particular value is reached or a condition remains or becomes true. VBScript supports four types of looping statements: Do... Loop, While... Wend, For Each... Next, and For... Next.

Do... Loop keeps looping as long as a condition is true or when a false condition becomes true. For example:

```
Sub IterateIt()
    Dim ItNum
    ItNum = 0
    Do Until ItNum = 10
        ItNum = ItNum + 1
    Loop
    MsgBox "ItNum is finally " & ItNum"
End Sub
```

The initial value of ItNum is set in the third line. The fourth line, which starts the Do... Loop, states that looping continues until ItNum equals 10. The fifth line is a formula that adds 1 to ItNum, so ItNum will have succeeding values of 1, 2, and so forth, until it reaches the top value of 10 and the loop ends. The following line displays the current value of ItNum in a message box, and Loop marks the end of the loop lines. As long as ItNum is not equal to 10 (that is, ItNum is false), the lines within the loop continue to process.

The For... Next and For Each... Next statements also use counters to automate processing. The For... Next counterpart to the prior Do... Loop is:

```
For k = 0 To 10 Step 1
    ItNum = ItNum + k
    MsgBox "ItNum is now " & ItNum & "
Next
```

The Step keyword enables you to set a value by which the variable is increased or decreased. For Each... Next enables you to write individual statements for multiple items in an array.

While... Wend keeps looping as long as a condition is true. Use Do... Loop instead.

TAKE NOTE

MULTIPLE IF... THEN... ELSE STATEMENTS

You can write a script that tests several instances of If... Then... Else statements. Simply replace the Else that normally starts the last branching formula with an ElseIf, which ends the current If statement and starts another.

CROSS-REFERENCE
Chapter 14 introduces you to client- and server-based scripts and other contents of an ASP document.

FIND IT ONLINE
Use Internet Explorer to view the VBScript examples linked from **http://mavweb.net/vbs/toc.asp**.

Listing 15-7: Testing Weather Conditions

```
<HTML><HEAD>
<TITLE>How's the Weather?</TITLE>
</HEAD><BODY>
<% Dim Temp
Temp = 30
If Temp <= 32 Then
  Response.write "It's freezing out here!"
ElseIf Temp > 32 Then
  Response.write "It's warming up."
End If %>
</BODY></HTML>
```

① Set the temperature to 30 degrees.
② Display text if the temperature is freezing...
③ Or text if the temperature is above freezing.

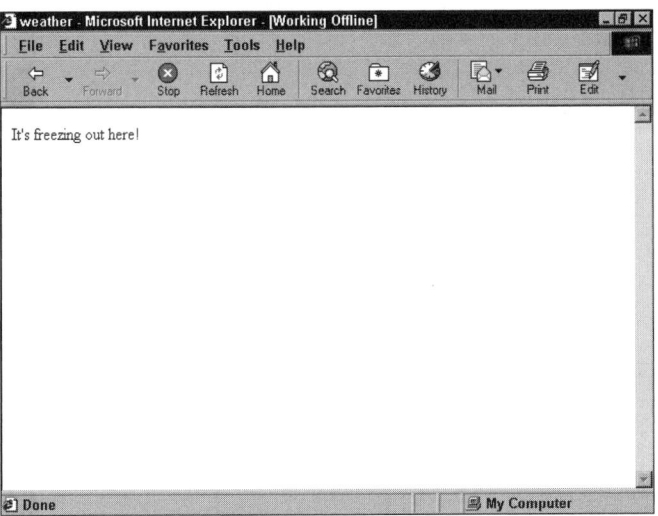

▶ The text in your browser window proves the accuracy of the script.
You can test the script by changing the temperature to above
freezing.

Listing 15-8: A Looping Example

```
<HTML><HEAD>
<TITLE>Loopy Loop</TITLE>
</HEAD>
<BODY>
<% Dim ChangeNum, Counter
For ChangeNum = 1 To 10 Step 2
Counter = Counter + ChangeNum
Response.Write "The current count is " _
& Counter
Response.Write ".  "
Next
Response.Write "The final count is " _
& Counter
%>
</BODY></HTML>
```

1 Accumulate successive values of ChangeNum automatically.
2 Add the current ChangeNum value to the current Counter
total.
3 Display the current Counter value continually.
4 Display the final Counter count in a message box.

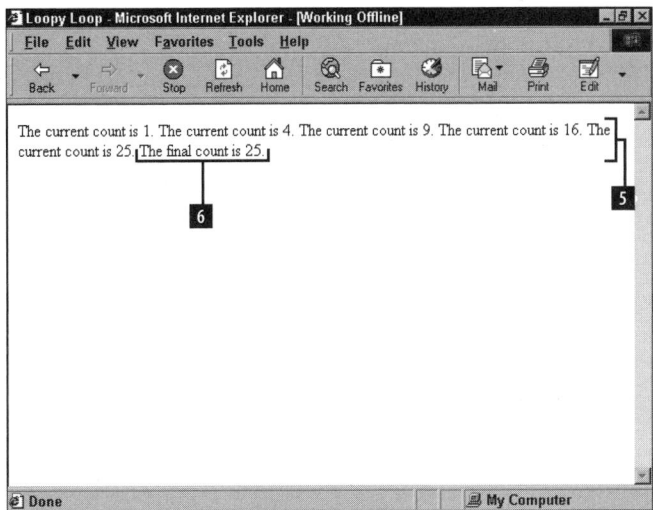

5 Display the current Counter value continually.
6 Display the final Counter count in the last sentence.

Building VBScript Programs

VBScript is a subset of Microsoft's Visual Basic, which is a full-featured programming language. Most programs start with the naming of constants and variables and the setting of initial values. Then, the logic and calculations begin. The same thing happens with long scripts embedded within ASP pages. The only difference is that the VBScript program is broken from time to time by HTML statements just to control the look of the Web page. For example:

```
<%
Dim YesOrNo, CurValue
CurValue = "No"
For YesOrNo = 1 to 8
  If Color(YesOrNo) = :"Blue" Then
    CurValue = "Yes"
    Exit For
  End If
Next
If CurValue = "Yes" Then
%>
The color is blue
<% Else %>
Blue is not on this list
<% End If %>
```

The example checks whether Blue is among the eight items on a list. If the script finds Blue, it ends the For... Next statement before the count has completed by interpreting the Exit For statement. Exit For sends the processor to the first line after the For... Next statement. Because in the following line, CurValue equals Yes, *The color is blue* appears. If Blue doesn't appear on the list after the eighth item, the count has reached the end. Because CurValue does not equal Yes, *Blue is not on this list* is displayed. Remember that the <% and %> delimiters indicate the start and end of scripts in ASP document. So you'll see that the VBScript script is interrupted by HTML statements — namely, *The color is blue* and *Blue is not on this list*.

TAKE NOTE

TROUBLESHOOTING VBSCRIPT-BASED ASP PAGES

When VBScript scripts don't work, troubleshoot by asking yourself these three basic questions:

1 Is the file containing the script located in a folder that the server recognizes?
2 Does the file have an .asp file extension?
3 Is the server active?

If the results of the script still don't appear, check both the script and the ASP document for errors. When you are a novice encountering problems, it's a good idea to write a simple script within a short ASP page. When that works properly, add more lines to your script — testing after each addition.

LEARNING ABOUT THE VBSCRIPT FUNCTION PROCEDURE

A subroutine is a *procedure*, a series of VBScript statements enclosed within start and end statements — in the case of a subroutine, the Sub and End Sub statements. The Function procedure, which starts with the Function statement and ends with the End Function statement, is similar to the Sub procedure. A typical Function procedure looks something like this example from the Microsoft VBScript tutorial:

```
Function Celsius(fDegrees)
    Celsius = (fDegrees – 32) * 5 / 9
End Function
```

and the resulting converted temperature is displayed as follows:

```
Response.Write "The Celsius temperature
is " & Celsius(fDegrees) & "
```

CROSS-REFERENCE

Chapters 16 and 17 discuss other scripting languages: JScript, JavaScript, ECMAScript, and PerlScript.

FIND IT ONLINE

A VBScript tutorial starts at **http://msdn.microsoft.com/scripting/vbScript/doc/vbswhat.htm.**

Listing 15-9: A VBScript Program

```
<HTML><HEAD>
<TITLE>Warehouse Matching System</TITLE>
</HEAD><BODY>
<% Sub Barre ←①
   Response.Write "order from Denny "
   Response.Write "at Barre, 555-555-1200." ←②
End Sub ←③
Sub Reno ←①
   Response.Write "order from Mary "
   Response.Write "at Reno, 555-555-1201." ←②
End Sub ←③
Sub Tampa ←①
   Response.Write "order from Sam "
   Response.Write "at Tampa, 555-555-1202." ←②
End Sub %>
<H4>Warehouse Matching System</H4>
                                    ←③
Every year, we will change the
warehouses from which you can order
manufacturing inventory. This year's
locations are listed on this page.
<H5>Handlebars</H5>
For handlebars,
<% Call Tampa %> ←④
<H5>Frames</H5>
For aluminum frames,
<% Call Reno %><BR>
For titanium frames,  ←④
<% Call Tampa %> ←④
<H5>Saddles</H5>
For saddles,
<% Call Barre %> ←④
<H5>Sprockets</H5>
For sprockets,
<% Call Tampa %> ←④
</BODY></HTML>
```

① *Start a subroutine.*

② *Provide information about a warehouse.*

③ *End the subroutine.*

④ *In VBScript, call a subroutine.*

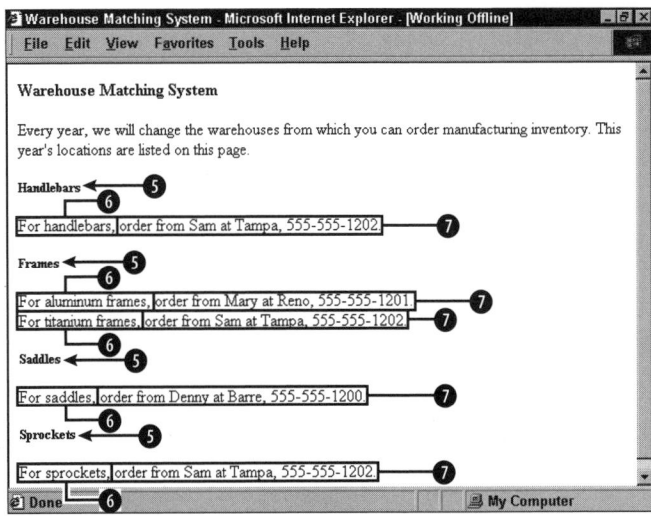

⑤ *Insert a heading for a piece of inventory.*

⑥ *Start a sentence.*

⑦ *The rest of the sentence comes from a subroutine.*

Personal Workbook

Q & A

1 What is VBScript's full name? What is VBScript's origin?

_____

_____

_____

2 Can VBScript scripts run on a client computer?

_____

_____

_____

3 What is a constant? What VBScript statement do you use to specify a constant?

_____

_____

_____

4 What is a variable?

_____

_____

_____

5 What is a conditional statement?

_____

_____

_____

6 What is a subroutine? How do you mark the beginning and end of a VBScript subroutine?

_____

_____

_____

7 What is a looping statement?

_____

_____

_____

8 What type of looping statement keeps looping as long as a condition is true or when a false condition becomes true?

_____

_____

_____

ANSWERS: PAGE 507

1 Go online and using the Microsoft VBScript Language Reference, learn ten VBScript functions.

2 Write a VBScript script that uses VBScript date and time constants to list the days of the week. Be sure to insert spaces or line breaks between the days.

3 Write a VBScript script that separates a text string into three individual components.

4 Write a VBScript script that fills a page with your favorite motto.

5 Write a VBScript script that produces ten random numbers. (Hint: Look up the Randomize statement.)

6 Go online and find three sources of VBScript scripts.

✔ You have been assigned to write an ASP page template that inserts information, such as today's date or the current date and time, at the bottom of every page.

✔ As a novice Web page writer for a developer of HTML and ASP sites, your first assignment is to convert a set of HTML documents with VBScript scripts to ASP pages.

✔ As an HTML-to-ASP page converter, write a set of procedures for helping novices convert pages.

✔ You are a third-grade teacher with your own Web site. For your students, write a VBScript program that displays a multiplication table within the cells of an HTML table.

Visual Quiz

This HTML document includes a VBScript script that has not been tested. Correct the errors, and convert the document to an ASP page.

```
visual quiz 15 - Notepad
File  Edit  Search  Help
<HTML>
<HEAD>
<title>Visual Quiz 15</title>
</HEAD>
<BODY>
<SCRIPT LANGUAGE="VBSCRIPT"
    RUNAT=SERVER>
Dimm Arrividerci, Adios
Greeting = "Hi There"
Adios = "aloha"
Document.Write Greeting
Document.Write Adios
Doucment.Write "Goodbye Again"
</SCRIPT>
</HTML>
```

CHAPTER 16

Introducing JScript, JavaScript, and ECMAScript

JScript, JavaScript, and ECMAScript are nearly identical scripting languages that are distant relatives of the Java programming language. When you incorporate scripts from these languages into your HTML or ASP documents, your Web pages can become active and you will actually be able to communicate with visitors to your site. JScript, JavaScript, and ECMAScript are languages that experienced programmers will find it easy to learn and to use. If you are a Java, C, or C++ programmer, you will definitely know the underlying structure and logic of these scripting languages.

JScript is bundled with both PWS (see Chapter 3) and IIS (see Chapter 4). So, the focus of this chapter (and all of the examples) is on JScript. However, because ASP is an open platform, you can use JavaScript or ECMAScript scripts, too. You'll just have to download the language to use it successfully with your ASP pages. Although JScript, JavaScript, and ECMAScript are virtually the same language, you may have to make minor changes in your code if you move from one of these languages to another.

Because JScript is a complex scripting language, this chapter cannot provide detailed information. For more detailed information about JScript, go to Microsoft's scripting site (**http://msdn.microsoft.com/scripting/**) and click on the JScript link. At the JScript site, you'll find a tutorial and a comprehensive language reference.

The tasks in this chapter introduce the basic JScript components — starting with the most fundamental and ending with general programming concepts. In fact, the chapter almost completely echoes Chapter 15 and its VBScript features.

In the first task, you'll be introduced to JavaScript, JScript, and ECMAScript. The second task shows you how to include JScript scripts in your HTML and ASP pages. Then, you'll find out how to use variables in your VBScript.

In the fourth task, you'll discover how to change the flow of document-processing from the usual top-to-bottom: You'll find out about JScript's conditional statements and looping statements. In the final task, you'll learn how to combine all your learning into simple JScript programs.

Throughout the chapter, Take Notes cover JScript features. The chapter features many JScript examples. As you read through this chapter, you can compare the JScript examples with the VBScript examples in Chapter 15. Each code listing in this chapter has a VBScript counterpart in Chapter 15.

Learning about the Types of Java-Based Scripting Languages

I n the preceding chapter, you learned how easy it is to write VBScript scripts. JavaScript, JScript, and ECMAScript, which are all closely-related scripting languages based on the Java programming language, might be right up your alley if you have programming experience in Java, C, or C++.

JavaScript

JavaScript was developed by Netscape Communications and Sun Microsystems and is the original Java-related scripting language. JavaScript was originally designed to be incorporated into Web pages read by the Netscape Navigator browser. JavaScript allows Web developers to produce dynamic documents and enables programmers to call routines written in Java, C, and C++.

JScript

After the inception of JavaScript, Microsoft developed JScript, which is virtually identical to JavaScript. JScript was able to run on the Microsoft Internet Explorer and read programs and applets written for Internet Explorer. JScript is bundled with ASP in both the IIS and PWS servers, so you don't have to make sure that it is on your computer system.

ECMAScript

Until recently, the only central JavaScript standard has been maintained by Netscape. In 1997, the European Computer Manufacturers Association (ECMA), a standards organization (**http://www.ecma.ch/**), released the first standard, known as ECMA-262 or ECMAScript. ECMAScript incorporates most — but not all — JavaScript features. JScript fully conforms to the ECMAScript standard. Although ECMAScript is a standard, Web browsers do not fully support it at this point. You can download ECMAScript manuals from **ftp://ftp.ecma.ch/ecma-st/e262-doc.exe** (Microsoft Word format) or **ftp://ftp.ecma.ch/ecma-st/e262-pdf.pdf** (Adobe Acrobat Reader format), or order a free CD-ROM (which is updated every six months).

TAKE NOTE

▶ RECOGNIZING SOME IMPORTANT DIFFERENCES BETWEEN JSCRIPT AND VBSCRIPT

As you will discover throughout this chapter, there are many differences between JScript and VBScript.

Perhaps the most critical difference is that JScript is case-sensitive, which means that you must enter elements of the language exactly as they appear in a JScript language reference (for example, `Date`). In contrast, VBScript is completely case-insensitive, so `DATE`, `date`, `Date`, and even `daTe` are all proper.

Another difference is that you should end every JScript line with a semicolon (`;`), which is not the case with VBScript lines. The lack of a semicolon may cause an error message or end of processing.

▶ LEARNING ABOUT JSCRIPT METHODS

The JScript language includes *methods*, which are keywords that act as attributes for objects. For example:

```
warning.fontsize(+2)
```

increases the size of the font for any occurrence of the `warning` object. JScript provides many methods, ranging from those that set color to those that perform mathematical calculations, and from those that set dates and time to those that place an HTML anchor (the `A` element) and name with a selected object.

CROSS-REFERENCE

To learn the basics of HTML and XML and the planning and design of Web documents, refer to Chapter 5.

FIND IT ONLINE

Microsoft's scripting home page (**http://msdn.microsoft.com/scripting/**) has links to JScript resources.

Listing 16-1: A Scripted HTML Document

```
<HTML><HEAD>
<TITLE>Display the Date and Time</TITLE>
</HEAD><BODY>
<H2>Display the Date and Time</H2>
<SCRIPT LANGUAGE="JSCRIPT" RUNAT=SERVER>
<!--
datetest=new Date();
//-->
</SCRIPT>
<P>The date and time are
<SCRIPT LANGUAGE="JSCRIPT" RUNAT=SERVER>
<!--
document.write(datetest);
//-->
</SCRIPT>
.
</BODY></HTML>
```

1 Start the script with the SCRIPT element.

2 Identify the language as JScript.

3 Declare the datatest variable.

4 Write datatest in the document.

Listing 16-2: A Counterpart ASP Page

```
<%@ LANGUAGE=JScript %>
<HTML><HEAD>
<TITLE>Display the Date and Time</TITLE>
</HEAD><BODY>
<H2>Display the Date and Time</H2>
<% datetest=new Date(); %>
<P>The date and time are
<% Response.Write(datetest); %>
.
</BODY></HTML>
```

5 Start the script with the <% delimiter.

6 Change Document to Response, an ASP keyword.

7 Enclose datetest within parentheses and always end with a semicolon.

8 Complete the script with the %> delimiter.

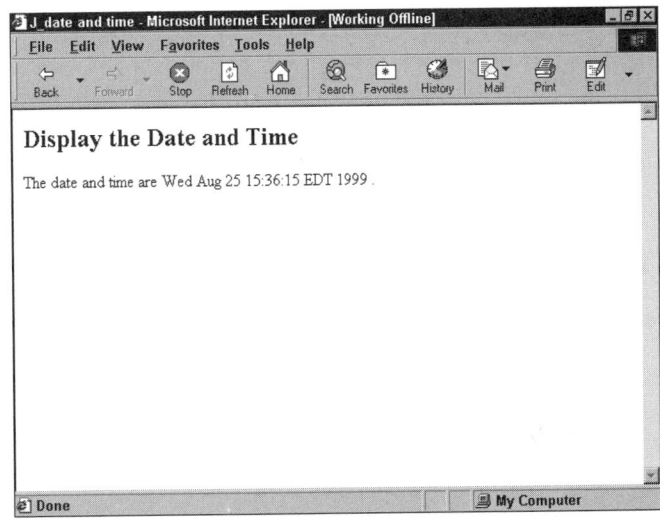

▶ The resulting document displays the sentence, which combines text and scripting results and ends with a period — all on one line.

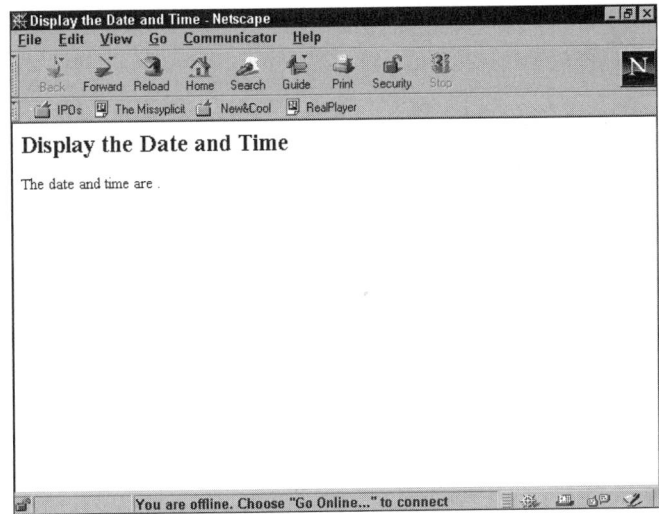

▶ Without PWS running, Netscape Navigator does not support ASP. So, this figure shows incomplete results.

Including JScript in Your Documents

Include JScript scripts differently in HTML and ASP pages. In HTML documents, you use the SCRIPT element and its attributes to mark the beginning and end of the script section, name the scripting language, and possibly give the location at which the script should run. For example:

```
<SCRIPT LANGUAGE="JSCRIPT"
    RUNAT=SERVER>
<!--
    Hello = "Hello, World! ";
    Num01 = 123456;
    Date01 = " 8-6-70";
//-->
</SCRIPT>
```

In the example, the start and end tags mark the scripting section. The LANGUAGE attribute states that JScript is the language in which the script is written. RUNAT states that the script is run on the server. The <!— and //—> delimiters are comments that prevent older non-scripting browsers from interpreting the script as document text. The spaces at the end of the Hello, World! value and at the beginning of 8-6-70 separate one variable from another when they are written. Make sure that you end each JScript line with a semicolon.

VBScript is the default scripting language for ASP. So, identify JScript explicitly as follows:

```
<%@ LANGUAGE=JScript %>
```

However, there is no need for a RUNAT attribute because ASP runs on the server. So, after declaring JScript in the first line of the document, the preceding code would look like this in an ASP page:

```
<%
    Hello = "Hello, World! ";
    Num01 = 123456;
    Date01 = " 8-6-70";
%>
```

TAKE NOTE

LEARNING ABOUT JSCRIPT OPERATORS

JScript provides sets of computational, logical, bitwise, assignment, and miscellaneous operators to calculate or test values. Expressions within parentheses are processed before expressions outside parentheses. Then operators are evaluated in the following order: field access (.), array indexing ([ ]), and function calls (( )); increment (++), decrement (--), unary negation (-), bitwise NOT (~), and logical NOT (!); multiplication (*), division (/), and modulo division (%); addition of numbers (+), subtraction of numbers (-), and string concatenation (+); bitwise left shift (<<), bitwise right shift (>), and unsigned right shift (>>); less than (<), less than or equal to (<=), greater than (>), and greater than or equal to (>=); equal to (==), not equal to (!=), identical to (===), and not identical to (!==); bitwise AND (&); bitwise XOR (^); bitwise OR (|); logical AND (&&); logical OR (||); conditional (? :); and assignment (=), assignment with operation (OP=), and multiple evaluation (,).

LEARNING ABOUT JSCRIPT DATA TYPES

In Chapter 15, you learned that VBScript has one data type that encompasses several variants. In contrast, JScript has six data types. The **Number** type can be positive or negative integers expressed in decimal, hexadecimal, or octal; positive or negative floating-point numbers, which can be expressed in scientific notation; *NaN* (not a number); and positive or negative infinity or 0. **String** is a variable-length character string starting at 0 (""). **Object** simply indicates an object. **Boolean** has a value of either True or False. **Undefined** has no initial value, and **Null** represents no valid data.

CROSS-REFERENCE
In Chapter 6, you can learn about elements, attributes, and other basic parts of Web documents.

FIND IT ONLINE
The JavaScript Reference is at **http://developer.netscape. com/docs/manuals/communicator/jsref/contents.htm.**

Listing 16-3: Displaying Various Values

```
<%@ LANGUAGE=JScript %>
<HTML><HEAD>
<TITLE>Show Various Values</TITLE>
</HEAD>
<BODY>
<% Hello = "Hello, World";
Response.Write(Hello); %>
<P>
<% FixNum = 1000000;
Response.Write(FixNum); %>
<P>
<% DateA = "4-17-67";
Response.Write(DateA); %>
</BODY>
</HTML>
```

❶ Mark the beginning of the script.
❷ Declare a variable and give it a value.
❸ Write the variable in your document.
❹ Insert a paragraph break.

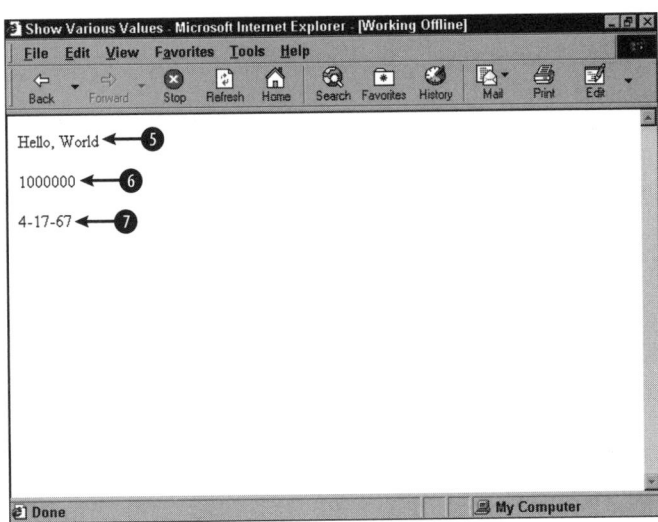

❺ Write a string.
❻ Show an integer.
❼ Display a date.

Listing 16-4: A Simple Calculation

```
<%@ LANGUAGE=JScript %>
<HTML><HEAD>
<TITLE>Calculate Some Numbers</TITLE>
</HEAD><BODY>
<%
Salary = 50000;
Bonus = 900;
Income = Salary + Bonus;
Response.Write(Salary); %>
<BR>+
<% Response.Write(Bonus); %>
<HR NOSHADE ALIGN="LEFT" WIDTH="45">
<% Response.Write(Income); %>
</BODY></HTML>
```

1 Implicitly declare three variables and give values to two of them.
2 Income is the result of adding Salary and Bonus.
3 Insert a horizontal-rule as an underline.
4 Write the Income.

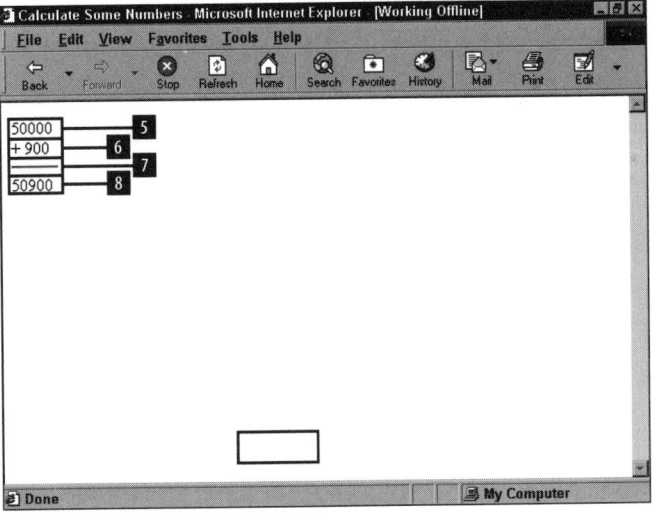

5 Write the salary.
6 Include the bonus.
7 Insert a horizontal-rule underline.
8 Display the results of the calculation.

Using JScript Variables

In Chapter 15, you learned that a variable is a user-defined name that represents varying data of all types — characters, digits, character strings, and so forth. (Note that the prior facing-page examples include variables.)

In JScript, when you give a variable a value, you state implicitly that the variable exists. For example:

```
ColorIt = "Red";
```

The name of the variable is on the left side of the equal sign, and its value is on the right. It's important to note that you should only declare a variable one time in a Web document — even one that incorporates several scripts.

You can use an array to declare multiple values for a variable. For example:

```
ColorIt = new Array(6);
ColorIt[0] = "Red";
ColorIt[2] = "Blue";
ColorIt[3] = "Green";
ColorIt[5] = "Cyan";
```

The first line of the example declares an array of seven variables, starting at 0 and ending at 6. Then four of the seven variables are given values. Be sure that you enclose the item number within brackets ([ ]), which are the characters that represent the array-index operator. And, as always, end each line with a semicolon.

What if you want to declare a variable without giving it a value until later in the Web document? Simply precede the variable declaration with the var keyword:

```
var ColorIt;
```

Of course, you can precede every variable with the var keyword. For example:

```
var ColorIt = "Red";
```

This example ensures that everyone knows you are declaring a variable. Variables also take multiple values:

```
var several = "Red", "Celtics", "Knicks";
```

Variables can even include a formula to be calculated as well as subvariables:

```
var ComputeThis = 50, count, frammis = 6;
```

So, you can see that a single variable can include numbers, text, and even other variables with their own values.

Names of JScript variables must follow certain rules: A name cannot be a reserved JScript keyword, cannot contain spaces, and must be unique. In fact, the more unique a name is, the less likely you will have to change it if JScript developers add another reserved keyword to the list.

TAKE NOTE

▶ QUESTIONING THE EXISTENCE OF JSCRIPT CONSTANTS

As you read through Chapter 15, you probably discovered that it's easy to confuse constants with variables in VBScript. You can see that there is little difference by looking at the following VBScript statements:

```
Dim Hello
Hello = "Howdy"
```

```
Const Hello = "Howdy"
```

Regardless of how you declare it, the resulting value for Hello is *Howdy*. For this and other reasons, JScript does not have a keyword with which you set the value of a constant explicitly.

▶ COMMENTING YOUR SCRIPTS

Regardless of the scripting language that you use, it's a good idea to add comments to your documents. In JScript, precede a single comment line with //. To add multiple-line comments, precede the first line with /* and end the last line with */.

CROSS-REFERENCE

To get an introduction and overview of Web forms and databases, refer to Chapter 12.

FIND IT ONLINE

A page of up-to-date JavaScript resources is located at http://www.jsworld.com/.

Listing 16-5: Concatenated Strings

```
<%@ LANGUAGE=JScript %>
<HTML><HEAD>
<TITLE>Examples of Strings</TITLE>
</HEAD><BODY>
<% StrFirst = "Sandra";
StrMiddle = "E.";
StrLast = "Eddy";
StrName = StrFirst += StrMiddle +=
StrLast;
Response.Write(StrName); %>
<P>
<% NameArray = new Array("Sandra", "E.",
"Eddy");
JndString = NameArray.join(" ")
Response.Write(JndString); %>
</BODY></HTML>
```

① Join the strings with the add-by-value (+=) operator.

② Create an array of strings.

③ Join the strings with the join method.

④ Insert a space between each string.

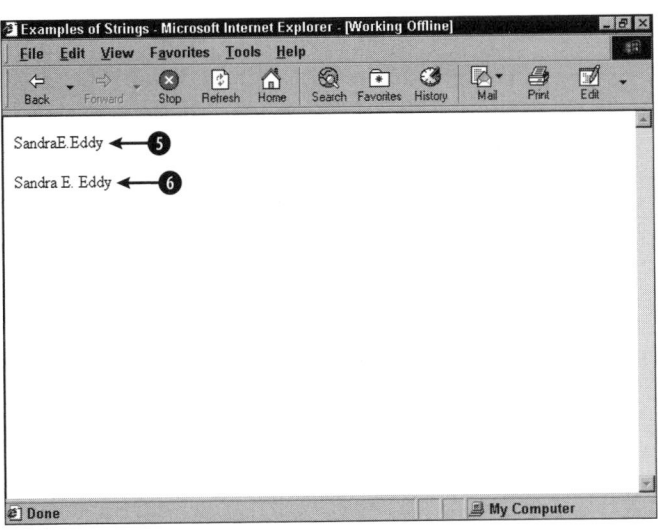

⑤ These strings that run together are joined by add-by-value operators (+=).

⑥ These joined strings are separated by spaces.

Listing 16-6: A Single String

```
<%@ LANGUAGE=JScript %>
<HTML><HEAD>
<TITLE>Examples of Strings</TITLE>
</HEAD><BODY>
<% StrFirst = "Sandra";
StrMiddle = " E. ";
StrLast = "Eddy";
StrName = StrFirst += StrMiddle += StrLast;
response.write(StrName); %>
</BODY></HTML>
```

▶ If you want to join three variables quickly, insert spaces before and after the middle variable.

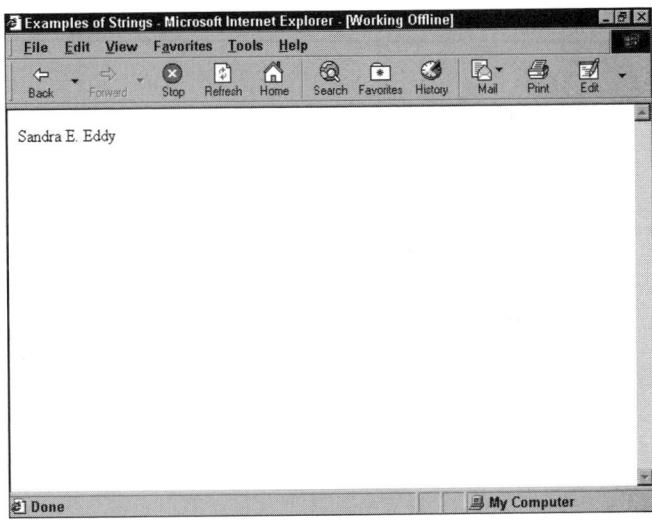

▶ This figure displays the single string. There is no need to concatenate strings if you need to work quickly.

Using JScript Control Structures

I n simple Web documents, processing starts at the top and ends on the last line of the document. In Chapter 15, you learned about conditional statements, which branch to different parts of the document. Conditional statements are designed to interrupt the top-to-bottom flow. The following JScript conditional statement differs a great deal from Microsoft's VBScript Tutorial example cited in Chapter 15:

```
function FixDate() {
    var myDate = "2/13/95";
    if (myDate < Date())
    myDate = Date();
}
```

In the first line, `function` is a keyword that indicates the beginning of a section of script that is processed as a unit. (Remember that in VBScript, the keyword was `Sub`, which represented the beginning of a subroutine.) Most of the remaining part of the function looks almost exactly the same as the VBScript subroutine: The second line declares a variable named `myDate` and gives it a date value. The following two lines set the conditions for processing: If `myDate` is less than the current system date and time, change `myDate` to the current system date and time. Otherwise, end the function. At this point, processing continues — at the line following the line from which the subroutine was called. Notice the presence of braces (`{ }`), which enclose the entire function. When a variable is declared within a function, it only applies to the function.

Chapter 15 also introduced you to looping statements, which automate one or more calculations. JScript supports three versions of looping statements: `for`, `while`, and `for... in`.

The `for` statement keeps looping as long as a condition is true. Look at this example from the Microsoft JScript Language Reference:

```
for (i = 0; i < 10; i++)
{
    j *= i;
}
```

In the first line of the statement, the initial value of `i` is set to 0, `i` is tested to find out if it is less than 10, and `i` is added (`++`) by 1. In the third line (within the braces), `i` is multiplied by itself (`*=`) to result in `j`. As long as `i` is less than 10, the lines within the loop are processed repeatedly.

The `while` statement is almost the opposite of the `for` statement. In contrast to the `for` statement, which initializes the expression and keeps looping as long as a condition is true, `while` loops until a condition is false. So, if a condition starts out false, processing within the `while` loop will never occur.

TAKE NOTE

▶ **LEARNING ABOUT THE `for... in` STATEMENT**

The `for... in` statement displays properties for objects named within. So, you can show characteristics of graphics, windows, and so forth to demonstrate familiarity with a visitor's Desktop or to repair a broken script.

▶ **USING JAVASCRIPT'S `do... while` LOOP**

JavaScript 1.2 (and greater) supports `do... while` loops, which continue to process as long as a condition is true.

```
do {
    one or more statements
}
    while
        one or more conditions
```

At this point, the JScript language does not include `do... while` loops.

CROSS-REFERENCE
You can learn about client- and server-based scripts and other contents of an ASP document by reading Chapter 14.

FIND IT ONLINE
You can find many JavaScript and JScript examples at http://www.infodial.net/support/javascript/index.htm.

Listing 16-7: Testing Weather Conditions

```
<%@ LANGUAGE=JScript %>
<HTML><HEAD>
<TITLE>How's the Weather?</TITLE>
</HEAD><BODY>
<% var Temp = 30;  ❶
if (Temp <= 32)
   response.write("It's freezing!");  ❷
else
if (Temp > 32)
   response.write("It's warming up.");  ❸ %>
</BODY></HTML>
```

❶ Set the temperature to 30 degrees.

❷ Display a message if the temperature is freezing...

❸ Or a message if the temperature is above freezing.

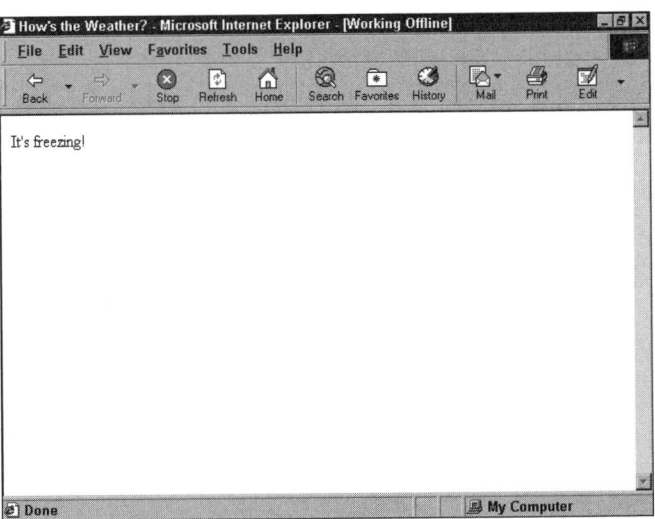

▶ The message shows that the Temp variable is set to a freezing temperature. You can test this script by changing the value of Temp in the script.

Listing 16-8: A Looping Example

```
<%@ LANGUAGE=JScript %>
<HTML><HEAD>
<TITLE>Loopy Loop</TITLE>
</HEAD><BODY>
<% Counter = 0;
for (ChangeNum = 1;
     ChangeNum < 10;  ◀1
     ChangeNum = ChangeNum + 2)

   {
     Counter += ChangeNum;  ◀2      3
     Response.Write("The current count is
" + Counter);
     Response.Write(".   ");
}
Response.Write("The final count is  ◀4
".concat(Counter));
Response.Write("."); %>
</BODY></HTML>
```

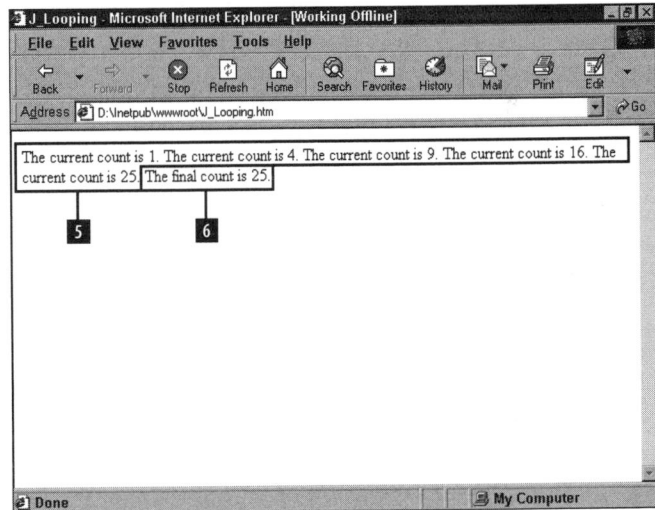

1 Initialize and set limits for ChangeNum.

2 Add the current ChangeNum value to the current Counter total.

3 Display the current Counter value continually.

4 Display the final Counter count.

5 Display the current Counter value continually.

6 Display the final Counter count.

Building JScript Programs

When you combine all JScript features, you can actually write real JScript programs — as long as they remain within ASP pages. You can interrupt JScript scripts with HTML statements that format and perform other similar functions. A sample page segment might look something like this:

```
<%
CurValue = "No";
for YesOrNo = 1 to 8
  if (theColor(YesOrNo) = "Blue"
    CurValue = "Yes"); %>
<P>The color is blue
<% else
  {
    if (CurValue = "No");
%>
<P>Blue is not on this list
<% } %>
<% function computer(w, x, y, z) {
  Response.Write("The computer is " + x)
  Response.Write(".") }
computer("IBM", "Dell", "Mac", "HP") %>
<H2>Testing a Counter</H2>
<FONT FACE="courier new">
<%
for (var i = 1; i <= 5; i++) {
  Response.Write("i = " + i);
  Response.Write("." + "<BR>"); } %>
</FONT>
```

The example displays a heading and then performs a function that writes the name of a computer (IBM, Dell, Mac, or HP), depending on the selected array member (w, x, y, or z). After another heading and a change of font, the example tests a counter, displaying the current counter value as it changes. So you can see that the JScript script is interrupted by HTML statements — namely, the headings

and the font change. Notice that the <BR> element is incorporated into the next to last line of the example.

As you will discover in Part 4, one of the best uses of scripting is to get a response from an individual filling in a form. Here's part of an HTML form:

```
<FORM ACTION="thanks.asp"
      METHOD="post">
Type your name:<BR>
<INPUT type="text" name="getName"
size="40"><BR>
Type your email address:<BR>
<INPUT type="text" name="getEmail" size="30">
<P><INPUT type="submit" VALUE="Submit">
<INPUT type="reset">
</FORM>
```

The difference between this and other HTML forms is that when the person filling in the form clicks the Submit button, the thanks.asp document appears. In that document, you can include a script that can gather information into a form. For example:

```
<BODY>
<H2>Thanks for signing up.</H2>
Starting next Monday, you will receive our
weekly e-mail newsletter on running your own
money-making business at home.
<%
email = request.form("getEmail");
%>
</BODY></HTML>
```

The document displays a thank-you message to the person who filled in the form. Then, using the JScript script within the <% and %> delimiters, the filled-in value of the getEmail variable is added to a predefined form.

CROSS-REFERENCE

Chapters 15 and 17 discuss other ASP-supported scripting languages: VBScript and PerlScript.

FIND IT ONLINE

Read about JScript and JavaScript differences at **http://shell.nanospace.com/~markst/jscript/jsdiff.htm.**

Introducing JScript, JavaScript, and ECMAScript

CHAPTER

16

Listing 16-9: A JScript Program

```
<HTML><HaEAD>
<TITLE>Warehouse Matching System</TITLE>
</HEAD><BODY>
<% function Barre() { ←❶          ❷
   Response.Write("order from Denny ");
   Response.Write("at Barre, 555-555-1200.");
} ←❸
function Reno() { ←❶              ❷
   Response.Write("order from Mary ");
   Response.Write("at Reno, 555-555-1201.");
} ←❸
function Tampa() { ←❶             ❷
   Response.Write("order from Sam ");
   Response.Write("at Tampa, 555-555-1202.");
} %> ❸
<H4>Warehouse Matching System</H4>
Every year, we will change the warehouses
from which you can order manufacturing
inventory. This year's locations are
listed on this page.
<H5>Handlebars</H5>
For handlebars,
<% Tampa(); %> ❹
<H5>Frames</H5>
For aluminum frames,
<% Reno(); %>
<BR>      ❹
For titanium frames,
<% Tampa(); %> ❹
<H5>Saddles</H5>
For saddles,
<% Barre(); %> ❹
<H5>Sprockets</H5>
For sprockets,
<% Tampa(); %> ❹
</BODY></HTML>
```

❶ Start a function.

❷ Provide information about a warehouse.

❸ End the function.

❹ In JScript, call a function.

TAKE NOTE

LEARNING ABOUT THE JSCRIPT `function` STATEMENT

In the preceding chapter, you learned about subroutines, which are a series of self-contained VBScript statements enclosed within the `Sub` and `End Sub` statements. JScript's `function` statement, which starts with the `function` keyword, a function name, optional arguments separated by commas, and a left brace (`{`) and ends with a right brace (`}`), is similar to a subroutine. Like a subroutine, a function can be called from within a script in the Web document at any time. Then, the statements enclosed within the function statement are processed. Finally, at the end of processing, control returns to the calling script.

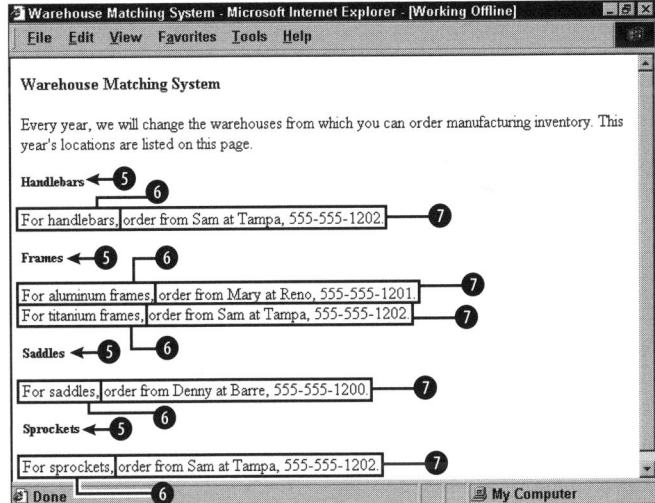

❺ Insert a heading for a piece of inventory.

❻ Start a sentence.

❼ The rest of the sentence comes from a function.

Personal Workbook

Q & A

1 Can JavaScript call routines written in Java?

_____

_____

_____

2 Are JavaScript, JScript, and ECMAScript bundled with IIS and PWS?

_____

_____

_____

3 What does the acronym ECMA represent? What does ECMA do? What is another name for ECMAScript?

_____

_____

_____

4 What is a JScript method?

_____

_____

_____

5 What is the JScript operator for incrementing? For the indexing of arrays? For a logical AND?

_____

_____

_____

6 When you declare a variable in JScript, do you use the `Dim` statement?

_____

_____

_____

7 How do you declare multiple values for a variable?

_____

_____

_____

8 What are the differences between the `for` and `while` statements?

_____

_____

_____

ANSWERS: PAGE 508

EXTRA PRACTICE

1. Go online and using the Microsoft JScript Language Reference, learn ten JScript functions.

2. Write a JScript script that uses JScript date and time constants to list the days of the week. Be sure to insert spaces or line breaks between the days. (How do this and the following three scripts differ from the counterpart VBScript scripts in the Extra Practice in Chapter 15?)

3. Write a JScript script that separates a text string into three individual components.

4. Write a JScript script that fills a page with your favorite motto.

5. Write a JScript script that produces ten random numbers.

6. Go online and find three sources of JScript scripts.

REAL-WORLD APPLICATIONS

✔ As a novice Web page writer for a developer of HTML and ASP sites, your first assignment is to convert a set of HTML documents with JScript scripts to ASP pages.

✔ Your company has asked you to research and write a proposal recommending whether to use VBScript scripts or JScript scripts in its ASP pages. Include advantages and disadvantages for both languages.

✔ Your company has reviewed your recommendations and decided to convert many of its VBScript scripts to JScript scripts. You are responsible for managing the conversion.

✔ You are a third-grade teacher with your own Web site. For your students, write a JScript program that displays a multiplication table within the cells of an HTML table.

Visual Quiz

This HTML document includes a JScript script that has not been tested. Correct all the HTML and JScript errors, and convert the document to an ASP page.

```
visual quiz 16 - Notepad
File  Edit  Search  Help
<HTML>
<HEAD>
<title>Visual Quiz 16</title>
</HEAD>
<BODY>
<SCRIPT LANGUAGE="VBSCRIPT"
    RUNAT=SERVER>
Greeting = "Hi There
Adios = "aloha"
Document.Write Greeting;
document.write("Adios")'
Doucment.write("Goodbye Again");
</SCRIPT>
</BODY>
</HMTL>
```

CHAPTER **17**

MASTER
THESE
SKILLS

▶ **Adding New Scripting Languages to ASP**

▶ **Moving from Perl to PerlScript**

▶ **Using PerlScript in Simple ASP Projects**

▶ **Taking Advantage of Perl's Variable Types**

▶ **Applying Perl's Tools to Common Web Development Processes**

▶ **Moving Common Gateway Interface (CGI) Scripts to ASP**

Using Other Scripting Languages: PerlScript and More Possibilities

While JavaScript and VBScript are enough for many developers, Active Server Pages was designed to be extensible enough to let developers add their own scripting languages. ASP itself provides a framework into which different language components can be connected — not a limited set of tools with only a single approach to scripting.

Perl, an established staple of Web development, has been the foundation of thousands of Common Gateway Interface (CGI) scripts across the Internet. ActiveState's Perl distribution includes PerlScript, a bridge between Perl and Active Server Pages that lets you use Perl to manipulate ASP objects, process input, and generate output. Developers already using Perl can use PerlScript and work in a familiar environment, or developers that need Perl's powerful tools for processing strings can sprinkle PerlScript into their Active Server Pages when needed.

Perl offers a wide variety of tools for handling the text at the core of Web transactions, and many of the tools are accessible without learning all the details of "obfuscated Perl." While Perl can seem intimidating at times, with odd syntax and different ways of handling common situations, the amount of Perl needed to build a functional Active Server Page is often minimal and not difficult to learn.

Perl's regular expression handling often provides a more concise and powerful set of tools for processing information coming in or going back out from Web users. This key tool set can be used easily in an ASP environment with PerlScript.

Sites that have used CGI scripts for their Web site automation will also find PerlScript useful as a handy tool for moving from the fairly basic interface provided by CGI to the more sophisticated interface ASP provides. While the conversion process may not be instantaneous, especially for more complicated scripts, PerlScript provides a relatively easy way to avoid rewriting a CGI script's core logic and move from CGI to ASP without introducing swarms of new bugs.

Adding Scripting Modules to ASP

Microsoft's COM object model and the architecture of IIS make it possible to plug different scripting languages (as well as components providing extra functionality) into Active Server Pages. The scripting languages are treated as components, fitting into a set of rules Microsoft has provided for interacting with the scripting interfaces in Internet Explorer, Internet Information Server, and the Windows Scripting Host.

All of these tools use a generic interface that allows scripts access to their internal object structures and allows them to manipulate those structures without requiring the objects to know anything about the language manipulating them. As a result, you can write scripts for the same object in many different scripting languages, and the object should appear the same to all of them. (There may be differences in the capabilities of the scripting languages themselves, but the objects with which they work don't need to know anything about this.)

Microsoft provides JavaScript and VBScript as part of the core IIS package, but PerlScript is available from ActiveState as an easy-to-add component. PerlScript connects Active Server Pages (or any other Windows scripting application) to the full set of capabilities provided in the Perl language. Although most PerlScripts are likely to use only a subset of Perl (and this book only has room to cover a subset), the full capabilities of Perl are available.

ActiveState has built a scripting module that connects Perl to Microsoft's scripting interfaces, giving developers an efficient way to connect Perl to the more sophisticated objects and scripting approaches of ASP. Developers who have been building Common Gateway Interface (CGI) scripts in Perl also get the benefit of an ISAPI (Internet Server Application Interface) interface to Internet Information Server, which lets their Perl CGI scripts run far more quickly than they did under the earlier model. Both modules are additions to the core Perl distribution, providing Windows-specific functionality for the multi-platform scripting language. Also, both modules are installed easily with the standard ActivePerl installer, as shown on the opposite page.

Although Perl is a scripting language, it has a different heritage from JavaScript and VBScript. JavaScript was designed expressly for use on the World Wide Web, while VBScript is a version of Microsoft's Visual Basic cut down to meet Web needs efficiently without too much complexity. Perl was originally a tool for UNIX system administration, providing support for a text-oriented command-line approach. PerlScript isn't a cut-down version at all. PerlScript provides developers with all the power (and potential complexity) of Perl, providing only a gate to Perl — not a reduced scripting language.

This approach has some significant advantages. Almost all of the modules that can be used with Perl can also be used with PerlScript. (The exceptions are usually modules that are specific to a non-Windows operating system.) Some of the more commonly used modules (like CGI.pm) aren't necessary with PerlScript, but some (like XML::Parser) provide functionality for which lots of Perl-specific code has already been written. The use of prefabricated Perl modules can simplify your job as much as the built-in ASP objects. Often, these modules come with source code, making it possible to customize them to your needs quickly and easily.

TAKE NOTE

ADDING SCRIPTING LANGUAGES BEYOND PERL

A number of other scripting languages, notably Python and Tcl, are also in common use among Web developers. While both of these languages have hooks to Java development, neither yet sports an ASP interface. If you want to use these with ASP, you need to build it yourself or convince members of these active open source communities that this should be a priority.

FIND IT ONLINE

You can download the ActiveState Perl distribution (including PerlScript) at **http://www.activestate.com/**.

Using Other Scripting Languages: PerlScript and More Possibilities

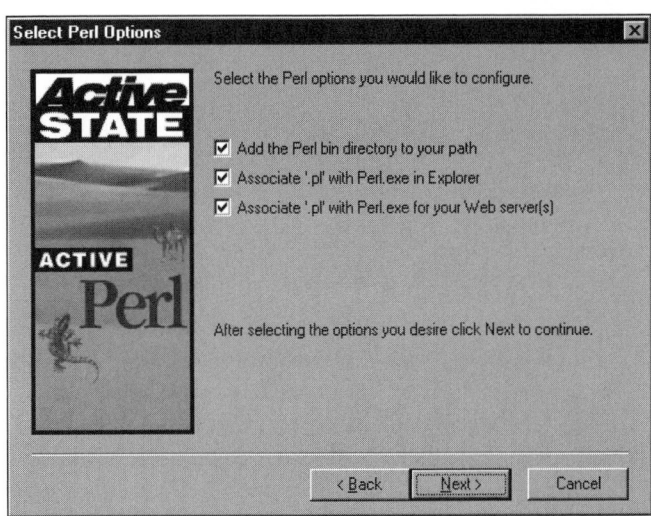

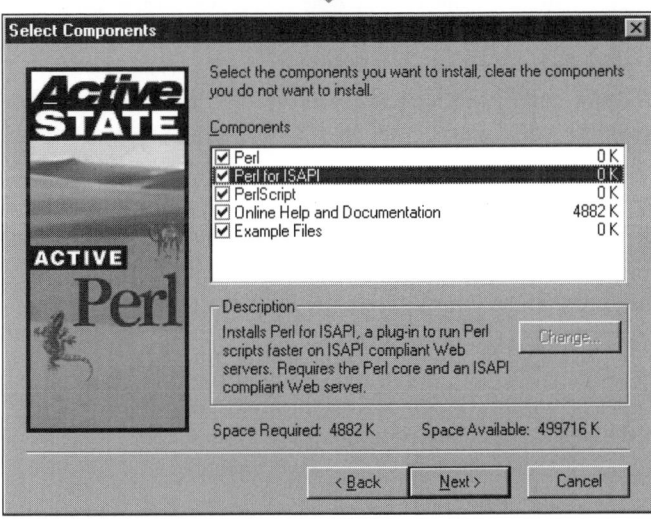

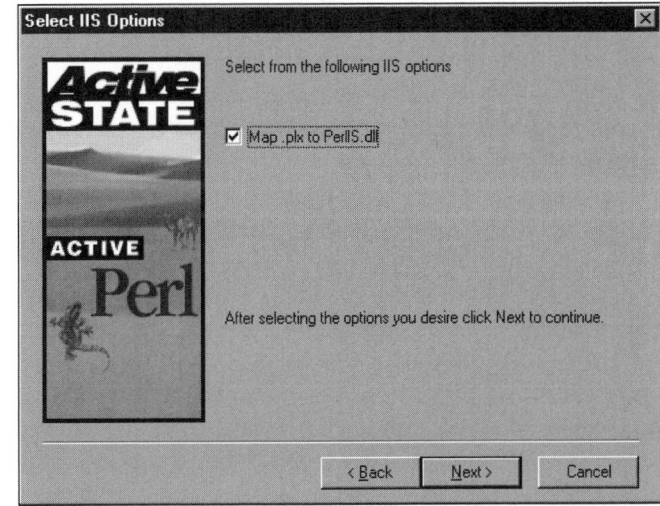

▶ PerlScript is installed as part of the ActivePerl setup. You must install the core Perl distribution to be able to use PerlScript. Remember, you may need to restart your computer at the end of this process.

▶ After the usual licensing acceptance, a briefing on the installation process, and directory selection, you'll need to choose the components you want to install. You must install at least Perl and PerlScript.

▶ If you want to be able to test your Perl scripts from the command line or use Perl in a CGI environment, make sure to check all of these boxes. If PerlScript is all you need, you may not need to establish these connections.

▶ If you want to use the Perl ISAPI option to run your CGI scripts within Internet Information server, select this option. After this, you'll be presented with a list of all of your choices and installation will commence.

Learning about PerlScript and Perl

Perl began as a general administrative tool for UNIX systems, and has evolved to an even more general language with powerful tools for manipulating text. The name Perl can stand for either Practical Extraction and Report Language, or Pathologically Eclectic Rubbish Lister. Both of those approaches fit quite well into the world of Web development.

One of the best things about Perl is that it is available for free, and that enormous quantities of supporting code are also available for free. (The discussion on the opposite page explains how and why this approach works so well.) There have been a few differences over the years between the Windows, UNIX, and Macintosh versions of Perl, but most of those differences have been addressed, and most Perl code can move comfortably between the various environments.

Perl's creator, Larry Wall, claims that "Perl is designed to make the easy jobs easy, without making the hard jobs impossible." Perl looks very much like C and UNIX shell scripts, and has pulled in pieces from a wide variety of sources. Perl is a glue language, intended more as a tool for managing and connecting resources than as a tool for building objects from the ground up. This approach has led to a multifaceted language with a powerful combination of features for processing, filtering, mixing, and generating information — a good match for the needs of the average Web script, though Perl was created long before the Web existed.

Perl is extremely text-oriented. Information in variables is stored as text and converted (for example, to do math) as necessary. Any information can be treated as text, and the search-and-replace tools Perl provides work on numbers and database results as well as inputs provided by users. Regular expressions, a key tool for matching strings, provide a compact representation that can precisely locate particular textual information and enable quick processing.

Perl has a reputation for being unreadable. While it does have the potential for complexity and confusion — there are actually "obfuscated Perl" contests — there is no need for beginners to abbreviate their code or take advantage of some of Perl's quirky control structures. Especially in the context of PerlScript, where ASP is providing much of the underlying functionality, the Perl syntax and tools can add clarity and convenience to scripts rather than add layers of additional complexity. If you and your fellow developers value clarity, you can build readable, maintainable, and manageable pages using PerlScript as easily as you can with JavaScript or VBScript.

Perl provides advanced functionality that goes well beyond the needs of the average ASP developer — object creation, modules for database manipulation, XML parsing, on-the-fly interpretation of generated code, and powerful tools for managing files and processes. All of these tools are readily available if you need them, and the Perl community is constantly developing more modules, generally freely available, that provide even more capabilities. As a continuing project itself, Perl is currently on Version 5 and still moving forward. (The major releases are stable — while Perl is a perpetual work-in-progress, the completed work is safe to use.)

All of these tools can be accessed from PerlScript as well as Perl. However, if you'd like to write Perl programs for your Web site rather than Active Server Pages using PerlScript, the ActiveState Perl distribution provides ISAPI support that enables you to connect your Perl scripts to Internet Information Server more efficiently than with the standard CGI connections.

FIND IT ONLINE

The CPAN archives hold an enormous number of Perl modules, many of which are constantly updated. Visit **http://www.perl.org** to explore an enormous toolkit.

Using Other Scripting Languages: PerlScript and More Possibilities

▶ **PERL AND OPEN SOURCE DEVELOPMENT**

PerlScript brings a different aspect of Web development to the Microsoft-centered world of Active Server Pages. Perl comes from the wilder world of open source development and free distribution. While its creators undoubtedly make money on their book and consulting deals, Perl itself is distributed at no charge, complete with source code. Users can modify and redistribute the main distribution without having to pay Perl's developers anything.

Perl itself is distributed under two licenses — developers can choose either license. The first, the GNU Public License, requires free redistribution of both Perl and any code built on top of the Perl package. (This does not include code written using Perl, but extensions to the language core itself.) The GNU Public License is a commonly used license for open source software that is used notably for Linux and the GNU suite of compilers and tools. The second, the Artistic License, is more flexible, enabling developers to market closed-source projects based on Perl, provided they follow a set of rules.

The two ports of Perl for Windows 95 and NT are called Perl for Win32 and ActivePerl. Perl for Win32 is maintained by the core Perl team, and uses the same licensing terms as the main Perl packages. Source code is available, Perl for Win32 can be freely redistributed, and developers can choose the license they want.

ActivePerl is also free, though not open source. You need to use this port in order to use PerlScript. ActiveState's Community License is more restrictive. While this port is built on the main Perl distribution, source code for some key parts (including PerlScript and the ISAPI module) isn't available. You can't redistribute it without paying fees to ActiveState; these fees keep that particular project going.

ActiveState's Community License provides details on what kinds of redistribution, generally within your own organization, is permitted. (You can always point people to the ActiveState site or the Comprehensive Perl Archive Network (CPAN) archives so they can get their own copy, of course.)

ActiveState is something of a broker between the open source Perl community and Microsoft, performing services such as connecting Perl to ASP via PerlScript, and connecting Perl to IIS via the Perl ISAPI bridge. ActiveState provides the Perl distributions that Microsoft includes in its Windows NT resource kits, and the existence of a strong Windows NT port of Perl often helps UNIX administrators manage otherwise unfamiliar systems.

Perl modules are typically licensed under the same terms as Perl itself — the Artistic License and the GNU Public license. The CPAN archives contain enormous amounts of code, giving you access to pre-built libraries that you can modify to meet your needs if necessary. If you build some especially spectacular code yourself (and your employer will let you release it), you can return your contribution to the community by releasing it through CPAN. While most PerlScript applications glue together components and help pass information from one component to another (or back to the user), you may find that you've written a great module in Perl that you'd like to share. Among other things, you may find yourself getting contributions once you release it!

The Perl community is an extremely active group, ready and willing to help. While ActiveState provides some key tools for using Perl with ASP in particular, you shouldn't forget the existence of this very large and supportive community, in which sharing code is an ordinary but extremely fruitful way of doing business. Although Active Server Pages are developed within the confines of a proprietary set of tools on a proprietary Web server that runs on a proprietary operating system (for the most part, with some exceptions noted in Chapter 4), you can still take advantage of the hard work and enthusiasm of the open source community.

Including PerlScript in ASP

Internet Information Server assumes by default that all scripts in ASP files are in VBScript. As most ASP programmers seem to use VBScript, this is usually a convenience. For the PerlScript programmer, however, this default can be a bit of a nuisance. Fortunately, there are a number of ways to tell IIS that your scripts use PerlScript, each of which is appropriate in slightly different circumstances.

If all (or most) of your scripts for an entire site use PerlScript, Internet Information Server's Management Console will let you change the default language used for scripting. Buried deep within the properties dialog for Web sites and virtual directories is an option that sets the default language used for all scripts within that directory. This means, for instance, that you could have a PerlScript directory in which all of the scripts use PerlScript, and a VBScript directory in which all of the scripts use VBScript. The default value can be set at a number of levels, from all the sites for a server down to a single subdirectory at the end of a directory tree.

To set a default scripting language, select Properties for the area that you want to modify. Within the Properties dialog will be a tab whose name includes the word "directory" — it may be "home directory", "virtual directory", or just "directory". Click the Configuration button to open the Application Configuration dialog. The App Options tab contains the settings you need to change the default scripting language. The figure shows how to set PerlScript as your default scripting language.

ASP will also recognize a "language preprocessor" statement that must appear as the first line in your document. The @LANGUAGE preprocessor enables you to select an alternate scripting language to be the default for a entire ASP file, though not the entire application. If you have a single file that uses PerlScript in an application primarily built on VBScript or JavaScript, the @LANGUAGE preprocessor is probably the easiest way to handle things. (This is especially convenient if you're porting a CGI application.) To set the default scripting language to PerlScript, the following line must be the first line in the program:

```
<%@LANGUAGE = PerlScript %>
```

You can only use one language on a page for floating code that just appears between the `<%` and `%>` delimiters. However, you can include functions written in multiple languages on the same page using the SCRIPT element and its RUNAT and LANGUAGE attributes. SCRIPT elements may run on either the browser or the server — ASP will process the script on the server if and only if the RUNAT attribute of the SCRIPT element is set to `'SERVER'`. Typically, you'll want to create subroutines when you take this approach. The LANGUAGE attribute may be set to VBScript, JavaScript, or PerlScript, as appropriate. Including PerlScript functions in an Active Server Page that uses another scripting language by default will require this approach. An example of this kind of language-mixing is shown on the opposite page.

This approach makes it possible to mix and match different languages on the same page, though doing so is rarely a good idea. Programmers who know one language may be baffled when they encounter the other, making it difficult to maintain the application. Unless you have a very good reason for including multiple languages, one language per page is generally the best way to handle multi-language development. Sometimes it is possible to use PerlScripts from a library that has been thoroughly tested in conjunction with scripts in a page in another language, but typically it's better to stick with one language you're certain that all of your developers can understand.

Like their fellow JavaScripts and VBScripts, PerlScripts may be included with a Server-Side Include, which makes it easy to share common library files across a large number of ASP documents.

CROSS-REFERENCE

For more on server-side includes, see Chapter 14.

Using Other Scripting Languages: PerlScript and More Possibilities

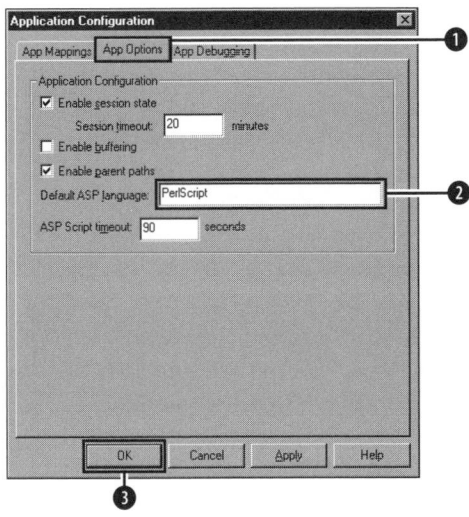

❶ *To change the default scripting language used by an ASP application, open the Application Configuration dialog for a given directory.*

❷ *Enter **PerlScript** in the Default ASP language dialog box.*

❸ *Click the OK button.*

```
<%@ LANGUAGE = PerlScript %>
<HTML>
<HEAD><TITLE>PerlScript Page</TITLE>
</HEAD>
<BODY BGCOLOR="#FFFFFF">
<H1>PerlScript Demo</H1>
<P>Using the code:
<PRE>$Response->write("Hello world!");</PRE>
will generate:
<%
$Response->write("Hello world!");
%>
</BODY>
</HTML>
```

▶ *Using the @LANGUAGE preprocessing directive lets you write your code directly in PerlScript, wherever it appears in your document.*

```
<HTML>
<HEAD><TITLE>Mixed Script Page</TITLE>
</HEAD>
<BODY BGCOLOR="#FFFFFF">
<H1>Mixed Script Demo</H1><H3>
<% PerlHello()
   VBHello() %>
<SCRIPT LANGUAGE="PerlScript" RUNAT="SERVER">
sub PerlHello {
$Response->write("PerlScript says Hello!<BR>");}
</SCRIPT>
<SCRIPT LANGUAGE="VBScript" RUNAT="SERVER">
sub VBHello
Response.write("VBScript says Hello!")
end sub
</SCRIPT></H3></BODY></HTML>
```

▶ *By using SCRIPT elements with the RUNAT and LANGUAGE attributes, you can put different types of script together.*

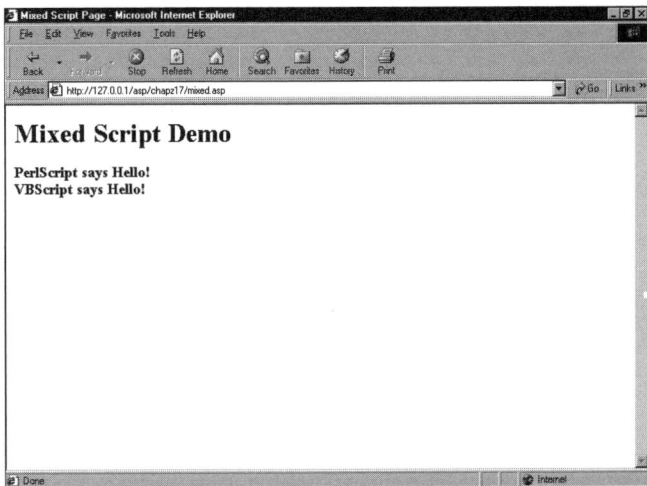

▶ *The Mixed Scripts sample produces messages from VBScript and PerlScript on the same page.*

Using PerlScript Variables (Part 1: Variable Types)

PerlScript offers a wide variety of variable types, from simple strings through arrays to associative arrays and eventually objects — everything that its parent language, Perl, offers. The notations and varieties of variables in Perl can sometimes be bewildering, especially at first, but the basics are fairly simple. Most Active Server Pages will only need the basics, plus access to the core ASP objects and possibly a Perl module or two.

The simplest Perl variables are called *scalars*, and may contain strings or numbers. (There isn't much formal data typing in Perl.) Scalar names always begin with the dollar sign ($) and a letter, and may contain letters, numeric digits, or underscores. `$this_is_my_number_1_variable` is a legal scalar name, but `$@#X!` is not. You can perform mathematical operations on scalars, concatenate them, process them with functions, or explore and rebuild them with regular expressions. Scalars are a generic variable type that can hold a single value.

Perl also provides *arrays*, a set of values referenced by number. An array is basically a group of variables — usually scalars, but sometimes arrays or hashes — in sequence, and can be processed either as a unit or by exploring its scalars one by one. Array names follow the same rules as scalar names, except that they start with an at sign (@) rather than a $. An array might be named `@myArray`, for example. To access the fourth element of the array `@myArray`, you use a scalar-like notation: `$myArray[3]`. (Arrays in Perl start counting at 0, so 3 identifies the fourth member of the array.) Using −1 as the counter returns the last entry in the array, and you can find out how many elements `@myArray` has with `$#myArray`.

A more sophisticated set of tools enables you to reference values in a set by key value. Called associative arrays or hashes, this type of variable enables you to store a set of scalars (or arrays, or hashes) and retrieve them using names rather than numbers. The names of associative arrays follow the same rules as scalars, except that they begin with % — `%myHash`, for example. Accessing a scalar value associated with a key is much like accessing an array value, but uses curly braces and a string rather than square brackets and a number: `$myHash{'keyValue'}`.

Keeping track of these different types, especially when Perl uses the $ notation for all of them, can be difficult. A simple rule can help keep them straight, however. Whenever you encounter a variable starting with $, check to see what follows it. The three variables below may look similar, but they reference a scalar value, an element of an array, and an element of an associative array:

```
$myValue
$myValue[2]
$myValue{'2'}
```

Perl also includes a large number of built-in variables, much like ASP includes a set of built-in objects. `$_` is the default input, a value that makes possible a large number of handy shortcuts. In general, the value of `$_` is the last value that Perl returned or selected, making it easy to iterate through a list without creating placeholders for the pieces of that list. Other built-in variables include `$.`, which contains the current line number of the most recently read file (helping you find your way through the file), `$]`, which returns the version number of the Perl instance being used, as well as a number of separators and flags. While you won't need to use most of these built-in variables, they do give Perl a level of flexibility most scripting languages don't provide. Some of them (`$_` in particular) can lead to code that's hard to read if you're not a Perl expert, so use them with care.

CROSS-REFERENCE

Perl 5 Desktop Reference, by Johann Vromans (O'Reilly, 1996) is a handy reference to Perl and PerlScript.

FIND IT ONLINE

You can find lots of PerlScript-specific information at **http://www.perlscripters.com/**.

Using Other Scripting Languages: PerlScript and More Possibilities

```
<%@ LANGUAGE = PerlScript %>
<HTML>
<HEAD><TITLE>Fun with Scalars</TITLE>
</HEAD>
<BODY BGCOLOR="#FFFFFF">
<H1>Scalars Demo</H1><H3>
<% $string1="Hello";
   $string2="world!";
   $value1=34;
   $value2=27; %>
<%= ($string1." ".$string2) %><BR>
Value1: <%=$value1%><BR>
Value1++: <%=$value1++%><BR>
Value1 after ++: <%=$value1%><BR>
Value1 + Value2: <%=$value1+$value2%><BR>
Value1 . Value2: <%=$value1.$value2%><BR>
</H3></BODY></HTML>
```

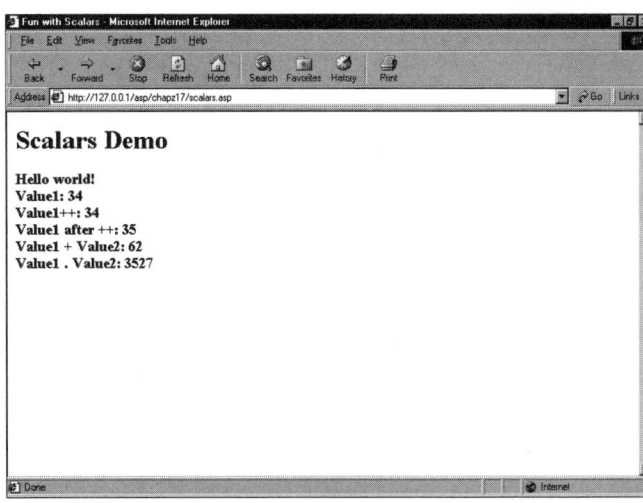

▶ *This sample code demonstrates many of PerlScript's operators for working with scalars*

```
<%@ LANGUAGE = PerlScript %>
<HTML>
<HEAD><TITLE>Fun with Hashes and Arrays</TITLE>
</HEAD>
<BODY BGCOLOR="#FFFFFF">
<H1>Hash and Array Demo</H1>
<% #don't start with an @ sign
@days = (Sun, Mon, Tues, Wed, Thurs, Fri, Sat);
%fullnames = (Sun, Sunday, Mon, Monday, Tues,
Tuesday, Wed, Wednesday, Thurs, Thursday, Fri,
Friday, Sat, Saturday);
 %>
<TABLE>
<TR><TH>Abbrev</TH><TH>Full Name</TH></TR>
<% foreach $day (@days) { %>
<TR><TD><%= $day %></TD><TD>
<%= $fullnames{$day}%></TD></TR>
<% } %></TABLE>
</BODY></HTML>
```

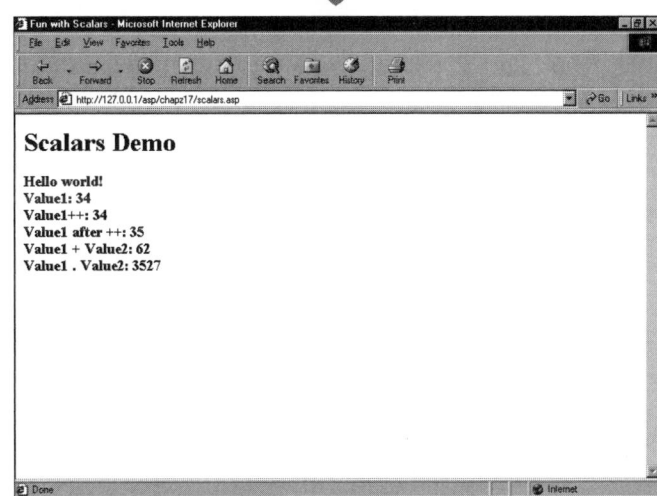

▶ *PerlScript and ASP can process scalar variables and present the results as HTML.*

▶ *ASP and PerlScript together can produce simple pages that display considerable amounts of information processed in arrays and hashes.*

▶ *Accessing and manipulating PerlScript's arrays and hashes is fairly intuitive, once you learn the conventions demonstrated here.*

Using PerlScript Variables (Part 2: Objects)

Like VBScript and JavaScript, Perl (and PerlScript) is not object-oriented, though it can be used to create and manipulate object structures. Objects came late to Perl, with Version 5, but Perl is quite capable of both supporting a variety of objects (including the core ASP objects) and creating object structures itself (as many of the Perl modules do).

In PerlScript ASP applications, it's very unlikely that you'll need to set up your own objects. Creating objects is a somewhat complicated process. Perl's creators use a fairly loose definition of object ("Referenced Thingy") that makes it easy to integrate Perl code into objects but can be a little difficult to get used to if your background includes stricter object-oriented languages, like Java or C++. Fortunately, you don't need to know how to create objects to use the ASP objects or the various objects produced by Perl modules.

Manipulating objects, reading and modifying their properties, and calling their methods is a constant part of ASP development. Object invocations look a little different in PerlScript than they do in VBScript or JavaScript, but the basic concepts are similar. Instead of using a period (.) to separate the parts of an object reference, use `->` (called the "Infix dereference operator") when you're working with Perl. The core ASP objects have the same names, though they need to be preceded by a dollar sign — such as `$Response` for Response, and `$Request` for Request. Other objects will have the names you assigned them and the methods and properties created by the package that defines them.

Object properties can be treated as ordinary variables, and displayed in the HTML using the `<%= %>` delimiters. For example:

```
<%= $Request->QueryString%>
```

would insert the query string that came with a request into the HTML output.

PerlScripts may also use the `Write` method of the Response object to write to the HTML output:

```
<% $Response->write('Hello!'); %>
```

would write `Hello!` to the HTML output. Just like VBScript and JavaScript object handling, method calls and property references may be combined:

```
<% $Response->write("The query string is ".$Request->QueryString);%>
```

You'll also see two colons (::) used in many Perl modules. This notation describes a package contained inside of another package that provides access to nested structures within packages, rather than within objects. `XML::Parser` refers to the Parser package, which itself is part of the XML package. `XML::Expat` is also part of the XML package, but is a separate package from `XML::Parser`. While these aren't object references, they are often used in conjunction with object references to make use of the objects inside of a particular package.

TAKE NOTE

▶ **THERE'S MORE THAN ONE WAY TO REFERENCE AN OBJECT**

Once you become more familiar with the intricacies of Perl objects, you may want to use a different notation — the "indirect object" form, in which the method name precedes the object name and the `->` is skipped. You should probably start with the object-oriented syntax, however, as it is much closer to the JavaScript and VBScript examples from which you often work in an Active Server Pages environment.

CROSS-REFERENCE
For more on Perl's objects, see Chapter 5 of Larry Wall and Randall Schwartz's *Programming Perl, 2nd Edition* (O'Reilly and Associates, 1997).

FIND IT ONLINE
For a quick introduction to creating your own object structures in PerlScript, see **http://www.perlscripters.com/Beginner/default. asp?Which=OOP.**

Using Other Scripting Languages: PerlScript and More Possibilities

```
<%@ LANGUAGE = PerlScript %>
<% $Response->CacheControl("Public"); #use
Response object to control caching %>
<HTML>
<HEAD><TITLE>ASP, PerlScript, and the Response
Object</TITLE>
</HEAD>
<BODY BGCOLOR="#FFFFFF">
<H1>ASP, PerlScript, and the Response
Object</H1>
<P>This text was written as regular HTML.</P>
<% $Response->write("<P>This text was written
using \$Response->write.</P>");%>
<P>If you look closely at $Response, you'll see
it contains <%= "$Response" %> or something
similar.</P>
<% $output="<P>This text was written through a
variable.</P>"; %>
<%= $output %>
</BODY></HTML>
```

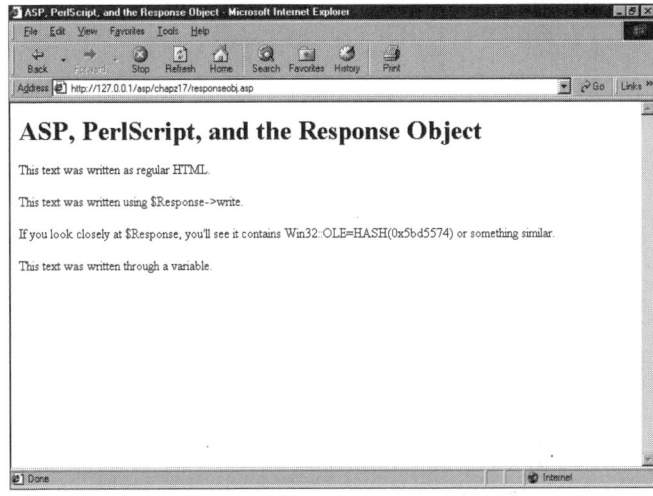

▶ Although the syntax looks a little different, PerlScript is capable of accessing the same object structures with which VBScript and JavaScript work.

```
<%@ LANGUAGE = PerlScript %>
<HTML>
<HEAD><TITLE>ASP, PerlScript, and the Request
Object</TITLE>
</HEAD>
<BODY BGCOLOR="#FFFFFF">
<H1>ASP, PerlScript, and the Request Object</H1>
<P>Your IP address is <%=$Request-
>ServerVariables("Remote_Host")%>.</P>
<P>The query string attached to your request was
<%=$Request->QueryString()%>.</P>
<P>You said <%=$Request->QueryString("perl")%>
to Perl and
find scripting <%=$Request-
>QueryString("scripting")%>.</P>
</BODY></HTML>
```

▶ PerlScript can access any ASP object structure that VBScript and JavaScript can, making it easy to reach into the Request object and pull out details about the user request.

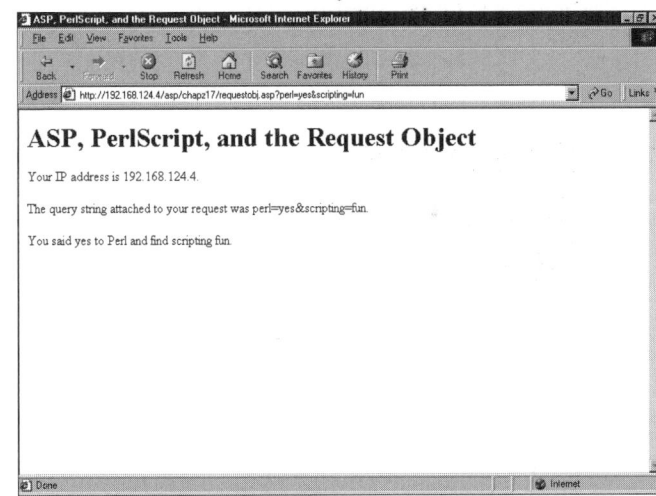

▶ This entire page was written using the PerlScript code at left, demonstrating how to manipulate core ASP objects.

▶ PerlScript code can also read and manipulate ASP object structures, letting scripts print out the server variables information as a list.

Using PerlScript Control Structures

Perl (and therefore PerlScript) provides a wide range of control structures. Perl supports `if/then/else` statements in a wide variety of forms, as well as `unless`, `while`, `until`, `for`, `foreach`, `continue`, and even the infamous `goto`. Perl also has structures that are useful for controlling code that may not work — in Perl parlance, code that may "die" — allowing for exception handling. We can't explore all of Perl's many possibilities in two pages, but you'll have enough to write your PerlScripts.

The simplest control structures are the `if` and `unless` constructs. `if` statements test an expression to see if it is true, and if so, executes a block of code.

```
if (expression) block
```

Expressions are placed in parentheses, and typically do tasks such as testing for equality, while blocks are placed in curly braces and contain commands. Like much of Perl, if your needs are simple, this can be reorganized into:

```
expression1 if expression2
```

(Because it's an expression, not a block of code, *if expression1* will need to be an expression with side effects, like `$counter++`.) The `unless` statement works pretty much the same way, though in reverse: the block of code (or the first expression) will only get executed if the expression turns out to be false:

```
unless (expression) block
expression1 unless expression2
```

Both `if` and `unless` support `else`, to provide code that gets executed if their conditions aren't met. `if` also supports `elsif`, which provides code that gets executed if the initial condition isn't met but a second condition is met. For example:

```
if ($myMood eq "grumpy") {
        $Response->write("It's okay, really");
} elsif($myMood eq "silly") {
        $Response->write("Heh heh heh");
} else {
```

```
        $Response->write("Don't know about
that.")}
```

The `else` is the last thing executed, returning its reply only if the conditions for the initial `if` and all the following `elsif`s aren't met.

Perl also offers a variety of looping structures. Basically, Perl will execute a block of code until a set of conditions are met that indicate that it's time to move on. Perl's `while` and `until` structures operate this way, as well as its `do...while` and `do...until` structures.

The `while` and `until` structures use similar syntax in their basic form:

```
while (expression) block
until (expression) block
```

These two structures are essentially the same, except that `while` will execute the block if `expression` evaluates to true, while `until` will execute the block if `expression` evaluates to false.

The `do...while` and `do...until` structures are similar, except that the block of code will always be executed at least once, to whatever expression may evaluate. Because of this, `expression` is saved for last, appearing after the block:

```
do block while (expression)
do block until (expression)
```

Sometimes you just want to execute a loop a given number of times, rather than base its execution on the value of a given expression. Perl's `for` loop offers this functionality using syntax that looks much like C:

```
for (expression1; expression2; expression3;)
block
```

The initial value of the counter is set in *expression1*, the condition that indicates the loop should continue is described in *expression2*, and the action that should be taken (on the counter) is in *expression3*. For example, a loop that counts from zero to 19 and terminates might look like:

```
for ($count=0; $count<20; $count++;) {
        $Response->write("Counter
value:".$count." ");
}
```

Other times, you want to step through an array or a collection, checking each item as you go. While you could find out how many items are in the target and then set up a `for` loop, Perl offers the handy `foreach` statement. The `foreach` statement handles all of the overhead, counting the items for you. The general form is:

```
foreach var ListOrDefault block
```

The `foreach` statement can take a variable (an array, for instance). This variable will be used to provide access to the members of the specified list. If no variable name is provided, the block will have to reference the values in the list through `$_`. The list itself may be an array variable, a hash variable, or an explicit list in parentheses, with list items in quotations and separated by commas. If no list is provided, `foreach` will use the default variable `$_` for its source list.

For example, to iterate through the array `@array` and print its contents, you could write:

```
foreach $value (@array) {
        $Response->write("Value:".$value." ");
}
```

If you didn't want to create the throwaway `$value` variable, you could write:

```
foreach (@array) {
        $Response->write("Value:".$_." ");
}
```

Perl also enables you to add labels to blocks of code, including `while`, `until`, `for`, and `foreach` statements. Labels are identifiers followed by colons, and are typically written in uppercase to make them stand out more clearly. (Labels must start with letters and may contain letters, digits, and underscores.) Labels make it possible for Perl to have a `goto` statement, the bane of many programmers. In a Perl program, you can jump to a labeled block of code by saying:

```
goto labeledBlock;
```

Perl also offers last, next, and redo statements that enable you to move around within labeled control structures.

Another feature of Perl that isn't technically a control structure, but is often used as one, is the combination of the `die` and `eval` functions that provides exception handling. Both of these functions have a slightly blackened reputation. The `die` function enables programmers to return a message when something catastrophic happens, halting execution — not something you normally want to see in a Web script. The `eval` function was targeted as a major security hole, because of its original use as a way to interpret Perl commands in strings at run time. If used improperly, crackers could feed a page raw Perl commands and break into the system running the flawed code.

The combination of `eval` and `die`, however, can make the best of both tools without exposing your code to the perils of either tool used alone. Putting a code block within an `eval` function enables the code to execute safely, returning the error message produced by the `die` function as the variable `$@`. Code can then look like:

```
$neededValue=eval { #dangerous code };
if ($@) {
  # error handling
} else {
  # continue on happily
}
```

The `die` function is quite simple, taking a list (typically just a string) that contains the error message:

```
die "Catastrophic error here!";
```

Typically, you call `die` as the result of some kind of failed condition check, not just by itself.

While most PerlScript code is too simple to require extensive use of `eval` and `die` constructs, you may need it if you start to work with files or network connections directly, and particularly with certain modules (notably XML::Parser) that use `die` to return a message when the input they receive doesn't meet the requirements.

Using PerlScript Regular Expressions

Regular expressions are one of the most powerful features in the Perl and PerlScript arsenal. By combining a small set of Perl operators with a basic syntax for matching strings, you can create comprehensive search-and-replace and text processing applications. While regular expressions may look a little odd at first, and some can remain difficult to read, they provide enormous capabilities in a compact package.

Two key operators are commonly used with regular expressions: `m//` and `s///`. The matching operator, `m//`, is used to determine if a string contains a pattern that matches the regular expression. The substitution operator, `s///`, goes another step beyond that, enabling you to replace those matched patterns with your own content. The syntax for the matching operator is:

`m/pattern/options`

The options are listed in the first table on the opposite page. The matching operator will return the string (or strings, if the g option is used) the pattern matched, or true, depending on the program context. The syntax for the substitution operator is similar:

`s/pattern/replacement/options`

Note that the replacement text must be a string, not a pattern. The substitution operator returns the number of substitutions made (sometimes treated as true), or zero if there weren't any (sometimes treated as false).

The text to be matched or substituted is connected to the matching or substitution operator by the `=~` or `!~` (which negates the returned value) operator:

`($name=~m/George/)`

This expression will return true if `George` is anywhere in the value contained by `$name`.

The patterns are built out of normal alphanumeric characters, with variable names interpolated, and a set of special characters and switches. Simple patterns built out of letters and digits are easy to work with. For example, to check whether a response (`$response`) includes the letter y, a typical way of determining whether a user typed some variant of `yes`, you could check:

`($response=~m/y/i) # i ignores case`

If this returns true, there's a y in there somewhere. Checking that the y is at the beginning of the string takes a little more work — the "metacharacter" of the caret ^. To check that the string begins with y or Y, use:

`($response=~m/^y/i) # i ignores case`

CROSS-REFERENCE

For complete details on regular expressions, see Jeffrey Friedl's *Mastering Regular Expressions* (O'Reilly, 1997).

Metacharacters are listed in the second table on the opposite page. If you ever need to match a metacharacter (say you're looking for real carets), you can escape it with the backslash. To match a caret, use \^. To match a backslash, use \\. You can also use the parentheses to group characters into "atoms", making it easier to process the precise chunks of text you need.

Quantifiers, enclosed in curly braces, enable you to specify how many times an atom must be matched. If a single number appears in the braces (like {3}), the atom must match that number of times exactly. If a comma follows a single number (like {2,}), the pattern must match *at least* that many times. If two numbers appear (like {2,4}), the atom must appear at least the first number of times but no more than the second. An asterisk (*) means that the atom must appear zero or more times, a plus sign (+) means that the atom must appear one or more times, and a question mark (?) means that the atom may appear zero or one times — just like XML content models!

A backslash before a letter gives it special meaning, as shown in Table 3 on the opposite page. The set of tools presented here is just a start, but it should get you started. The capabilities of regular expressions are nearly endless.

Continued

Table 17-1: COMMON OPTIONS FOR THE M// AND S/// OPERATORS

Letter	Implication
g	"global" match — find (or replace) all occurrences of the pattern in the document.
i	"insensitive" match — ignore case of letters.
m	"multiple line" match — treats multiline input as a set of lines.
o	"only compile once" — makes searching quicker if the pattern won't change.
s	"single line" match — treats multiline input as a single long line.
x	"extended" match, using extended regular expressions, which can contain whitespace formatting.
e	evaluates the replacement text before making the replacement. (s/// only.)

Using PerlScript Regular Expressions *Continued*

Table 17-2: METACHARACTERS USED IN REGULAR EXPRESSION MATCHING

Metachar	Usage
\	Used to "escape" the other characters or create backslash character sequences
|	"Or" — lets patterns match multiple atoms.
( )	Parentheses group atoms into larger atoms.
[ ]	Allows scrambling of the characters.
{ }	Used to indicate quantifiers.
^	Used to assert that an atom must appear at the start of a string, or to negate.
$	Asserts that an atom must appear at the end of a string, or to interpolate variables.
*	The atom must match zero or more times.
+	The atom must match one or more times.
?	The atom must match zero or one times.
.	Represents any number of characters.

Table 17-3: COMMONLY USED BACKSLASHED CHARACTERS AND THEIR MEANINGS

Letter	Implication	Letter	Implication
\A	Matches beginning of string	\n	Newline
\a	Alarm (matches beep characters)	\r	Carriage return
\b	Matches on a word boundary	\s	A whitespace character
\B	Matches except on a word boundary	\S	A non-whitespace character
\d	Any digit (0–9)	\t	Tab
\D	Any non-digit	\w	An alphanumeric character (letters + _)
\e	Escape	\W	Any non-alphanumeric character
\f	Formfeed	\Z	Matches end of string
\G	Matches starting where previous match ended		

TAKE NOTE

ANOTHER WAY TO DO REPLACEMENT

If you just want to make a string all lowercase or strip out duplicate characters, the `tr///` operator can be easier than working with the full regular expression pattern matching. It takes a list of things for which to search and a list of things with which to replace them, which is great when you need to do simple things. `$lowercase=~tr/A-Z/a-z/;` will make the value of `$lowercase` purely lowercase (if you're using a language like English). This strategy is quick and easy and less prone to errors, though it isn't as powerful.

Using Perl in ASP and CGI

CGI — the Common Gateway Interface — and ASP are, in many ways, competing technologies. The Common Gateway Interface is a standard that works across hundreds of different Web servers on many different platforms (including Microsoft's IIS), while ASP performs the same tasks in a primarily Windows-centric way that takes advantage of core Microsoft technologies. Even using PerlScript in Active Server Pages is still considerably different than writing CGI scripts in Perl, thanks to completely different approaches and supporting software.

Despite the competition between technologies and the very different appearance of the actual code, the gap is bridgeable. ActiveState's ActivePerl distribution combines the Perl ISAPI module, for running CGI scripts unmodified at much higher speed, and PerlScript. PerlScript provides an opening you can use to migrate your Perl code into ASP. Going the other direction, from ASP pages into CGI scripts, is typically much more difficult than moving from CGI to ASP, but careful separation of your logic from your output generation code can make it easier.

An instant (though not extremely efficient) port of CGI scripts to ASP is available in the Win32:ASP::CGI module from Lennart Borgman. This module can be extremely helpful in two important cases: where you need to move your CGI program into an ASP environment immediately, or where you need to keep your code portable among platforms. Win32::ASP::CGI enables you to write three-line PerlScript Active Server Pages that reference your CGI script. When executed, the information in the Request object is converted to a form CGI script will understand, and the output of the CGI script is routed to the Response object. These conversions (especially the first) can take some processing, especially if your CGI program then converts that information to its own internal format using tools like those provided in the CGI.pm library. Still, the processing hit may be less important than the cross-platform capabilities produced with this strategy.

If you want to make a full conversion, there's a lot more work to do. The ease of converting code from CGI to ASP is fairly directly proportional to the degree of separation between your logic and your CGI-specific code. If you used the CGI.pm module for Perl, you need to find calls to CGI.pm and replace them with their ASP equivalents. You can still use portions of CGI.pm, the portions that generate HTML, but you'll need to replace print statements with calls to `response.write`. In some cases (like cookie management), you'll probably need to rewrite some of your logic if you want to take advantage of ASP's built-in capabilities. In other cases, you may be able to get away with leaving code alone.

Converting complex CGI scripts that mix code processing input from the CGI interface with logic can be incredibly difficult, especially if the authors took advantage of Perl's many tools for minimization. A large CGI to ASP conversion project that has to work with tightly-written but tightly-integrated code may require either massive resources or a different toolset, like the Win32:ASP:CGI module or all the way back to the PerlISAPI option, bypassing ASP altogether. If necessary, you can write new Active Server Pages that process the information generated by or received by the CGI scripts, enabling you to extend the application without rewriting it. However, maintaining applications written in multiple environments can cause a lot of headaches.

TAKE NOTE

PROGRAMMING STYLE COSTS

While most programmers have their own preferences for how their code should look, encouraging a clean separation between the logic of your application and the interfaces that move information to and from that logic will make it much easier to move the code later. If you're always looking for that extra bit of efficiency, you may find yourself having to rewrite lots of code later.

FIND IT ONLINE

The Win32::ASP::CGI module is available from **http://www.PerlScripters.com**, in their modules area.

Do I Want to Learn Perl?

Developers already using Perl for other projects will find PerlScript easy to learn, while other developers will need to figure out whether learning Perl is worth their time. Perl's reputation as a particularly cryptic language may scare possible users away.

Your site's needs are probably the most important driving factor (though your resume may factor in as well). If your site is mostly a data collection or brochure-oriented site, VBScript and JavaScript probably provide as much or more functionality as you'll need, built-in and well-documented. If, however, your site is spending much of its time processing user requests (for example, to help direct them to parts of your site that seem especially relevant to their needs), Perl's text processing capabilities can be very helpful. Regular expressions can simplify text processing and searching dramatically, even though their syntax may seem daunting.

One approach that may work for Perl neophytes is to include PerlScript modules in their Active Server Pages when (and only when) they need Perl's text-handling prowess. VBScript and JavaScript can both call PerlScript subroutines. Perl code can be isolated in library modules maintained by those with more knowledge about Perl, and their behavior clearly described. Documentation is critical, as mixing languages within projects often generates chaos. Starting with regular expressions — complex and odd-looking though they may seem — is probably the quickest way to take advantage of PerlScript's unique capabilities. While the rest of Perl's structures may be interesting, Perl's regular expression support is really what separates it from the rest of the pack.

Learning Perl can be a lot easier if you focus on the parts you need first, building small examples and integrating them with code you already understand.

Integrating ASP with Other Environments

While PerlScript provides a convenient way to integrate your ASP development with both prior Perl work and future uses of your Perl code, it still leaves open many questions about integration between Active Server Pages and other Web development environments. While using multiple environments to create a single Web application is unusual, requiring developers with many skills to create and maintain them, large-scale applications often have to combine contributions of different types from different groups.

Some cases are relatively simple. Netscape's Web Servers, for example, contain a scripting environment called "Server-Side JavaScript." While SSJS uses different object models, the core JavaScript code, if separated from the code integrating it with the environment, is easy to move to and from ASP, much like CGI Perl code and PerlScript.

In other cases, integrated development may not be possible or easy, and you'll need to build applications that can share resources and keep track of information among themselves. Cookies, described in Chapter 25, can help you assign keys to users that different applications can use to reference information in a relational database, for example. Similarly, form information and query strings can help you pass information from application to application through the user's browser.

Integration is a fairly common problem. While it would be nice to think that every problem can be solved using the same tools (and some companies insist that the same set be used for every project), reality often intrudes. You may find hidden opportunities in what seems like an extended problem. As the Web continues to grow, expect to encounter more and more of these types of problems, and expand your toolkit for handling them.

Personal Workbook

Q & A

1 Describe the relationship of PerlScript to Perl.

_____

_____

_____

2 Where can you find the PerlScript distribution?

_____

_____

_____

3 How do you tell IIS to use PerlScript for all of the code in a document?

_____

_____

_____

4 Can you use COM objects with PerlScript Active Server Pages?

_____

_____

_____

5 How can I make my CGI programs run under IIS?

_____

_____

_____

_____

_____

6 Where can I find more Perl modules to use with Active Server Pages?

_____

_____

_____

_____

_____

7 Which operators use regular expressions?

_____

_____

_____

_____

ANSWERS: PAGE 509

EXTRA PRACTICE

1. Download the ActivePerl distribution and install Perl, PerlScript, and Perl ISAPI.

2. Build a simple page that takes two numbers from a form and adds them together.

3. Visit **http://www.perl.com** and explore the world of Perl resources.

4. Practice using regular expression operators on files from the Perl command line.

5. Rewrite the `for` and `foreach` statements using other statement structures.

6. Rewrite some JavaScript or VBScript pages in PerlScript.

REAL-WORLD APPLICATIONS

✔ Users are complaining that your checkbox-based site doesn't give them enough flexibility. How could you use PerlScript to improve your site's functionality?

✔ You're moving your site from an old Web server to a brand-new Windows NT Server-based system. You need to preserve all of your CGI scripts. How would you go about doing this?

✔ Your team includes three people with previous JavaScript experience and two people with Perl experience. The target platform for your application is Internet Information Server. How do you get your developers to work together quickly?

✔ After spending months polishing a Web site for a soon-to-be-released product, Marketing informs you that the product name has changed. What Perl feature can help you avoid manual search-and-replace?

CHAPTER 18

MASTER THESE SKILLS

▶ Figuring Out What Tools Work Where

▶ Detecting Browser Versions from the Server

▶ Taking Advantage of a "Safe" Server Environment

▶ Presenting the Same Page in Multiple Versions

▶ Transforming Documents to Meet Client Needs

Supporting Various Browsers and Other Fine-Tuning

In every chapter of this book thus far, you have added to your knowledge of server technologies, Windows operating systems, HTML and XML, scripting languages, and — of course — the primary subject, ASP. When you plan, design, and develop Web pages, you have to juggle several difficult factors: selecting a markup language, choosing a stylesheet technology, and predicting the browsers with which visitors to your site will view the pages that you have spent days and months producing. You can control the first two of these factors, but how do you plan for all the browser possibilities? Fortunately, the current features and behavior of the two most popular browsers — Microsoft Internet Explorer and Netscape Navigator — are well-known. You can always create pages for these two browsers alone, but you'll miss part — admittedly a small one — of your prospective audience.

What if you hear about a new release of a browser? How do you investigate and adjust your pages to take advantage of its new features? This chapter shows you how you can stay current. After you read through the tasks in this chapter and create versions of the examples in this chapter, you can modify your pages to take advantage of new browser features.

Although this chapter focuses on the importance of browsers to Web pages, you'll also discover other important aids to building outstanding pages. First, you'll get an overview of ASP tools — the software that will help you develop pages and scripts and, at the same time, save you hours of work. Speaking of ASP software, the Browser Capabilities Component, which is bundled with the IIS and PWS servers, is a utility that lists browser information: its name, version, and technologies that it supports. The Browser Capabilities Component is covered in the second task. The third task discusses security features beyond those set for the IIS and PWS servers yet basic for most computer networks. The following task presents ways in which you can tailor pages for a variety of browsers: You'll find out how to write documents that include separate sections for each browser. Finally, you'll discover how to transform documents from one markup language to another, from HTML to ASP, from one stylesheet to another, and from a word-processing format to an HTML document.

Figuring Out What Tools Work Where

Now that you have enough information about building ASP pages, you can learn the fine points of document creation and editing. Up to now, you have seen how to use a text editor, such as Windows Notepad, to write document text and script codes. However, if you have any experience producing letters and memoranda, you know that a text editor is not enough. To develop good-looking documents, you need the best word processing program — for its formatting "skills" and predefined layouts. So, when you have day-by-day responsibilities for producing Web documents, you should find a set of software tools to make your work easier and the results better-looking.

Like word processors, HTML editors help you write the HTML statements in your documents. An HTML editor adds boilerplate statements automatically — especially in the HEAD section. Most HTML editors have a friendly user interface with shortcut buttons to commonly-used features and functions. Some editors enable you to open two windows simultaneously: a WYSIWYG (what you see is what you get) window, in which you can see what a visitor will see, and a source window, in which you can view the underlying HTML code. An HTML editor knows the attributes for each element and the proper syntax. If you make a wrong choice, chances are the editor will issue an error message immediately. When you save a document, an editor automatically appends the `.htm` or `.html` file extension. Finally, developers of HTML editors usually bundle all sorts of interesting applets, page-design templates, and page objects.

Scripting editors exist, but probably the most helpful scripting resources are the code samples available at some ASP sites (see Table 18-1 on the facing page and see the Find It Online notes throughout the book). The list seems to be growing weekly. Why write it yourself if someone has already written and tested it?

To maintain a significant presence on the Web, you need to test your pages to ensure that most browsers will be able to display them in their entirety. For example, visitors to your site should be able to view the results of your scripts — calculations, responses to their input, graphics, and even scripted animations. If scripts are written in a language that a particular browser cannot interpret, the pages will be incomplete to visitors using that browser. Because ASP is an open-platform technology, you don't have to worry about your server-side pages. However, if you plan on combining both server-side and client-side pages, browser compatibility is a big issue. For more information, see the following task.

Of course, in order to test your code, you should install some browsers on your computer or a client computer on your network. The two most popular are Microsoft Internet Explorer and Netscape Navigator. It's a good practice to view documents using other browsers as well.

TAKE NOTE

FINDING WHAT YOU WANT AT MICROSOFT.COM

For novice searchers, finding resources on the Microsoft Web site can be daunting. There are two ways to get good information, via Products and Search links on the home page (**http://www.microsoft.com/**).

Use the All Products or specific product links to search for a Microsoft application and browse through links at that site. You can learn about system requirements, download white papers, and find links to related programs.

Use the Search link to look for articles, tips, and hints about a topic or program. To search, click Search, enter a keyword or phrase, choose search criteria, and select the search category. Your best choice as a Web page developer is Developer Resources.

CROSS-REFERENCE
Appendix G lists programs for creating HTML and XML documents, scripts, and ASP pages.

FIND IT ONLINE
See a browser cheat sheet at **http://msdn.microsoft.com/workshop/essentials/versions/cheatsheet.asp**.

Supporting Various Browsers and Other Fine-Tuning

Site	URL	Description
ASP Alliance	http://www.aspalliance.com/	Articles, advice, listservs, and links to ASP magazines
ASP Forums	http://www.aspforums.com/	Links to messages about ASP as well as downloads and more
ASP Resource Index	http://www.aspin.com/index/default.asp	The Yahoo of ASP sites, with a multitude of links
ASP Webring	http://www.asp101.com/webring/	A Web ring of many ASP sites — most informative and some commercial
ASPfree.com	http://www.aspfree.com/main.asp	A site with a long menu of choices and demos of scripts
ASP-Help	http://www.asp-help.com/	Links to many resources including a code library and databases
ASPWire	http://aspwire.com/	Links to up-to-date ASP news and articles
aspZone.com	http://www.aspZone.com/	An online magazine for advanced ASP developers
LearnASP	http://www.learnasp.com/	Links to many free tutorials and lessons
Niblack	http://www.niblack.com/	A commercial site with how-to's, reference materials, and news
PowerASP	http://www.powerasp.com/	Links to code snippets, hints, code wizards, a newsletter, and more
Stevenator's ASP Column	http://www.aspalliance.com/stevesmith	Links to a FAQ, tutorials, samples, personal applications, and more
Ultimate ASP Resources	http://www.ultimateasp.com/ultimate/home/default.asp	Links to free downloads, tutorials, references, a discussion group, and more

Table 18-1: SELECTED ASP WEB SITES

Detecting Browser Versions from the Server

When you install the IIS or PWS servers (see Chapters 2 and 3, respectively), the Browser Capabilities Component (`browscap.ini`) and its code (`browscap.dll`) are added to a system folder on the server computer. For Windows NT computers, the files are located in the `\WinNT\System32\InetSrv\` or a subfolder. For the Windows NT Workstation computers, you'll probably find the files in `\WINNT\System32\InetSrv`. For Windows 98 computers, the files are in `\Windows\System\Inetsrv`. To view your `browscap.ini` file, simply double-click it.

Let's examine the following block of statements from a `browscap.ini` file:

```
[Netscape 4.00]
browser=Netscape
version=4.00
majorver=4
minorver=00
frames=TRUE
tables=TRUE
cookies=TRUE
backgroundsounds=FALSE
vbscript=FALSE
javascript=TRUE
javaapplets=TRUE
ActiveXControls=FALSE
beta=True
```

The first five lines name the browser and provide version-number information. For example, `majorver` indicates the number of the current major version (the 4 to the left of the period), and `minorver` states the number of the current minor version (the 00 to the right of the period). The remaining lines state whether the version of the browser supports various features or technologies: `TRUE` indicates support, and `FALSE` signals a lack of support. The

`beta=True` statement says that this version is a beta release. So, you can see that Netscape 4.00 (which, by the way, is a recent — but not current — version of Netscape Navigator) supports the use of frames, tables, cookies, JavaScript, and Java applets, but does not support background sounds (the use of the Microsoft extension, `BGSOUND`), VBScript, or ActiveX controls.

To use `browscap.ini` in your documents to find out what the current crop of browsers can do or even to provide special sections of code for certain browsers, insert the following line of VBScript in the BODY section of an ASP page:

```
<% Set browseIt = Server.CreateObject ("MSWC.BrowserType") %>
```

The VBScript `Set` statement names an object variable (`browseIt`) and creates an object (`Server.CreateObject`) using the reserved name `MSWC.BrowserType` or progid.

In the next task, you'll learn how to use `browscap.ini` to customize your pages for different browsers.

TAKE NOTE

KEEPING BROWSCAP.INI CURRENT

How can you be sure that you have the latest version of `browscap.ini`? At cyScape's BrowserHawk page (**http://www.cyscape.com/browscap/**), you can download `browscap.ini` or cyScape's commercial version, BrowserHawk(tm), which automatically detects new browsers without having to be updated. If you decide to download `browscap.ini` from this page, you can fill in a form to receive e-mail notifications of file updates. Another `browscap.ini` download site is Asp Tracker (**http://asptracker.com/**).

CROSS-REFERENCE

To learn about ASP's other installable components, browse through the chapters in Part 4.

FIND IT ONLINE

Read about the Browser Capabilities Component at **http://msdn.microsoft.com/mastering/free/mwd64/mwd9800347.htm**.

Listing 18-1: A Browser-Detection Example

```
<HTML><HEAD>
<TITLE>What Can Your Browser Do?</TITLE>
</HEAD><BODY>
<% Set browsit=Server.CreateObject("MSWC.BrowserType") %>  ←①
<H4>Your Browser's Attributes Are:</H4>
<% response.write "Browser Name: "
response.write browsit.browser %>  ←②
<BR>
<% response.write "Version: "
response.write browsit.version %>  ←③
<BR>
<% response.write "Does it support VBScript? "
response.write browsit.vbscript %>  ←④
</BODY></HTML>
```

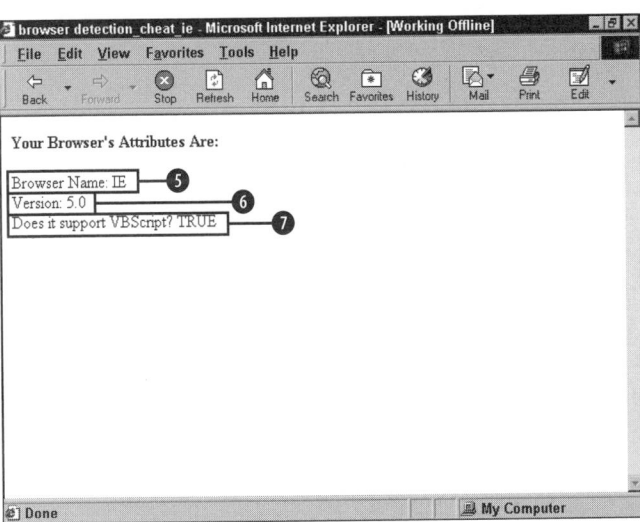

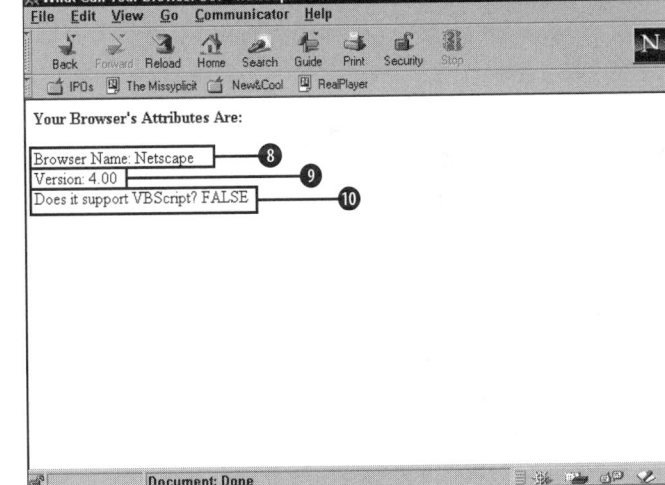

① Enable the Browser Capabilities Component.

② Write a heading and browser name.

③ Write a heading and the version number.

④ Answer a question about VBScript support.

⑤ Write a heading and browser name.

⑥ Write a heading and the version number.

⑦ Answer a question about VBScript support.

⑧ Write a heading and browser name.

⑨ Write a heading and the version number.

⑩ Answer a question about VBScript support.

Taking Advantage of a "Safe" Server Environment

In Chapters 2 and 3, you read an overview of computer system security and learned how to set security features for the IIS and PWS servers. If you are running ASP pages on IIS, you have several security options. Securing PWS is a somewhat minimal task. This task discusses some of the other measures that you can use to protect your Web site and its pages when information flows between the server and the client. Table 18-2, on the facing page, lists security resources on the Web. Each entry in the table includes the address of the resource and a brief description.

Most of the information transmitted between client and server computers is simply ASCII text: Anyone who intercepts it can read it without requiring any translation. One of the ways that software developers address plain-text transfer is to encrypt the data during transmittal and decrypt it after it reaches its destination. *Encryption* is a process that changes the text characters into a code that is unreadable. Obviously, *decryption* is the process by which the encrypted information is converted to its original characters.

A *key* uses secret knowledge for encrypting and decrypting. There are two key technologies: secret or symmetric key and public key. *Secret key* uses the same key for both encryption and decryption. *Public key* uses two keys, one public (for encryption) and one private (for decryption). A variation of public-key technology is the Digital Signature Algorithm (DSA), which applies to digital signatures rather than encryption or decryption. A *digital signature* uses encryption and authentication to gain access to a document or file.

Another security process is *authentication*, which is a process by which user information — such as an identifier, password, or digital signature — is validated by the computer or network, usually by matching it against a list of identifiers and passwords.

A digital *certificate* associates a name with a public key. A certificate can also include an expiration date, the name of the organization that issues the certificate, and other information that will allow verification of the individual holding the certificate.

Even without special security measures, the IIS server runs a series of "tests" on a client trying to gain access. It checks the address and domain of the client and the user's identity. It makes sure that IIS and NTFS permissions have been granted. Finally, it finds out whether the Custom handler permits access. Remember that both IIS and PWS keep logs of activities, so that you have a record of permitted and denied accesses.

TAKE NOTE

LEARNING ABOUT SECURE SOCKETS LAYER

Secure Sockets Layer (SSL) is a Netscape-developed protocol that guards security in Internet-based data transfers. SSL works as follows: The client computer contacts the server computer. To authenticate the client, the server sends a certificate. The client decrypts the certificate, issues a secret key for the current session, and starts sending information to the server. First, the server encrypts the session key with its public key, and then it encrypts the information. SSL is built into most browsers.

Occasionally when you download secure information, you see a prompt that states that your browser must have 128-bit security. This is an SSL message that means that the session key must be 128 bits long, rather than the typical 40 bits. Essentially, the longer the key, the more difficult it will be for a hacker to decrypt. The latest versions of Internet Explorer and Netscape Navigator support the use of 128-bit session keys. However, the U.S. government limits the export of 128-bit keys to countries in North America. Microsoft's Gated Cryptography (SGC) is an SSL extension that enables 128-bit keys for financial institutions around the world.

CROSS-REFERENCE

Chapter 25's "Learning About Secure Connections" task discusses some advanced security measures.

FIND IT ONLINE

At **http://msdn.microsoft.com/workshop/essentials/versions/ hess0602.asp**, make your site browser-compatible.

Table 18-2: SECURITY RESOURCES ON THE WEB

Resource Name	Address	Description
Frequently Asked Questions about Today's Cryptography	`http://www.rsa.com/rsalabs/faq/`	A 216-page FAQ, with a glossary, on cryptography
Public Key Cryptography Standards	`http://www.rsa.com/rsalabs/pubs/PKCS/`	Publications about public-key cryptography standards
Netsurfer Focus: Computer and Network Security	`http://www.netsurf.com/nsf/v01/01/nsf.01.01.html`	A set of articles about security with good links
Secure Sockets Layer	`http://home.netscape.com/security/techbriefs/ssl.html`	An article about SSL from its originator
Server Gated Cryptography (SGC)	`http://www.microsoft.com/security/tech/sgc/default.asp`	The home page for Microsoft's SGC, which is an extension of SSL
New to Security?	`http://www.microsoft.com/security/new.asp?ID=2`	A directory of links to security papers
Security Basics	`http://www.microsoft.com/security/resources/security101wp.asp`	A white paper on security basics
The Basics of Security	`http://www.microsoft.com/workshop/server/feature/server033198.asp`	An article on security with ASP, IIS, and Microsoft Site Server in mind
Security & Cryptography	`http://www.microsoft.com/workshop/security/default.asp`	A page with links to Authenticode, cryptography, and Certificate Server Architecture pages
Securing Networked Systems	`http://www.cert.org/sepg99/index.htm`	A security presentation from an important security group
Security Tools: Information and Sources	`http://www.cert.org/other_sources/tool_sources.html`	Links to several FTP and Web sources
W3C Security Resources	`http://www.w3.org/Security/`	W3C's security home page, with many links

Presenting the Same Page in Multiple Versions

It's difficult to balance the desire to develop your Web pages using the latest technologies with a concern about how many browsers will not be able to read pages because they do not support those technologies. As you have seen in the "Detecting Browser Versions from the Server" task, even the latest versions of two popular browsers are not completely compatible. Obviously, you cannot satisfy all your visitors all the time, but you probably want to use the latest and greatest ASP and HTML tools.

If you have developed many HTML documents, you know that you can use the NOFRAMES element to enclose no-frames sections — for the visitors to your site who use browsers that do not support frames. The <NOFRAMES> start tag and </NOFRAMES> end tag form a type of simple subroutine (for you VBScript users) or function (for JSCRIPT users). If a browser supports frames, it processes the content of the HTML frames tags. A browser that does not support frames "drops through" the frames tags and content to the NOFRAMES section.

As you learned in the preceding chapters in this part, you can write scripts that include subroutines or functions that are self-contained and are not processed until they are called from within the same or different scripts within a document. You can use this type of scripting to write document sections that are processed when a particular browser views a document. For example, you can write one subroutine or function for browsers that are frames-compliant and another for browsers that do not support frames.

In the "Detecting Browser Versions from the Server" task, you learned how to set the browscap.ini file from within an ASP page to get and display information about browsers. You can use that browser information to automate the branching to particular subroutines or functions. For example, when a visitor links to your page, you can use browscap.ini to check a browser's version number. If it is not the latest and greatest, your page can prompt a visitor to download the browser and build in a link to the browser's home page. Or, you can write a script that asks browscap.ini whether a browser supports frames (TRUE). If so, the browser processes the following lines of the document. If the browser does not (FALSE), the script branches to a "noframes" section.

The reliability of a Web page that uses browscap.ini data to test a browser depends completely on how recently browscap.ini has been downloaded or edited. For more information, refer to the Take Note in the previous task.

TAKE NOTE

▶ INTRODUCING THE GLOBAL.ASA FILE

When you add scripts to a Web page, it approaches the level of a program; it becomes a Web application or application object. As a matter of fact, each ASP virtual directory is known as an application: Every file in that directory is part of the application object. Each application, in turn, has its own global.asa file, which is a text file you can edit to include variables that control events that are processed when an application or session starts or ends.

▶ EXITING A VBSCRIPT SECTION EARLY

The Exit statement enables you to exit a VBScript section before it is programmed to end. For example, if a variable matches a desired unique value, why continue checking other values or dropping down to the next section. Instead, you may want to stop processing and return to the line after the line that jumped to the section. VBScript provides the following flavors of Exit: Exit Do exits a Do... Loop, Exit For exits a For... Next or For Each... Next loop, Exit Function exits a Function, Exit Property exits a Property, and Exit Sub exits a Sub. There is no Exit statement in JScript.

CROSS-REFERENCE
To learn about using **global.asa**, read the "Using the global.asa File" in Chapter 22.

FIND IT ONLINE
Learn to write for multiple browsers at **http://msdn.microsoft. com/workshop/essentials/versions.multi.asp**.

Listing 18-2: A Frames Example with Scripting

```
<% Set browsit=          ◄❶
Server.CreateObject("MSWC.BrowserType")
If browsit.Frames Then %>   ◄❷
<HTML><HEAD>
<TITLE>A Framed Page</TITLE>
</HEAD>
<FRAMESET ROWS=25%,75%>
<FRAME SRC="FRAME1.HTM FRAMEBORDER="0"Ł   ◄❸
        SCROLLING="no">
<FRAME SRC="FRAME2.HTM FRAMEBORDER="0">
</FRAMESET></HTML>
<& Else %>
<HTML><HEAD>
<TITLE>A Page without Frames</TITLE>   ◄❹
</HEAD><BODY>You have a frameless browser.
</BODY>
<& End If &></HTML>
```

❶ Enable the Browser Capabilities Component.
❷ Write a script for frames browsers.
❸ Define a frameset and its frames.
❹ Write script and a document for non-frames browsers.

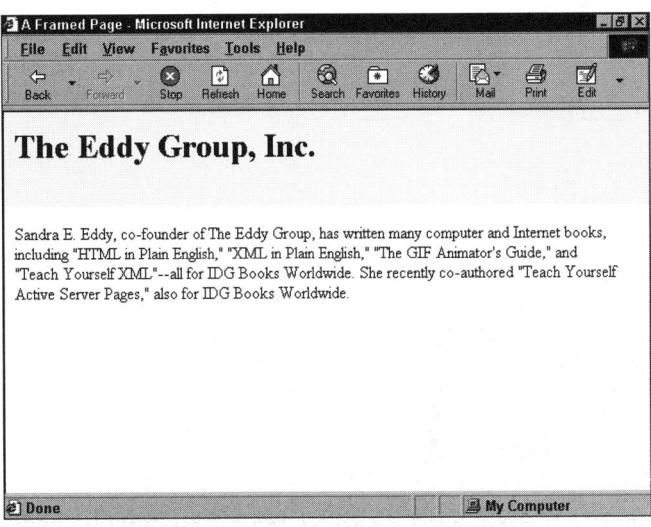

▶ This figure shows the results of the scripting when it is read by a browser that supports frames.

Listing 18-3: A Frames Example without Scripting

```
<HTML><HEAD>
<TITLE>Frames and No Frames</TITLE>
</HEAD>
<FRAMESET ROWS=25%,75%>
<FRAME SRC="FRAME1.HTM FRAMEBORDER="0"Ł
        SCROLLING="no">          ◄❺
<FRAME SRC="FRAME2.HTM FRAMEBORDER="0">
</FRAMESET>
<NOFRAMES>  ◄❻
You have a frameless browser.
</NOFRAMES></HTML>   ◄❼
```

❺ Define a frameset and its frames.
❻ Start a no-frames section with the <NOFRAMES> start tag.
❼ And complete the section with the </NOFRAMES> end tag.

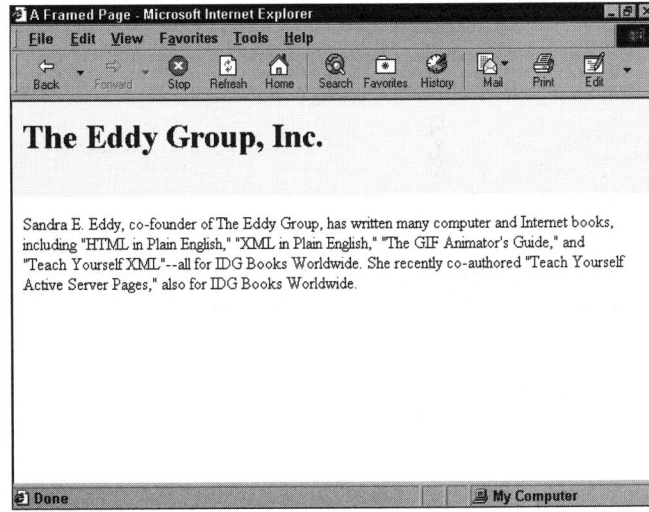

▶ Without a script and with the NOFRAMES element, a browser that supports frames shows the same results.

Transforming Documents to Meet Client Needs

The *Microsoft Press Computer Dictionary* defines *transform* as follows: "To change the appearance or format of data without altering its content; that is, to encode information according to predefined rules."

When you develop documents for the Web, transforming a document means that it is "translated" from the markup language in which it is written to another language. Transformation can happen in the following ways.

XML processors often transform XML documents to HTML. One reason for this is that most Web browsers cannot read XML. Another reason is that XML documents must be formatted with a stylesheet to be viewed; HTML elements provide styles for selected objects on a page. So when a document is transformed to HTML, the number of people who can view a document increases dramatically.

People often transform their SGML or XML documents by attaching a different DTD. Sometimes, this is done to add elements to an existing language. At other times, the document developer is finished testing a document against a test DTD and wants to move the document to a production DTD. Or, a developer has discovered a new DTD that defines a markup language for his or her industry. In fact, a new version of HTML — with additional elements — and a new DOCTYPE line at the top of a document, in effect, "attaches" a new DTD to that document.

When you rename an `.htm` or `.html` file to `.asp`, you actually start the transformation from HTML to ASP. Then for sections of script, you can change the `<SCRIPT>` and `</SCRIPT>` tags to the `<%` and `%>` delimiters. Finally, make sure that your server is up and running, and process the ASP page using the server computer rather than the browser software on the client.

Attaching a different external stylesheet to an ASP page or HTML document transforms it, even though the basic HTML language remains unchanged. For example, you can display paragraphs in a block format rather than an indented first line, or change the font and point size of headings or body text.

Sometimes, you rely on your regular word processor to transform a formatted document to HTML. When you do this, you will probably want to edit and even delete some of the resulting HTML code, which may be excessive. (See the before-and-after examples on the facing page.) At this point, it's a good idea to add comments to the document, too. As a result, you may save your visitors a few nanoseconds of loading time. In addition, those who maintain your documents will be able to read and edit the documents more easily.

Any time you transform a document from one language, application, or style to another, be sure to improve the document to make it easier to read or more pleasant to view.

TAKE NOTE

STANDARDIZING TRANSFORMATION WITH XSL

The XML Stylesheet Language (XSL) is an XML grammar whose documents are constructed in the same way as XML documents. XSL consists of two parts: a language that transforms documents and a vocabulary for applying formats to documents. In XSL, you can transform a document from the default unformatted XML markup and other content to one that meets predefined corporate or department standards. This enables a company or department to present identically formatted printed or online document sets to their clients or to the public. Every memorandum will look the same as any other, and all letters to clients will have the same layout, fonts, and point sizes. XSL uses rules that specify sections of the starting document, and then instruct a processor how to change and format those sections. For more information about using XSL to transform documents, see Chapter 27.

CROSS-REFERENCE
Review Chapter 27 in order to learn how to use XSL to transform documents.

FIND IT ONLINE
Read about using updated browsers at **http://msdn.microsoft. com/workshop/essentials/versions/hess022398.asp.**

Listing 18-4: A Word-Processing Document Transformed to HTML

```
<HTML><HEAD>
<META Name="Generator" Content="Application"></META>  ◀─ ❶
<TITLE>Body</TITLE> ❷
</HEAD><BODY BGCOLOR="#FFFFFF">  ❸      ❹
<UL><UL><FONT SIZE="4" FACE="Arial"><B>The Eddy Group, Inc.</B></FONT></UL></UL>  ◀─ ❷
<UL><UL><FONT SIZE="4" FACE="Arial"><B></B></FONT><FONT SIZE="3" FACE="Book
Antiqua">The Eddy Group, Inc., has been in existence since 1991. Its primary
business is writing computer and Internet books for prominent
publishers.</FONT></UL></UL>  ◀─ ❷
<UL><UL><FONT SIZE="3" FACE="Book Antiqua"><I>The Eddy Group's co-founders are
Sandra E. Eddy and E. A. Schnyder.</I></FONT>
</BODY></HTML>
        ❷
```

Listing 18-5: The Edited HTML Document

```
<HTML><HEAD>
<META Name="Generator"
Content="Application"></META>
<TITLE>Body</TITLE>
</HEAD><BODY BGCOLOR="#FFFFFF">
<FONT SIZE="4" FACE="Arial"><B>The Eddy Group,
Inc.</B></FONT>   ❺       ❻
<P><FONT SIZE="3" FACE="Book Antiqua">The Eddy
Group, Inc., has been in existence since 1991.
Its primary business is writing computer and
Internet books for prominent publishers.
<P><I>The Eddy Group's co-founders are Sandra
E. Eddy and E. A. Schnyder.</I></FONT>
</BODY></HTML>
   ❺
```

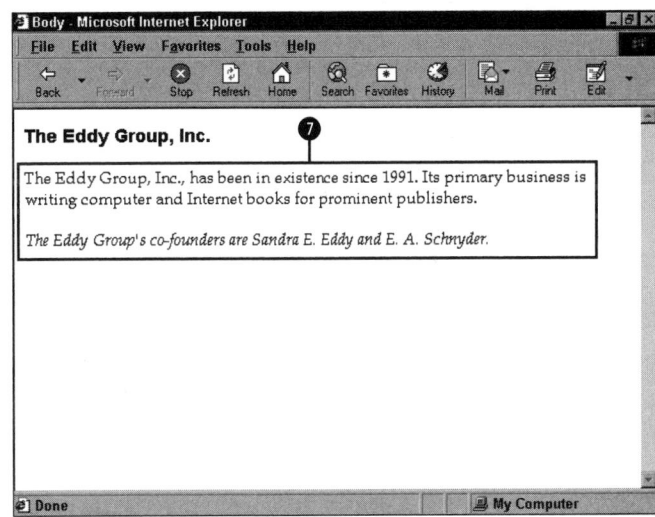

❼ Paragraph breaks were added. A different font was applied.

❶ This part of the document needs no changes.

❷ The word processor doubled <UL> and </UL> tags,

❸ Duplicated FONT elements,

❹ And added a set of <B> and </B> tags without text.

❺ Paragraph breaks were added.

❻ A different font was applied.

Personal Workbook

Q & A

1 What is the Browser Capabilities Component? What does it do?

_____

_____

_____

2 What are installable components? Name the installable components that are bundled with IIS and PWS.

_____

_____

_____

3 What is encryption?

_____

_____

_____

4 What is a key? Name the two key technologies.

_____

_____

_____

5 What is authentication?

_____

_____

_____

6 What is `global.asa`?

_____

_____

_____

7 How can you end a VBScript section early?

_____

_____

_____

_____

8 What is transformation?

_____

_____

_____

_____

ANSWERS: PAGE 509

Supporting Various Browsers and Other Fine-Tuning

EXTRA PRACTICE

1. After downloading a new version of `browscap.ini`, search the file for information about your active browser.

2. Go online and get more information about digital signatures.

3. Find and download one or two trial versions of script editors from online sites.

4. Using a word processor, write a home page for your business. Then save the page as an HTML document, and edit that document (if necessary).

5. Create a document that includes two parallel sections of your choice, one written in VBScript and the other in JScript. Write a script to branch to one section, depending on a certain condition.

REAL-WORLD APPLICATIONS

✔ Your department has assigned you to update `browscap.ini` biweekly.

✔ Your company wants you to investigate software that you can use to write your ASP pages. Review the available programs and suites and write a report to management.

✔ Although your non-profit organization has a limited budget, it wants to take advantage of ASP and other new Web technologies. After reviewing the technologies and available shareware, write a proposal.

✔ You are in charge of converting some of your company's reports, which were written on a word processor, to the Web. Convert, edit, and enhance the reports using ASP and other technologies.

Visual Quiz

This is the result of a transformation from a word processor file to an HTML document. Improve the title. Convert the heading to a large point size. Remove extra elements and default attributes, and improve the format of the document.

_____

_____

_____

_____

_____

```
visual quiz 18 - Notepad
File  Edit  Search  Help
<HTML>
<HEAD>
<META Name="Generator" Content="Lotus Word Pro"></META>
<TITLE>Body</TITLE>

</HEAD>

<BODY BGCOLOR="#FFFFFF">

<H2>A Sample HTML Page</H2>
<P>
<P>This page shows samples of HTML elements.
<P>
<P>This is a bulleted list.
        <UL TYPE="disc">
                <LI>Computers
                <LI>Printers
                <LI>Zip Drives
        </UL>
This is a numbered list.
        <OL>
                <LI>Start the engine.
                <LI>Put it into gear.
                <LI>Take your foot off the brake.
                <LI>Hit the gas pedal.
        </OL>

</BODY>
</HTML>
```

PART

IV

Contents of 'Desktop'

Name

My Computer

Network Neigh

Internet Explore

Microsoft Outloo

Recycle Bin

My Briefcase

3252-9

3259-6

3261-8

3262-6

3281-2

3286-3

DE Phone List

Device Manager

In

Iomega Tools

Using Objects and Databases

At this point in *Teach Yourself Microsoft Active Server Pages 3*, you have a basic understanding of the ASP architecture and both markup and scripting development. You should also have a development server ready with which to test your Active Server Pages. In this part of the book, you will learn how to build dynamic Web pages that integrate that architecture, script, and markup.

The next nine chapters will give you an overview of the objects that ASP provides as a foundation set, as well as show you where to find (or perhaps develop) more objects that meet your needs more closely. You'll learn how to process the information that users send through forms, and generate replies that combine their requests with your own documents and databases. You'll learn about the intricacies of setting up connections to relational database systems, and how to manage those connections to get your users their information most efficiently. By using some of ASP's built-in tools, you'll be able to get information into and out of databases reliably, supporting multiple simultaneous users without requiring complex code. You'll learn how to track users and provide customized information without requiring redundant information entry or password authentication. After a brief tour of what Microsoft's new XML tools bring to ASP, you'll conclude with an overview of the many application architectures you can build with your newfound tools.

CHAPTER **19**

MASTER
THESE
SKILLS

▶ **Learning about ASP and Object-Oriented Development**

▶ **Accessing and Manipulating Objects**

▶ **Working with the Request Object**

▶ **Working with the Response Object**

▶ **Learning about the Server, Application, and Session Objects**

▶ **Working with the Err object**

Using Built-In ASP Objects

In this chapter, you'll learn to take advantage of the many facilities that Active Server Pages provides for building complex, interactive, Web-based applications. In addition to its support for processing scripts within HTML documents, Internet Information Server (IIS) provides a set of tools that you can use to process information sent by the user and the information going back to the user. IIS also provides more general tools for storing application-wide, server-wide, and user-specific information across multiple transactions.

The key to this functionality is objects. While Active Server Pages isn't an object-oriented development environment, scripts can access objects written using Microsoft's COM specification for components. Although you don't need to learn anything about COM itself or build COM objects, the COM specifications make it easy for your programs to take advantage of the capabilities other developers have built into their COM objects.

The Active Server Pages engine itself includes a foundation set of objects providing access to information sent over HTTP, and can be easily extended through the addition of other objects. The core set of objects provided by ASP is often enough to build a simple application, and nearly every application of any complexity will need to use these objects as well.

Mastering the basics of manipulating objects and learning more about your users' requests is an important first step on the way to building complete applications. By the end of this chapter, you should be able to access information sent to your server by your users and manage the responses sent back to them, thereby establishing a solid foundation to which you can add extra functionality. Your applications will be able to access the information sent by users through forms and links, and reply with customized responses.

Learning about ASP and Object-Oriented Development

Programmers who are used to traditional procedural and object-oriented development environments sometimes find Active Server Pages a strange hybrid of marked-up data, procedural code (the scripts), and object-oriented development (sometimes the scripts, but usually the COM objects). At the same time, Web developers who are used to mixing scripts with Web page content may still find the conventions that Active Server Pages uses to differentiate client-side and server-side scripts and objects confusing. As a result, it's probably a good idea to re-examine just what exactly goes into creating an ASP application.

While effective ASP development makes constant use of objects (and ASP is processed using objects whether you explicitly call them or not), ASP is definitely not an object-oriented development tool. ASP is much more of an object-manipulation tool, creating and using objects toward a particular goal: the creation of Web pages. The architecture of ASP is a combination of mostly familiar tools, knitted together with some simple conventions.

Active Server Pages are the control center for an entire framework of objects. Some, like Request, Response, and Object Context, exist only for the duration of a single HTTP transaction. Others, like Server, Application, and Session, provide context across multiple transactions, multiple users, and sometimes even multiple applications. As shown in the Active Server Pages diagram, the connections between these many objects provide context and content for your Web applications. You won't need to use all of these objects for every application, but if you need them, they're available.

Objects provide a consistent representation of the data that your pages are processing, providing a more sophisticated set of tools than the raw HTTP headers and a space for writing back to the user. Objects can be used to discover user needs, collect information, manage the presentation and transmission of that information, store the information for later use, and keep track of application-wide (and server-wide) information.

Fortunately, you don't need to know much about what goes on inside of these objects. You can treat them as black boxes, using scripting languages to get information into them and out of them. You can add other developers' objects to the collection that comes with ASP, and glue them into the overall framework with your scripts. Building Active Server Pages is typically a matter of figuring out which object provides the services you need, and integrating with your application by writing a small bit of script.

TAKE NOTE

STARTING SMALL

Don't let the seeming complexity of the ASP environment overwhelm you. The Request and Response objects are the most important and friendliest. You can build genuinely useful pages based on that subset, and move on to more complex architectures as necessary. Many developers have used ASP for small projects without even referencing the objects directly — ASP can be used effectively from any point on the learning curve.

OBJECTS AS BLACK BOXES

One of the best things about Active Server Pages, and about object development in general, is that you don't have to worry about what goes on inside the objects you use. Generally, I've found that the objects inside the ASP framework behave as documented — you don't need to worry about the core ASP framework generating bugs. If you have bugs, make sure that you're creating and referencing the objects correctly.

CROSS-REFERENCE

Information on adding new objects to your ASP environment is provided in Chapter 20.

FIND IT ONLINE

Microsoft provides an overview of the ASP environment at **http://msdn.microsoft.com/workshop/server/asp/ASPover.asp**.

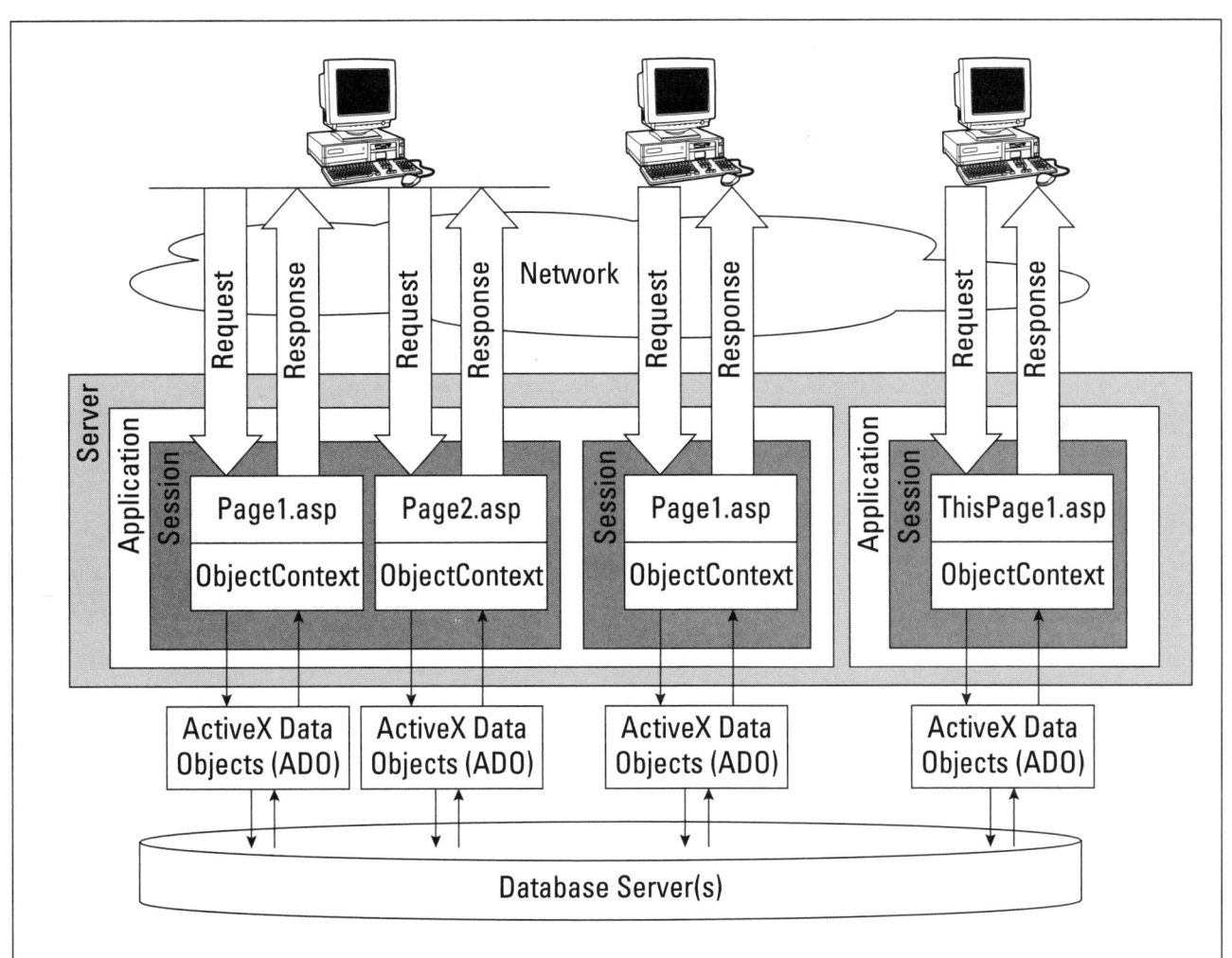

► *Active Server Pages operate at the core of a sophisticated set of objects.*

Accessing and Manipulating Objects

Active Server Pages can read (and sometimes write) object properties and collections, call object methods, and provide handlers for some object events. The syntax for accessing objects is fairly simple, and looks pretty much the same in both VBScript and JScript.

Object properties are always referenced with the name of the object followed by a period (.), followed by the name of the property. For example, to assign the value of the Request object's `TotalBytes` property to the `SmallrequestLength` variable, the code would look like:

```
requestLength=Request.TotalBytes
```

Similarly, properties (at least those which are writable) can also be assigned values through a similar mechanism. To set the `Buffer` property of the `Response` object to `True`, for example, the following code would be appropriate:

```
Response.Buffer=True
```

Some properties use a different syntax, taking values in a way that looks more like the following method calls. For example, the `CharSet` property of the Response object uses this syntax. To set the character set of your response to UTF-8 (a Unicode format commonly used by XML), you would use:

```
Response.CharSet("UTF-8")
```

instead of:

```
Response.CharSet="UTF-8"
```

We'll point out properties where this syntax is appropriate in the appropriate tables and examples.

Object collections provide you with access to properties using a reference to a string. The Request object, for example, keeps all of the server variables (commonly used in CGI development) in a collection called `ServerVariables`. To retrieve one of their values, you access the collection as a property named by a key string. For example, the following stores the IP address of the browser requesting the current page (known as REMOTE_ADDR) in a variable named `atIP`:

```
atIP=Request.ServerVariables("REMOTE_ADDR")
```

Collections are frequently used for information that may or may not be available depending on the nature of this particular transaction. Collections also provide a `Count` property that specifies how many values it contains, and information can be retrieved by numerical references as well as by key.

Method calls let you pass information to an object and have it perform some action. Sometimes the object returns a value to the code that called it, but sometimes the call is used simply to pass information to the object or have it take some action. The Response object, for example, has several methods, notably `Write`, that change the information sent back to the user but don't return any information to your program. To write information to the outgoing stream, you can call `Response.Write` with a string to add:

```
Response.Write "This is outgoing text."
```

(Parentheses are required around arguments when you call methods in JScript.) Some method calls return a value as well. The Server object contains a utility function for encoding content within a URL, for example. To URL encode a query string and store that value in the variable query, you could write:

```
query=Server.URLEncode("ASP objects")
```

The string "ASP objects" would be converted to "ASP+objects", making it possible to include it as a query string in a URL.

CROSS-REFERENCE

Events will be covered in relation to the objects that actually generate them (see Chapters 23, 26, and 27).

FIND IT ONLINE

For more information about manipulating objects, see: **http://msdn.microsoft.com/workshop/server/asp/comtutorial.asp.**

```
<HTML><BODY>
Query String: <%= Request.QueryString %><BR>
<PRE>
<%=Request.ServerVariables("ALL_HTTP")%>
</PRE></BODY>


<%
Response.Write "<HTML><HEAD><TITLE>"
Response.Write "Programmer's Page</TITLE>"
Response.Write "</HEAD><BODY>"
Response.Write ("<P>I wrote this page myself
through")
Response.Write " code directly.  No messing
around"
Response.Write " with mixtures of scripts and
markup!</P>"
Response.Write "<P>I can even do things like
include HTML"
Response.Write " samples easily using method
calls:</P><PRE>"
htmlEncode=Server.HTMLEncode("<HTML><HEAD>
<TITLE>")
Response.Write htmlEncode
Response.Write "<PRE></BODY>"
%>
```

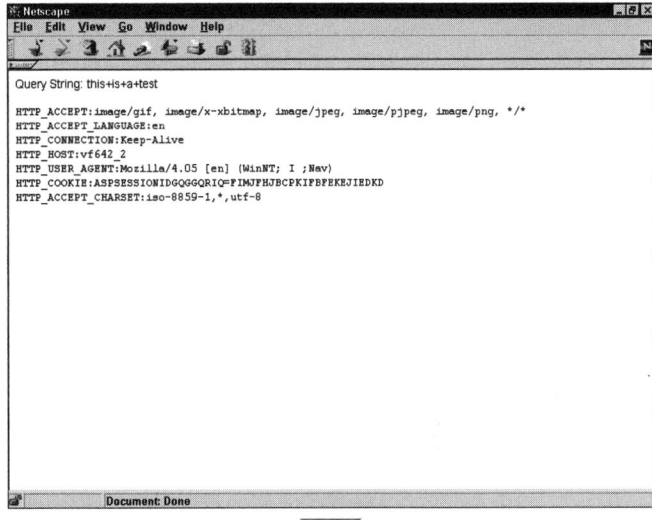

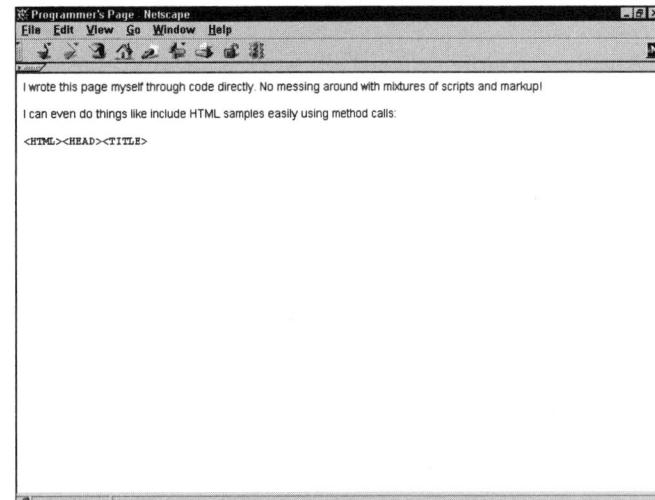

▶ Object properties and collections alone can be used to create a simple page that's useful for debugging.

▶ Object methods can be used to build pages with traditional procedural techniques. Note that the parentheses around the method arguments are optional, but don't interfere with the result.

Working with the Request Object

The Request object is a critical tool for connecting with your users. While static Web page development can rely on the connections established between pages with hyperlinks, Active Server Pages typically provide a much higher level of interaction. Many ASP sites rely on forms to collect information and help users navigate through them. Nearly every piece of information supplied by the HTTP protocol can be used in some situation. The Request object provides a complete representation of the information sent by users, including access to the raw material.

The Request object supplies most of its information through collections, which represent the contents of HTTP headers, information from forms, cookies, and other material. Most of the time, developers rely on ASP to process that information, thereby avoiding the tedious task of parsing material based on the lower-level standards. While you can do it the hard way if you need to (typically when you need to extract binary information sent as a file upload from a browser), the Request object's many collections have simplified most of that work.

The structure of the collections that the Request object provides definitely point ASP development toward the creation of single-purpose pages, designed to accept information from particular forms using particular protocols. Always expect to build pages that are designed for a single set of inputs and return the outputs you want. If you need to accept information in multiple formats, build multiple pages.

GET requests are mostly processed through the QueryString collection (which can also be retrieved as a property), while POST requests are processed through the Form collection. GET requests and query strings have an advantage in that they can be bookmarked. This capability makes it easier for the user to return to any point in your application. Some applications end up being a mix of both: GET for the lightweight work, POST for the heavy-duty forms processing.

You can use the QueryString collection to retrieve user information that comes from a GET. When the form is submitted, as in Listing 19-1, you can expect to get all the data back in the query string, appended to the URL, as follows:

```
mypage.asp?name=Susie&eMail=me@my.
com&notify=true
```

```
userName = Request.QueryString("name")
eMail = Request.QueryString("eMail")
add = Request.String("notify")
```

When the METHOD attribute of a form is a POST, the data comes wrapped in the HTTP headers. In this case, the QueryString collection is empty, and the values are placed in the Form collection. You can retrieve the <form> values as follows:

```
userName = Request.Form("name")
eMail = Request.Form("eMail")
add = Request.Form("notify")
```

Continued

Troubleshooting

Do not use the GET method if you expect the data entered by the user to exceed about 1,000 characters. Using the GET method to get larger amounts of data via an HTML form could cause undesired results.

CROSS-REFERENCE

Chapter 23 discusses in more detail how to process HTML forms.

FIND IT ONLINE

For more information about the Request object, see: **http://msdn.microsoft.com/library/sdkdoc/iisref/vbob5ulw.htm**.

Table 19-1: THE COMMON PROPERTIES, COLLECTIONS, AND METHODS OF THE REQUEST OBJECT

Collection	Description
ClientCertificate	All the information contained in the client's certificate, useful for identifying the person on the other end of your Secure Sockets Layer (SSL) connection.
Cookies	All available cookies. Will be covered in depth in Chapter 25.
Form	The fields of a form returned by a POST request. Cannot be used if the BinaryRead method has been called.
QueryString	The fields of a form returned by a GET request, or simply a query string appended to the URL in a link.
ServerVariables	The full set of variables available for this request, much as they appear in Common Gateway Interface (CGI) transactions. See Table 19-2.

Property	Description
TotalBytes	Contains the total number of bytes contained in the user's request. If you want to process the request manually with the BinaryRead method below, this property provides a stopping point.

Method	Description
BinaryRead	A method for collecting information directly from the HTTP request header by reading it in as a series of bytes. Cannot be used after the Form collection has been used.

Listing 19-1: Making a FORM using the GET Method

```
<form name="guestBook" action="response.asp" method="get">
<h2>Please fill our guest book.</h2>
<table width=60% cellspacing=0 cellpadding=4>
<tr><td>Name:</td><td><input type="text" name=uName size=50></td></tr>
<tr><td>eMail:</td><td><input type="text" name=eMail size=50></td></tr>
<tr><td><input type="radio" name="notify" value="yes" CHECKED>
        <input type="radio" name="notify" value="no"></td>
  <td>Do you want to be notified when the site changes?</td></tr>
<tr><td colspan=2><input type="submit" value="Register"></td></tr>
</table>
</form>
```

Working with the Request Object
Continued

A collection's `Count` property returns the number of items in the collection. This property tells you if there are multiple values, and provides a way to iterate through the Request object's collection. `Request.Form("guestBook").Count` would return the number 4 in Listing 19-1, with data entry fields, because the form's submit button is also considered a data entry field.

Developers who have grown accustomed to the Common Gateway Interface (CGI) approach to Web development will appreciate the `ServerVariables` collection, which provides access to information about the request in a format similar to that of CGI (see Table 19-2). The familiar header and server information is available, though developers need to remember that the ASP engine will preface any header it doesn't recognize with `HTTP_`. The `ServerVariables` collection provides a useful window for developers who need detailed access to the contents of authentication schemes, including basic authentication, Microsoft's authentication, and the information stored in digital certificates.

The `QueryString` and `Form` collections that you examined previously are only available in a single browser request. Each time the user requests any file from the server, the Request object's collections are updated with the information from that request. Occasionally, there is a need for more persistent data storage. To achieve this, the HTTP protocol specification introduced the concept of cookies.

A *cookie* is a packet of information sent by the browser to the server with each request. Data items within each cookie are available in the `Cookies` collection, which is accessed in a similar manner to the `QueryString` and `Form` collection.

When accessed through the Request object, cookies are read-only. You can only change cookie information using the Response object.

Security is currently a big issue on the Net. If you are concerned about security in your electronic transactions, one feature that is becoming increasingly available in browsers is access to the Secure Sockets Layer (SSL). When SSL is in use, the browser sends the server certificates that identify the client.

If you want to make use of this information in your Web pages, you can use the `ClientCertificate` collection. Accessing the information in the `ClientCertificate` collection follows a similar pattern to the other Request object collections.

TAKE NOTE

▶ COUNTING FORM ELEMENTS

Use `Request.Form(element).Count` to determine if the user has selected more than one item in a drop-down selection list. Also use the `Count` property to determine which submit button was pressed if you have multiple actions on your HTML form.

CROSS-REFERENCE
Chapter 25 discusses how to implement cookies in your Web application.

Table 19-2: COMMONLY USED SERVER VARIABLES

Server Variable	Use
ALL_HTTP	Returns all the header information that came directly from the request.
AUTH_PASSWORD	Returns the user's password if authentication was required and basic authentication (which doesn't use encryption) was used.
AUTH_TYPE	The authentication method used to validate the username and password.
AUTH_USER	The username of the current user, if authentication was required.
CONTENT_TYPE	The MIME content type of the data sent by the client. Typically, this will be `application/x-www-form-urlencoded`, but may change to `multipart/form-data` if file information is being uploaded.
HTTP_USER_AGENT	A string describing the client software, which can be used to send different content depending on browser capabilities.
LOCAL_ADDR	The TCP/IP address of the Web server receiving the request. If you are running your Web site across multiple servers, keeping track of this address can be critical.
QUERY_STRING	The query string that came as part of the request.
REMOTE_ADDR	The TCP/IP address of the client making the request.
REQUEST_METHOD	The HTTP method used for the request. Typically GET or POST, but HEAD, PUT, and DELETE are also possible.
SERVER_NAME	The server's TCP/IP address or resolvable DNS name. Useful for creating URLs pointing to this server.
SERVER_PORT	The TCP/IP port on which this server received the request. Typically 80, but is sometimes 8080, 8001, or 443, depending on configuration.
URL	The base URL that the client requested, without the query string.

Working with the Response Object

You just learned to use the Request object to extract information from forms and from the query string within the URL. Now, you will learn to use Response object to create HTML content dynamically. The Response object is used to add and alter HTTP headers, build page bodies dynamically, and redirect your clients to alternative pages automatically. In Table 19-3, you can see the common methods, properties, and collections implemented by the Response object.

The most obvious requirement for the Response object is for it to send back a page containing text, graphics, and other interesting content.

You can take advantage of the Response object's `Write` method to insert a string into the HTML stream that goes to the browser. For example:

```
Response.Write("You are visitor number " +
counter + ".")
```

You can construct strings in code and write them to the page. Using the `Write` method also makes your code more readable than interspersing HTML tags and `<% ... %>` throughout your Web page.

In some situations, it is extremely useful to be able to redirect your users to an alternative page, instead of the one they requested. If you are requiring a user ID and password to gain access to parts of your site, you might redirect users to the login page when they request an item that is in the password-protected area.

The first thing to note about redirection: It is tied up with the HTTP protocol. When the browser makes an HTTP GET request, it expects to receive headers informing the browser what is actually coming from the server. The browser can receive a redirection header, which tells the browser to go and get the information elsewhere. For example:

```
Response.Redirect "http://www.idgbooks.com"
```

Another useful feature is buffering, which enables you an extra degree of control over when a client receives information, as well as what a client receives. The `Buffer` property can have one of two values: true or false. If the property is set to true, all scripts in the current page execute before the first byte of data is written to the client. By default, buffering is set to false and data is written as it is made available by the server.

To use buffering, you must first set the `Buffer` property before the opening `<HTML>` tag.

```
<%@ language="JScript" %>
<% Response.Buffer = True %>
<HTML>
```

Setting the `Buffer` property alone gives you no advantage. However, by setting it to true, you have access to the auxiliary methods of `Clear`, `Flush`, and `End`.

`Response.Clear` erases any buffered output in the message body. The `Clear` method does not erase any previously set response headers. It is often used when an error occurs during the execution of a page.

Continued

TAKE NOTE

▶ RESPONSE.BUFFER

Use `Request.Form(element).Count` to determine if the user has selected more than one item in a drop.

CROSS-REFERENCE

Chapter 23 gives examples of using **Response.Buffer** and its properties.

FIND IT ONLINE

Wise ASP (**http://www.aspalliance.com/wiseasp/template. asp**) offers an article on how to layout your ASP script to avoid interspersing HTML tags and ASP delimiters.

Table 19-3: THE COMMON PROPERTIES, COLLECTIONS, AND METHODS OF THE RESPONSE OBJECT

Collection	Description
Cookies	Values of all the cookies to send to the browser.

Method	Description
Clear	Erases any buffered HTML output.
End	Stops processing the page and returns the current result.
Flush	Sends buffered output immediately.
Redirect	Instructs the browser to connect to a different URL.
Write	Writes a variable to the current page as a string.

Property	Description
AddHeader	Adds a new header to any that are already in the buffer.
Buffer	Indicates whether to buffer the page until complete.
CacheControl	Determines whether proxy servers are able to cache the output generated by ASP.
ContentType	HTTP content type for the response.
Expires	Length of time before a page cached on a browser expires.
ExpiresAbsolute	Date and time when a page cached on a browser expires.
Status	Value of the HTTP status line returned by the server.

Troubleshooting

Many of the properties and methods of the Response object are used to set HTTP response headers in the HTML stream. If page buffering is not on, any attempt to use these Response object properties to write headers after the initial <HTML> tag generates an error – all response headers must be written before any message body data is sent.

Working with the Response Object
Continued

You can dynamically send all buffered output back to the browser while still processing the page by using the `Response.Flush`.

During page processing, you may want to end processing the script immediately when a condition is met. These situations could include an error condition or some type of notification. `Response.End` immediately stops all script execution. If page buffering has been turned on for the page, it flushes the buffer before ending processing.

The Response object holds a `Cookies` collection that enables you to write values to the cookies that are sent back with your page. This code adds a cookie to a client's machine:

`Response.Cookies("UserShoeSize") = 12`

Cookies can also have properties relating to their lifetime and availability. If you do not set these explicitly, any information stored in them will be lost when the user shuts down their browser. You can also set various other properties of a cookie. These properties are domain, path, and secure (see Table 19-4). You will look at these properties in more detail later.

When a client requests a page on your server, the page is delivered to the browser where it is placed in the browser's cache and then displayed on the screen. If the browser can fulfill a page request using a local cached copy, it uses the cached version by default.

For most dynamic and transactional Web sites, the information in any given page changes frequently. Using the Response object, you can set an expiration date for your pages so that the browser knows when the cached copy has expired. In order to avoid this, you have to inhibit the browser's page caching. This can be accomplished by manipulating the Response object. There are different ways to disable page caching. All of these ways rely on addressing directives to the browser in the HTTP header. However, all browsers do not respond in the same way to the directives sent by the server, so it's a good idea to send more directives in order to inhibit caching for most browsers, as shown in Listing 19-2.

The first two lines of the code use `Response.AddHeader` to append header information to the HTTP header. The `Expires` and `ExpiresAbsolute` properties mark the current page with information about the duration of the page in the browser's cache. These lines must be inserted before any other code in the form page, because they refer to information put in the HTTP header that is sent to the browser before any other output.

A number of properties and methods are available in the Response object that enable you to write HTTP headers to the HTTP data stream. Many of the properties set a specific value for an HTTP header record.

Many Internet users connect to the Internet through a proxy server. If you do not want the page to be cached when a proxy server is used, set the `CacheControl` property to `Private`:

`Response.CacheControl = Private`

The `Content-Type` HTTP header is used to notify the client about what type of data is returned within the message body. The `ContentType` property of the Response object enables you to set the `Content-Type` header in your ASP script (see Table 19-5). By default, ASP provides the `text/html` content header.

Table 19-4: COOKIE ATTRIBUTES

Attribute	Description
Domain	An optional attribute that restricts the cookie being returned to only this domain.
Expires	A required date parameter that specifies the cookie's expiration.
Path	An optional parameter that restricts the cookie being returned only when the path is matched.
Secure	An optional attribute that requires the connection between the client and server to be secure before the cookie is written.

Listing 19-2: Setting Page Expiration

```
<%
Response.AddHeader "cache-control", "private"
Response.AddHeader "pragma", "no-cache"
Response.ExpiresAbsolute = #January 1, 1990
00:00:01#
Response.Expires=-1000
%>
```

Table 19-5: COMMON CONTENT TYPES

Content Types
Text/html
Image/JPEG
Application/x-www-form-encoded
Image/GIF
Application/x-cdf

Learning about the Server, Application, and Session Objects

The Server Object is one of the five built-in objects in ASP. The Server object contains basic properties and methods that are used in almost every Active Server Page that you will create. Table 19-6 lists the interfaces into the Server object.

Let's start with the single property of the Server object. The `ScriptTimeout` property enables you to terminate a script in order to protect itself from being overloaded, possibly by an infinite loop. This property defines the delay before the script will be terminated. To retrieve the current value, you can use Listing 19-3.

Have you ever had to write a document in HTML about HTML? Suppose you want to add the following line to Listing 19-3.

```
The previous information used the <%
=Server.ScriptTimeout %> property.
```

To get this code listing displayed as part of the page on the browser, rather than having it executed on the server, you have to replace the angle brackets with an escape sequence, which the browser can understand. An example escape sequence is `&lt;` for the less than character.

Fortunately, the Server object can help you out. The `HTMLEncode` method takes a string of text and converts any illegal characters it contains to the appropriate HTML escape sequence. For example, to produce your previous text correctly on a browser (without being interpreted as the actual property), you would use Listing 19-3.

The Server object's `URLEncode` method is similar to `HTMLEncode`, but takes a string of information and converts it into URL-encoded form, rather than HTML. All the spaces are replaced by plus signs (+), and certain other characters are replaced by a percent sign and their ANSI equivalent in hexadecimal.

```
<% =Server.URLEncode (varDynamicURL) %>
```

When dealing with Web sites, file paths are not always what they appear to be. The file pointed to by:

```
http://www.yourserver/com/default.asp
```

may have a physical path on the server of:

```
c:/inetpub/wwwroot/default.asp
```

but the page could also be stored on the server at any path. It is not usually possible to determine the location of a file from the URL used to access it.

Web servers never allow the browser to access a Web site's physical file system directly. The browser simply asks the Web server for the file and then accepts whatever it is given. This approach allows the Web server a large degree of freedom in how its files are stored and exposed to clients. In IIS, file requests are based on virtual roots. A virtual root is a directory in a Web site where a logical (URL) location in the Web does not necessarily correspond to its physical location as it relates to the root of the site.

To the Web developer, the difference is usually unimportant. However, certain things in ASP scripts could require you to know or find the physical location of a file when you have only its Web path. You can use `Server.MapPath` to provide file location information for use in your scripts. Its purpose is to translate the logical path information that may be used by a client browser into a physical path on the server. For example, if a script needs to know the actual physical location on disk of the application's virtual root, you could get the information with Listing 19-3.

Continued

FIND IT ONLINE

For more information about the next release of Windows 2000 server products, see: **http://www.microsoft.com/windows/server/Overview/intro/default.asp**.

CROSS-REFERENCE

Chapter 25 describes how to implement Application variables.

Table 19-6: THE COMMON PROPERTIES AND METHODS OF THE SERVER OBJECT

Property	Description
ScriptTimeout	Length of time a script can run before an error occurs in seconds.

Method	Description
CreateObject	Creates an instance of an object or server component.
HTMLEncode	Applies HTML encoding to the specified string.
MapPath	Converts a virtual path into a physical path.
URLEncode	Applies URL encoding (including escape chars) to a string.
Execute	A procedure call, executing whatever resource you pass it.
Transfer	Transfers page execution from one page to the next.
GetLastError	Returns a reference to an ASPError object.

Listing 19-3: Using the Response Object

```jscript
<%@ language="JScript" %>
<html>
<body>

<%
  // Using the ScriptTimeout property
  Response.Write("Script timeout is " + Server.ScriptTimeout + "seconds.")
%>
<%
  // Using the HTMLEncode method
  Response.Write("The previous information used the " +
     Server.HTMLEncode("<% =Server.ScriptTimeout %\>") + " property.")
<%
  // Using the MapPath method
  var vRoot = Server.MapPath("/orders")
  Response.Write("The orders application root is located at " +
     vRoot + ".")
%>

</body>
</html>
```

Learning about the Server, Application, and Session Objects *Continued*

The result in vRoot (virtual root) would be something like this:

```
C:\inetpub\wwwroot\orders
```

You could then use this information to create or modify documents on the fly using the `FileSystemObject` and `TextStream` objects.

The last of the Server object's methods is certainly the most useful for creating interesting applications. The Active Server Pages environment can be extended by the use of server components. To use the components in your scripts, you need to be able to instantiate them. This process create instances of the object they contain, so that you can use their methods and access their properties. You use `Server.CreateObject` for this task.

One of the components supplied with Active Server Pages is the Browser Capabilities component. See Listing 19-4 for how to create an instance of the Browser Capabilities object, using its `progID` of `MSWC.BrowserType`. You can then use the object's methods. If this code is run from Netscape Release 4, you get the output in the browser output from executing Listing 19-4.

The Server object has been spruced up with three new methods in IIS 5.0. The `Execute` method is literally a procedure call, executing whatever resource you pass it. The `Transfer` method is a functional direction controller, transferring page execution from one page to the next. The `GetLastError` method returns a reference to an ASPError object, which is also introduced in IIS 5.0.

The `Execute` command can be used to force execution of ASP file within one page. `Server.Execute` issues an execution request for a resource directly, rather than as a command from the browser.

The `Transfer` method addresses many of the problems of the `Response.Redirect` method, including efficiency. When the `Transfer` method is called, any session-level or application-level variables or objects assigned in the calling page up to the invocation of the method are available to the next resource. The `Response.Redirect` method requires that all content is buffered before calling the method, but `Server.Transfer` manages that issue, making the code to work with this method less burdensome.

The `GetLastError` method may be the best improvement to the Server object. `Server.GetLastError` returns an ASPError object in the event that an error has occurred in processing. The ASPError object is the first version of an error handling mechanism implemented in ASP, with a number of properties to provide information regarding the offending error. The `GetLastError` method's purpose is to return a reference to this object when applicable. There are three basic problems in ASP scripts that will generate an error captured by the ASPError object: preprocessing errors, such as an include file; compile errors, such as incorrect code; and runtime errors, which can be generated by incorrect data handling.

When IIS encounters one of these errors while processing an ASP request, the `Server.Transfer` method is called and the `500-100.asp` error page is requested. You can customize this default error page, and the ASPError object can be used on that customized error page to provide detailed information about the error that occurred.

Continued

Listing 19-4: Using `Server.CreateObject`

```jscript
<%@ Language="JScript" %>
<html>
<body>
<% main() %>
</body>
<html>
<script runat="server" language="JScript">
function main() {
  var objBrowser = Server.CreateObject("MSWC.BrowserType");
  Response.Write("The " + objBrowser.Browser + " " + objBrowser.Version + " supports ...");
  Response.Write("<ul>");
  Response.Write("<li>Javascript: " + objBrowser.Javascript);
  Response.Write("<li>Frames: " + objBrowser.Frames);
  Response.Write("<li>Cookies: " + objBrowser.Cookies);
  Response.Write("</ul>");
}
</script>
```

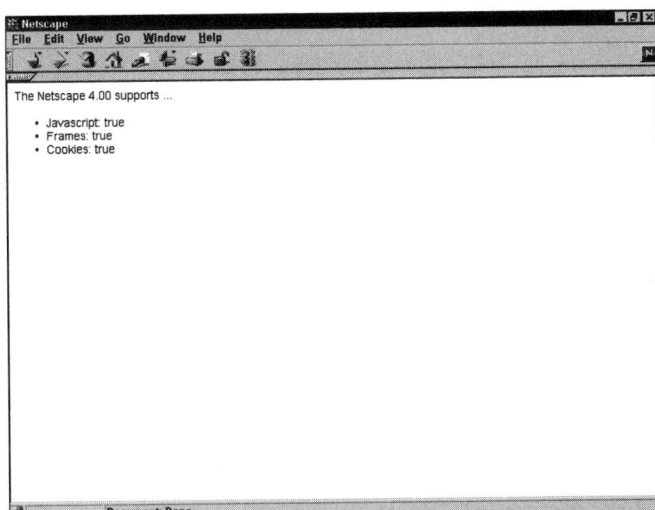

Listing 19-5: Using `Server.Transfer`

```vbscript
<script language="VBScript">
<% Response.Buffer = true %>
<html>
<body>
<% If Session("userAuthenticated") = false Then
  Server.Transfer("login.asp")
  End If
%>
<% ' Else continue processing your page %>
. . .
```

Learning about the Server, Application, and Session Objects *Continued*

Now that you have looked at the other objects in the overall Active Server Pages object model, you need to consider how an application built with ASP fits together. An application comprises all the files that can be referenced through a single virtual mapping, or aliased directory on the Web server.

The Application object can store information for use by script files, process requests, and respond to events.

Values are placed into the collection through simple assignment statements, placed anywhere in your application. For example,

```
Application("name") = Request.Form("name")
```

If you need to write code that executes when your Web application either starts or finishes, you need to put it into an event handler (see Listing 19-6). Because this sort of script requires a home, you place it in a particular file in the root directory of the virtual application, called `global.asa`.

The Application object has two collections (see Table 19-7) that enable you to browse through objects and variables.

The `Contents` collection contains a group of all of the items that have been added to the application through a script command. You can use the `Contents` collection to obtain a list of items that have been given application scope. The `Application Contents` collection contains those items that have been declared at the application level without using the `<OBJECT>` tag.

Using the Application object, the data values are global to the whole application, and are available in any of its pages. However, when you have data that needs to be shared between different pages, but not necessarily between different clients, you can make use of the Session object. Each client that requests a page from your application is assigned a Session object.

When you store information in the Session Object, the client that owns that session is assigned a sessionID, which can use used in your pages to identify them while they are browsing your site. The sessionID is assigned by the server, and is only available to you as a read-only property. The actual sessionID information is stored as a cookie with no expiry date, so that is expires when the client browser is closed.

The benefit of the Session object is that you can place information into it and retrieve that information at any point during the user's visit. This feature is implemented by using a collection similar to the Request and Response objects.

In ASP, there is a problem when storing arrays in a Session or Application object. All Session-level and Application-level variables are stored as variants. There is no way to store an array of variants. Instead, you have to use a variant array and store all of your values there. The following example shows how to do this:

```
Dim myArray()
ReDim myArray(3)
myArray(0) = "jscript"
myArray(1) = "vbscript"
myArray(2) = "perlscrpt"
' store array for later use
Session("scriptArray") = myArray


' Retrieve and use in (another) your page
tempArray = Session("scriptArray")
Response.Write "My favorite language is " +
tempArray(0) + "."
```

You create the `myArray` and `ReDim` to hold three elements. Then you assign your different values to each index in `myArray`, and then assign it directly to your Session variable `scriptArray`. You now have a variant array.

Later, in another request, you can retrieve the `Session("scriptArray")` to a local variable, then access it as normal using the indexes. You could access it using `Session("scriptArray")(3) = "newscript"`, but this incorrect method will result in loss of data.

Continued

Table 19-7: THE COMMON COLLECTIONS, EVENTS, AND METHODS OF THE APPLICATION OBJECT

Method	Description
Lock	Prevents other clients from modifying application properties.
Unlock	Allows other clients to modify application properties.
Remove	Deletes an item from the Contents collection.
RemoveAll	Clears the entire collection from memory.

Events	Description
OnStart	Occurs when a page in the application is first referenced.
OnEnd	Occurs when the application quits, after the Session_onEnd event.

Collection	Description
Contents	Contains all of the items added to the Application through the script commands.
StaticObjects	Contains all of the objects added to the Application with the <object> tab.

Listing 19-6: Creating Application Events with global.asa

```
<script language="VBScript" runat="server">
Sub Application_OnStart
  ' Your Application script logic for starting your app
  Application("startTime") = Now()
  Application("dbName") = "myDB"
  Application("dbID") = "internetGuest"
  Application("dbPwd")= "ig"
End Sub

Sub Application_OnEnd
  ' Your Application script logic for ending your app
End Sub
</script>
```

Learning about the Server, Application, and Session Objects *Continued*

The two Session object events, `onStart` and `onEnd`, are similar to those of the Application object. `onStart` occurs when a client browser first requests a document from the application's virtual directory. Because these events occur outside of any particular script, you again need to create the event handler routines with the `global.asa` file.

When you store information in the Session object, the client that owns that session is assigned a SessionID, which can be used in your pages to identify the client while it is browsing your site. The SessionID is assigned by the server, and therefore is read-only.

A session can end in two ways. The most direct way is by use of the Session object's `Abandon` method. This method ends the session immediately, and frees the resources it uses. Any code in the `Session_onEnd` event handler will now run.

The other way a session ends occurs when the client that owns the session does not make a request from the application within the `Timeout` property's time period. The default value is 20 minutes, but you can alter this setting on a per-session basis by changing the value of the `Session.TimeOut` property.

As with the Application object, the Session object has two collections, `Contents` and `StaticObjects`, which allow you to browse through objects and variables, created at the session scope(see Table 19-8).

Two new methods of the `Contents` collection are introduced with IIS 5.0: `Remove` and `RemoveAll`. The `Remove` method can be used to delete an item from the Contents collection. `RemoveAll` clears the entire collection from memory. These methods offer the advantage of letting you write more efficient code to manage server resources during script execution. The syntax is simple. With the `Remove` method, you simply reference either the variable name or its numeric place in the 1-based collection. The `RemoveAll` method will delete all items from your collection.

You can use the ObjectContext object to either commit or abort transactions managed by Microsoft Transaction Server (MTS) initiated by an Active Server Pages script. When an ASP contains `@TRANSACTION` directive, the page runs in a transaction and does not finish processing until the transaction either succeeds completely or fails.

The ObjectContext object implements two methods of the MTS ObjectContext object (see Table 19-9). The `SetAbort` method explicitly aborts the transaction. This causes MTS to prevent any updates to resources that were contacted during the first phase of the transaction. When the transaction aborts, the script's `onTransactionAbort` event will be processed.

Calling the `SetComplete` method does not necessarily mean that the transaction is complete. The transaction will only complete if all of the transactional components called by the script call `SetComplete`. In most instances, you will not need to call `SetComplete` within the script, as the script is assumed complete if it finishes processing with calling `SetAbort`.

CROSS-REFERENCE

Chapter 24 describes how to use the ObjectContext object and Microsoft Transaction Server.

Table 19-8: THE COMMON PROPERTIES, COLLECTIONS, METHODS, AND EVENTS OF THE SESSION OBJECT

Method	Description
Abandon	Destroys a Session object and releases its resources.
Remove	Deletes an item from the Contents collection.
RemoveAll	Clears the entire collection from memory.

Events	Description
OnStart	Occurs when the server creates a new session.
OnEnd	Occurs when a session is abandoned or times out.

Collection	Description
Contents	Contains all of the items added to the Application through the script commands.
StaticObjects	Contains all of the objects added to the Application with the <object> tab.

Property	Description
TimeOut	Sets the timeout period for the session state for this application, in minutes.

Table 19-9: THE COMMON METHODS AND EVENTS OF THE OBJECTCONTEXT OBJECT

Event	Description
OnTransactionCommit	Occurs after a transacted script's transaction commits.
OnTransactionAbort	Occurs if the transaction is aborted.

Method	Description
SetComplete	Declares that the script is not aware of any reason for the transaction not to complete.
SetAbort	Aborts a transaction initiated by an Active Server Page.

Working with the Err object

VBScript allows a mechanism for skipping past any run-time errors that might occur in your ASP application. This is a handy feature when you want your ASP application to continue execution, without displaying any error messages, even if the application generates any run-time errors. To do this, you use the On Error Resume Next statement.

In Visual Basic, there are several different ways of using the On Error statement to control how your code should react to any errors it encounters. Unfortunately, VBScript only contains one of these. By placing the statement On Error Resume Next at the beginning of your code routines, you instruct the script interpreter to ignore any errors it encounters and carry on processing.

The On Error Resume Next statement causes execution to continue with the statement immediately after the one that caused a run-time error. If the error is in a subroutine or function that you called from elsewhere in your code, this subroutine or function is terminated immediately and execution continues with the line in the main body of the code after the one that called it.

If the subroutine or function has its own On Error Resume Next statement, execution of its code continues after an error. Once execution leaves a subroutine or function, the On Error Resume Next statement within that routine is deactivated. You can think of it as being local to the routine.

You should always consider using On Error Resume Next at least in the main body of your script, so that you can trap an error that occurs in any of the procedures you may call.

If an error occurs in your ASP application, it is easy to determine the error number and description by using the Err object. All you need to do is insert the ASP statement On Error Resume Next before the ASP statements and then use the Err object, as shown in Listing 19-7, to access the error description and number.

The Err object stores information about run-time errors, and you can use it to create your own custom errors. Why would you want to do this? There are times when you might want to pass a custom error message back to the user. You can set the properties of the Err object (see Table 19-10) to any value you please, then call its Raise method to raise this error. This stops execution of the code and passes the error back to the ASP system.

The On Error Resume Next will trap any errors that might have left your pages in disaster. However, the problem is that your code might still be executing, even if an error did occur. Using the Err Object therefore will stop execution of your code.

If you are a Visual Basic programmer, you probably already understand the virtues of the Option Explicit statement. Visual Basic allows you to declare variables anywhere you like or, should you choose to, not define them at all. That means, by default, you do not have to declare variables before using them. Although this might seem like a great feature at first, it is actually a deceptive one that can lead to applications that are difficult to debug. Consider the application in Listing 19-8. What do you think is the outcome? If you think the outcome is $100000, you are wrong (see browser output).

Do you see why the ASP application produces erroneous output? The programmer typed the variable in your salary incorrectly. The Option Explicit statement is responsible for making sure you declare variables before using them. Should you, by accident, misspell a variable or forget to declare a variable, the VBScript points out your mistake so you can easily correct it. Do use Option Explicit in all your ASP applications and make it a point to declare variables before using them. The syntax is simple:

```
<% Option Explicit %>
```

CROSS-REFERENCE
Chapter 24 describes how to use the ObjectContext object and Microsoft Transaction Server.

Listing 19-7: Detecting Errors using the Err Object

```
<@ language="VBScript">
On Error Resume Next
' ... ASP body is here
If err.number > 0 Then
   Response.Write Err.Number
   Response.Write Err.Description
End If
```

Table 19-10: THE PROPERTIES AND METHODS OF THE ERR OBJECT

Method	Description
Clear	Clears all current settings of the Err object.
Raise	Generates a run-time error.

Property	Description
Description	Sets or returns a string describing an error.
Number	Sets or returns a numberic value specifying an error.
Source	Sets or returns the name of the object that generated the error.

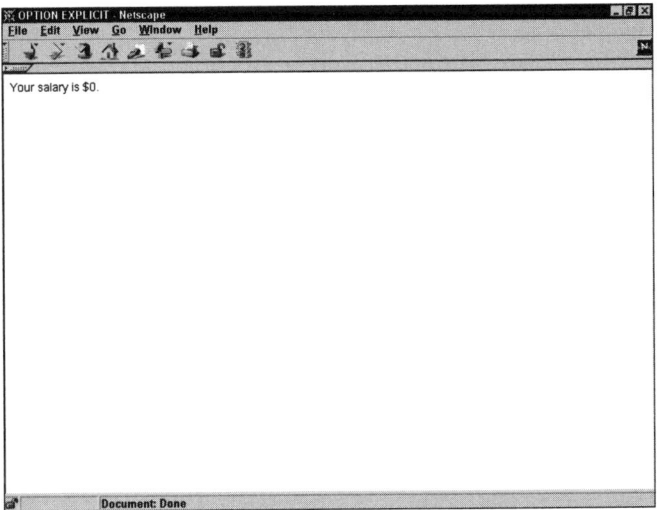

Listing 19-8: To Use or Not to Use Option Explicit

```
<@ language="VBScript">
<HTML>
<HEAD>
   <TITLE>Option Explicit</TITLE>
</HEAD>
<BODY>
<% DIM intYourSalary
   intYourSalary = 100000
   Response.Write("Your salary is $" & _
      CCur(intYorSalary) & ".<BR>")
%>
</BODY>
</HTML>
```

Personal Workbook

Q & A

1 What object and method is used to gain access to external objects?

_____

_____

_____

2 What will be the outcome of the following code?

```
<html>
<head>
<title>Moving On</title>
</head>
<body>
<% Response.Redirect "aBetterPage.asp"
%>
</body>
</html>
```

_____

_____

_____

3 How do you access the HTML form variable ("email") if the form is submitted to an ASP script with the POST method?

_____

_____

_____

4 What are spaces replaced with when using `Server.URLEncode`?

_____

_____

5 Show two different ways to retrieve the value of the variable email from an HTML form from the client's browser using the Request object.

_____

_____

_____

6 If the GET method is used to submit data in an HTML form to an ASP script, is there a limit placed on the size of HTML form data?

_____

_____

7 What method is recommended for submitting data from HTML forms to an ASP script?

_____

_____

_____

ANSWERS: PAGE 510

EXTRA PRACTICE

1 Write an ASP script that displays the IP address of the Web browser.

2 Write an ASP script that displays the full pathname of the ASP script.

3 How would you fix the code in Question #2?

4 Create an ASP script that redirects a user to your favorite Web site.

5 Write code that triples the current session's timeout value.

REAL-WORLD APPLICATIONS

✔ Write an HTML form and ask for a name and address. Write the name in a cookie and retrieve it the next time the page is executed.

✔ Create an `Application_onStart` and `Session_onStart` event to record the time that each was created. Display each on your Web page.

CHAPTER **20**

Installing Additional ASP Objects

In this chapter, you'll learn how to extend the capabilities of Active Server Pages well beyond the basic Web and database functionality built into the ASP engine. The tools described here enable you to build on top of that functionality, using syntax similar to the syntax used for the basic ASP objects. This extension mechanism will enable you to build complex code that runs more efficiently than scripts. Better still, if someone else has already created the tool you need, plugging it into ASP is easy.

We'll start with a brief overview of Microsoft's COM architecture, exploring how COM enables developers to mix and match components without having to understand their details. COM developers can build anything they want inside the "black box," so long as they provide an interface that ASP developers and other programmers can use to connect to that box.

COM's standard interface has created a market in components. Many components are available for free, while others provide advanced functionality that comes at a price. In either case, you can often save yourself a lot of time creating complex scripts or your own COM components by taking advantage of work someone else has already done.

Installing COM components is a bit mysterious, with connections to the Windows Registry and no central management console. We'll take a look at several ways you can install COM components (even when you don't know you're installing them) and how to make sure you've got everything set up properly for ASP. As you gather these components, you need to keep track of them. When you develop with only the core ASP objects, your ASP scripts remain very portable. When you add additional objects to the mix, your scripts will have new dependencies that can complicate upgrades and distributed processing. We'll explore strategies for keeping track of what your scripts need.

Finally, we'll take a look at what's involved in creating your own COM components. While creating components is a few levels up in programming difficulty from writing scripts, there may be times when you need to create your own set of components.

Learning about ASP and Components

We'll start with a brief overview of Microsoft's COM architecture, exploring how COM enables developers to mix and match components without having to understand their details. COM developers can build anything they want inside the "black box," so long as they provide an interface that ASP developers and other programmers can use to connect to that box.

Microsoft's Component Object Model (COM) has emerged over the last few years as Microsoft's preferred model for creating interchangeable components. COM succeeds OLE, DDE, ActiveX, and a number of other technologies. Windows is definitely COM's home environment, though there is some COM development for UNIX and Macintosh computers. Even within Windows, COM objects sometimes come in processor-specific flavors for the Intel and Alpha families of processors. (Always check to make sure you get the correct version when downloading components — these two are not compatible.)

COM objects are typically written in C++, though "wrappers" are available for Java classes and the products of other development environments. Many software applications (including Microsoft's Internet Explorer) are just sets of COM objects with an initialization routine that gets them started. Most Windows development environments include tools for creating COM objects.

In general, COM components can communicate with COM components, calling each other's methods and modifying each other's properties. For ASP, this means that scripts (which run in a COM-compliant scripting engine) have access to any COM object installed on the host server. It doesn't matter whether that COM object was installed with ASP, a spreadsheet, Internet Explorer, or hand-installed — all COM objects are available. It also makes it easier to move tasks from machine to machine.

COM objects have all the powers of regular programs. They can access the hard drive, modify the registry, communicate with other computers, or drive a graphical user interface. In ASP, COM components are most likely to be used for Input/Output (I/O) with the local system or with remote computers, or for specialized processing requiring the performance boost that compiled code can provide over interpreted script.

While Active Server Pages works well with components outside of its master set, it only sets up its core objects for developers. If you want to use components from other sources, you'll need to install and initialize them yourself. You'll also need to learn the component interfaces so that you can access them from your scripts.

TAKE NOTE

▶ ACTIVEX, COM, DCOM, AND SO ON.

Microsoft has changed the names of its components a number of times, often mystifying developers. The components you need for ASP use COM and also include ActiveX controls. Most of them are supplied as .dll files. As long as a component supports COM, it should work fine with ASP. COM+ will be the "new" COM for Windows 2000.

▶ COMPONENTS VS. OBJECTS

The terms *component* and *object* are often used interchangeably, but they aren't quite the same. A component is a piece of software that can be reused, while an object is typically a particular instantiation of that component. The Request object, for example, is an instantiation of a Request component inside the ASP engine that applies to a particular user request.

CROSS-REFERENCE
For a programmer's introduction to COM, see *Inside COM*, by Dale Rogerson (Microsoft Press, 1997).

FIND IT ONLINE
Microsoft provides a wide variety of COM resources at **http://www.microsoft.com/com/**.

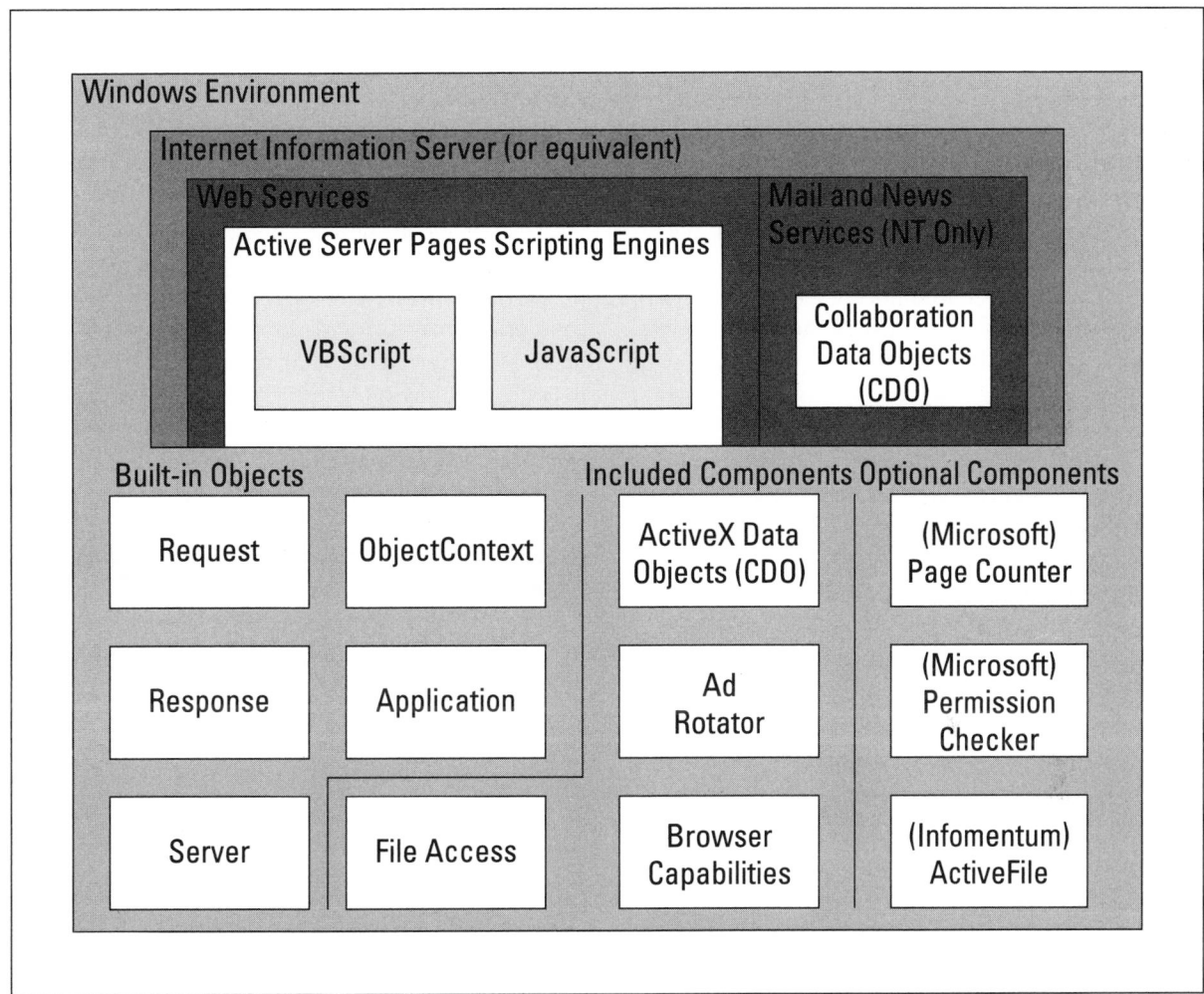

▶ *Active Server Pages operate at the core of a sophisticated set of objects, managing built-in objects, included components, and other components that may be added from a variety of sources.*

Finding New Components

COM is a great way to extend the capabilities of your Active Server Pages applications, but building your own COM components is a task better left to specialists. (If you're an experienced C++ programmer, of course, you probably qualify.) Many developers building Web sites have encountered the same set of problems, making it likely that someone has already built the pieces you need.

Microsoft has built a large number of components beyond the core ASP objects. Some, like the ActiveX Data Objects covered in the following chapter, are included with ASP, though they need separate initialization. A few, like the File Access components, are installed as part of the scripting environment that comes with ASP, though they aren't ASP-specific. Others require a separate download and installation process, however, more components are being included with Active Server Pages as Internet Information Server matures.

Microsoft isn't the only company building COM objects, however. A number of vendors have entered the market, producing components as freeware, shareware, and regular software. While you won't find these components listed in your average software catalog, specialty companies (like Programmer's Paradise) carry a large line of components.

Component development tends to focus on niche markets, with particular development companies working on tools that address a particular area. A number of companies create communications toolkits, an area where complexity led to specialized development tools even in the days of DOS. Many of the components available aren't suited to Active Server Pages development — graphical user interface toolkits, for example. (You can still use some of the graphics toolkits to generate graphics on the server and transfer them as GIF or JPG files, however.)

Many components rely on other components to accomplish their tasks. Infomentum's ActiveFile component, for example, relies on Microsoft's ActiveX Data Objects

component set to help it store files inside relational databases. Many components rely on parts of the Windows operating system (beyond the essentials of COM) to do their work. One of the key advantages of these components is the ease with which they can share resources, and the ease with which they can share themselves.

When evaluating different components, be sure to perform some basic stress testing before committing to a particular component, particularly those still in beta. While components may seem to behave perfectly well in a small development setting, building components that work well in larger-scale environments is a difficult task, especially when multiple dependencies are involved. Components can make your work much easier, but this magic bullet does require careful evaluation and implementation.

TAKE NOTE

▶ WORK IN PROGRESS

Microsoft is continually creating new components and building them into Internet Information Server with each new release. As a result, the list of Microsoft components is in constant flux, and each component is not always available.

▶ LICENSING ISSUES

Many products are composed of COM objects, but it isn't clear whether the use of those COM objects in an ASP environment is a violation of the product licensing. If you plan to use COM objects that came as part of a software application in your ASP development, you may want to contact the developer to make sure you aren't violating the terms of your license, especially if it is a single-user license.

FIND IT ONLINE

To explore a large catalog of components for sale, see **http://www.pparadise.com**.

Table 20-1: COM COMPONENTS AVAILABLE FROM MICROSOFT

Full Name	Internal Reference Name(s)	DLL	Usage
ActiveX Data Objects (ADO)	ADODB.Command ADODB.Connection ADODB.Error ADODB.Field ADODB.Parameter ADODB.Property ADODB.Recordset	msado15.dll	ActiveX Data Objects are a critical link between your scripts and information in databases that uses Microsoft's Open Database Connectivity (ODBC) drivers using OLE DB, yet another Microsoft database technology. ADO will be covered in depth in the following chapter.
Ad Rotator	MSWC.AdRotator	adrot.dll	The Ad Rotator enables you to define how often particular ads should appear according to rules you set in an external file. (You can use different files for different pages.)
Browser Capabilities	MSWC.BrowserType	browscap.dll	The Browser Capabilities component uses information provided in the browscap.ini file to identify the types of information that different browsers support. You can then serve different formats to different browsers based on the information that this component returns. (Updated `browscap.ini` files are available at **http://backoffice.microsoft.com/downtrial/moreinfo/bcf.asp**, or you can modify them yourself.)
Collaboration Data Objects	Many (see IIS documentation)	cdonts.dll	The Collaboration Data Objects for NT Server enable you to send or manage mail using the SMTP server included with IIS or the Microsoft Exchange Server. The version of CDO that is installed with IIS is intended only for use with Active Server Pages. CDO is only installed on the Windows NT Server Internet Information Server and is not available on Windows NT Workstation or Windows 95 or 98.
Content Linking	MSWC.NextLink	nextlink.dll	The Content Linking component allows you to link chains of documents using a list of pages. This component reads an external file to find the current page's location in the list, and lets you create links to the previous and next pages (with descriptions) automatically. Sites with large collections of sequential documents will find it especially useful.

Finding New Components

Continued

Table 20-1: COM COMPONENTS AVAILABLE FROM MICROSOFT *(continued)*

Full Name	Internal Reference Name(s)	DLL	Usage
Content Rotator*	IISSample.ContentRotator	controt.dll	The Content Rotator lets your pages change slightly each time they are loaded. The initialization file contains a weighted list of entries, and the component will choose one of those entries each time the page is loaded. Repeat visitors will find something new each time, at least until they've seen all the pieces.
Counters*	MSWC.Counters	counters.dll	The Counters component lets you create named counters for your pages which you can increment or decrement through code. You must create a single Counters component in your global.asa file, and then reference it from your other ASP pages. A counters.txt file will be maintained by the component.
File Access	Many (see IIS documentation)	scrrun.dll	The File Access component allows your programs to read and write files on your local and network hard drives. Use with caution.
MyInfo	MSWC.MyInfo	myinfo.dll	The MyInfo component enables you to create a list of named entries in an XML file. You can then reference this list anywhere on your site.
PageCounter*	IISSample.PageCounter	pagecnt.dll	This is a simpler version of the Counters component, which increments every time a page is loaded and displays the current count.
Permission Checker*	IISSample.PermissionChecker	permchk.dll	The Permission Checker is only available on Windows NT and requires that your site use Basic or Windows NT Challenge Response authentication. You can then use the HasAccess method to determine whether the user has access to particular files.

▶ *Those marked with an asterisk (*) are not installed with IIS 4.0, but may become part of IIS 5.0.*

Table 20-2: A SAMPLING OF COMPONENTS AVAILABLE FROM THIRD-PARTY VENDORS

Name	Source	Description
ATI UPS Server Objects	http://www.arealgem.com/ controlsweb/Whitepaper.asp? product=shipcalc	The ATI UPS ServerObjects connect your Active Server Pages to United Parcel Services' (UPS) shipping costs calculator, allowing your site to calculate shipping costs for orders.
Euro Conversion Component	http://www.softwing.com/euro/	This component provides currency conversion between the 11 national currencies participating in the European Monetary Union and the Euro. The component simplifies conversions between these currencies and the Euro, and provides a central file that can be used to revise the rates if needed.
A$Pcharge	http://www.bluesquirrel.com/ products/asp/asp.html	A$PCharge allows your site to accept and process credit cards. You can set up an account with Epoch, CyberSource, CyberCash, or iBill for your transactions, or use ICVerify software (sold separately) and a modem for more traditional direct credit verification.
ASP2XML	http://www.stonebroom.com/ asp2xml.htm	ASP2XML provides a direct route from ODBC data sources (including databases and documents such as Excel spreadsheets) to XML. ASP2XML provides a general shortcut for moving your database information to XML output.
Active Server Paint	http://www.coherentdata.com/ cvisual/aspaint/	This module enables you to generate JPEG, GIF, and BMP images as you need them, using information you supply through scripts. Active Server Paint is several steps beyond the simple rotation among static files provided by the Ad Rotator.
ASP Flash Turbine	http://www.blue-pacific. hexagon.net/aspturbine/	This component lets you create Flash files, which can be viewed in browsers with the Flash plug-in from Macromedia. Flash files are very small multimedia and graphics presentations.
ASPChart	http://www.serverobjects.com/ products.htm	Enables you to create charts in JPEG, PNG, and BMP graphics formats using scripts.
ImageSize	http://www.serverobjects.com/ products.htm	Returns the height and width of your graphics files, simplifying page creation and making it easier to change your sites without disrupting your users.
ASPPage	http://www.serverobjects.com/ products.htm	Connects your ASP application to alphanumeric paging using the TAP protocol. If you can stand it, your users can page you directly with this application.

Installing and Initializing New Components

Internet Information Server and the Active Server Pages engine handle the installation and initialization of their built-in components (notably the Request, Response, Server, Application, and ObjectContext components), but components that come from other sources take a bit more work to get started. Both installation and initialization may require some attention before you can make your components perform their duties.

Some components come with installers. Microsoft's Internet Information Server installer will add some components to your system; some of their other components also come with their own small installers; and several components from third parties have installers. Many components come as parts of other products. Internet Explorer 5.0, for example, includes an XML parser and XSL processor that can also be used with Active Server Pages. Occasionally, components arrive as a raw dynamically linked library (DLL) file, with no installer. Fortunately, the Regsvr32 command described on the opposite page can help you register these files and make them available for use by your scripts.

Once you've installed your components, they should be registered with your server and accessible by name. Unlike the built-in objects, however, you'll need to create instances of your components using the Server object's CreateObject method.

In VBScript, the syntax will be:

```
Set objInstance =
Server.CreateObject("progid")
```

(The Set is required when you are assigning an object to a variable name.) In JavaScript, the syntax will be:

```
objInstance = Server.CreateObject("progid");
```

In both cases, *objInstance* is a variable name you will use to reference the object once you create it, and *progid* is the name by which the component identifies itself within the Windows registry. After the component name, a specific object name will appear to identify which of the objects contained by the component is being created. To create an instance of the Microsoft Content Linking component in VBScript, you could use:

```
Set objContentLink =
Server.CreateObject("MSWC.NextLink")
```

In JavaScript, the syntax would be:

```
objContentLink =
Server.CreateObject("MSWC.NextLink");
```

Some objects require configuration files used at their initialization in addition to this simple instantiation. Microsoft's Browser Capabilities component, for example, uses a `browscap.ini` file that lists the capabilities of a wide variety of Web browsers. The MyInfo component, which enables you to keep information about your site accessible for easy reuse throughout the entire site, relies on a `myinfo.xml` file. This approach is most useful when all of the pages on a site need a consistent view of the information provided by this object. (Browser capabilities should not vary among Web pages, for instance.)

Other components may need configuration files, but only need to access them when a particular method is called. Microsoft's Ad Rotator component and Content Linking component are two examples of this approach, which is typically used if the object may need to behave differently when instantiated on different pages. In this manner, different portions of the same site can use material that was custom-built for their use, while sharing the same code that performs the action.

Make certain to read the documentation for each of your components to find out what, if any, configuration files are required. Sometimes components depend on particular configuration files, sometimes they need support in the `global.asa` file, and sometimes they need configuration from within the script.

CROSS-REFERENCE

To learn about instantiating objects in the **global.asa** file, see Chapter 22.

Installing COM Components Manually

Sometimes developers ship a raw file without installation instructions, or something happens to the registry and a component disappears. In such situations, Microsoft's bare-bones RegSvr32 program is a useful tool for registering (and unregistering) components.

RegSvr32 is hidden in the Windows system directory (typically C:\windows\system\ on Windows 95 and 98 computers, and C:\winnt\system32\ on Windows NT computers). RegSvr32 is a command-line tool that takes the name of a DLL file as an argument, and either installs or uninstalls the components in that file, depending on the switches you set. For example, to install the Ad Rotator component on a Windows NT Server, the command might look like:

```
C:\WINNT\system32>regsvr32
inetsrv\adrot.dll
```

If all went well (basically, if adrot.dll was in the right place), you'll get a dialog box announcing "DllRegisterServer in inetserv\adrot.dll succeeded." If not, you'll get a dialog box announcing that "Load Library(*filename*") failed."

To uninstall the component, you issue the same command, but with the /u switch:

```
C:\WINNT\system32>regsvr32 /u
inetsrv\adrot.dll
```

If the component file is in the right place, you'll get a dialog box announcing "DllUnregisterServer in inetserv\adrot.dll succeeded." This message will appear whether or not the component was ever actually installed. If you specify the wrong file, you'll get the same "Load Library" error described previously.

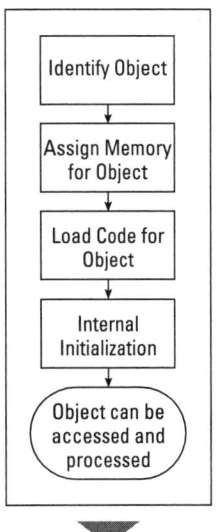

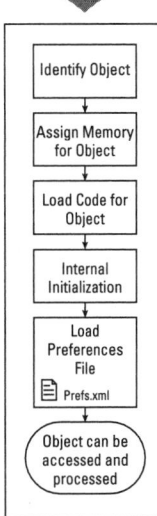

▶ *The initialization process for a simple component doesn't require the management of any external resources.*

▶ *More sophisticated components can take advantage of information stored in preferences files, though it takes an extra step when the object is initialized.*

Managing Your New Components

COM objects tend to accumulate over time. They are occasionally removed when applications are removed, but typically lie buried deep within the registry and the file system. While most developers won't need to dig too deep into the darker corners of Windows, there are times — especially when you're moving code from one server to another — when it is very useful.

For the most part, a standard server log (typically a notebook detailing changes made to a computer) provides enough management information for servers running a single Web application. Most ASP applications require the installation of Internet Information Server (or the equivalent), along with a few components that are easily tracked. The hardest part of using notebooks is keeping them accurate; it's easy to forget to take notes, especially if an installation goes sour. (You can keep the notebook on the computer, though it's harder to get to if the system crashes.)

Keeping track of which components are used by which application on a server running multiple Web applications can become a huge hassle if developers don't keep track of their tools. Searching code for object identifiers does work, if necessary, but it's generally much easier to keep a central log detailing dependencies. Logs shared by multiple developers are commonly managed along with the code in large projects, but for small projects, a paper notebook may be adequate.

If you don't have documentation, or you want to poke at the components on your system directly, the options provided with Windows itself are pretty thin. The RegSvr32 application described in the Installation task only enables you to add and remove components, without providing a list of the objects installed. You can find a list of the objects in the Windows registry using the RegEdit program. To find out which DLL file is associated with a particular component, you'll need to search under HKEY_CLASSES_ROOT for the name of your component. Once you find that key, open its CLSID sub-key, and write down that number. Then find the TypeLib key, which is also under HKEY_CLASSES_ROOT. The TypeLib key contains a list of class ID (CLSID) values, mapping them back to the DLL that contains that component. Once you find the DLL name, you can use the RegSvr32 program to uninstall your component or install it on a different system.

If poking at the registry isn't your thing, but you need to figure out the relations between your components, you may need to turn to a specialized COM manager like COM Explorer (4Developers), which is available as a thirty-day trial that can be extended by purchasing a license. COM Explorer provides a list of COM components (without the rest of the registry) and a set of tools for exploring and modifying their setup. COM Explorer gives you direct access to the information in the Windows registry without the information overload.

TAKE NOTE

▶ EDITING THE REGISTRY

Editing the registry is something you should do only when you know exactly what you're doing. None of the preceding tasks require you to make changes to your registry — let the RegSvr32 program do that for you. Only make changes to the registry if you absolutely have to, make backups beforehand, and then double-check every step before saving any changes. While most registry modifications aren't dangerous, accidents (like hitting the delete key in the wrong place) do happen. Be very, very careful any time you open this particular toolbox.

CROSS-REFERENCE
To learn more about the registry for Windows 98, *The Windows 98 Registry: A Survival Guide for Users*, by John Woram (IDG Books, 1998) is a good place to start.

FIND IT ONLINE
For more information about COM Explorer or to download a trial version, see: **http://www.4developers.com**.

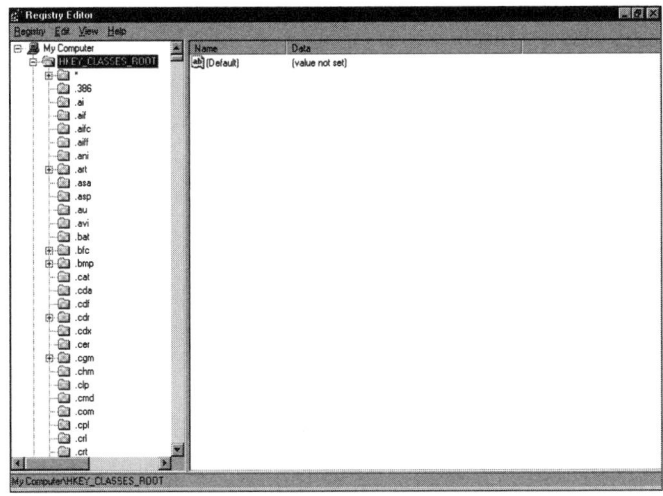

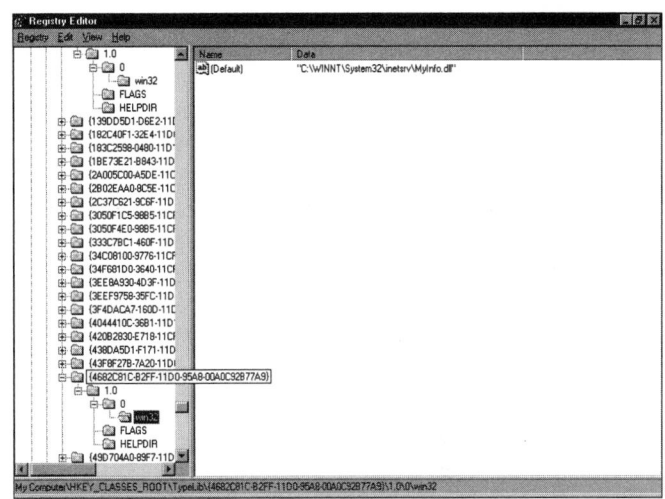

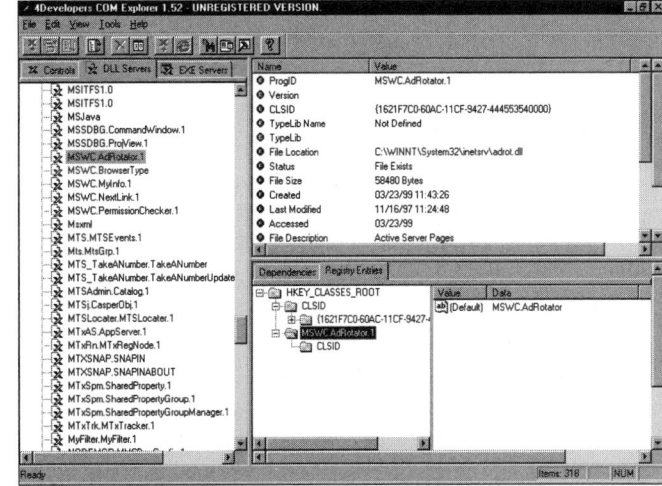

▶ Registry entries for COM controls are stored in the HKEY_CLASSES_ROOT subtree of the Windows registry.

▶ You can track down the CLSID number that Windows uses to manage components internally by finding its entry under the HKEY_CLASSES_ROOT subkey.

▶ Once you know the CLSID of the component you need to manipulate, you can find its source file in the TypeLib area under HKEY_CLASSES_ROOT.

▶ If direct registry manipulation isn't for you, commercial tools like COM Explorer can provide an in-depth view of the components available with considerably less digging.

Developing Your Own Components

While there are many Web-specific components available for ASP, there are many situations where the logic behind a particular application doesn't quite fit any of the implementations currently available. Sometimes, the core logic of your application is simply too complex for efficient processing with scripting. Other times, your application needs to communicate with resources that don't fit any of the tools that Active Server Pages provides.

If you fear that you've moved off the map of known Active Server Pages components, it may be time to open a larger toolkit and try building your own COM components. You'll need to invest in development tools and have a clear idea of how to use them (or hire someone who does), but the results may justify the extra cost of development. (If it's a component you can resell, other developers may be happy to pay off your development costs.)

While COM development does require some programming experience, many developers completed this task. A wide variety of tools are available from a wide variety of vendors in a number of different environments. While much COM development is done using C++, other environments, like Borland's Delphi (which uses Object Pascal) or Microsoft Visual Basic, provide more options for developers from different backgrounds. A number of tools will let you use Java objects in your Active Server Pages, either by creating COM objects directly (like Microsoft's Visual J++), or by wrapping your Java in some supporting code (like Sun's set of tools.)

If you decide your application needs a custom-built COM component, you'll need to spend some time analyzing your needs to determine which tasks belong to the component and which tasks are the domain of the supporting scripts. If the component is only going to be used for the Web, your task is a little bit simpler. However, because COM components can be reused for other applications as well, it may be worth examining how the object will integrate with other potential user environments.

Because of the different tools used to build COM components and the higher level of difficulty, COM development and Web implementations are often handled by different developers. While this arrangement works well up to a point — specialization does make sense in many situations — you need to make certain that your Web development team and your COM development team stay on the same track. Defining interfaces clearly at the beginning is a good start, but interfaces have been known to drift, and the results returned by the object may not always be exactly what was expected.

When the object is "finished," it's time for some heavy test runs. Developing your site around a COM component that doesn't perform well is a recipe for angry users and tired developers. If possible, use some form of automated testing tool to see how well the component performs and take care of all memory leaks. (Even a small memory leak can cause problems when a site gets busy, and performance that looks good when a site is only getting moderate traffic can become much worse as volume increases.) This may matter less for small sites, especially those on intranets, but some form of performance testing is usually an excellent idea.

TAKE NOTE

► DOCUMENTATION

When you create COM objects, it's especially critical to document them carefully and completely. Most COM object are distributed only as binaries, with no source code to help other developers find their way. Even if you keep the source code available, well-written documentation will make it much easier for Web site developers who aren't necessarily hard-core programmers to take advantage of your work.

CROSS-REFERENCE

For a developer's perspective on COM objects and how to build them, see *Essential COM*, by Don Box (Addison-Wesley 1998.)

FIND IT ONLINE

For more information about creating objects, see:
http://msdn.microsoft.com/developer/sdk/com.asp

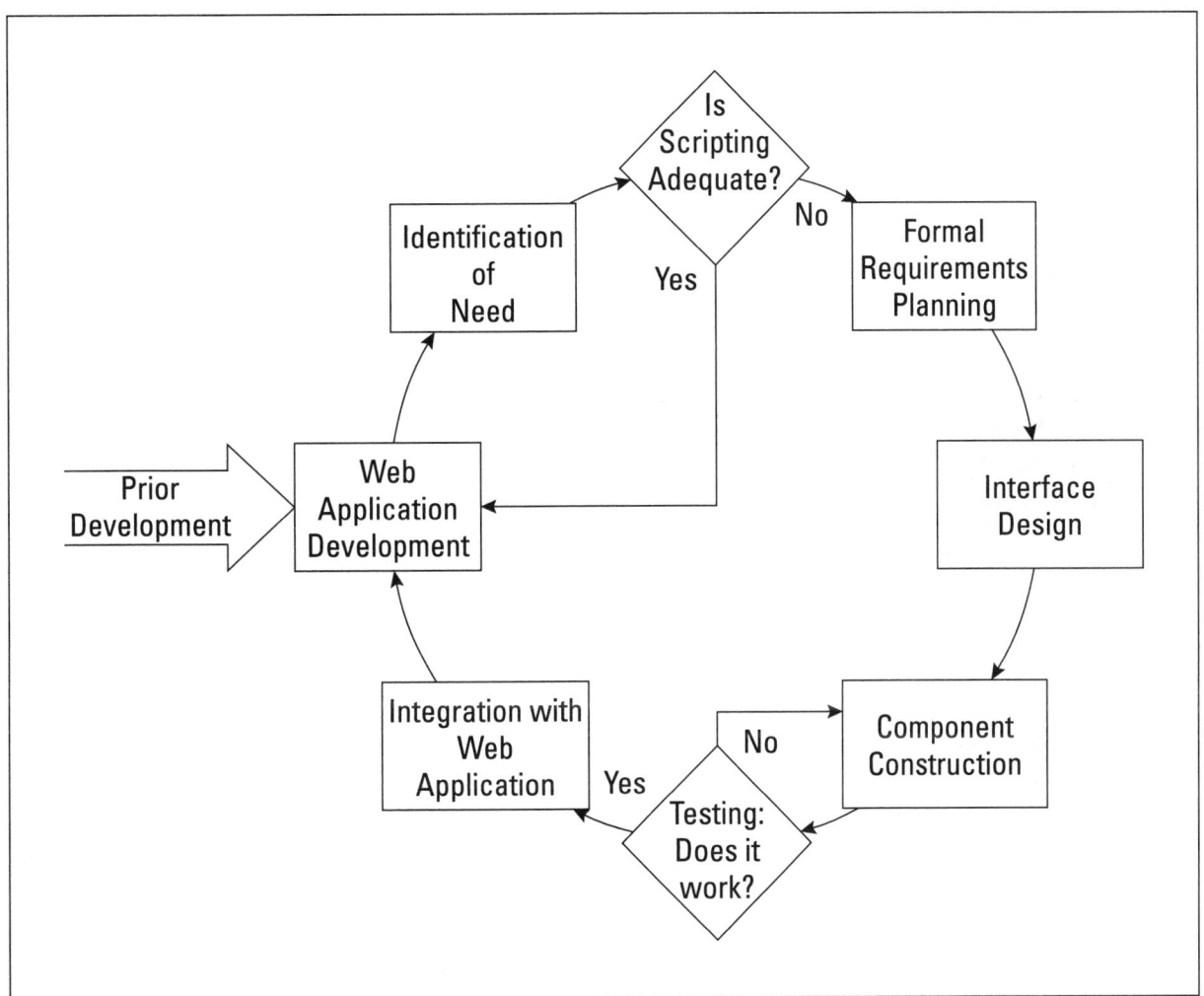

▶ *Whether one person or one thousand people are creating a Web application, it's worth taking the time to evaluate and implement the creation of new COM components carefully. A full planning process must evaluate whether the component is needed and what it must do, as well as specify and implement interfaces connecting that component to the scripts.*

Personal Workbook

Q & A

1 What advantages do component-based development systems offer?

_____

_____

_____

2 Which components are built-in to ASP and available with every request?

_____

_____

_____

3 Which built-in object do you use to instantiate objects based on installed components?

_____

_____

_____

4 Can you use COM objects from Internet Explorer with Active Server Pages?

_____

_____

_____

5 Which Windows utility can you use to install components from the command line?

_____

_____

_____

6 Where can I find more COM components to use with Active Server Pages?

_____

_____

_____

7 Where are initialization files for COM components stored?

_____

_____

_____

8 When do I need to build my own COM components?

_____

_____

_____

ANSWERS: PAGE 511

334

EXTRA PRACTICE

1 Download some trial versions of ASP components and install them.

2 Build a simple page that uses Microsoft's Ad Rotator component to send different graphics to users. (Documentation for Ad Rotator is included with IIS.)

3 Explore your Windows (or WinNT) system directory to find the many DLL files stored there.

4 Find the `browscap.ini` file using your computer's Find Files or Folders function. Examine the entries, and plan a page that delivers customized content that makes the most use of browser capabilities.

5 Visit Microsoft's site to find the latest on COM, DCOM, and COM+.

REAL-WORLD APPLICATIONS

✔ Your site looks good but performs poorly. What kinds of tasks might you consider moving from scripts to COM components?

✔ You have an intranet application that makes heavy use of ActiveX components. You need to make it usable for non-Windows computers. What components could simplify this task?

✔ Your old server is starting to collapse under your popular site's traffic, and you need to move your application to a new server. How do you figure out what needs to be moved for a smooth transition?

✔ You need to upgrade a COM component in your current application. What steps do you need to take to upgrade the component and integrate its new features?

Visual Quiz

The figure below shows the winnt\system32\inetsrv directory of an NT Server with Internet Information Server. Which files do you know contain COM components? Which files are initialization files for those components?

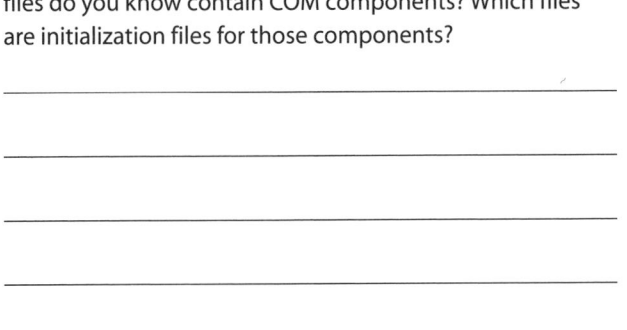

CHAPTER **21**

MASTER THESE SKILLS

▶ Learning about Data Sources

▶ Learning about Relational Databases

▶ Using Intermediaries to Connect to a Database

▶ Learning about SQL and Relational Databases

▶ Using ADO to Connect to Relational Databases

▶ Creating Web-Based Database Application Architectures

Using ActiveX Data Objects

Accessing data within the enterprise consistently is a challenge for today's business applications. Open Database Connectivity (ODBC) provides the first step toward overcoming this challenge by enabling applications to access relational databases. However, as developers and system architects want to include non-relational data sources and work in environments such as the Internet, they encounter the dilemma of either developing their own data-access paradigms, or working with application program interfaces (APIs) that are incompatible in the new environments. Microsoft ActiveX Data Objects (ADO), along with OLE DB, solves this dilemma by providing a single model that works with all data sources in a variety of environments.

The benefits of component DBMSs can be seen in the success of ODBC's database access interface. ODBC is provided as a means of accessing relational data from a diverse set of sources. ODBC uses a standard series of diverse set of sources and a standard series of functions and commands. With this approach, the programmer is shielded from coding the SQL requirements of each specific data source, thereby increasing productivity.

OLE DB takes ODBC a step further to providing a truly standard means of accessing data from diverse sources.

Whether you're creating a front-end database client or middle-tier business object using an application, tool, language, or even an Internet browser, ADO provides consistent, high-performance access to data. ADO is the single data interface you need to know for 1- to n-tier client-server and Web-based, data-driven solution development. Like many of its predecessors, such as DAO and RDO, ADO relies on an underlying layer of software to interact with a given data source. OLE DB is the underlying layer.

OLE DB technology is being positioned as the cornerstone of Microsoft's component database architecture. OLE DB technology is a set of OLE interfaces that provides applications with a standard means of accessing relational data from various information stores. These standard interfaces support specific elements of the data access functionality that is appropriate to the data source, enabling the data source to share its data.

Learning about Data Sources

Today, developers building database solutions face many challenges as they seek to integrate the variety of data found across most enterprises. More than ever, integrated database solutions need to access data stored in both Database Management System (DBMS) and non-DBMS information sources.

Common DBMS sources in today's workplace include mainframe databases such as IMS and DB2, server databases such as Oracle and SQL Server, and desktop databases such as Microsoft Access. Non-DBMS sources, on the other hand, include information stored in file systems, indexed-sequential files, e-mail, spreadsheets (Excel), project management tools, and any other type of data used regularly. See Architecture for Accessing Data Sources figure.

Just the thought of having to interface with all of these data sources within a single database solution is overwhelming. If you have worked with any of these data sources in the past, you will appreciate the challenge of becoming proficient with the tools and interface of just one package. As data storage continues to evolve, you will be faced with new challenges from new data formats.

Open Database Connectivity (ODBC) is provided as a means of accessing relational data from a diverse set of sources, using a standard series of functions and commands. With this approach, the programmer is shielded from having to code to the requirements of each specific data source.

OLE DB takes ODBC a step further to a truly standard means of accessing data from all of these diverse sources. Whereas ODBC is designed around accessing relational data sources, OLE DB is focused on providing access to any data, anywhere.

In order to access an ODBC data source through an ASP page, you need to register the data source with the server by defining the Data Source Name (DSN). There are three types of data source names, but primarily you will use the System DSN.

The system DSN stores connection information for the indicated database. System DSNs are available to all users of the computer for which it is defined, including Windows NT services. For this reason, it is the DSN ordinarily used with the Internet.

You can use the ODBC program in the Control Panel to register the data source with your server. The exact registration steps depend upon the type of database you are registering. See the figure and steps for registering a System DSN.

The preferred method, however, to connect to a Microsoft SQL Server database is to use the native OLE DB provider for SQL Server.

```
Set oConn =
Server.CreateObject("ADODB.Connection")
OConn.Open "PROVIDER=SQLOLEDB;DATA SOURCE =
yourServer; UID=guest; PWD=guest;
DATABASE=Northwind"
```

This OLE DB provider uses several parameters. The PROVIDER parameter is used to specify the name of the OLE DB provider to use for the connection. The DATA SOURCE parameter is used to provide the name of your SQL Server. The UID and PWD contain the login credentials to your SQL Server. And, finally, the DATABASE parameter is used to specify a particular database located on your SQL Server.

Instead of manually creating the connection string yourself, you can use the Microsoft Data Link to automatically create a file that contains the connection information. See figure and steps to create a new Data Link.

Continued

CROSS-REFERENCE
Chapter 2 introduces you to setting up Windows NT and Internet Information Server for ASP.

FIND IT ONLINE
Go to **http://www.microsoft.com/data** for complete and up-to-data information about ODBC and OLE DB.

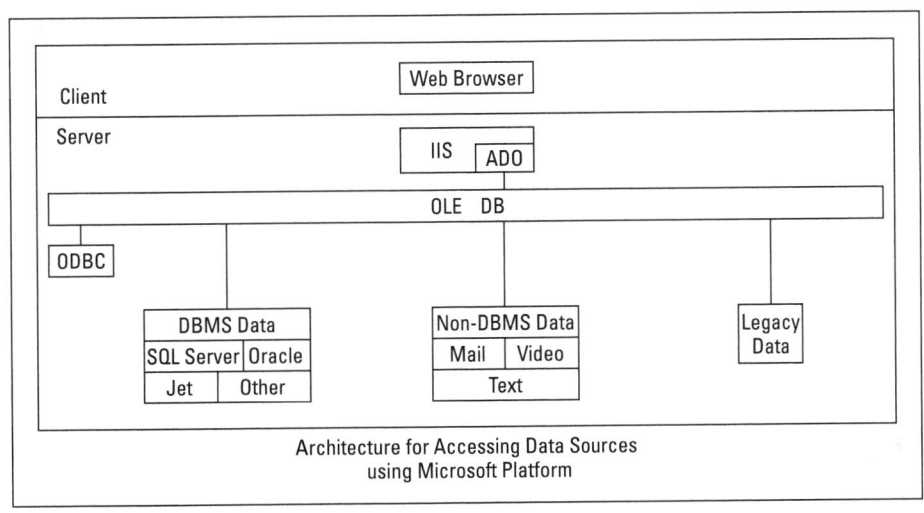

Architecture for Accessing Data Sources
using Microsoft Platform

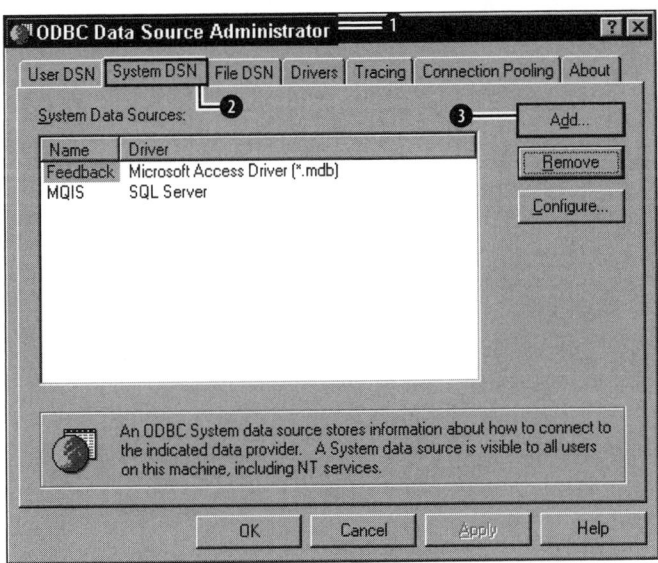

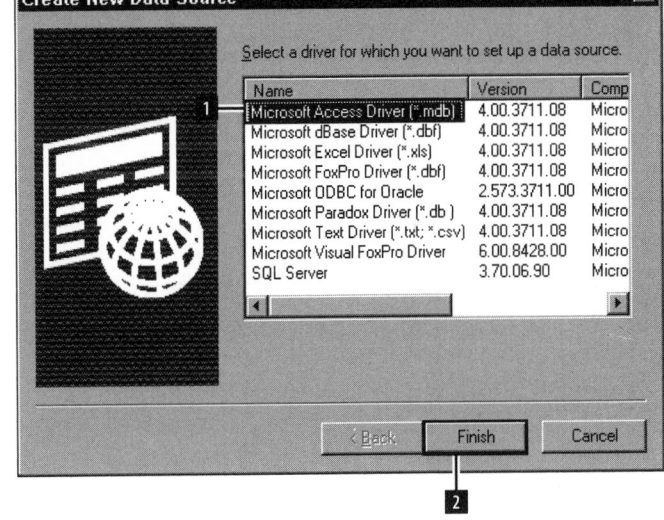

1 Launch the 32bit ODBC program from its icon in the Control Panel.

2 Click the System DSN tab.

3 Click the Add button to create a new System DSN.

1 To use an Access database, select the Microsoft Access Drive (*.mdb) entry from the list.\

2 Click Finish.

Learning about Data Sources

Continued

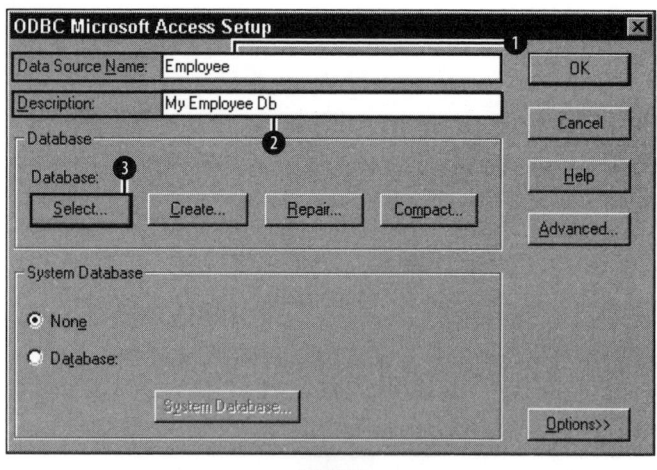

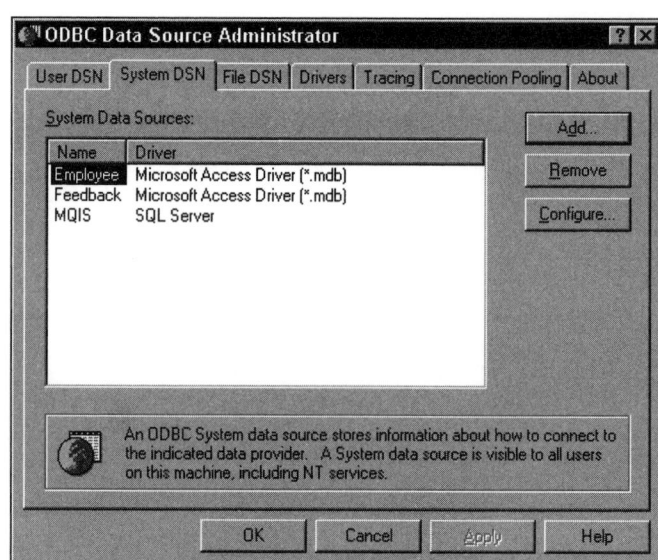

▶ *When you have entered all the details, click OK to return to the System DSN tab. Your System DSN will be shown and ready to use.*

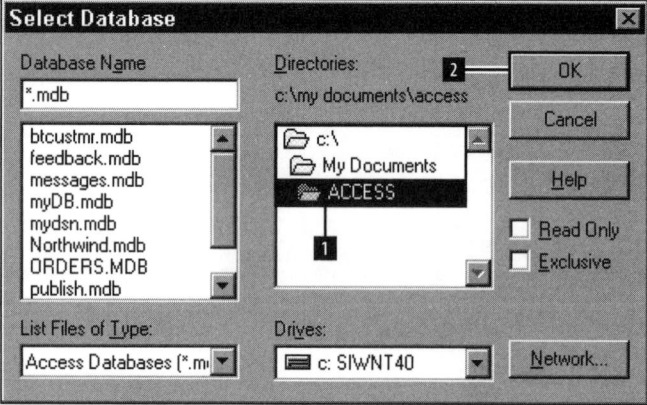

① *You now have to enter the name of the data. The Data Source Name (DSN) provides the name that your ASP scripts will use as a datasource parameter.*

② *Enter a description.*

③ *Click Select.*

▮ *You also need to select the path where your database resides.*

▮ *After you select your database, click OK.*

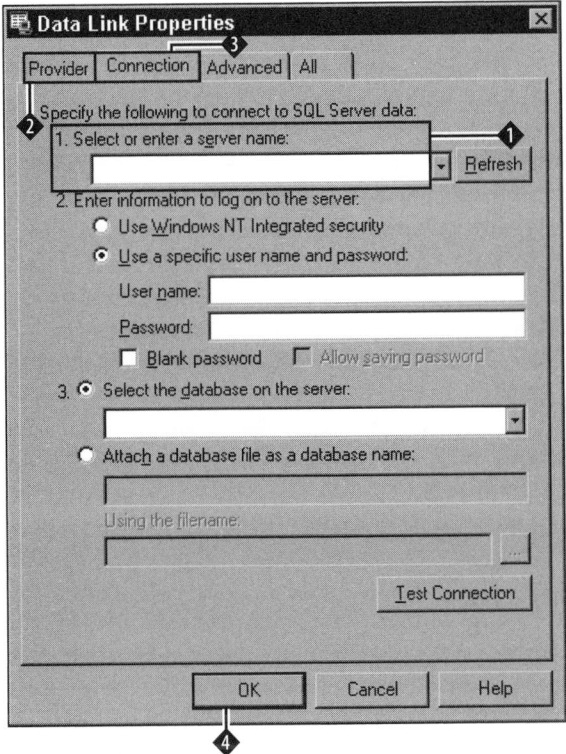

● *Right-click your Windows desktop and choose New and select Microsoft Data Link. You are provided with the opportunity to give your new Data Link a name.*

▶ *Double-click the new Data Link. This will launch the Data Link applet.*

● *Next, choose the data provider by choosing the Microsoft OLE DB provider for SQL Server from the Provider tab. Click Next.*

● *From the Connection tab, enter your server name, provide your authentication information, and select a particular SQL database to access.*

● *Click OK to save your new Data Link.*

```
<%
Set oConn =
Server.CreateObject("ADODB.Connection")
oConn.Open "File Name=c:\myDataLink.UDL
%>
```

▶ *You can open your database with the code listed above.*

Learning about Relational Databases

I n recent years, people have used the term *database* rather loosely, and as a result, the term has lost some of its usefulness. To some people, a database is any collection of data items. In this book, a database is defined as a collection of records.

A record is simply a representation of some physical or conceptual objects. For example, let's say that you want to keep track of a list of relatives. You assign a record for each relative. Each record, or relative, has multiple attributes, such as name, address, and telephone number.

Different as databases may be in size, they are almost always structured according to one of the three database models: hierarchical, network, or relational. DBMSs have evolved from hierarchical to network to relational models. Today, the relational model is most common database model.

Regardless of the size of the computer that hosts the database and whether the machine is connected to a network, the flow of information between the database and user is the same, as the figure depicts. The DBMS masks the physical details of the database storage so that the application only needs to know about the logical characteristics of the data, not how the data is stored.

Relational database management systems (RDBMS) offer the following benefits: **independence** of physical data storage and logical database structure, **variable and easy access** to all data, complete **flexibility** in database design, **reduced data storage** and redundancy, and **easier to maintain.**

Relational databases gain their flexibility from the fact that their data resides in tables that are largely independent of each other. You can add, delete, or change data in a table without affecting the data in the other tables, provided that the affected table is not a parent of any of the other tables.

A relational database is made up of one or more relations. A relation is a two-dimensional array of rows and columns. Most people are familiar with two-dimensional arrays of rows and columns in the form of electronic spreadsheets such as Microsoft Excel. You can store your data in a relation (a table). The Sample Relational Database Table shows a relational database table holding customer information. Every column in a database table embodies a single attribute of the table, such as name, address, or phone number. And each row in the table (a record) holds the data for a single customer.

A database consists of your data as well as metadata. *Metadata* is data that describes the structure of the data within a database. Because the database contains a description of its own structure, it is said to be self-describing.

A database is a representation of a physical or conceptual structure, such as your customer list. The accuracy of the representation depends on the level of detail of the database design. Too much detail is a waste of effort, time, and disk space. Too little detail may render the database useless. Decide how much detail you need now and how much you may need in the future — then provide your determined level of detail in your design. See steps for creating relational databases figure for additional guidelines.

CROSS-REFERENCE

In Chapter 23, you will learn how to integrate databases and Web pages.

FIND IT ONLINE

For managers of business-critical applications and data, go to http://www.intelligententerprise.com.

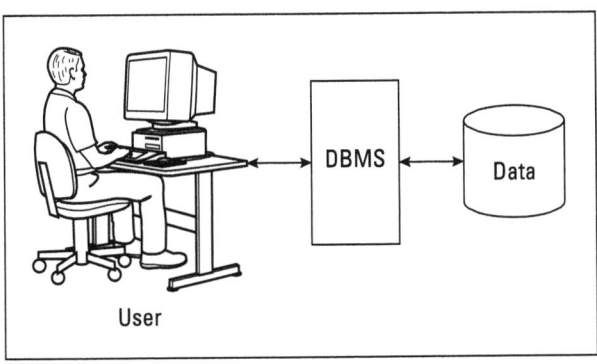

1 Decide what objects are relevant to the problem.

2 Determine which of these objects should be tables and which should be columns in tables.

3 Define tables according to your determination of how you need to organize the objects.

4 Optionally, you may want to designate a table column or a combination of columns as a key.

Table 21-1: SAMPLE RELATIONAL DATABASE TABLE

Customer ID	Company Name	Contact Name	Address	City	Postal Code	Country
101	Acme	Mike Smith	101 East St.	Pearl	21099	U.S.
2999	Niles	Jamie Turne	10 145th St.	NYC	10200	U.S.
3487	Bort	Ellen Teverovsky	8800 9th Ave.	Akers	34991	U.S.

Using Intermediaries to Connect to a Database

All ASP scripts are executed on the Web server. Each time a user visits an ASP page, its code is actually executed on the Web server and the results are sent back to the client browser. Unlike static HTML pages, ASP pages can easily offer dynamic content to users browsing a Web site because the page's contents are created dynamically.

To unleash the dynamic potential of ASP, you need to know how to build ASP applications that interface with databases. An ASP script can act as an intermediary to connect to your favorite database using ActiveX Data Objects (ADO).

After you create a DSN for your database, it is easy to use ADO to insert and retrieve database records. Here are the basic steps in your ASP script to use ADO:

First, create an interface from your Web-based ASP script to your database. The following ASP statement will create an instance of the ADO Connection object.

```
Set oConn =
Server.CreateObject("ADODB.Connection")
```

Then specify the database with which you want to work. This is done by using the Open method and specifying the DSN:

```
oConn.Open "DSN=MyDB;UID=guest;pwd=guest"
```

After establishing a connection with your database, the Execute method of the Connection object is used to issue SQL commands. SQL statements can be used to insert, delete, and retrieve database information. The syntax of the Execute method is straightforward:

```
oConn.Execute "SELECT name FROM authors"
```

After you have finished using the database, close the database connection. Closing database connections immediately after using them makes efficient use of your resources. However, opening and closing connections can cause performance problems because of the system overhead involved. So make sure that you close the connection once per page to optimize performance. The syntax for closing a database connection follows:

```
oConn.Close
Set oConn = Nothing
```

The following sections provide more detail about using ADO and SQL. Don't worry if you are still a bit confused about how to use ADO or SQL commands.

Remember that the ASP file itself is not what you aim to send to the browser. Instead, the ASP file is the result after the page has been interpreted on the Web server by the Active Server Pages system.

CROSS-REFERENCE

Chapters 23 and 24 describe how to get user input and how to display output from your database.

FIND IT ONLINE

Microsoft offers an overview of how to use ASP to connect to your database. See **http://msdn.microsoft.com/workshop/ server/asp/aspfeat.asp**.

Web Database Application using ASP

1.) Start with your database (or any OLE DB data source)

2.) Develop your ASP/Web-server logic to interact with database

3.) Use HTML forms to get user imputs

Troubleshooting

As long as several users do not access your database application at the same time, you will be fine using a desktop application, such as Microsoft Access. However, if you are building a Web database application that is used by many users simultaneously, consider a database application such as Microsoft SQL Server or Oracle, which are scalable to handle thousands of users. Generally, Access is limited to ten concurrent users.

Learning about SQL and Relational Databases

Both relational database theory and SQL originated in one of IBM's research laboratories. As IBM researchers performed early development on relational DBMS systems, they created a data sub-language to operate on these systems. They named it SQL (Structured English Query Language).

It's important to note that SQL isn't a procedural language. As a detailed description of how a task is accomplished, a procedural language operates on one record or one unit of data at time. Some familiar procedural programming languages include C, Cobol, and ADA. When they operate on data, procedural languages have certain characteristics.

SQL, on the other hand, is nonprocedural. To solve a problem by using SQL, you simply tell SQL what you want, instead of telling the system how to get you what you want. The DBMS decides the best way to reply to your request.

SQL often presents a problem for experienced programmers, who have to unlearn old habits developed while using procedural languages. This process is similar to learning recursion in a procedural language. At first, it is impossible to see programs recursively; then suddenly, it all makes sense.

The most recent version of the SQL standard is SQL-92 (ANSI Document No. X3.135-1992). SQL-92 is a major revision of SQL-89. The SQL command language consists of a limited number of commands that relate specifically to data handling. Some of these commands perform data-definition functions. Some perform data-manipulation functions and others perform data-control functions. See exhaustive List of SQL Statements.

TAKE NOTE

SQL3

The next version of the SQL, currently code-named SQL3, will incorporate procedural language facilities such as BEGIN blocks, IF statements, functions, and procedures. The SQL developers are adding these facilities so that you can store programs at the server, where multiple clients can optimize and use these programs repeatedly.

SQL contains everything you need to create, maintain, and provide security for a relational database. The part of SQL that you use to create databases is called the Data Definition Language (DDL). You perform database maintenance by using the Database Manipulation Language (DML). The Data Control Language (DCL) provides security for your database.

Continued

CROSS-REFERENCE
To learn more about designing SQL queries, browse through Chapter 23.

FIND IT ONLINE
Search the best SQL sites chosen by SQL Zone editors for professional developers at **http://www.sql-zone.com/**.

SQL Statements

ADD	DESCRIBE
ALLOCATE DESCRIPTOR	DESCRIBE UNIT
ALTER	DISCONNECT
ALTER DOMAIN	DROP
ALTER TABLE	ESCAPE
AUTHORIZATION	DISCONNECT
AVG	EXECUTE IMMEDIATE
BEGIN	FETCH
CHECK	FOREIGN KEY
CLOSE	GET
COMMIT	GET DESCRIPTOR
CONNECT	GET DIAGNOSTICS
CONTINUE	GO
COUNT	GOTO
COUNT(*)	GRANT
CREATE ASSERTION	HAVING
CREATE CHARACTER SET	INSERT INTO
CREATE COLLATION	MAX
CREATE DOMAIN	MIN
CREATE SCHEMA	OPEN
CREATE TABLE	ORDER BY
CREATE TRANSLATION	PREPARE
CREATE VIEW	REFERENCES
DEALLOCATE DESCRIPTOR	REVOKE
DEALLOCATE PREPARE	ROLLBACK
DECLARE CURSOR	SELECT
DECLARE CURSOR FOR	SET
DEFAULT	SUM
DELETE	UPDATE
DELETE FROM	

Learning about SQL and Relational Databases *Continued*

SQL's DDL provides you with everything you need to define a database completely, modify its structure after you create the database, and destroy the database after you no longer need it. Basic elements of DDL include tables, views, schemas, catalogs, and clusters.

Most DBMS systems provide a graphical tool for creating database tables. You can also create tables by using a SQL command, as in Listing 21-1. You should also use the guidelines in Guidelines in Creating Tables whether using a graphical tool or SQL commands directly.

The DDL does not deal with data itself. The DML is the part of SQL that operates on the data. Some DML statements read like ordinary English-language sentences and are easy to understand. However, if a DML statement includes multiple expressions, clauses, predicates, or subqueries, understanding what the statement is trying to achieve can be a real challenge.

You can use the following DML statements: INSERT, UPDATE, DELETE, and SELECT. The most common data manipulation task is to retrieve selected information from a database. You may want to retrieve the contents of one specific row out of thousands in a table.

The simplest use of the SELECT statement is to retrieve all the data in all rows of a specified table, as follows:

```
SELECT * FROM orders
SELECT orderNumber FROM orders
```

DCL statements protect the database from unauthorized access, harmful interaction among multiple database users, and power failures and equipment malfunctions. One example is to protect against equipment failure by using *redundancy*, which means having backups of your database and applications that can be loaded and run on a backup computer system.

You can also protect your database from other threats, such as interference from simultaneous access by multiple users. You can use constraints to help keep users from entering bad data. By using DCL, you can protect your data from most problems.

Indexes are an important part of any relational database. Indexes serve as pointers into the tables that contain the data of interest. By using an index, you can go directly to a particular record, without scanning the table one record at a time. For large tables, indexes are a necessity.

Amazingly, the SQL-92 specification doesn't provide a means to create an index. The RDBMS systems must provide their own implementation of indexes. Because these implementations of creating an index are not standardized, they will probably differ from one another.

FIND IT ONLINE
Oracle Technology Network (**http://technet.oracle.com**) is a valuable resource for building Oracle Internet applications.

FIND IT ONLINE
SQL Server Magazine, which contains articles, discussion forums, and software for developers, is located at **http://www.sqlmag.com**.

Listing 21-1: Using DDL — A Sample CREATE Table

```
CREATE TABLE Orders (
    OrderID       integer NOT NULL,
    CustomerID    integer NULL,
    EmployeeID    integer NULL,
    OrderDate     datetime NULL,
    RequiredDate  datetime NULL,
    ShippedDate   datetime NULL,
    ShipVia       int NULL,
    ShipName      varchar (40) NULL,
    ShipAddress   varchar (60) NULL,
    ShipCity      varchar (15) NULL,
    ShipRegion    varchar (15) NULL,
    ShipCountry   varchar (15) NULL)
```

❶ *Define the columns that each table must contain.*
❷ *Give each table a primary key that you can guarantee is unique.*
❸ *Make sure that every table in the database has at least one column in common with one other table in the database.*

Create Useful Indexes

Well-designed indexes can greatly enhance the performance of your application. Unfortunately, the reverse is also true. Poorly-designed indexes or no indexes at all can slow your application to a crawl. It is important to take indexing seriously and create useful indexes. The key is to provide the optimizer with a good selection of indexes and let it choose the one that makes the most sense for a given operation.

When you are determining which columns to include for indexes, consider how you will use the data. If you will be performing queries involving WHERE clauses, consider each column in the clause as a candidate for an index. Also, remember that column order is important when defining an index. As in the case of a composite key (a key composed of more than one column), you need to make the most distinguishing column the leftmost part of the index.

A few additional guidelines apply when designing your indexes. First, keep your indexes narrow. Try to avoid multicolumn, compound indexes. Instead, create a larger number of narrow indexes. This approach provides the optimizer with more possibilities from which to choose.

The most important thing to remember about choosing indexes is that empirical testing will be your best guide.

Using ADO to Connect to Relational Databases

ctiveX Data Objects (ADO) are a group of objects designed to provide a simple programming interface to databases. The Database Access Component hierarchy has three main objects (Connection, Recordset, and Command), and several collections of subsidiary objects (Parameters, Properties, and Errors).

Using the Connection object, you can establish an active connection that enables you to gain access to data stored elsewhere — generally in a database. To obtain records from this data source, execute SQL queries, or manipulate the data directly, you can use the Command object. The Recordset object gives you access to the data that is returned from executing an SQL query, a stored procedure, or by opening a table.

First, let's look at how you connect to a data source and manipulate the data.

Defining a connection to a database is a straightforward process. First, create an instance of the Connection object. Here is how you set up a Connection object that is capable of referencing a data source:

```
Set oConn =
Server.CreateObject("ADODB.Connection")
```

The Connection object provides methods and properties that enable you to work with it. See the Connection Object Methods table for more detail. These methods and properties fall into three groups: opening and closing a connection, executing a command on the data source specified by the connection, and controlling transactions.

Once you have created an instance of the Connection object using the Server's object CreateObject method, you are ready to start using it. However, it does not actually refer to anything yet. Next use the connection to open your data source so that you can access and manipulate its data. This step is achieved using the Open method, which is provided by the Connection object.

```
Set oConn =
Server.CreateObject("ADODB.Connection")
oConn.Open "DSN=MyDB;UID=guest;pwd=guest"
```

Use the Connection object's Execute method to carry out commands that change the data in your data source. The Execute method accepts a string containing an SQL statement, the name of a stored procedure, or the name of a table in the data source. The last simply returns a recordset containing all the data in that table.

Here is an example of using an SQL query directly:

```
Set oConn =
Server.CreateObject("ADODB.Connection")
oConn.Open "DSN=MyDB;UID=guest;pwd=guest"
oConn.Execute "DELETE bonus FROM authors "
```

Continued

CROSS-REFERENCE
To learn about other ASP objects, read Chapter 19.

FIND IT ONLINE
Access Microsoft's update to information about ADO at
http://www.microsoft.com/data/ado/default.htm.

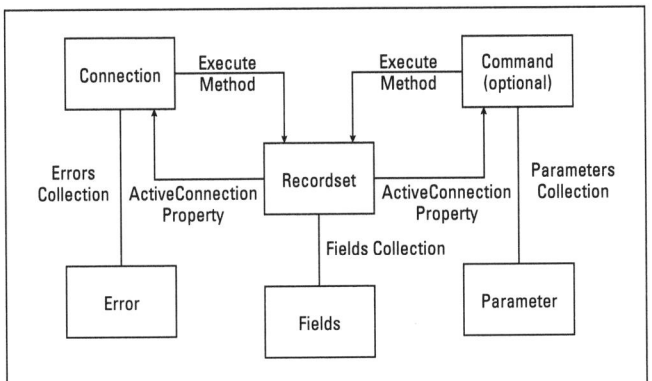

Table 21-3: THE CONNECTION OBJECT METHODS

Method	Decription
Open	Creates the database session. Usually the first method called.
Close	Closes the session, if one has been opened; generates an error if one has not.
Execute	Executes a query, SQL statement, or stored procedure. Useful for performing actions that do not return any records, such as deleting rows in a table.
BeginTrans	Begins a new database transaction.
CommitTrans	One of two ways to end a database transaction; tells the database that the entire operation was successful and all changes should be applied to the data.
RollbackTrans	The other way to end a transaction; this method informs the database that an error has occurred and all database operations since the BeginTrans should be undone.

Using ADO to Connect to Relational Databases *Continued*

Make sure to close a connection explicitly when it is no longer needed. Although a connection is closed when it goes out of scope, it is better to close the connection by design. You can call `Close` proactively and set the variable to `Nothing` when you know that you will no longer need a connection. This approach frees up resources before the connection actually goes out of scope. For example:

```
oConn.Close
Set oConn = Nothing
```

You can set the `CommandTimeout` property of the Connection object to determine how long to wait (in seconds) for execution of the query to finish. By default, the value is 30. If the value is set to 0, ADO will wait indefinitely until the operation has completed.

The use of transactions composes the last discussion item for the Connection object in this section. You may be familiar with this subject from other databases with which you have worked. When you need to perform a series of updates on a data source, you can improve efficiency by allowing the system to store up all the changes. You then commit the changes in one go, rather than writing each change individually to the records.

This principle has another advantage: Because the changes are not committed until you have completed all changes, you can always change your mind up to that point. This advantage is called rolling back the changes, and is used most often where an error occurs. Rather than having an undetermined number of changes to the data, you know that you can roll back all changes so that the data is not changed. The changes are only committed to the database if all the operations complete successfully (see Listing 21-2). The system that will do this is called Microsoft Transaction Server, and you will become familiar with it later in this book.

Thus far, when querying or updating a data source, you have used the Connection object to execute commands. The Command object represents one command to issue against a database connection, such as a SQL statement or stored procedure. The Command object is designed to handle the execution of these types of commands better than the `Execute` method of the Connection object (see Table 21-4 for common methods).

In this case, a connection is still established, but no intermediate connection variable is maintained. This approach is only efficient if you need the data from all the operations at the same time. If you are using the same connection for several operations, then you should create a separate Connection object, and perform successive operations with it.

The first step in using the Command object is to specify the `ActiveConnection` against which you want to use it.

```
Set oCmd =
Server.CreateObject("ADODB.Command")
oCmd.ActiveConection =
"DSN=MyDB;UID=guest;PWD=guest"
```

Continued

CROSS-REFERENCE

To learn about implementing transactions, please read Chapter 24.

Listing 21-2: Using Transactions

```
Set oConn = Server.CreateObject("ADODB.Connection")
oConn.Open "DSN=Northwind;UID=guest;pwd=guest"←❶
oConn.BeginTrans←❷
oConn.Execute "DELETE AuthorID FROM Authors WHERE StartDate < #1/1/1990#
oConn.Execute "DELETE AuthorID FROM Books WHERE StartDate < #1/1/1990#
If oConn.Errors.Count = 0 Then←❸
  oConn.CommitTrans
Else
  oConn.RollbackTrans←❹
End If
```

❶ First create and open your Connection.
❷ Begin executing your transaction logic.
❸ Using the Errors collection, determine if any errors occurred.
❹ Depending on whether errors occurred, either Rollback or Commit your transaction.

Table 21-4: THE COMMAND OBJECT METHODS

Method	Description
CreateParameter	Each command object has a collection of Parameter objects. This method adds a new parameter to that collection.
Execute	The main method of this object; it causes the command to be run against the data provider.

Using ADO to Connect to Relational Databases *Continued*

Once you have established the `ActiveConnection`, you can use the Command object in a similar way to the Connection object. Plus, you do not need to open the data source explicitly, or close it afterwards.

However, the different properties of the Command object enable you to specify some parameters outside the `Execute` method, and get more control over the operation (see Table 21-5). For example, you can set the `CommandText` and `CommandType` first, instead of specifying them in the `Execute` statement (see Listing 21-3).

In many cases, you will want to return some records via ADO in order to put some values into your page. For queries that return values, you must assign the results to a Recordset object.

You can create a recordset as the result of executing a query. This recordset can be from either the Command or Connection objects. You will recognize the syntax below as similar to the way you execute a query that does not return any records. The only difference is that you `Set` the result to refer to a Recordset object, and enclose the parameters in parentheses.

```
Set oConn =
Server.CreateObject("ADODB.Connection")
oConn.Open "DSN=Northwind;UID=guest;pwd=guest"
Set oRS = oConn.Execute("SELECT * FROM
Authors")
```

Alternatively, you can use the Command object to create your recordset:

```
Set oCmd =
Server.CreateObject("ADODB.Command")
oCmd.ActiveConection =
"DSN=Northwind;UID=guest;PWD=guest"
oCmd.CommandText = "SELECT * FROM Authors"
oCmd.CommandType = 1
Set oRs = oCmd.Execute
```

For a single access to your data source, in which you do not need to maintain a connection for several operations, you can create a recordset directly without going through the Connection or Command objects. The Connection is still created in the background automatically, just as when you used the Command object without specifically creating a Connection object first.

To create a recordset directly, you first have to create an instance of a Recordset object, using the `Server.Create Object` method. Then you can use the `Open` method of the Recordset object to fill the new recordset with values from the data source.

```
Set oRs =
Server.CreateObject("ADODB.Recordset")
oRs.ActiveConection =
"DSN=Northwind;UID=guest;PWD=guest"
oCmd.CommandText = "SELECT * FROM Authors"
oCmd.CommandType = 1
Set oRs = oCmd.Execute
```

Continued

TAKE NOTE

USING THE CONSTANTS DEFINITION FILE

To use the constant names in your code, you need to include a constants definition file in the page using a server-side include.

```
<!— #include file =
includes/Adovbs.inc" —>
```

Table 21-5: THE COMMAND OBJECT PROPERTIES

Property	Description
ActiveConnection	Returns or sets the Connection object that this command uses. (Each command object works against an associated database connection.)
CommandText	Holds the SQL statement or stored procedure to be executed by this object.
CommandTimeout	Serves the same purpose as the same property in the Connection object.
CommandType	Tells the data provider about the nature of the command text sent to it. It can have one of many values; two common values are Text(1) and Stored Procedure(4).
Name	Allows a name to be assigned to a command.
Prepared	Controls whether a compiled version of the command is generated before it is executed.
State	Identifies whether the current command is open or closed.

Listing 21-3: Using the Command Object

```
Set oCmd =   ←1
Server.CreateObject("ADODB.Command")
oCmd.ActiveConnection
"DSN=Northwind;UID=guest;pwd=guest"
oCmd.CommandText "DELETE AuthorID FROM←2
Authors
WHERE StartDate < #1/1/1990#"
oCmd.CommandType = 1←3
oCmd.Prepared = True←4
oCmd.Execute←5
Set oCmd.ActiveConnection = Nothing←5
```

1 Create the Command object and set the ActiveConnection property to the DSN that you want to use.

2 Set CommandText property to the SQL statement that you want to execute.

3 Setting CommandType property to 1 tells the Command that you are sending a SQL statement.

4 Set Prepared property to True to generate a compile version.

5 Execute and Close the ActiveConnection.

Listing 21-4: Using the Recordset Object

```
Set oRs =
Server.CreateObject("ADODB.Recordset")←❶
oRs.ActiveConection =
"DSN=Northwind;UID=guest;PWD=guest"
oCmd.CommandText = "SELECT * FROM Authors"
oCmd.CommandType = 1
Set oRs = oCmd.Execute
Do While Not oRS.EOF←❸
    ' vbscript application code
    oRS.MoveNext
Loop
❷
```

❶ By combining the Recordset object with a Do While loop, you can access every record in turn.

❷ Use a Do While because there may not be any records when you open the recordset.

❸ When you have no more records, EOF will be true.

Using ADO to Connect to Relational Databases *Continued*

Four cursor types are available when opening a Recordset object. The different cursor types have their own merits, and each one lends itself to particular uses. The code listings assume the default cursor type of `adOpenForwardOnly`. Appendix C lists a summary of the different types.

When you create a Recordset object and fill it with data, you will generally want to use it for something. You may want to move around from one record to another, edit existing records and add new ones, and extract data from the records. In order to perform these operations, you need to consider several aspects of how a recordset works.

The first step is to examine how you get the information from the recordset onto the Web page. You can think of the Recordset object as having the same structure as a table. In other words, the Recordset object consists of rows and columns. You can use five main methods to move around a recordset (see table for a summary).

The `Move` method moves a number of records in either direction, relative to the current record. The `Move` method also makes the new record to which it moves the current record. You can specify positive or negative numbers for the argument in order to move forward or backward.

```
oRs.Move 7
oRs.Move -4
```

The `BOF` property of a recordset is True when the current record pointer is positioned before the first record in the recordset. The `EOF` property is True when the current record pointer is beyond the last record. If there are no records in the recordset, both `BOF` and `EOF` are True. Before any operations are attempted, you should inspect the `BOF` and `EOF` properties when you first open a recordset in order to ensure that there is at least one record in it.

You can discern the number of records in a recordset using the `RecordCount` property. To loop through the records in a recordset, you generally use the `MoveNext` method (see Listing 21-4).

IIS 5.0 includes the latest release of ADO: Version 2.1. A new feature known as the Microsoft OLE DB Persistence Provider works with the Recordset object's `Save` and `Open` methods, enabling you to save a recordset to a file. The `Save` method adds an optional `adPersistXML` parameter, saving the file in XML format. The Web application can then reopen from that XML file and let that file be shared with other applications.

While an SQL query can apply the appropriate filters in building a recordset, you may need to locate a specific record. You can always accomplish this task by looping through the recordset to find the record that contains your value, but the `Seek` command now provides an efficient way of locating a record in a recordset. Using the Recordset's new `Index` property, you can move to records within a recordset quickly to locate the applicable row or rows.

In addition to the common properties and methods demonstrated in this chapter, there are many useful properties and methods. Appendix C lists the Recordset object's methods, properties, and collections.

TAKE NOTE

▶ PICKING THE RIGHT CURSOR FOR THE JOB

Choosing the correct SQL cursor has a direct impact on the success of your application. ADO provides four cursor options: forward-only, static, keyset, and dynamic.

Forward-only cursors are used when you only need to make a single pass through the data. They provide the fastest performance with least amount of overhead.

CROSS-REFERENCE

See Chapter 23 for more information on how to process a recordset.

Table 21-6: THE RECORDSET OBJECT METHODS

Method	Description
AddNew	Creates a new record in an updateable recordset.
CancelBatch	Cancels a pending batch update.
CancelUpdate	Cancels any changes made to the current or a new record.
Close	Closes an open recordset and any dependent objects.
Delete	Deletes the current record in an open recordset.
Move	Moves the position of the current record.
MoveFirst, MoveLast, MoveNext, MovePrevious	Moves to the first, last, next, or previous record in the recordset, and makes that the current record.
Open	Opens a cursor on a recordset.
Update	Save any changes to the current record.

Table 21-7: THE RECORDSET OBJECT PROPERTIES

Property	Description
AbsolutePage	The ordinal position of the current page.
AbsolutePosition	The ordinal position of the current record.
ActiveConnection	The connection object to which the recordset currently belongs.
BOF	True if the current record position is before the first record.
Bookmark	Returns a bookmark that identifies the current record uniquely, or sets the current record to the record identified by a valid bookmark.
EOF	True if the current record position is after the last record.
MaxRecords	Sets or returns the maximum number of records to return in the recordset.
RecordCount	The number of records currently in the recordset.

Creating Web-Based Database Application Architectures

New scenarios require access to information, and the complexity of that information continues to grow. Organizations previously had data on the mainframe and in various DBMSs. Now, important information is also found in mail stores, file systems, Web-based text and graphical files, and more. Thriving organizations will leverage all of this information by expanding — rather than replacing current UNIX and mainframe systems — to embrace client-server systems and the Internet.

Research has shown that there are four main criteria used in the decision-making process for judging and selecting database technologies and products.

First, customers don't plan to compromise their leading criterion, performance, for any other benefit. Similarly, services that augment the original capabilities of data providers must be held to the same standards: They must not stand in the way of native performance. And because applications and components must frequently scale to support hundreds or thousands of concurrently connected users, performance should be maintained as usage grows.

Second, customers want their database solutions to perform reliably. They use terms such as "rock-solid" and "fail-safe" to describe their requirements in this area. Underlying these statements is the need to minimize maintenance and support costs, and reduce the total cost of ownership.

Next, customers indicate that they are making strategic commitments to vendors of database technologies, and are looking for reciprocation. Customers describe their database decisions as "long-term," and purchase a string of database and related product releases. On the other hand, customers are very wary of becoming too dependent on a single vendor, a situation they term "vendor lock-in." Finally, new technologies should evolve gracefully from current technologies in order to avoid costly replacement of existing capabilities.

For customers, broad industry support is a more important gauge than the blessing of a standards body when choosing data access products. Broad industry support carries many benefits: safety in numbers, availability of skilled people to work with the products, and products that work together without expensive integration and customization.

Demands for this dynamic information has pushed Web computing to become a flexible and scalable (and sometimes complicated) implementation of multitier computing. Once you decide on your database products and technologies, you can begin to design the architecture.

A robust Web-based database application is a three-tier distributed application, including script-enabled HTML pages for the Web-based interface, a handful of ASP files for the business logic, and your database to manage the data.

Using ActiveX Data Objects

With the trend toward distributed computing in enterprise environments, it is important to have flexible and reliable communication among applications. Businesses often require independent applications that are running on different systems to communicate with each other and exchange messages, even though the applications may not be running at the same time. Applications built using a combination of ASP scripts communicating with cooperating components can interoperate with existing systems, applications, and databases.

Separating an application into several functional layers is certainly not a new idea. Until recently, however, distributed applications have been nearly impossible to put into effective practice using Windows.

Microsoft's IIS enables the development of Web-based business applications that can be extended over the Internet or deployed over corporate intranets. With IIS, Microsoft introduced a new paradigm to Internet transactional applications. Transactions are the plumbing that makes it possible to run real business applications with rapid development, easy scalability, and reliability.

The application-specific processing and business rules are maintained in the business logic tier. Business logic placed in ASP bridges the client environments and the data tiers.

Organizations of all sizes today are creating business solutions that leverage data from the desktop to the enterprise. As the types of data and types of access have proliferated, the challenge to create business advantage has remained paramount.

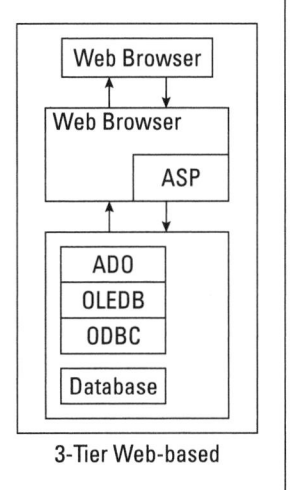

3-Tier Web-based

TAKE NOTE

▶ **ASKING THE RIGHT QUESTIONS**

The choice of data access technologies is strategic for organizations. Typically, factors such as the DBMS largely drive this choice. However, data access decisions are made for the long haul, and consequently need to be considered carefully. Here are some questions that you should ask when considering a data vendor:

▶ Is the vendor here to support me through several releases?

▶ Does the vendor have a strong and compelling strategy for data access, and does that strategy mesh with the goals of my organization?

▶ Has the vendor withstood the test of time by delivering strong products consistently in these markets?

▶ Likewise, has the vendor been able to succeed in these markets? Has the vendor proved its ability to deliver technological solutions and build market momentum, and garnered broad support for the technologies?

Personal Workbook

Q & A

1 What two properties should you check to see whether a recordset is empty?

_____

_____

_____

2 What type of DSN is recommended?

_____

_____

_____

3 How would you include the ADO constant definition file in your ASP page?

_____

_____

_____

4 Name three different data sources to which ASP can connect using ADO.

_____

_____

_____

5 How do you close Recordset and ADO Connection objects so that the resources used by these objects are returned to your system?

_____

_____

_____

6 Name two methods of the Connection object.

_____

_____

_____

7 What is the first step in using the Command object?

_____

_____

_____

8 What is the most widely accepted database model in use today?

_____

_____

_____

ANSWERS: PAGE 511

EXTRA PRACTICE

1. Write the ASP statement that instantiates the Connection object for data access.

2. Write a simple SQL statement to retrieve some records in the connection you just created.

REAL-WORLD APPLICATIONS

✔ Create a guestbook database with different attributes to store for your visitors using Access.

✔ Create an HTML page for a visitor to enter information and store it in your database.

CHAPTER **22**

MASTER
THESE
SKILLS

▶ **Using the Dictionary Object**

▶ **Working with the File System**

▶ **Using the Ad Rotator and Content Rotator Component**

▶ **Using the Content Linking Component**

▶ **Working with E-mail**

Using Built-In ASP Components

In previous chapters, you saw how Active Server Pages can use defined instances of objects on the server, and take advantage of the methods and properties that they provide.

In this chapter, we will examine objects that are available only on the server. These objects are provided by a special library file, Microsoft Scripting Runtime (`scrrun.dll`), which exposes the Scripting object. They can be used in various tasks and can work together with Active Server components.

You will also take a look at the Active Server components. In many ways, these components are like ActiveX controls, but they are designed for execution on the server. These objects enable you to change the page each time it is refreshed, add e-mail to Web applications, or access your server's file system if you have permission. These operations work whether or not the user's browser supports ActiveX objects, because the Web server does all the work.

In addition, you will learn how to display different HTML content dynamically with different frequencies using the Content Rotator component. Also, you will learn to make your Web site easier to navigate by using the Content Linking component.

Where do these components and objects come from? Some are provided as part of the Active Server Pages installation, while others are available for free or as a bought-in-product. Once you are familiar with using these components, you will have no trouble using other vendors' products in your pages.

Using the Dictionary Object

Think of the Dictionary object as being like an array, but with its own built-in intelligence that looks after the basic tasks of storing and manipulating the data. You do not have to worry about which row or column the data is in; you just access it using a unique key.

You will use the properties and methods supported by the Dictionary object to access the data items directly (see Table 22-1). You can create an instance of the Dictionary object using this JScript:

```
var dicFavorites;
dicFavorites = Server.CreateObject("Scripting.
Dictionary");
```

Once you have a new dictionary, you can add items to it:

```
dicFavorites.Item("team") = String(Request.
Form("userTeam"));
```

You can change the data stored in a Dictionary object by either changing the value of the key or the item of data associated with it. To change the value of the item with the key team, you could use:

```
dicFavorites.Item("team") = Request.Cookie
("userTeam");
```

If the key you specify is not found in the Dictionary object, a new key/item pair is created. If you try to retrieve an item using a key that does not exist, you get an empty string as well as a new key/item pair. To change the value of a key, and change the value of the corresponding item, use the Key property. To change the value of the existing key team, you could write:

```
dicFavorites.Key("team") = "Birds"
```

Two methods and a property are of particular interest when dealing with a Dictionary object. These enable you to iterate through all the key/item pairs stored in it. The Items method returns all the items in a Dictionary as a one-dimensional array, while the Keys method returns all the existing key values as a one-dimensional array. To find out the number of keys or items, you can use the Count property.

For example, you can retrieve all the keys and values from a Dictionary called dicObjectives using Listing 22-1. Notice that though the Count property holds the number of key/item pairs in the Dictionary, JScript and VBScript arrays always start at index 0. Therefore, we have to iterate through the array using the values 0 to Count −1.

TAKE NOTE

▶ TROUBLESHOOTING

An error will occur if you try to add a key/item pair when that key already exists, remove a key/item pair that does not exist.

FIND IT ONLINE

For utilizing the Dictionary object in VBScript, check out the following article: **http://www.4guysfromrolla.com/webtech/ 102898-1.shtml.**

Table 22-1: THE DICTIONARY OBJECT

Method	Description
Add key, item	Adds the key/item pair to the Dictionary.
Exists(key)	True if the specified key exists, False if not.
Items	Returns an array containing all the items in a Dictionary object.
Keys	Returns an array containing all the keys in a Dictionary object.
Remove(key)	Removes a single key/item pair.
RemoveAll	Removes all the key/item pairs.

Property	Description
Count	Returns the number of key/item pairs in the Dictionary. Read-only.
Item(key)	Sets or returns the value of the item for the specified key.
Key(key)	Sets or returns the value of a key.

Listing 22-1: Looping through a Dictionary

```
var counter = dicDelight.Count()          ❶
for (i = 0; i <= counter-1; i++) {        ❷
   tmpItem = String(dicDelight.Item(i));
   tmpKey = String(dicDelight.Key(i));    ❸ ❹
   if (tmpItem.length == 0)
Response.Write(" ");
   else {                                 ❺
     Response.Write(Key + ": " + tmpKey +
"<br>");
     Response.Write(Item + ": " + tmpItem
+ "<br>");                                ❺
   }
}
```

❶ Find out how many keys or items.
❷ Retrieve all the keys and values using a for loop.
❸ Store the value for this item.
❹ Store the value for the corresponding key.
❺ Write the values to the browser.

Working with the File System

You need to understand how to work with files on the server. Although a database is ideal for storing information in most cases, sometimes all you need is a simple plain text file to store some information.

Active Server Pages includes a rich set of methods, properties, and collections for working with files. By using ASP scripts, you have complete control over almost all aspects of the file system. To work with files, you use the File Access Component object, which uses the following objects:

- ▶ FileSystemObject works with the file system.
- ▶ TextStream reads and writes to a text file.
- ▶ File enables you to work with individual files.
- ▶ Folder enables you to work with file folders.
- ▶ Drive represents a disk or network share.

The File Access component has close to one hundred properties and methods. After reading the following section, you will understand how to use the most common and valuable methods and properties. The FileSystemObject object provides access to the computer's file system, enabling you to manipulate text files, folders, and drives from within your code. You can create an instance of the FileSystemObject in VBScript using the following code:

```
Set objFSO = Server.CreateObject("Scripting.
FileSystemObject")
```

The FileSystemObject contains one property, `Drives`, which returns a collection consisting of all the Drive objects available on the local machine. Each item of the `Drives` collection is a Drive object (see Table 22-2).

Listing 22-1 details how to use JScript to display a list of all the drives on your server, their drive letter, drive type,

and available sizes. See the figure on the facing page to see how the drive properties are displayed.

The FileSystemObject includes several methods for working with folders (see Table 22-3 for common methods). To use any of these methods, you must create an instance of the FileSystemObject object first.

Continued

Continued

TAKE NOTE

▶ PREVENTING ERRORS

If you run Listing 22-1 without a disk in your floppy drive or a CD in your CD drive, you will receive an error. You can get around this problem by using the isReady property to check whether media is present in the drive.

TAKE NOTE

▶ TROUBLESHOOTING

If you receive the following error when executing the a script, the IUSR_MachineName account does not have the correct permissions set to write the file:

```
Writing file ...
Server object error 'ASP 0177 :
800a004c'
Server.CreateObject Failed
/youraspfile.asp, line n
The operation completed successfully.
```

CROSS-REFERENCE

For more information about the `ServerVariables` collection, see Chapter 19.

FIND IT ONLINE

For information on how to use the FileSystemObject to perform standard Web site maintenance, see the following article: http://www.4guysfromrolla.com/webtech/090599-1.shtml.

Table 22-2: THE DRIVE OBJECT

Property	Description
AvailableSpace	Returns the amount of space available on specified drive.
DriveLetter	Returns the drive letter for the specified drive.
DriveType	Returns the value indicating the type of specified drive: 0 – Unknown, 1 – Removable, 2 – Fixed, 3 – Network, 4 – CD-ROM, 5 – RAM Disk
FreeSpace	Returns the amount of free space available on specified drive.
IsReady	Indicates whether a volume is ready to be used.
Path	Returns the path for specified drive.
RootFolder	Returns the Folder object representing the root folder of the specified drive.

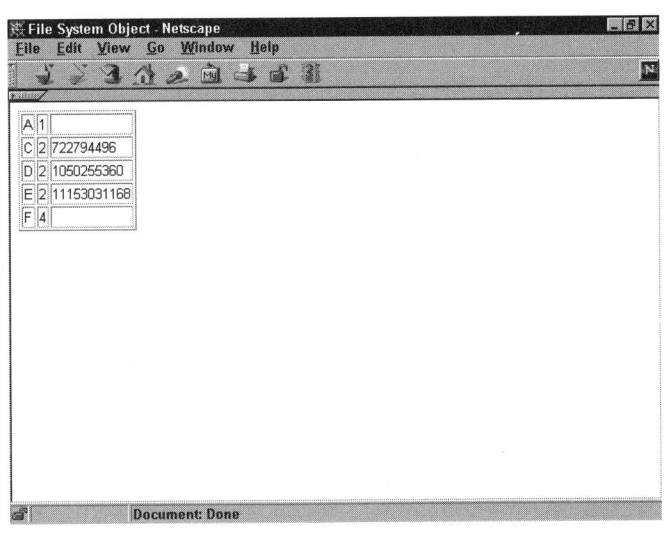

Listing 22-2: Using the FileSystemObject object

```jscript
<%@ language=JScript %>
<!DOCTYPE HTML PUBLIC "-//W3C//DTD HTML
4.0 Transitional//EN">
<html>
<head><title>File System
Object</title></head>
<body>
<table border=1>
<%
var fs =                              ❶
Server.CreateObject("Scripting.FileSystem
Object")
var dc = fs.Drives ←❷
var items = new Enumerator(dc); ←❸
while(!items.atEnd()) { ←❹
   i = items.item() ←❺
   Response.write("<tr>");
   Response.write("<td>" + i.DriveLetter +
"</td>");                          ❻
   Response.write("<td>" + i.DriveType +
"</td>");
   Response.write("<td>" +
i.AvailableSpace + "</td>");
   items.moveNext(); ←❼
}
%>
</table>
</body></html>
```

❶ Create the FileSystemObject Object.
❷ Retrieve the collection consisting of all Drive objects.
❸ Iterate through the Drives collection.
❹ Determine when the end of the collection is reached.
❺ Get one item from the collection.
❻ Write properties to the browser.
❼ Move to the next item in the collection.

Working with the File System
Continued

By using the TextStream object, ASP applications can access the server's file system. The TextStream object was designed to make it easy to manage text streams within ASP applications.

The TextStream object uses the FileSystemObject object to read and write text streams to files. To create and write to a text file, you must first create an instance of the FileSystemObject. In the next call, use the `CreateTextFile` method to return an instance of a TextStream object. Finally, use the `WriteLine` method to write data to the file:

```
Set fso = Server.CreateObject("Scripting.
FileSystemObject")
Set newStream = fso.CreateTextFile("d:\
temp\mytext.txt")
newStream.WriteLine("Hello, WWW.")
newStream.Close
```

This VBScript example creates a file named `mytext.txt` with the path `d:\temp\mytext`. The `WriteLine` method is used to send the single line of text to the file. See Table 22-4 for common methods and properties.

To read from a text file, you must first create an instance of the FileSystemObject. In the next call, use the `OpenTextFile` method to return an instance of a TextStream object. Finally, you can use the `ReadLine` method to read data from the file:

```
Set fso = CreateObject("Scripting.
FileSystemObject")
Set myStream = fso.OpenTextFile("d:\
temp\mytext.txt")
While not myStream.AtEndOfStream
 Response.Write myStream.ReadLine
Wend
myStream.Close
```

This VBScript script reads everything from the text file named `mytext.txt`. It outputs the contents of the file to the browser. If the file does not exist, the error File Not Found is returned.

To detect whether a file exists, you can use the `FileExists` method of the FileSystemObject. Simply pass the physical path of a file to this method, and it will return either True or False. Here is an example:

```
myPath = Request.ServerVarialbes("path_
translated")
Set fso = CreateObject("Scripting.
FileSystemObject")
If fso.FileExists(myPath) Then
 Response.Write("I found my way.")
Else
 Response.Write("I am lost.")
End If
```

The VBScript `while not .. wend` loop in this example moves through the contents of the file until the end of the file is reached.

Instead of using the `ReadLine` method to read through the contents of a file, you can use the `Read` method, which returns a specified number of characters from an open text file.

TAKE NOTE

▶ FINDING YOUR PATH

If you need to map the virtual path of a file to its physical path, you can use the `Server.MapPath` method.

Table 22-3: THE FOLDER OBJECT

Property	Description
Files	Returns the collection of Files contained in the folder.
IsRootFolder	Returns True if the specified folder is the root folder.
Name	Sets or returns the name of the specified folder.
Size	Returns the size of all files and subfolders contained in the folder.
SubFolders	Returns collection of all Folders contained in a specified folder.

Method	Description
CopyFolder	Copies a folder from one location to another. Syntax: `source, destination, [overwrite]`; where overwrite is a boolean.
CreateFolder	Creates the specified folder. Syntax: `FolderSpecifier`.

Table 22-4: THE TEXTSTREAM OBJECT

Property	Description
AtEndOfLine	Determines whether you are at the end of the line.
AtEndOfStream	Determines whether you are at the end of the text stream.

Method	Description
Read(n)	Reads text *n* character(s) at a time.
ReadLine	Reads an entire line of text.
WriteLine	Writes a string of characters followed with a carriage return.
SkipLine	Skips the current line and proceeds to the next line.

Using the Ad Rotator and Content Rotator Component

Advertising is big business on the Web as well as an effective way to make money on the Internet. In many cases, free services offered on the Web (such as search engines and electronic magazines) are free because they can make money by placing advertisements on their sites.

Here's a common problem: How can you display as many different advertisements as possible without coming up with a difficult algorithm?

Using the Ad Rotator component, you can create a Web page that chooses a random banner advertisement every time it is viewed. You can assign advertisements different weights so that they are displayed at different frequencies. You can also record the number of times an advertisement has been clicked to determine the advertisement's click-through rate. In addition, the ads and their locations are listed in a text file that can be changed on-the-fly to add or remove advertisements without making changes to your ASP script.

To create an instance of the Ad Rotator component:

```
var adRot = Server.CreateObject("MSWC.
AdRotator")
```

Once you create your adRot object, you can work with its properties and its single method (see Table 22-5). The first step is to decide on the width of the image border, the frame where you want the graphics to be displayed, and whether it accepts mouse clicks from the user.

```
adRot.Border = 0            // No border
adRot.Clickable = True      // Hyperlink
adRot.TargetFrame = "target =" "adFrm" "
```

Then, you need to insert the HTML for the graphic into the page that will be returned to the user. The GetAdvertisement method creates this HTML by getting details of the next advertisement to display from the rotator schedule file.

```
var tmpHTML
tmpHTML =
adRot.GetAdvertisement("ads\ad.txt")
Response.Write(tmpHTML)
```

The argument for the method is the location of the rotator schedule file relative to the current directory.

The next step is to create a rotator schedule file that the component uses to determine which ad to display. The rotator schedule file has two sections. In the first section, you provide general information about all the advertisements you want to display. In the second section, you specify the information for each advertisement. The two sections in this file are divided by an asterisk (*). See Table 22-6 for the layout.

Continued

FIND IT ONLINE

Here is an article on how you can use the Ad Rotator: **http://www.aspalliance.com/wiseasp/aboutadrotator. asp.**

FIND IT ONLINE

One way to begin selling banner advertisements easily for your Web site is to join an advertising network such as Flycast (**http://www.flycast.com**).

Table 22-5: THE AD ROTATOR COMPONENT

Property	Description
Border	Size of the border around the advertisement.
Clickable	Defines whether the advertisement is a hyperlink.
TargetFrame	Name of the frame in which to display the advertisement.

Method	Description
GetAdvertisement	Gets details of the next advertisement and formats it as HTML.

Table 22-6: THE AD ROTATOR PARAMETERS

Parameter	Description
REDIRECT	Virtual path and name of the program or ASP file that implements the redirection.
WIDTH	Width in pixels of the advertisement on the page. 440 is default.
HEIGHT	Height in pixels of the advertisement on the page. 60 is default.
BORDER	Border width around the advertisement in pixels. 1 is default.
*	
AdURL	Virtual path and filename of the advertisement image file.
AdHomeURL	Advertiser's home page URL. A hyphen can be used to indicate that there is no link.
Text	Text for display if the browser does not support graphics.
Impressions	A number indicating the relative weight that this advertisement should be given.

Using the Ad Rotator and Content Rotator Component *Continued*

The Redirect parameter specifies what page the user's browser will access if he or she clicks the ad.

```
[REDIRECT url]
```

If this parameter is used, the page specified should be a redirection file. If this parameter is not specified, the default is to send the user directly to the URL attached to the ad. The width, height, and border parameters specify the corresponding width, height, and border in pixels.

For each advertisement to be rotated, supply the four pieces of information described below the asterisk (*) in Table 22-6. The parameters in the table should be specified for each ad to appear in the prescribed location, and the parameters should follow each other, one on each line, with no blank lines in between. Listing 22-3 presents a sample rotator schedule.

If you want to log advertisement activity by recording each time an ad is clicked, the next step is to create the redirection file, which is accessed whenever a user clicks the displayed advertisement. The URL of this page is specified in the REDIRECT parameter of the rotator schedule file. The following ASP command would be placed in adhandler.asp, according to Listing 22-3:

```
Response.Redirect Request.QueryString("url")
```

This command will send the user to the correct URL for the banner that was clicked. If you want to save some more meaningful information, you can add your own necessary ASP script on this page. Just perform those actions before executing the redirection.

```
' Some database activity to record
'    user clickthrough rates
Response.Redirect Request.QueryString("url")
```

The Content Rotator component works much like the Ad Rotator component. A drive file, called a content schedule file, contains the information needed to show each rotating item. After the file is created, you are ready to use the component in your script.

The content schedule file, unlike the rotator schedule file, has no header information. There can be as many rotating entries as you need, each using the following syntax:

```
%% [#weight] [//comments]
your HTML string
```

First, you need to create an instance of the Content Rotator component. Then you can use the ChooseContent method to retrieve an HTML string:

```
<%
var ctRot = Server.CreateObject("MSWC.
ContentRotator")
=ctRot.ChooseContent("ctSchedule.txt")
%>
```

The GetAllContent method is useful for debugging a content schedule file. If you want to test the appearance of all entries in this file, you can use this method to view its contents before the entries are displayed to your Web site.

TAKE NOTE

▶ INSTALLING CONTENT ROTATOR

The Content Rotator is not installed automatically with IIS. You need to download it from the Microsoft Web site at **http://www.microsoft.com/ntserver/web** or install the IIS Resource Kit on your Web server.

▶ DISPLAY RICH MEDIA

You cannot use the Ad Rotator component to display rich media, including dynamic HTML. To display this type of advertisement, use the Content Rotator component.

Table 22-7: THE CONTENT ROTATOR COMPONENT

Method	Description
ChooseContent	Returns an HTML string.
GetAllContent	Returns all HTML strings.

Listing 22-4: Using a Content Rotator Schedule File

```
%%#5 // This is the first entry
<a href="reviews.asp">
Come and see the latest book reviews for
our newest books.
</a>
%%#5
<a href="news.asp">
For the latest Internet news click here.
</a>
%%#0 // This will not show because the
weight is 0. Temporarily disabled.
<a href=prizewinner.asp>
You are the lucky winner of a free book.
Click here to continue.
</a>
```

① *Two percent signs (%) start a new content listing.*

② *The number determines the relative weight of each content listing. This text will display five of ten times on average.*

③ *Pair of forward slashes (/) indicates a comment.*

④ *Text you want to insert.*

⑤ *Zero (0) weight entries will not be used.*

Listing 22-3: Using an Ad Rotator Schedule File

```
REDIRECT /adhandler.asp
WIDTH 400
HEIGHT 90
BORDER 0
*
http://www.sales.com/ads/blowout.gif
http://www.sales.com/
Visit our site!
50
http://www.cheap.com/ads/seasonal.gif
http://www.cheap.com/seasonal
See our end of season sales!
50
```

Using the Content Linking Component

One complaint about the World Wide Web has always been that all sense of order is lost. Users are free to click any link, and the order in which material is followed is not necessarily the order intended by the author.

Fortunately, the Content Linking component gives you an easy way to link pages in a site and maintain that linkage in the future.

The Content Linking component is a useful tool for sites that provide contents pages, which contain a list of links to other pages on the same site. The component matches the URL of the currently displayed page to a list of pages sorted in a text file on the server automatically, and can enable users to browse through the list of pages in forward or reverse order. In other words, even after the visitor has clicked a link in the contents page and is viewing one of the pages in the list, the component can still tell where that page is within the list.

Because the details are stored in a text file, maintaining the site and links between the pages becomes a matter of editing the text file. For example, you can change the order in which the pages are displayed, just by rearranging them in the Content Linking List file.

The Content Linking List file contains a simple list of page URLs, in the order they are to be displayed. You also supply matching descriptions, which are displayed in the contents page, and you can add comments to each one if required. These comments help identify links later, and are not visible to visitors. The file contains one line of text for each page. Each line consists of the URL, description, and comment, separated by the TAB character and ending with a carriage return. For example:

```
/default.asp Registering for A Class
/step1.asp Step 1: Get the Course Number
/step2.asp Step 2: Check for Availability
/step3.asp Step 3: Arrive Early for Appt
```

Listing 22-5 uses the `nextlink.txt` file to maintain a list of pages that are available on a Web site. The code will create a bulleted list of each page listed in your text file. Follow the steps to create a table of contents for your Web site. See Table 22-8 for a complete list of methods.

Table 22-8: THE CONTENT LINKING COMPONENT

Method	Description
GetListCount(list)	Returns the number of pages in the file list.
GetListIndex(list)	Returns the position of the current page in the file list.
GetNextURL(list)	Returns the URL of the next page in the file list.
GetNextDescription(list)	Returns the description of the next page in the file list.
GetPreviousURL(list)	Returns the URL of the previous page in the file list.
GetPreviousDescription(list)	Returns the description of previous page in the file list.
GetNthURL(list)	Returns the URL of the nth page in the file list.
GetNthDescription(list)	Returns the URL of the nth description in the file list.

Listing 22-5: Creating a Contents Page

```
var nextLink = Server.CreateObject("MSWC.NextLink"); ←❶
var strListFile = "nextlink.txt"; ←❷
var nLinkCount = nextLink.GetListCount(strListFile); ←❸

Response.Write("<ul>");
for ( var i=0; i < nLinkCount; i++ ) { ←❹
  Response.Write("<li><a href=" + nextLink.GetNthURL(strListFile, i) + ">"); ←❺
  Response.Write(nextLink.GetNthDescription(strListFile, i)); ←❻
  Response.Write("</a>");
}
Response.Write("</ul>");
```

❶ Create the NextLink object.
❷ Define the file that contains your links.
❸ Count the number of links.
❹ Use the `for` loop to get each link in the file.
❺ Get the URL and use in the `<A>` tag as the `href`.
❻ Get the description of the URL.

Working with E-mail

Many situations require you to send e-mail from your Web site. For example, if a user forgets their password, you may want to send that user an e-mail message containing their password. In this section, you will learn how to send e-mail messages from within your ASP script.

Microsoft has bundled both an SMTP server and a collection of objects for communicating with mail servers in the NT 4.0 Option Pack for Internet Information Server 4.0. SMTP will not run on Windows 95/98 with Personal Web Server.

The Microsoft SMTP Server does the basic job of sending and retrieving e-mail in accordance with the Simple Mail Transport Protocol. In some ways, it is very limited. The service does not support the Post Office Protocol (POP). On the positive side, the Microsoft SMTP Service is valuable for sending automated e-mail messages from your Web site.

To check whether the SMTP Service is installed and running on your server, open the Internet Service Manager (ISM) and see whether an icon labeled Default SMTP Site appears within the IIS folder (as shown in the figure on the facing page). If the icon does not appear, you should install the service by running the Windows NT Option Pack Setup program. If the service is installed but not running, you can start the service by selecting Action, Start.

The SMTP service, located in the InetPub/MailRoot directory, uses a Pickup directory to send mail. The service monitors the Pickup directory constantly for new e-mail messages. Whenever it finds an e-mail message, the service attempts to send it. If the service is unable to deliver the message immediately, it is kept in the Queue directory while the service attempts to keep delivering the message. If the e-mail message cannot be delivered and cannot be returned to the sender, the message is moved to the Badmail directory.

The most dependable and easiest method of using the SMTP Service to send e-mail is by using the Collaboration Data Objects (CDO). This can be accomplished with a function that can be included in all your pages that need to send e-mail (see Listing 22-6). This function accepts four parameters: the e-mail address of the sender, the e-mail address of the recipient, the subject, and the body of the message. See Table 22-9 for a list of properties and descriptions.

After the four parameters are selected, an instance of the NewMail object is created, the appropriate properties are set to the parameters, and the Send method is used to send the e-mail message. When using the NewMail object, you should be warned that a new instance of this object must be created for each message you send. If you need to send multiple e-mail messages from within a single Active Server Page, you must create and destroy multiple instances of the object to avoid receiving an error.

When sending e-mail messages, you will need to set the From address to an e-mail address with your domain. Otherwise, some e-mail servers may reject your messages automatically.

Also, when sending e-mail messages, you often want to send the message to multiple e-mail accounts. You can accomplish this task by separating the e-mail address of each recipient by a semicolon.

Continued

CROSS-REFERENCE

To learn about setting up Windows NT, see Chapter 2.

FIND IT ONLINE

To learn how to install and create additional SMTP sites on the same server, search for the Microsoft Knowledge Base Article ID Q183476 at **http://www.microsoft.com/search.**

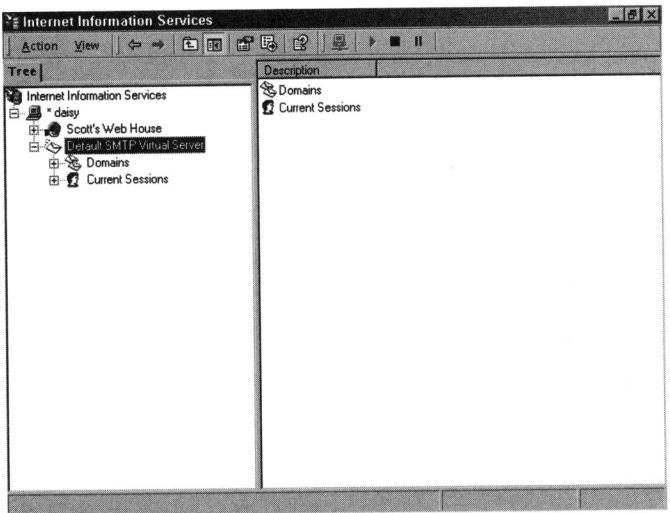

Table 22-9: THE NEWMAIL OBJECT

Property	Description
Body	Specifies the text that will appear as the body of the mail message.
BCC	Specifies any blind carbon copy recipients. BCC means that neither the original recipient nor anyone who was specified as a copy recipient knows that the BCC recipient has been sent a copy.
CC	Specifies any copy recipients.
From	Specifies the sender.
Importance	Sets the priority of a mail message.
Subject	Specifies the subject.
To	Specifies the recipient.

Method	Description
Send	Sends the mail to the Pickup directory of the SMTP service, where it will be processed.
AttachFile	Adds a file attachment to an e-mail message.

Working with E-mail *Continued*

A file attachment can be added to an e-mail message by using the `AttachFile` method of the NewMail object. The AttachFile method accepts three parameters: the full file path of the file to send, the name of the file as it will appear in the e-mail message (optional), and the encoding method that should be used to encode the file:

```
ObjMail.AttachFile(Source, [,FileName],
[,EncodingMethod])
```

Most, but not all, e-mail clients support messages priorities. For example, using Lotus Notes, you can send a message with Low, Normal, or High Priority. You can use the `Importance` property of the NewMail object to set the priority of a message. You can set the property to the following values: 0 – Low Importance, 1 – Normal Importance (default), 2 – High Importance.

When sending an e-mail message, you can indicate that a copy of the message should be sent to another e-mail address. There are two ways that you can send a copy of a message. When you send a message with a carbon copy, the main recipient of the message is able to view the e-mail address of the recipient of the carbon copy.

Alternatively, you can send a blind carbon copy. If you send a blind carbon copy, the main recipient of the message will not know that another copy of the message has been sent.

You can use the CDO to send messages that include HTML formatting and images. For example, you can include text with particular fonts and colors, custom background images, and HTML links.

You should be warned, however, that most e-mail clients do not fully support e-mail with either HTML formatting or images.

By default, the CDO sends e-mail messages as plain text. To send e-mail that contains HTML, you set two properties of the NewMail object:

```
objMail.MailFormat = 0
objMail.BodyFormat = 0
```

When the `MailFormat` property is set to 0, the e-mail is sent in MIME format. When the `BodyFormat` is set to 0, the e-mail message can contain HTML.

Listing 22-6: Using CDO

```jscript
<%@ Language=JScript %>
<html><head><title>Email Form</title></head>
<body><% main() %></body></html>

<script LANGUAGE="JSCRIPT" RUNAT="SERVER">
function write(str) {        ◀━❶
 Response.write(str + "\n");
}
function main() {        ◀━❷
 if (Request.Form("send").Count > 0)
sendTheMail();
 else showFeedbackForm();
}
function sendTheMail() {        ❻
 var fromEmailAddress =
String(Request.Form("fromEmailAddress"));
 var fromEmailName =
String(Request.Form("fromEmailName"));
 var toEmailAddress =
String(Request.Form("toEmailAddress"));
 var subject =
String(Request.Form("subject"));
 var body = String(Request.Form("body"));
 var objMail =        ◀━❼
Server.CreateObject("CDONTS.NewMail");
 objMail.To=toEmailAddress;
 objMail.From=fromEmailName
 objMail.Subject=subject;
 objMail.Body=body;
 objMail.importance=1;
 objMail.Send();        ◀━❽
 write("<h3>Your email has been sent.</h3>")
}
function showFeedbackForm() {        ❸
 write("<form name=form method=POST action=" +
  Request.ServerVariables("script_name") +
">");
 write("<input type=hidden name=toEmailAddress
value=admin@your.com>");
 write("<table border=0 cellPadding=3        ◀━❹
cellSpacing=0 width=100%>");
 write("<thead><tr><th colspan=2>Email
Form</th></tr>");
 write("<tbody><tr><td valign=top>Your Email
Address: </td>");
 write("<td><input name=fromEmailAddress
size=35 maxlength=50></td></tr>");
 write("<tr><td valign=top>Your Name: </td>");
 write("<td><input name=fromEmailName size=35
maxlength=50></td></tr>");
 write("<tr><td valign=top>Subject: </td>");
 write("<td><input name=Subject size=35
maxlength=50></td></tr>");
 write("<td vAlign=top>Body: </td>");
 write("<td><textarea NAME=body ROWS=2 COLS=15
WRAP=hard></textarea></td></tr>");
 write("<tr>");
 write("<td align=center colspan=2 >");
 write("<input type=submit value='Send  Email'
name=send>");        ◀━❺
 write("<input type=reset value=Clear
class=button></td></tr>");
 write("</table>");
}
</script>
```

❶ write() is a typing shortcut for writing to the browser.

❷ main() will check if the Send Email button was pressed using the Count property. If it was, then send the e-mail. If not, then present an HTML form to prepare an e-mail.

❸ The HTML form will call itself.

❹ Create an HTML form with the e-mail parameters.

❺ Name the submit button "Send" to check in main().

❻ Use Request.Form to retrieve the form elements.

❼ Create the CDO New Mail object and set the parameters.

❽ Send your e-mail.

Personal Workbook

Q & A

1 What property of the NewMail object is used to set the priority of an e-mail message?

_____

_____

_____

2 Can you use CDO to send things other than a regular text message?

_____

_____

_____

3 What does the Content Link file contain?

_____

_____

_____

4 What does the Ad Rotator component do?

_____

_____

_____

5 True or False. Advertisement images of any size can be cycled on a Web page using the Ad Rotator component.

_____

_____

_____

6 What property of the Dictionary object will show the number of key/item pairs?

_____

_____

_____

7 Which object provides access to the computer's file system?

_____

_____

_____

8 Which directory does SMTP use to send mail?

_____

_____

_____

ANSWERS: PAGE 512

EXTRA PRACTICE

1. Capture some banner ads and create an Ad Rotator Schedule file. Use the Ad Rotator component on your Web site.

2. Use the FileSystemObject object to determine which drives exist on your machine and display their properties.

3. If you have SMTP, create a feedback form and send the e-mail to your own e-mail account.

4. Go to Wise ASP Web site (**www.aspalliance.com/ wiseasp/**), and see how they use the Content Linking object with a drop-down box to contain all of their articles.

REAL-WORLD APPLICATIONS

✔ You are planning to create your own Web site. List all of your pages and descriptions in a file so that you can later use the Content Linking component.

✔ Create a drop-down box to use to jump around the Web site you just designed. Use the Content Linking file as the values.

CHAPTER **23**

MASTER THESE SKILLS

▶ Designing SQL SELECT Queries

▶ Building Queries from User Requests

▶ Making SQL Queries against a Database

▶ Building Documents from Query Results

▶ Post-Processing Query Results

▶ Breaking Down Roadblocks: Handling Queries Efficiently

▶ Managing Your Code: Structure Your ASP Pages

Integrating Databases and Web Pages: Output

The preceding chapters introduced you to ActiveX Data Objects (ADO). Now that you've had a chance to look at the features of ADO, this chapter will help you leverage ADO in your Web development efforts by introducing the building blocks to interacting with databases and manipulating its output.

It is important that you understand the structure of a typical SQL SELECT statement. When you structure your query, many considerations will affect your application's overall performance. Decisions ranging from how much data you will return to how you sort your data all have a tremendous impact on query execution. You will learn how to design SQL queries efficiently to interact with ADO.

You have learned the ways in which an ASP application can interact with users browsing a Web site. Preceding chapters introduced you to getting data from forms, using either the POST or GET method and the Form collection of the Request object. In this chapter, you will learn how to interact with a user's browser to build customized SQL SELECT queries.

In preceding chapters and sections, you learned how to set up the ADO Connection object and Recordset object to execute SQL statements. In this chapter, you will learn how to select a particular Recordset cursor to maximize performance and maximize functionality. You will also learn how to process the result set from your customized query in an efficient manner.

Because ASP is a scripting language, many programmers think they can forego up-front structuring. You will have more success with ASP if you address some high-level issues from the beginning. As a result, you will learn how to lay out your ASP script like a program.

Designing SQL SELECT Queries

The most frequent task against a database is retrieving selected information. You may want to retrieve the contents of one specific row out of thousands in a table. You may want to retrieve all the rows that satisfy a condition or a combination of conditions. One SQL statement, the SELECT statement, performs all these tasks for you.

The simplest use of the SELECT statement is to retrieve all the data in all the rows of a specified table. That task would look like this:

```
SELECT * FROM customers
```

The asterisk (*) is a wildcard character that means everything. In this context, the asterisk is a shorthand substitute for listing all the column names of the customers table. As a result of this statement, all the data in all the rows and columns of the customers table appear in your query results.

SELECT statements can be much more complicated than this example. In fact, some SELECT statements can be so complicated that they are virtually indecipherable. This potential complexity results from the fact that you can tack multiple modifying clauses onto the basic SELECT statement. The WHERE method is commonly used to restrict the rows that a SELECT statement returns.

For data to be useful, you must be able to separate the small amount you do want from the huge amount you do not want (see Table 23-1).

The modifying clauses available in SQL are FROM, WHERE, HAVING, GROUP BY, and ORDER BY. The FROM clause tells the database engine on which table or tables to operate. The WHERE and HAVING clauses specify a characteristic of the data that determines whether to include a particular row in the current operation. The GROUP BY and ORDER BY clauses specify how to display the retrieved rows. Table 23-1 provides a summary.

If you have more than one of these clauses, they must appear in the order of the Code Listing.

Continued

TAKE NOTE

▶ **HELPING YOU WRITE A QUERY**

Start with the SELECT clause, and write a list of what you want to see in the result set. This list will give a goal of what you want.

Put all the tables containing the columns needed to complete the SELECT list into the FROM clause.

Sometimes reversing the wording of the problem helps. For example, instead of saying "Give me all of the authors who live in NY," say "NY is the city where I want all of the authors." This may help you see the underlying logic.

Sometimes negating the wording of the problem helps. Instead of saying "Give me all the authors who made $10,000," say "Don't give me authors who made less than $10,000." It is often easier to find what you do not want than what you do want.

Remember to allow for NULLs creating UNKNOWN logical values. Always test your code with NULLs in all possible places.

CROSS-REFERENCE

Chapter 21 discusses how relational databases use SQL.

TAKE NOTE

AVOID BLOBS

Blobs (Binary Large Objects) are stored in your database as either text or image data types. Your database server does not store the Blob data on the data page along with the other fields in the row. Instead, it maintains a pointer to the Blob. This essentially means that storing data in Blobs will increase your storage requirements.

There are also functional limitations with Blobs. For example, if you were to use a WHERE clause to search on a text column, you are limited to using the LIKE operator. This can be very time-consuming and will add a lot of overhead to your application.

Before using a Blob field, consider the alternatives. If you want to store images in the database, you may find it more appropriate to store the images in the database, and simply maintain URLs that point to the images within the table. If you are storing lots of text data, you may find that rather than using a Blob field, you can denormalize the table and break the data into varchar (with a length of 255 text characters) fields.

Table 23-1: SQL MODIFYING CLAUSES

Modifying Clause	Description
FROM	Specifies from which tables to take data.
WHERE	Filters out rows that do not satisfy the search condition.
GROUP BY	Separates rows into groups, based on the values in the grouping columns.
HAVING	Filters out groups that do not satisfy the search condition.
ORDER BY	Sorts the results of prior clauses to produce final output.

```
SELECT column_list
  FROM table_list
  [WHERE search_condition]
  [GROUP BY grouping_column]
  [HAVING search_condition]
  [ORDER BY ordering_condition]
```

Designing SQL SELECT Queries
Continued

The WHERE clause is a filter that passes rows that meet the search condition and rejects those that do not meet the condition. The GROUP BY clause rearranges the rows that the WHERE clause passes according to the value of the grouping column. The HAVING clause is another filter that takes each group that the GROUP BY clause forms and passes those groups that meet the search condition, rejecting the rest. The ORDER BY clause sorts whatever remains after all the preceding clauses process the table.

The FROM clause is easy to understand if you specify only one table:

```
SELECT * FROM customers
```

This statement returns all the data in all the rows of every column in the SALES table. You can, however, specify more than one table in a FROM clause:

```
SELECT * FROM customers, orders
```

This statement forms a virtual table that combines the data from the customers table with the data from the orders table. Each row in the customers table combines with every row in the orders table to form a new virtual table. This virtual table contains the number of rows in the customers table multiplied by the number of rows in the orders table. In most cases, the majority of rows that form this virtual table are garbage. You can filter out the rest of the rows by using a WHERE clause.

A statement performs an operation, such as SELECT, only on table rows WHERE a stated condition is True. The syntax of the WHERE clause is:

```
SELECT column_list
  FROM table_name
  WHERE condition
```

The column list specifies which of the columns in the table you want to display. The statement displays only the columns you list. The FROM clause specifies from which table you want to display columns. The WHERE clause excludes rows that do not satisfy a specified condition. The condition may be simple or it may be compound.

The Code Listing provides examples of typical WHERE clauses.

The conditions that these WHERE clauses express are known as *predicates*. A predicate may be True, False, or unknown. The unknown case arises if one or more elements in the assertion are null. The comparison predicates in Table 23-2 are the most common, but SQL offers a number of others that increase your capability greatly to filter out a desired data item from others.

Here is an example of a compound SELECT statement:

```
SELECT customer_name, phone
 FROM customers
 WHERE contactTitle = 'president'
  AND country = 'portugal'
```

This statement returns the names and phone numbers of all customers who are presidents of their respective companies and reside in Portugal.

Sometimes you want to select a row if the value falls within a specified range. One way to make this selection is by using comparison predicates. You can, for example, formulate a WHERE clause to select all the rows in the orders table that have a value in the orderValue column greater than 40 and less than 100:

```
WHERE orders.orderValue >= 40
 AND orders.orderValue =< 100
```

Continued

TAKE NOTE

▶ **OPTIMIZE YOUR QUERIES**

When you structure your query, many considerations will affect your application's overall performance. Decisions ranging from how much data you will return to how you sort your data all have a tremendous impact on query execution. Apply good judgement when designing your queries and be sure to monitor and tune query performance regularly.

Some types of queries are more resource-intensive than others. Queries that return large result sets can become a bottleneck to your application and can create unnecessary network traffic. This becomes even more evident as you try to scale your application to more users. Instead, attempt to filter records based on user selections and only return the data that is absolutely necessary. Also, rather than using SELECT *, be sure to only include the columns that you need within your SELECT statement.

Certain query operators are also very resource-intensive. For example, IN, NOT IN, and OR queries can be very demanding on the server. The not equal comparison operator is another operator to avoid if possible. Certain column functions such as SUM can also take their toll on the server. If you must use these operators, pay close attention to how it is affecting your application's performance.

Table 23-2: SQL COMPARISON PREDICATES

Comparison	Symbol
Equal	=
Not equal	<> , !=
Less than	<
Less than or equal	<=
Greater than	>
Greater than or equal	>=

```
WHERE orders.custID = customers.custID

WHERE orders.shippingWeight > 100

WHERE orders.orderDate > 6/1/99
 AND orders.orderDate < 10/1/99

WHERE orders.ShippingCountry <> 'us'
```

Designing SQL SELECT Queries
Continued

Another way of specifying a range that includes the end points is to use a BETWEEN predicate:

```
WHERE orderValue BETWEEN 40 AND 100
```

This clause is functionally identical to the preceding example. This formulation saves some typing and is also perhaps a little more intuitive than the one that uses two comparison predicates joined by the logical connective AND.

If you use BETWEEN, you must be able to guarantee that the first term in your comparison is always equal to or less than the second term.

The IN and NOT IN predicates deal with whether a particular set includes their arguments. You may, for example, have a table that lists customers of certain geography. You can find those customers living on the West Coast:

```
SELECT customerName
 FROM customers
 WHERE state IN ('or', 'wa', 'ca')
```

The NOT IN version works the same way. Say you have customers in New York and Pennsylvania who are not eligible to receive your special promotional e-mail:

```
SELECT customerName
 FROM customers
 WHERE state NOT IN ('ny', 'pa')
```

You can use the LIKE predicate to compare two character strings for a partial match. Partial matches are valuable if you have some idea of the string for which you are searching, but do not know its exact form.

To identify partial matches, SQL makes use of two wild-card characters. The percent sign (%) can stand for any string of characters, zero or more characters in length. The underscore (_) stands for any single character.

The NOT LIKE predicate retrieves all rows that do not satisfy a partial match, including one or more wildcard characters.

You may want to search for a string that includes a percent sign or an underscore. In this case, you want SQL to interpret the percent sign as a percent sign and not as a wildcard character. You can write such a query by typing an escape character just prior to the character you want SQL to take literally:

```
SELECT customerAddr
 FROM orders
 WHERE customerAddr LIKE '#%'
 ESCAPE '#'
```

The NULL predicate finds all rows where the value in the selected column is null:

```
SELECT employeeName
 FROM employees
 WHERE bonus IS NULL
```

Often applying one condition in a query is not enough to return the rows that you want from a table. To meet these needs, SQL offers the logical connectives AND, OR, and NOT.

If multiple conditions must all be True before you can retrieve a row, use the AND logical connective:

```
SELECT employeeName
  FROM emplyees
  WHERE hireDate >= #1/1/2000#
  AND hireDate <= #2/1/2000#
```

This query will return all employees hired on January 1, 2000 up to and including February 1, 2000.

If any one of two or more conditions must be True to qualify a row for retrieval, use the OR logical connective:

```
SELECT orderID
  FROM orders
  WHERE product = 'tire'
  OR product = 'filter'
```

This query will return all order IDs that include products that have tire and filter included.

The NOT connective negates a condition. If the condition normally returns a True value, adding NOT causes the same condition to return a False value. If a condition normally returns a False value, adding NOT causes the condition to return a True value. Consider the following example:

```
SELECT employeeName
  FROM employees
  WHERE NOT (state = 'ny')
```

This query will return all employees not working in NY.

Table 23-3: SQL LIKE PREDICATE

SQL Predicate	Query Results
WHERE phone LIKE '410%'	410-555-1212
	410-666-3131
	410-777-5252
WHERE address LIKE '%85th%'	8928 85th Place
	142 85th Street
	101 185th Way
WHERE hireDate LIKE '1/1/9_'	1/1/90
	1/1/92
	1/1/95

Building Queries from User Requests

The information stored in the Request object collections originates from the client browser. It is then passed to the server. The server decodes all this information and makes it available through Request object's collections.

The browser can send specific information to the server in two ways.

Using the GET method:

```
<form method="get" ... >
```

Using the POST method:

```
<form method="post" ... >
```

When using a form to get data, you can use the GET method. The GET method is ideal for forms that return no more than a few dozen bytes of data. It is limited to about 2,044 bytes of data because the data submitted with it appears as a query string in the Web browser's URL text box.

When the GET method is used in an HTML form, an ASP application can easily determine the value of HTML form variables by using the `Request.QueryString()` method:

```
Request.QueryString("userID")
```

This code returns the value of the "userID" HTML form data entry field.

Listing 23-1 shows an example of using the GET method. The first If statement checks whether the HTML form has been filled in. If not, the HTML statements to create a form are displayed. If the HTML form has been filled in, the Else clause will retrieve the form data.

When the HTML form is submitted, the ASP script will call itself. You should notice how the data from the HTML form is submitted to the ASP application as part of the URL address string. For example:

```
yourserver.com/getMethod.asp?account=101022
```

In the Else statement, you should create instances of the Connection object and the Recordset object, respectively,

that are used in the rest of the example. The Connection object is then opened, as it is needed to open the Recordset object later. Then you must store the desired SQL statement into a variable for the Recordset object's `Open` method. This method takes two arguments: the SQL statement and the Connection object.

Notice how that you must use the `Request.QueryString()` method to get the value of the HTML form data field, `account`. Next, you should use the VBScript command `replace`. You need to replace all single quotes with two single quotes, because SQL will misinterpret a single quote within a text field.

After the recordset is open, you need to check the `RS.EOF` property, which will be false if the account was found in the recordset. Next you need to produce lines of HTML containing the values from the table columns of business, contact, and address for the account number entered on your original form. Make sure you close the Connection and Recordset objects when you finish your processing to free up their resources.

Continued

TROUBLESHOOTING

Developers tend to make several common mistakes when building SQL statements. To get around these mistakes, take the following steps:

▶ Text fields must have single quotes around the values.

▶ Fields with spaces in their names must be surrounded with open and close brackets [].

▶ Text fields with single quotes cannot be placed into SQL statements unmodified. You must transform a single quote (') to double single quotes (").

CROSS-REFERENCE

Chapter 19 introduces you to using the Request object.

Listing 23-1: The GET Method and `Request.QueryString`

```
<html>
<head><title>UsingFormGetMethod.asp</title></head>
<body>
<h3>This form uses the HTML GET Method to transfer data
back to the Web Server. </h3>
<% main() %>
</body>
</html>
<script runat="server" language="VBScript">
Sub main
If Request.QueryString("Account") = "" Then          ←①
 Response.Write("<form action=listing23-1.asp method=get name=dataForm>")
 Response.Write("Account #: <input name=account maxlength=25><p>")
 Response.Write("<input type=submit>")               ←②
 Response.Write("</form>")
Else
 Set conn = Server.CreateObject("ADODB.Connection")   ←④
 Set RS = Server.CreateObject("ADODB.Recordset")
 conn.Open "FILENAME = c:\myDataLink.udl;DATABASE=pubs"
 account = Request.QueryString("account")            ←⑥
 account = Replace(account, "'", "''")
 sql = "SELECT business, contact, address FROM accounts "   ←⑤
 sql = sql & "WHERE account = '" & account & "'"              ←③
 RS.Open sql,conn
 If Not RS.EOF Then               ⑦
  Response.Write(RS("business") & " " & RS("contact") & ".<br>")
  Response.Write(RS("address") & ".<p>")
 End If
 conn.Close()
/RS.Close()//
End If
End Sub
</script>
```

① *Check whether the HTML form has been filled in.*
② *If the HTML form is not filled in.*
③ *If the HTML form has been filled in.*
④ *Create instances of the Connection object and the Recordset object.*
⑤ *Store the desired SQL statement into a variable.*
⑥ *Use the* `Request.QueryString` *method to get the value of the HTML form data field.*
⑦ *Produce lines of HTML containing the values from the table.*

Building Queries from User Requests *Continued*

When you need to send large amounts of data, you should not use the GET method. Instead, use the POST method.

When the POST method is used in an HTML form, an ASP application can easily determine the value of HTML form variables by using the `Request.Form()` method, as in Listing 23-2.

Listing 23-2 presents an ASP application that is similar to Listing 23-1, except that the POST method is used instead of the GET method.

When the POST method is used in an HTML form, an ASP application can easily determine the value of HTML form variables by using the `Request.Form()` method.

The first If statement checks whether the HTML form has been filled in. If it has not, the HTML statements to create a form are displayed. If the HTML form has been filled in, the Else clause will retrieve the form data.

When the HTML form is submitted, the ASP script will call itself. You should notice that the data from the HTML form is not submitted to the ASP application as part of the URL address string. Instead, the data is part of the HTTP header.

In the Else statement, you should create instances of the Connection object and the Recordset object, respectively, that are used in the rest of the example. The Connection object is then opened, as it is needed to open the Recordset object later. Then you must store the desired SQL statement into a variable for the Recordset object's Open method. This method takes two arguments: the SQL statement and the Connection object.

Notice how Listing 23-2 uses the `Request.Form()` method to get the value of the HTML form data field, `account`. Next you should notice the VBScript command `Replace`. You need to replace all single quotes with two single quotes, because SQL will misinterpret a single quote within a text field.

After the recordset is open, you need to check the `RS.EOF` property, which will be false if the account was found in the recordset. Next, you need to produce lines of HTML containing the values from the table columns of business, contact, and address for the account number entered on your original form. Make sure you close the Connection and Recordset objects when you finish processing to free up their resources.

TAKE NOTE

▶ SUBMITTING FORMS

When the user submits the HTML form, the data in the HTML form is sent to the ASP application. A connection is established with the Web server to transfer the data only when the form's Submit button is clicked. ASP parses that data and gives you access to it by using the Request object.

Listing 23-2: The POST Method and `Request.Form`

```
<html>
<head><title>UsingFormPostMethod.asp</title></head>
<body>
<h3>This form uses the HTML POST Method to transfer data
back to the Web Server.</h3>
<% main() %>
</body>
</html>
<script runat="server" language="VBScript">
Sub main
If Request.Form("Account") = "" Then           ←❶
  Response.Write("<form action=listing23-2.asp method=post name=dataForm>")
  Response.Write("Account #: <input name=account maxlength=25><p>")
  Response.Write("<input type=submit>")           ←❷
  Response.Write("</form>")
Else
  Set conn = Server.CreateObject("ADODB.Connection")
  Set RS = Server.CreateObject("ADODB.Recordset")   ←❹
  conn.Open "FILENAME = c:\myDataLink.udl;DATABASE=pubs"
  account = Request.Form("account")←❻
  account = Replace(account, "'", "''")
  sql = "SELECT business, contact, address FROM accounts "
  sql = sql & "WHERE account = '" & account & "'"   ←❺
  RS.Open sql,conn
  If Not RS.EOF Then
    Response.Write(RS("Business") & " " & RS("Contact") & ".<br>")
    Response.Write(RS("Address") & ".<p>")
  End If
  conn.Close()
  RS.Close()←❸
End If
End Sub
</script>
```

❶ Check whether the HTML form has been filled in.

❷ If the HTML form is not filled in.

❸ If the HTML form has been filled in.

❹ Create instances of the Connection object and the Recordset object.

❺ Store the desired SQL statement into a variable.

❻ Use the `Request.Form` method to get the value of the HTML form data field.

❼ Produce lines of HTML containing the values from the table.

Making SQL Queries against a Database

Every use of a database requires a Connection object, which represents the actual session established with your database. In general, the Command object is used for working with more complex database actions. Simple queries and record manipulation are generally handled through the Recordset object.

Any group of records, whether it is the result of a query or the entire contents of a table, is represented by a Recordset object. You will use this object (which is the most complex of all objects) for almost all your data access. For most situations, though, it is used in a simple manner. Listing 23-3 demonstrates a common use of a recordset, retrieving and displaying the results of query.

In Listing 23-3, use `Response.Buffer` to tell the server to hold the buffer until it is flushed. Using `Response.Buffer` and `Response.Flush` to control the output to the browser greatly improves your response time. First, you need to create instances of the Connection object and the Recordset object that are used in the rest of the example. The Connection object is then opened, as it is needed to open the Recordset object later. Next, you need to store the desired SQL statement into a variable for the Recordset object's `Open` method. This method takes two arguments: the SQL statement and the Connection object.

After the recordset is open, copy the recordset collection values onto the client in the form of local variables. This strategy saves you a look-up operation on the collection each time you iterate through the collection values and will speed up your script.

A simple loop allows the entire contents of the recordset to be processed. In this case, you will use the `while` construct to contain the loop condition, `RS.EOF`, which is a property that will be true if the current record is past the last record in the recordset. Next, you need to produce a line of HTML containing the values from the table columns of fname, lname, and salary. Here is where you use `Response.Flush` to control your output buffer to the client's browser. Once every iteration, you will send your HTML to the browser. The extremely important `RS.MoveNext` line, which advances the record pointer and prevents an infinite loop from occurring, concludes the loop. Make sure you close the Connection and Recordset objects when you finish your processing to free up their resources.

CROSS-REFERENCE

In addition to the few simple properties and methods demonstrated previously, there are many others you should know. See Appendix C and Chapter 21.

CROSS-REFERENCE

Chapter 21 describes in detail how to use all the properties, methods, and collections of the Data Access component.

Listing 23-3: Using the Recordset Object

```
<%@ Language=JScript %>
<% Response.Buffer = true; %>←❶

<html>
<head><title>Displaying a Recordset</title></head>
<body>
<%
  var conn = Server.CreateObject("ADODB.Connection");
  var RS = Server.CreateObject("ADODB.Recordset");
  conn.Open(Application("dbName"),Application("dbID"),Application("dbPwd"));

  var sql;
  sql = "SELECT * FROM users \n";←❸
  sql+= "ORDER BY lname \n";

  RS.Open(sql,conn);

  if (!RS.EOF) {←❺
   var sFirstName = RS("fname");
   var sLastName = RS("lname");   ←❹
   var iSalary = RS("salary");
  }
  while (!RS.EOF) {←❺
   Response.Write(String(sFirstName) + " " + String(sLastName))
   Response.Write(" makes $" + String(iSalary) + ".<br>");
   Response.Flush;←❻
   RS.MoveNext();←❼
  }
  conn.Close();RS.Close()Ł
%>
</body>
</html>
```

❶ Use `Response.Buffer` to tell the server to hold the buffer until it is flushed.

❷ Create instances of the Connection object and the Recordset object.

❸ Store the desired SQL statement into a variable for the Recordset objects.

❹ Copy the recordset collection values onto the client.

❺ `RS.EOF` will be true when the current record is past the last record in the recordset.

❻ Use `Response.Flush` to control your output buffer to the client's browser.

❼ `RS.MoveNext()` advances the record pointer.

Building Documents from Query Results

O ne of the most time-consuming aspects of creating a Web site is the process of constructing and processing the information entered into HTML forms. This section provides some tips and tricks to make the task of working with HTML forms easier.

Text boxes, text area, radio buttons, check boxes, and select lists all have unique characteristics that pose special problems when you integrate them into your Active Server Page.

In building your ASP page, there will be instances when you want to assign a value to a variable for a text box or text area. For example, suppose you want to enable users to change their e-mail addresses, which are stored in a users table. Listing 23-4 takes a Recordset variable and assigns it to a form variable called `email`.

Notice that the listing calls `getStringField()`, which uses `Server.HTMLEncode`. Certain characters that a user can enter into an HTML form will corrupt the form if displayed. If a variable that contains quotation marks is assigned to the VALUE attribute, then the variable will be displayed incorrectly and the HTML will be corrupted. The `HTMLEncode()` method takes care of this problem by replacing all special HTML characters automatically.

Often, you need to fill in HTML forms that contain multiple groups of related information. For example, you can have a radio button group with two options, "Week" or "Less". You must give them a unique value, so that you can distinguish them when we come to access the HTML form collection:

```
<input type=radio name=shop value="week"> Week
<input type=radio name=shop value="unknown">
Less
```

When the browser submits the page, it only includes the values of radio button and check box controls that are selected. In the preceding example:

```
Control name 'shop' has the value 'week'
```

Radio buttons have the property of belonging to a group, where the user can only select one of them in that group. Clicking on one of the buttons clears the others in the same group. To tell the browser that they belong to a group, all we have to do is give them the same name attribute, but different value attributes, as we did in the preceding example.

Unlike in the case of a text box, you cannot use the value attribute to provide a radio box with a default value of CHECKED or 'not checked'. If you want the status of a check box to depend on the value of a variable, you must include additional logic in your ASP script. In Listing 23-4, you can determine whenever the Recordset value is equal to the radio group value and write CHECKED when appropriate.

You can use the same logic in the case of check boxes (see Code Listing).

Select lists have a similar function to radio buttons. You can use a select list to display a limited menu of options. Unlike radio buttons and check boxes, however, select lists use the SELECTED attribute to determine which option is listed.

CROSS-REFERENCE
Chapter 19 describes the different properties of the Server object, including `HTMLEncode`.

CROSS-REFERENCE
Chapter 12 describes how to build an HTML form.

Let's take a closer look at Listing 23-4. Let's assume that an ID is passed to this page in `Request.Form("userID")` from a preceding page. This HTML form will enable the user to change certain attributes about their account information, including name, e-mail address, shopping frequencies, and whether they want a newsletter.

Good page design isolates functionality into separate functions. Listing 23-4 uses `main()` to call all each isolated function in the script, which is the only client-side ASP. First, `useADO()` handles the SQL call to retrieve the user's information based on the `"id"` passed in. The Request.Form element accepts an argument named `"id"`. Then you need to create and open the Connection object. Next, you should build the SQL statement to execute using the `"id"`, and then execute the SQL command against the Connection object. The resulting recordset is then assigned to local variable RS back in the calling function.

`displayResults()` will display the HTML form with the Recordset data that was passed in. But first, you should guarantee that the `"id"` was found in the Recordset using the EOF property. If the `"id"` was not found, display an error message. Then exit out of the function, displaying only the error message.

The first part of the HTML form to create is the radio box controls. You can check the value of the Recordset column ("frequency") returned against the VALUE of the "shop" radio box. If the two values match, the radio box will be CHECKED.

The next part of the HTML form creates two text boxes that contain the user's name and e-mail. They are populated from the Recordset variables "name" and "email," respectively, into the VALUE attribute. Again, notice that the `getStringField()` method is a safe measure against bad data.

Finally, you create the submit button and close out the HTML form.

Continued

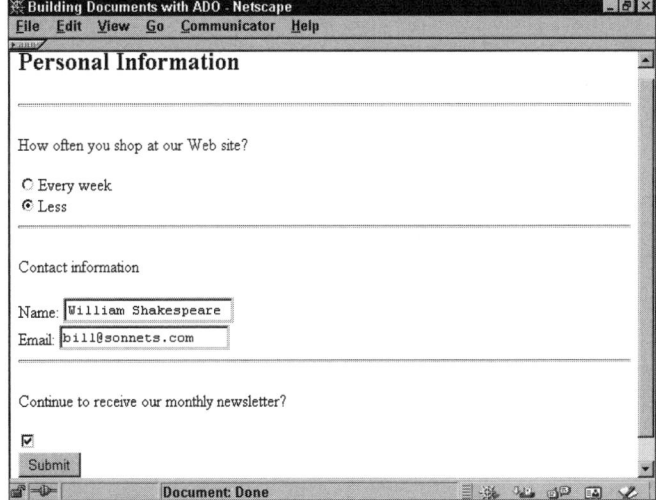

Building Documents
from Query Results *Continued*

Listing 23-4: Building HTML Forms from ADO

```
<%@ Language=JScript %>
<html>
<head><title>Building Documents with ADO</title></head>
<body> <% main() %> </body>
</html>

<script runat="server" language="JScript">

function main() {
 var RS = useADO(String(Request.Form("userID")));
 displayResults(RS);                                    ←①
 conn.Close();
}

function getStringField(theRSField)←②
{
 theStr = String(theRSField);
 if (theStr == "null" || theStr == "undefined")
  return "";
 else
  return theStr;
}

function useADO(id) {←③
 var conn = Server.CreateObject("ADODB.Connection")
 conn.Open(Application("dbName"),Application("dbID"),Application("dbPwd"))
 var sql;
 sql = "SELECT * FROM users where id = " + id
 return conn.Execute(sql);
}
```

① *Calls each isolated function in the script.*
② *A safe measure against bad data.*
③ *Handles the SQL call to retrieve the user's information based on the "id" passed in.*

Listing 23-4: Building HTML Forms from ADO (continued)

```
function displayResults(RS) {←❹
if (RS.EOF) {←❺
  Response.Write("Your information was not found.<br> \n");
  Response.Write("Please contact your administrator.<br> \n");
  return;←❻
}
Response.Write("<h2>Personal Information</h2> \n");
Response.Write("<form method=post action=processform.asp> \n");
Response.Write("<hr><p>How often you shop at our Web site?</p> \n");
Response.Write("<input type=radio name=shop value=week");
if (getStringField(RS("frequency")) == "week") Response.Write(" CHECKED ");
Response.Write(">Every week<br> \n");
Response.Write("<input type=radio name=shop value=unknown");                      ←❼
if (getStringField(RS("frequency")) == "unknown") Response.Write(" CHECKED ");
Response.Write(">Less<br> \n");
Response.Write("<hr><p>Contact information</p> \n");
Response.Write("Name: <input type=text name=userName maxlength=30");
Response.Write(" value=" + getStringField(RS("name")) + "><br> \n");       ←❽
Response.Write("Email: <input type=text name=email maxlength=50");
Response.Write(" value=" + getStringField(RS("email")) + "><br> \n");
Response.Write("<hr><p>Continue to receive our monthly newsletter?</p> \n");
Response.Write("<input type=checkbox name=news value=true");
if (getStringField(RS("newsletter")) == True) Response.Write(" CHECKED ");
Response.Write("><br> \n");
Response.Write("<input type=submit> \n");←❾
Response.Write("</form> \n");
}
</script>
```

❹ `displayResults()` *will display the HTML form with the Recordset data that was passed in.*

❺ *But first, you should guarantee that the "id" was found in the Recordset using the* EOF *property.*

❻ *Exit out of the function, displaying only the error message.*

❼ *Create the radio box controls.*

❽ *Create two text boxes that contain the user's name and e-mail.*

❾ *Create the submit button.*

Post-Processing Query Results

I n this section, you will learn how to use several of the advanced features of the Recordset object, so that you do not have to dump the entire result set back to the user. Any group of records, whether the result of a query or the entire contents of a table, is represented by the Recordset object. This is the object you will use for almost all your data access. In this section, you will learn how to perform such tasks as retrieving a count of records in a Recordset and scrolling through a Recordset.

After a Recordset is opened, you can determine the number of records that exist in the Recordset by using the RecordCount property. For example, the following listing uses a static cursor to obtain the record count. The RecordCount property is not supported by forward-only or dynamic cursors. When used with either of these cursor types, it always returns the value –1. You should avoid using the RecordCount property whenever possible because it always demands a rich cursor type.

```
<! --#include virtual="/adovbs.inc" -->
<%
Set conn =
Server.CreateObject("ADODB.Connection")
conn.Open "FILE
NAME=c:\myDataLink.udl;DATABASE=pubs"
Set RS =
Server.CreateObject("ADODB.Recordset")
RS.CursorType = adOpenStatic
RS.Open "SELECT * FROM authors", conn
Response.Write "And the survey says ... "
Response.Write RS.RecordCount
Response.Write " records."
%>
```

There are many situations in which you will need to provide a user with the means to page through the records in a Recordset. Suppose, for example, that you are creating an ASP script that displays all the books for sale in your warehouse. If you have hundreds of books, you might want to divide the books into multiple pages.

The Recordset object contains several properties for paging through a Recordset. By using these properties to divide the records in a Recordset into different pages, you can enhance the user's visit to your Web site. These properties include:

- ▶ AbsolutePage — sets or returns the current page of records;
- ▶ PageCount — returns the number of pages in a recordset;
- ▶ PageSize — sets or returns the number of records contained in a single page.

To divide a Recordset into pages, use the PageSize property to set the number of records in a page. Next, after opening the Recordset, use the AbsolutePage property to move to a particular page. Listing 23-6 is an example of how to divide your recordset into multiple pages.

Take note of a few things about Listing 23-6. First, notice that a variable named rowCount is used to limit the number of records displayed on a page. If this variable were not used, every page would contain both the records for the page and the records for all the pages. Also, notice that the VBScript CInt() function is used to convert the value passed in the URL string to an integer. If you do not do this, you may get unpredictable results. Finally, notice that the Recordset is not opened with a forward-only cursor. Unfortunately, this means that the paging properties can be inefficient.

TAKE NOTE

► USING CONSTANT DEFINITIONS

The adovbs.inc and adojavas.inc files were installed on your server when you installed Active Server Pages. The file contains a long list of constant definitions to use with ADO.

CROSS-REFERENCE

Chapter 21 describes how to create a database connection using OLE DB.

CROSS-REFERENCE

Chapter 21 describes the different properties, methods, and collections of the Recordset object in detail.

Listing 23-5: Paging through a Recordset

```
<% Response.Buffer = true; %>
<! --#include virtual="/adovbs.inc" --><html>
<head><title>Paging Through a Recordset</title></head>
<body> <% main() %> </body></html>
<script runat="server" language="VBScript">
Sub main
DIM currentPage, rowCount, i, title
If Request.QueryString("currentPage") = "" Then
  currentPage = 1
Else
  currentPage = Request.QueryString("currentPage")
End If
Set conn = Server.CreateObject("ADODB.Connection")
conn.Open "FILE NAME=c:\myDataLink.udl;DATABASE=pubs"
Set RS = Server.CreateObject("ADODB.Recordset")
RS.CursorType = adOpenStatic
RS.CursorLocation = adUseClient
RS.PageSize = 4
RS.Open "SELECT * FROM titles", conn
RS.AbsolutePage = cInt(currentPage)
Set rowCount = 0
Set title = RS("title")
While Not RS.EOF and rowCount < RS.PageSize
 Response.Write title & "<br>"
 rowCount = rowCount + 1
 Response.Flush
 RS.MoveNext
WEnd
Response.Write "<hr>"
for i = 1 to RS.PageCount
 Response.Write "<a href=recordset.asp?currentPage=" & i & ">" & i & "</a>"
End Sub
</script>
```

1. Determine the current page requested.
2. Limit the number of records that are displayed on a page.
3. Open your connection to the database and execute the query.
4. Bind the recordset variable to a local variable.
5. Loop through the recordset until EOF or the page is full.
6. Create a choice bar for the user to navigate throughout the recordset.

Breaking Down Roadblocks: Handling Queries Efficiently

If you are creating a database-driven Web site, you must devote a significant amount of time to monitoring and tuning your database and testing the efficiency of your SQL statements. Even minor adjustments can have dramatic effects in the speed of your Web site. This section assumes you are using Microsoft SQL Server 6.5 or 7.0, but the following principles apply to any RDBMS.

To tune your database effectively, you must have a method of measuring its current performance. Microsoft SQL Server includes several utilities for monitoring activity on your database and timing the speed of its queries.

To measure the speed of execution of your SQL queries, you can use Microsoft ISQL/w or Microsoft Query Analyzer, depending on which version of SQL Server you are running. Either of these utilities will show each of the steps that SQL Server follows to execute your query and the time required for each step.

To time the execution of a SQL statement with Query Analyzer, launch the program from the SQL Server group and choose Query, Current Connection Options. Next, select the option labeled Show Stats Time (see Current Connection Options of Query Analyzer). After this option is selected, whenever you execute a query using Query Analyzer, statistics for the query will be displayed along with the results of the query.

To view query statistics using ISQL/w, choose Query, Set Options. Next, select the option labeled Show Stats Time. For example, after executing the SQL statement:

```
SELECT * FROM authors
```

The Query Analyzer Results Window shows the statistics and results.

Your choice of indexes for your database tables has the greatest impact on the performance of your queries. When executing queries, you typically want to do everything possible to avoid a table scan. Table scans are bad because they force SQL Server to begin at the first row of a table and read each row to find the rows that match the query's search criteria. For example, to perform a table scan of a data table that contains a thousand records, SQL Server must read each and every row. When SQL Server uses an index, it can avoid reading the rows one by one.

Because indexes have such a dramatic impact on performance, you should experiment as much as possible with using different indexes on your database tables. After adding or removing an index, use ISQL/w or Query Analyzer to test the speed of typical queries against the table with the index. You should consider that adding too many indexes to a table may actually slow down operations, such as table updates and insertions, because the indexes for a table must be updated whenever the data in a table is updated.

SQL Server maintains statistics on the distribution of values in the columns of a database table. It uses these statistics to determine the indexes to use for retrieving information from a table when executing a query. These statistics are updated automatically. However, they can become inaccurate if the data in a table undergoes any type of dramatic change. If the statistics for a table become outdated, SQL Server will start to make poor choices when choosing query execution plans. You can use the Database Maintenance Plan Wizard to update statistics automatically for your database on a periodic basis.

CROSS-REFERENCE
Chapter 21 describes the fundamentals of relational databases.

CROSS-REFERENCE
Chapter 21 explains how to use the Recordset object.

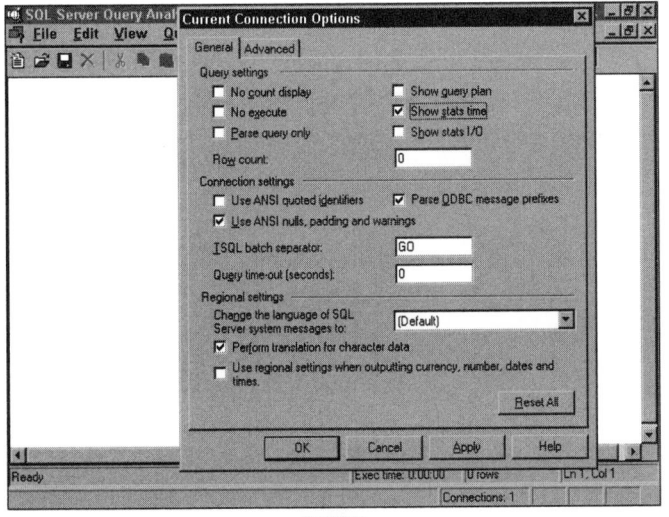

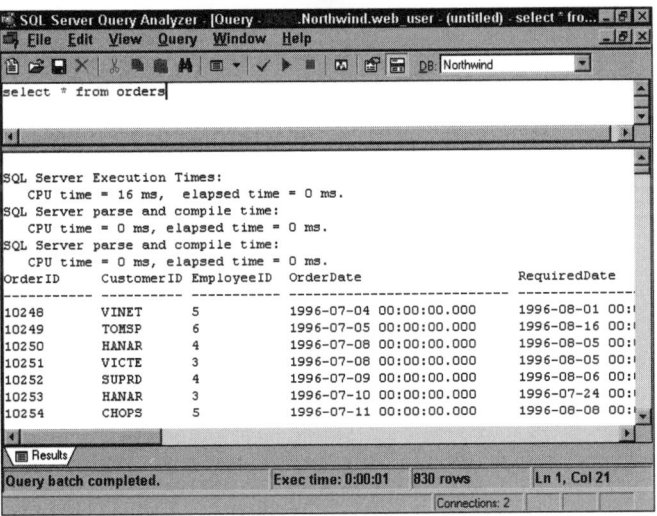

You should make another adjustment by using stored procedures. Executing SQL stored procedures from within your ASP scripts is almost always more efficient than executing equivalent SQL query strings. If you want to boost the performance of your Web site's database access, replace all your query strings with calls to stored procedures.

A stored procedure executes faster than a SQL string because a stored procedure is parsed and compiled only once, when it is first executed. In contrast, each and every time a SQL query string is executed, SQL Server must create a new query plan.

Continued

Breaking Down Roadblocks: Handling Queries Efficiently *Continued*

In preceding chapters and sections, you learned how to set up the ADO Connection object and Recordset object to execute SQL statements. In this section, you will learn how to select a particular cursor to maximize performance and functionality.

A Recordset is opened either implicitly or explicitly with a particular cursor and locking type. Understanding cursor and locking types is important for two reasons. First, using different cursor and locking types can have a dramatic effect on the performance of your ASP scripts. If you make the wrong choices, it can take forever for your ASP page to retrieve and display a list of database records. Second, certain properties of the Recordset object are available only when you use the correct cursor and locking types. For example, you must open the Recordset with the right cursor and locking type to retrieve a count of the records in a Recordset or to create a Recordset that contains updateable records.

When you execute a SQL query that returns a set of rows, the rows are delivered to your ADO application through a cursor. There are four different types of cursors that determine how the results of a query are delivered.

A forward-only cursor is the default cursor and provides the fastest performance. Forward-only cursors do not support backward scrolling; they allow only a single pass through the result set.

A static cursor reflects the state of the data in a table when the cursor is first opened. The cursor cannot detect whether rows in the underlying table have been updated or deleted or whether new rows have been added. Unlike a forward-only cursor, however, a static cursor can be used to scroll back and forth through the result set.

A keyset-driven cursor can detect certain (but not all) changes made to the underlying rows in a table. In particular, a keyset-driven cursor can reflect data accurately that has been updated. However, it cannot detect whether rows have been inserted or deleted by other users. A keyset-driven cursor supports scrolling.

A dynamic cursor is the richest cursor type. It can detect any changes made to a table by other users while the cursor is open. It also supports scrolling fully.

If you do not specify a particular cursor type when opening a Recordset object, SQL Server will return the records by using the forward-only cursor. This cursor type (which is specific to SQL Server) is very efficient. You will almost never have a compelling reason to use a richer type of cursor in your ASP script. However, you need to balance the need for performance against the need for particular Recordset properties.

TROUBLESHOOTING

You must be careful when retrieving text columns with a Recordset. To prevent blank records from being returned, you must list the text column as the last column in your SELECT statement, or you must open a cursor other than the default forward-only cursor.

TAKE NOTE

▶ USING FORWARD-ONLY

When the default cursor is opened, it is often called a *firehose* cursor, because the connection is kept open and the results of the query are blasted to your application as fast as possible.

TAKE NOTE

▶ CREATING A SCALABLE WEB SITE

If you want to create a scalable Web site, do not consider using Microsoft Access. Access is a desktop database and not a client/server database. This means that it was not designed to support the large number of simultaneous users that a modest public Web site receives. For example, Access does not support advanced multi-user locking, transaction logs, or efficient indexing.

Managing Your Code: Structure Your ASP Pages

Because ASP seems so simple, developers are sometimes tempted to build piles of spaghetti code. You will save yourself a lot of effort if you learn the development decisions that you should make when creating an ASP front end.

In a typical application front end, you will take some user input, validate it, call some business function(s), and then either display an error to the user or continue to the next page. A well-designed page will support both functions.

A page could do everything described above and still have a poor design. Page design should be the first thing you consider — whether it is structured and organized to help users do their jobs.

A typical bad page design has a programmatic flow straight through from the beginning of the page to its end (see Bad Page Design vs. Good Page Design). When you look at a page with this type of linear progression, it is hard to determine what the script does just by browsing it. Say the page lets users update their address information. To deduce this from a linear design, you would have to go to the end of the page, where the update is actually called.

A dependency-laden page structure makes it hard to add new logic. Adding it in the wrong place could mess up a variable that some code needed later, creating hard-to-find problems. You will face other issues with as well, such as no scoping of variables, no code reuse, and so forth.

Instead, for a good start in decomposing the page, begin by breaking it up with functions. You will isolate some functionality, gain scope control over some variables, and make the code easier to read.

Good page designs place isolated functionality into functions, which enables you to remove some of the clutter from the page.

The next step is to tie your functions together by adding a main processing procedure at the beginning of your script. This main processing procedure should be called as soon as you enter your script. Have `main()` call all the functions, handle errors, or return values from your page.

`main()` gives you a centralized location to see what is going on in your script. Because it removes a need for global variables, `main()` also supports better scoping of variables.

This structure makes ASP feel more like a real programming language — not just interpreted text. If you add logic to the page later, you can see the core of the functionality in `main()`, and can start new function calls with less impact on existing logic. You can also gain better reuse by having a function to display errors and calling it as needed, rather than replicating that code throughout the script.

CROSS-REFERENCE

Chapter 14 describes the breakdown of an ASP script.

```
┌─────────────────────┐
│   Bad Page Design   │
└─────────────────────┘
Send HTML
    <%
    %>
Get the user's input
    <%
    %>
Retrieve the user's information
    <%
    %>
If success then
    Display the results
Else
    Display the error
    <%
    %>
Display HTML input form
    <%
    %>
Validate input
Update user's information
    <%
    %>
If success then
    Display results
Else
    Display error
    <%
    %>
End HTML
```

```
┌─────────────────────┐
│   Good Page Design  │
└─────────────────────┘
<%
    Call Main
%>
    Main
        Call Get UserInput
        If first time then
                Call LookUpInfo
                Call DisplayForm
        Else
                Call ValidatInput
                Call UpdateInfo
                If Error then
                    Call DisplayError
                Else
                    Redirect
    End Main

    LookUpInfo
    End LookUpInfo

    Display Form
    End Display Form

    ValidateInput
    End ValidateInput

    DisplayError
    End DisplayError
```

TAKE NOTE

▶ APPLYING STANDARDS

You need standards for good page design and good ASP coding. Treat ASP like other programming languages. You should follow guidelines for variable naming, such as Hungarian notation.

If you are using VBScript, make sure every script has the "Option Explicit" keywords at the top of every page. This way, you must explicitly create every variable you want to use.

Minimize the scope of variables. With most of your logic in functions, you will rarely need global page scope variables. They may seem easier to use, but they will come back to bite you in the future.

Use VBScript's `On Error Resume Next` notation or use JScript's `Try .. Catch`. With this approach, ASP will not throw an error back to your browser. Instead, you can handle errors within your script.

Most likely, you expect ample documentation with comments and lots of white space. These characteristics promote maintainability, but because ASP is an interpreted environment, every line gets parsed. As a result, lots of comments and space will degrade performance. You need to strike a balance.

Personal Workbook

Q & A

1 Why must you limit the use of SELECT * statements?

_____

_____

_____

2 True or False. The `Recordset.RecordCount` property always returns the correct number of records.

_____

_____

_____

3 What are the modifying clauses available to the SELECT statement in SQL?

_____

_____

_____

4 If you are using VBScript, what keywords should you put at the top of every page to ensure that you declare each variable in your ASP script?

_____

_____

_____

5 Name two common mistakes that programmers tend to make when building SQL statements and how to get around them.

_____

_____

_____

6 What are the characters that SQL uses to identify partial matches? And how are they different?

_____

_____

_____

7 What factor has the greatest impact on the performance of your database and queries when designing your database?

_____

_____

_____

8 What is the firehose cursor?

_____

_____

ANSWERS: PAGE 513

EXTRA PRACTICE

1 Create an HTML form that retrieves a person's name and social security number. After they submit your form, display the information back to them.

2 Create an HTML form asking the user to search in the Northwind database for all customers (in the Customers table) who live in a particular city, such as Madrid.

3 Create an HTML form asking the user to search in the Northwind database for all customers (in the Customers table) whose company name starts with the letter *B*. You should use the % SQL wildcard.

REAL-WORLD APPLICATIONS

✔ Create an HTML form with a radio button group asking the user in which time zone they live. Create a custom response for each different time zone and display it when they hit Submit.

✔ Create an HTML form with check boxes asking what days of the week the user worked last week. Display the total days and each day the user checked with a custom message.

CHAPTER **24**

MASTER
THESE
SKILLS

▶ **Issuing Update Requests with SQL: Simple Model**
▶ **Learning about Transactions**
▶ **Learning about Microsoft Transaction Server**
▶ **Using the ObjectContext Object**
▶ **Implementing Transactions**

Integrating Databases and Web Pages: Input

Transaction processing involves spreading the logical and business rule processing over multiple applications. This chapter shows you how this approach works, and how it requires you to design your application differently from traditional client/server applications.

To understand Microsoft Transaction Server (MTS) and what it does, you need to understand one concept. This software should have been named Microsoft Component Server — not Microsoft Transaction Server. MTS is all about managing the way applications use components, and *not* just about managing transactions. Yes, transactions are a big part of many applications you write and MTS can help to manage these — but MTS also provides a useful service for applications that don't use transactions at all.

MTS 1.0 changed the way developers build server-centered applications by providing a component-oriented run-time environment that eliminates writing infrastructure code. MTS 2.0 extends the environment by providing powerful integration with Microsoft Internet Information Server 4.0 (IIS), transactional connectivity to Oracle and DB2 databases, transactional mainframe connectivity and the COM Transaction Integrator, and improved performance and manageability.

By combining IIS Active Server Pages with MTS, you can build powerful line-of-business and electronic commerce applications with interactive and dynamic Web-based interfaces. In fact, while ASP pages alone can implement a significant amount of calculations and database access, you should use ASP scripts for presentation management and MTS for application logic. This approach yields Web-based applications — built from reusable components — that can support a large number of users, perform complex calculations, and access multiple databases and other resources such as mainframe applications.

Issuing Update Requests with SQL: Simple Model

In this world, you can always count on change. Because the world is changing constantly, the databases used to model aspects of that world need to change, too. A customer may change his phone number. The quantity of some (or all) of your products will change. These are the kinds of typical events that require you to update a database.

One type of general component with which MTS deals is the data access component. The job of this component is used to provide a method for the system to interact with the data. SQL provides the UPDATE statement for interacting and changing data in a database. By using a single UPDATE statement, you can change one, some, or all the rows in a table. The UPDATE statement uses the following syntax:

```
UPDATE table_name
  SET column1 = expression1,
  column2 = expression2, ...
[WHERE predicates]
```

The WHERE clause is optional. This clause specifies the rows that you are updating. If you do not use a WHERE clause, all the rows in the table are updated. The SET clause specifies the new values for the columns that you are changing.

Customer lists change occasionally when people move or change their phone numbers, or especially when phone companies add new area codes. The Customers table is used as a data example (see Table 24-1). Suppose that Yang Wang of Chop-suey Chinese decides to move his business from Bern to Genève. You can update his record in the table by using the following update statement. Table 24-2 shows the changes.

```
UPDATE customers
  SET city = 'Genève',
  areaCode = '034214',
  telephone = '0897'
WHERE companyName = 'Chop-suey Chinese'
```

```
  AND contactName = 'Yang Wang'
  AND city = 'Bern'
```

You can use a similar statement to update multiple rows. Suppose London decides to add a new area code 420 to all numbers that begin with 171 555. You can update all your customers in the table by using a single UPDATE statement with the following statement. Table 24-2 shows the changes.

```
UPDATE customers
  SET areaCode = '420'
WHERE areaCode = '171'
  AND telephone LIKE '555*'
```

As time passes, some data gets old and loses its usefulness. You may want to remove some outdated data from a table. Unneeded data in a table slows performance, consumes memory, and can confuse users. You may want to transfer older data to an archive, for example. Then, you can delete that data from its original source. SQL provides for the removal of rows from database tables with the DELETE statement.

You can delete all the rows in a table by using a single DELETE statement, or you can restrict the deletion to only selected rows by adding a WHERE clause. The syntax is similar to the syntax of a SELECT statement, except that you use no specification of columns. If you delete a table row, you remove all the data in all the row's columns.

Suppose that Jonas Bergulfsen of Santé Gourmet (see Table 24-1) decides to go out of business in order to home-school his children. You can remove his record in the table by using the following delete statement. Table 24-2 shows the changes.

```
DELETE FROM customers
WHERE companyName = 'Santé Gourmet'
  AND contactName = 'Jonas Bergulfsen'
```

CROSS-REFERENCE

See Chapter 21 for learning about relational databases.

CROSS-REFERENCE

See Chapter 23 for designing SQL SELECT queries.

Table 24-1: ORIGINAL CUSTOMER TABLE

CompanyName	ContactName	City	AreaCode	Telephone
Around the Horn	Thomas Hardy	London	171	555-7788
Bon app'	Laurence Lebihan	Marseille	91	24.45.40
Chop-suey Chinese	Yang Wang	Bern	0452	076545
Consolidated Holdings	Elizabeth Brown	London	171	555-2282
Santé Gourmet	Jonas Bergulfsen	Stavern	07	98.92.35
Que Delícia	Bernardo Batista	Rio de Janeiro	21	555-4252
The Big Cheese	Liz Nixon	Portland	503	555-3612

Table 24-2: UPDATED CUSTOMER TABLE

CompanyName	ContactName	City	AreaCode	Telephone
Around the Horn	Thomas Hardy	London	420	555-7788
Bon app'	Laurence Lebihan	Marseille	91	24.45.40
Chop-suey Chinese	Yang Wang	Genève	0897	034214
Consolidated Holdings	Elizabeth Brown	London	420	555-2282
Que Delícia	Bernardo Batista	Rio de Janeiro	21	555-4252
The Big Cheese	Liz Nixon	Portland	503	555-3612

Learning about Transactions

Transaction processing has been around since the mainframe days. You may have heard of products such as CICS or Tuxedo. These products are examples of transaction processing systems, which provide transaction services to applications that use them. A number of attributes make up transaction processing.

A transaction is an atomic unit of work that either fails or succeeds. There is no such thing as a partial completion of a transaction. Because a transaction can be made up of many steps, each step in the transaction must succeed for the transaction to be successful. If any one part of the transaction fails, then the entire transaction fails. When a transaction fails, the system needs to return to its previous state before the transaction started. This is known as a *rollback*. When a transaction fails, then the changes that had been made are said to be rolled back. In effect, this acts in a similar way to our favorite key in word processing, Undo. The transaction processing system is responsible for carrying out this undo.

An application that is used with a transaction processing system is composed of components. These components fall into two general categories. The first type is an application component. The job of this component is to perform some type of business rule processing for the application. The other general type of component is the data access component. The job of this component is to provide a method for the system to interact with the physical data itself.

Each of the components that make up a transaction is developed as if it were a single-user component. In traditional multi-user application development, the developer needs to be aware of how multiple users are accessing a system. In transaction processing system, the system deals with the intricacies of multiple users accessing a particular piece of data. The transaction server handles all of the interactions so that each component can assume that it is the only one interacting with the system at any one time.

Now that you know about transaction processing, you need to understand why you would want to use it in developing your application. The ability to develop applications in a single-user mode, then use the transaction processing system to scale to hundreds or thousands of users is one reason. The transaction processing system also provides the support for automatic rollback of transactions that did not complete successfully.

Transactions are an essential tool for building server-centric applications from component software. To date, most applications have been developed as a monolithic application by a single team of developers where it is relatively easy to design transactions properly. But, as companies turn to component-based development, and use pre-built components developed by other companies, transaction protection becomes much harder to ensure.

FIND IT ONLINE

To learn more about transactions in MTS, visit **http://msdn.microsoft.com/library/backgrnd/html/msdn_transfaq.htm.**

For an example of a transaction processing system, let's consider a simple bank funds transfer application assembled from three components — Transfer, Credit, and Debit.

Assume that Transfer begins work by calling Debit and Credit. Debit succeeds and subtracts $100 from a database. Credit fails because its database was unable to commit successfully. Unless the developer of Transfer has programmed what to do if one of the components has failed, the application will withdraw $100 from the savings account without putting it in a corresponding checking account.

Although this scenario may be easy to correct in a three-component application, typical business applications involving hundreds of components running across multiple servers are unmanageable without transactions. With component-based development, an automatic distributed transaction infrastructure is the only way to address these issues in a cost-effective manner.

TAKE NOTE

▶ **ACID PROPERTIES**

Transaction processing systems ensure that transactions are atomic, consistent, isolated, and durable. This alleviates the developer from having to support these characteristics explicitly. (These characteristics are known as ACID, which is an acronym for atomicity, consistency, isolation and durability.)

The atomicity property identifies that the transaction is either completed fully, or the system is returned to its previous state before the transaction started.

A transaction enforces consistency in the system state by ensuring that at the end of any transaction, the system is in a valid state. If the transaction completes successfully, then all changes to the system will have been made properly, and the system will be in a valid state. If any error occurs in a transaction, then any changes already made will be rolled back automatically.

When a transaction runs in isolation, it appears to be the only action that the system is carrying out at one time. If there are two transactions that are both performing the same function and are running at the same time, transaction isolation will ensure that each transaction thinks it has exclusive use of the system.

A transaction is durable in that once it has been completed successfully, all of the changes it made to the system are permanent. These safeguards prevent the loss of information, even in the case of system failure.

Learning about Microsoft Transaction Server

The Web has emerged as an ideal vehicle for delivering line-of-business and electronic commerce applications to users. Browsers represent an easy way to present powerful and dynamic user interfaces with near-zero desktop footprint and maintenance costs. And Internet/Intranet networking now reaches almost every part of the world, making it possible to turn virtually any desktop into a high-powered presentation and user input device instantly.

Most Web servers now have mechanisms for accepting input from users, invoking an application, and returning a response. However, the process of handling application requests from Web servers is more difficult than it sounds.

Most Web servers provide little or no application infrastructure themselves. They can invoke an application or script, but it is up to the developer to provide basic services such as database access.

Most application development technologies that provide good infrastructure services don't integrate well with Web servers. For example, a common problem is maintaining information about users between browser requests in the connectionless world of the Web.

Microsoft Transaction Server (MTS), combined with IIS, can be used for building three-tiered applications with Web-based front ends. IIS provides facilities for delivering visual and interactive pages to browsers using Active Server Pages.

MTS makes transaction management transparent to the component developer. Developers do not have to write begin or end transaction statements into their application code. Developers can even use different tools and languages to build their components. When the component accesses a resource such as a database, message queue, or mainframe application, MTS enlists the resource in the transaction automatically. If the component calls another component, the called component also joins the transaction automatically. When all components in a transaction complete their work, MTS initiates a full two-phase commit to either commit or abort the work.

Transaction Server provides a facility for building distributed applications by enabling you to build functionality into a series of ActiveX server Dynamic Link Libraries (DLLs) and distribute them across your network. Transaction Server keeps track of where each of these DLLs is located, and performs all the communications between them and your application. This approach enables you to move your functionality modules to the most suitable computer on your network based on the processing load that each module will be requiring in order to service all the requests from applications needing the services of the module. You can even double up and place the same module on multiple computers and enable Transaction Server to load balance between the copies. This strategy provides you with the flexibility to take a complex processing module that might take several minutes to perform its tasks and place it on several computers. This way, if the copy of one computer was sitting idle while the copy of another computer was servicing two or three requests, and a new request came in, Transaction Server could direct the request to the idle copy of the module instead of the copy that was already busy.

Transaction Server also provides the capability to mix and match modules of functionality that are built in a number of different programming languages. Any language that can be used to build ActiveX server DLLs can be used to build modules for use with Transaction Server.

CROSS-REFERENCE

See Chapter 2 for more information on installing MTS.

FIND IT ONLINE

For the latest information on Microsoft Transaction Server, visit **www.microsoft.com/com/tech/mts.asp**.

Integrating Databases and Web Pages: Input

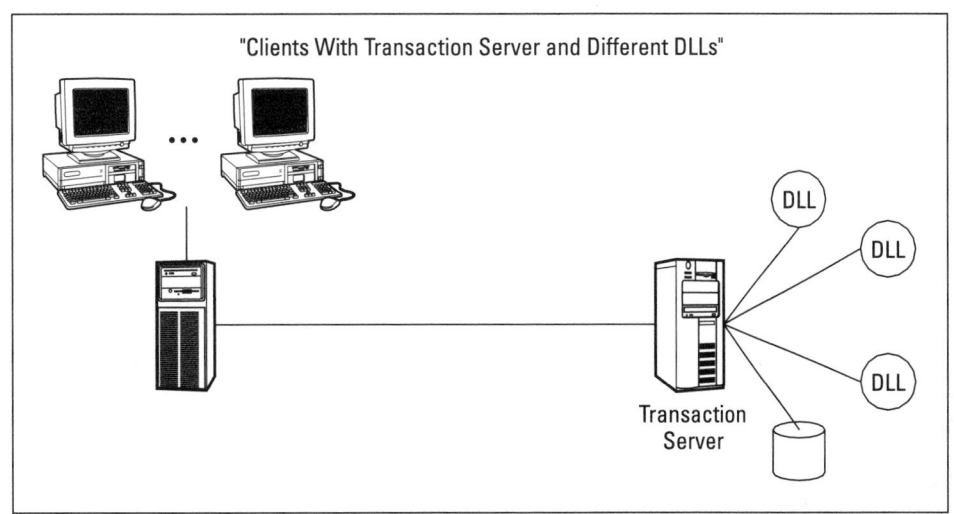

Using the ObjectContext Object

With Internet Information Server 4.0 and 5.0, ASP pages have a direct interface to controlling components in the Microsoft Transaction Server (MTS). This interface is made possible through the ObjectContext object. The ObjectContext object is used to help manage and define the conditions of an instantiated object managed by MTS. These conditions are used to help identify properties of the object, such as what process created the object or the completion time of the work unit. The context properties are used by the MTS to allocate resources to the instantiated object. To support transaction processing in your ASP, both of the components managed by MTS and the ASP must be configured properly.

The MTS manages components by setting four transaction properties, as shown in Table 24-3. These properties enable you to configure different levels of transaction support.

In order to use transaction-level processing, the Components property must be set to either "Requires a transaction", "Requires a new transaction", or "Support transactions".

ASP uses the Transaction directive (see Table 24-3) to initiate page-level transactional processing. When the scripting engine processes this directive, your ASP script is executed as a transaction on MTS. To initiate your pages as a transaction, use the following directive in the first line of your ASP script:

```
<%@ Transaction = Required %>
```

The interaction between the Web server and MTS enables direct commit and rollback of an MTS object directly from your ASP script. Now your application logic can be in an ASP script, while core-processing functionality is left to the MTS components.

The ObjectContext is used to identify when the object transaction is complete. In addition, you can control the object's completed task by accepting its results immediately, delaying the results temporarily, or rejecting the object's work completely. This capability to control whether the object's work is accepted is made possible through the `SetComplete` and `SetAbort` methods (see Table 24-4).

The `SetComplete` method is used to commit an MTS object's transaction as a success. The changes made by the object method on a resource are committed permanently. To accept changes made by your object, use the `SetComplete` method as in Listing 24-1.

Continued

CROSS-REFERENCE

For more information on setting up and configuring MTS to manage your components, please continue to the next section, "Implementing Transactions."

FIND IT ONLINE

To keep with up with Microsoft, check out **http://msdn.microsoft.com/library/partbook/asp20/html/theaspobjectcontextobject.htm**.

Table 24-3: MTS COMPONENT

Property	Description
Requires a transaction	Sets the component object to execute within the scope of the transaction.
Requires a new transaction	Sets the component object to execute only within its own transaction.
Support transaction	Sets the component object to execute within the scope of the client's transaction.

Table 24-4: OBJECTCONTEXT

Method	Description
SetComplete	Sets the work of an object as a success and accepts the changes to the resource permanently.
SetAbort	Sets the work of an object as a failure and returns the resource to its original state, neglecting any changes made to the resource.
Event	**Description**
OnTransactionCommit	Event triggered after the ObjectContext.SetComplete method is executed.
OnTransactionAbort	Event triggered after the ObjectContext.SetAbort method is executed.

Using the ObjectContext Object

Continued

The SetComplete method declares that the script is not aware of any reason for the transaction not to complete. If all components participating in the transaction also call SetComplete, the transaction will complete. The SetComplete method will be called implicitly when the ASP script reaches the end of the script, and SetAbort has not been called.

In Listing 24-1, if the transfer of $1500 is successful, then the SetComplete method finalizes the transfer of funds. However, if the funds were not available, the transaction is rolled back to its original state.

After the SetComplete method is executed, the OnTransactionCommit event, if available, is processed.

The SetAbort method is used to roll back changes as a result of an object method. When the SetAbort method is called, the object rejects the completed work and returns the transaction back to its original state. Listing 24-1 demonstrates the use of the SetAbort method to roll back transactions made by an MTS object.

After the SetAbort method is executed, the OnTransactionAbort event, if available, is processed on the script. If the subroutine is not available, your ASP script continues processing.

There is no method for an ASP script to determine explicitly if a transaction in which it is participating has aborted or committed. The ASP script must therefore use transaction events to determine and perform special processing if a transaction is being committed, or being aborted and rolled back. The ObjectContext object has two events just for this task that are triggered after the ObjectContext's methods are executed, as seen in Table 24-4.

Because the transaction is not committed until after the script reaches the end, this event will not be processed until the entire page is processed. The OnTransactionAbort method is called if the current transaction is being aborted. This method will be called immediately after any object participating in the transaction calls SetAbort. An example is shown in Listing 24-2.

Listing 24-2 initiates transaction processing using the Transaction = Required directive and executes the SetComplete method to trigger the OnTransactionCommit() event. If funds were moved properly, the ObjectContext.SetComplete method triggers the OnTransactionCommit() event to route the user to an ASP page called PrintBankRecept.asp. If the listing fails to transfer account information properly, the ObjectContext.SetAbort methods rolls back the transaction explicitly and executes the OnTransactionAbort() subroutine.

Integrating Databases and Web Pages: Input

Listing 24-1: Controlling Success and Failure with `ObjectContext`

```
<%@ Transaction = Required %>    ①

<%
Set acctTransfer = Server.CreateObject("Bank.Account")    ②
If acctTransfer.MoveMoney("credit", "debit", "1500") Then
   ' The money was moved successfully
   ObjectContext.SetComplete    ③
Else
   ' Unsuccessful transfer of money
   ObjectContext.SetAbort    ④
End If
%>
```

① *Initiates transaction processing.*

② *Instantiate your object.*

③ *If funds were moved properly, use* `ObjectContext.SetComplete` *to trigger the* `OnTransactionCommit` *event.*

④ *If funds were moved unsuccessfully, use* `ObjectContext.SetAbort` *to trigger the* `OnTransactionAbort` *event.*

Listing 24-2: Using `OnTransactionCommit`

```
<%@ Transaction = Required %>
<%
Sub OnTransactionCommit()    1
  Response.Transfer "PrintBankReceipt.asp"    2
End Sub
Sub OnTransactionAbort()    3
 Response.Transfer "PrintInvalidInformation.asp"
End Sub
%>

<%
Set moneyTransaction = Server.CreateObject("Bank.Account")
If moneyTransaction.MoveMoney("credit", "debit", "1500") Then
   ' The money was moved successfully
   ObjectContext.SetComplete
Else
   ' Unsuccessful
   ObjectContext.SetAbort
End If
%>
```

1 *Use the* `OnTransactionCommit` *and* `OnTransactionAbort` *events to use IIS 5.0's* `Response.Transfer` *to redirect the user.*

2 *Route the user to* `PrintBankRecept.asp`.

3 *Route the user to* `PrintInvalidInformation.asp`.

Implementing Transactions

Integrating Transaction Server into an Active Server Page application is similar to integrating custom components into an Active Server Page application. A few differences exist, such as any components are instantiated slightly differently from custom components. However, from this point on, the differences are hard to spot.

By using a simple bank account maintenance application included with Transaction Server, this section will cover how to integrate Active Server Pages with Transaction Server. This example enables the user to credit and debit small amounts to either of two accounts, as well as transfer funds between the two accounts.

Before you can register a custom component with Transaction Server, the component has to be built as in-process, ActiveX server DLL. After you have built your component as an ActiveX DLL, you need to register it with the Transaction Server before it can be used. You do this through the Transaction Server Explorer. When you have started the Transaction Server Explorer, you need to make sure the Distributed Transaction Coordinator (DTC) is running.

Before you can start registering components in Transaction Server, you must have a package into which you are going to install the components. Packages are logical groupings of objects that are generally used as a unit. You can create a package by following these steps.

From the Transaction Server Explorer, select the Packages Installed folder and right-click the mouse. Select New | Package from the pop-up menu. On the first screen of the Package Wizard, choose Create an Empty Package.

Next, type a name for the package. For the bank account maintenance package, call it Bank. Click the next button.

If the objects in the package need to run under a specific login account, select the "This user:" radio button and provide the user name and password. Otherwise, leave the default radio button selected.

Click the Finish button to complete the process.

Continued

TAKE NOTE

▶ SETTING SECURITY RESOURCES

A package can be configured so that all of the components within it run using a specific user account. This approach will enable you to configure the security settings of resources needed by the components so that the resources will always be available. The default setting, however, is for the components in the package to run using the user account of the application that calls them. This means that the calling application may not have full access to any resources needed by the components.

▶ SHORTCOMINGS IN MTS

The biggest shortcoming with MTS is that all of your processing is synchronous in nature. As a result, everything in the processing chain has to wait until everything else in the chain is complete before processing control can be returned to the calling application.

FIND IT ONLINE

For the latest information on Microsoft Transaction Server, visit **www.microsoft.com/com/tech/mts.asp**.

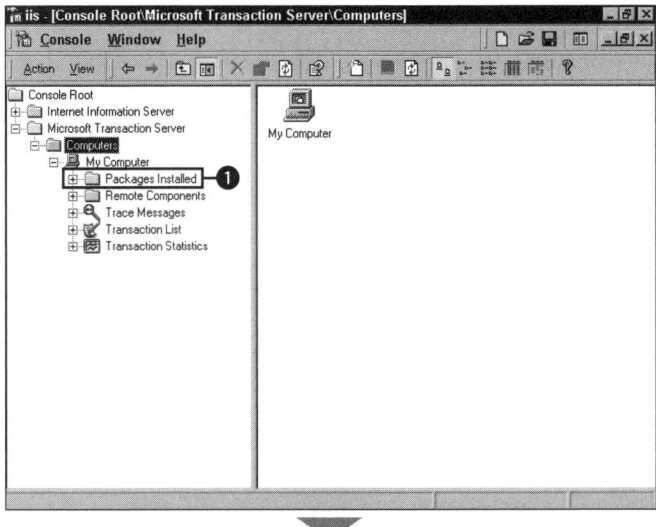

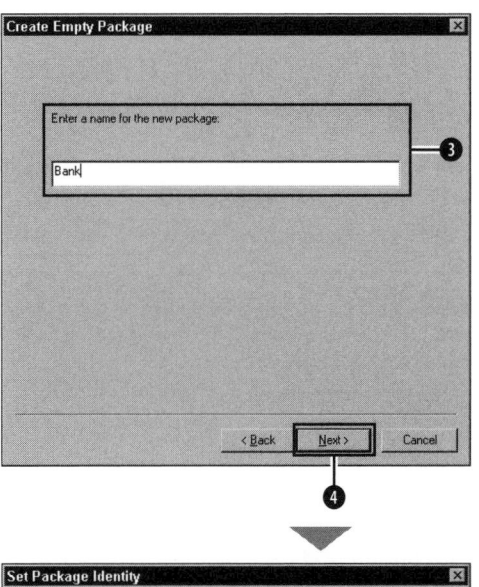

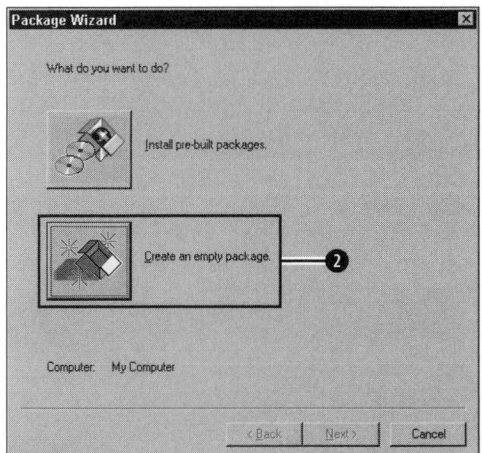

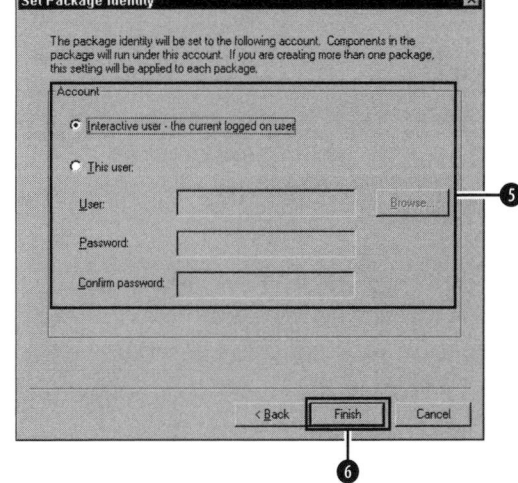

❶ Select the Packages Installed folder and right-click the mouse.

❷ Choose Create an empty package.

❸ Call this package Bank.

❹ Then click the Next button.

❺ Choose a login account.

❻ Click Finish.

Implementing Transactions
Continued

Once you have a package, you can install components into it. This is where you register the ActiveX DLLs that you have and will be creating. You can register your components with the following steps.

First, from the Transaction Server Explorer, select the Components folder in the package into which you want to install the components. In your case, this package is the Bank package that you just created. Right-click the Components folder. Select New | Component from the pop-up menu. On the first screen of the Component Wizard, choose Install new component(s).

Click the Add Files button, and then select the ActiveX DLL that you want to register.

When you return to the Install Components screen, the upper list box should show the DLL that you are installing, and the lower box should show all the classes within the DLL.

Click the Finish button, and the components will be installed in Transaction Server.

Select the components you just installed, one at a time, and right-click the mouse. Select Properties from the pop-up menu. On the Component Properties editor, select the Transaction tab, and select the transaction attribute desired for the currently selected component.

Creating Transaction Server components for use within an Active Server Page is similar to creating any other custom component for use within ASP. To instantiate Transaction Server components, according to Microsoft documentation, you should use `Server.CreateObject()`.

```
Set objMTX =
Server.CreateObject("Bank.Account")
```

After you create an instance of a Transaction Server component, you can call the component's methods much like you would call the methods of any other component. By referencing the component methods via the component itself, you can call any of the methods that have been exposed.

The best way to return information from Transaction Server components is through the use of the parameters to the component method. The standard return value of the method will be a success code to inform you whether the method was successful.

Continued

TAKE NOTE

▶ RECOMPILING ACTIVEX DLLS

Whenever you recompile any ActiveX DLL built-in Visual Basic, you need to refresh the component in Transaction Server. This task can be done by deleting the component from the Management Console, and following the same steps that you used to install the component originally. The component has to be re-registered with Transaction Server because the Visual Basic generates a new CLSID for each component in the DLL every time the DLL is compiled.

▶ BANK COMPONENT — RECEIVING AN ERROR

Unfortunately, the Bank Component that comes with Transaction Server does not integrate easily or straightforward into ASP. You have probably found that it doesn't work. The reason for this problem is that the VBScript in your ASP is passing all parameters to the Transaction Server components as Variant data types, while the components are expecting string and long data types. In order to get the sample to work, you need to modify the VB components to expect all method parameters to be Variant. Unfortunately, to explain this procedure is beyond the scope for this book. However, this example shows you how to implement a Transaction Server package from the code and installation steps.

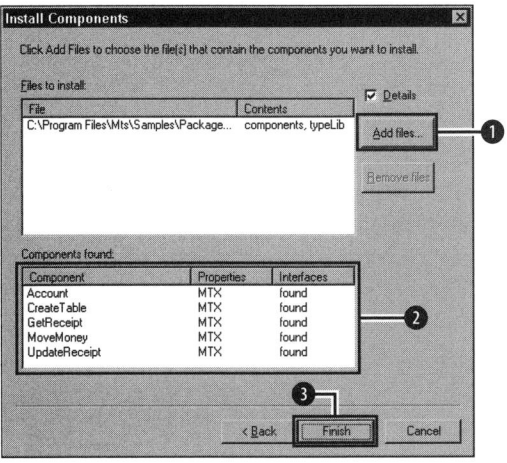

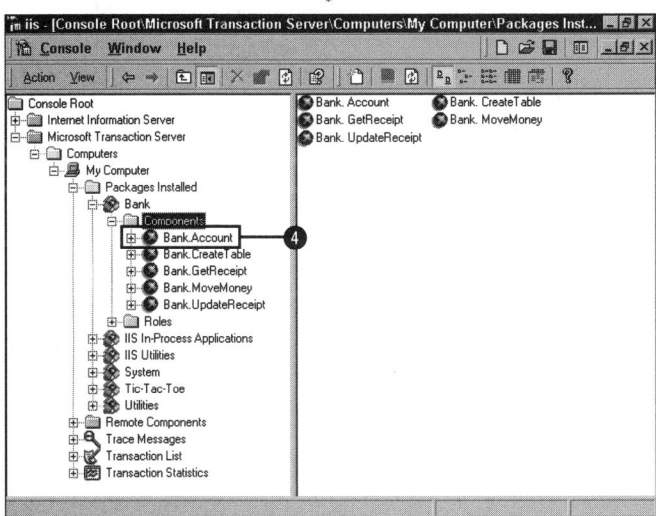

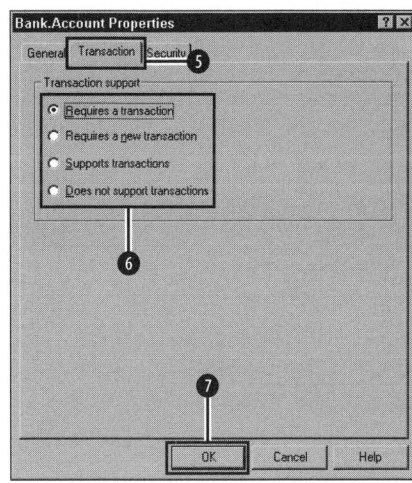

❶ Click the Add Files button, and then select the ActiveX DLL that you want to register.

❷ The lower box should show all the classes within the DLL.

❸ Click the Finish button.

▶ Note the components listed in the main window.

❹ Choose Bank.Account.

❺ On the Component Properties editor, select the Transaction tab.

❻ Select the transaction attribute desired for the currently selected component.

❼ Click OK to close the Bank.Account Properties window.

Implementing Transactions
Continued

You can get your first experience integrating ASP with Transaction Server components by using the Bank Account Maintenance application that is provided with Transaction Server and Option Pack 4. In order for this application to work, you will have to be familiar with Visual Basic. However, even if you don't know Visual Basic, please follow the example for the discussion even if you do not know VB.

The Bank Account Maintenance application that is provided as an example with Transaction Server consists of five classes. These classes, and their functionality, are listed in Bank Account Maintenance Classes Table.

In order to call the Bank Account Maintenance components through Transaction Server, you need to create a front-end using an HTML form. A simple version of this form is in function `processForm()` of Listing 24-3.

You will find the familiar `main()` in Listing 24-3. The `Count` property of `Request.Form` will determine if the Submit button was pressed. If Submit was pressed, Listing 24-3 calls `processForm()`. After the call to this function, `showForm()` is called.

`showForm()` creates an HTML form that will allow an interface into the Bank Account Maintenance component. Listing 24-3 creates the following FORM elements: Account Number as "primeAct," Amount ($) as amount, Transaction Type as "transType," Transfer Account as "secondAct," and Component as component. The transaction type radio buttons have the following values: credit, debit, and transfer. The component radio buttons had the following values: moveMoney and account. When the user hits Enter, the ASP script calls itself to use `processForm()`.

`processForm()` verifies that the user entered the proper combination of data and radio buttons. Once the data is verified, you use `CreateObject` to instantiate either the `Bank.Account` or `Bank.MoveMoney` program. If the `CreateObject()` is successful, the script will call the Transaction Server component.

Table 24-5: BANK ACCOUNT MAINTENANCE CLASSES	
Class	**Description**
`Bank.Account`	Performs the credit and debit actions on a specified account, returning the resulting balance.
`Bank.MoveMoney`	Calls all the other classes to perform complex actions.
`Bank.GetReceipt`	Generates sequential receipt numbers.
`Bank.UpdateReceipt`	Maintains the starting number of the next receipt number in the database.
`Bank.CreateTable`	Creates the necessary tables in SQL Server if the tables do not already exist.

Continued

Listing 24-3: Using Transaction Server and ASP

```
<html><head><title>Bank Account - Transaction Server</title></head>
<body><h2>Bank Maintenance</h2><% main() %></body></html>
<script runat="server" language="VBScript">
Sub write(str)
 Response.write(str + vbcrlf)
End Sub
Sub main()
 If Request.Form("submit").Count > 0 Then processForm()
 showForm()
End Sub
Sub processForm()
  dim rtnMsg
  If Request.Form("component") = "moveMoney" Then
    progID = "Bank.MoveMoney"
  Else
    progID = "Bank.Account"
  End If
```

❶ The Count *property of* Request.Form *will determine if the Submit button was pressed. If Submit was pressed then, the listing calls* processForm().

❷ *After the call to* processForm(), showForm() *is called.*

❸ processForm() *verifies that the user entered the proper combination of data and radio buttons.*

Implementing Transactions

Continued

Listing 24-3: Using Transaction Server and ASP (continued)

```
If Request.Form("transType") = "debit" Then
  transType = "debit"
  multiplier = "-1"
Elseif Request.Form("transType") = "credit" Then
  transType = "credit"
  multiplier = "1"
Else
  If (progID = "Bank.Account") Then
    rtnMsg = "Error. Please select MoveMoney to transfer funds."
  Elseif Request.Form("secondAct") = "" Then
    rtnMsg = "Error. Please enter an account to move money into."
  Else
    transType = "transfer"
    multiplier = "1"
    sndAct = Request.Form("secondAct")
  End If
End If
If Request.Form("primeAct") = "" Then
  rtnMsg = "Error. Please enter an account to credit or debit."
Else
  primtAct = Request.Form("primeAct")
End If
If Request.Form("amount") = "" Then
  transType = ""
  rtnMsg = "Error. Please enter a transaction amount."
Else
  trnAmount = Request.Form("amount")
End If
If transType <> "" Then
  Set objMTX = CreateObject (ProgID)  ◄─❹
  If objMTX is nothing Then
    transType = ""
    rtnMsg = "Error. Could not create the object."
  End If
End If
```

❹ *CreateObject to instantiate either the Bank.Account or Bank.MoveMoney.*

```
  If transType <> "" Then
   If Request.Form("component") = "account" Then
     objMsg = objMTX.Post(CLng(primeAct), (CLng(amount) * CLng(Multiplier)), rtnMsg)
   Else
   objMsg =
objMTX.Perform(CLng(primeAct),CLng(sndAct),CLng(amount),transType,rtnMsg)◄⑤
   End If
   End If
   write rtnMsg
End Sub
Sub showForm()
write("<form name=form method=POST action=" +◄⑥
Request.ServerVariables("script_name") + ">")◄⑦
write("<h3>Please enter any of the following information:</h3>")
write("<TABLE ALIGN=center WIDTH=70% CELLSPACING=0 CELLPADDING=3 BORDER=0>")
write("<tr><td>Account Number:</td>")
write("<td><input type=text maxlength=15 name=primeAct></td>")
write("<tr><td>Amount ($):</td>")
write("<td><input type=text maxlength=15 name=amount></td>")
write("<tr><td>Transaction</td>")
write("<td><input type=radio name=trans value=transfer CHECKED>Transfer")
write("<input type=radio name=trans value=credit>Credit")
write("<input type=radio name=trans value=debit>Debit</td>")
write("<tr></tr><td>Transfer Account:</td>")
write("<td><input type=text maxlength=15 name=secondAct></td>")
write("<tr><td>Component:</td>")
write("<td><input type=radio name=component value=moveMoney CHECKED>Move Money")
write("<input type=radio name=component value=act>Account</td>")
write("<tr><td><input class=button type=submit value=Submit name=submit></td> ")
write("</table>")
write("</form>")
End Sub
</script>
```

⑤ *Call the Transaction Server component.*

⑥ `showForm()` *creates an HTML form that will allow an interface into the Bank Account Maintenance component.*

⑦ *Once the user hits Enter, the ASP script calls itself to use* `processForm()`.

Personal Workbook

Q & A

1 What is a transaction?

_____

_____

_____

2 What SQL statement can you use to remove data from a table?

_____

_____

_____

3 What are the ACID characteristics of a transaction?

_____

_____

_____

4 What is the `SetAbort` method used for?

_____

_____

_____

5 How does ASP know to use page-level transactional processing?

_____

_____

_____

_____

6 Is the WHERE optional when using the UPDATE statement?

_____

_____

_____

_____

7 What are two competitors to Microsoft Transaction Server?

_____

_____

_____

_____

ANSWERS: PAGE 513

EXTRA PRACTICE

1 Build an @ statement to go at the top of your page that makes the page require a transaction and use JScript as its default scripting language.

2 Using the Northwind DB, write a SQL UPDATE statement to change any CITY from London to Berkshire. Then, write another UPDATE to change it back.

3 Using ADO, write an ASP script to display the records in the practice #2 to a Web page after each update.

CHAPTER **25**

Using Cookies, Sessions, and Passwords to Maintain State

Traditional network-based applications have always had one major advantage—the automatic maintenance of state by the network itself. By design, HTTP is a stateless environment. The client browser requests individual documents from the Web server, which in turn receives the request, processes it, returns a document, and discards the request. HTTP 1.0 does not provide any mechanism to associate a particular request with a previous request.

Whether you are maintaining lots of user-specific state data on the client or just a primary key, you need to pass data back and forth between the client browser and the Web server. If you are creating a Web application that involves something like a shopping cart, you must consider carefully how you want to build up and store state for each user across requests.

What do we mean by the term state? *State* is a combination of features between networking software and operating systems to recognize users continually after they log onto our application. One of the new features of HTTP 1.1 addresses some of these issues with regard to state, and will be discussed later in the chapter.

You can maintain state across Web applications by using cookies. A *cookie* is a small informational text string that is stored on the user's hard disk. Typically, when the client makes a request for a document on a server, the server returns a cookie. When the user returns to the same Web page, the browser sends that cookie back.

State can also be provided with ASP's automatic mechanism for maintaining state—Session variables. One caveat: ASP requires the browser to support and accept cookies in order to function properly.

Finally, state can be provided using a back-end database. The main advantages of storing state data in the back-end database are that the database is durable and you can store as much state information as you need. Storing state on the client has size limitations and raises security issues.

One of the primary reasons that you use state information is to identify individual users. You can use state information to change the behavior of our application based on the user's identity. More specifically, you may need to log users in, verify their passwords, and decide to which part of the application they need access.

Learning about State Management

The Web is basically a connectionless environment, in which a browser connects, gets its info, and then disconnects. This can make maintaining state a bit tricky. So when you start the design phase of our Web application, you need to ask yourself a simple question: Where are the places you can maintain user-specific state information in your Web application?

You regard the state of an application as the collection of variables that identify both the application itself and the period during which it is being used. There are three places where it may be appropriate to store state data. First, you can store state in the client tier, inside the HTML you send to the browser. Second, you can store state in the middle tier, inside the Web server. Third, you can store state in a back-end database.

The main advantage of storing state on the client is speed; you do not need to make time-consuming trips to a back-end database. However, storing state on the client has size limitations and raises security issues. Also, you may want to avoid storing potentially sensitive information on the user's computer. Moreover, the user may have browser security settings that prevent you from writing to their hard disk.

The easiest way to store state on the client is with cookies. Cookies are a general mechanism that can both store and retrieve information on the client side of the connection. ASP makes the task easier through the `Cookies` collections of the Request and Response objects.

Also, when you are designing a Web application for a site based on a single Web server, storing state inside the server using ASP Application and Session variables can make an easy and attractive solution.

However, if you have a Web form that uses session-based load balancing, storing data inside our ASP-enabled Web server doesn't work. Another concern with ASP session management is that it can unnecessarily waste precious resources such as processing cycles, memory, and network bandwidth.

The main advantages of storing state data in a back-end database are that the back-end database is durable and you can store as much state information as you need. Storing state on the client has size limitations and raises security issues. You should note that when you store state in a back-end database, you probably still would be required to maintain at least a minimal amount of state information on the client. For example, it's common to pass a client ID or a unique ID between the client and our Web server with each request. This approach will enable you to map a user to one or more records in our database.

When considering a back-end database, you should also consider: How much of a performance cost is there when you access the back-end database? Does the back-end database represent a significant performance bottleneck? If the answer is yes to either of these questions, you may consider reducing trips to the back-end database.

Here are a few other questions to consider during the design phase: How costly is it if user-specific state gets lost or corrupted? Do you want user-specific state information to be available when the user moves to a different machine? Do you need to store so much user-specific state that it will not fit in the cookie framework?

CROSS-REFERENCE

Chapter 22 introduces you to managing resources.

FIND IT ONLINE

The Internet Engineering Task Force (IETF) RFC 2109 provides information about state management at (ftp://ftp.isi.edu/in-notes/rfc2109.txt).

Using Cookies, Sessions, and Passwords to Maintain State

▶ ANOTHER CLIENT-SIDE TECHNIQUE

There is one other client-side state management technique that you should have up your sleeve to help maintain state. This technique involves the use of a hidden field in an HTML form. If a user will not accept cookies and you want to store more information, hidden fields may be our solution for you . Note that this technique requires the use of an HTML form and a Submit button.

```
<form action="page.asp" method="post">
  <input type="hidden" name="userID"
value="Joe User">
  <input type="submit" value="Submit
Your Request">
</form>
```

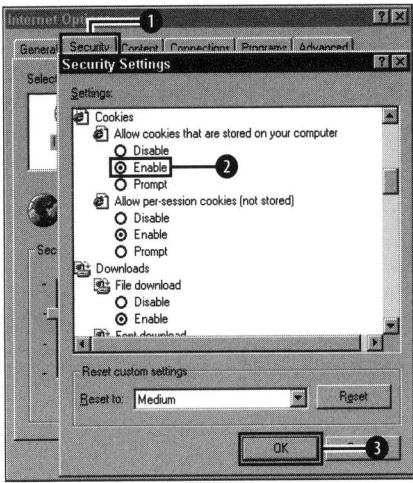

❶ *To enable cookies in Internet Explorer 5.0, select Tools @>Internet Options @> Security and click Custom Level.*

❷ *Scroll down and enable "Allow cookies that are stored on your computer."*

❸ *Click OK.*

Managing Cookies with ASP

Cookies have been around since the introduction of Netscape Navigator 1.1 in March 1995. However, their capabilities have only been exploited recently. Likewise, users have just recently recognized the potential loss of privacy in having a place on their own computer where persistent information could be stored.

In truth, there's nothing particularly frightening about cookies. Cookies could be used to track all input from a user and drop it in a database, but they don't inherently contain private information. They can only be associated with information users provide about themselves.

Fundamentally, a cookie is a long-text string associated with a domain and a path that the browser and server pass back and forth. Technically, the cookie is passed via an HTTP header and stored by the server in the client variable HTTP_COOKIE and by the browser in a local file.

The server can assign a number of cookies to the browser, with the following limits as documented, specified, and implemented by Netscape:

```
300 total cookies
20 cookies per domain matching pattern
4,096 characters per cookie, including the
variable name
```

The server can set or change the cookie's values, and ASP's Response object provides you with an interface for just this purpose. The Response object holds a `Cookies` collection to which you can write values. Single cookies are simple `CookieName` to `CookieValue` mappings. Some examples are included:

```
<% Response.Cookies("FavoriteCookie") =
"almond" %>
<% Response.Cookies("UserCity") =
"Washington, DC" %>
```

Cookies can also have properties relating to their lifetime and availability. If you don't set these properties intentionally, all information stored in them will be lost when the user shuts down their browser. If you want to store some information about the user that is still available later, you have to set an expiration date. See Listing 25-1 for a script that demonstrates how to store a cookie that was passed in from an HTML form.

Continued

Troubleshooting

```
Response object error 'ASP 0156:
80004005'
Header Error
Mypage.asp line#
The HTTP headers are already written
to the client browser. Any HTTP header
modifications must be made before
writing page content.
```

Does this error message plague you?

`<% Response.Buffer = true %>` needs to be added as the first line to any pages made by a HTML document that mixes header HTTP information and content.

CROSS-REFERENCE
Chapter 14 introduces you to HTTP document transmission.

FIND IT ONLINE
The Cookie Central Web site (**http://www.cookiecentral.com**) provides full information about cookies as well as updates to issues.

Listing 25-1: Creating Cookies with the Response Object

```
<%@ language=JScript %>
<% Response.Buffer=true%>

<script language=jscript runat=server>
/ Accept variables in the URL using the GET method
var lastname = Request.Querystring("lastname")
var firstname = Request.Querystring("firstname")

Response.Cookies("lastname") = lastname;
Response.Cookies("lastname").Domain =     Request.ServerVariables("Server_name");
Response.Cookies("lastname").Expires = "December 31, 2001";

Response.Cookies("firstname") = firstname;
Response.Cookies("firstname").Domain = Request.ServerVariables("Server_name");
Response.Cookies("firstname").Expires = "December 31, 2001";
</script>

<html>
<head>
<title>Having My Cookies</title>
</head>

<body>
<%
/*
     First time through the cookie is written.
     Second time through the cookie can be retrieved.
*/
Response.Write(Request.Cookies("lastname") + "<p>");
Response.Write(Request.Cookies("firstname") + "<p>");
%>

</body>
</html>
```

Managing Cookies with ASP
Continued

You can also set other properties of a cookie to restrict which servers can gain access to information stored in it. In other words, you can prevent other Web sites from gaining access to the cookie's information. These other properties include: `domain`, `path`, and `secure`.

Setting the `domain` to `/www.idgbooks.com/` would allow only pages existing on that particular network to receive the cookie from the browser. You can also be more specific by setting the `path` to `/catalog`. The final attribute, `secure`, indicates that the cookie should only be transmitted over a Secure Sockets Layer connection. That approach will enable you to store more private information and not worry about it being stolen.

If you need to produce a cookie dictionary, in which a cookie has several values, you just have to specify a key along with the cookie name. A few examples follow:

```
<% Response.Cookies("UserAddress")("City") =
"Annapolis" %>
<% Response.Cookies("UserAddress")("State") =
"MD" %>
<% Response.Cookies("UserAddress")("Zip") =
"21401" %>
```

Now that a cookie is created, how do you access it? Data items within each cookie are available in the `Cookies` collection of the Request object. When accessed through the Request object, the cookies are read-only. You can use the JScript code in Listing 25-2 to get all members of the `Cookies` collection.

Cookies can be reset by simply sending a cookie with the same variable name. Or, the `expires` property can be set to a previous day and time. When dealing with cookies, you have to make sure that you don't overwrite or reset existing information. To prevent errors, you should check the `haskeys` property of a cookie to determine whether you are dealing with a dictionary of several values or a single value. (See Listing 25-3.)

A few more significant problems are associated with using cookies. First, because cookies are stored on the client machine or kept in memory, they do not follow the user from machine to machine. Second, the cookie files are not protected, so it is possible to delete them from the client machine.

Also, the cookie file should not be edited by hand because browsers store cookies internally during a session. Netscape, for instance, doesn't write new cookies until the application is exited.

Cookies work great until you encounter users who have disabled cookie passing in their browsers. If you have a requirement to accommodate these users, you will not be able to store data on the client that will live across sessions of the browser. You must also come up with another technique to pass state data back and forth.

FIND IT ONLINE

The ActiveServerPages Web site (**http://www.learnasp.com/ learn/cookiesform.asp**) provides full information about reading and writing cookies using ASP.

Listing 25-2: Listing All Your Cookies — The Cookies Collection

```
<%
var cookies = new Enumerator(Request.Cookies);  ←❶
while (!cookies.atEnd ()) {  ←❷
  i = cookies.item();  ←❸
  Response.Write("Cookie: " + i + " is " +
Request.Cookies(i) + ".<br>");
  Cookies.moveNext();  ←❹
}
%>
```

❶ First, you assign your collection to a new instance of the JScript enumerator object.
❷ Using a `while` loop, you can check for the end of the collection with the `atEnd` method.
❸ In each iteration, you get one item from the collection with the `item` method.
❹ And finally, the `moveNext` method will take you to the next item in the collection.

Listing 25-3: Checking for HasKeys

```
<% bHasKeys =  ←❶
Request.Cookies("UserAddress").HasKeys %>  ←❷
```

1 bHasKeys is a boolean that will be set to true for our cookie, if it is a dictionary.
2 You can also iterate through the `keys` collection of the cookie dictionary to display all the cookie information.

Moving from Cookies to Sessions: Letting ASP Do the Work

SP Sessions provide an obvious solution for storing state information in our HTML.

An ASP Session object is created automatically for each user when they load an ASP document that is within the scope of a `global.asa` file. You can use the Session object to store information needed for a particular user session. Variables stored in the Session object are not discarded when the user jumps between documents within our application. Instead, these variables persist for the entire time that the user is accessing pages in our application.

The Session object is implemented by using a collection similar to the Request and Response objects. Values are placed in the collection through simple assignment statements. A sample of setting and retrieving values appears in Listing 25-4.

Create and run this listing several times, and notice how the number is increased by one each time. The value should start at the beginning again.

Also, you can store and maintain state values globally for all users using the Application object. The Application object has much in common with the Session object. The difference between the Session object and the Application object is scope. Information can be maintained in the Application object that is used across all the site's sessions.

Because there is only one application variable in memory, application variables are better than session variables, no matter how many users are on your site. Application variables can be a more convenient place to store central information and retrieve it fast.

Session variables, on the other hand, must be used with a word of caution. These variables can waste memory because they live until their timeout minutes have expired. Session variables also can waste threads if you put in any objects made by the `Server.CreateObject()`. Another word of caution for a Web site that uses several applications — all scripts within different virtual applications cannot read each other's session variables.

TAKE NOTE

▶ GLOBAL.ASA

In order to make Application and Session objects work in ASP, you use a single file for each application. `global.asa` contains the state of the application via the Application and Session object properties. This file resides in the application root directory on the server. A `global.asa` file is divided into four events:

- ▶ `Session_onStart()` — When each user begins a session for the first time, this event is triggered.
- ▶ `Session_OnEnd()` — When a current Session is abandoned by using the `Session.Abandon` method, or when it times out.
- ▶ `Application_onStart()` — When the first user accesses a file in our application, this event is triggered.
- ▶ `Application_onEnd()` — When the application is unloaded from the Web server, which is managed by the IIS snap-in to MMC.

CROSS-REFERENCE
Chapter 14 introduces you to the Request and Response objects.

FIND IT ONLINE
The Cookie Central Web site (**http://www.cookiecentral.com**) provides full information about cookies as well as updates to issues.

Using Cookies, Sessions, and Passwords to Maintain State

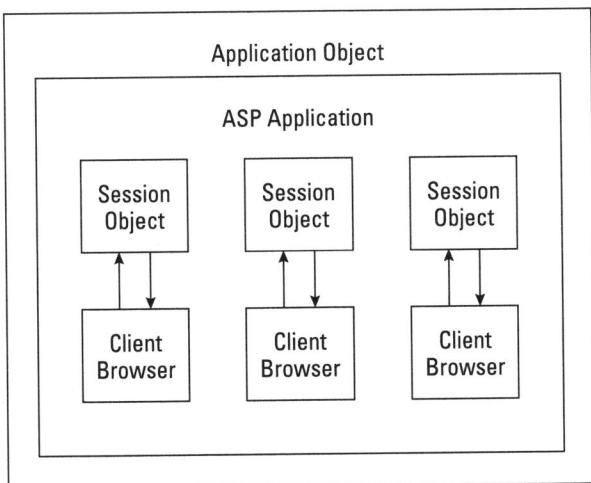

Listing 25-4: Storing Information in the Session Object

```
<html>
<head>
<title>Counting My People</title>
</head>

<body>
<%
Session("MyCounter") = Cint(Session("MyCounter")) + 1%>

<h3>Counter is up to: <% =Session("MyCounter") %> </h3>
</body>
</html>
```

① *Line 8 increments the value of* MyCounter.

② *You use the* Cint *function to convert an empty string to 0 for when the Session is initiated.*

Using the Session Object to Manage User Interactions

The benefit of the Session object is that you can place information into it and retrieve that information at any point during the user's visit. The Session object has a number of properties that provide more information about the current user, and thus enable you to manage their visit more accurately.

These properties can be examined and their values used to change the information presented to the user dynamically. In addition, the properties can change how the information is represented visually. The Session object also provides a method that enables the developer to force a session to end, regardless of the timeout value.

The `SessionID` value is a long value that identifies the session uniquely among all other sessions running on the same system. This value could be used as an identifying value for each user as they are using the system. A word of caution: the `SessionID` is only guaranteed unique within this current instance of the application.

Sessions expire or end when there has not been a request in however many minutes are set in `Session.Timeout`. The `Timeout` property is the time (in minutes) that the session can remain idle before it is terminated by the system. A session is considered idle as long as there are no new page requests or any requests to refresh the current page. The default value for this property is 20 minutes. If the application is a high volume site, the developer may want to set this number to a low value. This setting prevents resources from being consumed by users who have moved to other sites.

However, changing the `Timeout` property only affects the current session. It has no lasting effect. It is more efficient to modify the interval value through the IIS. Setting this property through code should be reserved for more dynamic uses. See figure.

Continued

TAKE NOTE

DETERMINING HOW THE SESSION OBJECT STARTS

For the Session object to function correctly, it is necessary to determine when a person's visit to the site starts and ends. The Web server does this by using a cookie. This particular cookie identifies an ASP `SessionID`, which the server then uses to maintain a set of information about that user. If the ID isn't there, it considers this request to be the start of a visit.

Troubleshooting

Session and Application events only happen when a client retrieves an ASP page. They are not triggered when an HTML page is retrieved. Make sure that your application depends on specific events occurring only within ASP pages.

CROSS-REFERENCE

Chapter 19 introduces you to the Session object.

FIND IT ONLINE

ActiveServerPages (http://www.activeserverpages.com/iishelp/iis/html/asp/intr12do.htm) provides full information about the Session object from Microsoft.

Using Cookies, Sessions, and Passwords to Maintain State

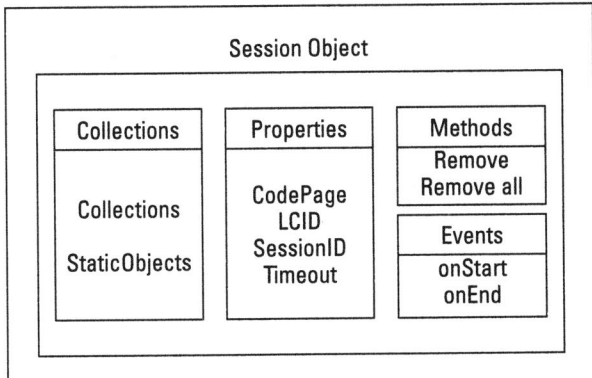

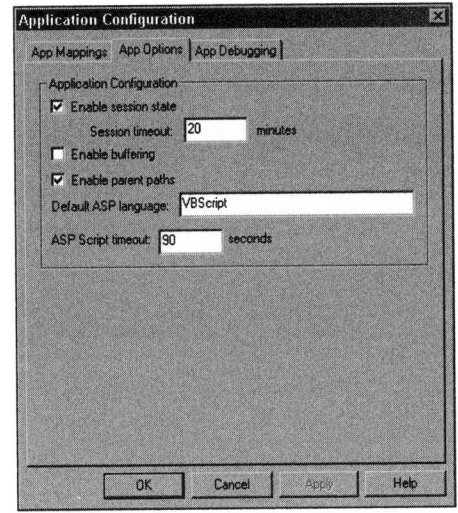

Listing 25-5: Session Variables

```html
<html>
<head>
<title>Session Variables</title>
</head>

<body>
<h3>The SessionID = <% =Session.SessionID %></h3>
<h3>The Timeout limit = <% =Session.Timeout %></h3>
</body>

</html>
```

Using the Session Object to Manage User Interactions *Continued*

If you want to force a session to end before its timeout value has been reached, then you can use the `Abandon` method. This method will destroy all of the objects that were allocated by the session and release their resources. When this method is called, the current script that is being processed will continue to be processed to completion. When the current script finishes, the `Session_onEnd()` event is fired.

The `CodePage` property of the Session object is used to determine which codepage is used to display the content that is generated by the ASP script. A *codepage* is the Windows term for a language-specific character set. Different languages and different locales may use different code pages.

To see how you can use local values stored in the Session object, refer to the simple script in Listing 25-5.

The `Contents` collection contains all of the items that have been established for a session without using the `<object>` tag. The collection can be used to determine the value of a specific session item, or to iterate through the collection and retrieve a list of all items in the session (see Listing 25-6).

The Application object has much in common with the Session object. Both objects exist so that you can maintain state, have a place to store information, and have the information persist for more than the life of one page.

Information used across all the site's sessions can be maintained in the Application object. See Listing 25-7 for an example of tracking the number of active sessions on a Web application.

The code in the `Application_OnStart` procedure just initializes the collection item for later use. The `Session_OnStart` procedure contains the `lock` and `unlock` methods of the Application object.

The Application object contains values that can be modified by multiple users. That characteristic means that it is possible for conflicts to occur. Take our preceding example: If two sessions started at the same time, then they both could execute the increment line. This would result in false or corrupted data being stored in this collection.

The `lock` and `unlock` methods prevent this type of problem from occurring. A call to `Application.Lock` does not return until it gets an exclusive hold on the Application object. Other attempts to issue that same command do not return until the session that locked the object calls `Application.Unlock`.

However, these calls bring their own problems. It is important to minimize the time that the Application object is locked because all other sessions requiring its use will be waiting. If you must perform a series of operations between two uses of the Application object, use multiple `Lock` and `Unlock` pairs to ensure the shortest possible locking time.

TAKE NOTE

MODIFYING THE GLOBAL.ASA

Modifying the `global.asa` file resets the application, all its information, and all the currently open sessions.

Listing 25-6: Session Contents Collection

```
<%
Dim Item
For Each Item in Session.Contents←❶
  Response.Write(Item & " = " &_
Session.Contents(Item) & "<br>")
Next
         ❷
%>
```

❶ Using the VBScript For .. Each construct, you can loop through
all values in a collection.

❷ Here Item is a variable that holds the value of one item the
Session object.

Listing 25-7: Using the Application Object —
`global.asa`

```
SUB Application_OnStart
  Application("Counter") = 0
END SUB

SUB Session_OnStart
  Application.Lock
  Application("Counter") =
Application("Counter") + 1
  Application.Unlock
END SUB

SUB Session_OnEnd
  Application.Lock
  Application("Counter") =
Application("Counter") - 1
  Application.Unlock
END SUB
```

Using Passwords: When You Know Your Users

One of the primary reasons that you use state information is to identify each user. They are already identified with ASP by a `SessionID`, but this item tends not be very useful. Instead, you will generally want to change the behavior of your application based on the user's absolute identity, a `userID`. This follows a similar practice to a normal, non-Web-based client/server application.

To prevent anonymous users from connecting to restricted content, you can configure your Web server to authenticate users. Authentication involves prompting users for unique user name and password information. IIS can be configured to allow authenticated access. For example, Windows NT Challenge/Response would require a valid Windows NT user account.

There are several authentication methods available to IIS administrators for controlling access to the server and files. These password authentication methods include Anonymous, Basic, Windows NT Challenge/Response, and digital certificates.

You can use the Directory Security property sheet of IIS MMC to configure our Web server's user identification security features, as shown in the figure. The Anonymous Access and Authentication Control option sets the anonymous access and authentication control methods to your server. Click Edit to select from the different authentication methods.

You can use Windows NT Challenge/Response user authentication to ensure that user names and passwords are encrypted before they are transmitted over the Internet. Although doing so improves security, there is a tradeoff. Note that Windows NT Challenge/Response user authentication does not encrypt information transmitted through the Internet; it encrypts only the user names and passwords.

Troubleshooting

At the time of this writing, only Internet Explorer supports Windows NT Challenge/Response user authentication. Use this method of authentication to improve security only if you you are certain that all of your users use Internet Explorer.

CROSS-REFERENCE

Chapter 2 introduces you to managing IIS and Windows NT security.

FIND IT ONLINE

This tutorial (**http://www.activeserverpages.com/learn/authenticatentcr.asp**) explains NT authentication.

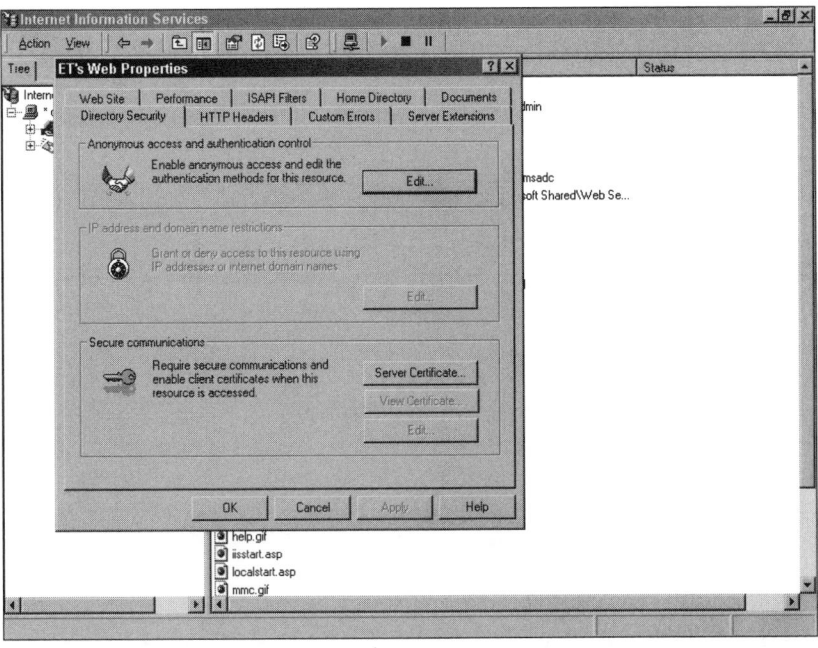

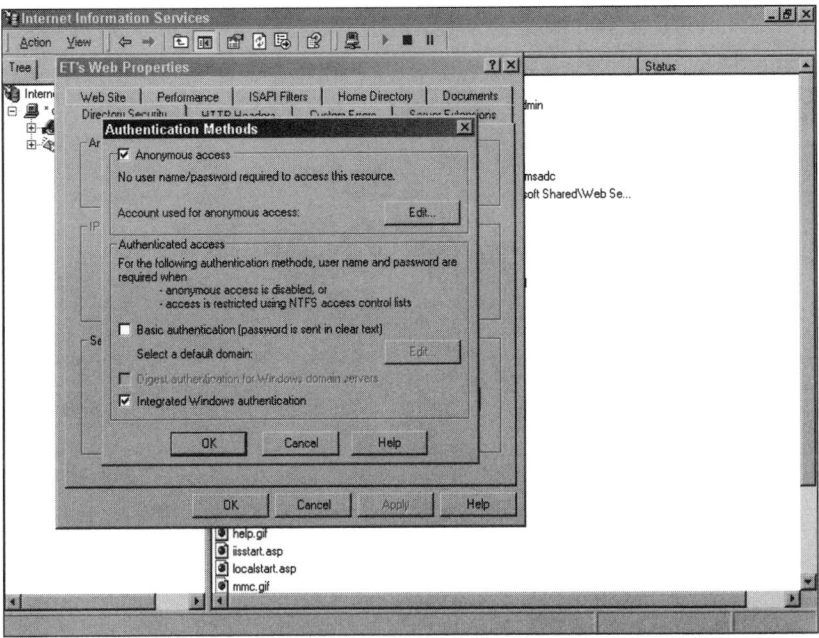

Building Pages Based on User Authentication

When using NT's authentication is not feasible, you can implement a standard HTML and ASP log-on type of dialog, and use the information the user provides within your application.

On the HTML form, the user will have to supply a user name and password and click a Submit button. See figure and Listing 25-8.

Most of the page is straightforward HTML, because it is not an ASP page. The opening tag of the HTML form specifies which file will be called to handle the form when Submit is clicked. In this case, the handler is `login_response.asp`, which doesn't need a path specified because it resides in the same directory as this form. The important detail to note in the input fields is the name assigned to these fields — that is how the values are retrieved from the `Request.Form` collection.

Next, you need to respond to the request by checking the following details. It makes sense to use the POST method for the form so that the information is not sent attached to the URL in the query string, but at least partly concealed within the HTTP header. The first step will be to verify who the user is, and decide if you already know them. Then, if you do know them, you can check to see if they supplied the correct password. This process involves three basic steps, and you will usually take the information from a database.

To see if the user already exists in your database, you just need to search for their user name in the appropriate table. Assuming you have a table Users with userName and userPwd as columns, you can use an ASP page and SQL query to extract the details, as in Listing 25-9.

Listing 25-9 attempts to retrieve the database record for the `userID` entered. In the listing, you create and then open a connection to the database. Next you open the recordset. Once you have the recordset, you first need to see if there was a record in it.

If this recordset does not exist, then it is not a valid `userID`, and the script displays an appropriate message. At most, there will only be one recordset, because the userName column would need to be unique. The easiest way to check if one recordset was returned is to check the values of BOF and EOF. Only if the recordset is empty will both values be True.

If the recordset does exist, then the next piece of logic checks whether the password entered is correct for this `userID`. The recordset you retrieved contains the password field as well. Because the password is stored from the form, it is just a straight comparison.

If it is not a match, another message is displayed. If it is a match, then code executes to place some values in the Session object where they can be used later. A message is then displayed that welcomes the user to the system.

Continued

CROSS-REFERENCE

Chapter 12 introduces you to processing a form.

FIND IT ONLINE

This tutorial (**http://www.aspalliance.com/flicks**) explains NT authentication.

448

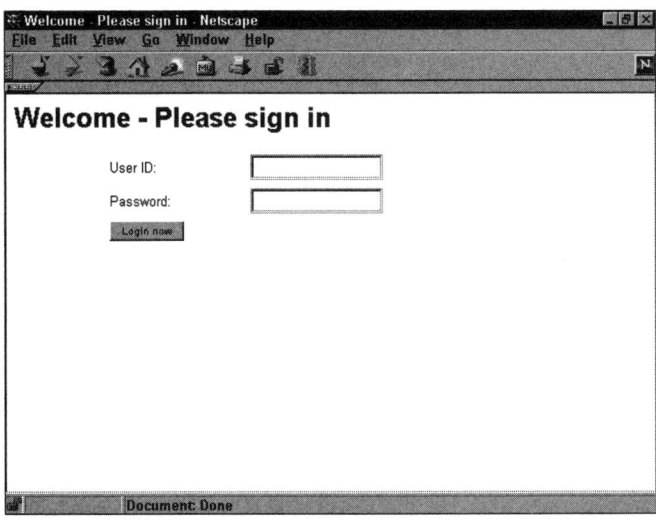

Listing 25-8: HTML Login Page

```
<html>
<head><title>Welcome — Please sign in</title><head>
<body>
<h1>Welcome — Please sign in</h1>
<form action="login_response.asp" method="post">
<div align="center">
<table border=0 cellspacing=4 cellpadding=4>
  <tr>
  <td>User ID:</td>
  <td><input type="text" size="20" name="UserName"></td>
  </tr>
  <tr>
  <td>Password ID:</td>
  <td><input type="password" size="20" name="UserPwd"></td>
  </tr>
  <tr>
  <td><input type="submit" name="login" value="Login"></td>
  </tr>
</table>
</div>
</form>
</body>
</html>
```

Building Pages Based on User Authentication *Continued*

Listing 25-9: ASP login_response Page

```
<html>
<head><title>User Login</title></head>
<body>
<%
Set oConn =
Server.CreateObject("ADODB.Connection")   ①
oConn.Open Application("dbName"),   ②
Application("dbUserID"), Application("dbUserPw")

Set sql = "SELECT * FROM Users " & _   ③
 " WHERE UserName = '" & Request.Form("UserName") & "'"
Set oRS = oConn.Execute(sql);

If (oRS.EOF or oRS.BOF) Then   ④
  Session("Authenticated") = false   ⑤
%>
<h2>User Does Not Exist</h2>
<h3><a href="login.asp">Try again</a></h3>
<%
Else
  If oRS("UserPwd") <> Request.Form("UserPwd")   ⑥
Then
    Session("Authenticated") = false
%>
<h2>User Password Is Incorrect</h2>
<h3><a href="login.asp">Try again</a></h3>
<%
  Else
```

```
    Session("Authenticated") = true ← ❼
    Session("UserName") = oRS("UserName")
%>
<h2>Login Successful</h2>
<h3><a href="mainpage.asp">Continue to the Main
Menu</a></h3>
<%
    End If
  End If
oConn.Close
oRS.Close
oConn = Nothing
oRS = Nothing
%>
</body>
</html>
```

❶ *Create the Connection object.*

❷ *Open the Connection object using the database information stored in the Application object.*

❸ *Build the SQL statement to retrieve the user name and password from our Users table.*

❹ *Once you execute the SQL statement within our connection, you check to see if a record was returned using* EOF *and* BOF.

❺ *If no record was returned, then the user does not exist in the Users table.*

❻ *If a record is returned and the* UserPwd *from Users does not match the HTML form element, then the password is incorrect.*

❼ *If the password does match, then set a Session variable to true. You will check this variable on every secure ASP page to verify that the user has already been authenticated.*

Learning about Secure Connections

After bandwidth, security is the biggest concern when creating active content on the Internet. IIS gives you a range of tools with which you can ensure Web site security. At the core of this security is Windows NT Server.

The starting point for strong Internet security is the operation system of any machine connected to it. Using IIS, strong levels of security were built into the core of Windows NT in order to meet and exceed certifiable security standards, such as the C2 security guidelines.

Users visiting commercial Web sites are sometimes reluctant to supply sensitive information, such as a credit card or bank account number. They fear that computer intruders will intercept this information. To address this type of security concern, you need to protect sensitive information transmitted over a network from all forms of interception and tampering.

IIS provides users with a secure communication channel by supporting Secure Sockets Layer (SSL) and RSA Data Security encryption on both the server and client.

The SSL 3.0 protocol, implemented as a Web server security feature, provides a secure way of establishing an encrypted communication link with users. SSL guarantees the authenticity of your Web content, while reliably verifying the identity of users accessing restricted Web sites.

The Internet (or an intranet) is a network of many machines, all communicating using TCP/IP protocol standards. SSL is a protocol layer that is located between the TCP/IP layer and the Application layer, which contains HTTP. See figure.

The SSL protocol secures data communication through server authentication, data encryption, and data integrity. SSL has the following benefits:

- ▶ Authentication ensures that data is sent to the correct server and that the server is secure.
- ▶ Data integrity ensures that the data received by the target has not been altered in any way.

Using SSL, however, does require an SSL digital certificate. A digital certificate is an item of information that binds the details of an individual or organization to their public key. The most widely accepted format for digital certificates is the X.509 standard, which is relevant to both clients and servers. If you can obtain access to someone's certificate, you have their public key.

In IIS, you can control whether SSL is required for access to a particular virtual server or folder. Plus, you can decide whether that server or folder requires a certificate.

But what stops anyone from creating a false certificate and pretending that they are someone else? The solution is Certificate Authorities (CAs). A CA is a commonly known third party, responsible for verifying both the contents and ownership of a certificate.

Client certificates usually contain identifying information about the user and the organization that issued the certificate (see Table 25-1).

TAKE NOTE

▶ USING ENCRYPTION

Encryption is the name given to the process of applying an algorithm to a message. The algorithm scrambles data in the message — making it very difficult to deduce the original method. Inputs to the algorithm usually involve additional secret data called *keys*, which prevents the message from being decoded.

CROSS-REFERENCE

Chapter 27 introduces you to placing Web architecture in a client-server context.

FIND IT ONLINE

Entrust, a useful CA for the creation of certificates that can be used for demonstration, is located at: **http://www.entrust.com**.

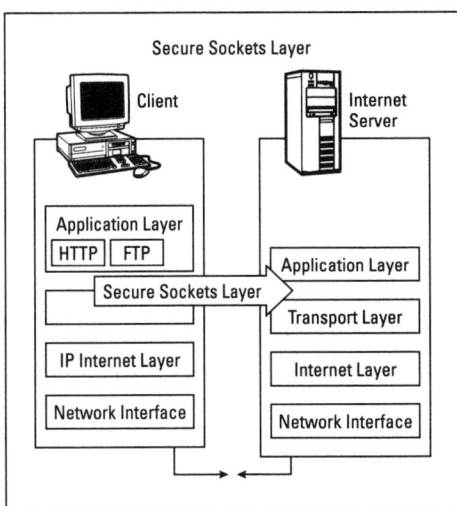

SSL Digital Certificate Information

Version
Serial Number
Signature algorithm ID
Issuer name
Validity period
Subject user name
Subject public key information
Issuer unique ID
Subject unique identifier
Extensions
Signature on the above fields

Personal Workbook

Q & A

1 Are cookies harmful to the user's computer?

_____

_____

_____

2 How do you delete a cookie?

_____

_____

_____

3 Which ASP object is used to create a cookie?

_____

_____

_____

4 Is there a limit to the number of cookies that can be created by a server?

_____

_____

_____

5 Name two things that can cause a user's session to end.

_____

_____

_____

6 What is the default time of a session?

_____

_____

_____

7 I want an object to be available to all my users. Does it matter whether I put it into the Application or Session object?

_____

_____

_____

ANSWERS: PAGE 514

EXTRA PRACTICE

1 Write the ASP statement to modify the Session timeout to ten minutes.

2 Rewrite the following code to minimize the time that the Application object is locked.

```
<%
Application.Lock
Set iTotalWages =
Application("totalWages")
For i  = 1 to numEmployees
iTotalWages = rs("wage") + iTotalWages
RS.movenext
Next i
Application("totalWages") = iTotalWages
Application.Unlock
%>
```

REAL-WORLD APPLICATIONS

✔ Develop an ASP page that uses an HTML form to collect a user's name and store it in a cookie. When the user visits the same ASP page, greet the user personally.

✔ Create another ASP page that deletes the previous cookie.

CHAPTER **26**

MASTER
THESE
SKILLS

▶ **Working with XML on the Server**

▶ **Generating XML Documents for XML-Aware Clients**

▶ **The Fine Art of Transformation — XSL**

▶ **Using Microsoft's XSL ActiveX Object in ASP**

▶ **Transforming from XML to HTML**

Managing XML with ASP

W eb server developers have typically focused on serving HTML and supporting resources (such as graphics) to Web browsers. Extensible Markup Language (XML) can use the same infrastructure to send information marked up using a variety of vocabularies. For the most part, generating and transmitting XML documents using ASP is much like generating and transmitting HTML. XML's greater flexibility and cleaner structures open new possibilities, however, which ASP is beginning to support.

Like HTML, XML documents are basically text files that combine content and markup. Generating these text documents is done the same way as generating HTML, with a small extra trick for setting the correct MIME content type. Similarly, static XML documents can be served easily from IIS, once you've added the proper MIME content type to the list of types the server understands.

XML provides developers with new options, however, and ASP can serve in a number of different roles. ASP applications can access the contents and structure of XML documents using Microsoft's XML parser and the access it provides to the W3C Document Object Model. Your Active Server Pages can use XML documents as source material, processing and (perhaps) responding to the content stored in those documents.

ASP can also use the Extensible Style Language (XSL) to transform static XML documents to HTML documents (so older browsers can have access to XML content), or even transform them to graphics using an XML-based graphic language, Microsoft's Vector Markup Language (VML). XSL is very new and still in development (Microsoft calls its implementation "experimental"), so we'll take a quick tour of its syntax and structures and demonstrate its possibilities.

Managing XML Documents on the Server

In many ways, XML documents are just like HTML documents — you can store them on your server as text files, edit them with both text editors and specialized tools, or generate them with ASP. The similarities make it easy to get started, but the differences have important implications.

The most fundamental difference is the MIME content-type identifier for XML — currently text/xml or application/xml, as opposed to text/html. To serve static XML documents (those that are stored as files on your Web site), you need to tell the server that those files are XML. You can tell IIS to identify documents with a particular file extension — you're not limited to .xml — following the steps on the opposite page.

Not all XML documents will have the MIME type text/xml or application/xml. Developers can create new types for files that "happen" to be based on XML. The W3C is working on a standard, Scalable Vector Graphics (SVG), that will probably end up with a MIME type of image/svg or image/svg-xml. Microsoft's Channel Definition Format (CDF) file use the MIME type application/x-netcdf. As your XML use becomes more sophisticated and you start serving multiple types of documents, you may want to look into registering MIME types for your XML documents and identifying them to your server as specific document types rather than "just" XML.

XML files can be stored as plain text files (just like HTML files), though new document stores, which typically manage preparsed versions of your XML documents, are on the way. Your existing file system can get you started, but if you find your collection of XML documents growing beyond your ability to manage them, you may want to look into a more sophisticated system from a third-party vendor.

TAKE NOTE

▶ NOT ALL XML IS THE SAME

XML can be used to hold information of many different sorts, from documents to graphics to databases. While the basic syntax — elements, attributes, and DTDs — is always the same, the structure and content of this information can be very different. XML is easy to store and process because of its structure and its roots in ordinary text files, but treating all XML documents identically may not be a good idea.

On some levels, you can process XML generically. If you're assembling documents from XML documents, you just need to know which information to extract — not what it means. XML's simple structures can help you find and use information without requiring you to understand its content. On the other hand, if you need to pull information from a set of database tables, you'll want to be able to tell the difference between the files that represent database tables and the files that represent graphs generated from those tables. This could mean a different file extension (.xml doesn't tell you enough), storage in separate directories, or code in your application that checks document types more thoroughly.

Whatever approach you finally take toward managing XML documents on the server, you'll probably find that different kinds of XML documents deserve the same kind of treatment that different document types get (like different file extensions). You will probably still want to keep a list of all the file types on your system that are based in XML in order to be able to use generic processing when possible. Parsing an XML file that doesn't contain the information you want typically causes less disruption than attempting to parse a binary file that isn't even XML.

FIND IT ONLINE

The IETF (Internet Engineering Task Force) manages MIME type registration. See RFC 2045 at **http://www.rfceditor.org** for more information on how to register your own MIME content types.

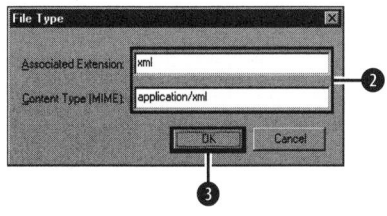

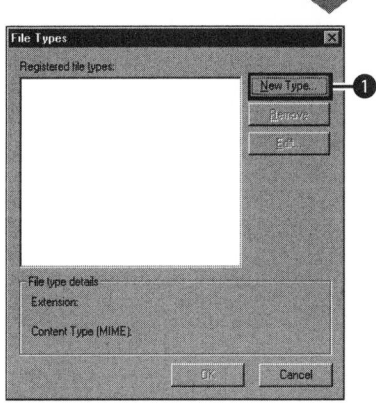

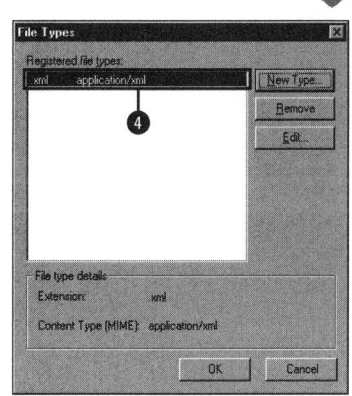

▶ You can edit and add MIME type headers from the HTTP Headers area of the properties box for whatever level of the Web site you consider appropriate.

❶ To add a new type (for XML, for instance), click the New Type button of the File Types dialog box.

❷ IIS depends on file extensions to assign MIME types. In the File Type dialog, enter the file extension (in this case, **xml**) you want to associate with a Content Type (in this case, **application/xml**).

❸ When you've entered both, the OK button will activate and you can click it to proceed.

❹ Your new content-type will appear in the File Types dialog when you're done, and IIS will now apply the new content type to appropriate files.

Generating XML Documents Using Familiar ASP Techniques

You can use Active Server Pages to generate XML documents on the fly, using user input, database information, or even other XML documents as sources of information. As more browsers come to support XML, this scenario will probably become more common. Fortunately, generating XML documents can be much like the HTML document generation that ASP was originally created to support.

When you're generating XML, you need to set the content-type explicitly — ASP expects all of the pages you generate to be text/html, which can leave your users with blank screens or a lot of run-on text, depending on their browser. Setting the MIME type to XML won't solve all of these problems, but will at least notify browsers that they're getting a different format than normal, forcing them to process the information as XML (if they can) or ask the user what they should do.

To set the content-type of a document, just set the Response object's `ContentType` property:

```
Response.ContentType="application/xml"
```

You can also set the character set information, as a supplement to the encoding declaration built into the XML document, using the Response object's `Charset` method:

```
Response.Charset="UTF-8"
```

Unless you have turned on response buffering, the content-type and character set of a document must be set *before* you start writing content to the document.

Checking the browser type to make sure clients can support your output is another good idea, especially if your application will be running on the Internet. As we'll see later in this chapter, this strategy can be used to determine whether to send XML and a corresponding XSL stylesheet to the client for processing or to do the processing on the server and send out HTML.

The only other significant difference between HTML and XML generation with regular ASP is the need to ensure that your documents are *well-formed*. This term means planning to include an end tag for every start tag, making empty elements end with />, and double-checking to make sure that <, >, and & characters don't appear in content. Checking output is often a difficult task to automate. You may need to generate sample output and set rules for the data that may be included in the information used as source material for your documents. There is no mechanical way to check your ASP documents to make sure they produce well-formed XML, though simple scripts based on tightly-regulated information sources can usually be checked by hand. While it is sometimes possible to build testing environments that generate every possible data and ASP combination and check the results, this just can't be done in cases where the data will be changed as the application is used. If this approach has too much uncertainty, you may want to try generating your XML through the DOM, as described in the following task.

It's important to remember that your Active Server Pages themselves will almost never be well-formed XML. The use of <% and %> as delimiters, as well as the use of <, >, and & within code, virtually ensure that your Active Server Pages will flunk an XML parsing test. However, this failure doesn't matter to your XML generation: what matters is the output, not the inputs (including your ASP code) that generated it.

This standard HTML form will collect information you'll be converting into XML.

The ASP code in Listing 26-2 looks much like the code ordinarily used to generate HTML, but with different element names.

CROSS-REFERENCE

Chapter 18 describes how to use browser detection, which can help you determine whether a client can support XML.

Listing 26-1

```html
<html><head><title>Forms to XML</title></head>
<body><h1>Address Collector</h1>
<form action="formxml.asp" method="POST">
<p>First Name:<input type="text"
name="firstname" size="20" /></p>
<p>Last Name:<input type="text"
name="lastname" size="30" /></p>
<p>Address 1:<input type="text"
name="address1" size="40" /></p>
<p>Address 2:<input type="text"
name="address2" size="40" /></p>
<p>City:<input type="text" name="city"
size="25" /> State/Province:<input type="text"
name="state" size="25" /></p>
<p>ZIP/Postal Code:<input type="text"
name="postalcode" size="15" /> Country:<input
type="text" name="country" size="25" /></p>
<p><input type="submit" name="Submit" /></p>
</form>

</body></html>
```

Listing 26-2

```asp
<%@LANGUAGE="JavaScript"%>
<%Response.ContentType="application/xml";%>
<?xml version="1.0"?>
<record>
<name><firstname><%=Request.Form.item("firstna
me")%></firstname>
<lastname><%=Request.Form.item("lastname")%></
lastname></name>
<address><line1><%=Request.Form.item("address1
")%></line1>
<line2><%=Request.Form.item("address2")%></lin
e2>
<city><%=Request.Form.item("city")%></city>
<state><%=Request.Form.item("state")%></state>
<postalcode><%=Request.Form.item("postalcode")
%></postalcode>
<country><%=Request.Form.item("country")%></co
untry>
</address>
</record>
```

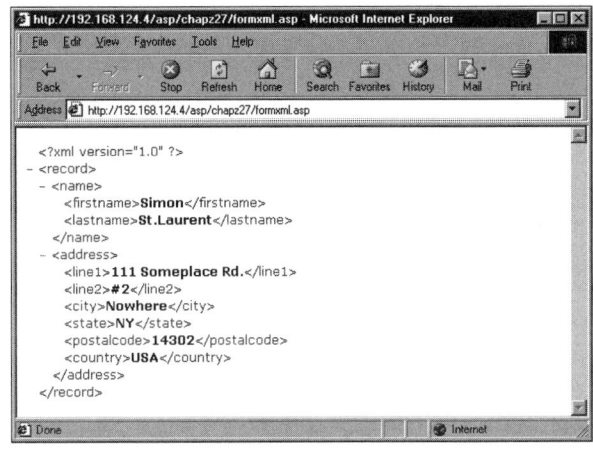

▶ *The output sent back to the user is XML (not HTML) generated dynamically.*

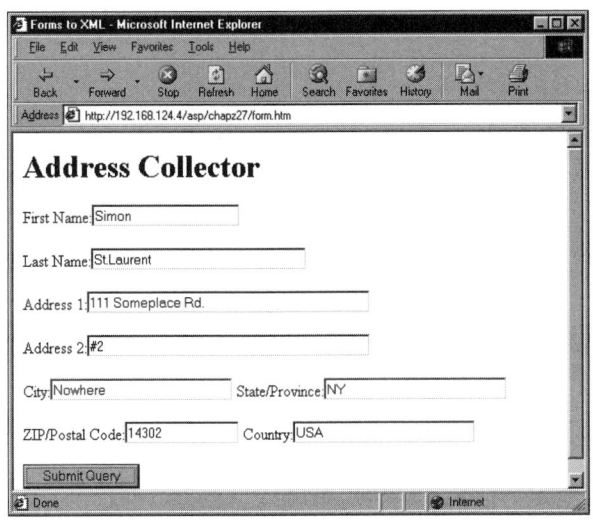

▶ *The form looks very familiar, and collects information as usual.*

Generating and Reading XML Documents with the DOM

The Document Object Model (DOM) got its start in the client-side battles between Microsoft and Netscape, but has found new use on the server side of Web development. The DOM enables you to work with documents as collections of elements and attributes, rather than as a stream of text. Effectively, the DOM presents a "processed" view of your documents, and enables you to manipulate your document as a set of objects. Microsoft's XML parser includes tools for opening documents, creating new documents, reading and writing the content of documents, and converting the document to a text stream.

To do anything with a Document Object Model, you need to create an appropriate object:

```
set
myDoc=Server.CreateObject("Microsoft.XMLDOM")
```

Once you have an object with which to work, you can load documents into the DOM:

```
myDoc.async=false
myDoc.load("sourcefile")
```

The `async` property tells the parser to process the entire file before returning control to the script.

Alternatively, you can create a root element within the DOM and build a document from scratch:

```
set
rootElement=myDoc.createElement("myRootElement
Name")
```

The DOM represents documents as a set of nodes, which may contain elements, attributes, text, and other XML components. The DOM provides an API for manipulating and reading those nodes, demonstrated on the opposite page. The DOM components follow similar rules to those imposed on XML documents: elements may contain attributes, text, other elements, comments, and processing instructions, while attributes may contain text — no sub-elements or other attributes.

While the `load` method reads an XML document, the `xml` method writes an XML document back out as a string, enabling you to present it as output in your ASP document:

```
Response.write(myDoc.xml)
```

Microsoft has provided a number of key extensions to the DOM. The functions for loading documents and writing documents back out are notable (and necessary) extensions, as the W3C's DOM standard doesn't provide any mechanisms for performing these basic functions. Another key extension Microsoft has provided enables you to use the pattern matching syntax for XSL (described in the next few tasks) with its DOM implementation, rather than having to navigate from node to node to node to find information.

Listing 26-3

```javascript
<%@LANGUAGE=JavaScript%>
<%Response.ContentType="application/xml";
sourceFile=Server.MapPath("prizewin.xml");
var myDoc=Server.CreateObject("Microsoft.XMLDOM");
myDoc.async=false;
myDoc.load(sourceFile);
var rootNode=myDoc.documentElement;

var entry=rootNode.firstChild ;
var nameNode=myDoc.createElement("name");
var firstNameNode=myDoc.createElement("firstname");
var firstNameText=myDoc.createTextNode(Request.Form.item("firstname"));
firstNameNode.appendChild(firstNameText);
var lastNameNode=myDoc.createElement("lastname");
var lastNameText=myDoc.createTextNode(Request.Form.item("lastname"));
lastNameNode.appendChild(lastNameText);
nameNode.appendChild(firstNameNode);
nameNode.appendChild(lastNameNode);
entry.appendChild(nameNode);
var addressNode=myDoc.createElement("address")
var line1Node=myDoc.createElement("line1")
var line1Text=myDoc.createTextNode(Request.Form.item("address1"));
line1Node.appendChild(line1Text);
addressNode.appendChild(line1Node);
var line2Node=myDoc.createElement("line2")
var line2Text=myDoc.createTextNode(Request.Form.item("address2"));
line2Node.appendChild(line2Text);
addressNode.appendChild(line2Node);

var cityNode=myDoc.createElement("city")
var cityText=myDoc.createTextNode(Request.Form.item("city"));
cityNode.appendChild(cityText);
addressNode.appendChild(cityNode);

var stateNode=myDoc.createElement("state")
var stateText=myDoc.createTextNode(Request.Form.item("state"));
stateNode.appendChild(stateText);
addressNode.appendChild(stateNode);
```

Continued

463

Generating and Reading XML Documents with the DOM *Continued*

Listing 26-3 *(Continued)*

```
var postalNode=myDoc.createElement("postalcode")
var postalText=myDoc.createTextNode(Request.Form.item("postalcode"));
postalNode.appendChild(postalText);
addressNode.appendChild(postalNode);

var countryNode=myDoc.createElement("country")
var countryText=myDoc.createTextNode(Request.Form.item("country"));
countryNode.appendChild(countryText);
addressNode.appendChild(countryNode);

entry.appendChild(addressNode);
Response.write(myDoc.xml)
%>
```

▶ *This ASP code will take the form data (generated by the form in the preceding task) and use the Document Object Model to combine it with the XML at the top right.*

Listing 26-4

```
<?xml version="1.0"?>
<letter>
<entry />
<greetings>Dear Fool,</greetings>
<p>You have won a million, trillion dollars!!!!!  In laminated game money, that is.  Please
contact us to collect your prize at +1 888 555 1212.  Shipping and handling fees of up to ten
thousand dollars may be required to collect your prize.</p>
<signoff>Hahahaha!</signoff>
<signature>the prize committee (we prys your money away from you!)</signature>
</letter>
```

▶ *With the DOM, it's easy to build a template document like the one shown here and add extra pieces in your ASP document.*

Listing 26-5

```
<%@LANGUAGE=JavaScript%>
<%Response.ContentType="application/xml";%>
<names><%
fileName=Request.QueryString("address");
sourceFile=Server.MapPath(fileName);
var myDoc=Server.CreateObject("Microsoft.XMLDOM");
myDoc.async=false;
myDoc.load(sourceFile);var entryCollection=myDoc.getElementsByTagName("lastname");
entries=entryCollection.length;

for (i=0; i<entries; i++) {
var inspection=entryCollection.item(i);
%>Last name: <%
var lastname=inspection.nodeName;

Response.Write(inspection.xml);
%>
<% } %>
</names>
```

▶ *You can also use the DOM to read in a file, extract the pieces you need, and spit them out in a new format.*

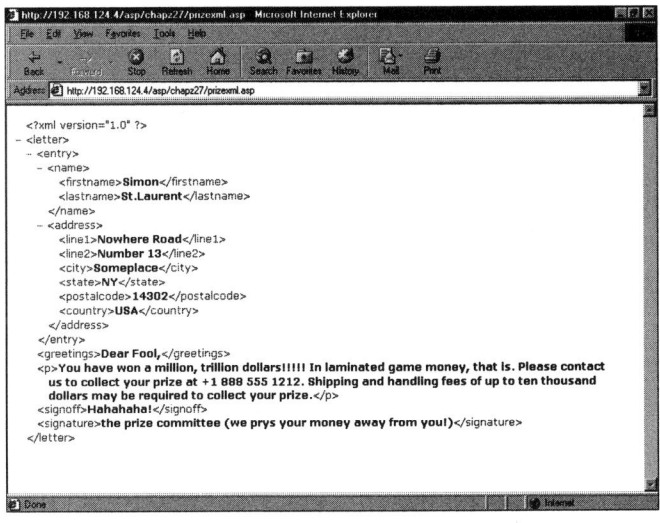

▶ *The output from this code combines the form information sent by the user with the XML document used as a foundation.*

Generating and Reading XML Documents with the DOM *Continued*

Listing 26-6

```xml
<entries>
<entry>
<name>
<firstname>William</firstname>
<lastname>Clinton</lastname>
</name>
<address>
<line1>1600 Pennsylvania Avenue</line1>
<line2>White House</line2>
<city>Washington</city>
<state>DC</state>
<postalcode>20000</postalcode>
<country>USA</country>
</address>
</entry>
<entry>
<name>
<firstname>George</firstname>
<lastname>Bush</lastname>
</name>
<address>
<line1>1600 Pennsylvania Avenue</line1>
<line2>White House</line2>
<city>Washington</city>
<state>DC</state>
<postalcode>20000</postalcode>
<country>USA</country>
</address>
</entry>
<entry>
<name>
<firstname>Ronald</firstname>
<lastname>Reagan</lastname>
</name>
<address>
```

```xml
<line1>1600 Pennsylvania Avenue</line1>
<line2>White House</line2>
<city>Washington</city>
<state>DC</state>
<postalcode>20000</postalcode>
<country>USA</country>
</address>
</entry>
</entries>
```

▶ *These addresses provide the raw material for the DOM extractor.*

Listing 26-7

```javascript
<%@LANGUAGE=JavaScript%>
<%Response.ContentType="application/xml";
sourceFile=Server.MapPath("prizewin.xml");
var myDoc=Server.CreateObject("Microsoft.
XMLDOM");
myDoc.async=false;
myDoc.load(sourceFile);
var rootNode=myDoc.documentElement;
var oldEntry=rootNode.firstChild ;

sourceFile=Server.MapPath("address.xml");
var mySubDoc=Server.CreateObject("Microsoft.
XMLDOM");
mySubDoc.async=false;
mySubDoc.load(sourceFile);
var entry=mySubDoc.documentElement;
rootNode.replaceChild(entry,oldEntry);
Response.write(myDoc.xml)
%>
```

▶ *In addition to reading and writing documents, the DOM lets you insert the contents of one document into the structure of another.*

Listing 26-8

```
<entry>
<name>
<firstname>William</firstname>
<lastname>Clinton</lastname>
</name>
<address>
<line1>1600 Pennsylvania Avenue</line1>
<line2>White House</line2>
<city>Washington</city>
<state>DC</state>
<postalcode>20000</postalcode>
<country>USA</country>
</address>
</entry>
```

▶ *This single address will be added to the form letter previously shown to create a new document.*

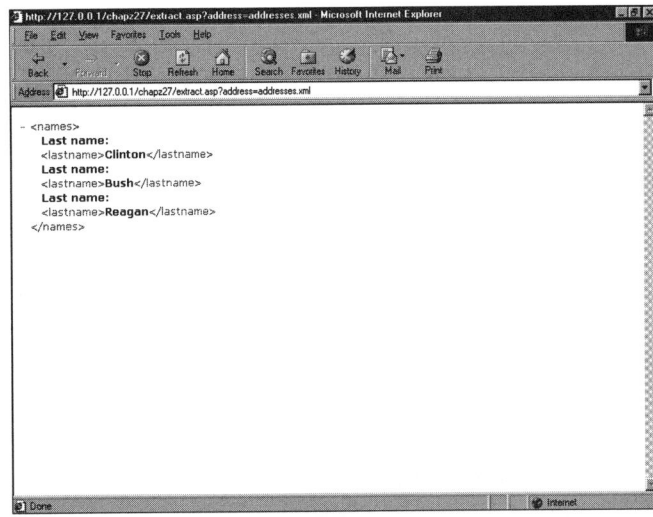

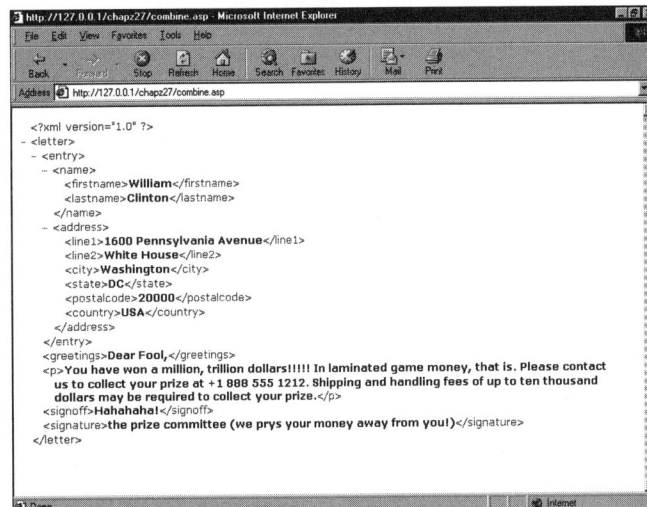

▶ *The extraction program has read in the XML document, pulled out the three lastname elements, and reported them in a new XML file.*

▶ *This looks like a single document (and it is), but it was built out of two separate XML documents that were combined in an ASP script.*

Learning about XSL Tree Construction and Transformations

Active Server Pages is a powerful tool for generating documents from a variety of data sources using procedural tools. There are times, however, when transformation is more appropriate than generations, and XML documents are designed to facilitate transformation from one XML vocabulary to another. The Extensible Style Language (XSL) provides a transformation-oriented vocabulary for handling XML-to-XML conversions, supplementing the procedural tools available in Active Server Pages.

XSL began as a proposal from Microsoft, ArborText, and Inso, and is currently a project under development at the World Wide Web Consortium (W3C). Microsoft released an experimental implementation with Internet Explorer 5.0. Although that implementation no longer matches the latest draft of XSL, it is the only implementation readily available for use with Active Server Pages at present. (Check the W3C at **http://www.w3.org/Style/XSL/** for the latest information on XSL, and with Microsoft for further recent implementations.) Using the Internet Explorer 5.0 implementation of XSL for production work is somewhat dangerous, and the language has already changed significantly, but it can get you started and may provide you with a good conceptual foundation even as the detail changes.

Unlike ASP, in which commands are used to fill in documents, XSL uses rules that identify portions of the original document and then provide information about what should be done with that information. In Active Server Pages, you build a document from a document plus information it calls into itself through function calls; in XSL, you build a document by matching portions of a document to a set of rules and transforming the information to a new form specified by those rules. Switching between these two approaches can be confusing — it requires a bit of a leap to make the transition.

You don't actually need to use ASP in order to use XSL. You can use an XSL processor built into client software (like Internet Explorer 5.0), if one is available. ASP can use the same XSL processor built into Internet Explorer 5.0, enabling you to use the same stylesheet on both sides of the client-server divide. For many simple examples, it's easiest to start by building XSL stylesheets and loading them into Internet Explorer 5.0 with an accompanying document. As your work becomes more complex, requiring transformation of documents generated with ASP, you may need to move your processing to the server.

An XSL processor requires two inputs: a source document and an XSL stylesheet. The XSL stylesheet may be connected to the document using a processing instruction included in the document, or it may be assigned separately (which is common in server-side processing). The source document is parsed, and the XSL stylesheet is parsed. The XSL processor looks through the parsed source document for structures that match those described by the XSL stylesheet. If the XSL processor finds matching structures, it applies the rules described in the XSL stylesheet to produce a result tree, which itself represents an XML document. Basically, the XML source document plus the XSL stylesheet yield a result document.

The XSL specification describes two areas: the transformation language (called XSL-T), and a formatting vocabulary for the result tree. In the current Microsoft implementation, only the transformation side is supported. The formatting vocabulary most commonly used is HTML, providing an easy path from new-style XML to old-style HTML.

FIND IT ONLINE

Microsoft's documentation for its XSL processor is available at **http://msdn.microsoft.com/xml/XSLGuide/default.asp**.

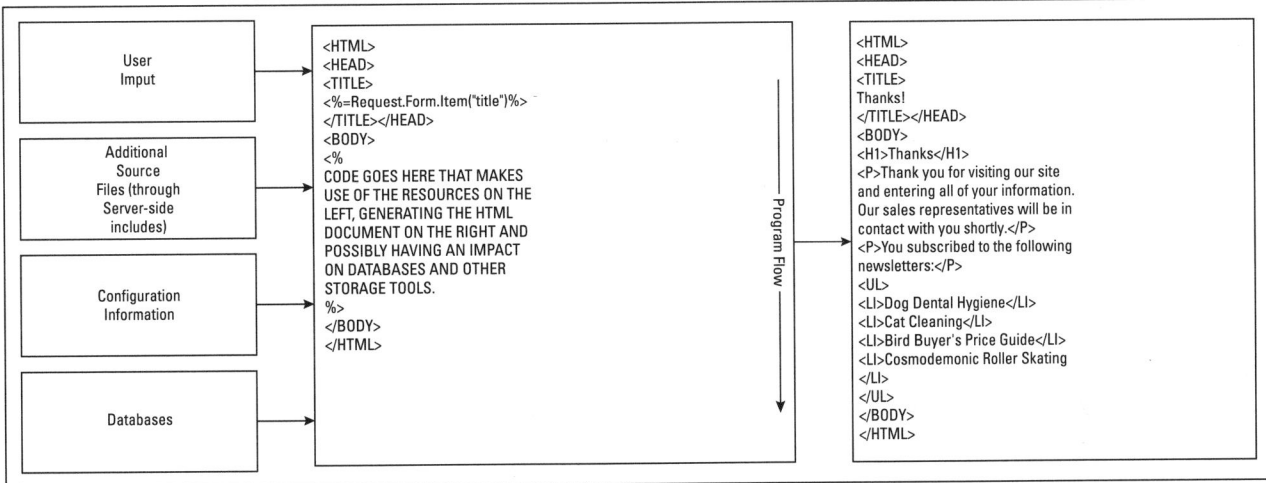

▶ Active Server Pages are effectively programs, designed to run in a particular order. Within those programs, developers can make calls to external resources to collect and modify information going into the construction of the page. ASP generally follows a procedural development model.

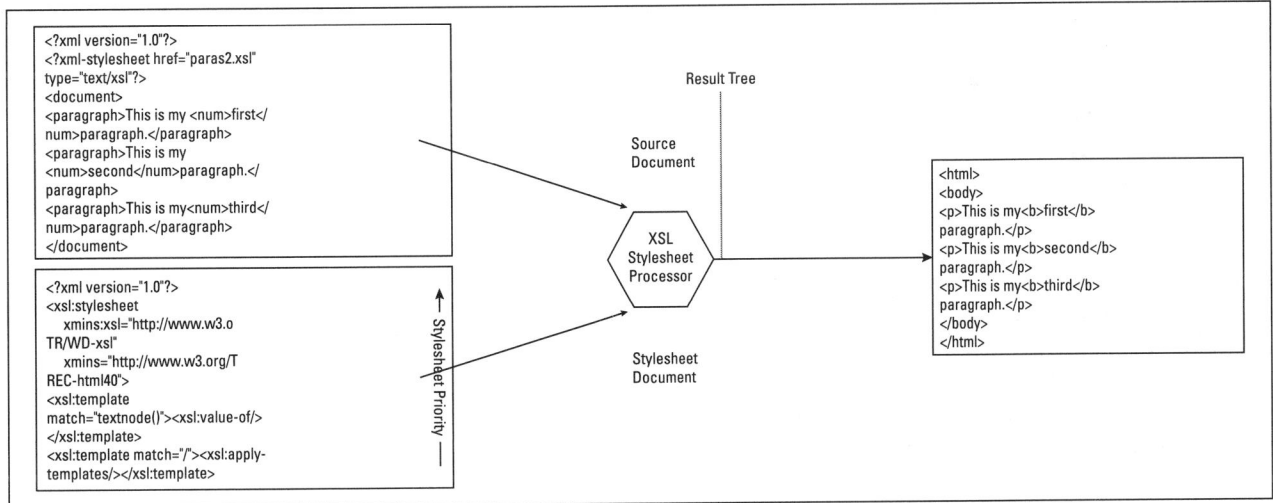

▶ XSL stylesheets are collections of rules, the order of whose application is dependent on the structure of the source document. Rather than running as a program to collect information and assemble it, XSL stylesheets describe transformations of an origin document. XSL generally follows a declarative development model.

Building a Simple XSL Stylesheet — Elements

While XSL is capable of some extraordinary transformations, many beginners find it difficult to get information even to appear in the browser the first few times they attempt XSL. While the basic concepts of matching patterns and applying rules are fairly simple, the details are frequently more complex. Because many XML-to-HTML transformations are actually quite simple, starting with a basic example will provide a solid foundation for many of the styles you'll need to create for your sites.

Our first document has a root element of DOCUMENT and three PARAGRAPHS:

```
<?xml version="1.0"?>
<?xml-stylesheet href="paras.xsl"
type="text/xsl"?>
<document title="Sample Document">
<paragraph>This is my <num>first</num>
paragraph.</paragraph>
<paragraph>This is my <num>second</num>
paragraph.</paragraph>
<paragraph>This is my <num>third</num>
paragraph.</paragraph>
</document>
```

The processing instruction in the second line connects this document to a stylesheet (`paras.xsl`) that has the MIME content type text/xsl, indicating to the browser that this stylesheet is an XSL stylesheet.

That XSL stylesheet needs to contain some declarations and rules describing how to transform the document above into an HTML document that the browser can display. The root element of the stylesheet begins an XSL stylesheet and provides namespace information that IE5 will use to identify the stylesheet as XSL and treat the results as HTML:

```
<?xml version="1.0"?>
<xsl:stylesheet
    xmlns:xsl="http://www.w3.org/TR/WD-xsl"
    xmlns="http://www.w3.org/TR/REC-html40">
```

The first rule (template) in the document matches the root element (/) and tells the XSL processor to apply further templates to its content:

```
<xsl:template match="/">
<xsl:apply-templates/>
</xsl:template>
```

The `match` attribute always identifies the element (or attribute) to be matched. The `xsl:apply-templates` element tells the XSL processor to apply further templates to the content of the matched element. The second template will match the document element and replace it with a basic HTML framework:

```
<xsl:template match="document">
<html><body>
    <xsl:apply-templates/>
</body></html>
</xsl:template>
```

Again, the `match` attribute identified the element to be matched, and the `xsl:apply-templates` element told XSL to continue processing the child elements. The contents of the document element will be processed by the rest of the rules, which in this case is only one:

```
<xsl:template match="paragraph">
    <p><xsl:value-of/></p>
</xsl:template>
```

Unlike `xsl:apply-templates`, `xsl:value-of` tells the XSL processor to add the text contained by the element and use it here, rather than processing child elements (if there are any, they will be flattened). The resulting document will look like:

```
<html><body>
    <p>This is my first paragraph.</p>
    <p>This is my second paragraph.</p>
    <p>This is my third paragraph.</p>
</body></html>
```

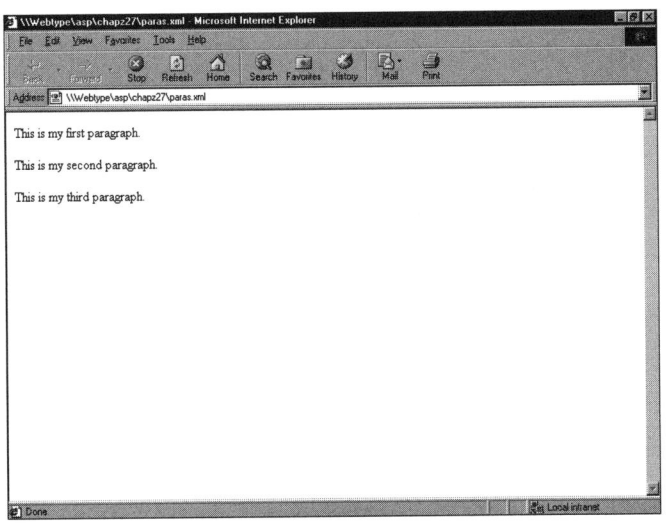

▶ XSL can transform XML to HTML for easy display in a browser. The results look like an ordinary HTML document.

▶ In the previous example, we "flattened" out the content of the paragraph elements. If we wanted to bold the content of the num elements, however, we'd have to do some extra work. We need to tell the processor to apply templates to the content of the paragraph elements, but don't want to lose the rest of the text. Fortunately, XSL has a textnode() option that matches text contained within the current element and enables you to display it. The following code below includes a rule for processing text nodes, and then uses the basic apply-templates and value-of constructs to build the element framework.

Listing 26-9

```
<?xml version="1.0"?>
<xsl:stylesheet
      xmlns:xsl="http://www.w3.org/TR/WD-xsl"
      xmlns="http://www.w3.org/TR/REC-html40">
<xsl:template match="textnode()"><xsl:value-
of/></xsl:template>
<xsl:template match="/"><xsl:apply-
templates/></xsl:template>
<xsl:template match="document">
<html><body><xsl:apply-templates/></body></html>
</xsl:template>
<xsl:template match="paragraph">
      <p><xsl:apply-templates/></p>
</xsl:template>
<xsl:template match="num">
      <b><xsl:value-of /></b>
</xsl:template>
</xsl:stylesheet>
```

Building a Simple XSL Stylesheet — Matching and Selecting

The simple XSL stylesheet processing described in the preceding section can take you a long way — provided that you're only processing simple elements that aren't too thoroughly mixed together. If you want to do things like move attribute values into your displayed content, restrict matches to particular hierarchies, or highlight information based on its position, you need to use more of the options that XSL provides for matching document information.

XSL provides special characters that match particular nodes, as shown here:

*	Matches any element.
.	Matches the current element.
..	Matches the parent of the current element.
/	Matches the root element when used alone; matches any child element when used in conjunction with another element.
//	Matches all descendants.
[number or end() or condition]	Matches the indicated iteration of a given element or an element meeting the *condition*.
@name	Matches the attribute of the current element named *name*.
|	Enables you to identify alternatives.

Note that the syntax for these XSL characters has changed in the official W3C XSL drafts and may change yet again. These will, however, work with Internet Explorer 5 and ASP.

The simplest change to the match attributes presented previously is to add hierarchies. For example, to match every paragraph that was a child of a document element (but only of a document element), the template would look like:

```
<xsl:template match="document/paragraph">
    <p><xsl:value-of/></p>
</xsl:template>
```

To match an element that has an attribute, preface the attribute name with @ and treat it as a child of the element:

```
<xsl:template match="document/@title">
```

To limit your matches to document elements whose title attribute is 'Sample Document', use the braces:

```
<xsl:template match="document/[@title='Sample
Document']">
```

The braces also enable you to select an iteration of an element (where zero is the first element). For example, to reference the second paragraph element, you could use:

```
<xsl:template match="paragraph[1]">
```

The vertical bar (|) character enables you to specify multiple possibilities in a match. This can be very useful when you're working with older information and you're not sure how (or if) it was capitalized. For instance:

```
<xsl:template match="h1 | H1">
```

These same rules can be used to select content for inclusion in the result. To grab an attribute from the element currently being processed — say, title — and add it to the content, use the @ character in front of the attribute name and use it as a select attribute's value:

```
<xsl:template match="document">
<html><body>
<h1><xsl:value-of select="@title"/></h1>
    <xsl:apply-templates/>
</body></html>
</xsl:template>
```

When the `xsl:value-of` element doesn't have a select attribute, it just uses the content of the element identified in the match statement. Fortunately, you're not limited to just the content of the element you've matched — you can grab the value of other elements and attributes in the surrounding document tree: children, parents, siblings, and their attributes. If it does have a select attribute, you can use it to grab information from other locations in the document tree, starting from your current location.

FIND IT ONLINE

Microsoft's tutorial on XSL patterns for the Internet Explorer 5 implementation is available at **http://www.msdn.microsoft.com/xml/XSLGuide/patterns-overview.asp**.

Managing XML with ASP

CHAPTER 26

One key rule to remember: Microsoft's XSL implementation gives priority to rules at the end of the stylesheet. If there are two possibilities, the last one is used.

Listing 26-6

```
<?xml version="1.0"?>
<?xml-stylesheet href="catalogfilter.xsl"
type="text/xsl"?>
<catalog owner="Joe">
<book title="ASP in an Hour">$19.95</book>
<radio manufacturer="Joe">$28.94</radio>
<cd title="Sounds of ASP">$9.49</cd>
<car manufacturer="Cars R Us"
model="RZ204">$29,996.00</car>
<donut flavor="jelly">$0.49</donut>
<donut flavor="glazed">$0.49</donut>
<mango>$0.75</mango>
<candy>
<bar type="Chocolate Munch"
picture="chocolate.gif">$0.25</bar>
<wafers type="Yummy Wafers"
picture="wafers.gif">$0.25</wafers>
</candy>
</catalog>
```

▶ XSL enables you to work with fairly "messy" XML, like the rough catalog above, and filter and format it into some kind of presentable manner.

Listing 26-7

```
<?xml version="1.0"?>
<xsl:stylesheet
    xmlns:xsl="http://www.w3.org/TR/WD-xsl"
    xmlns="http://www.w3.org/TR/REC-html40">

<xsl:template match="/"><xsl:apply-
templates/></xsl:template>
<xsl:template match="catalog">
<html>
<head><title>
    <xsl:value-of select="@owner"/>'s Catalog
```

```
</title></head><body>
<h1><xsl:value-of select="@owner"/>'s
Catalog</h1>
            <xsl:apply-templates/>
</body></html>
</xsl:template>


<xsl:template match="book | cd">
    <p><b><xsl:value-of select="@title"/></b>
    <xsl:value-of/></p>
</xsl:template>


<xsl:template match="donut">
    <p><b><xsl:value-of select="@flavor"/>
donut</b>
    <xsl:value-of/></p>
</xsl:template>

</xsl:stylesheet>
```

▶ This stylesheet will provide a general format to the catalog (with a title and headline) and filter its contents to present only key items — such as books, CDs, and donuts.

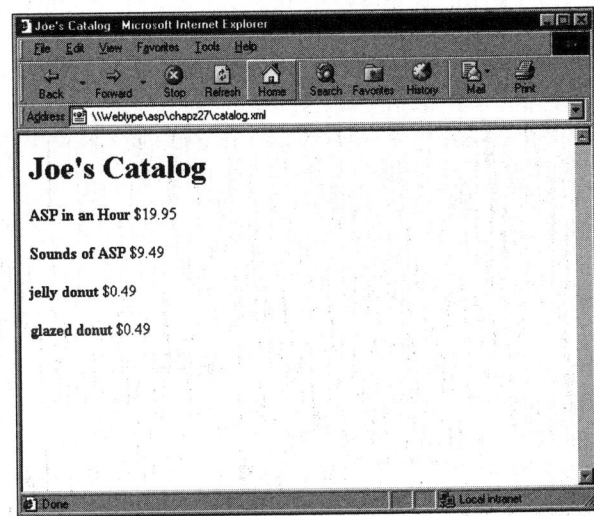

▶ This stylesheet turns the mess above into a reasonably nice HTML presentation of a catalog.

473

Building a Simple XSL Stylesheet — Writing Markup and Other Features

With a basic grasp of match patterns and a couple of tools for building documents, you can build many HTML documents, even ones with complex formatting. There are still a couple of possible hitches, though. First, we need to be able to create attributes using values found in the original XML document. Assigning attribute values from information in the origin document makes it possible to do things like create IMG elements, in which the critical information is stored in attribute values. The `xsl:attribute` element enables you to create attributes within the current element:

```
<xsl:template match="image">
<img>
<xsl:attribute name="src">
<xsl:value-of select="@location"/>
</xsl:attribute>
</img>
</xsl:template>
```

This code would create (in the result document) an img element with a src attribute whose value came from the location attribute of the image element in the source document.

XSL provides several other similar options: `xsl:text` for creating text, `xsl:element` for creating elements, `xsl:pi` for creating processing instructions, and `xsl:comment` for creating comments. These extra tools enable you to assemble well-formed documents easily, and operate like `xsl:attribute` as shown in the preceding example.

Another XSL element type, `xsl:copy`, is a convenient tool for moving XML structures from the origin document to the result document verbatim, without making any changes. If your stylesheet is simply rearranging existing XML, rather than transforming it to a new vocabulary, this capability can be very useful. The `xsl:copy` element is used exactly like `xsl:value-of`, using the select attribute (if present) to identify which information should be included in the result document. (If the information to be included is just text, `xsl:copy` may produce the same

results as `xsl:value-of`.) An `xsl:copy` example is shown on the opposite page.

XSL also provides tools for processing sets of elements. The `xsl:for-each` element enables stylesheet designers to describe processing when the number of instances of a particular match is unknown. The `xsl:for-each` element must be used within `xsl:template` rules, though in some ways the use of its select attribute feels more like the `xsl:template` element's match attribute.

```
<xsl:template match="document">
<xsl:for-each select="paragraph">
<p><xsl:value-of/></p>
</xsl:for-each>
</xsl:template>
```

Microsoft's implementation of XSL supports two simple conditional methods (`xsl:if` and `xsl:choose`) for processing XSL, thereby enabling you to determine if more complex conditions are met. This implement also supports a set of run-time functions that enable you to format numbers, create numbering within documents, and determine your location within the document tree. The XSL subset provided within Internet Explorer 5 — not to mention the entire subject of XSL — deserves a book of its own. If you need more XSL than has been covered here, we recommend exploring Microsoft's online resources or buying one of the many excellent books covering XSL.

The stylesheet in Listing 26-12 uses the `xsl:for-each` element to provide a special display for the contents of the candy element from the catalog on the preceding page.

The stylesheet in Listing 26-13 builds on the grouping by adding pictures of the candies.

Listing 26-12

```
<?xml version="1.0"?>
<xsl:stylesheet
    xmlns:xsl="http://www.w3.org/TR/WD-xsl"
    xmlns="http://www.w3.org/TR/REC-html40">
```

CROSS-REFERENCE

If you need a reference to Internet Explorer 5's implementation of XML, see *Professional Style Sheets for HTML & XML* (Boumphrey) Wrox Press 1998.

FIND IT ONLINE

For more on Microsoft's "Advanced Features," see **http://www.msdn.microsoft.com/xml/XSLGuide/xsl-advanced.asp**.

```
<xsl:template match="/"><xsl:apply-
templates/></xsl:template>
<xsl:template match="catalog">
<html>
<head><title>
    <xsl:value-of select="@owner"/>'s Catalog
</title></head><body>
<h1><xsl:value-of select="@owner"/>'s
Catalog</h1>
        <xsl:apply-templates/>
</body></html>
</xsl:template>

<xsl:template match="candy">
<hr />
<h2>Special Candy!</h2>
    <xsl:for-each match="//">
    <p><b><xsl:value-of select="@type"/></b>
<xsl:value-of/></p>
    </xsl:for-each>
<hr />
</xsl:template>
</xsl:stylesheet>
```

Listing 26-13

```
<?xml version="1.0"?>
<xsl:stylesheet
    xmlns:xsl="http://www.w3.org/TR/WD-xsl"
    xmlns="http://www.w3.org/TR/REC-html40">

<xsl:template match="/"><xsl:apply-
templates/></xsl:template>
<xsl:template match="catalog">
<html>
<head><title>
    <xsl:value-of select="@owner"/>'s Catalog
</title></head><body>
<h1><xsl:value-of select="@owner"/>'s
Catalog</h1>
        <xsl:apply-templates/>
```

```
</body></html>
</xsl:template>

<xsl:template match="candy">
<hr />
<h2>Special Candy!</h2>
    <xsl:for-each match="//">
    <p>
    <img>
    <xsl:attribute name="src">
        <xsl:value-of select="@picture"/>
    </xsl:attribute> </img>
    <b><xsl:value-of select="@type"/></b>
<xsl:value-of/></p>
    </xsl:for-each>
<hr />
</xsl:template>

</xsl:stylesheet>
```

▶ *Images give the catalog a bit of extra flair.*

Using the XSL ActiveX Object to Convert XML to HTML on Demand

While using XSL stylesheets to display and transform XML in the browser is useful and exciting, it only works (at present) with Internet Explorer 5. To present that information to other browsers, we need to perform the transformation on the server. Fortunately, we can use the tools that Microsoft has provided for its browser — as COM components — through Active Server Pages. The XSL ActiveX Object can take a document and a stylesheet, and return the output as text that you can send out to users.

Using XSL with Active Server Pages requires you to create two DOM objects: one for the original document, and one for the style document. You can create these documents either by loading files or by generating the DOM's contents with a script. (This latter approach means that you can build XML documents, and transform them to HTML on the server if your browser doesn't support XML.) Once you have the two documents, you can use the `transformNode` or `transformNodeToObject` methods to generate output you send to the browser.

A typical session using `transformNode` might look like:

```
<%
sourceFile=Server.MapPath("src.xml")
styleFile=Server.MapPath("style.xsl")
set
srcDOM=Server.CreateObject("Microsoft.XMLDOM")
srcDOM.async=false
srcDOM.load(sourceFile)
set
styleDOM=Server.CreateObject("Microsoft.XMLDOM")
styleDOM.async=false
styleDOM.load(styleFile)

Response.Write(srcDOM.transformNode(styleDOM))
%>
```

To use `transformNodeToObject` (which Microsoft claims will improve performance), the last line would change to:

```
sourceDOM.transformNodeToObject(styleDOM,
Response)
```

In either case, you may want to set the content-type before writing your response if you're sending output that is anything other than HTML.

> ## TAKE NOTE
>
> ### ▶ THE DOM AND/VS. XSL
>
> A number of XSL's critics have pointed out that there really isn't anything you can do with XSL that you can't do with the DOM API. (There are things you can do with the DOM that are difficult or impossible to do with XSL, though they are done rarely.) Both approaches work with XML documents as trees; in fact, Microsoft blurs the two approaches by using the DOM for its XSL processing and by providing XSL-like pattern-matching capabilities for its DOM implementation.
>
> The difference in style between the two approaches is what drives programmers to choose. If you're most comfortable with writing procedural code (scripts), you'll probably prefer to work with the DOM. If you're more comfortable creating documents, you'll probably prefer XSL. Both approaches work well, and the two can be used together when necessary. Frequently, you'll use procedural code to build a document structure using ASP and the DOM, and XSL to transform it to other formats when necessary. That approach may be easier than writing multiple ASP programs or trying to access database information through experimental XSL-based query languages. If you prefer one or the other, stick with it and use it; just don't try to convince other developers that your approach is the "right" approach.

FIND IT ONLINE

Microsoft offers a Visual Basic tool for building XSL patterns at
http://www.msdn.microsoft.com/downloads/samples/
internet/xml/xsl_pattern_builder/default.asp.

Listing 26-14

```
<?xml version="1.0"?>
<?xml-stylesheet href="paras2.xsl"
type="text/xsl"?>
<document>
<paragraph>This is my <num>first</num>
paragraph.</paragraph>
<paragraph>This is my <num>second</num>
paragraph.</paragraph>
<paragraph>This is my <num>third</num>
paragraph.</paragraph>
</document>
```

▶ *Even though this XML file is simple, older browsers won't recognize it. We'll use some trickery to get around that problem.*

Listing 26-15

```
<%
xmlFile="paras.xml"
set theBrowser=Server.CreateObject("MSWC.
BrowserType")
if ((theBrowser.browser="IE") and (theBrowser.
majorver>4)) then
Response.Redirect(xmlFile)
else sourceFile=Server.MapPath(xmlFile)
set
sourceDOM=Server.CreateObject("Microsoft.XMLDOM")
sourceDOM.async=false
sourceDOM.load(sourceFile)
set
styleDOM=Server.CreateObject("Microsoft.XMLDOM")
styleFile=Server.MapPath("paras2.xsl")
styleDOM.async=false
styleDOM.load(styleFile)
Response.Write(sourceDOM.transformNode(styleDOM))
end if
%>
```

▶ *This browser detection code looks for recent versions of IE. If the browser is older or not IE, we go ahead with the transformation. If the browser is a recent version of IE, we'll redirect it to the original XML, avoiding a lot of server-side processing.*

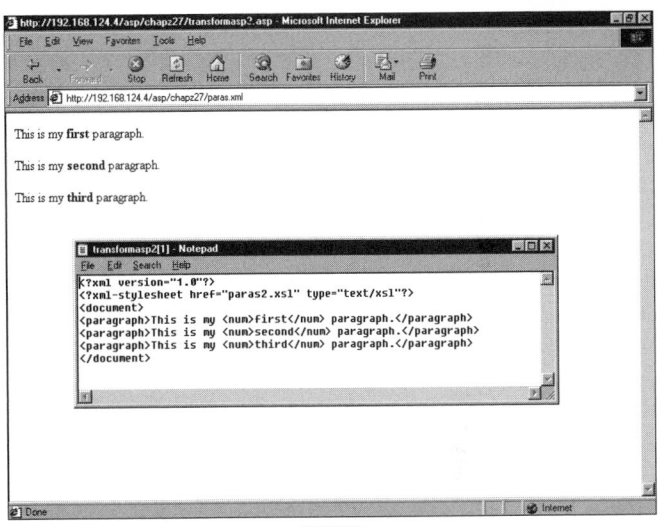

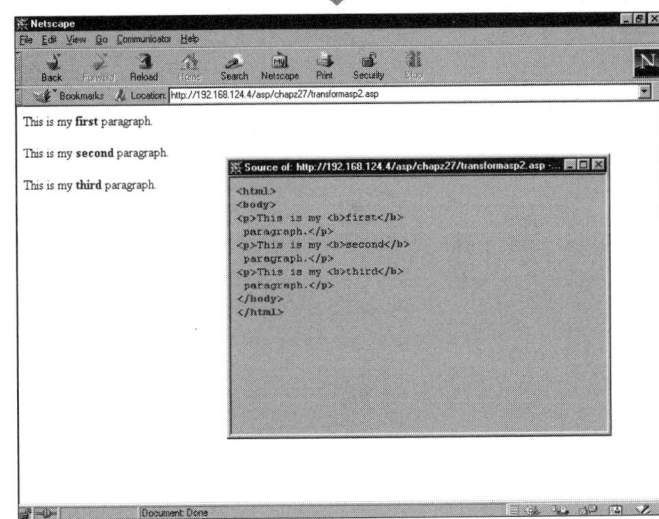

▶ *When Internet Explorer 5.0 or later gets the XML, it does the stylesheet processing itself, presenting it properly but still seeing the XML as the source.*

▶ *When older browsers visit the site, the server performs the conversion and these browsers see HTML as the source document.*

Personal Workbook

Q & A

1 How can I identify XML so that browsers will recognize it?

_____

_____

_____

2 To which browsers can I send XML directly?

_____

_____

_____

3 What does the DOM let me do?

_____

_____

_____

4 Why would I want to convert XML to HTML?

_____

_____

_____

5 Does XSL annotate your documents or transform them?

_____

_____

_____

_____

6 How can I install XSL support for ASP?

_____

_____

_____

_____

7 Can I send XML to non-browser applications?

_____

_____

_____

_____

ANSWERS: PAGE 515

1 Write an XSL stylesheet that converts HTML lists (LI) to paragraphs (P).

2 Write an XSL stylesheet that removes IMG elements but leaves the rest of the document intact.

3 Visit the W3C site (**www.w3.org/TR**) and check out the latest version of the XSLT specification. Figure out what you'll need to change to make your IE5-based code work with the latest version.

4 Write a catalog application that uses an XSL stylesheet to filter information at the user's request.

5 Write a bit of DOM code that generates an XSL stylesheet dynamically.

✔ You need to send information from your Web server to a management server that checks your site periodically. Figure out how to send traffic information to the management server using an XML format.

✔ You have to send database information to users in four countries. Figure out how to support the country-specific information using XSL stylesheets.

✔ You have to provide an interface to a mainframe that sends information as delimited text files. Figure out how best to convert these files to XML using ASP and/or XSL.

CHAPTER **27**

MASTER
THESE
SKILLS

▶ **How Web Applications Can Be Integrated with Tools**

▶ **Planning for the Next Generation of Multitier Web Applications**

▶ **Analyze Browsers and the Client's Impact on Server-Side Programming**

▶ **Break Down the Job of the "server" into Its Many Components**

▶ **Create Architectures for the Next Generation of Web Applications**

Creating Client-Server Web Applications

Active Server Pages enable you to combine many different functions into a single block of code, and it's easy to think of your ASP files as "the application." While this approach will work wonderfully for many different Web development tasks, making ASP work as a foundation for large-scale application development requires stepping back from your code to look at what you've built and where the connections between components are made.

The Web has turned the world of corporate and large-scale software development upside down. Web developers with a variety of skills and different skill levels now operate where a small staff of highly specialized programmers and system administrators once held court. The "client-server revolution" of the early 1990s has turned into a Web development frenzy, for better or worse.

Active Server Pages can provide a central arena for controlling the relationships between data storage and processing on the server and data entry, manipulation, and exploration on the client. While Active Server Pages is certainly a programming environment, in many ways ASP is better described as an interface between the information storage and processing capabilities of the server and the viewing, entry, and editing capabilities of the client.

Moving from the basic foundations of ASP, which you've explored throughout this book, to a sophisticated appreciation of those tools requires examining those tools again and figuring out how best to use them. By writing code that reflects the architecture of the larger project your Active Server Pages represent, you can simplify the design process, make changes less painful to implement, and create applications that can be easily extended to support new user and back-end needs.

ASP is a powerful tool with incredible potential for integrating a wide variety of computing tools. By making the shift from writing code that just gets a job done to creating an application that integrates a variety of tools, you'll find yourself better able to work with tools as they arrive and address those tools to a wide variety of application needs.

Web Architecture in a Client-Server Context

When the Web first arrived, it was a new way to distribute documents to a wide audience at very low cost. The relative simplicity of HTML and the groundswell of free and cheap browsers and Web servers rapidly carried the Web beyond its academic origins. "Brochureware," Web sites that presented information about organizations and products, laid the foundation for the commercial Web as we know it today. At the same time, companies started using internal Webs — intranets — to distribute internal information along similar lines. As these two lines of evolution matured, it became clear that the Web needed to be more than a presentation medium, and extra tools for increasing its interactivity, like forms and CGI, grew more important.

At the same time that the Web was expanding, an older set of "client-server" tools had been bringing new capabilities to large scale systems, enabling developers to create more modular and (theoretically) scalable applications than had been possible in the older mainframe-based text terminal approach. Client-server tools relied heavily on server-side databases for storage and client-side applications for integration with familiar user interfaces. "Middleware" often eased the connection between client and server, but wasn't always needed. This architecture made it possible to build sophisticated interfaces to information stored in a central repository, and let programmers distribute processing. If a task (like searching a database) was better performed on a server, the server could do it. If the task was better performed on a client (like drawing a graph from the results of that search), the client could do it. Arguments over how best to partition applications and which tools to use were both loud and critically important.

As exciting as client-server computing is, it had some drawbacks. Both clients and servers were typically custom-built applications that had to integrate a number of tools. While many of the components of the server end could be bought off the shelf (like databases), most of the client had to be built anew each time. Deciding how best to partition often caused problems among large groups of developers building these applications. All of this led to a high price tag for both construction and maintenance on applications built using this exciting new paradigm.

The Web promised one important improvement over client-server: lower costs for cross-platform applications. By using a generic Web browser and generating HTML on the server, the Web approach eliminated almost the entire cost of building and testing client software. While developers and users paid for these savings in reduced functionality, this approach worked very well for a large number of applications, and adequately for many more. The dramatic reductions in cost and complexity offered by the Web opened up new possibilities, and gave system administrators more direct control over the distribution and maintenance of applications.

Active Server Pages is an important ingredient in this low-cost environment, making it possible for developers to integrate information from a variety of sources and present them as HTML — or, now, XML. While the low-cost route may have taken the Web far, users still demand enhanced functionality. Fortunately, the next generation of Web tools — which can still use ASP as a key component — can provide that functionality without requiring drastic changes in the way Web developers work.

TAKE NOTE

CONVERTING CLIENT-SERVER TO ASP AND BACK

If your client-server application was written as a set of ActiveX components, you may be able to connect those components directly to your Active Server Pages. Similarly, if you had custom components built for your Active Server Pages, you may be able to reuse them in client-server applications.

CROSS-REFERENCE

For a broad view of client-server development, see *The Client-Server Survival Guide (3rd Edition)*, by Robert Orfali, Dan Harkey, and Jeri Edwards (Wiley, 1999).

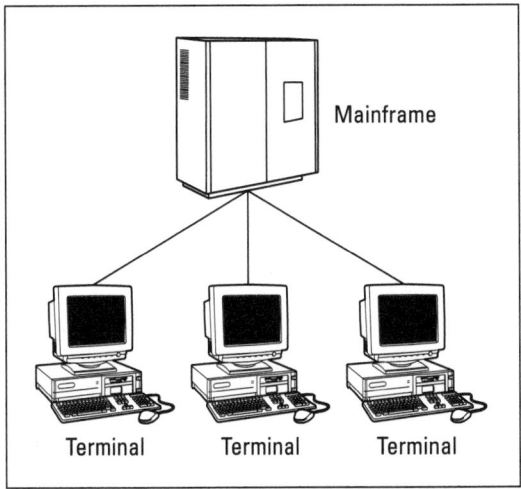

Mainframe

Terminal   Terminal   Terminal

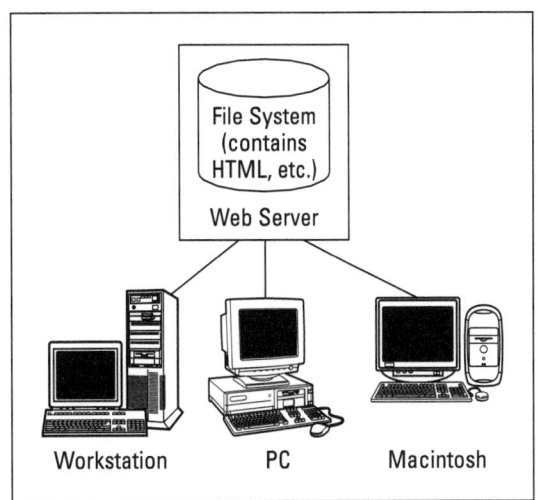

File System (contains HTML, etc.)

Web Server

Workstation   PC   Macintosh

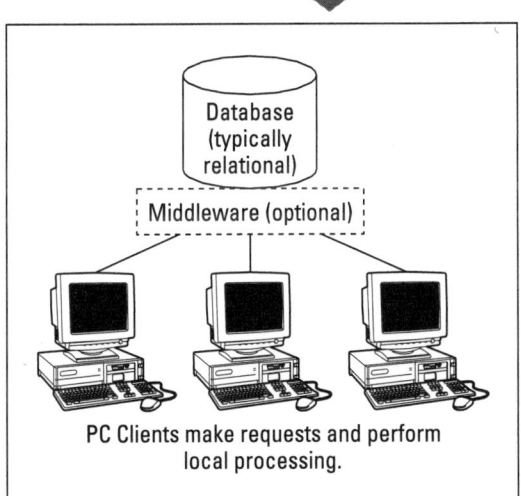

Database (typically relational)

Middleware (optional)

PC Clients make requests and perform local processing.

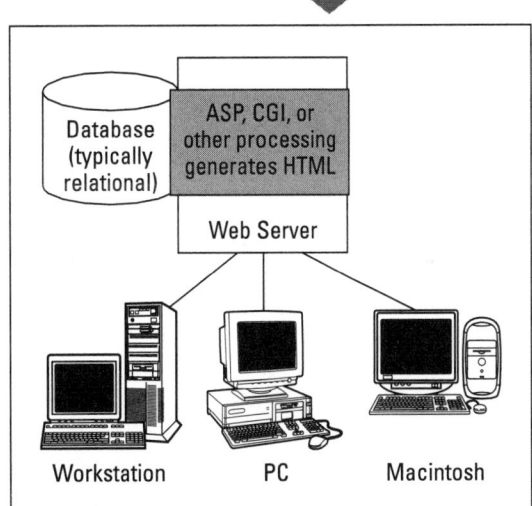

Database (typically relational)

ASP, CGI, or other processing generates HTML

Web Server

Workstation   PC   Macintosh

▶ Mainframe terminals were the original means of sharing centrally stored information with a large group of people.

▶ Client-server applications let developers provide more sophisticated access to information stored on centrally managed systems.

▶ The Web originally gave users access to centrally stored files, letting them create documents and share them.

▶ As the Web developed, more applications began using databases to store key information and built programs connecting those databases to a standard Web interface.

XML, HTML, and Distributed Applications

When HTML first appeared (and even today), many people insisted on calling it a programming language. HTML is merely a format that applications can use to exchange information. While you can edit HTML by hand (and its vocabulary is indeed a markup language), HTML by itself is passive, a set of information that can be processed by applications that understand it. HTML is also a weakly defined language with a limited vocabulary, making it possible — indeed likely — that multiple applications will interpret the same code differently or different code the same. HTML is a "terminal" (or final) format — once information is stored in HTML, it's very hard to extract the meaning of that information from the HTML. It can be copied into another terminal format — like RTF or Microsoft Word — but it's very hard for an application to do something with HTML beyond display and storage.

XML opens up enormous new possibilities for Web applications. Instead of generating "terminal" output, Web applications (including ASP) can generate marked-up information that client applications can then process in a more sophisticated way. XML is transformable, processable, and transferable, while HTML is more often salvageable, if anything. XML promises to give the Web the same kind of power that the client-server model promised, but built using standardized low-cost components.

XML's tight syntax and customizable vocabulary make it possible for information to go through multiple levels of processing between the server and end-users. What might start out as a raw table could be analyzed and turned into a graph anywhere along the way; users could even store information they retrieved from an XML document locally, and pass it to another processor later for further analysis. XML opens up the Web client-server approach so that there are processors, displays, and storage, not just a terminal-like application entirely controlled by the server.

Building on this approach could lead to more sophisticated hybrid client/server applications. Active Server Pages can be run on any Windows 95, 98, or Windows NT computer, making it possible to build "micro-applications" that present a Web interface to certain aspects of a user's machine. This makes it possible for a computer to retrieve and process information at the request of the user, and then make that information available to other users on the network, who may continue the processing. While there is still likely to be a distinction (in processing power, if nothing else) between clients and servers, applications can be distributed this way without the same requirement for a central node managing all of the work.

Web-based applications have suffered for years under the constantly increasing load they've been asked to carry. While technologies like ASP and IIS are available for free, the hardware on which to run them (and the operating system) is not. By taking advantage of underutilized "client" computers, it may indeed be possible to get more work accomplished without purchasing more equipment or having to change technologies. While distributed processing isn't going to cure all problems — and may in fact introduce new ones — it does make it easy to shift work from the server to the client and may give users considerably more control over the results they get.

Another aspect of XML's promise is its independence from any particular technology. XML is generic — applications can easily read XML, regardless of the computer on which they may run. IBM mainframes can share XML information with Windows NT servers. Active Server Pages applications can send XML to Java applications without having to worry about the intense competition between the makers of these two technologies. While it can't do everything, XML does open a lot of new doors to old-time Web development strategies.

FIND IT ONLINE

For more information on emerging and established XML data formats, see **http://www.schema.net**.

Creating Client-Server Web Applications

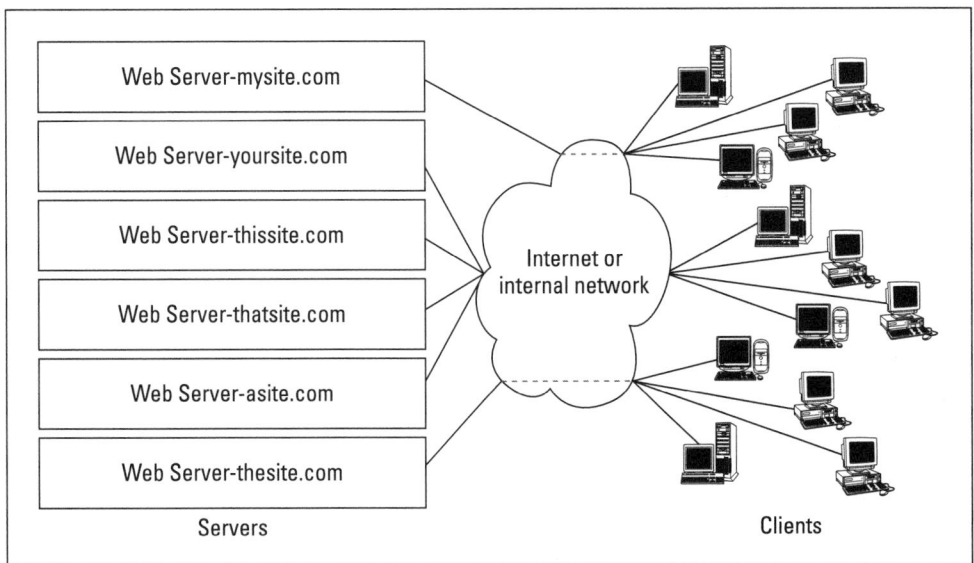

▶ *In the early days of the Web, the distinction between Web servers and browser clients was extremely clear. Web servers were storage and distribution points for information that users explored with browsers.*

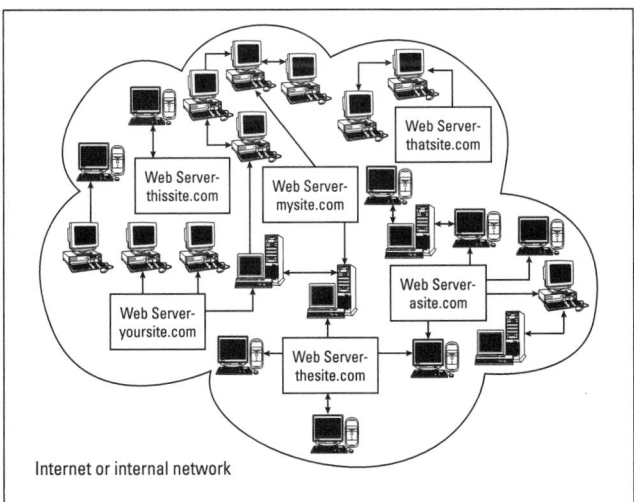

▶ *The rapid growth of XML and its potential for easy transformation opens up new possibilities in distributed computing, where the main distinction between "servers" and "clients" is size, rather than functionality. Clients can now analyze and redistribute information themselves.*

485

Analyzing the Client: How Thin? How Heavy?

Web developers have treated the browser as a screen on which they can project information, enable the user to interact with some of that information (through tools like client-side JavaScript), and collect more information (through forms). The browser has provided a "thin" client capable of presenting information more attractively than the old terminal screens used for mainframe applications, but generally with the same or lower level of interactivity. Although browser vendors have pushed hard to add programmability to their browsers through initiatives like Dynamic HTML, most information processing still takes place on the server, using tools like Active Server Pages.

The advent of XML and the emergence of small devices have broadened the market for Web-based development beyond the original Web browser market. Small Web clients, built into devices like cellular phones, Windows CE devices, and Palm Pilots, aren't capable of handling everything that HTML browsers can do, especially tasks like scripting and graphics support. At the same time, software that looks like a Web browser and uses HTTP to request information may in fact be an enormous application in its own right, collecting and scouring information or presenting it to users in a much more sophisticated way than the average HTML browser.

This significant change in the range of software that may be accessing your Web site should make you consider customizing your content more thoroughly. While browser-detection may have seemed like a small consideration in a world where browsers were mostly comparable, content negotiation is suddenly much more important in a world where the entire concept of a "Web client" is much more amorphous and considerably more flexible.

Both more powerful and less powerful clients offer opportunities for performance enhancement. If a client is capable of doing more of its own processing using XML, then an ASP processor that feeds it straight XML is going to be quicker, and the files probably smaller, than a processor that converts it to HTML. If a client can't handle graphics at all, why bother sending the files? Although most of the portable browser solutions rely on proxy servers that strip out unusable information, "smart" programs that understand what their customers can use thereby can reduce bandwidth consumption significantly and improve server performance.

Developers creating complete application environments — with control over both the server and the client — have many more architectural options as a result of this wider range of clients. Rather than generating graphs on the server and transmitting them as graphics, application developers can pass smaller files to clients, and rely on the clients' otherwise underutilized processing power to reduce the load on the server and create a more customizable experience for the user. Similarly, if developers know in advance that small clients are an important target, they can establish categories of information that are appropriate for different levels of clients and use them to generate appropriate transfers of information.

Although ASP has definitely benefited from the "thin client, powerful server" mentality created by the triumph of the Web interface, it is completely capable of continuing beyond this initial phase and working with clients of many sizes. There are some problems with the new clients that are more difficult to solve than with prior all-Microsoft solutions. Many of the custom components used by ASP could work on the client side as well, making it possible to shift processing rapidly if the client was also a Microsoft browser on a recent Microsoft operating system — a fairly common expectation on many corporate networks. The new possibilities — Java applications as clients, large-scale agent applications scouring the Web for useful information, and handheld devices, not all of them Microsoft — are more of a challenge, but still rich with possibilities.

CROSS-REFERENCE

For more on browser detection tools, see Chapter 18.

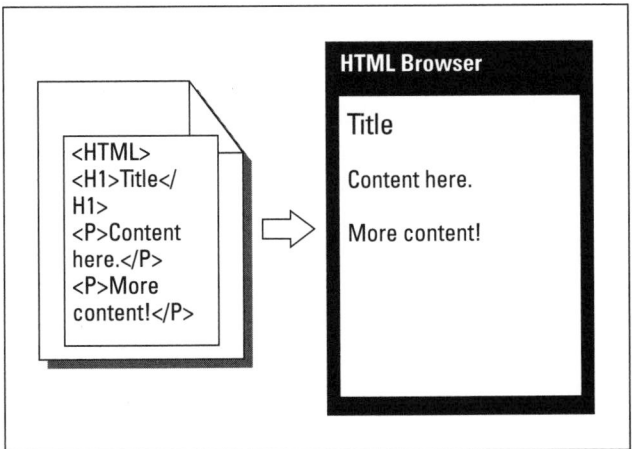

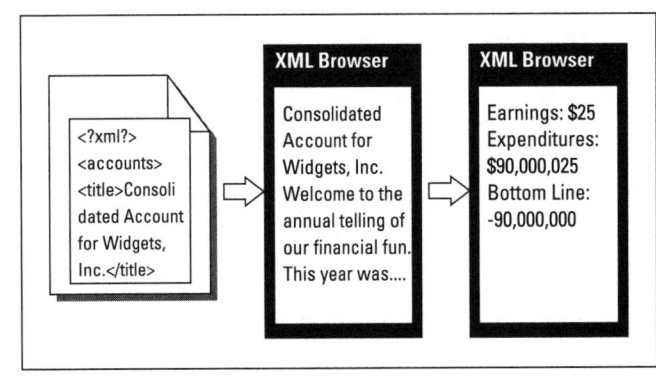

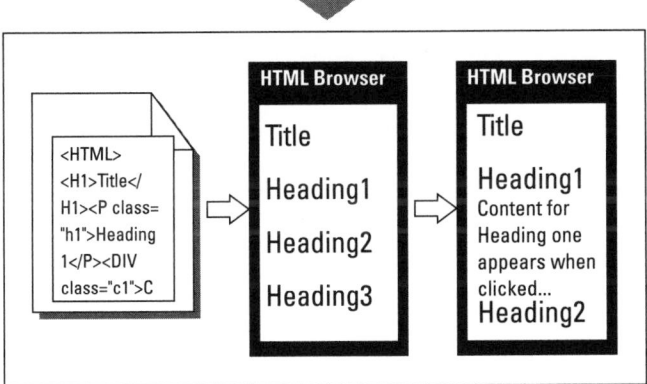

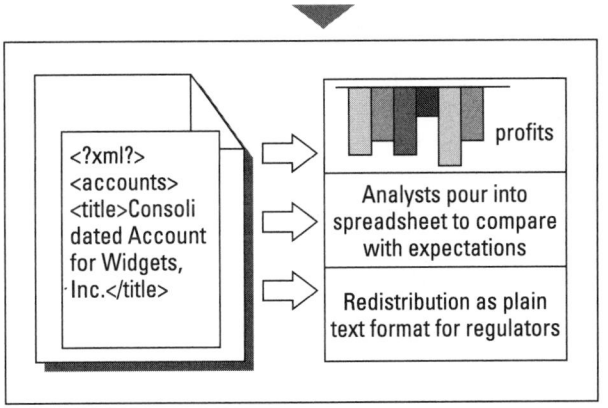

▶ *HTML browsers typically load a document and present it to you in just one way: the way they initially interpret it.*

▶ *HTML browsers that support Dynamic HTML enable you to interact with the document and change its appearance at run time. Typically, this is used for tasks like the expanding outline shown above.*

▶ *XML browsers are capable of displaying the same core information set through different style sheets, allowing for a much broader range of presentation possibilities — including filtering.*

▶ *Clients receiving XML aren't limited to presenting it. They can present it, store it, analyze it, or republish it in a different form.*

Using the Server as Repository and Data Manager

As clients become more capable of processing information on their own, the role of the server must change as well. The change probably won't be drastic, and many traditional HTML browsers will remain in operation, but developers may want to reconsider how they structure their applications to make it easier to separate processing from information storage. Active Server Pages may come to seem like a control room and staging area rather than the "application" itself.

Smarter clients (and clients that simply want less information) can relieve the server of much of the application logic they've needed to support, and even reduce the number of bytes that need to be transmitted per request. This doesn't mean that there's less work for ASP developers to do — it just provides an opportunity to make applications more efficient and better organized.

Servers provide a central point of contact between the client and processing and storage on or behind the server. Servers offer several key features that make interactive Web development possible. First, servers typically provide lots of storage, either in the file system (for lots of HTML, ASP, XML, graphics, and other files) or in databases. Second, servers keep track of users across multiple transactions, letting developers manage "state" as users move through a site. Web servers also provide processing and manage connectivity to other back-end resources.

It isn't always easy to build your applications so that storage, state, information processing, and connectivity are all kept separate. ASP is capable of handling all of these tasks and its structure encourages you to blend all of them into large complex structures that are often difficult to break down again into smaller pieces.

A different approach to Web application development may help you build ASP applications today that are ready for tomorrow's challenges. Thinking about scalability and ways to distribute your application early can make your life much easier if your application hits the big time and is swamped with hits. Simply being able to sort out your application logic from the Web page creation makes it easier to build more efficient components if needed, moving your core logic from interpreted scripting to compiled components. Keeping your state maintenance logic — your session and cookie handling — separate from the body of your documents will enable you to build larger systems that maintain state across multiple servers, if necessary.

Connectivity deserves special attention, especially because security issues crop up whenever an internal system is exposed to the world. While it may not create large problems to gather request information through a Web form and present it to mailing list software as a large text file, riskier situations like credit card handling and exposing databases for editing need a much closer look. Many Active Server Pages act as gateways, connecting users to sensitive internal services. By separating the code that establishes these connections from the code that presents results to the user, you can build applications that can change if the demands for back-end processing or security change.

Breaking down programs this way in Active Server Pages is somewhat difficult, because the whole style of ASP — interspersed code and markup — tends to encourage putting all of your logic into a single page. It doesn't have to be that way, though. You can use server-side includes to connect your ASP documents to modules that exist outside of the page itself, and reuse those modules across multiple documents. This approach may make it easier to convert your script modules to components, by building up a library of common logic kept separately from the demands of individual pages.

CROSS-REFERENCE

Server-side includes (SSIs) are discussed in more detail in Chapter 14.

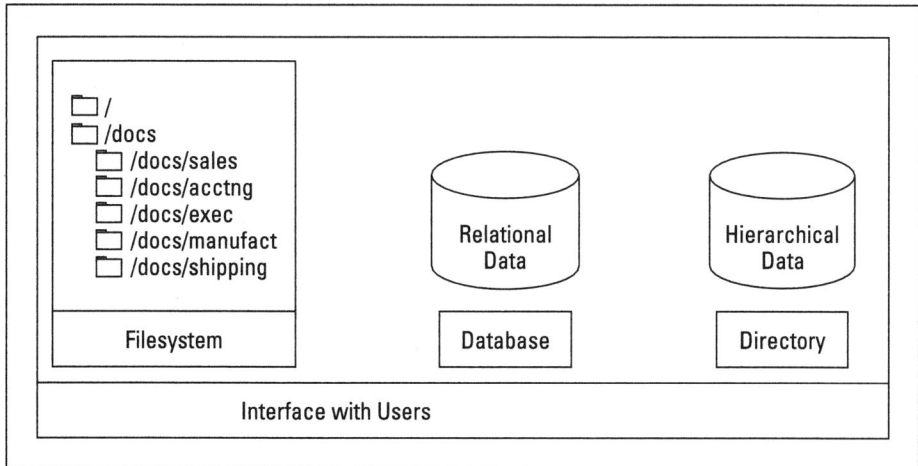

▶ *Treating a server as a large common repository for information gives you a single system that needs to be managed while providing many users with a reliable storehouse.*

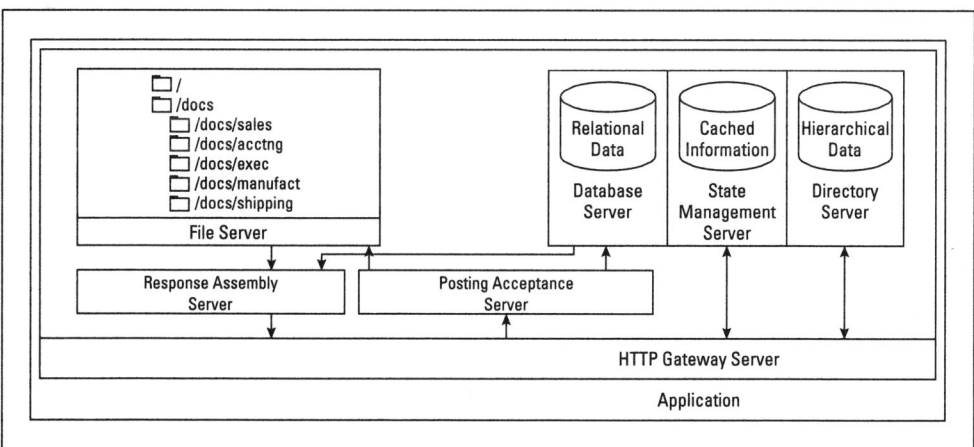

▶ *Making an application scale smoothly may require the integration of multiple servers. In this case, different components have been assigned to different servers, allowing each server to focus on a particular aspect of request processing.*

Multitier Web Applications: ASP as Middleware

Most ASP applications that reference databases operate as three-tier applications: the Web server is the client, the database is the repository, and the Active Server Pages act as middleware, helping the two ends of the conversation interact. In more sophisticated applications, the Active Server Pages themselves interact with middleware, going through extra levels of processing to get information that has already been filtered, transformed, or assembled. As client-side applications start to take advantage of XML and the potential it offers for additional processing, even more layers of processing may appear between the original data source and the view the user finally receives.

Active Server Pages can be an excellent tool for managing the flow of information between these various processors. ASP provides a gateway, using the well-understood and ubiquitous HTTP protocol, between the inside (servers) and the outside (clients). ASP is there to let you interpret all the information received via HTTP so that your servers can use it, and to format the information you're sending out to clients in a way that they can understand. ASP is your gatekeeper, organizer, and mediator. Even if you move from treating ASP as the "application" to considering it the "gateway," ASP has an enormous amount of functionality to offer projects of many scales.

As gatekeeper, ASP can "pre-qualify" your users before giving them access to sensitive information. ASP can provide a Web interface to tools like Microsoft's Active Directory, helping you build more security and more levels of security into your application than authentication alone will provide. Based on information about your users, you could build applications that provided sales data to all of the people in the sales department, but customized the view to show only their own sales in detail and a rough picture of everyone else's sales. Someone else in the company might get the same pages, but with everyone's sales in detail, and someone else might get profit information as well as revenue information.

As organizer, ASP can help you coordinate your back-end services to work smoothly with your client software's expectations. ASP can combine results from multiple sources, or use results from one set of tools to make requests of another. By doing this work in ASP, on the server end, you can take advantage of the much larger bandwidth resources on internal networks to avoid having to make multiple requests on the lower-bandwidth networks that typically connect clients to servers.

As mediator, ASP can help users reach the back-end services they actually need, presenting them with options customized to their requests. Active Server Pages can be combined with cookies to build "smart" pages, which learn which resources users actually need and make those resources more readily available. In conjunction with the gatekeeper function, the mediator function can help you avoid needless processing and produce "just-in-time" pages with minimum wasted effort.

By building your ASP application as a set of components with particular roles, rather than just building pages that work a particular way, you can maximize efficiency and flexibility, developing reusable systems rather than one-shot solutions. ASP is a powerful tool you can use to address many different problems, even when the needs of a particular problem seem very different. As glue, ASP provides integration services that let you manage resources and connect users to information in ways that weren't possible with older models of computing. ASP enables you to present a coherent face to the world. That world may be the public, or it may be employees of a particular company, but ASP offers you the opportunity to give that world the information it wants while giving you control over who gets it and how.

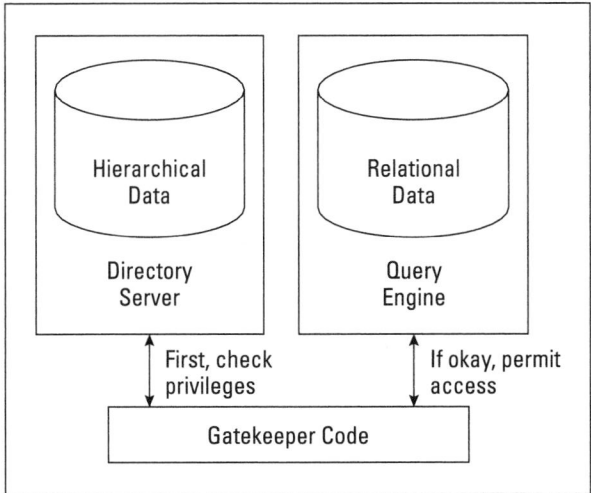

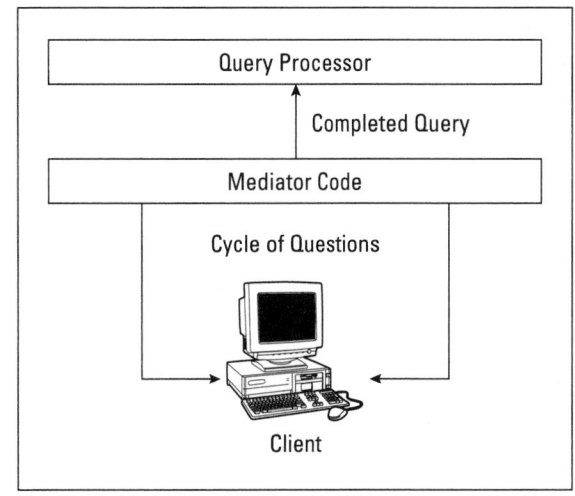

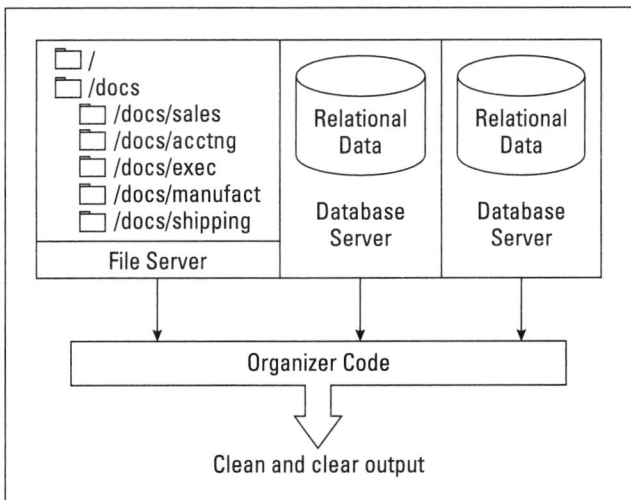

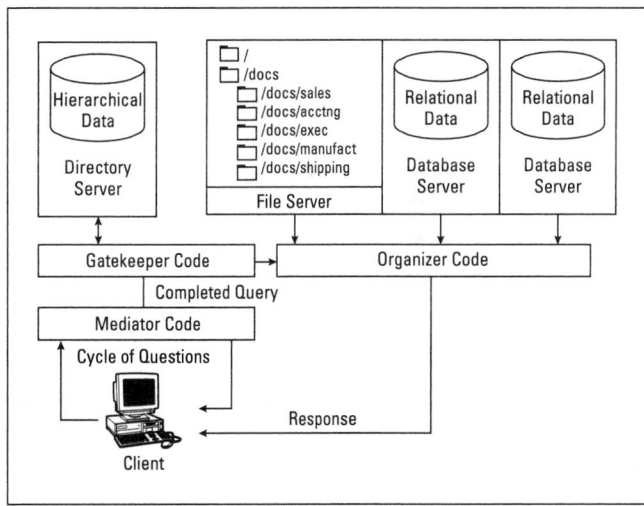

▶ *Active Server Pages can act as a gateway, controlling access to sensitive information in conjunction with a directory server or another authentication database.*

▶ *Active Server Pages can organize the results returned by multiple back-end databases or queries, presenting users with a seamless facade covering what are actually several different data sources.*

▶ *Active Server Pages can act as a mediator, developing queries from user input to build a more appropriate (though perhaps more complex) query than would normally be used.*

▶ *By combining the gatekeeper, organizer, and mediator functions, an application can give users secure, friendly, and appropriate access to information.*

Personal Workbook

Q & A

1 How might the emergence of handheld Web browsers affect your ASP applications?

_____

_____

_____

2 How might the emergence of more powerful and specialized browser-like clients affect your ASP applications?

_____

_____

_____

3 What key advantage helped the Web blossom in the client-server development environment?

_____

_____

4 Can Active Server Pages communicate with Java clients?

_____

_____

5 How can I reuse code modules in ASP?

_____

_____

_____

_____

6 How can I keep track of user preferences?

_____

_____

_____

_____

7 Can ASP technology be used on client computers?

_____

_____

_____

_____

ANSWERS: PAGE 515

Creating Client-Server Web Applications

1. Examine a simple ASP application, such as one that collects user information. How can you break down its functionality?

2. Build a simple ASP application that sends XML to the client and lets the client choose the style sheet.

3. Build a simple database application that assigns users privileges based on their authentication name.

4. If you can borrow or buy a Palm or WinCE device, explore its potential for connecting to the Internet.

5. Examine a complex client-server application. Determine how you could rebuild it using ASP and an XML-aware client.

6. Build an ASP application that combines information from two or more data sources.

✔ After you add graph-generating software to an ASP application, demand slows your performance to a crawl. How could you move this processing to the client?

✔ You have five different databases and a credit-card clearing operation to connect to users. How would your ASP application handle this?

✔ The company that built a client-server application for your firm went out of business without finishing the client end. How can you connect users to the server quickly?

✔ You run a small site presenting news reports to automated agents and the occasional human being. How do you set up ASP to customize those reports based on the requesting software?

Personal Workbook
Answers

Chapter 1

See page 18

1 **What does *ASP* mean? What does it do?**

A: ASP means Active Server Pages. ASP manages all of the technologies, executes them, and converts them to HTML code that almost any browser can handle.

2 **What does IIS represent? What is *IIS*?**

A: IIS is the Microsoft Internet Information Server. IIS is a full-featured Web server that runs on a Windows NT computer.

3 **What does PWS represent? What is *PWS*?**

A: PWS is the Personal Web Manager. PWS is a small Web server that runs on your own personal computer or on the Windows NT Workstation.

4 **How do HTML documents and ASP pages differ?**

A: HTML documents run on a browser. ASP pages run on a server and are viewed on a browser.

5 **What is a *server-side script*?**

A: A server-side script is a script that is interpreted by the server rather than the browser.

6 **What is *scalability*?**

A: Scalability is an application's ability to expand the system to allow for higher numbers of pages and/or visitors to the site.

7 **What delimiters do you use to identify ASP code to a server?**

A: Use the <% delimiter to mark the beginning of ASP code and the %> delimiter to mark the end.

8 **What does *HTTP* represent? What does HTTP do?**

A: Hypertext Transport Protocol (HTTP) is the protocol that enables one computer to send a hypertext document to another computer on the World Wide Web.

Visual Quiz

Q: Circle the beginning of each section of scripting code. Circle the end. Mark the lines that are the same in HTML and ASP.

A: In ASP pages, scripting code starts with the <% delimiter and ends with %>. The lines that are the same in HTML and ASP are the first five lines, the first set of script lines, the third-level heading (starting with <H3>), the paragraph (starting with <P>), and the last two lines.

Chapter 2

See page 34

1 **Who needs to be involved in planning an Internet Information Server installation?**

A: As many people as possible, including system administrators, developers, and content creators.

495

Personal Workbook Answers

2 Where can you download and learn about Internet Information Server?

A: Microsoft's Web site.

3 Which protocol does NT Server use to transmit information over the Internet?

A: TCP/IP, the Transmission Control Protocol/Internet Protocol.

4 Which protocol does Internet Information Server use to support Web traffic?

A: HTTP, the Hypertext Transport Protocol.

5 Which scripting language does Active Server Pages use by default?

A: VBScript, a simplified version of Visual Basic.

6 What tool do you run to administer Internet Information Server?

A: The Internet Service Manager.

7 Why do you need to secure Web servers on internal networks?

A: Sadly, many security breaches are the result of inside jobs, perpetrated by employees rather than outside crackers. Every site with access to important information needs some protection.

8 What TCP/IP port does HTTP use? What TCP/IP port does secure HTTP use?

A: Regular HTTP uses port 80. Secure HTTP uses port 443.

Visual Quiz

Q: Microsoft Management Console lets you control much more than just ASP. Given the opening screen below, how would you zero in on the ASP controls for your Web site named WowScript and turn off the display of full debugging messages for ASP?

A: Open the Internet Information Server Folder under Console Root. Inside, open the server name with your site on it. Then open Default Web Site and look for the WowScript site. Right-click on it and select Properties from the pop-up menu. In the Virtual Directory tab of the Properties dialog box, click the Configuration button. In the Application Configuration dialog box that appears, select the App Debugging tab and select the Send text error message to client radio button. (You can type in your own message if you like.) Then click the OK button on all of these dialog boxes to close them and save your changes.

Chapter 3

See page 48

1 On what platforms can you use the Personal Web Server?

A: PWS is a Web server for the Windows NT Workstation, Windows 98, and Windows 95.

2 What are two ways that you can use PWS?

A: You can use PWS to host a small Web site or to test the Web pages that will be posted to another server.

3 What is *TCP/IP* and what does it do?

A: Transmission Control Protocol/Internet Protocol is two sets of protocols for data communications between computers with the same or different operating systems.

4 What program do you need to install on your computer before installing PWS?

A: To properly install PWS, Internet Explorer 4.01 (or greater) must already be installed on your computer.

5 What is the name of the user interface for PWS?

A: The Personal Web Manager is PWS's user interface.

496

6 **How do you start a guided tour of PWS?**

A: To start a PWS tour, open the Personal Web Manager and click on the Tour icon.

7 **Are the PWS help files stored at an online site?**

A: No; the help files are located on your computer.

8 **How do you control access to your entire Web site?**

A: To stop access, click on the Stop button on the Main window. To restore access, click on Start.

Visual Quiz

Q: Look at the figure and answer these questions. How would you make your Web site unavailable? How would you take a tour of PWS? When did the current PWS session start? How would you display a chart that illustrates the requests per hour? How would you set permissions for a particular directory?

A: Make the Web site unavailable by clicking on the Stop button. Tour PWS by clicking on the Tour icon. The current PWS session started at 10:18 a.m. Display a chart that illustrates the requests per hour by selecting Request per Hour from the View Statistics drop-down list box. To set permissions for a particular directory, click on the Advanced icon, select the desired directory, click on the Edit Properties button, and fill in the Edit Directory dialog box.

Chapter 4

See page 60

1 **Who needs to be involved in choosing your ASP deployment environment?**

A: As many people as possible, especially system administrators and developers.

2 **Where can you download and learn about Chili!Soft ASP?**

A: http://www.chilisoft.com.

3 **What services does Chili!Soft ASP provide to non-Microsoft Web servers?**

A: A complete set of tools for processing Active Server Pages, including scripting languages, Active Data Objects access, and all the built-in ASP objects.

4 **What extra functionality does Chili!Beans provide?**

A: The ability to instantiate and access Java beans much like COM objects are used in Microsoft's ASP.

5 **What ASP features may vary among different Web server platforms?**

A: Server variables and file name and access conventions are two of the most common. Depending on the ASP environment used, different objects, methods, and properties may or may not be available.

6 **How does Halcyon Software's iASP work across different servers and platforms without platform- or server-specific configuration?**

A: iASP is a Java servlet, and can be used on any platform that supports Java and servlets.

7 **Which of the ASP alternatives explored here is open source?**

A: OpenASP, from the ActiveScripting Organization.

8 **Why is it a good idea to install Chili!Soft ASP on off-hours?**

A: You'll need to stop the Web server and restart the entire server.

Chapter 5

See page 76

1 **What do *HTML* and *XML* stand for?**

A: HTML represents the Hypertext Markup Language, and XML represents the Extensible Markup Language.

PERSONAL WORKBOOK ANSWERS

2 **What is a *hypertext link*?**

A: A hypertext link is underlined or highlighted text on which someone browsing through a document can click to jump to other parts of the same document or a completely different document.

3 **What is a *DTD*?**

A: A DTD, or document type definition, specifies the rules for creating documents, contains declarations for markup, default values, and ranges of values.

4 **What is the difference between HTML and XML?**

A: Every component of the HTML language is defined in an SGML DTD. XML is an SGML subset, so you can use XML to create DTDs for custom languages.

5 **What is an *element*?**

A: An element is the markup that instructs a Web browser or processor how to use particular chunks of an HTML or XML document.

6 **What are *start tags* and *end tags*?**

A: Start tags and end tags enclose element names and mark the beginning and end of selected pieces of an HTML or XML document.

7 **What are *attributes*?**

A: Attributes fine-tune the behavior of an element and allow you to change a color, set a value, name the selection, or provide a URL.

8 **What is the difference between markup and character data?**

A: Markup, which is the logical structure of a document, instructs browsers and other processing programs on how to organize and format parts of the document. Character data, which is the physical structure of the document, is all the non-markup content of a document.

Visual Quiz

Q: **Identify the markup and character data in this HTML document. Underline each markup item, and circle the content.**

A: The markup is the entire first line, `<HTML>`, `<HEAD>`, `<TITLE>`, `</TITLE>`, `</HEAD>`, `<BODY>`, both instances of `<P>`, `<B>`, `</B>`, `<STRONG>`, `</STRONG>`, both instances of `</P>`, `<I>`, `</I>`, `<EM>`, `</EM>`, `</BODY>`, and `</HTML>`. The content is everything else in the document; in other words, the text within the start tags and end tags.

Chapter 6

1 **How does a browser or processor identify markup in a document?**

A: Browsers and processors identify markup by looking for delimiters, such as < and >.

2 **How does a processor identify a particular type of markup?**

A: In a DTD, reserved keywords, such as `!ELEMENT` and `!DOCTYPE`, indicate particular types of markup.

3 **What does EBNF stand for?**

A: EBNF standard for Extended Backus-Naur Form (EBNF) notation.

4 **List five EBNF delimiters or connectors.**

A: Some EBNF delimiters are <, >, ", ', (,), [,], and ^. EBNF connectors are , and |.

5 **What is the *root element*?**

A: The top element in a document is the root element.

6 **What are *child elements*?**

A: Child elements are the remaining elements in a document; they are children of the root element.

7 What is an *inline element*?

A: An inline element's content flows from the previous element to the following element without a line break.

8 What is a *block element*?

A: A block element's content starts on a new line and triggers another line break at the end of its display.

Visual Quiz

Q: Identify components in this XML document. Where is the XML version? Mark the symbol that starts the DTD and the symbol that ends the DTD. What is the name of the root element? Circle the root's child element declarations. Circle the children of one of the child elements. Circle the part of the document that will be displayed. Mark one start tag and one end tag. Identify the empty element and show its location in the output text. Circle the entity references.

A: The XML version is `1.0`. The symbols that start and end the DTD are `[` and `]`. The name of the root element is `report`. The child elements declarations are:

```
<!ELEMENT logo    EMPTY>
<!ELEMENT head1   (#PCDATA)>
<!ELEMENT head2   (#PCDATA)>
<!ELEMENT text    (bold|ital)>
```

The children of one of the child elements are `bold` and `ital`. The part of the document that will be displayed are *Introduction* and *Our company has big plans for this year. The following report will go into the details.* Start tags are `<head1>`, `<logo>`, `<head2>`, and `<text>`. End tags are `</head1>`, `</logo>`, `</head2>`, and `</text>`. The empty element is `logo`. Its location in the output text is:

```
<logo src="corplogo.gif"/>
```

The entity references are:

```
<!ENTITY   file01   SYSTEM "file01.doc">
```
and
```
<!ENTITY   file02   SYSTEM "file02.doc">
```

Chapter 7

See page 108

1 Does an HTML document ever include an internal DTD?

A: No. HTML documents sometimes contain an opening line that "calls" an external DTD — a predefined DTD that declares all HTML's elements, attributes, and entities.

2 Do XML documents always include an internal DTD?

A: Yes. XML documents can either have a minimal internal DTD that only refers to an external DTD subset or an internal DTD in which all the elements, attributes, entities, and other markup components are declared.

3 What does the first line of an HTML document look like?

A: The first line of many HTML documents looks something like this: `<!DOCTYPE HTML PUBLIC "-//W3C//DTD HTML 4.0//EN">`.

4 What does the document type declaration of an XML document with an external DTD look like?

A: The document type declaration of an XML document with an external DTD looks as follows: `<!DOCTYPE book SYSTEM "book.dtd">`.

5 What delimiters mark the beginning and end of an internal XML DTD?

A: Start an internal DTD with `[`, and end it with `]`.

6 What declarations can the XML declaration contain?

A: The XML declaration contains the version number, and can include standalone and encoding statements.

Personal Workbook Answers

7 **In a list of child elements, what does the comma separator indicate? What does the pipe indicate?**

A: A comma separator forces the selection of child elements in a set order. The pipe separator allows child elements to be chosen in any order.

8 **What happens when an XML parser encounters an entity reference in a document?**

A: When an XML parser encounters an entity reference, it quickly replaces it with replacement text enclosed within the associated entity declaration.

Visual Quiz

Q: Mark the many things that are wrong with this DTD.

A: The 11 things are

1 The current version of XML is 1.0.
2 The first line does not end with a > delimiter.
3 In the third line, the root element is misspelled.
4 Also in the third line, you cannot declare an element (chap) twice.
5 In the fifth line, a pipe character should separate head1 and head2.
6 The heading1 element declaration does not agree with the head1 listing within the root element.
7 The h2 element declaration does not agree with the head2 listing within the root element.
8 Although the declaration for the text element is correctly written, the commas force a document writer to use normal text, boldface text, and italicized text — one time only and in that order. Use the pipe symbol and add an asterisk to each element (normal*|bold*|ital*).
9 The element declaration norm does not agree with the normal listing within its parent element.
10 The sum element is not listed within the root or another parent element.
11 The end of a DTD should end with one greater-than symbol — not two.

Chapter 8

See page 128

1 **What sets the structure of all HTML and most XML documents?**

A: The DTD sets the structure of all HTML and most XML documents.

2 **What is the name of the first line in many HTML documents and the second line in an XML document?**

A: The first line in many HTML documents and the second line in an XML document is the document type declaration.

3 **What is *metadata*? What HTML element do you use to mark metadata?**

A: Metadata is author, date, or keyword information about the current document entered in the HEAD section at the top of the document. Use one or more META elements to name the author or editor, the creation date or latest edit date.

4 **How do you insert an element in a document? Where do you place attributes and attribute values? Where do you insert character data?**

A: To insert an element in a document, enter a start tag and an end tag. Inside the start tag, add applicable attributes and values. Between the start tag and end tag, enter appropriate character data.

5 **What is the basic rule for embedding a child element under a parent element?**

A: A child element must be completely enclosed within its parent; elements should never overlap.

6 **Write a sample empty element as it appears in an XML document.**

A: A sample XML empty element would look like this:
```
<img src="sample.gif"/>
```

7 Where is a general entity located? Where is a parameter entity?

A: A general entity appears in the body of a document. A parameter entity is located in a DTD.

8 What is a *locator*?

A: A locator is the character-string part of a linking element that names the location of the target.

Visual Quiz

Q: How would you write this HTML document? Use the H1, H3, H6, IMG, P, and A elements. Note that the image is 40 pixels by 40 pixels. [Hint: The URI for Dell is http://www.dell.com/, and the URI for Compaq is http://www.compaq.com/.]

A: The code for this HTML document would look something like this:

```
<!DOCTYPE HTML PUBLIC
    "-//W3C//DTD HTML 4.0//EN">
<HTML>
<HEAD>
<TITLE>Visual Quiz 8</TITLE>
</HEAD>
<BODY>
<H1>A Top-Level Heading</H2>
<H3>A Lower Heading</H3>
<H6>The Lowest Heading of All</H6>
<IMG SRC="redarrow.jpg" height="40"
width="40">
<P>This is one paragraph.</P>
<P>This is another.</P>
<P>Will you buy a
<A href="http://www.dell.com/">
Dell</A>
 or a
<A href="http://www.compaq.com/">
Compaq</A>
 computer?
</BODY>
</HTML>
```

Chapter 9

See page 142

1 What are the basic components of a list?

A: A list has a start tag followed by a number of single or paired list items and, at the end, an end tag.

2 What is the difference in the appearance of items on ordered and unordered lists?

A: Items on ordered lists are preceded by numbers or letters; items on unordered lists are preceded by bullets.

3 Should items on an ordered list be arranged in a particular order?

A: Items on an ordered list should be arranged in a specific sequence, each step depending on the prior one.

4 Can you nest a combination of ordered and unordered lists?

A: Yes. You can compose nested tables of ordered and unordered lists.

5 How do you change the number type or bullet type for a list?

A: Change a number type using the `type` attribute.

6 How do you insert a list in an HTML or XML document?

A: To add a list to a document, begin with a start tag, followed by single or paired list items, and complete the list with an end tag.

7 What is another name for a definition list?

A: Another name for a definition list is glossary.

8 What are the two child elements of a definition list?

A: The child elements of a definition are the definition term and the definition description.

Personal Workbook Answers

Visual Quiz

Q: How would you code this as an HTML document?

A: You could code an HTML document as follows:

```
<!DOCTYPE HTML PUBLIC
    "-//W3C//DTD HTML 4.0//EN">
<HTML>
<HEAD>
<TITLE>Visual Quiz 8</TITLE>
</HEAD>
<BODY>
<H1>Read Me First</H1>
Before you start assembly, perform the
following steps:
<OL>
<LI>Unpack the plastic bag containing the
screws.</LI>
<LI>Count the screws:</LI>
<UL>
<LI>6 1" Phillips</LI>
<LI>10 3/4" Phillips</LI>
<LI>4 1/2" Phillips</LI>
<LI>6 1" Standard</LI>
</UL>
<LI>Check the wooden components.</LI>
<UL>
<LI>6 2x4 — 24" long</LI>
<LI>1 30"x"60" table top</LI>
<LI>2 4"x60" supports</LI>
<LI>6 1" Standard</LI>
</UL>
<LI>Make sure that you have four
casters.</LI>
<LI>Have a Phillips head and standard
screwdriver, rubber mallet, sledgehammer,
bandages, and soft cotton cloths on
hand.</LI>
</OL>
</BODY>
</HTML
```

Chapter 10

See page 156

1 **What components make up a table?**

A: A table is composed of horizontal rows and vertical columns. The *cells*, which are the intersections of rows and columns, contain the actual data.

2 **What are the main table elements in the HTML 4.0 specification?**

A: The main table elements are TABLE, CAPTION, TR, TH, and TD.

3 **What is the characteristic of a *row-centric* table?**

A: Information is added to a row-centric table row by row.

4 **What is the primary difference between an HTML table and an XML table?**

A: Because you define the elements in XML, an XML table can be either row-centric, column-centric, or neither.

5 **When you include both HTML and XML markup in the same document, how should you show the difference?**

A: Many developers use uppercase HTML elements and attributes and lowercase XML elements and attributes.

6 **What elements do you use to define table cells?**

A: Use the TH and TD elements to divide a table into heading cells and data cells, respectively.

7 **How do you split a table into head, foot, and body sections?**

A: Use the THEAD, TFOOT , and TBODY elements to split a table into head, foot, and body sections, respectively.

8 **What attribute of the TABLE element shows or hides borders around a table and its cells?**

A: Use the border attribute to show or hide borders around a table and its cells.

502

Personal Workbook Answers

Visual Quiz

Q: How would you construct this table? [Make sure to properly align the contents of every cell.]

A: You could construct the table as follows:

```
<TABLE BORDER="4" RULES="all" CELL-
PADDING="5" CELLSPACING="0">
<TR>
   <TH>Employee</TH>
   <TH>Address</TH>
   <TH COLSPAN="3" ALIGN="center">
      Distance</TH>
</TR>
<TR>
   <TH></TH>
   <TH></TH>
   <TH><I>Tom</I></TH>
   <TH><I>Dick</I></TH>
   <TH><I>Harry</I></TH>
</TR>
<TR>
   <TD><B><I>Tom</I></B></TD>
   <TD>Main Street</TD>
   <TD ALIGN="center">-</TD>
   <TD>2 miles</TD>
   <TD>4 miles</TD>
</TR>
<TR>
   <TD><B><I>Dick</I></B></TD>
   <TD>Maple Lane</TD>
   <TD>2 mile</TD>
   <TD ALIGN="center">-</TD>
   <TD>6 miles</TD>
</TR>
<TR>
   <TD><B><I>Harry</I></B></TD>
   <TD>Ray Way</TD>
   <TD>4 miles</TD>
   <TD>6 miles</TD>
   <TD ALIGN="center">-</TD>
</TR>
</TR>
<CAPTION ALIGN="bottom">
<I>Car Pooling Table</I>
</CAPTION>
</TABLE>
```

Chapter 11

See page 172

1 What is a *frame*?

A: A frame is a small window that displays an entire or partial Web document.

2 What is a *frameset*?

A: A frameset is a set of frames.

3 Does XML support the use of frames and framesets?

A: The current version of XML does not support the use of frames.

4 What does the HTML FRAMESET element do?

A: Using the FRAMESET element, you can define the number of frames in a frameset, set the percentage of the window devoted to each frame, and specify certain characteristics for the set.

5 What does the HTML FRAME element do?

A: The FRAME element names the URI for the target document that will appear in the frame and provides attributes with which you can affect the look and content of the frame.

6 What start and end tags do the **<FRAMESET>** and **</FRAMESET>** tags replace in HTML frameset documents?

A: In a frameset document, the <FRAMESET> and </FRAMESET> tags replace the <BODY> and </BODY> tags.

PERSONAL WORKBOOK ANSWERS

7 What attribute do you use to control the display of a scroll bar in a frame? From what values can you choose for this attribute?

A: Use the `scrolling` attribute to insert or hide a scroll bar. Enter `scrolling="yes"` to always insert a scroll bar, `scrolling="no"` to omit a scroll bar, or `scrolling="auto"` to insert a scroll bar if the document content is greater than the limits of the frame.

8 When you have a frames site, how do you deal with browsers that do not support frames?

A: Whenever you design a set of frames-based Web documents, you should always include a "no-frames" section using HTML's `NOFRAMES` element.

Visual Quiz

Q: How would you code this frameset?

A: You could code this frameset as follows:

```
<!DOCTYPE HTML PUBLIC "-//W3C//DTD HTML
4.0//EN">
<HTML>
<HEAD>
<TITLE>Frames</TITLE>
</HEAD>
<FRAMESET COLS=50%,*>
    <FRAME SRC="frame1.htm">
    <FRAMESET ROWS=50%,*>
        <FRAME SRC="frame2.htm">
        <FRAMESET COLS=50%,*>
            <FRAME SRC="frame3.htm">
            <FRAME SRC="frame4.htm">
        </FRAMESET>
    </FRAMESET>
</FRAMESET>
</HTML>
```

Chapter 12

See page 188

1 What types of databases should online retailers use at their sites?

A: Retailers should use customer-information databases and inventory databases.

2 What is a *database field*?

A: A field contains one piece of information.

3 What is a *database record*?

A: A record is composed of a group of related fields.

4 What is a *form*?

A: A form enables you to enter information into database records.

5 What is a *control* in an HTML form?

A: A control is an individual component within a form.

6 List the HTML control types.

A: HTML control types are the checkbox, file select, hidden, menu, object, radio button, reset, submit, multiple-line text box, and the single-line text box.

7 What HTML element starts and ends a form?

A: The `FORM` element marks the start and end of a form.

8 What is an *extension*?

A: An extension is an element that *extends* beyond the current HTML version but is not an "official" part of the version.

PERSONAL WORKBOOK ANSWERS

Visual Quiz

Q: How would you code this HTML input form? Use the `checked` attribute for the American radio button. Use the `value` attribute to label the command buttons. [Hint: For other help, look at the element declarations on some of the facing pages in this chapter.]

A: One way to code the HTML input form is as follows:

```
<!DOCTYPE HTML PUBLIC
    "-//W3C//DTD HTML 4.0//EN">
<HTML>
<HEAD>
<TITLE>Visual Quiz 12</TITLE>
</HEAD>
<BODY>
<H1>Visual Quiz 12</H1>
<P>Choose a menu:</P>
<FORM action="cgi-bin/form-example"
method="post">
<INPUT type="radio" name="American"
checked><B> American<B><BR>
<INPUT type="radio" name="Italian"><B>
Italian</B><BR>
<INPUT type="radio" name="French"><B>
French</B><BR>
<INPUT type="radio" name="Chinese"><B>
Chinese</B>
<P>What's your full name?
<INPUT type="text" name="name"
size="40"></P>
<P>What's your email address:
<INPUT type="text" name="email"
size="30"></P>
<P><INPUT type="submit" value="Send
Form">
<INPUT type="reset" value="Clear
Form"></P>
</FORM>
</BODY>
</HTML>
```

Chapter 13

See page 206

1 When you associate a stylesheet with an HTML or XML document, what happens?

A: When you associate a stylesheet with a document, you can govern the appearance of that document.

2 What is the main difference between stylesheets for HTML documents and those for XML documents?

A: XML does not allow for formatting and enhancing elements and attributes: all the XML documents designed for output onscreen or in printed format *must* be associated with stylesheets.

3 What does *CSS* represent? What is the latest version of CSS?

A: CSS represents cascading stylesheets. CSS is in its second version at the time of this writing.

4 What does *XSL* represent? Is XSL an official specification?

A: XSL represents Extensible Style sheet Language. XSL is currently a working draft.

5 What is a style-sheet *rule* made up of?

A: A style-sheet rule is composed of two parts: The *selector* is the HTML or XML element to which the rule applies, and the *declaration* consists of the property (similar to an attribute) and the value — both within brackets.

6 What is the *baseline*?

A: The baseline is the invisible line on which a character sets in a line of text.

PERSONAL WORKBOOK ANSWERS

7 **What is the *x-height*?**

A: The x-height is the measurement of the body of a low-ercase character from the top of the character down to the baseline.

8 **What CSS properties set spaces between words and between characters?**

A: The `letter-spacing` property sets the space between two characters. The `word-spacing` property determines the space between two words.

Visual Quiz

Q: Identify the bad syntax in this stylesheet.

A: On the first line, `.doc`, which is most likely a word-processing document extension, should not be the extension of a background image; the most popular image extensions for Web pages are `.gif` and `.jpg`. The margin property line should end with a semi-colon, which indicates the end of a particular property but not the set of properties for an element. The `text-indent` property does not include an underscore. `P.title` is the proper way to represent the title class of the `P` element. The `margin` property incorrectly contains five margins, which is one margin over the limit. The proper use of the identifier selector is `P#135`. `Tms New` is probably not the name of a valid font. Although you can surround Courier with quotation marks, there is no reason to. Use quotation marks to enclose names composed of two or more words.

Chapter 14

See page 226

1 **What is the main difference between HTML documents and ASP pages?**

A: HTML documents are run on the client, and ASP pages are run on the server.

2 **What are *server-side includes*?**

A: Server-side includes (SSIs) are commands with which you can add a file, provide information, or specify how to use an object in your ASP pages.

3 **What is the only SSI supported by ASP?**

A: The only SSI supported by ASP is `#INCLUDE`.

4 **What are *objects*?**

A: Objects are variables made up of their definitions and any associated data.

5 **Name five of HTML 4.0's intrinsic events.**

A: HTML 4.0's intrinsic events are `onblur`, `onchange`, `onclick`, `ondblclick`, `onfocus`, `onkeydown`, `onkeypress`, `onkeyup`, `onload`, `onmousedown`, `onmousemove`, `onmouseout`, `onmouseup`, `onreset`, `onselect`, `onsubmit`, and `onunload`.

6 **What are *packets*?**

A: Packets are bundles of data of varying sizes that are transmitted from one computer to another.

7 **What does the `document.write` command do?**

A: The `document.write` command displays a document object onscreen.

8 **What is ASP's counterpart to the `document.write` command?**

A: The `response.write` command is the ASP counterpart to `document.write`.

Visual Quiz

Q: This is an HTML document that needs its architecture addressed. Edit the document so that it is easier to understand.

A: One way of editing the document is as follows:
```
<HTML>
<HEAD>
<TITLE>A Sample HTML Document</TITLE>
```

```
</HEAD>
<BODY BGCOLOR="white">
<H1>Lists</H1>
Thanks for visiting. On this page, you'll
see an
<A HREF="http://www.eddygrp.com/OL">or-
dered list</A> and an
<A HREF="http://www.eddygrp.com/UL">
unordered list.</A>
<H3>An Ordered List</H3>
<OL>
    <LI>Do this step.</LI>
    <LI>Then do this step.</LI>
    <LI>Do it all over again starting at
the top.</LI>
</OL>
<H3>An Unordered List</H3>
<UL>
    <LI>Planes</LI>
    <LI>Trains</LI>
    <LI>Automobiles</LI>
    </UL>
<CENTER>
    <IMG SRC="scene.gif">
</CENTER>
</BODY>
</HTML>
```

Chapter 15

See page 240

1 What is VBScript's full name? What is VBScript's origin?

A: VBScript's full name is Visual Basic Scripting. VBScript is a subset of Microsoft's Visual Basic, which in turn is an updated and sophisticated version of the BASIC programming language.

2 Can VBScript scripts run on a client computer?

A: VBScript scripts run either on the client computer or the server.

3 What is a *constant*? What VBScript statement do you use to specify a constant.

A: A constant is a value that never changes. Specify constants with the Const statement.

4 What is a *variable*?

A: A variable is a user-defined name that represents varying data of all types.

5 What is a *conditional statement*?

A: A conditional statement includes two or more branches to different sections of a script.

6 What is a *subroutine*? How do you mark the beginning and end of a VBScript subroutine?

A: A subroutine is a section of script that is processed as a unit. Mark the beginning and end of a VBScript subroutine with the Sub and End Sub statements.

7 What is a *looping statement*?

A: A looping statement enables a Web processor to repeatedly calculate a formula nested within the loop until a particular value is reached or a condition remains or becomes true.

8 What type of looping statement keeps looping as long as a condition is true or when a false condition becomes true?

A: A Do... Loop keeps looping as long as a condition is true or when a false condition becomes true.

PERSONAL WORKBOOK ANSWERS

Visual Quiz

Q: This HTML document includes a VBScript script that has never been tested. Correct the errors, and convert the document to an ASP page.

A: One way of correcting this document is as follows:

```
<HTML>
<HEAD>
<TITLE>Visual Quiz 15</TITLE>
</HEAD>
<BODY>
<%
Dim Arrividerci, Adios
Arrividerci = "Hi There"
Adios = "Aloha"
Response.Write Arrividerci %>
<BR>
<% Response.Write Adios %>
<BR>
<% Response.Write "Goodbye Again" %>
</BODY>
</HTML>
```

Chapter 16

See page 254

① Can JavaScript call routines written in Java?

A: Yes. JavaScript can call routines written in Java.

② Are JavaScript, JScript, and ECMAScript bundled with IIS and PWS?

A: Of JavaScript, JScript, and ECMAScript, only JScript is bundled with IIS and PWS.

③ What does the acronym *ECMA* represent? What does ECMA do? What is another name for ECMAScript?

A: ECMA is the European Computer Manufacturers Association. ECMA is a standards organization. ECMA-262 is another name for ECMAScript.

④ What is a JScript *method*?

A: A method is a keyword that acts as an attribute for an object.

⑤ What is the JScript operator for incrementing? For the indexing of arrays? For a logical AND?

A: The JScript increment operator is ++, the operator for array indexes is [ ], and for logical AND is &&.

⑥ When you declare a variable in JScript, do you use the `Dim` statement?

A: No. JScript does not support the `Dim` statement.

⑦ How do you declare multiple values for a variable?

A: Use an array to declare multiple values for a variable.

⑧ What are the differences between the `for` and `while` statement?

A: The main difference between the `for` and `while` statements is that the `for` statement loops as long as a condition is true, and `while` loops until a condition is false. Another difference is that a `for` statement initializes and increments an expression, and `while` does not.

Visual Quiz

Q: This HTML document includes a JScript script that has never been tested. Correct all the HTML and JScript errors, and convert the document to an ASP page.

A: You could convert this HTML document into an ASP page as follows:

```
<HTML>
<HEAD>
<TITLE>Visual Quiz 16</TITLE>
</HEAD>
<BODY>
<%
Greeting = "Hi There";
Adios = "aloha";
response.write(Greeting);
```

```
response.write(Adios);
response.write("Goodbye Again");
%>
</BODY>
</HMTL>
```

Chapter 17

See page 276

1 Describe the relationship of PerlScript to Perl.

A: PerlScript is a module that connects Perl (all of it, not a subset) to Microsoft's scripting hosts.

2 Where can you find the PerlScript distribution?

A: At http://www.activestate.com.

3 How do you tell IIS to use PerlScript for all of the code in a document?

A: Use the @LANGUAGE preprocessing directive.

4 Can you use COM objects with PerlScript Active Server Pages?

A: Yes, it all works the same. You'll need to use Perl's object syntax ($Response->write() rather than Response.write(), for example), but the names and operations are the same.

5 How can I make my CGI programs run under IIS?

A: You can use the Win32::ASP::CGI module, or just run them using the Perl ISAPI functionality that comes in the PerlScript distribution.

6 Where can I find more Perl modules to use with Active Server Pages?

A: The CPAN archives, at http://www.perl.com.

7 Which operators use regular expressions?

A: The m// and s/// operators, as well as Perl's split function. Note that tr/// does *not* use regular expressions.

Chapter 18

See page 290

1 What is the *Browser Capabilities Component*? What does it do?

A: The Browser Capabilities Component is a utility that lists browser information: its name, version, and technologies that it supports.

2 What are *installable components*? Name the installable components that are bundled with IIS and PWS.

A: Installable components are applets that are part of the set of software bundled with the server. Installable components include an advertisement rotator, page counter, ActiveX Data Objects (ADO), and the Browsers Capabilities Component.

3 What is *encryption*?

A: Encryption is a process that changes the text characters into a code that is unreadable.

4 What is a *key*? Name the two key technologies.

A: A key uses secret knowledge for encrypting and decrypting. There are two key technologies: secret or symmetric key and public key.

5 What is *authentication*?

A: Authentication is a process by which user information is validated by the computer or network, usually by matching it against a list of identifiers and passwords.

6 What is *global.asa*?

A: The global.asa file is a text file that you can edit to include variables that control events that are processed when an application or session starts or ends.

7 How can you end a VBScript section early?

A: The Exit statement enables you to exit a VBScript section before it is programmed to end.

PERSONAL WORKBOOK ANSWERS

8 What is *transformation*?

A: Document transformation is the translation of a document from the markup language in which it is written to another language.

Visual Quiz

Q: This is the result of a transformation from a word processor file to an HTML document. Change the title to a better one. Convert the heading to a large point size. Remove extra elements and default attributes, and improve the format of the document.

A: The improved document could look something like this:

```
<HTML>
<HEAD>
<TITLE>A Sample HTML Page</TITLE>
</HEAD>
<BODY>
<H2>A Sample HTML Page</H2>
<P>This page shows samples of HTML
elements.
<P>This is a bulleted list.
<UL TYPE="disc">
    <LI>Computers
    <LI>Printers
    <LI>Zip Drives
</UL>
This is a numbered list.
<OL>
    <LI>Start the engine.
    <LI>Put it into gear.
    <LI>Take your foot off the brake.
    <LI>Hit the gas pedal.
</OL>
</BODY>
</HTML>
```

Chapter 19

See page 318

1 What object and method is used to gain access to external objects?

A: Server.CreateObject

2 What will be the outcome of the following code?

```
<html>
<head>
<title>Moving On</title>
</head>
<body>
<% Response.Redirect "aBetterPage.asp"
%>
</body>
</html>
```

A: An error would be generated because the Redirect method writes an HTTP response header, and all headers must be written before the first content data is sent to the client.

3 How do you access the HTML form variable ("email") if the form is submitted to an ASP script with the POST method?

A: You display the email HTML form variable by using the following ASP statement:
`<% =Request.Form("email") %>`.

4 What are spaces replaced with when using Server.URLEncode?

A: All the spaces are replaced by plus signs (+).

5 Show two different ways to retrieve the value of the variable email from an HTML form from the client's browser using the Request object.

A: Request.Querystring("email") or Request.Form("email")

6 If the GET method is used to submit data in an HTML form to an ASP script, is there a limit placed on the size of HTML form data?

A: Yes. Do not use the GET method if you expect data entered by the user to exceed about 1,000 characters.

7 What method is recommended for submitting data from HTML forms to an ASP script?

A: The POST method is recommended for submitting data from HTML forms to an ASP script. You have the potential to lose data using the GET method if the user submits a form with too much data.

Chapter 20

See page 334

1 What advantages do component-based development systems offer?

A: Easy extensibility through cheap and easily reusable components.

2 Which components are built-in to ASP and available with every request?

A: The Request, Response, Server, Application, and ObjectContext components.

3 Which built-in object do you use to instantiate objects based on installed components?

A: The Server object and its CreateObject method.

4 Can you use COM objects from Internet Explorer with Active Server Pages?

A: Yes, they use the same interfaces. Not all of IE's objects will be useful, of course.

5 Which Windows utility can you use to install components from the command line?

A: RegSvr32.

6 Where can I find more COM components to use with Active Server Pages?

A: Microsoft provides a number for free, sites like www.asp101.com provide links to vendors, and catalogs like Programmer's Paradise offer a wide selection.

7 Where are initialization files for COM components stored?

A: It depends on the component. Not all components have initialization files, but those that do typically find the file in the same location as the DLL containing the component. Check the documentation for each component.

8 When do I need to build my own COM components?

A: If scripting isn't adequate for the task, and you can't find any component that someone else has built that addresses your needs, it may be time to explore COM development.

Chapter 21

See page 360

1 What two things should you check to see whether a recordset is empty?

A: You should check both the BOF and EOF properties of the recordset. If both are true, then the recordset is empty.

2 What type of DSN is recommended?

A: There are three types of DSNs, but primarily you will use the System DSN. System DSNs are available to all users of the computer for which it is defined, including Windows NT services. For this reason, it is the DSN ordinarily used with the Internet.

PERSONAL WORKBOOK ANSWERS

3 How would you include the ADO constant definition file in an ASP page?

A: You can include the ADO constant definitions file easily by copying it to the Includes directory of your Web Server's document root directory and using the following statement at the beginning of the ASP page:

```
<!–# virtual = "\includes\adovbs.inc" –>
```

4 Name three different data sources, that ASP can connect to using ADO.

A: DBMS sources: Oracle, SQL Server, Microsoft Access. Non-DBMS sources: indexed-sequential files, email, spreadsheets (Excel), project management tools.

5 How do you close Recordset and ADO Connection objects so that the resources used by these objects are returned to your system?

A: You can proactively call Close and set the Connection variable to Nothing when you know that you will no longer need a connection. This frees up resources before it actually goes out of scope.

6 Name two methods of the Connection object.

A: Choose two from the following: Open, Close, Execute, BeginTrans, CommitTrans, and RollbackTrans.

7 What is the first step in using the Command Object?

A: The first step in using the Command object is to specify the ActiveConnection you want to use it against.

```
Set oCmd = Server.CreateObject("ADODB.
Command")
oCmd.ActiveConection = "DSN=Northwind;
UID=guest;PWD=guest"
```

8 What is the most widely accepted database model in use today?

A: Today, the most widely accepted database model is the relational model.

Chapter 22

See page 380

1 What property of the NewMail object is used to set the priority of an email message?

A: You can use the Importance property of the NewMail object to set the priority of a message.

2 Can you use CDO to send things other than a regular text message?

A: You can use the CDO to send messages that include HTML formatting and images.

3 What does the Content Link file contain?

A: The Content Linking List file contains a simple list of page URLs, in the order they are to be displayed.

4 What does the Ad Rotator component do?

A: Using the Ad Rotator component, you can create a Web page that chooses a random banner advertisement every time it is viewed.

5 True or False. Advertisement images of any size can be cycled on a Web page using the Ad Rotator component.

A: All advertisements to be rotated in an area must be exactly the same size.

6 What property of the Dictionary object will show the number of key/item pairs?

A: The Count property holds the number of key/item pairs in the Dictionary object.

PERSONAL WORKBOOK ANSWERS

7 **Which object provides access to the computer's file system?**

A: The FileSystemObject object provides access to the computer's file system, allowing you to manipulate text files, folders and drives from within your code.

8 **Which directory does SMTP use to send mail?**

A: The SMTP service uses a Pickup directory to send mail and is located in the InetPub/MailRoot directory.

Chapter 23

See page 408

1 **Why must you limit the use of SELECT * statements?**

A: You should not use a SELECT * statement to retrieve all the records in a table. Instead, use a SQL statement to filter the data. As much as possible, get the database server to select and filter the data for you.

2 **True or False. The Recordset.RecordCount property always returns the correct number of records.**

A: False. The RecordCount property is not supported by forward-only or dynamic cursors. When used with either of these cursor types, the RecordCount property always returns the value -1.

3 **What are the modifying clauses available to the SELECT statement in SQL?**

A: The modifying clauses available in SQL are FROM, WHERE, HAVING, GROUP BY, AND ORDER BY.

4 **If you are using VBScript, what keywords should you put at the top of every page to ensure that you declare each variable in your ASP script?**

A: If you are using VBScript, make sure every script has the "Option Explicit" keywords at the top of every page. This way you must explicitly create every variable you want to use.

5 **Name two common mistakes programmers tend to make when building SQL statements and how to get around them.**

A: When building SQL statements, there are several common mistakes developers tend to make. To get around these mistakes, take the following steps: Text fields must have single quotes around the values; Fields with spaces in their names must be surrounded with []; Text fields with single quotes cannot be placed into SQL statements unmodified. You must transform a single quote, ', to double single quotes, ''.

6 **What are the characters that SQL uses to identify partial matches? And how are they different?**

A: To identify partial matches, SQL makes use of two wildcard characters. The percent sign (%) can stand for any string of characters, zero or more characters in length. The underscore (_) stands for any single character.

7 **What factor has the greatest impact on the performance of your database and queries when designing your database?**

A: Your choice of indexes for your database tables has the greatest impact on the performance of your queries.

8 **What is the firehouse cursor?**

A: When the default cursor is opened, it is often called a firehose cursor. Because the connection is kept open and the results of the query are blasted to your application as fast as possible.

Chapter 24

See page 430

1 **What is a transaction?**

A: A transaction is an atomic unit of work that either fails or succeeds.

513

PERSONAL WORKBOOK ANSWERS

2 **What SQL statement can you use to remove data from a table?**

A: You can delete all the rows in a table by using a single DELETE statement, or you can restrict the deletion to only selected rows by adding a WHERE clause.

3 **What are the ACID characteristics of a transaction?**

A: Transaction processing systems ensure that transactions are atomic, consistent, isolated, and durable. These characteristics are known as ACID, which is an acronym for atomicity, consistency, isolation and durability.

4 **What is the SetAbort method used for?**

A: Sets the work of an object as a failure and returns the resource to its original state, neglecting any changes made to the resource.

5 **How does ASP know to use page-level transactional processing?**

A: ASP uses the Transaction directive to initiate page-level transactional processing. When the scripting engine processes this directive, your ASP script is executed as a transaction on MTS. To initiate your pages as a transaction, use the following directive in the first line of your ASP script: <%@ Transaction = Required %>

6 **Is the WHERE optional when using the UPDATE statement?**

A: The WHERE clause is optional. This clause specifies the rows that you are updating. If you do not use a WHERE clause, all the rows in the table are updated.

7 **What are two competitors to Microsoft Transaction Server?**

A: The two closest competitors to MTS are CORBA-compliant Object Request Brokers (ORBs) that support the Object Transaction Service and Sun's Enterprise JavaBeans strategy.

Chapter 25

See page 454

1 **Are cookies harmful to the user's computer?**

A: Cookies are actually helpful to the user because they enable Web application developers to make it easier for users to use the Internet.

2 **How do you delete a cookie?**

A: Set the cookie's expiration date attribute to a date that has already passed, as follows: Response.Cookie("userName").Expires = "December 31, 1990"

3 **Which ASP object is used to create a cookie?**

A: The Response object is used to create a cookie.

4 **Is there a limit to the number of cookies that can be created by a server?**

A: Yes, each server can create only 20 cookies.

5 **Name two things that can cause a user's session to end.**

A: Any two of these answers: The session can time out, you can call Session.Abandon or the Web server stops running.

6 **What is the default time of a session?**

A: 20 minutes.

7 **I want an object to be available to all my users. Does it matter whether I put it into the Application or Session Object?**

A: Yes and no. Placing it in either object will make it available to all your users. The difference is memory usage. If you create an object and add it to the Session object's collection, you are creating a copy for every single session. Placing it in the Application object makes it available to everyone, but only a single copy is required.

Personal Workbook Answers

Chapter 26

See page 478

1 How can I identify XML so that browsers will recognize it?

A: Map a MIME content-type of text/xml or application/xml to your XML file extensions.

2 Which browsers can I send XML to directly?

A: Internet Explorer 5.0 or later will accept XML. Netscape's 'Mozilla' will also accept XML, though it will probably use a different set of XSL tools.

3 What does the DOM let me do?

A: The Document Object Model lets you manipulate document information as a set of components rather than as a single stream of text.

4 Why would I want to convert XML to HTML?

A: When you need to present XML, you can use cascading style sheets (which work only on Internet Explorer 5 or later and Mozilla), or you can convert it to HTML.

5 Does XSL annotate your documents or transform them?.

A: XSL transforms your documents into new 'result' documents.

6 How can I install XSL support for ASP?

A: Install Internet Explorer 5 on your server or download the XML processing DLLs from Microsoft.

7 Can I send XML to non-browser applications?

A: Of course! Just make sure that your site doesn't transform it to HTML on the server.

Chapter 27

See page 492

1 How might the emergence of handheld Web browsers affect your ASP applications?

A: Smaller clients tend to ignore much of the information sent to them, possibly making many of your transfers redundant.

2 How might the emergence of more powerful and specialized browser-like clients affect your ASP applications?

A: Your server may be able to let the application handle some of the processing, reducing the server's load and giving the user more control.

3 What key advantage helped the Web blossom in the client-server development environment?

A: Price. Web development, and still is, much cheaper than most other forms of networked information processing.

4 Can Active Server Pages communicate with Java clients?

A: Yes, as long as ASP can understand the requests made by the Java clients and the Java clients can process the information (typically XML) sent by ASP.

5 How can I reuse code modules in ASP?

A: Server-side includes will let you store code modules centrally and use them in multiple ASP pages.

6 How can I keep track of user preferences?

A: You can use a database, a directory, or a tool like Microsoft's Site Server.

7 Can ASP technology be used on client computers?

A: Certainly, if they run one of Microsoft's Web servers or a competing ASP environment. This is a large step toward distributed computing.

Appendix B
HTML Elements

This appendix lists alphabetically arranged HTML elements from HTML 4.0 as well as Netscape and Microsoft extensions. For detailed reference information about HTML, refer to *HTML in Plain English*, by Sandra E. Eddy and also published by IDG Books Worldwide. Also, be sure to check the pages at W3C, which sets the standard for HTML. W3C's home page is located at **http://www.w3.org/**.

HTML 4.0 ELEMENTS

!	Inserts a non-displaying comment in a document. (This is actually an SGML element.)
!DOCTYPE	States the document type. Other information includes the HTML version, and the language in which the DTD is written. (!DOCTYPE is actually an SGML element.)
A	Specifies a link from which you can jump to an *anchor*, or target, to which you can jump within the current document or in another document.
ABBR	Formats a selected abbreviation in a style that is determined by the browser with which you are viewing the document.
ACRONYM	Formats a selected acronym in a style that is determined by the browser with which you are viewing the document.
ADDRESS	Formats selected author address information — particularly e-mail addresses — in a style that is determined by the browser with which you are viewing the document.
APPLET	Embeds a Java applet within a document. This is a deprecated element; use the OBJECT element instead.
AREA	Specifies the area — including coordinates, actions, and shapes — of a client-side image map.
B	Applies boldface to selected text. You can use the STRONG element to enable a browser to apply boldface or some other emphasis to selected text.
BASE	Defines the base (absolute) URL for the current document. This element is valid only within the HEAD section.
BASEFONT	Defines the base (default) font size, color, typeface, and/or language for a document. This is a deprecated element; specify the default font characteristics by using a stylesheet.
BDO	Specifies the direction of selected text — left to right or right to left — and/or the language in which it is written.

HTML Elements

BIG	Changes selected text to a font size that is larger than the current font size.
BLOCKQUOTE	Formats selected text as a long quotation in a block format. In contrast, you can use the Q element to format short, inline quotations.
BODY	Marks the beginning and end of the *body*, or the displayed contents, of the document. This is one of two parts of a typical document; use the HEAD element to mark the part of the document that describes the document, including the title, author name, creation and/or modification dates, and keywords.
BR	Starts a new line of text.
BUTTON	Inserts a three-dimensional script-operated button in a form.
CAPTION	Places a caption above or below the table with which it is associated.
CENTER	Centers a line of text between the left and right margins. This is a deprecated element; use a stylesheet to align selected lines instead.
CITE	Formats a selected book or paper title or the name of an expert in a style that is determined by the browser with which you are viewing the document.
CODE	Formats selected text as a monospace, computer-code font. The selection's font is determined by the browser with which you are viewing the document.
COL	Aligns one or more columns in a table.
COLGROUP	Groups one or more table columns in order to apply formats.
DD	Formats a definition description in a definition list. Each DD description must have a counterpart DT term.
DEL	Marks deleted text as a deletion. Deletion marks are analogous to revision marks in a word-processing document.
DFN	Formats selected text as a definition. The selection's font is determined by the browser with which you are viewing the document.
DIR	Marks the beginning and end of a directory list. This is a deprecated element; use another type of list element.
DIV	Marks the beginning and end of a division within a document.
DL	Marks the beginning and end of a definition list, which is made up of one or more pairs of list items (DD and DT elements).
DT	Formats a definition term in a definition list. Each DT term must have a counterpart DD description.
EM	Emphasizes selected text, usually with italics — depending on the browser with which you view the text. You can use the I element to ensure that italics are applied to a selection.
FIELDSET	Defines a group of input controls in a form (IE extension).
FONT	Assigns a typeface, font size, or color to selected text. This is a deprecated element; specify font characteristics by using a stylesheet.
FORM	Marks the beginning and end of a fill-in form.
FRAME	Defines one frame within a set of frames.

HTML 4.0 ELEMENTS *(continued)*

FRAMESET	Specifies a set of frames on the computer desktop.
H1 — H6	Formats selected text as one of six levels of boldface headings. The H1 element marks the highest level (with the greatest font size), and H6 marks the lowest (with the smallest font size).
HEAD	Marks the beginning and end of the part of the document that describes the document, including the title, author name, creation and/or modification dates, and keywords. This is one of two parts of a typical document; use the BODY element to mark the beginning and end of the displayed contents of the document.
HR	Inserts a horizontal line (rule) to separate two sections of a document.
HTML	Identifies the beginning and end of an HTML document.
I	Italicizes selected text. You can use the EM element to enable a browser to apply italics or some other emphasis to selected text.
IFRAME	Defines one inline, floating frame within a set of frames (IE).
IMG	Specifies an inline image to be inserted in a document.
INPUT	Specifies an input field — text box, check boxes, radio buttons, images, command buttons, or image — in a form.
INS	Marks selected text as an insertion. Insertion marks are analogous to revision marks in a word-processing document.
ISINDEX	States that this HTML document is an index with a single text input field. This is a deprecated element; use a form instead.
KBD	Formats selected text as a monospace, keyboard-input font. The selection's font is determined by the browser with which you are viewing the document.
LABEL	Labels an input control in a form.
LEGEND	Adds a caption to a fieldset.
LI	Defines an item in an ordered (OL) or unordered (UL) list.
LINK	In the HEAD section, displays a link to another HTML document.
MAP	Marks the beginning and end of a client-side image map.
MENU	Identifies a menu list in a form. This is a deprecated element; use another type of list instead.
META	Provides meta information for a document, including a title, author name, creation and/or modification dates, and keywords.
NOFRAMES	Codes frame alternates for browsers that do not support the use of frames.
NOSCRIPT	Codes script alternates for browsers that do not support the use of scripts.
OBJECT	Embeds a multimedia object, such as an image, video file, or sound file, in a document.
OL	Marks the beginning and end of an ordered (numbered) list.
OPTGROUP	Groups related menu items in a form's menu.
OPTION	Inserts a menu item in a form's menu.
P	Indicates the start and end of a new paragraph.
PARAM	Specifies parameters and runtime values in order to render an object onscreen.

HTML ELEMENTS

HTML 4.0 ELEMENTS *(continued)*

PRE	Formats selected text as a monospace, computer-code font. The selection's font is determined by the browser with which you are viewing the document. Whitespace and returns are preserved. (Preformatted)
Q	Formats selected text as a short, inline quotation. In contrast, you can use the BLOCKQUOTE element to format selected text as a long quotation in a block format.
S/STRIKE	Strikes through selected text. S and STRIKE are both deprecated elements.
SAMP	Formats selected text as a monospace, program-output font. The selection's font is determined by the browser with which you are viewing the document. Used for code samples.
SCRIPT	Inserts a script in a document.
SELECT	Inserts a menu in a form.
SMALL	Changes selected text to a font size that is smaller than the current font size.
SPAN	Marks the beginning and end of a section within a document.
STRONG	Emphasizes selected text, usually with boldface — depending on the browser with which you view the text. You can use the B element to ensure that boldface is applied to a selection.
STYLE	Starts and ends selected text in order to apply a style. The STYLE element overrides a linked cascading style sheet.
SUB	Moves the selected characters below the baseline on which other characters sit and applies a smaller font.
SUP	Moves the selected characters above the baseline on which other characters sit and applies a smaller font.
TABLE	Marks the beginning and end of a table.
TBODY	Marks the beginning and the end of the body of a table.
TD	Marks the beginning and end of the data in a table cell.
TEXTAREA	Inserts a multi-line text-input area in a form.
TFOOT	Marks the beginning and the end of the footer rows at the bottom of a table.
TH	Marks the beginning and end of heading data in a table cell.
THEAD	Marks the beginning and the end of the header rows at the top of a table.
TITLE	Specifies a title for the current HTML document. Insert the title in the HEAD section of the document.
TR	Marks the beginning and end of a table row, which contains table-heading data, table data, or both.
TT	Formats selected text as a monospace, teletype font. The selection's font is determined by the browser with which you are viewing the document. A fixed width format.
U	Underlines selected text. This is a deprecated element because underlined text can be confused with link text.
UL	Marks the beginning and end of an unordered (bulleted) list.
VAR	Formats selected text as a variable, usually italicized. The selection's font and emphasis is determined by the browser with which you are viewing the document.

This section lists Microsoft extensions. Some of these may become part of the HTML standard in the future. In the meantime, note that many browsers do not support Microsoft extensions.

MICROSOFT EXTENSIONS

BGSOUND	Includes a background sound that plays when the page is displayed.
EMBED	Embeds an object in a document (IE 3.0 and later versions).
MARQUEE	Adds a scrolling marquee to a document.
NOBR	Turns off automatic word wrap and line breaks except for those caused by the BR, P, or WBR elements.
NEXTID	Creates a unique identifier.

This section lists Netscape extensions. Some of these may become part of the HTML standard in the future. In the meantime, note that many browsers do not support Netscape extensions.

NETSCAPE EXTENSIONS

BLINK	Blinks text off and on.
ILAYER	Defines an inflow layer that overlaps other content onscreen.
KEYGEN	Generates a public key.
LAYER	Defines a layer of HTML content that overlaps other content onscreen.
MULTICOL	Formats multiple columns.
NOEMBED	Codes embed alternates for browsers that do not support embedding.
NOLAYER	Codes a layer alternate for browsers that do not support the use of layers.
SERVER	Includes a JavaScript compiled by LiveWire in a document.
SPACER	Formats horizontal and/or vertical whitespace in a document.
WBR	Inserts a line break, if needed, within a no-break (NOBR) line.

Appendix C
ASP Object Reference

Active Server Pages derives its rich functionality from the use of seven inherent objects. These objects do not have to be explicitly instantiated but are directly built into Active Server Pages. These objects have their own predefined roles and each has its own properties, methods, and events. These objects form the foundation of ASP development. ASP, in IIS 5.0, now has a new error-handling capability so that you can trap errors in a custom error message .asp file. You can use the ASPError object to obtain information about an error condition that has occurred in an ASP script. The ASPError object is returned by the Server.GetLastError method. The following provides a summary of each object's functionality.

APPLICATION OBJECT

Collection	Description
Contents	Contains all of the items that have been added to the application through script commands.
StaticObjects	Contains all of the objects added to the session with the tag.

Method	Description
Conents.Remove	The Contents.Remove method deletes an item from the Application object's Contents collection.
Contents.RemoveAll	The Contents.RemoveAll method deletes all items from the Application object's Contents collection.
Lock	The Lock method prevents other clients from modifying Application object properties.
Unlock	The Unlock method allows other clients to modify Application object properties.

Event	Description
Application_onEnd	The Application_OnEnd event occurs when the application quits, after the Session_OnEnd event.
Application_onStart	The Application_OnStart event occurs before the first new session is created, that is, before the Session_OnStart event.

ASP Object Reference

SERVER OBJECT

Property	Description
ScriptTimeout	The amount of time that a script can run before it times out.

Method	Description
CreateObject	Creates an instance of a server component.
Execute	Executes an .asp file.
GetLastError	Returns an ASPError object that describes the error condition.
HTMLEncode	Applies HTML encoding to the specified string.
MapPath	Maps the specified virtual path, either the absolute path on the current Server or the path relative to the current page, into a physical path.
Transfer	Sends all of the current state information to another .asp file for processing.
URLEncode	Applies URL encoding rules, including escape characters, to the string.

ASPERROR OBJECT

Property	Description
ASPCode	Returns an error code generated by IIS.
Number	Returns the standard COM error code.
Source	Returns the actual source code, when available, of the line that caused the error.
FileName	Indicates the name of the .asp file that was being processed when the error occurred.
LineNumber	Indicates the line within the .asp file that generated the error.
Description	Returns a short description of the error.
ASPDescription	Returns a more detailed description of the error if it is an ASP-related error.

RESPONSE OBJECT

Collection	Description
Cookies	The values of cookies sent in the HTTP request.

RESPONSE OBJECT *(continued)*

Property	Description
Buffer	Indicates whether page output is buffered. For IIS version 5.0 and later, the default value is True. Otherwise, the default value is False for versions of IIS up to and including 4.0.
CacheControl	Determines whether proxy servers are able to cache the output generated by ASP.
Charset	Appends the name of the character set to the content-type header.
Expires	Specifies the length of time before a page cached on a browser expires.
ExpiresAbsolute	Specifies the date and time on which a page cached on a browser expires.
IsClientConnected	Indicates whether the client has disconnected from the server.
PICS	Sets the value for the pics-label response header, to indicate the PICS content rating.
Status	Returns the value of the status line returned by the server.

Method	Description
AddHeader	Sets the HTML header name to value.
AppendToLog	Adds a string to the end of the Web server log entry for this request.
BinaryWrite	Writes the given information to the current HTTP output without any character-set conversion.
Clear	Erases any buffered HTML output.
End	Stops processing the .asp file and returns the current result.
Flush	Sends buffered output immediately.
Redirect	Sends a redirect message to the browser, causing it to attempt to connect to a different URL.
Write	Writes a variable to the current HTTP output as a string.

REQUEST OBJECT

Collection	Description
ClientCertificate	Contains the values of fields stored in the client certificate that is sent in the HTTP request.
Cookies	Contains the values of cookies sent in the HTTP request.
Form	Contains the values of form elements in the HTTP request body.
QueryString	Contains the values of variables in the HTTP query string.
ServerVariables	Contains the values of predetermined environment variables.

ASP Object Reference

REQUEST OBJECT *(continued)*

Property	Description
TotalBytes	Read-only; specifies the total number of bytes the client is sending in the body of the request.

Method	Description
BinaryRead	Retrieves data sent to the server from the client as part of a POST request.

SESSION OBJECT

Collection	Description
Contents	Contains the items that you have added to the session with script commands.
StaticObjects	Contains the objects created with the <OBJECT> tag and given session scope.

Property	Description
CodePage	The code page that will be used for symbol mapping.
LCID	The locale identifier.
SessionID	Returns the session identification for this user.
TimeOut	The timeout period for the session state for this application, in minutes.

Method	Description
Abandon	Destroys a Session object and releases its resources.
Conents.Remove	Deletes an item from the Contents collection.
Contents.RemoveAll	Deletes all items from the Contents collection.

Event	Description
Session_onEnd	Occurs when a session is abandoned or times out.
Session_onStart	Occurs when the server creates a new session. The server processes this script prior to executing the requested page.

OBJECTCONTEXT OBJECT

Method	Description
SetAbort	Declares that the transaction initiated by the script has not completed and the resources should not be updated.
SetComplete	Declares that the script is not aware of any reason for the transaction not to complete. If all components participating in the transaction also call SetComplete, the transaction will complete.

Event	Description
OnTransactionAbort	Occurs if the transaction is aborted. When the OnTransactionAbort event occurs, IIS will process the script's OnTransactionAbort subroutine, if it exists.
OnTransactionCommit	Occurs after a transacted script's transaction commits. When the OnTransactionCommit event occurs, IIS will process the script's OnTransactionCommit subroutine, if it exists.

ActiveX Data Objects (ADO) enables you to write an application to access and manipulate data in a datasource through an OLE DB provider. ADO's primary benefits are high speed, ease of use, low memory overhead, and a small disk footprint. There are seven objects in the ADO object model:

COMMAND OBJECT

Collection	Description
Parameters	Contains all the Parameter objects of a Command object.
Properties	Contains all the Property objects for a specific instance of an object.

Property	Description
ActiveConnection	Indicates to which Connection object the specified Command or Recordset object currently belongs.
CommandText	Contains the text of a command that you want to issue against a provider.
CommandTimeout	Indicates how long to wait while executing a command before terminating the attempt and generating an error.

ASP Object Reference

COMMAND OBJECT (continued)

Collection	Description
CommandType	Indicates the type of a Command object.
Name	Indicates the name of an object.
Prepared	Indicates whether or not to save a compiled version of a command before execution.
State	Describes the current state of an object.

Method	Description
CreateParameter	Creates a new Parameter object with the specified properties.
Execute	Executes the query, SQL statement, or stored procedure specified in the CommandText property.

ERROR OBJECT

Property	Description
Description	A descriptive string associated with an Error object.
HelpContext	Indicates the help file and topic associated with an Error object.
HelpFile	Indicates the help file and topic associated with an Error object.
NativeError	Indicates the provider-specific error code for a given Error object.
Number	Indicates the number that uniquely identifies an Error object.
Source	Indicates the name of the object or application that originally generated an error.
SQLState	Indicates the SQL state for a given Error object.

ERRORS COLLECTION

Property	Description
Count	Indicates the number of objects in a collection.

Method	Description
Clear	Removes all of the objects in a collection.
Item	Returns a specific member of a collection by name or ordinal number.

CONNECTION OBJECT

Collection	Description
Parameters	Contains all the Parameter objects of a Command object.
Properties	Contains all the Property objects for a specific instance of an object.

Property	Description
Attributes	Indicates one or more characteristics of an object.
CommandTimeout	Indicates how long to wait while executing a command before terminating the attempt and generating an error.
ConnectionString	Contains the information used to establish a connection to a data source.
ConnectionTimeout	Indicates how long to wait while establishing a connection before terminating the attempt and generating an error.
CursorLocation	Sets or returns the location of the cursor engine.
DefaultDatabase	Indicates the default database for a Connection.
IsolationLevel	Indicates the level of isolation for a Connection.
Mode	Indicates the available permissions for modifying data in a Connection.
Provider	Indicates the name of the provider for a Connection.
State	Describes the current state of an object.
Version	Indicates the ADO version number.

Method	Description
BeginTrans	Begins a new transaction.
Close	Closes an open object and any dependent objects.
CommitTrans	Saves any changes and ends the current transaction. It may also start a new transaction.
Execute	Executes the specified query, SQL statement, stored procedure, or provider-specific text.
Open	Opens a connection to a data source.
OpenSchema	Obtains database schema information from the provider.
RollbackTrans	Cancels any changes made during the current transaction and ends the transaction. It may also start a new transaction.

ASP Object Reference

PARAMETER OBJECT

Collection	Description
Parameters	A Parameters collection contains all the Parameter objects of a Command object.

Property	Description
Attributes	Indicates one or more characteristics of an object
Direction	Indicates whether the Parameter represents an input parameter, an output parameter, or both, or if the parameter is the return value from a stored procedure.
Name	Indicates the name of an object.
NumericScale	Indicates the scale of numeric values in a Parameter or Field object.
Precision	Indicates the degree of precision for Numeric values in a Parameter object or for numeric Field objects.
Size	Indicates the maximum size, in bytes or characters, of a Parameter object.
Type	Indicates the operational type or data type of a Parameter, Field, or Property object.
Value	Indicates the value assigned to a Field, Parameter, or Property object.

Method	Description
AppendChunk	Appends data to a large text or binary data Field or Parameter object.

PARAMETERS COLLECTION

Property	Description
Count	Indicates the number of objects in a collection.

Method	Description
Append	Appends an object to a collection.
Delete	Deletes an object from the Parameters collection.
Item	Returns a specific member of a collection by name or ordinal number.
Refresh	Updates the objects in a collection to reflect objects available from and specific to the provider.

PROPERTY OBJECT

Property	Description
Attributes	Indicates one or more characteristics of an object.
Name	Indicates the name of an object.
Type	Indicates the operational type or data type of a Parameter, Field, or Property object.
Value	Indicates the value assigned to a Field, Parameter, or Property object.

PROPERTIES COLLECTION

Property	Description
Count	Indicates the number of objects in a collection.

Method	Description
Item	Returns a specific member of a collection by name or ordinal number.
Refresh	Updates the objects in a collection to reflect objects available from and specific to the provider.

FIELD OBJECT

Collection	Description
Properties	A Properties collection contains all the Property objects for a specific instance of an object.

Property	Description
ActualSize	Indicates the actual length of a field's value.
Attributes	Indicates one or more characteristics of an object.
DefinedSize	Indicates the defined size of a Field object.
Name	Indicates the name of an object.
NumericScale	Indicates the scale of Numeric values in a Parameter or Field object.
OriginalValue	Indicates the value of a Field that existed in the record before any changes were made.
Precision	Indicates the degree of precision for Numeric values in a Parameter object or for numeric Field objects.

FIELD OBJECT (continued)

Property	Description
Type	Indicates the operational type or data type of a Parameter, Field, or Property object.
UnderlyingValue	Indicates a Field object's current value in the database.
Value	Indicates the value assigned to a Field, Parameter, or Property object.

Method	Description
AppendChunk	Appends data to a large text or binary data Field or Parameter object.
GetChunk	Returns all or a portion of the contents of a large text or binary data Field object.

FIELDS COLLECTION

Property	Description
Count	Indicates the number of objects in a collection.

Method	Description
Item	Returns a specific member of a collection by name or ordinal number.
Refresh	Updates the objects in a collection to reflect objects available from and specific to the provider.

RECORDSET OBJECT

Property	Description
AbsolutePage	Specifies in which page the current record resides.
AbsolutePosition	Specifies the ordinal position of a Recordset object's current record.
ActiveConnection	Indicates to which Connection object the specified Command or Recordset object currently belongs.
BOF	Indicates that the current record position is before the first record in a Recordset object.
Bookmark	Returns a bookmark that uniquely identifies the current record in a Recordset object or sets the current record in a Recordset object to the record identified by a valid bookmark.
CacheSize	Indicates the number of records from a Recordset object that are cached locally in memory.

RECORDSET OBJECT *(continued)*

Property	Description
CursorLocation	Sets or returns the location of the cursor engine.
CursorType	Indicates the type of cursor used in a Recordset object.
EditMode	Indicates the editing status of the current record.
EOF	Indicates that the current record position is after the last record in a Recordset object.
Filter	Indicates a filter for data in a Recordset.
LockType	Indicates the type of locks placed on records during editing.
MarshalOptions	Indicates which records are to be marshaled back to the server.
MaxRecords	Indicates the maximum number of records to return to a Recordset from a query.
PageCount	Indicates how many pages of data the Recordset object contains.
PageSize	Indicates how many records constitute one page in the Recordset.
RecordCount	Indicates the current number of records in a Recordset object.
Source	Indicates the source for the data in a Recordset object (Command object, SQL statement, table name, or stored procedure).
State	Describes the current state of an object.
Status	Indicates the status of the current record with respect to batch updates or other bulk operations.

Method	Description
AddNew	Creates a new record for an updatable Recordset object.
CancelBatch	Cancels a pending batch update.
CancelUpdate	Cancels any changes made to the current record or to a new record prior to calling the Update method.
Clone	Creates a duplicate Recordset object from an existing Recordset object.
Close	Closes an open object and any dependent objects.
Delete	Deletes the current record or a group of records.
GetRows	Retrieves multiple records of a Recordset into an array.
Move	Moves the position of the current record in a Recordset object.
MoveFirst, MoveLast, MoveNext, MovePrevious	Moves to the first, last, next, or previous record in a specified Recordset object and makes that record the current record.
NextRecordset	Clears the current Recordset object and returns the next recordset by advancing through a series of commands.

RECORDSET OBJECT (continued)

Method	Description
Open	Opens a cursor.
Requery	Updates the data in a Recordset object by re-executing the query on which the object is based.
Resync	Refreshes the data in the current Recordset object from the underlying database.
Supports	Determines whether a specified Recordset object supports a particular type of functionality.
Update	Saves any changes you make to the current record of a Recordset object.
UpdateBatch	Writes all pending batch updates to disk.

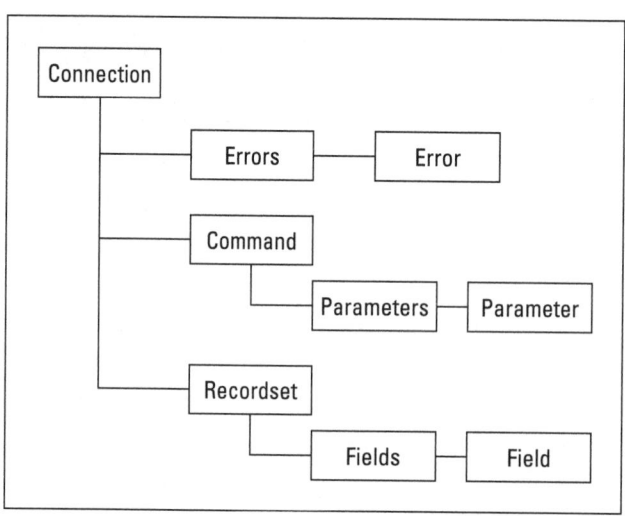

Appendix D
Language Codes

This appendix lists language name codes based on those in the ISO 639: 1988 standard. Language names are listed alphabetically. Note that when you use a language code in a document, it is common practice to enter it in lowercase. In contrast, the country code is usually expressed in uppercase (see Appendix E).

ISO 639 LANGUAGE CODES

Language	Code	Language	Code	Language	Code
Abkhazian	ab	Bulgarian	bg	Frisian	fy
Afan	om	Burmese	my	Gaelic (Scottish)	gd
Afar	aa	Byelorussian	be	Galician	gl
Afrikaans	af	Cambodian	km	Georgian	ka
Albanian	sq	Catalan	ca	German	de
Amharic	am	Chinese	zh	Greek	el
Arabic	ar	Corsican	co	Greenlandic	kl
Armenian	hy	Croatian	hr	Guarani	gn
Assamese	as	Czech	cs	Gujarati	gu
Aymara	ay	Danish	da	Hausa	ha
Azerbaijani	az	Dutch	nl	Hebrew	iw
Bashkir	ba	English	en	Hindi	hi
Basque	eu	Esperanto	eo	Hungarian	hu
Bengali	bn	Estonian	et	Icelandic	is
Bhutani	dz	Faroese	fo	Indonesian	in
Bihari	bh	Fiji	fj	Interlingua	ia
Bislama	bi	Finnish	fi	Interlingue	ie
Breton	br	French	fr	Inuktitut	iu

Language Codes

Language	Code	Language	Code	Language	Code
Inupiak	ik	Norwegian	no	Swahili	sw
Irish	ga	Occitan	oc	Swedish	sv
Italian	it	Oriya	or	Tagalog	tl
Japanese	ja	Oromo	om	Tajik	tg
Javanese	jw	Pashto	ps	Tamil	ta
Kannada	kn	Persian	fa	Tatar	tt
Kashmiri	ks	Polish	pl	Tegulu	te
Kazakh	kk	Portuguese	pt	Thai	th
Kinyarwanda	rw	Punjabi	pa	Tibetan	bo
Kirghiz	ky	Quechua	qu	Tigrinya	ti
Kirundi	rn	Rhaeto-Romance	rm	Tonga	to
Korean	ko	Romanian	ro	Tsonga	ts
Kurdish	ku	Russian	ru	Turkish	tr
Laotian	lo	Samoan	sm	Turkmen	tk
Latin	la	Sangho	sg	Twi	tw
Latvian	lv	Sanskrit	sa	Uigar	ug
Lingala	ln	Serbian	sr	Ukrainian	uk
Lithuanian	lt	Serbo-Croatian	sh	Urdu	ur
Macedonian	mk	Sesotho	st	Uzbek	uz
Malagasy	mg	Setswana	tn	Vietnamese	vi
Malay	ms	Shona	sn	Volapuk	vo
Malayalam	ml	Sindhi	sd	Welsh	cy
Maltese	mt	Singhalese	si	Wolof	wo
Maori	mi	Siswati	ss	Xhosa	xh
Marathi	mr	Slovak	sk	Yiddish	ji
Moldavian	mo	Slovenian	sl	Yoruba	yo
Mongolian	mn	Somali	so	Zhuang	za
Nauru	na	Spanish	es	Zulu	zu
Nepali	ne	Sudanese	su		

Appendix E
Country Codes

This appendix lists country name codes based on those in the ISO 3166 standard. Country names are listed alphabetically. Note that when you use a country code in a document, it is common practice to enter it in uppercase. In contrast, the language code is usually expressed in lowercase (see Appendix D).

ISO 3166 COUNTRY CODES

Country	Code	Country	Code
Afghanistan	AF	Bahrain	BH
Albania	AL	Bangladesh	BD
Algeria	DZ	Barbados	BB
American Samoa	AS	Belarus	BY
Andorra	AD	Belgium	BE
Angola	AO	Belize	BZ
Anguilla	AI	Benin	BJ
Antarctica	AQ	Bermuda	BM
Antigua and Barbuda	AG	Bhutan	BT
Argentina	AR	Bolivia	BO
Armenia	AM	Bosnia Herzegovina	BA
Aruba	AW	Botswana	BW
Australia	AU	Bouvet Island	BV
Austria	AT	Brazil	BR
Azerbaijan	AZ	British Indian Ocean Territory	IO
Bahamas	BS	Brunei	BN

COUNTRY CODES

Country	Code	Country	Code
Bulgaria	BG	Egypt	EG
Burkina Faso	BF	El Salvador	SV
Cambodia	KH	Equatorial Guinea	GQ
Cameroon	CM	Eritrea	ER
Canada	CA	Estonia	EE
Cape Verde	CV	Ethiopia	ET
Cayman Islands	KY	Falkland Islands	FK
Central African Republic	CF	Faroe Islands	FO
Chad	TD	Fiji	FJ
Chile	CL	Finland	FI
China	CN	France	FR
Christmas Island	CX	France, Metropolitan	FX
Cocos Islands	CC	French Guiana	GF
Colombia	CO	French Polynesia	PF
Comoros	KM	French Southern Territories	TF
Congo	CG	Gabon	GA
Cook Islands	CK	Gambia	GM
Costa Rica	CR	Georgia	GE
Cote D'Ivoire	CI	Germany	DE
Croatia	HR	Ghana	GH
Cuba	CU	Gibraltar	GI
Cyprus	CY	Greece	GR
Czech Republic	CZ	Greenland	GL
Denmark	DK	Grenada	GD
Djibouti	C	Guadeloupe	GP
Dominica	CM	Guam	GU
Dominican Republic	DO	Guatemala	GT
East Timor	TP	Guinea	GN
Ecuador	EC	Guinea-Bissau	GW

ISO 3166 COUNTRY CODES *(continued)*

Country	Code	Country	Code
Guyana	GY	Liberia	LR
Haiti	HT	Libya	LY
Heard and McDonald Islands	HM	Liechtenstein	LI
Holy See (The Vatican)	VA	Lithuania	LT
Honduras	HN	Luxembourg	LU
Hong Kong	HK	Macau	MO
Hungary	HU	Macedonia	MK
Iceland	IS	Madagascar	MG
India	IN	Malawi	MW
Indonesia	ID	Malaysia	MY
Iran	IR	Maldives	MV
Iraq	IQ	Mali	ML
Ireland	IE	Malta	MT
Israel	IL	Marshall Islands	MH
Italy	IT	Martinique	MQ
Jamaica	JM	Mauritania	MR
Japan	JP	Mauritius	MU
Jordan	JO	Mayotte	YT
Kazakhstan	KZ	Mexico	MX
Kenya	KE	Micronesia	FM
Kiribati	KI	Moldova	MD
Korea, North	KP	Monaco	MC
Korea, South	KR	Mongolia	MN
Kuwait	KW	Montserrat	MS
Kyrgyzstan	KG	Morocco	MA
Laos	LA	Mozambique	MZ
Latvia	LV	Myanmar (Burma)	MM
Lebanon	LB	Namibia	NA
Lesotho	LS	Nauru	NR

COUNTRY CODES

Country	Code	Country	Code
Nepal	NP	Saint Lucia	LC
Netherland Antilles	AN	Saint Vincent and The Grenadines	VC
Netherlands	NL	Samoa	WS
New Caledonia	NC	San Marino	SM
New Zealand	NZ	Sao Tome and Principe	ST
Nicaragua	NI	Saudi Arabia	SA
Niger	NE	Senegal	SN
Nigeria	NG	Seychelles	SC
Niue	NU	Sierra Leone	SL
Norfolk Island	NF	Singapore	SG
Northern Mariana Islands	MP	Slovakia	SK
Norway	NO	Slovenia	SI
Oman	OM	Solomon Islands	SB
Pakistan	PK	Somalia	SO
Palau	PW	South Africa	ZA
Panama	PA	South Georgia and The South	GS
Papua New Guinea	PG	Sandwich Islands	
Paraguay	PY	Spain	ES
Peru	PE	St. Helena	SH
Philippines	PH	St. Pierre and Miquelon	PM
Pitcairn	PN	Sudan	SD
Poland	PL	Suriname	SR
Portugal	PT	Svalbard and Jan Mayen Islands	SJ
Puerto Rico	PR	Swaziland	SZ
Qatar	QA	Sweden	SE
Reunion	RE	Switzerland	CH
Romania	RO	Syria	SY
Russian Federation	RU	Taiwan	TW
Rwanda	RW	Tajikistan	TJ
Saint Kitts and Nevis	KN	Tanzania	TZ

ISO 3166 COUNTRY CODES *(continued)*

Country	Code	Country	Code
Thailand	TH	United States	US
Togo	TG	Uruguay	UY
Tokelau	TK	Uzbekistan	UZ
Tonga	TO	Vanuatu	VU
Trinidad and Tobago	TT	Venezuela	VE
Tunisia	TN	Vietnam	VN
Turkey	TR	Virgin Islands, British	VG
Turkmenistan	TM	Virgin Islands, U.S.	VI
Turks and Caicos Islands	TC	Wallis and Futuna Islands	WF
Tuvalu	TV	Western Sahara	EH
Uganda	UG	Yemen	YE
Ukraine	UA	Yugoslavia	YU
United Arab Emirates	AE	Zaire	ZR
United Kingdom	GB	Zambia	ZM
United States Minor Outlying Islands	UM	Zimbabwe	ZW

Appendix F
Software Webliography

The Internet contains a growing number of Web-development resources, including downloadable freeware, shareware, and trial versions of software, as well as fact sheets and other information about the programs and the organizations that develop them. The following list describes the categories of available resources:

Commercial programs: These full-featured programs are the most expensive; however, the company developing the programs can often afford to add more "bells and whistles" and user-friendliness. You can often download a trial or demonstration version so that you can "try before you buy."

Trial versions: Many commercial software publishers provide these incomplete or limited programs, also known as *demonstration programs* (or demos), that you can preview before buying. A trial version may be an older version of the program, may expire on a particular date, or may not include all the features of the commercial software.

Shareware programs: These programs usually contain every feature and function: you are expected to buy a license after you try the program for a set number of days. In return, the author may send you program disks, a license, manuals, and notices of problems, fixes, and new releases.

Freeware programs: These programs are available at no cost from an altruistic developer or as a first-rate marketing effort. Freeware programs, which can be "lite" versions of commercial or shareware programs, can be just as good as their commercial or shareware counterparts.

This appendix lists software that can help you develop ASP pages, write the HTML and XML documents on which you base your ASP pages, and manage Web sites. Each entry in the appendix includes the program name, a brief description, and the URL for a Web page from which you can gather more information.

ASP Software

This section of the appendix lists selected software that supports the development of ASP pages.

Active Date Publisher (**http://www.brantek.com/products/adp.html**) is an editor that generates ASP code.

Active Server Paint (**http://www.cvisual.com/aspaint/**) lets your Active Server Pages generate GIF, JPEG, and BMP images.

ActiveState Perl (**http://www.activestate.com**) is a Perl distribution that allows you to use PerlScript in your Active Server Pages or use ISAPI for direct and efficient connections to Perl.

ActiveFile (**http://www.infomentum.com/**) enables file compression and decompression and directory manipulation from within ASP pages.

ASP Express (**http://www.aspexpress.com/aspexpress.asp**) is an ASP and HTML editor.

ASP-Beautify (**http://www.paessler.com/tools/ASPBeautify/index.htm**) is a shareware program that formats and indents ASP pages.

Software Webliography

ASP-Edit (**http://www.tashcom.com/software.html**) is an ASP editor that allows you to insert statements, functions, server variables and statements, VBScript statements, and SQL statements.

ASP Flash Turbine (**http://www.blue-pacific. hexagon.net/aspturbine/**) lets you generate graphics for Macromedia's Flash plug-in using ASP.

A$PCharge (**http://www.bluesquirrel.com/ products/asp/asp.html**) is a commercial program that processes credit cards at e-commerce sites.

ASP Chart (**http://www.serverobjects.com/ products.htm**) is a set of components for producing charts in JPEG, PNG, and BMP formats.

ASP2XML (**http://www.stonebroom.com/ asp2xml.htm**) is a set of components for producing XML from databases.

ASPLightning (**http://www.infomentum.com/ asplightning**) encapsulates ASP source code.

ASP Page (**http://www.softartisans.com/ softartisans/aspstudio.html**) connects your Active Server Pages to your pager, allowing users to page you on a beeper.

ASPStudio (**http://www.softartisans.com/ softartisans/aspstudio.html**) is a suite of many utilities that support ASP page development and enhancement.

ATI-UPS Server Objects (**http://www.arealgem. com/controlsweb/Whitepaper.asp?product=shipcalc**) allows your site to calculate United Parcel Service (UPS) shipping rates.

Chili!Soft ASP (**http://www.chilisoft.com/**) provides developers with a complete environment for hosting ASP pages on various servers.

Cool ICE (Internet Commerce Enabler) (**http://www. marketplace.unisys.com/coolice/**) manages Web documents and services on intranets and the Internet.

DameWare ActiveX Component Packs (**http:// www.dameware.com/**) are collections of ActiveX controls.

Dreamweaver (**http://www.macromedia.com/ software/dreamweaver/index_gif.html**) enables the development, design, and production of professional Web sites.

EuroConversion (**http://www.alphasierrapapa .com/componentcenter/euro/**) provides your ASP site with conversions between the Euro and 11 other currencies.

I-ASP (**http://www.halcyonsoft.com**) is a commercial Java-based environment for running Active Server Pages.

Ike M Kimiko HTML Editor (**http://www.ike-m. com/en/products/kimiko/index.asp**) is an HTML editor that supports ASP pages, JavaScript, VBScript, Server Side Includes, ActiveX, and more.

Microsoft Visual InterDev (**http://msdn. microsoft.com/vinterdev/**) is a commercial Web-development application that supports scripting and ASP.

NetObjects ScriptBuilder (**http://www. netobjects.com/products/html/nsb3.html**) enables the development of client-side and server-side scripts.

OpenASP (**http://www.activescripting.org**) provides ASP support on a number of non-Microsoft Web servers, notably Apache, and is open source.

PerlScripters.com (**http://www.perlscripters. com**) is a site for discussion and support of ASP PerlScript projects, hosting sample code, modules (like Win32::ASP::CGI), documentation, and more.

PowerDesigner (**http://www.sybase.com/ products/powerdesigner/**) is a suite of products with which you can develop Web pages.

Programmer's Paradise (**http://www.pparadise. com**) is a site that sells a wide variety of COM components you can integrate with ASP.

WebSite Professional (**http://website.oreilly. com/ws2_main.cfm**) is a suite of Web server tools that support the newest technologies, including Active Server Pages, VBScript, JScript, and Perl.

HTML Editors

This section of the appendix lists selected HTML editors.

1-4-All HTML Editor (**http://www.mmsoftware. com/14All/**) is an HTML editor for Windows.

Adobe PageMill (**http://www.adobe.com/ prodindex/pagemill/main.html**) is a commercial HTML editor for Windows and Macintosh.

ANT_HTML (http://telacommunications.com/ant/) is a document conversion tool for Windows and the Macintosh. Both shareware and trial versions are available.

AOLPress (http://www.aolpress.com/press/index.html) is an HTML editor for Windows and Macintosh.

Aspire-x (http://www.aspire-x.com/html/index.htm) is an HTML editor for Windows.

AsWedit (ftp://sunsite.doc.ic.ac.uk/packages/www/asWedit/) is a UNIX-based program that edits HTML for X Windows and Motif systems.

ATRAX the Web Publisher (http://www.winwareinc.com/atrax.html) is a shareware HTML editor for Windows.

BBEdit (http://www.barebones.com/|bbedit.html) is a commercial HTML editor for Macintosh.

BigM WebSite (http://www.geocities.com/CapitolHill/2519/WEBWRITE.HTM) is a freeware HTML editor for Windows.

City University HTML Editor (http://web.cs.city.ac.uk/homes/njw/htmltext/htmltext.html) is a freeware X Windows and UNIX HTML editor.

CoffeeCup HTML Editor (http://www.coffeecup.com/editor/) is an HTML editor for Windows.

DiDaPro (http://www.faico.net/dida/) is an HTML editor for Windows.

FlexED (http://nt.infoflex.com.au/flexed/flexed.htm) is a shareware HTML editor for Windows.

Hippie 98 (http://www.hippie98.com/) is a Windows-based HTML editor that supports JavaScript and ActiveX controls.

HomeSite (http://www.allaire.com/Products/HomeSite/) is a commercial HTML editor for Windows.

HotDog (http://www.sausage.com/hotdog5/overview.html) is an HTML editor for Windows.

HoTMetaL PRO (http://www.softquad.com/products/hotmetal/index.html) is a commercial HTML editor for Windows, Macintosh, and UNIX.

HTML Assistant Pro (http://www.brooknorth.com/products/) is an HTML editor for Windows.

HTML Author (http://www.salford.ac.uk/iti/gsc/htmlauth/summary.html) is a Microsoft Word template that you can use to create and edit HTML documents on Windows.

HTMLed (http://www.ist.ca/htmled/) is a shareware HTML editor for Windows.

HTML-Ed (http://www.wilmington.net/bmtmicro/catalog/html-ed.html) is a shareware HTML editor for OS/2.

html-helper-mode (http://www.santafe.edu/~nelson/tools/) is an HTML editor for UNIX.

HTML Notepad (http://www.cranial.demon.co.uk/htmlnote/home.htm) is a shareware HTML editor for Windows.

HTMLpad (http://www.intermania.com/htmlpad/index.html) is a shareware HTML editor for Windows.

The HTML Wizard (http://www.gnv.com/HTMLWizard/) is an HTML editor for OS/2.

LiquidFX (http://www.psylon.com/) is an HTML editor for Windows.

Microsoft FrontPage (http://www.microsoft.com/frontpage/) is a commercial HTML editor for Windows and Macintosh.

MyInternetBusinessPage (http://www.mybusinesspage.com/) is a shareware HTML editor for Windows.

NetObjects Fusion (http://www.netobjects.com/products/html/nf4.html) is a commercial HTML editor for Windows.

PageSpinner (http://www.optima-system.com/pagespinner/) is a shareware HTML editor for Macintosh.

Simple HTML Editor (S H E) (http://www.lib.ncsu.edu/staff/morgan/simple.html) is a HyperCard stack with which you can create HTML documents on a Macintosh.

SpiderPad (http://www.sixlegs.com/) is an HTML editor for Windows.

TC-Director (http://www.tashcom.com/software.html) is a shareware HTML editor for Windows.

SOFTWARE WEBLIOGRAPHY

tkHTML (**http://www.starfleet.com/liem/tkHTML/tkHTML.html**) is a shareware HTML editor for UNIX.

Web Elite (**http://www.safety.net/webelite/**) is a shareware HTML editor for Windows.

WebExpress (**http://www.mvd.com/webexpress/index.htm**) is an HTML editor for Windows.

Web Media Publisher (**http://www.wbmedia.com/publisher/**) is a shareware HTML editor for Windows.

Web Weaver (**http://www.mcwebsoftware.com/webweav.html**) is an HTML editor for Windows.

WebWorks Publisher (**http://www.quadralay.com/**) converts FrameMaker documents to HTML. Windows, Macintosh, and UNIX versions are available.

World Wide Web Weaver (**http://www.miracleinc.com/Products/W4/**) is a shareware HTML editor for Macintosh.

XML Editors and Suites

This section of the appendix lists selected XML editors and suites.

ADEPT Editor (**http://www.arbortext.com/**) is an SGML and XML editor that works like a word processor.

ADEPT Publisher (**http://www.arbortext.com/**) is a suite of Web document creation and publishing SGML and XML documents.

Adobe FrameMaker+SGML (**http://www.adobe.com/prodindex/framemaker/prodinfosgml.html**) is a commercial suite for SGML and XML documents.

Astoria (**http://www.chrystal.com/products/astoria.htm**) manages the content of SGML and XML documents.

Balise (**http://www.balise.com/products/balise/index.htm**) is a commercial development system for SGML and XML documents.

Bladerunner (**http://www.xmlecontent.com/**) is an XML editor for e-business documents.

CLIP! (**http://www.t2000-usa.com/product/clip_index.html**) is an editor that supports the development of valid XML documents.

Documentor (**http://www.excosoft.se/products/products.html**) is an SGML and XML editor.

EditTIME (**http://www.timelux.lu/EditTIME3/EditTIME.htm**) is an XML editor and processor.

S4-Desktop (**http://www.i-4-i.com/products/s4desk.htm**) is a suite of products that enable the creation and editing of SGML and XML documents. Also included is a library of functions.

WebWriter (**http://www.stilo.com/**) is a commercial XML editor.

XED (**http://www.ltg.ed.ac.uk/~ht/xed.html**) is an XML document-instance editor.

XMetal (**http://www.softquad.com/products/xmetal/xml-intro.html**) is an XML editor.

XML Authority (**http://www.extensibility.com/**) is a commercial XML DTD and schema editor.

XML Pro (**http://www.vervet.com/**) is an XML editor.

Web Site Software

This section of the appendix lists selected Web site software.

Adobe GoLive (**http://www.adobe.com/prodindex/golive/main.html**) is a commercial Web site creator and manager for Windows and Macintosh.

ASP Today (**http://www.asptoday.com**) contains columns that will bring you practical ASP related techniques, tips and tricks, in a focused format.

The CPAN Archives (**http://www.perl.org/**) is a set of Perl modules that goes well beyond Web sites, but should help you accomplish whatever your site needs to do in Perl.

Microsoft Visual Studio (**http://www.microsoft.com/vstudio/**) is a commercial suite of enterprise-development tools for Windows.

Wise ASP — A JScript/ASP Resource (**http://www.aspalliance.com/wiseasp/**) is a compilation of articles and examples that explains many of the topics and issues that come up when using JScript over VBScript.

Glossary

active server pages (ASP)
Microsoft technology that allows developers to create dynamic Web pages that execute on a server rather than a client computer and are viewed with a Web browser. See *client* and *server*.

ActiveX Data Objects
The high-level data access programming interface to the underlying OLE DB data access technology implemented using the Component Object Model.

ancestor
A higher-level element, such as a parent, in a family tree of elements. See *child*, *descendant*, and *parent*.

anchor
The starting link that refers to another location within the current document or within another document; the ending link to which a starting link refers; the target and/or source of a link.

application
A group of Active Server Pages (ASP) scripts and components that perform a related set of tasks.

application object.argument
A constant, variable, or expression passed to a function or procedure.

application root
The root directory for an application; all directories and files contained within the application root are considered part of the application.

application scope
A way of making data available to all users of an application from all pages of a Web application. A variable or an object instance is given application scope by storing it in the Active Server Pages (ASP).

atomicity
A feature of a transaction considered or guaranteed to be indivisible. Either the transaction is uninterrupted, or, if it fails, a mechanism is provided that ensures the return of the system to its state prior to initiation of the transaction.

attribute
A setting that affects the behavior of and further defines an element. Attributes can change or specify formats, alignments, text enhancements, paragraphs, or other parts of an SGML, HTML, or XML document.

authentication
The process by which the system validates a user's logon information. A user's name and password are compared against an authorized list, and if the system detects a match, access is granted to the extent specified in the permission list for the user.

Glossary

B

basic authentication
An authentication protocol supported by most browsers, including Internet Explorer. It is a method of authentication that encodes user name and password data transmissions.

boolean
Of, pertaining to, or characteristic of logical (true or false) values. Many languages directly support a Boolean data type, with predefined values for true and false; others use integer data types to implement Boolean values, usually (although not always) with 0 equaling false and "not 0" equaling true.

browser
Also called a Web browser. A client interface that enables a user to view HTML documents on the World Wide Web, another network, or the user's computer; follow hyperlinks among them; and transfer files.

buffering
Functionality of ASP that temporarily stores all output generated by a script until script execution is complete, then sends it to a client.

C

cache
A special memory subsystem in which frequently used data values are duplicated for quick access. A memory cache stores the contents of frequently accessed RAM locations and the addresses where these data items are stored.

call
To transfer program execution to some section of code (usually a subroutine) while saving the necessary information to allow execution to resume at the calling point when the called section has completed execution.

cascading style sheets
Sets of style sheets that enable Web developers to change documents' format and appearance. See *CSS1* and *CSS2*. See also *DSSSL* and *XSL*.

certificate, client
A digital certificate that functions in a way similar to a driver's license or passport. Client certificates can contain detailed identification information about the user and organization that issued the certificate.

certificate, digital
An encrypted file, containing user or server identification information, that is used to verify identity; also called an authentication certificate. When issued to users, a digital certificate is called a client certificate. When issued to a server administrator, it is called a server certificate.

certification authority
An entity that issues, manages, and revokes certificates.

character
A single unit of information; a letter, digit, or symbol.

child
An element or other object that is nested under a parent element or object; a subelement of an element. See *ancestor*, *descendant*, *nested*, and *parent*.

class ID (CLSID)
A universally unique identifier (UUID) that identifies a COM component. Each COM component has its CLSID in the Windows registry so that it can be loaded by other applications.

client
A user's computer, which makes requests of a server program or server computer. *Client-side* programs and scripts run on the client computer. The browser program runs Web pages on the client computer. See *server*.

client-server
A style of development where applications are divided between a central *server* and distributed *clients*, typically on users' desks. Additional *middleware tiers* sometimes perform processing between the client and server.

COM
The Component Object Model, Microsoft's model for creating and using reusable components. It is a standard of interoperability that allows applications to communicate with one another.

commit
The phase in a transaction when all interactions are finalized and the persistent state of the underlying database is changed.

Common object request broker architecture (CORBA)
A specification developed by the Object Management Group in 1992 in which pieces of programs (objects) communicate with other objects in other programs, even if the two programs are written in different programming languages and are running on different platforms.

compile time
The time during which a program is translated from source language into machine language.

content type
The type of file (such as text, graphic, or sound), usually indicated by the file name extension (such as .txt, .gif, or .wav, respectively).

cookies
A means by which, under the HTTP protocol, a server or a script can maintain information on the client computer. Cookies are small text files which are stored in the user's browser by the Web server.

corba
See *common object request broker architecture.*

cryptology
A field science involving the transmission of information in an encoded form so that only an intended recipient can decode the information and reveal its meaning. Encoded information is commonly said to be encrypted.

CSS1
The first standard for cascading style sheets; a simple set of rules to format and enhance text, paragraphs, and documents. See *cascading style sheets* and *CSS2.*

CSS2
The second standard for cascading style sheets; adds to the CSS1 base a set of styles for visual browsers, aural devices, printers, Braille devices, and so on, as well as styles for table layout, internationalization features, and more. See *cascading style sheets* and *CSS1.*

cursor
A piece of software that returns rows of data to an application. A cursor on a resultset indicates the current position in the resultset.

D

data provider
Software that implements Object Linking and Embedding Database (OLE DB) methods and interfaces.

data source
The name that applications use to request a connection to an Open Database Connectivity (ODBC) data source. It specifies the computer name and (optionally) database that the data source name (DSN) maps to.

data tier
A logical layer that represents a computer running a Database Management System (DBMS).

Glossary

deadlock
In databases, a situation in which two or more processes are prevented from continuing while each waits for resources to be freed by the continuation of the other.

default document
The document sent by the server when no specific document was requested.

delimiter
A character that indicates the start and end of a string or other piece of information. For HTML, the usual delimiters are less-than (<) and greater-than (>) symbols. The <% and %> delimiters mark the beginning and end of scripts in ASP pages.

descendant
All the elements or other objects that are nested under a parent element or object; subelements of the element. See *ancestor, child, nested,* and *parent.*

dll
See *dynamic link library.*

DOM
Document Object Model, an API developed by the W3C for accessing the content of XML and HTML documents.

DSSSL
Document Style Semantics and Specification Language; ISO 10179: 1996. An international style-sheet standard. DSSSL-O is a custom subset of DSSSL for online documents. See also *cascading style sheets* and *XSL.*

DTD
Document Type Definition; used in XML 1.0 to describe document structures for use in validation.

dynamic link library (DLL)
A feature of the Microsoft Windows family of operating systems that supports executable routines — usually serving a specific function or set of functions — to be stored

separately as files with the file extension name .dll, and to be loaded only when called by the program that needs them.

ECMAScript
The European Computer Manufacturers Association standardized this scripting language, also known as *JavaScript.*

element
A label with which you define part of a Web document. An element starts with a start tag (`<elementname>`), includes an element name, may contain subelements and contents with which you vary the results of the element, and ends with an end tag (`</elementname>`). See end tag, start tag, and subelement.

e-mail
A system whereby a computer user can exchange messages with other computer users (or groups of users) through a communications network.

empty element
An element that has no content between the start tag and the end tag but is a placeholder for future document content, such as an image or a line break. See *element, end tag,* and *start tag.*

encryption
A way of making data indecipherable to protect it from unauthorized viewing or use, especially during network transmission

empty tag
A tag used to abbreviate an element that has no textual content. The format of an empty tag is <elementname/?>, and attributes may be included.

end tag
The part of a Web-document statement that indicates the end of an element and its contents. The format of an end tag is `</elementname>`, in contrast to the start tag format, `<elementname>`. An end tag does not include attributes. In XML, an empty element can be made up of both a start tag and an end tag (`<elementname/>`). See *element* and *start tag*.

entity
A special character; a single unit, or item. Entity is an all-purpose term that can also refer to a specific content — ranging from a single character to an entire file.

expires header
An expiration date or time for a file sent by a server; the expiration information is used by proxy servers and browser caches.

form
In Web publishing, a Web page or portion of a Web page that is filled out by the user and sent back to the server for processing.

global.asa
A file that stores information about an IIS application such as initialization in structures, and objects that have been given application scope.

globally unique identifier (guid)
In COM, a 16-byte code that identifies an interface to an object across all computers and networks.

home directory
The root directory for a Web site, where the content files are stored. Also called a document root or Web root.

home page
The initial page of information for a collection of pages, a Web site or section of a Web site.

J

JavaBeans
An object model being developed by SunSoft that is targeted to interoperate with a variety of other object models, including COM and CORBA.

JavaScript
A scripting language that uses a C- or Java-like syntax.

JScript
The Microsoft open implementation of JavaScript. JScript complies with the ECMA 262 language specification.

K

keyword
A reserved word; a word or phrase that is a unique part of a language, such as HTML or VBScript, and therefore is unavailable for other uses within that language. See *reserved word*.

GLOSSARY

L

link
A highlighted and/or underlined word or phrase (or a graphic), that, when clicked on, takes you to one or more particular places in another document or one or more sections of the current document.

M

markup
Commands that define attributes, such as formats and enhancements, and describe the document. In XML and HTML documents, the commands with which the document is marked up are known as *elements*. The term *markup* refers to the marks that editors make on manuscripts to be revised. See *end tag*, *entity*, and *start tag*.

media type
The type of file and its contents, formatted as *file type/file format*. Examples include text/HTML and video/mpeg. Also called content-type or MIME type.

method
A procedure (function) that acts on an object.

middleware
Software that helps two participants in a transaction understand each other. Middleware performs a wide variety of functions, including filtering, formatting, and breaking down information into more easily processed components.

N

nested
A command line (including attributes) that is inserted completely within another command line.

O

object linking and embedding database (OLE DB)
Data-access interfaces providing consistent access to SQL and non-SQL data sources across the enterprise and the Internet.

object request broker (orb)
In client/server applications, an interface to which the client makes a request for an object. The ORB directs the request to the server containing the object and then returns the resulting values to the client.

ODBC
See *open database connectivity.*

OLE DB
See *object linking and embedding database.*

open database connectivity (ODBC)
An application programming interface that enables applications to access data from a variety of existing data sources. A standard specification for cross-platform database access.

orb
See *object request broker.*

P

parameter
A value passed in a function call.

parent
An element or other object under which other elements or objects are nested. In XML, an element is a parent of a subelement. See *ancestor, child, descendant,* and *nested.* See also *root.*

PerlScript
A tool from ActiveState that allows you to write Active Server Pages using the Perl scripting language.

process
In Windows, an object consisting of an executable program, a set of virtual memory addresses, and a thread; in UNIX, a synonym for thread.

Public-key encryption
An asymmetric scheme that uses a pair of keys for encryption: The public key encrypts data, and a corresponding secret key decrypts it. For digital signatures, the process is reversed: The sender uses the secret key to create a unique electronic number that can be read by anyone possessing the corresponding public key, which verifies that the message is truly from the sender.

R

recordset
A set of information, organized as a collection of fields, returned by a query against a database.

redirection
The process of writing to or reading from a file or device different from the one that would normally be the target or the source. Can be used to automatically send a user from an outdated URL to a new one.

Registry
A central hierarchical database in Windows used to store information necessary to configure the system for one or more users, applications, and hardware devices.

Regular Expression
A standard syntax for creating strings that can be used to determine whether the target of a match contains a pattern. Used extensively by *PerlScript.*

reserved word
A word or term used by a program or language for its own statements, declarations, and so on. Examples of reserved words in scripting are AND and OR. See *keyword.*

RSA
A public-key encryption standard for Internet security.

S

scope
In programming, the extent to which an identifier, such as a constant, data type, variable, or routine, can be referenced within a program. Scope can be global or local. Scope can also be affected by redefining identifiers, such as by giving the same name to both a global variable and a local variable.

script
A kind of program that consists of a set of instructions for an application or utility program. A script can be embedded in a Web page.

Glossary

script engine
A program that interprets and executes a script.

Secure sockets layer (SSL)
A protocol that supplies secure data communication through data encryption and decryption. SSL uses RSA public-key encryption for specific TCP/IP ports. It is intended for handling commerce payments.

server
A computer that serves client computers. *Server-side* programs and scripts and ASP pages run on the server computer. See *client*.

server certificate
A unique digital identification that forms the basis of a Web server's SSL security features.

Simple Mail Transfer Protocol (SMTP)
A TCP/IP protocol for sending messages from one computer to another on a network. This protocol is used on the Internet to route e-mail.

SQL
Structured Query Language. A language for managing relational database structures commonly used for getting information in and out of database structures.

SSL
See *Secure Sockets Layer*.

start tag
The part of an HTML or XML statement that indicates the start of an element and its contents. The format of a start tag is `<elementname>`, in contrast to the end tag format, `</elementname>`. In XML, an empty element can be made up of both a start tag and an end tag (`<elementname/>`). See *element* and *end tag*.

string
A group of one or more characters, usually text, enclosed within delimiters such as double quotation marks and sometimes given a unique name as identification. See *delimiter* and *identifier*.

style
One property or instruction in a style sheet. See *style sheet*.

style sheet
A set of instructions with which a word-processing or Web document is laid out or formatted. Style sheets format characters, paragraphs, pages, documents, and sets of documents. See *cascading style sheets*, *style*, and *XSL*.

tag
See *element*. See also *end tag* and *start tag*.

three-tier architecture
Divides a networked application into three logical areas: the user interface layer, the business logic layer, and the database layer.

tier
A layer in a distributed application. Two-tier applications are typically only a client and server, directly connected, while a three-tier application relies on a layer in the middle to help the client and server communicate. ASP is often used as a middle tier between a database server and a Web browser client.

transaction manager
A system service responsible for coordinating the outcome of transactions in order to achieve atomicity. The transaction manager ensures that the resource managers reach a consistent decision on whether the transaction should commit or fail.

two-tier architecture
See *client/server*.

URI
Uniform Resource Identifier. The Internet address of an anchor. A URI can be either a URL (absolute link) or a partial address (relative link), or a URN (Uniform Resource Name). See *URL* and *URN*.

URL
Uniform Resource Locator. An Internet address composed of the protocol type (such as `http:`, `ftp:`, or `gopher:`), the name of the server to be contacted (such as `www.w3.org`), the directories or folders (such as `/pub/WWW/Provider/`), and the optional filename (for example, `homepage.xml`). See *URI* and *URN*.

URN
Uniform Resource Name. An identifier that can contain a variety of information, including one or more URLs. See *URI* and *URL*.

V

VBScript
A scripting language based on Microsoft's Visual Basic programming language.

W

W3C
World Wide Web Consortium. The organization that develops standards for the World Wide Web and contributes to XML, HTML, and stylesheet standards.

whitespace
The "empty" sections of a document that do not include text or graphics. Use style sheets to add whitespace to a document to highlight headings and particular text and graphics, to improve the look of the document, and to make its text easier to read. See *cascading style sheets* and *style sheets*.

XML
Extensible Markup Language. A "child" or subset of SGML and a markup language that coexists with both SGML and HTML. XML enables complex hyperlinks, supports long documents, and allows users to define their own elements.

XSL
Extensible Style Language. A style sheet language designed specifically for XML, which is currently under development. See *cascading style sheets*.

Index

A

Index

Index

Index

B

back-end database, 434
back-end services, 490
background properties, 103, 198-199
background-attachment, 199
background-color, 199
background-image, 199
background-position, 199
background-repeat, 199
backslash, 271
backward scrolling, 404
backward-slash separator, 54
balance sheets, 146
Bank Account Maintenance application, 426
bank account number, 452
bank funds transfer application, 415
Bank.Account, 426
Bank.CreateTable, 426
Bank.GetReceipt, 426
Bank.MoveMoney, 426
Bank.UpdateReceipt, 426
banner advertisement, 370
banners, 103
BASE, 102, 112
base-10 system, 118
base-16 system, 118
BASEFONT, 102
baseline, 192, 202, 204
Basic Authentication method, 446
BASIC programming language, 229
batch files, 224
batching, 218
BCC, 377
BEGIN blocks, 346-347
BeginTrans, 351
Beyond the Bones of HTML, 71
BGCOLOR, 146
BGSOUND, 282

Bibliography Handbook, 140
BigNoseBird.Com Site Guide, 71
binary, 118
Binary Large Objects (Blobs), 385
BinaryRead, 301
bitwise AND, 246
bitwise left shift, 246
bitwise NOT, 246
bitwise operators, 246
bitwise OR, 246
bitwise right shift, 246
bitwise XOR, 246
BLOCKQUOTE, 202
BODY element, 82, 217, 377
BodyFormat, 378
BOF property, 356-357
boilerplate, 280
boldface, 66, 82, 86, 150
Bookmark, 357
Boolean, 234, 246
border, 150, 199, 200, 371
border-bottom, 199
border-bottom-width, 199
border-color, 199
border-left, 199
border-left-width, 199
border-right, 199
border-right-width, 199
border-style, 199
border-top, 199
border-top-width, 199
border-width, 199
Borland, 332
bottom, 202
BR, 102
brackets, 80
British English, 74
brochure-oriented site, 275
browscap.dll, 282, 325
browscap.ini, 282, 286, 328

Index

Index

Continued

Index

E

Index

Index

F

False, 232
fantasy, 204
FETCH, 347
field access, 246
file, 122, 366
File Access Component object, 326, 366
file extension, 458
File select control type, 178
File Transfer Protocol (FTP), 8, 16, 176
FileExists, 368
Files, 369
FileSystemObject, 6, 310, 366, 368
firehose cursor, 405
firewall, 30
float properties, 200-201
floating-point number, 234
flow objects, 194
Flush, 304-305
Folder, 366
folder name, 122
FONT, 150, 192, 201
font-family, 201, 204
font-size, 201, 204
font-style, 201, 204
font-variant, 201, 204
font-weight, 201, 204
fonts, 180
For Each... Next, 236
for statement, 250
for... in statement, 250
For... Next, 236
FOREIGN KEY, 347
Form collection, 300-301
form controls, 120

form-handling program, 184
formatting, 114, 280
formfeed, 273
forms
    controls, 178, 182
    creating, 180
    definition, 178
    processing, 184
    user input, 182
forward slash, 472
forward-only cursor, 356, 404
forward-slash separator, 54
fragment identifier, 124
FRAME, 102, 159, 162
frameborder, 162
frames
    attributes, 162
    border, 168
    column-centric, 162
    content, 164
    escape, 164
    modifying, 168
    non-frames content, 170
    order, 164
    row-centric, 162
    setting up, 162
    support, 159
    targeting, 166
FRAMESET, 159-160, 217
free downloads, 26
FreeSpace, 367
From, 377
Front Page Extensions, 26
FrontPage 2000, 52
FrontPage Server Extension, 13
FTP. *See* File Transfer Protocol (FTP)
function calls, 246
Function procedure, 238

567

Index

Index

Index

L

LABEL, 217
labels, 180
lang, 106, 151
LANGUAGE attribute, 246
languages, 444
Lark and Larval, 127
Latin character set, 74, 96
layouts, 280
LearnASP, 281
left bracket, 96
less than, 89, 246
less than or equal to, 246
letter-spacing, 201
licensing, COM objects, 324
line feeds, 186
line-height, 201, 204
link, 66, 72, 102, 112, 122
LINK element, 196
Linux, 5, 8, 52, 261
Listing 22-1, 366
lists
    definition, 132, 140
    nesting, 138
    ordered, 132, 134
    simple, 132
    types, 132
    unordered, 132, 136
list-style, 201
list-style-image, 201
list-style-position, 201
list-style-type, 201
Load Library, 329
loading, 216
LOCAL_ADDR, 303
locator elements, 124
locator link, 122
Lock, 313, 444

locking types, 404
logical AND, 246
logical NOT, 246
logical operators, 232, 246
logical OR, 246
logical structure, 66
login credentials, 338
login_response.asp, 448
logo, 154
Long, 234
looping statements, 236, 250
Lotus Notes, 52, 88, 378
lowercase, 273

M

Macintosh, 12, 103, 260, 322
MailFormat, 378
mailto, 122
Main window, PWS, 42
main(), 406, 426
mainframe databases, 338
mainframes, 212
Mainsoft Mainwin package, 54
maintaining state, 425, 434
majorver, 282
Management Console, 424
MAP element, 166
MapPath, 309
margin, 116, 198, 203
margin-bottom, 203
marginheight, 162
margin-left, 203
margin-right, 203
margin-top, 203
marginwidth, 162
marked-up data, 296
markup, 66, 80

Index

Index

Index

Index

Index

Continued

Index

my2cents.idgbooks.com